Affirming Students' Right to Their Own Language

A Co-publication of the National Council of Teachers of English and Routledge

"This book is as much about redefining what it means to be human as it is about redefining language and education. [It] responds to the question of how our current definitions of language define human beings in the world. . . . The defining criteria are questioned with a focus on students' language rights, language policies, and pedagogical practices. [*Affirming Students' Right to Their Own Language*] provides us with new ways and definitions of being human beings in the world."

David Bloome, Ohio State University, From the Foreword

How can teachers make sound pedagogical decisions and advocate for educational policies that best serve the needs of students in today's diverse classrooms? What is the pedagogical value of providing culturally and linguistically diverse students greater access to their own language and cultural orientations?

This landmark volume responds to the call to attend to the unfinished pedagogical business of the NCTE Conference on College Composition and Communication 1974 Students' Right to Their Own Language resolution. Chronicling the interplay between legislated/litigated education policies and language and literacy teaching in diverse classrooms, it presents exemplary, research-based practices that maximize students' learning by utilizing their home-based cultural, language, and literacy practices to help them meet school expectations.

Pre-service teachers, practicing teachers, and teacher educators need both resources and knowledge about language variation in PreK-12 classrooms and effective strategies that enable students to use their own language in the classroom while also addressing mandated content and performance standards. This book meets those needs.

Jerrie Cobb Scott is Professor of Urban Literacy and Director of the Reading Center at the University of Memphis.

Dolores Y. Straker (deceased) was Dean of the Raymond Walters College at the University of Cincinnati.

Laurie Katz is Associate Professor of Early Childhood Education at Ohio State University.

Visit the Routledge website at **www.routledgeeducation.com**
Visit the National Council of Teachers of English website at **www.ncte.org**

Affirming Students' Right to Their Own Language

Bridging Language Policies and Pedagogical Practices

A Co-publication of the National Council
of Teachers of English and Routledge

Edited by

Jerrie Cobb Scott
University of Memphis

Dolores Y. Straker
University of Cincinnati

Laurie Katz
Ohio State University

Routledge
Taylor & Francis Group

NEW YORK AND LONDON

National Council of
Teachers of English

First published 2009
by Routledge
270 Madison Ave, New York, NY 10016

Simultaneously published in the UK
by Routledge
2 Park Square, Milton Park, Abingdon, Oxon OX14 4RN

Routledge is an imprint of the Taylor & Francis Group, an informa business

National Council of Teachers of English
1111 West Kenyon Road
Urbana, IL 61801-1096
NCTE Stock Number 00856

© 2009 Taylor & Francis

Typeset in Minion by
Swales & Willis Ltd, Exeter, Devon
Printed and bound in the United States of America on acid-free paper by
Sheridan Books, Inc.

Library of Congress Cataloging-in-Publication Data
Affirming students' right to their own language: bridging language policies
and pedagogical practices/edited by Jerrie Cobb Scott, Dolores Y. Straker,
and Laurie Katz.
    p. cm.
    Includes bibliographical references and index.
    1. Native language and education–Cross-cultural studies.   2. Education,
Bilingual–Cross-cultural studies.   3. English language–Study and
teaching–Political aspects–Cross-cultural studies.   I. Scott, Jerrie Cobb.
II. Straker, Dolores Y. (Dolores Yvonne), 1947–2008.   III. Katz, Laurie.
IV. National Council of Teachers of English.
LC201.5.A44 2008
428.0071'2–dc22   2008021686

ISBN10: 0–8058–6348–6 (hbk)
ISBN10: 0–8058–6349–4 (pbk)
ISBN10: 1–4106–1813–7 (ebk)

ISBN13: 978–0–8058–6348–2 (hbk)
ISBN13: 978–0–8058–6349–9 (pbk)
ISBN13: 978–1–4106–1813–9 (ebk)

This book is dedicated to the memory of our dear friend, colleague, and co-editor, Dolores Yvonne Straker (1947–2008). It is our hope that this book will inspire others to follow in Dolores's footsteps of walking the talk of affirming students' right to their language and of taking broad steps to create policies that support effective teaching practices for the ethnically and culturally diverse students of our national and global learning communities.

Contents

Foreword: 3/5 of a Language?   xi
DAVID BLOOME

Preface: Unmasking Support of Students' Language Rights   xvii
Acknowledgments   xxiii

PART I SETTING THE CONTEXT   1

1 **Cross-Currents in Language Policies and Pedagogical Practices**   3
   JERRIE COBB SCOTT, DOLORES Y. STRAKER, AND LAURIE KATZ

2 **Perspectives on Language Policies and Pedagogical Practices**   18
   Interview 1: Issues in Global and Local Language Policies
   JOEL SPRING

   Interview 2: An Insider's View of African American Language
   Policies and Pedagogies
   GENEVA SMITHERMAN

   Interview 3: The Law of Language in the United States
   CHRISTINA M. RODRÍGUEZ

   Interview 4: What Teachers Need to Know to Educate English
   Language Learners
   MARY CAROL COMBS

PART II EDUCATIONAL POLICIES, ATTITUDES, AND
UNFULFILLED PROMISES   39

3 **The Hidden Linguistic Legacies of Brown v. Board and No**
   Child Left Behind   41
   JOHN BAUGH AND AARON WELBORN

4   Portraits, Counterportraits, and the Lives of Children:
Language, Culture, and Possibilities   54
RICK MEYER

5   Restore My Language and Treat Me Justly: Indigenous
Students' Rights to Their Tribal Languages   68
DOROTHY AGUILERA AND MARGARET D. LECOMPTE

6   Power, Politics, and Pedagogies: Re-Imagining Students'
Right to Their Own Language Through Democratic Engagement   85
VALERIE KINLOCH

7   Exploring Attitudes Toward Language Differences: Implications
for Teacher Education Programs   99
LAURIE KATZ, JERRIE COBB SCOTT, AND XENIA HADJIOANNOU

8   Positionality: Using Self-Discovery to Enhance Pre-Service
Teachers' Understanding of Language Differences   117
NANCY RANKIE SHELTON

9   Beyond the Silence: Instructional Approaches and Students'
Attitudes   132
DAVID E. KIRKLAND AND AUSTIN JACKSON

PART III   TOWARD A PEDAGOGY OF SUCCESS IN CLASSROOMS   151

10   "We Have Our Own Language as Well as the Languages We
Bring": Constructing Opportunities for Learning Through a
Language of the Classroom   153
BETH V. YEAGER AND JUDITH L. GREEN

11   "Taylor Cat is Black": Code-Switch to Add Standard English to
Students' Linguistic Repertoires   176
REBECCA S. WHEELER

12   There's No "1" Way to Tell a Story   192
LAURIE KATZ AND TEMPII CHAMPION

13   Culturally Responsive Read-Alouds in First Grade: Drawing
Upon Children's Languages and Cultures to Facilitate Literary
and Social Understandings   206
JEANE COPENHAVER-JOHNSON, JOY BOWMAN, AND
ANGELA JOHNSON RIETSCHLIN

14 Developing Culturally Responsive Teacher Practitioners
Through Multicultural Literature   219
TAMARA L. JETTON, EMMA SAVAGE-DAVIS, AND MARIANNE BAKER

15 Educating the Whole Child: English Language Learners in a
Middle School   232
MARI HANEDA

16 New Chinese Immigrant Students' Literacy Development:
From Heritage Language to Bilingualism   247
DANLING FU

17 High Stakes Testing and the Social Languages of Literature
and Literate Achievement in Urban Classrooms   262
DOROTHEA ANAGNOSTOPOULOS

PART IV GLOBAL PERSPECTIVES ON LANGUAGE DIVERSITY
AND LEARNING   273

18 Possibilities for Non-Standard Dialects in American
Classrooms: Lessons from a Greek Cypriot Class   275
XENIA HADJIOANNOU

19 The Writing on the Wall: Graffiti and Other Community
School Practices in Brazil   291
ANA CHRISTINA DASILVA IDDINGS

20 The Social Construction of Literacy in a Mexican Community:
Coming Soon to Your School?   303
PATRICK H. SMITH, LUZ A. MURILLO, AND ROBERT T. JIMÉNEZ

21 Multilingualism in Classrooms: The Paritetic School System
of the Ladin Valleys in South Tyrol (Italy)   319
GERDA VIDESOTT

22 Educational Policies and Practices in Post-Apartheid South
Africa: The Case for Indigenous African Languages   329
NKONKO M. KAMWANGAMALU

23 Meaningful Early Literacy Learning Experiences: Lessons
from South Africa   345
CAROLE BLOCH

24 India's Multilingualism: Paradigm and Paradox   360
    ZARINA MANAWWAR HOCK

**Afterword: Reflections on Language Policies and Pedagogical
Practices**   376
JACQUELINE JONES ROYSTER, JERRIE COBB SCOTT,
AND DOLORES Y. STRAKER

Author Biographies   388
Author Index   403
Subject Index   411

Foreword: 3/5 of a Language?

DAVID BLOOME

A definition of language is always, implicitly or explicitly, a definition of human beings in the world. (Williams, 1977, p. 21)

If Williams is correct, then it is important to ask how our current definitions of language define human beings in the world. But before we can ask that question, we have to ask where, when, and how definitions of language occur. Once we have asked these questions, we can ask a third question. How might we redefine language and in so doing redefine ourselves and our students as human beings in the world? These three questions constitute the core of this book.

I begin by briefly discussing three locations in which language is defined: law and official policies, the social institutions of our society, and music/art. These are not the only locations for defining language, but an examination of these three areas can provide key thematic insights about the defining of language. I examine these three locations as a way to frame how we might redefine language and in so doing redefine ourselves and our students as human beings in the world.

Locations for Defining Language

Law and Government Policy

Although the Constitution of the United States does not name an official language for the nation, laws in more than 25 states have attempted to create that effect, if not legal standing. Many scholars, activists, and politicians have criticized the legal movement toward establishing "English Only" laws and policies (e.g., Auerbach, 1993; Crawford, 1992; Macedo, 2000; McCarty, 2003). They argue that such laws and policies marginalize those who do not speak English or who are not fully fluent in English and undermine efforts to maintain cultural heritage. And, further, they argue that such laws and policies are counterproductive to the goal of educating for academic excellence and of educating all children and adults to become fluent users of Standard English (e.g., Dixon, et al., 2000; Garcia & Curry-Rodriguez, 2000).

Although the critique and these arguments are not to be disregarded, they overlook one important aspect of these laws and policies: the dichotomizing of languages into official and unofficial ones (if not in law, in policy and practice). This dichotomizing can be viewed as a dividing practice, a subtle, nearly invisible way of producing power relations among groups of people (cf., Foucault, 1980) that seems to be "naturalized" (cf., Fairclough, 1992).

It makes "common sense" to have an official language, a lingua franca, so that people from diverse backgrounds can communicate with one another, creating social cohesion. To suggest something other than this common sense would be tantamount to irrationality. But, this common sense needs to be examined, if not challenged. For example, we might ask if the establishment of official and unofficial languages produces official and unofficial people. In my city, Columbus, Ohio, not unlike cities across the United States, few members of the safety forces (police, fire, emergency healthcare) speak a language other than English. We have had tragedies occur because of the safety forces' inability to communicate with residents (*Columbus Dispatch*, 2007).

Some would argue that the moral of such tragedies is that everyone should learn English, which places the blame of the tragedy on the victims themselves for not speaking English. But others would argue that, in reality, not everyone speaks English neither will it ever be the case that everyone will. For them, the moral of such tragedies is the need to embrace multilingualism as law and policy. They argue that the pursuit of "English Only" laws and policies and the consequential dichotomizing of people into those who are official and those unofficial are to blame. They reject the premise of national unity and social coherence through monolingualism and the prioritizing of nationalism over human needs and welfare. Official people get to participate in a democracy, get police, fire, and medical protection, and have rights protected by law. Unofficial people are marginalized by laws and policies promoting an official language and are thereby made more vulnerable to tragedies for which they themselves get blamed. It is as if the failure to speak fluent Standard English is a sin for which people must be punished.

The alignment of the dividing practices of official and unofficial languages, official and unofficial people, and righteous and sinful people ignores government laws and policies that have produced large-scale migration especially of those who are poor and lacking education. Economic globalization, wars and military actions, and huge economic disparities across borders force people to migrate. Such migration involves many countries, not just the United States. Sometimes this migration is from rural areas to the cities and sometimes it is across borders. Regardless, it is hypocritical to label such migration voluntary and similarly to label those who cross borders without documentation criminal and illegal when they seek to escape the poverty and violence produced by government laws and policies over which they have no control. The question to ask, therefore, about laws and policies that have dichotomized languages into official and unofficial ones are not just about their production of official and unofficial people, but also how they define those who make such laws and policies.

Social Institutions

The social institutions of our society are also places where language gets defined. The chapters in this book focus primarily on the institution of schools, but language also gets defined in banks, churches, medical offices, businesses, and other social institutions. The primary definition of language in these social institutions in the U.S. is race. That is, varieties of English are aligned with different races and organized hierarchically. Those varieties of English associated with white, northern, middle- and upper-class communities are perceived as better than those varieties of English associated with groups such as African Americans, Mexican and other Latino communities, Southerners, and people from working-class backgrounds. The strength of such a definition of language is indicated by the plethora of courses for people in business to help them eliminate their "accent."

Recognition of a racialized definition of language permeates classrooms where teachers emphasize the importance of learning Standard English. With few exceptions, even those teachers who recognize the legitimacy of non-Standard varieties of English emphasize Standard English, justifying their practice as providing students with access to the "money" language. Such educational practices define language as a tool such that switching back and forth across varieties of English is simply a matter of a technical skill that can be taught through contrastive analysis, modeling, immersion, among other pedagogies.

It is common sense to teach students the language of "money" and of dominant society, banishing other languages in school (and sometimes at home) in service of the goal of access to money and dominant society. Anyone who would argue against such teaching would seem either irrational or racist (even to ask if the equation of speaking Standard English with access is empirically so beyond individual cases). Yet, it is important to examine and perhaps challenge the dichotomous framing of language teaching as either providing access or denying access.

To define language as simply a technical skill, as only a vehicle for communication, is to isolate language from history and meaning. The history of English is not just a history of vowel shift, but it is also a history of political and social events. In the 1780s, changes in spellings and word usage further demarked a separation between the U.S. and Britain. Enslaved Africans were forced to take on Anglicized names. Under Jim Crow laws and culture (and even after), grown men were called "boy" or by their first names when circumstances would otherwise require an honorific such as Mr. or Dr. and the use of the family name. And there is also the history of the word "nigger" and other words used to demean individuals and a whole people. There are similar historical dimensions to words and language associated with ethnic groups other than African Americans as well as a history of language associated with women and gays and lesbians. In brief, every word—even a simple greeting—brings with it a deep history which is as much a part of that word as its denotative meaning.

Parts of the histories of English are bound to how language produces social identities. The language we speak indexes our community membership. Each of us belongs to multiple communities, and as we shift languages across communities our social identities shift. Yet, memberships in these language communities are not without cost. These communities make demands of us; they require us to adopt ways of speaking, thinking, feeling, acting, and valuing. They demand we adopt their histories. But moving across these communities and their histories can be problematic. Not all communities are compatible with each other. Some communities encroach on others, exploiting them for their own benefit or forcing a redefinition. Crossing the boundaries of these communities may require a "double consciousness" (cf., Dubois, 1903). And, as novelists and scholars have shown, such double consciousness can have detrimental effects on individuals and communities.

The common sense view of language as merely a technical skill makes invisible the problematic relationships of communities to each other, their power relations, and the existence of double consciousness. And while it is not necessarily the case that all people from diverse communities experience double consciousness and while it is not necessarily the case that those who do engage in double consciousness experience alienation, some do and the potential for alienation exists for all. Young people from marginalized communities are especially vulnerable as they work out for themselves their social identities and their relationships to home, school, peers, family, and future work communities. They work out these relationships through language.

Music/Art

We tend to think of music and art as locations where the imagination and new ways of expression can challenge established views. And this is true, at least partially. Whether it is in hip hop or jazz, visual art street murals or body art, or in verbal art spoken word, rap, poetry slams, or other forms of artistic expression, some artists have created new definitions of language. These new definitions of language are closely tied to the experiences of those denied access to more established forms of expression and frame meaning as social critique. In more academic terms, the definitions of language found in such artistic forms eschew the formalism of the decontextualized aesthetic (cf., Volosinov, 1929/1973).

Yet, at the same time that music and art provide locations for some artists to produce new definitions of language, music, and art are also used to reflect and stabilize extant definitions of language. The story of *My Fair Lady* is iconic: learning proper English turns a working-class flower girl into lady. Whether on television, radio, iPod, or in the movies, mass media representations of criminals, gang members, and comic fools often speak non-Standard English, while representatives of "justice" and "morality" speak more prestigious varieties of English. While it may no longer be the case that in mass media art forms that the heroes wear white hats and the villains wear black ones, they speak varieties of English associated with being white and Black (or non-white), respectively. Language becomes a definition of people portrayed in modern morality plays with familiar narratives.

Redefining Language

How might we redefine language and in so doing redefine ourselves and our students as human beings in the world? In response to mass media definitions of language and its use in defining people as consumers, there has been an "underground" movement of culture jamming. Culture jamming seeks to undercut the corporate–consumer culture of Western nations such as the United States through acts of sabotage, parody, and education, creating a "'*détournement*' a perspective-jarring turnabout in [people's] everyday life" (Lasn, 1999, p. xvii).

In part, that's what the 1974 Resolution by the National Council of Teachers of English and the Conference on College Composition and Communication on affirming students' rights to their own language is—a *détournement*. And given the definitions of language produced by government laws and policies, social institutions, and the mass media, among others, it is not surprising that the resolution has met strong opposition. In our daily lives we rarely question the language of consumerism and the increasing acquisition of things. We rarely question our social and racial hierarchies even when we find ourselves and our children at the lower end. We rarely question the substitution of market value for meaning; and we rarely question how our definitions of language define what it means for us to be human beings in the world. The chapters in this book are as much about redefining what it means to be human as they are about redefining language and education.

What we have then is a book that responds to the question of how our current definitions of language define human beings in the world. The book shows that our current definitions of non-dominant languages have too often been defined in terms of unofficial human beings who are largely perceived as being less than human. The defining criteria are questioned in this book with a focus on students' language rights, language policies, and pedagogical practices. It provides us with new ways and definitions of being human beings in the world.

References

Auerbach, E. (1993). Reexamining English Only in the ESL Classroom. *TESOL Quarterly*, 27, 1, 9–32.

Columbus Dispatch. (2007). Girl, 4, Drowns; 911 Call Fell Short. May 2. (Available at www.dispatch.com/dispatch/content/local_news/stories/2007/05/02/drowning.ART_ART_05-02-07_B1_EM6I JLK.html.)

Crawford, J. (Ed.) (1992). *A Source Book on the English Only Controversy*. Chicago, IL: University of Chicago Press.

Dixon, C., Green, J., Yeager, B., Baker, D., & Franquiz, M. (2000). "I Know That": What Happens when Reform Gets Through the Classroom Door. *Bilingual Research Journal*, 24, 1 & 2. (Available at brj.asu.edu/v2412/abstractt.html.)

Dubois, W. E. B. (1903/1989). *The Souls of Black Folk*. New York: Pocket Books.

Fairclough, N. (1992). *Discourse and Social Change*. Cambridge: Polity.

Foucault, M. (1980). *Power/Knowledge*. New York: Pantheon Books.

Garcia, E. E., & Curry-Rodriguez, J. (2000). Education of Limited English Proficient Students in California Schools. *Bilingual Research Journal*, 24, 1 & 2. (Available at brj.asu.edu/v2412/abstractt.html.)

Gutierrez, K., Banquedano-Lopez, P., & Asato, J. (2000). "English for the Children": The New Literacy of the Old World Order, Language Policy and Educational Reform. *Bilingual Research Journal*, 24, 1 & 2. (Available at brj.asu.edu/v2412/abstractt.html.)

Lasn, K. (1999). *Culture Jam: The Unloading of America*. New York: Eagle Book Brook/William Marrow & Co.

Macedo, D. (2000). The Colonialism of the English Only Movement. *Educational Researcher*, 29, 3, 15–24.

McCarty, T. (2003). Revitalizing indigenous languages in homogenizing times. *Comparative Education*, 39, 2, 147–163.

Volosinov, V. (1929/1973). *Marxism and the Philosophy of Language* (trans. L. Matejka & I. Titunik). Cambridge, MA: Harvard University Press.

Williams, R. (1977). *Marxism and Literature*. Oxford: Oxford University Press

Preface: Unmasking Support
of Students' Language Rights

The depiction of two masked faces on the cover of this book represents, for us, a metaphor for the number of years that too many have worn the mask that "grins and lies" as Paul Lawrence Dunbar puts it in his poem "We Wear the Mask." We attempt in this book to unmask the many faces of language policies and pedagogical practices that have surfaced over time in support of the rights of students to use their primary language and culture as resources for learning. It is the unmasking of support for minority language rights in 2003 that stands as the central motivation for and focus of *Affirming Students' Right to Their Own Language: Bridging Language Policies and Pedagogical Practices.*

In 2003 the National Council of Teachers of English (NCTE) affirmed the Students' Right to Their Own Language (SRTOL) resolution that was passed by the Conference on College Composition and Communication (CCCC) in 1974. Why, nearly 30 years later, was the SRTOL resolution given new life? The short answer is that unfortunately, many of the same conditions that SRTOL was intended to address in the early 1970s have re-emerged with an intensity that cannot be ignored. One such issue then, as now, is the performance gaps between mainstream and non-mainstream students. Then, as now, evidence that performance gaps are due in part to the different language and cultural patterns that non-mainstream students bring to the classroom surrounds us.

Today we know a great deal more about language diversity and education than we did three decades ago; yet, many of the recent educational policies threaten to lower the access of non-mainstream students to their language, to high-quality instruction, and to equitable educational opportunities. Rationally, then, this book attempts to pull together much of what we know in a way that enables professional educators to make sound pedagogical decisions and advocate for educational policies that make sense in relation to the realities confronted in our increasingly diverse classrooms. We believe that this can be done if professional educators have a fuller understanding of the relationships between educational policies and pedagogical practices.

In support of the reaffirmation of SRTOL, the members of the 2003 NCTE Commission on Language felt that this time around, responses to the SRTOL resolution should address what commission member Geneva Smitherman has called the "unfinished business" of SRTOL—the praxis, or practice, dimension of giving non-mainstream students the same type of access to their language and cultural orientations that is built into the curriculum for mainstream students. In its broadest sense, then, the purpose of this book is to address the praxis dimension of the Students' Right to Their Own Language.

This book responds to the call to take care of some of the unfinished pedagogical business of the Students' Right to Their Own Language (SRTOL) resolution. It reveals some of the unfulfilled promises of legislated/litigated educational policies, and it demonstrates the value of giving students access to their own language and cultural patterns as a means of improving the quality of learning and reducing the performance gap between non-mainstream and mainstream students.

The value of presenting the book at this time is that some of the most widely discussed pedagogical challenges today have to do with language diversity in classrooms. Teacher educators complain that teachers in training know very little about how to manage language and cultural diversity in the classroom, and practicing teachers complain that their teacher education programs failed to prepare them for the realities of today's language diverse classrooms. These concerns are closely aligned with the concerns that led to the creation of the SRTOL resolution in the first place, suggesting that it is quite timely to:

- revisit the key tenets of the SRTOL resolution;
- take stock of the legislated/litigated educational policies that support or challenge the major tenets of SRTOL;
- examine the progress we have made in the pedagogical arena with respect to instructional issues addressed by SRTOL in the classroom; and
- provide a global perspective on how other nations have and are dealing with issues of language diversity.

All are considered important aspects of the unfinished business of the SRTOL resolution.

One problem that is widely acknowledged by professional linguists, socio-linguistics, ethnographers, and language/literacy educators is that educators are limited in their access to practical information about effective, evidence-based instructional strategies for second language/dialect speakers. Much of what has been written in response to SRTOL has focused on composition, especially at the post-secondary level. This volume gives teachers and teacher educators immediate access to ways to more fully tap into the unforgettable promises of a pedagogy of success for linguistically and culturally diverse students in PreK-12 classrooms. Thus, the primary audiences for this book are teacher educators and pre- and in-service teachers who need and want to further their technical and practical knowledge of language and cultural variation and its effects on students from preschool to post-secondary levels.

This book also has much to offer professors who teach language-based courses in education (early, middle, secondary levels), introductory linguistics courses, as well as courses on urban education, English language learners, English/language arts, language/cultural diversity and schooling, and educational policies. Each of these groups will find the research-informed articles that draw heavily on teacher/action research and policy-oriented research to be highly useful. The research reported throughout the book makes it especially appealing to both professional and student researchers who are involved in or searching for timely topics and effective research methodologies that warrant further interrogation. Finally, it is our hope that this volume will serve as a resource for professional development consultants who are often called on to provide training in the areas of language diversity, including bi-dialectalism, bi- and multilingualism, and bi-literacy.

Overview

Affirming Students' Right to Their Own Language: Bridging Language Policies and Pedagogical Practices is organized into four parts. Part I focuses on language policies and implications for education. Part II focuses on language policies and attitudes as impediments to fulfilling the promises for equal educational opportunities to high-quality instruction for all students. Part III presents hands-on strategies for giving students access to their primary language and cultural orientations to foster more meaningful, effective learning. Numerous instructional strategies are provided that can make real the promises of policies that claim to remove educational inequities. Part IV returns to language policies and pedagogical practices but from a global perspective. Shared are strategies for managing language diversity in the classroom and for preserving the rights of minority language groups through legislated-litigated policies. At the end of the book, we offer some reflections on the language policies and pedagogical practices presented in this volume.

In short, issues of language policy and pedagogical practices are interwoven throughout the book, giving the reader a glimpse of problems and solutions that have evolved over time to redress problems of educating students well in a society where diversity is becoming more the norm than the exception to the norm.

To provide a glimpse of the parts of the book and how they fit together, we offer here a fuller description of the contents of the book. The book opens with the foreword, "3/5 of a Language?" This bold question sets an interrogating tone that is found throughout the book. The preface prepares the reader for a book that is about defining language, even minority languages and dialects, as uniquely human qualities of people who live in a world with authentically equal rights to language, especially rights to their own language.

Just as the preface sets an interrogative tone, Part I provides the context for the book. Chapter 1, "Cross-Currents in Language Policies and Pedagogical Practices," chronicles the development of litigation, legislation, and related resolutions provided by professional organizations, including the SRTOL resolution, with special attention to the key tenets of the SRTOL resolution.

Chapter 2, "Perspectives on Language Policies and Pedagogical Practices," consists of interviews with prominent scholars who offer their perspectives on past and present language policies and pedagogical practices. The interviews begin with Joel Spring, whose pioneering work on language policies, including policies of relevance to indigenous Native Americans, provides a broad context for understanding language policies both in the United States and abroad. Geneva Smitherman, widely known for her work on minority dialect/language rights and her scholarly contributions to describing the structural and rhetorical patterns of African American languages, continues the conversation with a focus on language and educational issues that affect the African American community. The interview with Christina M. Rodriguez, an attorney whose professional experiences with and in-depth knowledge of litigated-legislated language policies, brings clarity to complex aspects of language and the law. The interview with Mary Carol Combs, known for her wealth of research and pedagogical experiences, responds to a question of critical importance to this book: What do teachers need to know in order to better accommodate the learning needs of minority language speakers? Combs' response to this question provides a direct link between the language policies discussed in the other three interviews and the pedagogical chapters of the book.

Part II, "Educational Policies, Attitudes, and Unfulfilled Promises," further explicates the language policies discussed in Part I of the book. Chapters 3–5 link educational policies to the unfulfilled promises of educational policies, while Chapters 6–9 link language attitudes to the unfulfilled promises of educational practices. The central theme that runs throughout this section is that the unfulfilled promises of educational policies and negative attitudes toward language differences can and should be rectified by providing all students access to their own language and cultural orientations and to high- quality, equitable educational opportunities.

Part III, "Toward a Pedagogy of Success in Classrooms," presents exemplary language/literacy teaching practices across the spectrum of preschool to post-secondary classrooms. Chapter 10 opens the section with a research-based description of ways to develop nurturing classroom environments in language-diverse classrooms. In Chapters 11–14, the authors continue to draw on their research-based experiences to describe linguistically and culturally responsive teaching strategies in the areas of code-switching, storytelling, read-alouds, and multi-cultural literature. Chapters 15 and 16 look specifically at strategies for English language learners in the middle grades. Part III ends with a discussion of the debilitating effects of high stakes testing on literate achievement in urban class-rooms. Drawing on their research, the authors make linkages between research and practice while providing hands-on instructional strategies that can be immediately adapted for use in classrooms. The central theme that runs throughout Part III is that a pedagogy of success, grounded in the use of students' language and community-based knowledge as resources, can and should yield instruction that is not only effective and productive, but also meaningful and engaging.

Part IV, "Global Perspectives on Language Diversity and Learning," describes effective practices used beyond our national boundaries to address critical issues of language diversity. Emphasis is placed on lessons that can be learned from the global community for improving language and language arts instruction in diverse settings in the United States. Chapters 18–21 focus on pedagogical topics that reveal how language diversity is managed in different countries, including bi-dialectalism in a Greek community, community-based teaching practices in Brazil, home and school literacy practices in a Mexican community, and multilingualism in the Ladin Valleys of Italy. Chapters 22–24 combine policy and pedagogical topics and address issues of indigenous languages in South Africa and India where English serves as the medium of instruction in many schools. The chapters in Part IV make clear the naturalness of bi-dialectalism, multilingualism, and bi-literacy in other nations and reveal the shared tensions across nations, including the United States, about how to deal with language policies that defend the rights of speakers of minority languages in education.

The Afterword, "Reflections on Language Policies and Pedagogical Practices," by Jacqueline Jones Royster, Jerrie Cobb Scott, and Dolores Straker, provides an introspective response to the essays in the volume. It describes recurring themes throughout the volume with a view towards highlighting what the book suggests about the current state of language policies and pedagogical practices and about future directions in language policies and pedagogical practices for minority dialect/language speakers.

Giving credence to the ideas of the authors while inviting readers to generate their own responses, most chapters end with questions and activities for further exploration. This allows readers, particular those using the book in college courses, to involve students in interactive discussions about the text. This volume treats not only language policies or pedagogical practices, but uniquely links policies and practices. Moreover, this volume consistently responds to the recent demands for evidence-based pedagogy. Informed by research conducted jointly by teachers and teacher educators, this book demonstrates the power of collaborative endeavors in creating new knowledge and the availability of a large body of research-based literature that describe and explain the instructional efficacy of giving students access to their own language and cultural orientations in the teaching and learning process. We hope readers will appreciate seeing aspects of what we are calling a "pedagogy of success" within the context of educational policies, research, and theories that are used to drive and support approaches to language-literacy instruction that work well in minority dominant and language-diverse classrooms.

Acknowledgments

We want first to acknowledge the five years of support given to the making of this book by members of the NCTE Commission on Language. The commissioners have not only authored chapters of the book, but also hosted sessions featuring contributors to this volume at national conferences. Throughout the book there are recurring themes toward establishing directions for future actions that affirm students' rights to their language and bridge educational policies to pedagogical practices. A special note of gratitude goes to those who have worked graciously and diligently with us from the beginning conceptualization phase of the book to the final production: Anna Christina DaSilva Iddings, Xenia Hadjioannou, Kandi Hill-Clarke, Ezra Hyland, Valerie Kinloch, Richard Meyer, Nancy Rankie Shelton, and Geneva Smitherman.

David Bloome, President of NCTE during the initial conceptualization of the book, was highly supportive and graciously accepted our invitation to write the Foreword of the book. Zarina Hock, who was senior editor at NCTE during the early preparatory stages of the book, posed questions and provided frank and serious feedback that added greatly to the content of the book. Her interest continued even into her retirement with the contribution of a chapter on India.

We gratefully acknowledge our editor, Naomi Silverman, for her patience, guidance, and support of the project. Her commitment inspired us to work diligently through multiple edits and to ensure that the voices of a diverse group of contributors would be heard on both the national and international level.

Each of the editors has received continuous support from supportive staff at their institutions. For the support of our staff and graduate assistants, we remain highly grateful. Finally, we acknowledge being responsible for any oversights that have been made along the way but remain hopeful that this book will not only provide some answers, but also invite further interrogation, discussion, and action regarding what it means from a policy and pedagogical perspective to give students the right to their own language and culture as a means of improving learning for all students, especially those who are speakers of minority dialects and languages.

I
SETTING THE CONTEXT

1

Cross-Currents in Language Policies and Pedagogical Practices

JERRIE COBB SCOTT, DOLORES Y. STRAKER, AND LAURIE KATZ

Changes in pedagogical practices, practices of the pedagogical practices, are often influenced by changes in educational policies. In the case of policies related to minority language rights in education, legislated and litigated language policies are of particular significance. It is not uncommon for the ebb and flow of educational policies to be at odds with the flow of pedagogical practices, thereby creating cross-currents in legislated-litigated language policies and pedagogical practices. This book evolved out of an interest in the cross-currents created by the Students' Right to Their Own Language Resolution (SRTOL), best described as an attempt by a professional organization (College Composition and Communication of the National Council of Teachers of English) to inform and influence educational policies and teaching practices related to the language rights and education of minority students. One could say that the SRTOL resolution created cross-currents, as it was at odds with the existing flow of education policies and teaching practices.

The two main reasons for presenting this book are (1) to address the issue of how best to translate the SRTOL resolution into practical pedagogical solutions, and (2) to enhance readers' conscious awareness of the cross-currents between language policies and pedagogical practices that affect what happens in classrooms on a daily basis. Central to the content of this book are the key tenets of the SRTOL resolutions and the layers of cross-currents between language policies directed at minority language rights and pedagogical practices that enhance the learning of speakers of minority dialects and languages. The purpose of this chapter, then, is to provide a context for reading not only the chapters in the book, but also the larger sociopolitical context within which the content is presented.

The first part of this chapter provides a historical context for reading the chapters on language policies. We present a timeline of language-related legislation and litigation, followed by a brief description of chapters in the book that explain language policies and related pedagogical practices. The second part of this chapter places the SRTOL in an historical context. We present a timeline of language-based resolutions, followed by a brief description of chapters that demonstrate ways that developing and practicing teachers can actually give students access to the fundamental rights called for by the SRTOL Resolution: (a) the right to access education for social, political, and economic participation in society; and (b) the right to access education in the student's primary language or mother tongue.

Bridging Language Policies to Pedagogical Practices

Citizens of the United States often view this nation as a monolingual one; however, the historical patterns tell a different story. The struggle for minority dialect and language rights has had a long and varied history, dating back at least to the compulsory ignorance laws that barred enslaved African Americans from becoming literate. The timeline presented here gives a sense of critical historical periods for legislated and litigated language polices. In Part II of the book, the authors discuss the unfulfilled promises of minority language policies. We briefly describe the chapters in order to provide a context for reading the book.

A Timeline of Minority Language Policies

In the U.S. the sources of language diversity can be linked to three major groups: African American, indigenous peoples, and immigrant populations. In the interest of pinpointing critical times that are of relevance to minority language rights, the timeline is divided into five periods: (1) 1740 to 1845; (2) 1845 to 1905; (3) 1905 to 1954; (4) 1964 to 1980; and (5) 1980 to the present. The timeline and discussion are informed largely by Wiley's (2002) historical description of language rights in education in the United States.

1740 TO 1845

From 1740 to 1845, each of the aforementioned groups was affected in different ways. Compulsory ignorance laws for enslaved Africans were imposed under colonial rule and retained in the slave codes of the United States. This meant that enslaved Africans were barred from becoming literate until 1865. In addition, Whites were fined and punished if caught teaching African Americans. Indigenous Native American peoples were given the right to literacy under the Civilization Fund Act of 1819. This legislated act provided for education with English as the medium of instruction and for the development of practical skills among indigenous Native American peoples. Mission schools were established for some Native American groups to promote the speaking of English and the acceptance of Anglo values. By 1822 a Cherokee writing system was developed, and Cherokee schools succeeded in promoting the Cherokee language and developed Cherokee–English bi-literacy. With respect to immigrants, early immigrants of German descent operated bilingual English–German schools in the Midwest from 1840 to 1850. For example, Pennsylvania passed a law allowing the use of German as a medium of instruction in public schools, and Ohio passed a law allowing for German and English to be used as the medium of instruction in public schools.

1845 TO 1905

Over the next 60 years, the tolerance for different languages declined, due in part to territorial annexations that dramatically increased the number of indigenous groups. Texas was annexed in 1845, and by 1846 Washington, Oregon, and Idaho were annexed. Then came the treaty of Guadalupe Hidalgo and Mexican Cession in 1848, followed by the Gadsen Purchase in 1853, the annexation of Hawaii in 1898 and Puerto Rico in 1901. What this amounted to was the incorporation of indigenous resident populations under U.S. territorial and later state laws. The Native Americans, by way of contrast, lost autonomy and governance over their schools. Among the Cherokee, there was a gradual decline in literacy as a result of the policy of compulsory Americanization, and English-medium instruction continued into the 1930s. During this same period, German immigration peaked and school related English Only laws were passed, aimed primarily at German Catholics. These laws were ultimately repealed in Illinois and Wisconsin. Regarding African Americans, the now infamous 1896 case of Plessy v. Ferguson upheld the doctrine of "separate but equal," a litigated act that legalized segregated schools, thereby restricting African Americans' rights to access education for social, political, and economic participation in society.

1905 TO 1954

From 1905 to 1923, large waves of immigrants from southern and eastern Europe entered the United States, in part because immigration laws, which were restructured on the basis of national origin, favored people of European descent. Increased numbers of immigrants, undoubtedly coupled with the defeat of Germany and its allies by the United States and its allies in World War I, contributed to the loss of the German language's favorable status in the United States. The major impact was that instruction in German gradually declined, and by the end of World War I (1914 to 1918), instruction in German was banned. A number of states passed laws officially designating English as the language of instruction and restricting the use of non-English languages as the medium of instruction. The restrictive policies brought about concerns, leading eventually to the 1923 Supreme Court ruling in the case of Meyer v. Nebraska (1923), which overturned the ban on instruction in German and other "foreign" languages. During this same time period, other rulings also overturned the ban on instruction in languages other than English, including the 1927 case of Farrington v. Tokushige (1927).

Regarding indigenous languages, the Supreme Court ruled that any attempt by the territorial governor of Hawaii to restrict instruction in community-based schools in Japanese, Chinese, and Korean was unconstitutional. This legitimized the efforts of heritage schools to provide instruction in native languages and reversed the English Only rule regarding the medium of instruction. However, the situation was different for indigenous Native Americans. The Native American Termination Policy renewed restrictions on the use of Native American languages in the schools. The situation for African Americans was tempered by a greater degree of tolerance. In 1954 the famous Brown v. Board of Education ruling reversed the Plessy v. Ferguson (1896) "separate but equal" ruling, thereby ending legal segregation in schools and providing protection from various forms of discrimination, excluding protections for minority languages rights.

1964 TO 1980

Other protections from discrimination were to come with the 1964 Civil Rights Act, the 1965 Immigration Act, the 1968 Bilingual Education Act, and Phase II of the Tribal Restoration Act. Civil Rights laws and immigration reform provided legal protection from discrimination. At least four Supreme Court cases held that school districts must accommodate the needs of language minority students. The Lau v. Nichols case (1974) received a favorable ruling that called for schools to accommodate the needs of children of Chinese descent. Transitional bilingual education was the remedy prescribed in three other cases: Serna v. Portales Municipal Schools (1974), Rios v. Read (1978), and the U.S. v. Texas (1981). In Chapter 2 (Interview 3), Christina Rodríguez provides a provocative overview of language-related litigated cases.

In 1979, a Federal court ruled in the case of Martin Luther King, Jr. Elementary School v. Ann Arbor School District Board that the school district must take the language of African American English speakers into account in teaching them to read in Standard English. This case has been heralded as a landmark decision, as this was the first time that a ruling was made in relation to children who spoke a dialect other than Standard English. The other cases had to do with different languages, including the 1981 case of Castañeda v. Pickard (1981), which established criteria for acceptable program remedies. In Chapter 2 (Interview 2), Geneva Smitherman clarifies the key issues in the King case, as well as the Oakland Ebonics situation, both of which dealt with African American English.

1980 TO THE PRESENT

This brings us to the current period, which is marked by intolerance for language diversity. In 1981, the English Only Movement was formally reinvented. It called for the designation of English as the official language of the nation, reflecting a restrictive and anti-immigration sentiment. The English Only Movement goes further in its defense of English as the official language of the United States, for its advocates call for an Amendment to the Constitution of the United States. In the United States, language rights have been treated largely through legislation and litigation, as this discussion demonstrates. Joel Spring discusses the particularities of English Only and the lack of constitutional protections for minority languages in Chapter 2 (Interview 1).

Regarding immigrants, the Federal government has put in place mechanisms that can potentially replace bilingual education with English Only, thereby restricting students' access to the resources provided by their primary languages. Regarding indigenous groups, vestiges of symbolic tolerance of Native American languages are present today, but without the force of strict reinforcements. So, what of the descendants of enslaved Africans? At best, African Americans have been thrown into the at-risk category where their language is given little consideration in redressing problems of school failure.

Putting a pedagogical face on the anti-bidialectal/bilingual move is the 2000 No Child Left Behind Legislation, which some see as an attempt to force schools into practices that stifle the preservation and further development of a multilectal/ multilingual society. And this seems to be working well from a pedagogical perspective, for many teachers and school districts have made accountability measures, including the passing of high stakes tests, a priority that leaves little time for taking the language and cultural orientations of a diverse student population into account. Moreover, many of today's curriculum standards address diversity in a politically polite but non-demanding manner.

Thus far, we can see that the three major sources of language diversity in the United States are the dialects of English that grew out of the enslavement of Africans, the languages of indigenous peoples, and the languages of early settlers and new immigrants to the country. At the very least, this overly simplistic timeline of legislation and litigation sheds some light on the language rights of minority students that are claimed by the SRTOL resolution and makes clear the cross-currents that have occurred between language policies and pedagogical practices. A closer look at the chapters in Part II of the book will further explain our current situation, pointing to existing cross-currents between language policies and pedagogical practices that impede progress towards fulfilling the unfulfilled promises for improving the education of minority language/dialect speakers.

Unfulfilled Promises

In the opening chapter of Part II, Baugh and Welborn focus primarily on African Americans, critically reviewing issues of legislation and litigation from Brown v. Board of Education to the No Child Left Behind (NCLB) mandates. They argue that while both promised relief to problems of educational inequities, neither dealt in a straight forward way with the hidden linguistic legacy of African Americans. The judicial perview of Brown v. Board of Education was narrowly defined and focused largely on the desegregation of facilities. The more recent NCLB legislation is shortsighted in that it is overly dependent on high stakes test results to serve as the equalizer of past inequities and present school failures. Many of the authors in this volume criticize the NCLB mandates as the driving force behind (a) test-driven curricula, (b) an upsurge of ineffective, reductionists approaches to teaching and learning in general, (c) the reinforcement for the English Only Movement, and (d) the creation of disincentives for considering the heritage language of students in instruction.

In Chapter 4, Meyer takes a close look at language policies that affect teaching practices with minority language groups, especially Native Americans. He argues that the policy framework has become so narrow that it does not allow an accurate portrayal of our diverse student population. Instead of accepting the portrayal of students and schools as being in a crisis state, Meyer unveils counterportraits of diverse students that shed light on ways of repositioning children to move towards high-quality educational experiences and teachers to make increasingly well-informed decisions about language and literacy pedagogy.

Focusing primarily on indigenous language groups, Aguilera and LeCompte (Chapter 5) provide an historical overview of legislation that has undermined the sovereign rights of indigenous students and demonstrate how their research on the language immersion instructional approach enhanced the social, emotional, and academic success of indigenous students who are typically thought to be on a path to educational failure.

Across these three chapters, references are made to each of the aforementioned source groups of today's language diverse population: African Americans, indigenous Native Americans, and immigrants. This enables the reader to better see the rise and fall of promises within legislated and litigated policies for these groups. The sustaining power of the promises is evidenced in our current era where the promise of leaving no child behind turns on its face as a near guarantee that speakers of minority dialects and languages are the first to be left behind.

Affirming Students' Language Rights

The Students' Right To Their Own Language (SRTOL) resolution, first drafted in 1972 and adopted by members of the Conference on College Composition and Communication in 1974, evolved in the midst of social and political upheavals over the civil rights movement that called into question issues of educational equity, justice, and liberation for "marginalized" people. The work on the SRTOL resolution was intended to address and better account for the language rights of students, particularly students from communities publicly labeled as disadvantaged, poor, working class and Black. The SRTOL sought to bring to the attention of policymakers and educators the language differences of ethnic groups who were victims of marginalization. As with SRTOL, other language-centered resolutions sought to find ways to give marginalized students access to the linguistic and cultural resources that emanate from their primary language and the homes and communities in which they live.

For mainstream students, language teaching and schooling are experienced as an enculturative process, where learning experiences are crafted to build on and expand what students bring to school. For minority language students, language teaching and schooling have often been experienced as an acculturative process, where learning experiences are crafted to help non-mainstream students to master the norms of mainstream groups. Advocates of SRTOL felt that traditional methods of teaching neither consciously recognized that instruction offered to all students actually built on the language and cultural orientations of mainstream students, nor seriously addressed the need for alternate approaches to instruction for students of non-mainstream language backgrounds. It happens that the tasks of challenging traditional ways of doing things and of giving students alternative routes would take multiple trials. Throughout the reading of this book, then, it is important to pay attention to the multiple ways in which the trials have created cross-currents between policies and practices and to decipher from the trials the course of action that will work best to address the realities confronted in the classroom and in the world.

The 1974 SRTOL resolution called attention to the language rights of dialect speakers, but with the 2003 reaffirmation of the SRTOL resolution, it now calls attention to evolving conditions, theories, research, and practices beyond those addressed in the original resolution. A variety of related solutions reflect various cross-currents between minority language rights and educational practices that are referenced in many of the chapters in this volume. It is useful then for the reader to know what these resolutions are, how they complement the major tenets of the SRTOL resolution, and how thoughts and actions have moved beyond the original SRTOL tenets. We first provide a timeline of resolutions, followed by a synopsis of how the chapters of this book address key aspects of the SRTOL resolution.

A Timeline of Resolutions

In this chronicle of resolutions, we describe the 1972 SRTOL resolution and five related documents: (1) the 1974 SRTOL position statement on SRTOL; (2) the 1986 Position Statement on English as the Official Language (English Only); (3) the 1988 Language Policy Resolution; (4) the CCCC's 2003 reaffirmation of the 1972 SRTOL resolution; and (5) the NCTE 2003 Resolution reaffirming the 1972 SRTOL resolution.

The SRTOL resolution states:

> We affirm the students' right to their own patterns and varieties of language—the dialects of their nurture or whatever dialects in which they find their own identity and style. Language scholars long ago denied that the myth of a standard American dialect has any validity. The claim that any one dialect is unacceptable amounts to an attempt of one social group to exert its dominance over another. Such a claim leads to false advice for speakers and writers, and immoral advice for humans. A nation proud of its diverse heritage and its cultural and racial variety will preserve its heritage of dialects. We affirm strongly that teachers must have the experiences and training that will enable them to respect diversity and uphold the right of students to their own language. (1974, pp. 2–3)

Clearly, some of the same conditions that the SRTOL resolution was designed to address are present today, and they are becoming more complex as new non-English speaking students and new external mandates become integral parts of the U.S. schooling landscape. The following tenets can be deduced from the SRTOL resolution:

1. Negative attitudes toward students' language arise from mythological understandings and erroneous views of inherently inferior or superior dialects of English.
2. Attitude adjustments depend partially on enriching understandings of the role that power and dominance play in validating and assigning status to languages and dialects and the use of language as a device for social control.
3. Teachers need to be trained to (a) avoid transmitting misguided, uninformed advice about language to students, (b) respect diversity, (c) use alternative approaches to language/literacy instruction, and (d) support minority students' language rights.

4. The nation should develop a sense of pride in preserving its rich language and cultural heritage.

In 1974, a position statement was published with the intent of responding to "some of the questions the resolution will raise" (1974, p. 3), as is further explained in the rationale for the position statement:

> The members of the Committee realized that the resolution would create controversy and that without a clear explanation of the linguistic and social knowledge on which it rests, many people would find it incomprehensible. The members of the Executive Committee, therefore, requested a background statement which would examine some common misconceptions about language and dialect, define some key terms, and provide some suggestions for sounder, alternate approaches. (p. 3)

Consequently, in this special issue of the *College Composition and Communication Journal*, questions are posed and responses provided to questions of relevance to language attitudes, language/literacy teaching and learning, and relationships between language and social mobility. And, it likely served as precursor to a question that has gained currency of late—what do teachers need to know about language in order to better accommodate the needs of students of diverse language backgrounds?

In 1986 the heavy focus given to dialects in the SRTOL statement was extended to languages in other resolutions. The Position Statement on English as the Official Language (Conference on College Composition and Communication) was a response to the English Only Movement, as the following background statement and resolution show:

> **Background:** A movement throughout the United States in the 1980s to establish English as the official language, within individual states and in the nation as a whole, raised concern among educators and others, worried that it could lead to discriminatory actions toward American speakers of other languages:
>
> > **Resolved** that NCTE condemn any attempts to render invisible the native languages of any Americans or to deprive English of the rich influences of the languages and cultures of any of the peoples of America;
> >
> > That NCTE urge legislators, other public officials and citizens to actively oppose action intended to mandate or declare English as an official language or to "preserve," "purify," or "enhance" the language. Any such action will not only stunt the vitality of the language, but also ensure its erosion and in effect create hostility toward English, making it more difficult to teach and learn. (NCTE Resolutions, n.d.)

In 1987, another response to the English Only Movement came from the English Plus Information Clearinghouse (EPIC) in Washington, D.C. As reported by

EPIC, the English Plus concept "holds that the national interest can best be served when all persons of our society have access to effective opportunities to acquire strong English proficiency plus mastery of a second or multiple languages" (Paragraph 3). Opposing the English Only Movement and supporting the English Plus concept are a variety of groups, including civic, religious, and professional organizations. New Mexico, Washington, and Oregon passed "English Plus" laws in order to protect the use of languages other than English and encourage the study of foreign languages. Both Hawaii and Louisiana have official polices aimed at preserving languages and cultures.

In 1988 (and updated in 1992) the CCC pinned the National Language Policy Resolution. Again, the background and resolution will serve as a backdrop for many of the chapters in this volume that deal with issues of bi- and multilingualism:

> **Background:** The National Language Policy is a response to efforts to make English the official language of the United States. This policy recognizes the historical reality that, even though English has become the language of wider communication, we are a multilingual society. All people in a democratic society have the right to education, to employment, to social services, and to equal protection under the law. No one should be denied these or any civil rights because of linguistic differences. This policy would enable everyone to participate in the life of this multicultural nation by ensuring continued respect both for English, our common language, and for the many other languages that contribute to our rich cultural heritage:
>
> **Resolved** that CCC members promote the National Language Policy adopted at the Executive Committee meeting on March 16, 1988. This policy has three inseparable parts:
>
> 1. To provide resources to enable native and nonnative speakers to achieve oral and literate competence in English, the language of wider communication.
> 2. To support programs that assert the legitimacy of native languages and dialects and ensure that proficiency in one's mother tongue will not be lost.
> 3. To foster the teaching of languages other than English so that native speakers of English can rediscover the language of their heritage or learn a second language. (NCTE Resolutions)

In very precise terms, the language policy resolution states that what is wrong with the English Only legislation is that it is unnecessary, unrealistic, educationally unsound, unfair and dangerous, invasive, counterproductive, and unconstitutional.

In 2003 the CCC's executive committee reaffirmed its original SRTOL resolution, and the NCTE passed the resolution, reaffirming the CCC's position statement. NCTE's 2003 affirmation of the SRTOL Resolution is preceded by a background statement:

Background: Since the adoption of the two resolutions in the early 1970's events in public schools and in public policy related to language variation and education have validated the principles of the resolutions. Most notable among these events have been the controversies surrounding policies and practices in several school districts, including Ann Arbor, Michigan, and Oakland, California.

Because issues of language variation and education continue to be of major concern in the twenty-first century to educators, education policymakers, students, parents, and the general public. (Notes of the Commission on Language, 2003)

BE IT RESOLVED that NCTE affirms the resolution on Students' Right to Their Own Language. (NCTE Resolutions)

We can see from this events timeline that critical issues about language moved beyond the social conditions associated with the civil rights movement to social conditions associated with the English Only Movement. Consequently, issues of dialect differences were extended to issues of language differences. Since non-English speakers were entering schools in large numbers, attention was expanded to include concerns over the academic success of students who have come to be called English Language Learners (ELLs) or English Learners (ELs).

The cross-currents are readily apparent in debates over how best to address the needs of minority dialect/language speakers. While some of the chapters in this volume treat issues having to do with bidialectalism, others focus on issues having to do with bilingualism. Just as resolutions continued to evolve in response to changes in social events, the academic arena also changed. In looking at the key SRTOL tenets treated in this book, one sees numerous examples of how SRTOL calls attention to itself as well as to issues beyond those treated in the original SRTOL resolution.

SRTOL and Beyond

To provide a more specific context for framing the reading of the chapters in this book, the eight major SRTOL tenets just listed are grouped into three categories: (1)attitudes toward language, (2)alternate teaching approaches, and (3)the restoration and preservation of the rich multilectal (multiple dialects) and multilingual heritage of the country.

Attitudes toward Language

Language attitudes cover the SRTOL tenets that address myths about inherently superior and inferior dialects and teacher respect for dialect and language differences. Attitudes are treated most directly in Part II of the book. In Chapter 7, Katz, Scott, and Hadjioannou review research on language attitudes, verifying that the conditions addressed by the tenets of SRTOL continue to exist, i.e. negative teacher attitudes toward non-mainstream dialects are linked to myths about standard dialects and inherently superior or inferior dialects. However, Katz and her colleagues move the discussion beyond *language attitudes* to *language ideologies*.

In Chapter 8, Shelton looks at ways to change negative teacher attitudes. She pushes the discussion beyond attitudes to include *language awareness*, beginning with preservice teachers' discoveries of variations in their own language and moving on to explorations of authentic language samples. In Chapter 9, Kirkland and Jackson demonstrate how even the progressive contrastive analysis approach to oral language development, which alert students to structural differences between non-Standard and Standard English, can lead to problems of self-identity. Their discussion shifts attention to *students' attitudes* toward their own language, rather than teachers' attitudes toward students' language.

Related to the issues of attitudes is the question of how languages or dialects attain their high or low status. Beyond being literate about the differential status of languages and dialects, the prevailing view in this book is that students and teachers should be guided to make discoveries about the mechanisms that help determine how language status is achieved. And so, critical literacy is offered as a partial solution to understanding language status. In Chapter 6, Kinloch demonstrates how she uses a critical literacy approach to guide students in their discovery of the power of dominance in determining which languages and language uses attain high status. A critical literacy approach is also suggested by Katz, Scott, and Hadjioannou (Chapter 7) and by Kirkland and Jackson (Chapter 9).

Again, while these chapters call attention to the key tenets of SRTOL having to do with language attitudes, they also move the issues beyond attitudes to language-based ideologies, language awareness, a critical awareness of how dialects and languages attain their status. In reading the chapters on attitude, then, it is important to attend to the relationships between language attitudes and language ideologies, language awareness, and self-identity, as well as to the use of a critical literacy approach to helping students and teachers reach a fuller understanding of language/dialect status.

ALTERNATE TEACHING APPROACHES

Regarding teacher preparation, the SRTOL tenets call for training that will provide alternate approaches to language variation in the classroom. Part III responds to this call, demonstrating again that SRTOL calls attention to itself and beyond with regard to classroom environments and pedagogical strategies. Central to employing alternate approaches to instruction is ensuring that the alternate approaches not only respect, but also use students' home/heritage language as teaching and learning resources and as a means of moving from a pedagogy of failure to a pedagogy of success.

It is important to point out that one of the reasons for respecting students' home language is that the home language or mother tongue is assumed to be directly connected to one's identity or ethnicity. The abandonment of one's heritage language could represent a betrayal of one's identity or ethnicity. Thus, respecting students' heritage language will ideally have the dual effect of enhancing learning as well as fulfilling identity-driven motivations to learn. Beyond associating self-identity with membership in a single ethnic or language community, many have begun to consider membership in multiple communities, including the classroom community. As most readers will readily agree, the extent to which a classroom operates like a community determines if and how much learning takes place. Since classrooms are often made up of students of diverse ethnic and language groups, a typical questions asked by teachers is how am I to create a sense of community with the multiple identities that are present in my language diverse classroom?

In Chapter 10, Yeager and Green call attention to overlapping identities and language practices in classrooms with students from such diverse heritage language backgrounds as English, Spanish, Portuguese, and Vietnamese. Drawing on their research of classrooms, Yeager and Green examine the ways in which teachers who work with linguistically and culturally diverse students discursively construct multiple languages as resources for developing a common classroom language. The chapter also shifts the gaze beyond sociolinguistics to interactional ethnography, demonstrating how interactional ethnography can provide a multilayered, multiscaled way of reconstructing classroom life where members from different language backgrounds create a common language.

There has been much controversy over the practicality of utilizing dialect- or language-specific strategies, as opposed to utilizing adaptive strategies that modify those strategies already being used. The typical teacher question is which one works best? The chapters in Part III suggest that the answers rest not with either-or choices but with both-and possibilities, depending on the classroom situation and the needs of the students. Therefore, with a view toward encouraging teacher decision making and giving teachers choices, both types of instructional strategy are provided in Part III of the book.

Dialect-specific strategies are presented by Wheeler (Chapter 11) in her presentation of the contrastive analysis approach to helping students learn to "code-switch" between their home dialect and Standard English. Katz and Champion (Chapter 12) focus on dialect-specific strategies in their demonstration of different ways that African American and Haitian children tell stories. Language-specific strategies are presented by Fu (Chapter 16) in her examination of new immigrant students and the back and forth switching between two languages found in students' writing. The language-specific strategies continue with Haneda (Chapter 15) in her discussion of English language learners in middle school. On the other hand, adaptive strategies are described in relation to read-alouds by Copenhaver-Johnson, Bowman, and Rietschlin (Chapter 13), in relation to multicultural literature by Jetton, Savage-Davis, and Baker (Chapter 14), and in relation to literature teaching by Anagnostopoulos (Chapter 17).

The chapters in Part III also call attention to but move beyond the theoretical frameworks that informed the original SRTOL tenets having to do with teacher preparation. The traditional and behaviorist oriented approaches to learning were thought to inform deficit orientations to teaching language minority students. A continuum of theoretical frameworks has emerged, ranging from behaviorists to constructivist explanations of learning and teaching. The extreme view of traditionalists was that all instruction should be geared toward teaching Standard English, while the extreme view of behaviorists would be that attention should be focused on what children are to learn, making it unnecessary to attend to students' language backgrounds. The cognitive view holds that learning is developmental; therefore, all have the capacity to develop if given the right circumstances. The sociocognitive view, which is associated with constructivist pedagogy, is that prior language and experience are essential to learning. And so, the experiences associated with students' home/heritage language and culture provide a bridge to new learning. Without a doubt, the sociocognitive and constructivist views directly support the argument that students' home language and culture are an integral part of their prior knowledge. Thus, we now have support for the SRTOL tenets that can be explained in terms of sociocognitive theories of learning where prior knowledge, including knowledge of home-based language and literacy strategies, is essential to building new knowledge.

The chapters in Part III denounce deficit-oriented thinking and are grounded in constructivist pedagogy, whether directly stated or not. Katz and Champion caution against using a deficit approach to evaluating young children's storytelling strategies and offer a sociocognitive framework for understanding variations in the narrative structures of African American and Haitian children. Danling Fu challenges the deficit-oriented assumption that limited capacity to use English accounts for the language-switching' (diglossia) used by English language learners. She offers sociocognitive explanations of language switching linked to situational variants that trigger language choices. Anagnostopoulos demonstrates the drawbacks of a test-driven literature program and the efficacy of a Bakhtinian model for enhancing understanding of literature and giving students greater access to their home/heritage language and culture.

PRESERVATION AND RESTORATION OF THE MULTILECTAL HERITAGE OF THE COUNTRY

The SRTOL tenets speak to the value of preserving the nation's rich store of language and cultural diversity as a means of preparing teachers to understand and support minority students' right to their own language. From a pedagogical perspective, language preservation practices may be hidden in plain view in the U.S., but they are highly visible in other nations. The chapters in Part IV speak directly to ways that other countries have managed bidialectalism and mulilingualism in schools and preserved heritage languages in communities. It is important to read Part IV with a view toward answering this question: What lessons can I as an individual or we as a nation learn from the experiences of the global community about preserving and managing diversity?

On managing bidialectalism, Hadjioannou (Chapter 18) demonstrates how the Greek Cypriot Dialect, a non-Standard dialect, is managed in the classroom along with the Standard Greek dialect. Students use the Greek Cypriot dialect without sanctions, and teachers use the Greek Cypriot dialect for certain types of conversational exchange. Apparently, teachers consciously use the Greek Cypriot dialect to support learning. In a sense, the Greek situation makes use of home or community language in the schools.

In Brazil, *Projecto Aprendiz* (Project Apprentice), a community-based program, actually translated the Freirian principles, many of which are espoused in U.S. reform initiatives, into practice. As demonstrated by Iddings (Chapter 19), a decaying urban area in São Paulo, Brazil, was transformed into a vibrant community school through the creation of sociocultural spaces where the various languages and voices of children could be heard and honored, and the right of expression made sovereign. In short, the authentic use of language contributed to the transformation of individuals as well as the community. Notably, the community took the lead with teaching and learning.

Regarding the growing number children of Mexican descent in U.S. schools, Smith, Luz, and Jiménez (Chapter 20) pose a rhetorical question: Are children of Mexican heritage in your schools or coming to your schools soon? The statistics say "Yes." And these authors offer descriptions of ways in which schools in the U.S. can utilize the literacy practices of students' home to enhance instruction in the schools. Moreover, Videsott (Chapter 21) demonstrates how a school district in Italy prepares teachers to accommodate the needs of a trilingual student population.

On restoring indigenous languages, Kamwangamalu (Chapter 22) moves us to South Africa where the paradoxes over how failures to restore indigenous languages through education can result in a long suffering, slow death of indigenous African languages. Interestingly enough, he views the elite class of South Africans as partners with the ruling classes of colonial intruders in the crime of language death. Not to be overlooked, however, are efforts to revive and restore the indigenous languages of South Africa. Bloch (Chapter 23) details the actions of the Project for the Study of Alternative Education in South Africa (PRAESO) to not only better manage the multilingual situation in schools, but to do so with a view toward restoring, growing and celebrating the indigenous languages of South Africa. The final chapter treats the preservation of heritage languages in India. In Chapter 24, Hock demonstrates how ethnicity is associated with one's heritage language in India, regardless of the types of schools attended. In addition to revealing the naturalness of multlingualism in India, Hock also points to paradoxes confronted by multilingual countries.

There are, indeed, lessons to be learned from the global community about the need for and ways to manage and preserve language diversity. Part IV moves the key tenets of SRTOL beyond the boundaries of the United States to the global community where bidialectalism and bilingualism are widely accepted and considered the norm, but they are managed in very different ways. As well, the restoration and preservation of indigenous languages are often protected in the constitution as well as in educational policies, but the mechanisms for doing so vary considerably and have their own cross-currents to be resolved. Looking beyond our immediate boundaries is at least one of the promising ways of exploring alternative ways of affirming students' rights to their own language and bridging educational policies to pedagogical practices.

References

Brown v. Board of Education, 347 U.S. 483 (1954).

Castañeda v. Pickard, 648 F.2d 989 (5th Cir.1981).

Conference on College Composition and Communication. (1974). Students' Right to Their Own Language [electronic version]. *College Composition and Communication*, 25, 1–65.

———. (1988, 1992). National Language Policy. Retrieved December 27, 2007, from http://www.ncte.org/cccc/resources/positions/123796.htm.

English Plus Information Clearinghouse. (1987). The English Plus Alternative. Retrieved December 28, 2007, from http://ourwolrd.compuserve.com/homepages/JWCRAWFORD/EPIC.htm.

Farrington v. Tokushige 273 U.S. 284, 298 (1927).

Lau v. Nichols, 414 U.S. 563, 565 [1974].

Martin Luther King Jr. Elem. Sch. v. Ann Arbor Sch. Dist. Bd., 473 F. Supp. 1371 (E.D. Mich. 1979).

Meyer v. Nebraska, 262 U.S. 390 (1923).

National Council of Teachers of English. (1986). On English as the "Official language." Retrieved December 28, 2007, from http://www.ncte.org/about/over/positions/category/lang/107499.htm.

———. (2003). On Affirming the CCCC "Students' Right to Their Own Language." Retrieved December 27, 2007, from http://www.ncte.org/about/over/positions/category/lang/114918.htm.

No Child Left Behind Act 2001. (2002). P.L. 107-119. Retrieved January 15, 2007, from http://www.ed.gov/policy/elsec/let/esea02/107-110.

Plessy v. Ferguson, 163 U.S. 537 (1896).

Rios v. Read, 480 F. Supp. 14 (E.D.N.Y. 1978).

Serna v. Portales Mun. Schs., 499 F.2d 1147 (10th Cir. 1974).

Students' Right to Their Own Language. (1974). *College Composition and Communication*, 25, 1–32.

U.S. v. Texas, 506 F. Supp. 405 (E.D.N.Y. 1978).

Wiley, T. G. (2002). Accessing Language Rights in Education: A Brief History of the U.S. Context. In J. W. Tollefson (Ed.). *Language Policies in Education.* Mahwah, NJ: Lawrence Erlbaum Associates, Inc.

2

Perspectives on Language Policies and Pedagogical Practices

Interview 1: Issues in Global and Local Language Policies

Joel Spring

Question: How do language policies in education create inequalities among learners?

There are a lot of different levels to that question. One is a global level. For instance, the way to approach this is to look at the birth of Esperanto in the 19th century. Esperanto was designed, among other things, to create world peace. One of its goals was to create an international language that could easily be learned by everyone in society so that you wouldn't have growth of inequality, where there would be some who didn't know the international language and there would be some who did. Unfortunately, Esperanto never took hold. That leaves us with the choice of two global languages right now, English and Mandarin. So in many countries where they're not English speaking, those who speak English are the ones in terms of class who are able to move into the international corporations and global economy. So, on a global scale, we are seeing the difference between those who know English and those who don't know English, or those who know Mandarin and those who don't know Mandarin. Then, in a particular nation, any subset within the nation who doesn't participate in the dominant language, obviously, has a level of dispossession from the economy and the political system. And, then of course it depends on what happens in the schools with the learning of the non-dominant language speakers.

Question: What occurs when a country's language policies are intended to promote equality and those goals aren't actually realized?

There are two countries that come to mind. If we look at the U.K., in a global sense in terms of colonial policy, the British wanted to impose their culture for the purposes of controlling a nation like India. So, English became a standard for bureaucracies in India and other British colonies. Many of those colonists traveled to England to absorb the culture. You could say British intentions on the surface were "oh, we're going to let everyone participate in the great language of the world and read the great literature." Lord Macaulay said Sanskrit was only worth a shelf compared to all the British literature.

But that's changed recently. Now, English as a global language is being learned in India for economic reasons and not for cultural reasons. The British thought they were doing good. If you asked them, they were civilizing the uncivilized. But in fact, they were bringing them in under hegemonic control of the monarchy.

For instance, in call centers in India that handle phone calls from a variety of international businesses from software to airlines, workers are learning English not because of colonial domination but because of the global economy. And the argument from a lot of linguists is that they're learning English for the purposes of "economic advancement." In the process, they're using textbooks to learn English that contain traditional Hindi stories and mythologies. And when they watch television, they watch American television, but it's either dubbed or subtitled in Hindi. So, it's really a complicated situation.

Another example is the groups that were conquered by the United States. The government tried to eradicate languages and cultures with the claim, "We're doing this for your good so that you can become part of the United States." This resulted in creating subclasses within the population. I think of particularly when Puerto Rico was conquered in 1898, the Native Americans when they were conquered, Hawaii when it was conquered, and in the Mexican–American War when most of the southwest including California and Texas was lost by Mexico. And in all of those situations, the educational policies of the United States government was to replace, at least to attempt to replace those languages, with English. And, again using the rhetoric, "Oh this was for their good", when in fact it just created subgroups within the population.

Question: You often hear the argument that it's important for persons in the United States whose primary language is other than English to learn English for economic reasons. You don't hear much about maintaining one's primary language for cultural reasons.

This is due to the success of the conservative English Only language movement which became embodied within the No Child Left Behind legislation. When the bilingual education movement began in the 50s, it was for the purpose of maintaining culture. And the groups involved in that were the Native Americans, Puerto Ricans, Hawaiians, and Mexican-Americans. And they saw bilingual education not as a way to learn English but as a way of maintaining their languages and their cultures. And after the bilingual education act was passed in the 1960s, there was immediate reaction to that by conservatives in the form of the English Only Movement.

When we get to No Child Left Behind, when it was passed in 2001, signed in 2002, what happens is that the conservatives win. They eliminate the Office of Bilingual Education and replace it with the Office of English Acquisition.

Question: Do you think there is a cultural divide between people who believe it's important to learn English for economic reasons and those who believe it's important to maintain one's primary language for cultural reasons?

The two can flow together. Arthur Schlesinger Jr. recently died. He was a major advocate eliminating multicultural education. He argued that the founding fathers actually represented the highest political and economic ideals and created institutions that are the foundation of the United States. For him, learning English and learning American culture, were very important for maintaining traditional American society.

Most immigrant populations in the United States, like other global workers, want to learn English so that they can participate fully in the economic system. And so, it's important to provide those people who want to learn English with the opportunity to learn it. But at the same time, then the question comes up, "Well, what about people who also want to maintain their own language as a culture?" And that's where the school, where it becomes an issue for the school, whether it does that or not. The No Child Left Behind sort of closed the door for a while on that argument.

I believe in language and cultural rights. There is a compulsory educational law that requires people to go to school. Furthermore, under the Lau decision, the schools already have an obligation to assure that students learn English. However, there's no obligation to maintain the language and culture of minority groups.

Learning English does not result in speaking the same English. There are world Englishes. Nigerian English is different from Indian English. Also, English and cultural instruction can vary depending on the global job. When Indians are trained for call centers, they're trained according to what call center they're going to be working for. If they're going to be working for a call center that serves with Australians, they will be trained to understand and speak in an accent that is Australian and learn a smattering of Australian culture, or something about Australia. In reality, what is left of the British Empire's drive to make English the global language is Englishes. It is sometimes difficult for Americans to understand other Englishes.

Question: Well, do you think then, when you look at an English learner who is in a fifth grade classroom, that she get's training in English relevant to a particular region?

That would seem logical. If you were in Alabama and you were learning English, you would probably speak a dialect of English very similar to the traditional Southern English while learning to spell in American English, as opposed to say British English.

The same thing holds for Spanish, which is another major imperialist language. There are many varieties of spoken Spanish resulting from the Spanish Empire.

Question: English has been the dominant language but there's evidence that this might change. What languages will be dominant within the context of globalization?

The competitive language right now is Mandarin. In fact, more people speak Mandarin than speak English. And, Mandarin is mentioned in the People's Republic of China Constitution. It's supposed to be the national language. Now there are a lot of different languages in China, but the national language is Mandarin. So, some people will argue that's the major competitive language.

It appears that English will continue to dominate. It's the language of the internet. The majority of scholarly articles in the world are published in English. Pilots have to learn English for flying. You can go down the whole list of things that make English dominant today. It looks like it will remain a global language.

And so, U.S. schools and No Child Left Behind seems to have just taken on a policy that the rest of the world is going to speak English, so we don't have to worry that much about foreign language training. And in the recent agenda from the Department of Education on world competitiveness and on language issues, stress is placed on the teaching of languages that have military and security interests, such as Arabic.

Question: What impact does the power of the group have on what becomes the most competitive language? I mean, right now the U.S. is a world power, do we expect a power shift?

It appears that for historic reasons, English will continue to be dominant. It's not just because of the actions of the United States, it's really more because of the actions of the British, particularly in the 19th and early 20th century . . . that for those historic reasons at this point, it appears to be English. Now, there have been competitors in the past, especially from European colonialists. One was France, which is really upset. French didn't become a global language. And in fact, in a recent meeting of former colonies in Vietnam, the only common language the participants had was English, not French.

But power is important. And I say that it has gotten to a point where it may be that no other language will really suffice and that English has become independent, in a way, from any particular nation. It's now a global economic language. The other country that tried to make its language dominant and that saw itself as an imperialist power was Russia. Russia went through a Russiafication program when they imposed the learning of Russian on their vast empire. The other country was Japan. Japan tried to impose Japanese on its colonies and throughout World War II. The learning of Japanese was required in Korea, Taiwan, and Manchuria. Japan hoped Japanese would be the global language.

We could hope for a simpler language to learn. Most countries, not all but most, are mandating the study of English in schools. You begin to see the development of social classes based on the knowledge of English. Between those who know English and those who don't. Knowledge of English is important for participating in the global economy.

Question: Could you speak more about the role of the so-called 'New Englishes' in the process of globalization?

Going back to the term Englishes, if you grow up in Nigeria and you learn English, even though your English is different from that of a person in India, you'll still know enough English to participate in an international corporation and sell your oil.

Question: So the idea of the new Englishes is making sure that you can communicate or you have the ability to be a part of the power structure, or to be part of the whole economic sphere?

That's generally why people in other countries now choose to learn English. And that doesn't mean that there isn't resentment and resistance. After all those who think "We have to learn this language to be able to work for this oil company" are bound to build resentments.

Question: Do you see any evidence of resentment across the country by English speakers who are being forced to learn Spanish in areas of the U.S. that are dominated by Spanish speakers? Or, does the learning of Spanish on a broader scale mean we're kind of giving in to a kind of bilingualism for the future or something?

Considering Spanish as a language that is popular to learn in the United States, the argument for that began, I would say, in the 1890s with arguments for including more Spanish in American schools. However, those arguments were offered in the context of trade with South America and Central America where Spanish was thought to be necessary and in terms of pan-American interests. Today, it's becoming a reality that a large part of the population is Spanish. So that in the United States, there is that sort of competitive situation going on. But in reality, people might learn Spanish but at this point, the global economy is primarily using English. To a certain extent, I can see in the No Child Left Behind policies, the English acquisition part, knowledge of Spanish helps in teaching kids English.

Question: What other key issues regarding language should teachers know so they can better understand the present and the future in terms of language policies and practices?

Well, it depends on what your goal is. In other words, it's hard for me to get my mind around that question because of the question of intentionality. First, teachers should understand a little bit about the history of language policy in the United States and U.S. schools so they understand what the debate is about. Many teachers don't truly understand that the debate is also over language and culture. So, the question becomes what part of that debate that you personally want to pursue. Now, I'm an advocate of language and cultural rights worldwide. So, I have proposed an amendment to the United States Constitution that would be an education amendment. You know, there's no mention of education in the U.S. Constitution. But every modern constitution written since World War II defines education as a right. And that's where we get into school finance issues here because it's not in the Constitution . . . so I would be in favor of including in an amendment the right to maintain your culture and your language so that we don't have policies like English Only, which are now part of No Child Left Behind. I have written a book on the globalization of educational rights including language rights. Teachers should learn about this, but I'm sure that what they learn varies from school to school, or from course to course, depending on who's teaching or whether it's been mandated in the college to teach about educational rights and language policies.

Question: Could you talk a bit more about the amendment that you're proposing?

In most constitutions written since the beginning of the 20th century education is considered a right. When the U.S. Constitution was written, public schooling and education was not considered that important and consequently was never mentioned in the Constitution. So, when school finance came up, for example the one from Texas, the Supreme Court refused to review it because they said: "Hey, this is not part of the Constitution. Education is not mentioned in the Constitution; this is something that should be handled by the states." And so, we've never had a ruling at the Federal level that people have to be provided with equality of educational opportunity regarding the financing of schools. So, that's how I started thinking about an amendment to the constitution. My next step was to think about other things that I would make a part of the amendment. Having a Native American background, I've been very concerned about language and culture, particularly the destruction that took place with Native American language and culture. And so, looking at that and then worldwide policies, I thought a very important part of that amendment would be that people have a right to their culture and language in schools.

Question: How do some policies marginalize some students while granting privileges to others?

I would say that the current No Child Left Behind legislation marginalizes some students. We could go through a whole range of ways that teachers can marginalize students, and they can immediately marginalize them by not recognizing or giving help or trying to offer support for students for whom English is a second language and not a first language. Again, I want to stress that under the No Child Left Behind legislation the emphasis is no longer on maintaining other languages and cultures, except possibly for Native Americans. The goal of the legislation is to make everyone monocultural and monolingual. But this could change overnight. Diane Ravitch, a conservative advocate and one time supporter of No Child Left Behind, recently gave a speech to the American Association of Colleges for Teacher Education. You wouldn't believe it. She doesn't want the legislation reauthorized. She's calling for more arts in the schools, and she's really abandoned the whole conservative agenda that went into No Child Left Behind.

Interview 2: An Insider's View of African American Language Policies and Pedagogies

Geneva Smitherman

Question: What do you think was the key impact on pedagogical practices in the court case of Martin Luther King School v. Ann Arbor School District?

First, for the historical record, let me state the formal name of this Federal court case: *Martin Luther King Junior Elementary School Children, et al. v. Ann Arbor School District Board.* The case was filed in 1977 in the Federal courthouse, which happens to be located in Detroit, Michigan, and the trial took place in Detroit during the month of July, 1979. The lawyers brought me on board right after they filed the suit in July of 1977, and for the next two years I worked closely with them, attended several of the pre-trial hearings, interviewed and tape recorded the children, and in early 1979, I pulled together a team of linguists and educators from around the country who came to Detroit to testify in the trial on behalf of the plaintiff children and their parents.

Now, I know yall ain ask me to talk about the case in detail, but one thing I think it's important to note is that the case was not originally about language. Although most people have come to know this as the "Black English" case, that was not the main issue that brought those Green Road housing project parents to file suit against the Ann Arbor School Board. Rather, the main concern of these single Black female household heads was poor, inadequate, improper pedagogical practices and policies. King School was not educating their kids, most of whom were boys. (So the problem we see in Black education today, with Black boys being undereducated and oh so many not graduating, dates back quite a number of years.) Instead of the teachers educating their kids and, especially for these parents, instead of the teachers teaching their kids how to read, King School just called them "learning disabled" and placed them in special classrooms and groups. One of these special classroom groups was speech therapy, which is how the language angle eventually got worked into the case.

During the two years of hearings and meetings before the trial, Judge Joiner dismissed the improper labeling and other educational issues and left us with only the language angle, which was contained in a one-sentence provision in the 1974 Equal Educational Opportunity Act (EEOA). This provision makes it a violation for any state to deny equal educational access to students due to their race, color, sex, national origin, and/or the state's "failure to overcome language barriers that impede equal participation by its students in its instructional programs." The case focused solely on language, one crucial educational impact we had hoped would have never got litigated. And so today, nearly three decades later, large and disproportionate numbers of Black boys are still being placed in special education classes. Forgive the digression, but this is one of the main reasons that our "victory" in the King court case is filed in the bittersweet section of my memory bank.

So, what impact did this "Black English" court case have on pedagogical practices? One thing—and in retrospect, this seemed to have happened pretty quickly—was a policy change among speech therapists and pathologists working in the schools. They stopped placing Black kids in speech therapy classes for their use of patterns of African American language (AAL). A great deal of private and public funding and professional research resources were focused on developing valid instruments and clinical assessments that would allow speech professionals to differentiate Black kids who were language impaired from those who were simply normal speakers of their AAL/home language. And certification standards and ethics criteria were developed to penalize and/or deny licenses to school speech therapists/pathologists in violation of these professional standards.

In the English language arts world, there was a revival of the teacher training programs, workshops, seminars, etc., on AAL and linguistic diversity in general, that had been so prevalent in school districts during the 1960s and early 1970s. With all of the national (and international) media focused on King, school districts across the nation took notice and got scared that they might be next to be sued by parents and kids. So they got busy. For a few years in the 1980s, there were mad [that is, a lot of] language workshops for teachers in many school districts. In some of these districts, maybe in many of them, the lessons learned had an impact on instruction as language arts teachers began to de-emphasize rote grammar and usage drills and simplistic notions undergirding the "national mania for correctness," as one sociolinguist put it years ago, and instead began to emphasize and incorporate lessons about writing as process, about content logic, reasoning, variety of expression, development of ideas, etc.—in short, about the things that are really fundamental in communication and in students' journey toward literacy. In fact, the Academic English Mastery Program (AEMP) in the Los Angeles Unified School District and the Standard English Proficiency (SEP) program in several other Cali school districts, were started shortly after 1979, the year of the King decision. The AEMP, especially, is great! Props to Dr. Noma LeMoine, the visionary who brought this program into being. It deals not only with AAL speaking kids but all English language learners and teaches from a code-switching, bilingual, cultural, historical literacy perspective.

But now it's 2007, and like so many socio-educational reforms in the U.S.—in, as hip hop artist Eminem called them, these "divided states of embarrassment"—language training programs and creative language instructional energies done fell off. When it comes to AAL and other non-dominant languages and varieties, when it comes to issues of linguistic diversity, when it comes to fundamental knowledge and practices about what it means to learn and teach and know language and literacy, too many teachers today ain got a clue. And the teacher preparation programs, the pre- and inservice professional development programs that are charged with preparing these teachers to meet the challenge of what has become an even more diverse, multilingual, multidialectal world than in the King era—well, I ain gon name no names, but sooooooo many of these programs is jes plain pitiful.

Question: Why were people so emotionally charged during the Oakland case? What was occurring in the political climate at that time? What impact did the Oakland case have on pedagogical practices?

Okay, first, before somebody git it twisted, there wasn't an "Oakland case," i.e., in the sense of a court case, like with King v. Ann Arbor. The situation in Oakland involved a resolution that the Oakland School Board issued on December 18, 1996. Oakland's "Ebonics resolution" committed the board, and by extension, its teachers, to a recognition and acknowledgement that the primary, home language of its African American students was "Ebonics" and that this language should be used as the medium of instruction in school subjects and to teach those students "Standard English." Folks heard this new (to them) name, "Ebonics" and something about Ebonics and Black kids and school, and all hell broke loose. The term "Ebonics" actually dates back to 1973 and was coined by Black psychologist Robert Williams at a conference. In its original conceptualization, Ebonics was used to label all of the African–European language mixtures—including pidgins and creoles— that had developed out of enslavement and colonialism. Although in the popular mind "Ebonics" is equated solely with the mixture that developed in the U.S., that is an imprecise, and some linguists argue, an inaccurate formulation. For one thing, linguists in this camp consider the African language dimension as the primary base of the language. Since there are several other languages and regions classified under the Ebonics language tree, I use the term "U.S. Ebonics" to reflect this conceptualization.

Of course didn nobody bother to read the Oakland School District's African American Task Force's report, background for the Oakland Board's Ebonics resolution, nor to read/learn about the abysmal achievement level and status of Black kids in the Oakland Schools. And with the media in charge, nobody bothered to read the Ebonics resolution itself, which is how come they-own know bout the commitment to "facilitate their [Oakland Black students'] acquisition and mastery of English language skills" [from the resolution].

The Oakland resolution involved not simply language, but the language of Black kids—hence, the emotional reaction. Race, and anything to do with race, is still a hot button issue in the U.S. Folks were just as emotionally charged during the period of the "Black English" case two decades before Oakland. I will never forget the Black woman journalist who said, in her article about the King case, that the children could learn to read if their mothers would get the books in and the boyfriends out. Despite all the claims of a "colorblind" society today, race is still paramount in the social consciousness, thought and behavior of both Blacks and Whites. Everybody jes be playin like race and skin color don't count. But incident after incident keep poppin up to let us know that, as Cornel West say, "race matters." Last year (2006), in the sixth year of this 21st century, in Jena, Louisiana, when a Black student, with permission from school administrators, sat under the "White tree" at his high school; White kids hung nooses from the tree. The Black students protested this segregation, one Black kid was beaten up for attending an all-White off-campus party (that he had been invited to), a White kid pulled a shotgun on him and two of his friends at a store, etc., etc. The upshot of this well-worn tale is that six Black kids—the "Jena Six"—are now facing criminal charges and prison. The White students were only given 3-day suspensions.

In the case of the Oakland Ebonics resolution, the race language element angered middle class Blacks as well as Whites—in part because what it called attention to was a painful reminder of the fact that we are still two separate societies, which the Kerner Commission, in its report on "civil disturbances" of the period, warned us about way back in the late 1960s. The Black middle class continues to be ambivalent about Black language and culture. And today there is an ever widening generational and class gap in African America, which was sadly evident in the national Black community's varying reactions to Oakland's resolution. For example, compare the hip hop magazine, *The Source's*, coverage of this event with national media coverage of the objections of Maya Angelou, who made her name using U.S. Ebonics in her poetry and fiction, and Reverend Jesse Jackson, who rhymes and preaches in U.S. Ebonics. After talking to Stanford linguist John Rickford when he made the trip out to Oakland, Jesse had a change of heart.

Now, it's not that middle-class Bloods don't speak African American language/ U.S. Ebonics. In their private social gatherings, they can be heard using many of the rhetorical and semantic styles, as well as some of the syntactical and phonological patterns of AAL. This is a reflection of the "linguistic push–pull" that I first described back in the 1970s. The "political climate," then, can best be described as a racialized one; so it was in 1977, in 1996, and today in 2007.

I am not aware of any significant impact that the Oakland Ebonics resolution had on pedagogical practices. Certainly it did serve to once again sound the clarion call about the issue of Black English in schools and society. Additionally, some amount of Federal funding—one source (who insisted on anonymity) says it was about a million dollars—was eventually allocated to the educational situation in Oakland. This grant served primarily to fund the research of one or two linguists who gathered language data on kids in some of the Oakland schools. I am vague on this because it was all kept on the loh loh, and I haven't seen any published reports of this work.

Question: What do you think is the most significant event in the history of the development of Black English and why?

I'm still waiting for it. Seriously. However, if you force me to just arbitrarily pick something, I would say two events: (1) the King case and (2)African American language use in hip hop.

The King case is significant because it brought AAL out of the academic and hood closets and wrote its name into the legal history of this country. King was, after all, a unique court case in the annals of Black civil rights legislative history. Further, because of the voluminous and prolific media coverage, both nationally and internationally, people who had not given much thought to "Black English" or language in general, who had just taken language for granted all their lives, were forced to think about the role of language, not only in education but in daily life, e.g., What does it mean to talk a certain way? Why does it matter? What does language have to do with learning the "three rs"? Why do Black folks talk a certain way and White folks another certain way? But then what about Blacks and Whites talking in the South? Is there a connection between a certain way of talking and your intelligence? etc., etc. These are just some of the questions and issues that were raised among educators, policymakers, and just plain everyday people in beauty and barbershops, at family reunions, in church, and in other venues in the Black community.

The use of African American Language by hip hop artists has created a venue for creative development and linguistic innovations in "Black English." One young scholar, both a hip hop head and journalist, as well as a Stanford-trained socio-linguist, H.Samy Alim, has done some very important research and scholarship showcasing the contribution of hip hop to the contemporary advancement and development of AAL. Further, because of the global dispersion of hip hop, features and patterns of AAL are now known, used and spoken in Germany, Japan, the Caribbean, South America, Nigeria, South Africa, France, the Netherlands, and other places far removed from the home of U.S. slave descendants.

Interview 3: The Law of Language in the United States

Christina M. Rodríguez

Question: How do language policies in education create inequities for participants of differing language minority communities?

The public schools are required by law to ensure equal access to education for all linguistic minority students. In Lau v. Nichols in 1974, the Supreme Court found that the San Francisco schools had violated their obligations under Title VI of the Civil Rights Act of 1964 by failing to provide adequate English language instruction for students of Chinese parentage (Lau v. Nichols 1974). Since Lau, Department of Education regulations have obligated schools to fulfill the decision's promise, and today's No Child Left Behind Act requires local schools to provide language instruction that increase English language proficiency and overall academic achievement.

But despite an elaborate legal framework intended to guide the decision making of local school districts in pursuit of these equality goals, inequities inevitably arise, for two primary reasons. First, linguistic minorities who make up a small percentage of a local school district's population can be more difficult to serve directly. Not only is Federal funding contingent on the percentage of English language learners (ELLs) in the student population, resources in the form of qualified teachers are also less plentiful for students whose native languages are not widely spoken minority languages like Spanish or Mandarin. In school districts with deeply diverse student populations, moreover, smaller minorities are less likely to be served with programs tailored specifically to their needs and with teachers adept in that minority's language. That said, among the pathologies attributed to bilingual education is the isolation of linguistic minority students from the larger student population for years at a time—a fate more likely to affect students who come from a heavily represented minority group, namely Spanish speakers.

Second, and more important, because ELLs are more likely to attend poor performing or under-resourced schools, their educational development is more likely to suffer as the result of general inequities in the system. Language programs often disserve ELLs not because bilingual education is an inherently flawed method of instruction, but because of "inept, passive-aggressive, or outright hostile administration," (Suárez-Orozco, Roos, & Suárez-Orozco, 2000, pp. 189–190), tendencies compounded by lack of funding and overcrowding. This larger problem of educational inequity is made worse by the persistence of de facto segregated schools. And, in the case of language minorities in particular, uneven access to quality language instruction is exacerbated by the fact that immigrant children today, in unprecedented numbers, live in parts of the United States today with little to no experience educating ELLs (Waters & Jiménez, 2005). Indeed, the dramatic rise in the number of ELLs in the so-called new immigration states, such as Georgia and North Carolina, fuels state and local efforts to crack down on illegal immigration, in large part because the rising ELL population is taxing the public schools in unfamiliar ways.

Question: Most people want to participate in the institutions of civic life, so it is important to provide them with the opportunity to learn English. At the same time, what language rights does one have if she wants to maintain her own culture through language?

To the extent that a right to protect one's culture exists, it can be located in the principle of intimate, familial association recognized as part of the ordered liberty guaranteed by the Due Process Clause of the Fourteenth Amendment. In Meyer v. Nebraska, a foundational case protecting this liberty interest, the Supreme Court struck down a state law that prohibited the teaching of any modern language other than English before the ninth grade. The court recognized not only the liberty of the language teacher to engage in instruction, as well as the student's right to acquire knowledge, but also the parent's right to control his or her child's education. The court thus acknowledged that parents have a "profound interest in cultural transmission," (Rodríguez, 2006) and that parental autonomy has served as the vehicle through which cultural pluralism has persisted in the United States (Minow, 2000). In a sense, Meyer acknowledges that a language lives or dies in the educational sphere, and that parents and local school officials should be free to elect the culture they pass on to their children.

This negative liberty is limited as a means of preserving culture through language, however—a limitation evident when we compare the American approach to the language rights protected by the constitution of Canada. The Charter of Rights and Freedoms establishes that French and English have equal status throughout Canada, reflecting a constitutional commitment to the survival of both languages. Among the mechanisms for preserving the minority French language is the constitutional guarantee of the right to an education in one's mother tongue, whether French or English, and the corresponding right to minority-run schools. No analogous right exists in U.S. law. Though parents and schools cannot be prohibited from teaching languages other than English, the state is simply not obligated to provide affirmative assistance in linguistic or cultural maintenance.

The negative liberty the U.S. Constitution affords is not trivial. It protects the rights of language minorities in the private sphere to maintain institutions such as foreign language presses, and to use non-English languages freely. These very basic rights have been denied language minorities around the world throughout history: the Kurds in Turkey and Catalan speakers in Franco's Spain are but two examples of groups whose languages have been banned altogether. But the right to preserve one's language remains largely a private right in the United States, one the state affirmatively supports only to the extent that language minorities win recognition of their linguistic interests through the political process.

The civil rights laws do provide some protection for those whose preference or natural inclination is to speak a language other than English. An Executive Order issued by President Clinton and reaffirmed by President Bush interpreted Title VI of the Civil Rights Act of 1964 to require all recipients of Federal funds to make their programs accessible to non-English speakers, and the Equal Employment Opportunity Commission has interpreted Title VII of the same Act to make English Only workplace rules presumptive violations of the law. States such as California and Illinois also have passed laws that restrain employers' authority to restrict the languages their employees may speak. These protections arguably enable language minorities to use and maintain their languages in the public sphere, and they require public entities to structure their institutions to make space for language minorities. But, as I explain later, most of these protections are transitional in nature, or intended to facilitate language minorities' move into the English speaking mainstream, not to recognize the right of linguistic minorities in and of themselves.

Question: What key issues should teachers know so they can better understand the present and the future with respect to language policies and practices?

Bilingual education is often discussed as if it represents a single method of instruction, in contradistinction to its opposite of English immersion. In reality, a range of language instruction programs exist, and even so-called English immersion programs function more effectively when staffed by teachers who can communicate with students in their native languages. What is more, though acquisition of English language fluency and literacy is of utmost importance, an English-at-all costs mentality should not be permitted to dictate the choice of a language instruction methodology, if that methodology would otherwise sacrifice the development of students' analytical capacities in other areas.

The testing regime implemented by the No Child Left Behind Act encourages the tendency to focus on short-term English language gains at the expense of long-term overall achievement. As the result of Federal mandates, local school districts and teachers may find that they have no choice but to prioritize forms of instruction that yield better immediate test results, regardless of their long-term pay off. But it is crucial not to lose sight of the long-term implications of policy choices designed to meet immediate external pressures.

Research on the success rates of various forms of language instruction is neither as thorough nor as comprehensive as necessary to sustain a true consensus about which methods work best. The success of a particular form of instruction is likely to depend on the language minority in question, as well as the resources—both monetary and human—available to particular school districts. In a resource-poor district, for example, an English immersion program may be the best option.

That said, evidence supports the conclusion that students schooled in well-run bilingual programs outperform their peers educated in English Only classrooms (Krashen, 1999), and that well-designed and properly resourced bilingual programs work best at promoting English language literacy in the long term, as well as at ensuring cognitive development and achievement in other subjects (Thomas & Collier, 2003). Bilingual education programs that lack trained teachers, adequate instructional materials, and community support are, not surprisingly, less likely to be successful.

The lesson from the empirical literature is that the critiques of bilingual education that tar all bilingual programs with the same brush reduce complex questions to political sound bites and should therefore be regarded with skepticism. At the end of the day, the investment of public resources, as well as administrative confidence, in the education of ELLs remains the key to improving the quality of education language minorities receive, whether the form of instruction chosen involves heavy or limited reliance on the students' native languages.

It is also worth noting that, in the language instruction debate, little if any value is placed on the retention of the native language, or on the fostering of bilingualism. But many parents and school officials across the country have recognized bilingualism's benefits by adopting dual language programs, which school language minorities and native English speakers together, promoting retention of native languages and extending the benefits of bilingualism to all students. The Center for Applied Linguistics estimates that over 300 such programs existed in 2006. Large cities such as Miami and Seattle, and small towns such as Beardstown, Illinois, and Jacksonville, Texas, have jumped on this bandwagon.

Evidence suggests that bilingually schooled children, regardless of their native language, demonstrate higher levels of long-term achievement than their mono-lingually schooled peers (Thomas & Collier, 2003). When designed to meet the needs of ELLs, dual language programs also address perhaps the greatest drawback to bilingual instruction—the isolation of language minorities from the rest of the student population. To be sure, dual language programs addressed to ELLs and not simply to children with preexisting bilingual capacity will have to be designed with ELLs' pressing need to learn English in mind. But parents, schools, and teachers should be open to this increasingly popular form of experimentation.

In addition to producing educational benefits, dual language programs have participatory or democracy-enhancing benefits (Rodríguez, 2006). Such programs integrate language minority students while helping them retain ties to the cultures of their parents and communities. Such programs also enable native English speakers to connect to and develop a sense of affiliation with subgroups within the larger body politic, thus increasing connections across group lines and helping to normalize the presence of linguistic minorities in American society—an essential component of immigrant integration. Relatedly, dual language instruction exposes native English speakers to the experience of learning a new language, or of having to operate in a language one does not fully control, likely enhancing empathy with and tolerance of language minorities. And, on an instrumental level, because dual language programs equip native English speakers and language minorities alike with the invaluable skill of bilingualism, they enhance all students' educational profiles, better equipping them to operate in a multiethnic country and a globalized economy.

Question: In your brief, you discuss institutions of civic life such as the courtroom, the classroom, the workplace and the administrative state. Would you discuss how giving students access to their own language is important to their participation in these spheres of civic life.

We must begin from the premise that our linguistic profile is defined by what I call the mutability continuum of language (Rodríguez, 2006). Even as the children and grandchildren of immigrants become native English speakers, the ongoing entrance of new immigrants will ensure that speech communities made up of non-English speaking immigrants, their English speaking descendants, and a range of bilinguals in between will continue to populate our society. Even the second and third generation descendants of immigrants, who will inevitably be English dominant, will retain ties to linguistically diverse speech communities. As a result, we have an interest in facilitating at least three types of communication: communication within linguistic minority communities; communication among individuals from different communities; and communication between subcommunities and the body politic generally. Language minority students growing up in the United States and being educated in our public schools are uniquely positioned to engage in each of these forms of communication, or to serve as the bilingual bridges that will help to keep our society woven together.

Finally, though the benefits of being able to communicate in English across groups and with the mainstream are substantial and well appreciated, the importance of staving off language loss is not. But children's loss of their capacity to speak a home language can have dramatic implications for family relations, introducing distance into the parent–child relationship and undermining the ability of parents to pass on values, skills, and advice (Fillmore, 2005). Language loss also separates children from the larger social networks that make up the world in which they reside. For many immigrant groups, affiliation with the minority community is crucial to the accumulation of social capital necessary for survival and social development in a new society. As new research on the phenomenon of so-called segmented assimilation is demonstrating, for some immigrant children, remaining closely connected to immigrant networks increases the chances of educational and economic success, because of the stability and community such closeness provides (Portes & Zhou, 2005). Nurturing bilingualism fosters this connection and is thus essential to the successful adaptation and development of many immigrant students.

Question: You state that "Courts have not understood the 'right' in question as a right to language, but as a right to the English language." Would you mind discussing that statement in more detail.

Language rights in the American context are transitional rights, or rights belonging to individuals unable to speak English. In contrast to the language rights protected under the Canadian constitution, which include the rights of French and English speakers to interact with the state in their mother tongue, language rights in the United States largely cease to exist once one has acquired English speaking ability.

In the context of bilingual education, for example, it is understood that children from language minority groups in the public schools have a civil rights interest in language instruction that promotes English language proficiency and overall academic achievement. The right is thus to an equal educational opportunity, not a right to maintain or preserve the mother tongue. With one outlying and dated exception, the Federal courts have never interpreted this civil rights imperative to require bilingual or bicultural education. Instead, they have required school districts to use their judgment about the best means to promote English language acquisition. Courts evaluate those judgments based on a three-part test. School must base their language instruction program on a legitimate educational theory recognized as sound. The program must be implemented effectively, and schools must devote resources and personnel to ensuring that the theory becomes reality. And the program must be evaluated after a trial period to ensure that the school does not persist in ineffective methods of instruction (Castañeda v. Pickard). The touchstone for evaluation is success in promoting English language proficiency alongside academic achievement, which is measured through English language testing, not in terms of native language maintenance.

Federal and state statutes protect various other language rights, but as with the right to educational opportunity, they are rights intended to assist those in the process of learning English, not to protect the interests of language groups qua language groups. Perhaps the most widely known and controversial example of this sort of transitional language right is the Voting Rights Act's requirement that jurisdictions whose language minority populations surpass a set threshold provide bilingual ballots and oral voting assistance during elections. This amendment was added to the Act in 1975 to address language minorities' effective exclusion from the polls, particularly in Texas, and was seen as compensation for the failure of the public schools to teach English adequately to language minorities. Bilingual ballots remain required by law today and are justified by the theory that all citizens, regardless of their linguistic abilities, should be able to participate in democracy. But they would no longer be necessary as a matter of law were English universally used.

In a similar vein, the importance of enabling participation by language minorities was recognized by President Clinton when he issued the Executive Order mentioned earlier. Pursuant to the order, law enforcement, healthcare providers, state and local governments, and all other recipients of Federal funds must therefore make a reasonable effort to provide for translation and interpretation of their services. This obligation is only triggered, however, when a fund recipient serves a community made up of a substantial number of limited English proficient individuals. In other words, bilingual services are contingent upon the existence of large communities of people unable to speak English; they do not attach to all language minorities.

To characterize language rights in the United States as instrumental rather than substantive is not to undermine their importance (Rubio-Marín, 2003). The bread and butter of the English Only Movement is opposition to instrumental language rights, on the ground that they slow assimilation. States and localities around the country have adopted official English laws, many of which would deny translated and interpreted services to non-English speakers.

Despite its popularity, the English Only approach obscures a crucial but under-appreciated fact: the process of learning English takes time. As a result, instrumental language rights are essential to the efficiency and openness of a democratic society, particularly in an era of high immigration. Though some English Only measures are motivated by understandable cost concerns, the outright refusal to provide even basic translation or interpretation presents public health and safety risks. Securing parental involvement in the schools also depends on schools having the capacity reach out to and communicate with parents. Finally, it is inhumane to expect people to operate at all times in a language they do not understand or have not mastered, particularly during moments of emergency and great vulnerability. For those who are newly arrived in the United States, the world can seem inscrutable. Making institutions accessible invites people to engage them, leaving us all better off.

The desire among immigrants to learn English is insatiable. ESL classes are oversubscribed, and to keep pace with current immigration trends, more classes are needed. But abandoning our commitment to instrumental language rights would only succeed in isolating precisely those whom we should be making the greatest effort to integrate into our society.

References

Castañeda v. Pickard, 648 F. 2d 989, 1009 (5th Cir. 1981).

Fillmore, L. W. (2005). When Learning a Second Language Means Losing the First. *The New Immigration: An Interdisciplinary Reader*, 302–306.

Krashen, S.(1999). *Condemned Without a Trial: Bogus Arguments Against Bilingual Education*. Portsmouth, NH: Heinemann.

Lau v. Nichols, 414 U.S. 563 [1974].

Meyer v. Nebraska, 262 U.S. 390 (1923).

Minow, M. (2000). *About Women, About Culture: About Them, About Us*. Cambridge, MA: Daedalus, 125.

Portes, A., & Zhou, M. (2005). The New Second Generation: Segmented Assimilation and its Variants. In M. Suárez-Orozco, C. Suárez-Orozco, & D. Q. Hilliard (Eds.). *The New Immigration: An Interdisciplinary Reader.* London: Routledge.

Rodríguez, C. (2006). Language and Participation. *California Law Review,* 94, 687.

Rubio-Marín, R. (2003). Language Rights: Exploring Competing Rationales. In W. Kymlicka, & A. Patten (Eds.). *Language Rights and Political Theory.* Oxford: Oxford University Press.

Suárez-Orozco, M., Roos, P. D., & Suárez Orozco, C. (2000). Law and School Reform: Six Strategies for Promoting Educational Equity (pp. 160–204). In J. Heubert (Ed.). *Cultural, Educational, and Legal Perspectives on Immigration: Implications for School Reform.* New Haven, CT: Yale University Press.

Thomas, W. P., & Collier, V. P. (2003). *A National Study of School Effectiveness for Language Minority Students' Long-Term Academic Achievement.* Washington, DC: U.S. Dept. of Education.

Waters, M. C., & Jiménez, T.R. (2005). Assessing Immigrant Assimilation: New Empirical and Theoretical Challenges. *Annual Review of Sociology,* 31, 105, 107.

Interview 4: What Teachers Need to Know to Educate English Language Learners

Mary Carol Combs

Question: What is the missing information that teachers need to have in order to better educate children of different language and cultural backgrounds?

As the numbers of English Language Learners (ELLs) in U.S. schools increase, teachers are becoming more concerned about meeting the needs of students who are acquiring English as a second and, sometimes, third language. These students are turning up in classrooms, and teachers often do not know how to teach them effectively. They know they have to change their instructional practices to reach ELLs, but don't always know where to begin.

In my graduate and undergraduate teacher preparation courses at the University of Arizona, the effectiveness question comes up all the time, and we may spend the entire semester exploring it. Of course, because teachers themselves have diverse interests and experiences, and teach a variety of subjects and age groups, they will approach this question in different ways. Nonetheless, there is strong agreement among them that effective teachers of ELLs are aware of second language acquisition theories, and consistently use sheltered strategies to make their English instruction more comprehensible, and incorporate culturally relevant content into their teaching.

Teachers sometimes have the perception that all they need to do to improve their instruction for ELLs is to alter how they teach, that is, to incorporate so-called "sheltered strategies" that might make their teaching more comprehensible. Strategies such as slow but natural speech, clearly enunciated speech, repetition and paraphrasing, visual reinforcement of academic content through the use of graphic organizers, controlled vocabulary, and frequent checks for comprehension, etc. (Echevarria & Graves, 2007; Echevarria, Vogt, & Short, 2004; Lessow-Hurley, 2005). I'm not saying that the strategies aren't critical—they absolutely are and they can go a long way toward helping ELLs understand subject matter. In fact, I spend a lot of time teaching these strategies, first, because they are useful, but also because knowing how to use them gives teachers more confidence.

I would add two additional requirements to this list: first, the need to "discover" one's students and, second, an interest in social justice.

Discovering One's Students

But effectiveness also means knowing as much as possible about the lives of students. I recommend that teachers make a concerted effort to learn as much as they can about the backgrounds—or "funds of knowledge"—of their students (González, Moll, & Amanti, 2005). Carlos Ovando, Ginger Collier, and I discussed this aspect of good teaching in our book, *ESL and Bilingual Classrooms* (2006). As mentioned earlier, teachers should be aware of students' first and second language proficiencies and their "cultural profiles." We provided a framework for teachers to organize information about their culturally and linguistically diverse students, essentially, a list of topics for teachers to investigate. While the list is incomplete, it provides a place to start (Ovando, et al., 2006, p. 32).

Background Topics Relevant to All Language Minority Students

- Immigrant or native born status.
- Socioeconomic profile, including educational level of parents.
- Rural versus urban backgrounds.
- Parents' aspirations for themselves and their children, including expectations for schools.
- Types of racial or ethnic prejudice that students may have experienced.
- Attitudes toward maintenance or revitalization of home language and culture.

Background Topics Relevant to Immigrant or Refugee Students

- Country of origin.
- Length of residence in the United States.
- Extent of ties with home country.
- Political and economic situation in region from which they emigrated.
- Reasons for emigration.
- Other countries lived in prior to arriving in the United States.
- Amount and quality of schooling in L1 prior to arriving in the United States, including the extent of math and science training as well as literacy.
- Languages other than English and their home language to which the students have been exposed.

School Observations

- Activities students enjoy or dislike, as a reflection either of cultural values or of their own personalities.
- Students' nonverbal communication.

- Students' comments on life in the United States, if immigrants, or comments about majority culture, if indigenous minorities.
- Signs of positive and negative adjustment in peer relationships.
- Comments that indicate a desire to share something of their home background.
- Comments that reflect students' developing concept of their ethnic identity.
- Students' own notions of the purpose of bilingual or ESL instruction as it relates to their own education.

Use of Literature, Media, Classes, and In-Service Opportunities and Participation in the Life of Ethnic Communities

- Gathering information from a wide variety of resources.
- Being alert to possible biases or distortions in materials or presentations.
- Distinguishing between descriptions of traditional cultural patterns and contemporary patterns.
- Cross-checking and relating what has been learned with the experiences of your own students and their families.

If students have been in U.S. schools already, data about students' language proficiencies, academic achievement, or demographic backgrounds may be available in their cumulative files. Teachers can also obtain important information by speaking with the students' previous teachers. Because immigrant families often experience high rates of mobility within or between school districts, however, student cumulative files may be incomplete and former teachers hard to locate.

If this is the case, information about students can probably best be gained through home visits or other opportunities for informal social contact. These opportunities can be a rich source of knowledge about students' lives. If there is a language barrier between teachers and families—usually the case—home visits can still be meaningful if there are extended family members or family friends who can translate. Personal contact with families outside of the school context can be very rewarding. It is well worth the time and effort.

Social Justice

Teaching for social justice is another aspect of teacher effectiveness, though admittedly less tangible than the other features already discussed. How does one define the concept of social justice, for instance or, indeed, develop a social justice agenda? How do teachers teach for social justice in the current era of high stakes standardized testing and Federal and state pressure to "close the achievement gap"? How can teachers incorporate multicultural, multilingual content into the rigid, "teacher-proof" reading programs that schools are increasing adopting? These are difficult but legitimate questions which my students and I try to explore in our class discussions.

Over the years it has been my privilege to have worked with many excellent teachers. These individuals are dedicated, resourceful, and creative masters of their content areas. I have also come to the conclusion that what sets the truly exceptional teachers apart from the merely competent, are their acknowledgement that schooling, under the right circumstances, can be emancipatory. These teachers respect the linguistic and cultural resources of their students, and as the title of this book suggests, strongly affirm students' right to their own language. They are also the ones who take the time to build trust with students, establish a collaborative community of practice (Wenger, 1998), and create a "dialogic space" within the classroom for students to explore, to question, and to critique. Good teachers sympathize with the economic and legal challenges faced by many immigrant families; exceptional teachers will advocate for families and students, even when doing so risks real consequences. For instance, a teacher who believes in social justice for her immigrant students or English language learners will refuse to ask them about their legal status, even when state and local measures may expect or require them to do so. (Note that legal residence is not currently a requirement for attendance in U.S. public schools. School districts are precluded from inquiring about students' immigration status because of the Supreme Court's decision in Plyler v. Doe, a case that tested a Texas state law withholding state funds from school districts serving indocumented students.)

References

Arizona Revised Statutes, Title 15 (Education), Section 3.1 (English Language Education for Children in Public Schools), 751-756.01.

Echevarria, J., & Graves, A. (2007). *Sheltered Content Instruction: Teaching English Language Learners with Diverse Abilities*, 3rd edn. Boston, MA: Pearson/Allyn & Bacon.

——, Vogt, M. E., & Short, D. (2004). *Making Content Comprehensible for English Learners: The SIOP Model*, 2nd edn. Boston, MA: Allyn & Bacon.

González, N., Moll, L. C., & Amanti, C. (2005). *Funds of Knowledge: Theorizing Practices in Households, Communities, and Classrooms*. Mahwah, NJ: Lawrence Erlbaum Associates, Inc.

Lave, J., & Wenger, E. (1991). *Situated Learning: Legitimate Peripheral Participation*. Cambridge: Cambridge University Press.

Lessow-Hurley, J. (2005). *The Foundations of Dual Language Instruction*, 4th edn. Boston. MA: Pearson/Allyn & Bacon.

Ovando, C., Combs, M. C., & Collier, V. (2006). *Bilingual and ESL Classrooms: Teaching in Multicultural Contexts*, 4th edn. Boston, MA: McGraw-Hill.

Plyler v. Doe, 457 U.S. 202 (1982).

Wenger, E. (1998). *Communities of Practice: Learning, Meaning, and Identity*. Cambridge: Cambridge University Press.

II
EDUCATIONAL POLICIES, ATTITUDES, AND UNFULFILLED PROMISES

3

The Hidden Linguistic Legacies of Brown v. Board and No Child Left Behind

JOHN BAUGH AND AARON WELBORN

Over half a century ago, the Supreme Court reversed itself and ruled that, in the context of a long history of racial and educational apartheid, separate schools were inherently unequal. Brown v. Board (1954) was hailed as the case that would lead to educational equity for African Americans. True equity, however, has rarely been achieved. At the time, the legal battle was being waged over the inadequate and inequitable conditions of schools that African American students were confined to. Since then, we have come to understand that separation is only one aspect of educational inequality. There are numerous in-school and out-of-school disparities that must also be taken into account, most of them neither addressed by the Supreme Court's decision nor adequately dealt with since. Among the most important is access to the language of wider communication—which is to say, Standard English proficiency.

The passage of President Bush's No Child Left Behind Act (NCLB) in 2002 was intended to recognize and correct the various problems (English proficiency among them) that contribute to the existence of widespread "achievement gap" among racial, ethnic, and economic groups. Like the Brown case, NCLB was initially greeted as a landmark of civil rights law with far-reaching significance, particularly for poor, marginalized, and minority populations. Civil rights activists, Congressional Black caucus members, democrats and republicans alike pointed to the measurable benefits the legislation would have for students of color, students with disabilities, those from low-income families, and those with limited proficiency in English. Essentially, the law proposes to level the educational playing field by holding schools accountable for all students' progress, particularly those students whose academic needs have traditionally been overlooked. To that end, NCLB puts pressure on schools to raise test scores across the board, certify that all teachers are highly qualified, and provide parents with more options if their schools can't meet the new standards—all worthy goals, to be sure. Despite its good intentions, however, the sweeping 600-page act has created a host of problems that were largely unforeseen by its authors and early advocates. These problems are so disproportionately hard on non-dominant groups, and so serious from a linguistic point of view, that the "cure" proposed by NCLB may actually be worse than the disease.

The discussion that follows is aimed at exploring the linguistic dimensions of racial reconciliation and education reform in the context of Brown v. Board and

NCLB, two of the most sweeping Federal measures aimed at providing an equitable education for African Americans and other historically disadvantaged groups. We hope to show how, in both instances, the unique linguistic legacy of slavery has been largely overlooked—to the considerable detriment of slave descendants. In part, this disregard can be attributed to prevailing misconceptions about African American vernacular English (AAVE) and the educational needs of AAVE speakers. The lack of linguistic understanding among educators and policymakers has led to negative academic outcomes for AAVE speakers, creating a situation strikingly inconsistent with the stated goals of No Child Left Behind. Without a more thoughtful consideration of linguistic diversity in Federal and state regulations, meaningful education reform will continue to elude us, and AAVE speakers will continue to be left behind in American schools.

The Linguistic Significance of Brown v. Board

Strictly speaking, Brown v. Board was about race and space, not language. The case attempted to overturn the system of de jure racial segregation that had flourished under the doctrine of "separate but equal" public facilities for Whites and African Americans, as established by the Supreme Court's earlier decision in Plessy v. Ferguson (1896). Because Brown was about segregated public spaces, there was no compelling legal need in the course of the trial to discuss the linguistic consequences of slavery—to say nothing of the social stigma that most Whites felt (and still feel) toward the linguistic practices of African Americans. Unequal access to common educational resources was the issue at hand, not unequal proficiency in the language of common communication. Yet the two are, in fact, inseparable, and educational reforms that ignore this fact are not likely to bring about the racial harmony and academic equity they were intended to achieve.

Most Americans view the acquisition of Standard English proficiency as a matter of choice, having little to do with racial heritage. Opportunities to learn it are perceived to be abundant and available to everyone, especially in our media-saturated culture. If you work hard enough and pay attention, you can speak, read, or write as well as anyone else and enjoy the same opportunities, or so the argument goes. But learning does not take place in a vacuum, and this line of reasoning ignores the effects of 500 years of history. The individual's struggle to succeed in the land of opportunity is a defining aspect of the American dream, but that dream is not yet fully realized for those of us who trace our ancestry to enslaved Africans.

The linguistic legacy of slave descendants of African origin differs from that of every other immigrant group that has come to the United States (Baugh, 1983, 1999, 2000; Labov, 1972; Rickford & Rickford, 2000; Smitherman, 2000; Wolfram & Thomas, 2002). As forced immigrants, or what Ogbu (1978, 1992) calls "involuntary caste-like" minorities, slaves did not have the luxury of gradually transitioning into English. Whereas the vast majority of U.S. immigrants came here with fellow speakers of their native tongue, bringing the language and customs of their homeland with them, slaves were linguistically isolated on capture and purposefully grouped with strangers who did not speak the same language. Whereas European immigrants could profit from their own labor, maintain a family, and expect to be afforded the same basic legal protections as everyone else, slaves could expect no such considerations. As chattel they were subject to immediate sale, a practice that destroyed families and plunged slaves speaking mutually unintelligible languages into further linguistic isolation. Whereas the typical European immigrant was able to attend public schools, slaves were statutorily denied access to schools and literacy. Even when that access was finally granted, it was only done so in a limited fashion, and in racially segregated schools.

These circumstances collectively produced tremendous linguistic schisms between slaves and other Americans, schisms that were only widened by the effects of legally sanctioned racial segregation throughout the country. Long before Brown v. Board, Dred Scott learned in another Supreme Court case that he had no rights "as a Negro" whose ancestors had been imported to America, overturning the verdict of a St. Louis jury in 1850 that had voted to grant him his freedom. At the time of the trial, when Blacks were overtly oppressed throughout the country, there was little need to call attention to linguistic differences among America's White and Black residents. With greater things at stake, such as personal freedom, such differences might have seemed beside the point. But are they still?

No reasonable person could look at this history and deny that the combined legacies of slavery, de jure segregation, and substandard schooling could have profoundly negative consequences for the descendants of African slaves. The linguistic consequences have been especially dramatic. In terms of language practices, African Americans have blended much more slowly into the melting pot than other immigrant groups. Likewise, the linguistic behavior of slave descendants has received harsher criticism than other ethnic varieties when compared to the European-based "American" standard. This sort of criticism is not confined to the United States. Prejudice against Black language usage can be found throughout South America, the Caribbean, and Central America, among other places where slave descendants have settled (Baugh, 1983, 1999, 2004; Hymes, 1971). However, because so many people, including many in the educational professions, have come to equate "Black" language usage with "improper," "broken," or "sloppy" usage, the historical factors that contribute to those usage differences have often been forgotten.

When it comes to language dialects, claims that some varieties are more "proper" or "correct" than others are based on social attitudes rather than linguistic facts. For almost as long as the study of language has been around, linguists have been saying that language varieties and dialects are merely different from each other, yet entirely consistent and rule governed within themselves. Without a doubt, the concept of Standard English is a useful one, especially in the realm of education. But even this "standard" comprises a range of dialects, as demonstrated by the considerable regional differences in pronunciation, grammatical patterns, and vocabulary that characterize the speech of our members of Congress, who hail from every state in the union. Standard English in the South sounds different from Standard English in the North, which in turn sounds different from Midwestern Standard English (Kretzschmar, et al., 1993). In broader perspective, American Standard English contrasts sharply in many ways from the Standard English spoken in Great Britain, Australia, and India (Preston, 1996). In fact, there is no universal standard.

There is, however, a shared understanding among members of a speech community of what the "standard" dialect is for their group. Often that dialect is closely associated with educated people and economic power (Wolfram, Adger, & Christian, 1999). By the same token, non-standard dialects are accorded lesser worth. It is important to stress that these are value judgments, not linguistic facts. From a scientific point of view, speaking a vernacular dialect does not indicate linguistic deficiency or poor learning skills, nor does it impede cognitive development (Wolfram, et al., 1999). Because Standard English proficiency is a matter of social acceptability and power, children should be encouraged to learn it. However, their vernacular dialects should be respected as part of their identity.

The belief that AAVE is "incorrect" or "ungrammatical" is inconsistent with empirical evidence to the contrary and incompatible with American ideals of tolerance and pluralism. Be that as it may, the fact is that AAVE has been devalued since the time of slavery, and those who speak with a strong non-standard dialect face considerable difficulty acquiring Standard English literacy. To succeed in school, AAVE speakers must master academic knowledge and skills while developing proficiency in a second dialect at the same time. This is not an easy task. The lack of linguistic understanding for minority students among educators only compounds the problem and reinforces barriers to academic achievement.

As for the linguistic significance of Brown v. Board, its chief significance lies primarily in its lack of consideration of these linguistic facts. In this respect, it falls in line with most Federal educational policies that ignore the problem of helping African Americans achieve greater Standard English proficiency. Of course, as stated earlier, the issue under judicial review was narrowly focused. Surely, Thurgood Marshall and his colleagues were not thinking about the linguistic legacy of the African slave trade. Neither could they predict how long that legacy would endure and the problems it would present for future generations. There can be no doubt that formidable linguistic hurdles confront many slave descendants in the United States and other nations in North and South America. We must not forget that the seeds of this problem were sown during slavery, and that from a linguistic point of view, the institution of slavery has not been completely overcome.

The Linguistic Significance of No Child Left Behind

Without a more complete understanding of linguistic diversity in schools, we are unlikely to escape the historical pattern of neglecting students from non-dominant linguistic backgrounds. The Federal No Child Left Behind Act (NCLB) was intended to break that pattern, at least in spirit. In reality, it has made little progress toward that goal, and in many respects threatens to set us back further.

Criticism of NCLB has come from many corners and covers a wide range of issues, from complaints that it is insufficiently funded (Crawford, 2004) to allegations that it actually promotes privatized education (Karp, 2004). Objections have been raised over the worth of high stakes standardized testing (Darling-Hammond, 2004), the gradual narrowing of the curriculum (Wood, 2004), and the unfair penalization of teachers and schools for factors beyond their control (Novak & Fuller, 2003). Recently, several states opposed to the law have hauled the Department of Education into court, citing a passage in the legislation's fine print that prevents states from having to spend their own money in order to meet NCLB requirements (Dillon, 2005). A new law in Utah actually seeks to supersede the Federal regulation by requiring schools to spend as little state money as possible on fulfilling NCLB's mandates (Will, 2005). The ultimate outcome of these challenges remains to be seen, but whatever the result, it is likely that NCLB will continue to face resistance until it undergoes significant revisions.

Proponents of the law cite NCLB's unprecedented Federal mandate that states raise the achievement levels of low income and minority children to the same heights as their more privileged counterparts. Indeed, this is the law's greatest virtue: it forces educators to pay more attention to those children who need it most. The biggest drawback, however, is the *kind* of attention that must be paid. NCLB's primary method for improving schools is to keep them focused on short-term test scores, backed up by the threat of Federal sanctions if those scores fail to rise fast enough. Test scores are quantifiable; they provide a scientific and easy-to-grasp means of measuring success. However, as Darling-Hammond (2004, p. 9) observes: "The biggest problem with the NCLB Act is that it mistakes measuring schools with fixing them." In most cases, the most formidable educational obstacles America's children face are not tests, but rather unequal resources, substandard schools, critical shortages of teachers trained to meet their needs, and—especially relevant to this discussion—unequal proficiency in Standard English. NCLB does little to address these fundamental problems.

In order to appreciate the linguistic implications of NCLB, particularly for speakers of AAVE, it will be helpful to look at some of the troubling issues the law has raised related to the education of minorities and English language learners, or what NCLB refers to as limited English proficient (LEP) students. How schools are being "held accountable" for these students, and the racial and linguistic implications of that accountability system, have proven to be especially thorny issues under the NCLB plan for America's schools.

Penalizing Diversity

Under NCLB, 100% of all students enrolled in schools receiving Federal aid must be able to pass state tests by the year 2014. To keep schools on pace toward that goal, NCLB requires states to develop their own formula for gauging "adequate yearly progress," or AYP. AYP is the graduated rate of improvement schools must maintain in order for 100% of their students to pass state tests within the 2014 timeframe. Besides developing an AYP formula for the total population of students enrolled in school, schools are required to set and meet separate AYP targets for up to nine student subgroups:

- Whites
- African Americans
- Asian/Pacific Islanders

- Native Americans
- Latinos
- other ethnicities
- students with disabilities
- students from low-income families
- limited English proficient (LEP) students.

Students who fall into multiple subgroups (that is, a Spanish speaking special education student from a low-income family) may be counted multiple times, with their test scores counting towards multiple AYP targets. Statistically insignificant subgroups (that is, fewer than 10 Native Americans in a large metropolitan high school) need not be counted.

These "disaggregated" data constitute one of the reasons why NCLB initially won a measure of broad support. Breaking with a long tradition of Federal education policy that ignored racial and socioeconomic inequalities, NCLB takes an express interest in the education of minorities, economically disadvantaged children, nonnative speakers of English, and other groups historically at risk of falling through the cracks of the American education system. The idea is that disaggregating test scores will identify which segments of a school's population show the greatest room for improvement so that teachers can concentrate their efforts there. In theory, this is unquestionably a step in the right direction. When combined with the elaborate accountability provisions set up under NCLB, however, the implications are less favorable.

If a single subgroup within a school misses its AYP target for two consecutive years—even if every other subgroup comes in with flying colors—that school will be labeled "needing improvement" and face an escalating series of sanctions. Sanctions can range from using Federal funds to pay for student transfers, to firing school staff, to administrative reorganization, to the imposition of private management, and ultimately to school closure.

One thing that quickly became evident after NCLB took effect was that, by these rules, thousands of schools across the country would soon be branded as "needing improvement." Moreover, a disproportionate percentage of them would serve large low-income and minority populations (Novak & Fuller, 2003). Clearly, schools with more student subgroups have more performance targets to hit, which is the same thing as saying that the larger and more culturally diverse a school is, the more likely it is to be identified for improvement under NCLB. A school in the suburbs with a predominantly White, middle-class student body and few statistically significant subgroups has fewer AYP requirements to meet than an urban school with significant numbers of racial and ethnic minorities, students with disabilities, children from low-income families, and LEP students. This frequently cited "diversity penalty" leads to a situation in which, as Crawford (2004, p. 5) puts it, "schools are being 'held accountable' for the demographic profile of their students."

The disparate effect of NCLB on schools with diverse populations was predicted by researchers and critics of the law before any sanctions took effect (Erpenpach, Forte-Fast, & Potts, 2003; Novak & Fuller, 2003; Sunderman & Kim, 2004). Now that most states are beginning to identify school districts for sanctioning, those predictions are proving painfully accurate. A study of school districts across seven states found that "districts identified as needing improvement under NCLB enrolled more minority and low-income students than districts making adequate progress. They also enrolled substantially higher percentages of English Language Learners" (Tracey, Sunderman, & Orfield, 2005, p. 7). Urban school systems, which are highly segregated for Black and Latino students, were over-represented among underperforming districts. Ironically, the very schools NCLB was ostensibly designed to help are the same ones slated to receive the first round of sanctions.

The problem is not limited to urban areas, either. It should not be news to anyone that, despite desegregation efforts made possible by the Brown decision over 50 years ago, there has been a steady trend towards racially resegregated schools in many parts of the country. The trend is most visible in the South, long home to a majority of African Americans and now at the center of a growing Latino migration. A recent study by the Harvard Civil Rights Project (Orfield & Lee, 2005) reports that currently in the South "more than three quarters of Latino students (78 percent) attend majority minority schools, followed closely by 71 percent of black students." Often these schools are characterized by concentrated poverty and high dropout rates. A related study cites that, overall, 46% of all Blacks and Latinos in the South attend schools where "graduation is not the norm" (Civil Rights Project, 2005). For many students of color and low-income children, such conditions do not represent a considerable improvement over those that existed prior to Brown v. Board. As Darling-Hammond (2004, p. 23) observes: "In a growing number of states, high school completion rates for African-American and Latino students have returned to pre-1954 levels."

There is little evidence to suggest that sanctioning these schools will improve their standing. Even if better schools are available nearby, NCLB gives them strong incentives to turn away poorly performing transfers, for fear of jeopardizing their own AYP ratings. A telling example of this dilemma was seen in September 2005 when U.S. Secretary of Education Margaret Spellings refused to ease testing and accountability requirements for schools in Texas and other states that took in children displaced by Hurricane Katrina (Garan, 2005; Lacoste-Caputo, 2005). That schools should have to fear sanctions for accommodating victims of a natural disaster is bad enough; that those sanctions might be enforced regardless is much worse. Despite provisions in the law-waving NCLB requirements in the event of "exceptional or uncontrollable circumstances, such as a natural disaster" (NCLB, Section 1111(b)(3)(C)(vii)), the only schools to receive Federal exemptions were those blown away by the storm. This is just one argument against an inflexible accountability program as the sole means of improving public education. There are many others.

Ignoring Resource Inequities

Perhaps NCLB's greatest weakness is that it fails to acknowledge or propose a remedy for the tremendous resource inequities that exist between schools, between school districts, and between students themselves, yet it requires everyone to meet the same achievement levels. Imposing a strict, top-down, one-size-fits-all standard ignores glaring social and economic disparities that exist across the country. As Darling-Hammond (2004) notes:

> Unlike most countries that fund schools centrally and equally, the wealthiest U.S. public schools spend at least ten times more than the poorest schools— ranging from over $30,000 per pupil at the wealthy schools to only $3,000 at the poorest. These disparities contribute to a wider achievement gap in this country than in virtually any other industrialized country in the world. (p. 6)

Money is one kind of resource. Language is another. If NCLB's impact on schools serving economically disadvantaged and minority students appears counter-productive, the situation regarding limited English proficient (LEP) students is no better.

The literature on teaching and evaluating LEP learners under the new guidelines imposed by NCLB is both considerable and conclusive. We will not delve here into the numerous assessment problems these guidelines have created, since they are described effectively elsewhere (Abedi, 2004; Batt, Kim, & Sunderman, 2005; Crawford, 2004; Coltrane, 2002; Hill & DePascale, 2003). The general picture is summed up accurately by Abedi (2004): "Measurement of the academic achieve-ment of LEP students is much more complex than what the NCLB legislation conceives." For the purposes of this discussion, the LEP subgroup deserves examination for two reasons. First, it is one of the fastest growing subgroups in the country. According to the National Center for Education Statistics, the number of schoolchildren who spoke a language other than English at home more than doubled (from 3.8 million to 9.9 million) between 1979 and 2003, while total student enrollment grew only a fraction of that. Looking at the total U.S. popu-lation, the latest census data shows that 47 million U.S. residents—nearly one in five—do not consider English their home language. As a result, Crawford (2005a, para. 6) notes: "the United States is more linguistically diverse than at any time since the early 1900s." This is remarkable in a country with a reputation for mono-lingualism. Second, the situation of LEP students under NCLB has instructive similarities with the educational plight of AAVE speakers.

Although the U.S. Department of Education insists that it does not advocate an "English Only" policy on educating LEP children, the approach outlined under NCLB essentially amounts to the same thing. NCLB allows states to assess LEP students in their native language for up to 3 years in reading. Most states, however, have not developed native language assessments (Batt, et al., 2005). Nevertheless, the law requires LEP students to take the same standardized tests as everyone else and have their scores recorded for accountability purposes, regardless of language barriers. Not surprisingly, schools with large numbers of LEP learners are more likely to be "held accountable" than schools with comparatively few, since a higher percentage of their students are not making "adequate yearly progress" on standardized tests (Batt, et al., 2005). Although some LEP children are able to learn English quickly, research shows that it typically takes between 5 and 7 years—not

2—to learn the academic English used in most standardized tests (August & Hakuta, 1997). This is only a ballpark figure. There is no "standard" learning curve when it comes to acquiring a second language. As with other developmental processes, numerous variables come into play, including historical, economic, and environmental circumstances. NCLB does not take such variables into account.

The current pressure on teachers to drill the language of standardized tests into their LEP students, and to do so quickly, is one reason why the National Association for Bilingual Education (NABE) has come out strongly against NCLB. Whatever native language skills these students bring to the classroom are of little importance under NCLB, neither is there time or incentive to develop these skills when test preparation is the order of the day. As one participant at the 2005 NABE conference put it: "The message to bilingual teachers everywhere is: They are going to be judged on how fast they can get their children out of bilingual education" (as cited in Antonio & Zehr, 2005, p. 13). Previous legislation (that is, the Improving America's Schools Act of 1994) had given Federal funding priority to schools whose LEP programs fostered proficiency in English alongside proficiency in the child's native tongue. This was supported by solid research and proven practices demonstrating that cultivating bilingual skills leads to superior academic achievement over the long term (Crawford, 2005a). NCLB shifted Federal priorities, effectively giving funding preference to schools that can most efficiently replace native language skills, rather than add to them. At a time when the United States has a critical need for individuals who are highly proficient in both English and other languages, this kind of English Only linguistic mindset is irrational, to say the least.

Equally distressing is the widespread disregard for the educational difficulties of students who speak non-Standard English. Heretofore, we have been focusing on traditional LEP students for whom English is not native. Little has been said, however, about the legal definition of limited English proficiency. NCLB characterizes an LEP student as someone "who was not born in the United States or whose native language is a language other than English," and "whose difficulties in speaking, reading, writing, or understanding the English language may be sufficient to deny the individual—(i) the ability to meet the State's proficient level of achievement on State assessments . . . (ii) the ability to successfully achieve in classrooms where the language of instruction is English; or (iii) the opportunity to participate fully in society" (NCLB, Section 9101 (25)). Students who speak AAVE are not considered traditional LEP students, neither should the two be confused. But neither are AAVE students native speakers of Standard English. Indeed, many AAVE speakers' difficulties with Standard English are sufficient to deny them the ability to pass standardized tests, the ability to achieve in Standard English Only environments, and the "opportunity to participate fully in society." Not all dialects are perceived as equal from a social or educational point of view. Therein lies the necessity for educational policies targeted to AAVE speakers' needs.

Can some African American students be considered part of a language minority group, even though English is their native tongue? Dialect differences would seem to justify an answer of "Yes." Why? Because the native dialect of AAVE speakers represents a language barrier to full participation in school (Baugh, 1995).

However, NCLB excludes AAVE speakers from consideration, presumably on the grounds that, as Fix and Zimmerman (1993, p. 12) argue: "Limited English proficiency is not a measure of a person's proficiency in his or her native language." AAVE speakers differ from their traditional LEP counterparts largely in their ability to understand spoken Standard English. However, comprehension of Standard English, in the face of other language barriers and linguistic discrimination, does not in itself imply that AAVE speakers have the same academic advantages as students who speak Standard English natively.

The essential point boils down to the fact that NCLB was never intended to apply to non-Standard English speakers. not to say that an educational solution is impossible for speakers of AAVE. A close linguistic parallel to the AAVE situation can be found in Hawaii, where the indigenous language was suppressed and the imported variety of English underwent a process of pidginization (Baugh, 1995, 2000). Although there are considerable differences between African Americans and Hawaiians, they share a similar linguistic tradition of non-Standard English that has, at least partially, stood as a barrier to educational success.

Legislators from Hawaii were able to convince the Federal government that native Hawaiians needed Federal educational support. There are striking parallels between the justification for such support in Hawaii's case and the case of non-Standard English speaking African slave descendants. Both groups were "involuntary caste-like" minorities. Both groups were denied the use of their indigenous language and subsequently performed poorly in schools—once they were given the opportunity to attend schools. And both groups faced linguistic discrimination due to the fact that they spoke a non-Standard vernacular of English. Clearly, the two groups differ greatly in terms of the magnitude of the linguistic problem. As a series of islands, Hawaii's language difficulties are confined to one state, physically isolated from the mainland. The linguistic legacy of slavery is far more pervasive throughout the country and goes back to the birth of the nation. Hawaii is a young state, and from the beginning of statehood Hawaiians were able to make greater use of the legal system to redress the historical oppression of native Hawaiians. Until recently, courts were an unreliable source of legal relief for Blacks.

Despite these differences, the essential similarities hint at educational solutions. The Federal aid to Hawaii was based on linguistic evidence that demonstrates linguistic differences between Hawaiian Pidgin English (HPE) and Standard English. At present, there is a strong movement in Hawaii to revive the indigenous language and preserve the native culture as much as possible. Federally assisted bidialectal education programs have contributed to this effort. The potential benefit of the Hawaiian programs can be credited largely to the respect afforded the students' mother tongue, a fact that stands in sharp contrast to the situation of African slave descendants. With very few exceptions, this overt sense of respect is still missing in the education of AAVE students.

Some educators have remarked that language development is a low academic priority for poor AAVE speakers because of myriad other social problems they face in daily life. The paradox of this statement lies in the fact that good education is critical to breaking perpetual cycles of poverty, and linguistic skills are a good indicator of the likelihood of academic success. AAVE students need instructional methods that will enable them to acquire Standard English literacy skills, while at the same time fostering a healthy respect for their dialect differences as an important aspect of identity and evidence of linguistic expertise. Valuing dialect differences can help young people who are struggling with pervasive negative stereotypes toward their own culture. It can help them not only to explore their heritage and associate more closely with fellow speakers of the same dialect, but also to overcome value judgments about "standard" language usage with a sense of pride in their community.

To be fair, NCLB makes a step a right direction by bringing added attention to racial and language minorities and increasing accountability for their performance. If these groups are underperforming and their achievement results are publicized, officials might take the necessary steps to help them succeed at higher levels. However, whatever potential benefits the law may have are being jeopardized by its emphasis on equalizing test scores rather than resources, its unreasonable and unfair treatment of schools serving diverse populations, and its lack of assistance for speakers of AAVE and other non-Standard varieties of English in achieving Standard English proficiency. In the spirit of the beleaguered rancher who once exclaimed: "You can't fatten cattle if you just weigh 'em," we must not mistake quantitative measurements for qualitative solutions. Neither should we place too much confidence in test-driven mandates as a means of advancing educational prospects for low-income students who, for whatever reason, lack fluency or proficiency in the dominant linguistic norms.

Discussion Questions and Activities

1. Define grammatical from a linguistic perspective and from a social perspective. Argue for or against the claim that African American Vernacular English (AAVE) is linguistically equivalent to Standard English.
2. Considering the debates over the No Child Left Behind legislation, describe changes in the legislation that you feel would yield better results for teachers and children.
3. Think about schools in your community. What evidence do you see of desegregation and/or resegregation patterns? Should the patterns be changed? If so, why? If not, why not?
4. Examine at least two articles on the English Only Movement. Based on your knowledge of and experience with the English Only Movement, discuss the potential positive and negative aspects of it.

References

Abedi, J. (2004). The No Child Left Behind Act and English Language Learners: Assessment and Accountability Issues. *Educational Researcher*, 33(1), 4–14.

Antonio, S., & Zehr, M. (2005). Bilingual Educators Ratchet up Criticism of NCLB Law. *Education Week*, 24(21), 13.

August, D., & Hakuta, K. (Eds.) (1997). *Improving Schooling for Language Minority Children: A Research Agenda*. Washington, DC: National Academy Press.

Batt, L., Kim, J., & Sunderman, G. (2005). *Limited English Proficient Students: Increased Accountability under NCLB.* Cambridge, MA: Civil Rights Project at Harvard University.

Baugh, J. (1983). *Black Street Speech: Its History, Structure, and Survival.* Austin, TX: University of Texas Press.

——. (1995). The Law, Linguistics, and Education: Educational Reform for African American language minority students. *Linguistics and Education,* 7, 87–105.

——. (1999). *Out of the Mouths of Slaves: African American Language and Educational Malpractice.* Austin, TX: University of Texas Press.

——. (2000). *Beyond Ebonics: Linguistic Pride and Racial Orejudice.* New York: Oxford University Press.

——. (2004). Standard English and Academic English (Dialect) Learners in the African Diaspora. *Journal of English Linguistics,* 33(1), 1–13.

Brown v. Board, 347 U.S. 483 (1954).

Civil Rights Project at Harvard University. (2005). *Confronting the Graduation Rate Crisis in the South.* Cambridge, MA: The Civil Rights Project at Harvard University.

Coltrane, B. (2002). *English Language Learners and High-Stakes Tests: An Overview of the Issues. ERIC Digest.* Retrieved December 1, 2005, from http://www.ericdigests.org/2003-4/high-stakes.html.

Crawford, J. (2004). *No Child Left Behind: Misguided Approach to School Accountability for English Language Learners.* National Association for Bilingual Education. Retrieved November 22, 2005, from http://www.nabe.org/documents/policy_legislation/NABE_on_NCLB.pdf.

——. (2005a). *Heritage Languages: Tapping a "Hidden Resource."* National Association for Bilingual Education. Retrieved November 22, 2005, from http://www.nabe.org/research/multi.html.

——. (2005b). *Making Sense of Census 2000.* National Association of Bilingual Education. Retrieved November 22, 2005, from http://www.nabe.org/research/demography.html.

Darling-Hammond, L. (2004). From "Separate but Equal" to "No Child Left Behind": The Collision of New Standards and Old Inequalities. In D. Meier, & G. Wood (Eds.). *Many Children Left Behind.* Boston, MA: Beacon Press, pp. 3–32.

Dillon, S. (2005). Teachers' Union and Districts Sue over Bush Law. *New York Times,* April 21, A1.

Erpenbach, W., Forte-Fast, E., & Potts, A. (2003). *Statewide Educational Accountability under NCLB.* Washington, DC: Council for Chief State School Officers.

Fix, M., & Zimmerman, W. (1993). *Educating Immigrant Children: Chapter 1 in the Changing City.* Washington, DC: Urban Institute.

Garan, E. (2005). Will Katrina Topple No Child Left Behind? *Education Week,* 25, 36–38.

Hill, R., & DePascale, C. (2003). Reliability of No Child Left Behind Accountability Designs. *Educational measurement: Issues and Practice,* 22(3), 12–20.

Hymes, D. (Ed.) (1971). *Pidginization and Creolization of Languages.* Cambridge: Cambridge University Press.

Karp, S. (2004). NCLB's Selective Vision of Equality: Some Gaps Count more than Others. In D. Meier, & G. Wood (Eds.). *Many Children Left Behind.* Boston, MA: Beacon Press.

Kretzschmar, W., McDavid, V., Lerud, T., & Johnson, E. (Eds.) (1993). *Handbook of the Linguistic Atlas of the Middle and South Atlantic States.* Chicago, IL: University of Chicago Press.

Labov, W. (1972). *Language in the Inner City: Studies in the Black English Vernacular.* Philadelphia, PA: University of Pennsylvania Press.

Lacoste-Caputo, J. (2005). Schools with Evacuees Risk Academic Rankings. *San Antonio Express-News,* September 16, 5B.

No Child Left Behind Act of 2001. (2002). P.L. 107-110. Retrieved December 2, 2005, from http://www.ed.gov/policy/elsec/leg/esea02/107-110.pdf.

Novak, J., & Fuller, B. (2003). *Penalizing Diverse Schools? Similar Test Scores,but Different Students Bring Federal Sanctions.* Policy Analysis for California Education. Retrieved December 2, 2005, from http://pace.berkeley.edu/policy_brief_03-4_Pen.Div.pdf.

Ogbu, J. (1978). *Minority Education and Caste.* New York: Academic Press.

——. (1992). Understanding Multicultural Education. *Educational Researcher,* 21, 5–14, 24.

Orfield, G., & Lee, C. (2005) *New Faces, Old Patterns? Segregation in the Multiracial South.* Cambridge, MA: The Civil Rights Project at Harvard University.

Plessy v. Ferguson, 163 U.S. 537 (1896).

Preston, D. R. (1996). Where the Worst English is Spoken. In E. Schneider (Ed.). *Focus on the USA.* Amsterdam: John Benjamins.

Rickford, J. R., & Rickford, R. (2000). *Spoken Soul: The Story of Black English.* New York: John Wiley & Sons, Inc.

Smitherman, G. (2000). *Talkin that Talk: Language, Culture, and Education in African America.* New York: Routledge.

Sunderman, G., & Kim, J. (2004). *Inspiring Vision, Disappointing Results: Four Studies on Implementing the No Child Left Behind Act.* Cambridge, MA: The Civil Rights Project at Harvard University.

Tracey, C., Sunderman, G., & Orfield, G. (2005). *Changing NCLB District Accountability Standards: Implications for Racial Equity.* Cambridge, MA: The Civil Rights Project at Harvard University.

U.S. Department of Education, National Center for Education Statistics. (2005). *The Condition of Education 2005*, NCES 2005-094. Washington, DC: U.S. Government Printing Office.

Will, G. (2005). In Utah, No Right Left Behind. *Washington Post*, November 11, A25.

Wolfram, W., Adger, C.T., & Christian, D. (1999). *Dialects in Schools and Communities.* Mahwah, NJ: Lawrence Erlbaum Associates, Inc.

Wolfram, W., & Thomas, E. R. (2002). *The Development of African American English.* Oxford: Blackwell.

Wood, G. (2004). A View from the Field: NCLB's Effects on Classrooms and Schools. In D. Meier, & G. Wood (Eds.). *Many Children Left Behind.* Boston, MA: Beacon Press.

4

Portraits, Counterportraits, and the Lives of Children: Language, Culture, and Possibilities

RICK MEYER

We have not far to look for suffering. It's in the streets, fills the air, lies upon our friends. Faces of pain look at us from the newspaper, from the TV screen. We know them: black man swinging in the warm wind, sealed cattle cars rumbling through the bitter cold, the glare of Auschwitz at midnight. . . . Many of us have never known this kind of misery, have never felt a lash or club, never been shot at, persecuted, bombed, starved—yet we suffer too. (Wheelis, 1973, pp. 3–4)

In this chapter, I consider the right of students to their own language as that right is influenced by the broader social, cultural, psychological, economic and, most importantly, policy contexts in which they live. I do this by presenting the official portraits of non-dominant culture students, portraits painted by formal and dominant institutions and agencies. The portraits (painted with words) are a vehicle to argue that the linguistic *suffering* that students experience in schools and in the greater society is one part of the greater silent suffering that they endure. I also paint counterportraits that demonstrate the talents and strengths of these same students; counterportraits are unofficial, meaning they carry little influence or prestige when held up to dominant culture policy. Students' compliance to the rigidly limiting linguistic demands of school may be one part of their official portrait as citizens. The quality of their linguistic lives, the opportunities denied them because of their linguistic origins, and the greater social contexts in which they live shape the shades, hues, tones, and nature of their official and unofficial portraits.

Growing Tension/Growing Suffering

The right of children to speak the language or dialect in which their mother loves them seems as senseful and important as the rights to eat, be safe, and enjoy the benefits of quality healthcare. Yet, in the present policy climate of the No Child Left Behind Act (NCLB), the intolerance for variations in language and dialect that periodically emerges in the U.S. is clearly once again upon us. The many assumptions about language and dialect that saturate NCLB in Reading First (the section of NCLB that specifically lays out the way reading instruction will occur) and the bilingual chapters of the law, make it clear that differences are not officially acceptable. Most notably, the sections of NCLB that deal with bilingual children provide textual evidence that the goal of NCLB is to have no child left bilingual (Meyer, in press). The systematic intense phonics programs that are being thrust upon teachers and children, offered under the guise that they are based on scientifically reliable and replicable research, are, in reality, ways in which students and teachers are forced into being compliant and passive consumers of programs that are actually quite void of well-researched literacy pedagogy (Strauss, 2005). These programs rely on the dominant dialect and language as they force children into hearing and reproducing sounds and words, orally and in writing, that are lacking in both meaning and the richness and vitality of what language is and what it is for (Meyer, 2001).

Gutiérrez, Rymes, and Larson (1995) provide a deeper understanding of what is occurring when students are denied the right to their own language. They refer to school curriculum as "first space" in which the official texts (canons) of school are taught in order to enculturate students into the perpetuation of the status quo. First space is a place in which students learn, sometimes bluntly and other times quite subtly, who has power, which texts matter, and which ways with words (Heath, 1983) have prestige and power as they concomitantly learn that their language or dialect (if different from the dominant) does not matter. Gutiérrez, et al. describe second space as the language and learning space students know and live outside of school. Third space is "the social space within which counter-hegemonic activity, or contestation of dominant discourses, can occur for both students and teachers" (p. 451). Third space is the space of social justice, critical questions, and the facing of difficult and real issues about language, curriculum, and more. Yet third space is increasingly rare because students' achievement on tests is inextricably tied to school funding and other high stakes that reside in first space policies.

Coles (2003) points out that the "bad science" in Reading First-funded programs does benefit those seeking to further a specific view of reading. The Department of Education Office of the Inspector General (2006) uncovered significant corruption in this regard. The actual scores used to compose a portrait of teachers and schools and children as failing have changed little over the past 30 years (Berliner & Biddle, 1995), a reality that suggests that the crisis in education is manufactured. The profit motive is driving the supposed crisis as publishers take advantage of a frantic climate in which schools seek programs to serve as boxed panaceas for the policy-induced deficits of their students and teachers (Altwerger, 2005). The "one size fits all" (Ohanian, 1999) orientation of these programs demands that students bracket non-dominant languages and dialects. Spring (2008) suggests that the manufactured crisis in public education has the destruction of public schools as it ultimate goal. He also points out the ease with which education is used as a political torch that politicians hold up and claim to understand. One can't help but wonder about who is served when public schools are portrayed as defective.

The argument for the perpetuation of structured programs based on policies that often deny children the use of the rich funds of linguistic knowledge they bring to school (Moll, Amanti, Neff, & Gonzalez, 1992) is this simple: our schools are failing, we need to fix them, the economy is at stake, and so is our very survival as a nation. That view of schools is a portrait painted by special interest groups (publishers; those interested in privatizing public education) that profit when schools are labeled as defective.

Policies exerting a stronghold on our schools reflect claims that the urgent need for workers fitting within the global market demand that we put aside thoughtful (and progressive) ideas and return to the basics. The argument is that differences must be homogenized into a single mainstream. Only through homogenization can we dissolve the differences brought about by poverty, poor teaching, and defective learners. The belief is that everyone should be taught phonics. Everyone should learn Standard English. Everyone should become a "good" American, meaning that we all look alike, sound alike, work alike, make good money, are well cared for, and have traditional families and values. Our president is, then, the ultimate father figure who will lead us out of this quagmire and accept no excuses for failure (Lakoff, 2002). When the argument is framed this way—a way that says all must succeed and we can leave no child behind—those that disagree are portrayed as absurd, un-American and anti-children.

The arguments in favor of high stakes testing, labeling schools, linguistic and cultural homogeneity, and the return to the past achieve an important, though often ignored goal: They leave children feeling defective, broken, and incompetent. The "defective" and "broken" feelings are the result of daily acts of aggression that non-dominant students feel. These are usually not physical assaults, but rather subtle but constant reminders that certain groups speak right, have privilege, deserve privilege, have access, and have entitlements while other groups do not. These regular insults to the essence of who students are, where they are from, and how they speak, learn and relate are microaggressions; microaggressions are defined as "subtle, stunning, often automatic, exchanges which are 'put downs' of Blacks [or other non dominant groups] by offenders" (Pierce, Carew, Pierce-Gonzalez, & Wills, 1978, p. 66). Each day in school, non- dominant students' understanding of who they are is psychically chipped away, a chipping that affects the portraits they compose of themselves within the world and their subsequent actions that grow from these portraits. Microaggressions lead to microtrans-formations (Wolfe, Martens, & Meyer, 2003) of the self as a citizen, student, speaker, reader, writer, and thinker. Poet Jimmy Santiago Baca (1987) felt this etching away of self to the point of believing what others told him about himself. He wrote about himself and his sense of efficacy as that sense grew from the many microaggressions he experienced in school and in the world (Jimmy Santiago Baca, 1987, p. 9):

Everything hoped for in my life
was a rock closed road
where I had left my identity . . .

Microaggressions push students towards beliefs about what is right and wrong linguistically, socially, culturally, economically, and in terms of identity. The push towards homogeneity is a push towards monodimensionality, the dissolution of difference, self-doubt, and even self-hatred. It is a push against a multicultural and multilingual country that is multidimensional. First space microaggressions are the forum in which students learn whose values matter and whose do not. Some face becoming complicit in their own cultural and linguistic demise as they succumb into compliance with the linguistic demands of their schooling. Others develop behaviors that are typically considered maladaptive and are labeled as defiant, confrontative, and incapable of learning. Any commitments to their language and culture are viewed as dissent, an activity not welcomed within the present policy climate.

Throughout this chapter I will suggest that the frame around our children has become so small it does not allow an accurate portrayal of their rich linguistic diversity. Not only are languages and dialects at risk, the very lives and minds of our children are at risk, which means that we are all at risk. We are at risk of having increasingly dissatisfied angry groups that feel they have little left to lose. The urgency of this 'at-riskness' is not mine alone. It is evidenced in a treaty (convention) signed by almost every nation that belongs to the United Nations. The United Nations Convention on the Rights of the Child (as cited in Andrews & Kaufman, 1999) demands children have certain rights relevant to their dialect, language, culture, creativity, and identity.

> States parties undertake to respect the right of the child to preserve his or her identity, including nationality, name and family relations as recognized by law without unlawful interference (Article 8, Paragraph 1, p. 221).

> The child shall have the right to freedom of expression; this right shall include freedom to seek, receive and impart information and ideas of all kinds, regardless of frontiers, either orally, in writing or in print, in the form of art, or through any other media of the child's choice (Article 13, Paragraph 1, p. 223).

> States parties shall respect the right of the child to freedom of thought, conscience and religion (Article 4, Paragraph 1, p. 223).

> States parties recognize the right of every child to a standard of living adequate for the child's physical, mental, spiritual, moral, and social development (Article 27, Paragraph 1, p. 227).

> In those states in which ethnic, religious, or linguistic minorities or persons of indigenous origin exist, a child belonging to such a minority or who is indigenous shall not be denied the right, in community with other members of his or her group, to enjoy his or her own culture, to profess and practice his or her own religion, or to use his or her own language (Article 30, p. 228).

The U.S. is one of only two member nations that have not ratified the Convention, the other being Somalia, a country that has only recently initiated a centralized government. In the following sections, I paint two portraits of the children in my state. I use New Mexico as the exemplar because it is where I live and because the children of this state are the ones I see in classrooms when I do research. These are the children and teachers that I work with in the schools. They are the children whose families I have come to know and appreciate. It will become quite clear that my state and our country as a whole violate the U.N. Convention.

Politics, Policy, and One Portrait

In painting portraits, portraitists find *context* crucial to their documentation of human experience and organizational culture. By context, I mean the setting—physical, geographic, temporal, historical, cultural, and aesthetic—within which the action takes place. Context becomes the framework, the reference point, the map, the ecological sphere; it is used to place people and action in time and space and as a resource for understanding what they say and do (Lawrence-Lightfoot & Davis, 1997, p. 41).

In New Mexico, statistics have saturated the palate used to paint the official portraits of our children. I will refrain from including every statistic because, quite frankly, the litany of deficits outlined by the data becomes sufficiently visible with a limited number of examples.

In 2005, 49% of New Mexico's fourth graders scored below basic reading level on the National Assessment of Educational Progress (NAEP, 2005); 38% of the state's eighth graders scored "below basic"; 23% of the state scored below basic in writing in 2002. The 2005 NAEP percentages for fourth graders' reading scores were disaggregated by ethnicity and are presented in Table 4.1 (Nations' Report Card, 2005).

Note the closeness in percentages of students in the below basic and at basic categories and poverty levels, something that official portraitists (agencies) do not like to face. The relationships between performance and income level do not matter in the official portrait. Overall, 80% of fourth graders were at or below proficient; this portrays a state with severe reading problems.

NCLB created policy that relies on state-level tests to grade schools and districts. The policy demands that all children will be at proficiency in reading and math by

TABLE 4.1 National Assessment of Educational Progress of Fourth Grade Students in Reading in New Mexico, 2005

Category of Student	Overall Score	% below Basic	% at Basic	% Proficient	% Advanced
All students	207	49	31	17	4
White	225	28	36	28	8
Indian	N.r.	N.r.	N.r.	N.r.	N.r.
Black	206	50	26	21	4
Hispanic	199	57	29	12	2
Poor	199	58	29	12	1
Non-poor	225	29	35	28	8
Male	203	53	30	14	3
Female	211	44	32	19	5

Determined by eligibility for free/reduced lunch.

the time they complete high school. That proficiency level refers specifically to performance on the state-level tests. Schools that do not make adequate yearly progress towards that goal of proficiency for all students are sanctioned (punished) in ways including forced change of curriculum and forced changes in faculty. In 2005 519 schools in New Mexico made adequate yearly progress (AYP); this represents 67% of the state's schools. However, 249 (33%) schools did *not* make AYP. Fifty five of the 89 districts of the state (62%) did not make AYP, and 132 schools moved into the "needs improvement" category because of their lingering on the list of not making AYP for more than the allowable number of years (New Mexico Public Education Department factsheet, 2005).

The official, policy-generated portrait of underperforming and underachieving children and teachers is the one hung up for display at staff development meetings at which teachers are told to comply with often ridiculous programs (Meyer, 2001) that will supposedly remediate the problems. Margaret Spellings, Federal Secretary of Education, tells parents: "Today, school children enjoy new benefits and expectations under the No Child Left Behind Act, the U.S. law for K-12 education. These include a quality education, regardless of one's country of origin or language spoken at home" (United States Department of Education, 2005, p. 1). On page seven of that same document, readers are told: "Do not accept excuses from your school if your child isn't learning to read." With the notions of "no more excuses" and "no child left behind" built as the frame around the portrait, the work is done. The portrait clearly shows our schools are broken and with the resounding cry of "no child left behind" the government is working to *fix* them by using policy to dissolve students' languages and cultures. The portrait of schools and children in crisis is depressing and it casts a shadow across the work that teachers do. Some teachers either begin to believe or comply with official portraits that show their students as *failing* or *not proficient* and accept the statuses of *in corrective action, restructuring,* or *not making adequate yearly progress*. These terms are like dark shadows seeping through the portraits of individual children and specific contexts.

Teachers learn from this portrait, complete with frame, that the children they teach are disadvantaged, defective and deficient. It becomes the teachers' job, they are told, to overcome children's deficits, defects, and disadvantages. Further, relying on the executive summary of the report of the National Reading Panel (2000a), staff developers and corporations offer programs based on what they are calling "scientifically based reading research." They use this term because it is clearly articulated in the No Child Left Behind Act that only such programs will be funded. Therein is the final layer of finish on the frame and portrait. The idea that we are relying on *science* to fix the problems in this portrait. No one in their right mind would disagree with a scientific approach to such a complex problem.

In summary, the official portrait is policy driven and influences decisions made at the state and district levels that directly influence teaching practices and the lives of students in schools. Programs are adopted and enacted in order to be in compliance, but the programs do not address the needs of the students. Teachers feel forced to abandon professional decision making and become compliant technicians.

The Counterportrait

Many educators respond to the national call for higher scores by complying with curricular decisions in which they have little or no say. Curriculum decisions by deferral is a deprofessionalizing move but many teachers make that move in order to retain their jobs. The national, state, and local portraits of children exert huge pressures for pedagogical compliance. However, there are counterportraits on which teachers might rely to make decisions about their teaching and for making cases for instruction that is specific to the needs of their students. Further, such educators argue for social programs beyond the school site because of the contents of the counterportrait.

The importance of contexts in the portraiture of children is at the heart of counterportraits. Counterportraits offer compositions in contrast to those painted by dominant agencies such as the Federal Department of Education or state-level statistics about performance. One way that counterportraits accomplish their composing is by considering data often ignored or factored out by mainstream portraitists. Thus, counterportraits offer information to complicate, shed light on, and in other ways recompose the portraits of children, teachers, and schools with the ultimate goal of repositioning children and teachers, moving them away from a mentality that blames and towards one that might honor and enhance the quality of their lives and experiences in and out of school.

Perhaps readers recall oldtime movies that began with a completely darkened screen and then a pinpoint of light appears at the center that gradually opens until the entire scene is visible. Moviemakers refer to that as "irising out." The official portrait of the children in my state is irising out that stops before the entire scene is available to the viewer. It's as if the moviemaker starts with the darkened screen, shows us children and teachers and schools in a very limited way, and then stops. In this counterportrait, I will open the iris further to show the full landscape in which the portraits of children and teachers must be considered.

New Mexico is the first state to be a majority of minorities: 50% of the children in the state are Hispanic; 33% of the state's children are White; 12% are Native American; 2% are Black; 2% are "other," and 1% is Asian/Pacific Islander (U.S. Census, 2000). Of the Hispanic children, 47% speak Spanish as their first language; 44% of the Native American children in our state speak a language other than English (Navajo, Keres, Towa, and Tewa are among the most popular) (New Mexico Voices for Children, 2003). In 2004, 37% of the children in my state were living in families in which no parent had a full-time job; 23% lived in homes in which the household head was a high school dropout (Kids Count News, Casey, 2006).

The U.S. government (Federal Register, 2005) defines the Federal Poverty Level (FPL) in the contiguous United States as $19,350 for a family of four. But, 25% of New Mexico's children live in poverty (that is 129,300 children); of those nearly half (57,000) are deeply poor. Deeply poor families are ones in which the income is less that half of the Federal Poverty Level. New Mexico has the nation's highest rate of child poverty (NM Voices for Children, 2003). Food insecurity is defined as "uncertain or limited availability of adequate supplies of nutritional and safe food" (Ecohealth, 2006). In my state, the mean for food insecurity and food insecurity with hunger in 2002–2004 was 15.8%, a full 4.4% above the U.S. average. Food insecurity with hunger averaged 4.9% in New Mexico for that same period of time (1.3 percentage points above the national average). According to *Hunger in America* (2005) "only four in 10 low-income children who receive school lunch also get school breakfast . . . only 2 in 10 low-income children who receive school lunch also receive summer food when school is out." Yet 11% of Native American mothers in our state work full time and year round and *still* live in poverty; 20% of Hispanic mothers living in poverty received public assistance and over half of them remained in poverty. Even with public assistance, family incomes were not raised to or above the poverty threshold (NM Voices for Children, 2003).

The income and nutritional portraits of so many children in my state are bleak and the health issues are not much brighter: 40% of the Native American children in New Mexico do not have health insurance; 17% of Hispanic and 16% of Whites don't either. Although we know that (only) 36% of employers offer health coverage to employees, many workers choose not to enroll because they need the take-home salary that would be lost to co-payments for inclusion in such a plan (NM Health Policy Commission, 2003). This creates situations in which emergency room care becomes the primary caretaker for many families. Minor medical conditions are not treated unless they develop into severe situations. Children have chronic infections, low-grade fevers, and other symptoms with which they learn to live, but not necessarily learn.

New Mexico graduated one Native American physician and 18 Hispanic physicians in 2002–2003 (State Health Facts, 2003). Teachers are not the only individuals who may or may not choose to learn about different cultures. Physicians often do not know how to deal with cultural differences. For example, one doctor working with Hmong patients suggested that the "preferred method of treatment was high-velocity transcortical lead therapy." When asked what that meant, the doctor responded that "the patients should be shot in the head" (Fadiman, 1997, p. 63).

In New Mexico, infant mortality rates from 1990–1999 were 7.3%. Thus we have children living in families where they and their siblings and parents are hungry, infants perish, and health issues are not addressed because of lack of money.

These are conditions that create huge amounts of stress leading to the high rate of domestic violence, drug use, and alcohol abuse in the state. Our state averages one teen suicide a day (Casper Star Tribune, 2005). We have a rate of 80 teen deaths by accident, homicide, and suicide per 100,000 teens in the state. Our suicide rate is twice the national rate for teens and suicide is the third leading cause of death among young in our state. Statistics from 2001 indicate that one in five adolescents in New Mexico had seriously considered killing themselves and one in ten had attempted suicide.

In summary, the unofficial portrait is not currently considered by policymakers but is a reality in classrooms, schools, and communities. Teachers that consider this portrait in their practice teach against the grain, from a critical literacy (Bomer, 2001), and may be threatened with charges of insubordination (Meyer, 2001).

No Simple Dichotomy

The two portraits presented so far in this chapter are not the only portraits on which teachers rely in making decisions about language use in the classroom. The first portrait paints a picture of almost untenable academic performance; the second offers insurmountable social, health, and nutritional issues that often leave teachers feeling hopeless and helpless. Yet there are many more portraits available as evidenced by the very children teachers see in their classrooms. The specificity of children demands that teaching be artistic and aesthetic, in addition to being well informed about content. Artistic teaching is not currently acceptable by Federal policies that call for teaching based on policy-approved programs. Artistic classrooms rely on a definition of science much more elaborate than the one described in the report of the National Reading Panel (2000b). The definition in that report limits the portraits of reading instruction to programs that are approved far from the realities of the site at which they are implemented.

In order to acquire Federal funding, many districts are using generic programs, which do more than misunderstand reading, they hurt children (Coles, 2003; Ohanian, 1999) because of the program's view of what is acceptable language. Generic programs are those that are produced for large-scale distribution and profit, often ignoring the specific portraits onto which they will be applied. Further, the limited research base of these programs (limited by government intervention into the nature of research) demands that programs ignore the specific ways in which certain cultural groups learn (McCarty, 2002; Philips, 1971).

Educators feel the pressure of being stuck between the two portraits I have described. The pressure they feel intensifies as they seek to address local needs with generic programs and find the connection to practice impossible. Frustrated teachers might blame the children; reflective and well-informed teachers blame the programs and policies. Teachers know that they cannot effectively teach children who are in pain, poorly nourished, or suffering the spiritual and psychological trauma that accompanies the stress of poor living conditions aggravated by the demand that only one language and dialect is appropriate and acceptable for success in school. There are examples of successful programs that address the issues of these conditions and work to develop relationships with children and their communities in ways that honor culture (Kitchen, Velázquez, & Myers, 2000). However, such programs are typically large grants with limited funding periods—when the funding expires, so do the successes.

It is simply not sufficient to tell teachers and children "no more excuses" unless there are systematic and sustained changes to policies influencing social conditions accompanied by a deep respect for the professional decisions that informed teachers can make at the local level. The portraits of children and their communities need to be brightened by culturally appropriate support for a better quality of life ("better" as defined by the community itself).

The Possibilities

We Know What Really Works, So . . . No More Excuses!

The most consistent predictor of school success continues to be family level of income. When a family's income is sufficient for a decent quality of life, many of the conditions necessary for learning blossom. A decent level of income means that a family has ongoing medical care for minor and major ailments. They eat nutritious meals, work reasonable hours, have time to spend with their family, and have time to develop a sustained relationship with the school. Karp (2004) suggests that adequate yearly progress (AYP) be applied to the economy rather than to a school's performance.

AYP as an economic principle becomes *yearly increment in personal income* (YIPI). YIPI demands that every family in the state reach the present median income (just under $35,000 in New Mexico) within 12 years by making annual increases in their income. During each of the 12 years a child is in first through twelfth grade, the child's family must earn increases in annual income equal to one-twelfth of the difference between their present income and the 2005 median income. The AYP model of school achievement punishes the schools, teachers, and children if yearly goals are not met. In the YIPI model, the state's industries and any for-profit organizations or groups are responsible for economic progress. If they have employees whose incomes do not reach their yearly goals, the companies could be taxed so their employees do reach their YIPI goals. This would ensure that workers make YIPI so they are eventually all "proficient" in earning. Any Federal agencies that are housed in the state are also part of the formula. In New Mexico, the labs that make atomic weapons, the military bases, and other Federal installations would not be immune. If YIPI were enacted, no families will be at 100% or less than the FPL by 2009. By 2011, no families will have incomes less than 150% of the FPL. By 2014 every family in the state will be at the 2005 median income level.

One important and ongoing claim about AYP is that it will directly influence the economic outlook of our country. If the children can read better, they will go farther in their education, get better jobs, be better workers, eventually make higher salaries, and have a better quality of life. The American dream will become a reality. If our government truly believed that increases in test scores would do all this, we would see significant evidence of this belief as we looked around the state. Let us consider the university at which I work. New Mexico had an overall high school graduation rate of 65% in 2000 (Greene, 2001). But let's assume that all 509,122 children presently in the state will graduate. Spreading them out over 12 years makes 28,285 graduates per year. Of our highest performers, 10% leave the state to attend college. If only 20% of the remaining graduates attend the University of New Mexico, that would mean an incoming class of 5091 students, compared to the 3200 who entered fall 2005. We better get building and hiring! We're not initiating industrial or technological growth, supporting housing growth, increasing the number of physicians available for regular medical care, or dealing with a myriad of other social improvements in anticipation of these smart and healthy readers. Our state government does not seem committed to preparing the canvas to paint the new picture of our highly educated youth and the Federal government fares even worse. In October of 2005, the U.S. Senate voted against increasing funding to Head Start, against increasing Pell grants to help the needy access higher education, against increasing funding for the Individuals with Disabilities Education Act, and against funding for after-school programs (Albuquerque Journal, 2005).

Perhaps it is time for teachers to cry out "No more excuses!" No more excuses for policies not supporting social programs that enhance the intellectual vitality of young children. No more excuses for not funding high-quality after-school programs for children. No more excuses for children being hungry. No more excuses for children not having the regular medical attention they deserve. No more excuses for funding cuts to schools, libraries, public parks, and other public facilities. No more excuses for minimum wages that prohibit a high quality of family life. No more excuses for poor pay for teachers. No more excuses for not initiating building and hiring in anticipation of more students entering post-secondary settings.

The success of children in New Mexico, the amazingly high number of schools not in corrective action or facing sanctions is something at which we should marvel in light of the conditions discussed in the second portrait. Yet the reality of the daily lives of the children that arrive at classrooms and schools throughout the state could leave some teachers feeling hopeless. Van Manen (1986) suggests that teacher burnout is not the result of working hard; it occurs when teachers reach the point at not being able to answer the question, "What's the use?" But there is hope.

The Hope is in the Local Portrait

Hope is multifaceted and involves at least these four ideas:

1. an awareness of the situation in which one is living;
2. a belief in and sense of the potential for change, which means an idea that possibilities exist;
3. a vision for change, which means not only imagining that things can be different but also imagining what that difference might look like;
4. a sense of potential for agency, even entitlement.

This last idea is about the sense of self as having instrumentality within one's world.

Hope brings with it a sense of empowerment. Empowerment is assumed sometimes, taken other times, but never given. We can't empower anyone; we can only participate in helping to compose conditions under which hope can flourish and be realized as we move it from potential to actualization. If we say we will empower someone, we're assuming an arrogant and hegemonic stance because *giving* suggests we can take away at will, too. I can't empower you. I can work to help create the conditions under which our voices—all of our voices, including our students'—can and will be heard.

Right now we're living in a time of backlash. Gutiérrez (2001) calls it "backlash pedagogy" (p. 568), which is based in backlash curriculum and backlash policy. We're being pushed into compliance and pushing back seems unviable, as it did during the civil rights movement, the labor movement, and the women's movements. Each of these movements had many faces, facets, and players. Now it is time to show the faces of our students, our teaching and learning conditions, and our schools and communities. We need to show the portraits—the full portraits—and not be silenced by the drive of corporations to make profits on the backs of our children. If our classrooms are becoming sweatshops for corporations, we need to show those portraits. If tests are not measuring what our children are doing, we need to show other portraits. If we feel as though we are blaming our students for poor performance, we need to untangle that story and take the blame away from the victims.

All four facets of hope are needed for change to be directional, rather than a random revolution that has no vision of life beyond the ending of the status quo. Change is the part of hope that is enacted, but the change needs to be rooted in dreams and visions that have social justice and the ideals of democracy at the center. The work of most of us as teachers and researchers is not at the policy level. We work at the local level, composing portraits and examining and critiquing them for accuracy and honesty. It is our voices as teachers—informed by the linguistic, cultural, social, political, and spiritual realities of our students—that will change the portraits of our students into one that is hopeful, accurate, and productive. When the counterportraits are presented, and truth is brought to the canvas in the form of light and hope, our students' linguistic and cultural lives will be embraced for the powerful resources they are.

Discussion Questions and Activities

1. Study and write your own state's official and unofficial portraits of children and schools. Consider various sources of information: state department of education website, website of the Annie E. Casey Foundation, the Children's Defense Fund, interviews with teachers, families, and other community members.
2. Study moments in history when non-dominant groups gained rights and opportunities. Consider the women's movement (suffragettes and more recently), civil rights in the U.S. and other countries, unions in U.S. factories, child labor and more. Make connections to the present oppressive policies affecting teachers and children.
3. Learn more about critical literacy and the changing nature of language arts instruction. Interview teachers, families, and community members, and read Bomer (2001). Compose a philospohy statement about your teaching of reading and writing reflective of your beliefs and the current political climate in which schools dwell.

References

Albuquerque Journal. (2005). How Our Congressional Delegation Voted. October 10.
Altwerger, B. (Ed.) (2005). *Reading for Profit: How the Bottom Line Leaves Kids Behind.* Portsmouth, NH: Heinemann.
Andrews, A. B., & Kaufman, N. H. (1999). *Implementing the UN Convention on the Rights of the Child: A Standard of Living Adequate for Development.* Westport, CT: Praeger.

Baca, J. S. (1987). *Martín & Meditations on the South Valley.* New York: New Directions Books.
Berliner, D., & Biddle, B. (1995). *The Manufactured Crisis: Myths, Frauds, and the Attack on America's Schools.* Reading, MA: Addison-Wesley.
Bomer, R. (2001). *For a Better World: Reading and Writing for Social Action.* Portsmouth, NH: Heinemann.
Casper Star Tribune. (2005). Retrieved October 29, 2005, from http://www.casperstartribune.net/articles/2005/07/10/news/regional/b338294a1e12eda5872570390078ea41.txt.
Coles, G. (2003). *Reading the Naked Truth: Literacy, Legislation and Lies.* Portsmouth, NH: Heinemann.
Ecohealth. (2006). Retrieved May 5, 2006, from www.ecohealth101.org/ glossary.html.
Fadiman, A. (1997). *The Spirit Catches You and You Fall Down: A Hmong Child, Her American Doctors and the Collision of Two Cultures.* New York: Farrar, Straus, & Giroux.
Federal Register. (2005). Retrieved November 5, 2005, from http://www.gpoaccess.gov/fr/index.html.
Greene, J. (2001). *High School Graduation Rates in the United States* (Revised, April 2002.). Retrived October 29, 2005, from http://www.baeo.org/. Washington DC: Black Alliance for Educational Options.
Gutiérrez, K. (2001). What's New in the English Language Arts: Challenging Policies and Practices, Y Qué? *Language Arts,* 78(6), 564–569.
——, Rymes, B., & Larson, J. (1995). Script, Counterscript, and Underlife in the Classroom: James Brown versus Brown v. Board of Education. *Harvard Educational Review,* 65(3), 445–471.
Heath, S. (1983). Ways with Words: Language, Life, and Work in Communities and Classrooms. Cambridge: Cambridge University Press.
Hunger in America. (2005). Retrieved October 22, 2005, from http://www.hungerinamerica.org/.
Karp, S. (2004). NCLB's Selective Vision of Equality: Some Gaps Count More than Others. In D. Meier, A. Kohn, L. Darling-Hammond, T. Sizer, & G. Wood (Eds.). Many Children Left Behind: How the No Child Left Behind Act is Damaging Our Children and Our Schools. Boston, MA: Beacon Press.
Kids Count News. Retrieved October 16, 2006, from the website of the Annie E. Casey Foundation: http://www.aecf.org/kidscount.
Kitchen, R., Velázquez, D., & Myers, J. (2000). Dropouts in New Mexico: Native American and Hispanic Students Speak Out. Paper presented at the Annual Meeting of the American Educational Research Association, New Orleans, LA (ERIC Document Reproduction Service No. ED440795).
Lakoff, G. (2002). Moral Politics: How Liberals and Conservatives Think. Chicago, IL: University of Chicago Press.
Lawrence-Lightfoot, S. & Davis, J, (1997). The Art and Science of Portraiture. San Francisco: Jossey-Bass.
McCarty, T. L. (2002). A Place to be Navajo: Rough Rock and the Struggle for Self-Determination in Indigenous Schooling. Mahwah, NJ: Lawrence Erlbaum Associates, Inc.
Meyer, L. (in press). *No Child Left Bilingual.* Portsmouth, NH: Heinemann.
Meyer, R. (2001). *Phonics Exposed: Understanding and Resisting Systematic Direct Intense Phonics Instruction.* Mahwah, NJ: Lawrence Erlbaum Associates, Inc.
Moll, L., Amanti, C., Neff, D., & Gonzalez, N. (1992). Funds of Knowledge for Teachers: Using a Qualitative Approach to Connect Homes and Classrooms. *Theory into Practice,* 31(1), 132–141.
National Assessment of Educational Progress. Retrieved October 2, 2005, from http://nces.ed.gov/nationsreportcard/.
National Reading Panel. (2000a). *Teaching Children to Read: An Evidence-Based Assessment of the Scientific Research Literature on Reading and its Implications for Reading Instruction. Executive Summary.* Washington, DC: National Institutes of Health.
——. (2000b). *Teaching Children to Read: An Evidence-Based Assessment of the Scientific Research Literature on Reading and its Implications for Reading Instruction. Report of the Subgroups.* Washington, DC: National Institutes of Health.
Nation's Report Card. (2005). Retrieved October 12, 2005, from http://nationsreportcard.gov/.
New Mexico Health Policy Commission. (2003). Retrieved October 4, 2005, from http://hpc.state.nm.us/.
New Mexico Public Education Department. (2005). Fact Sheet. Retrieved April 15, 2007, from http://www.ped.state.nm.us/div/acc.assess/Accountability/ayp 2005.html#2005.

New Mexico Voices for Children. (2003). Retrieved October 12, 2005, from http://www.nmvoices.org/.

Ohanian, S. (1999). *One Size Fits Few: The Folly of Educational Standards.* Portsmouth, NH: Heinemann.

Philips, S. (1971). Participant Structures and Communicative Competence: Warm Spring's Children in Community and Classroom. In C. Cazden, V. John, & D. Hymes (Eds.). *Functions of Language in the Classroom.* New York: Teachers College Press.

Pierce, C., Carew, J., Pierce-Gonzalez, D., & Wills, D. (1978). An Experiment in Racism: TV Commercials. In C. Pierce (Ed.). *Television and Education.* Beverly Hills, CA: Sage.

Spring, J. (2008). No Child Left Behind as Political Fraud. In H. Johnson, & A. Salz, (Eds.). What is Authentic Educational Reform? Pushing Against the Compassionate Conservative Agenda. Mahwah, NJ: Lawrence Erlbaum Associates, Inc.

State Health Facts. (2003). Retrieved October 5, 2005 from http://www.statehealthfacts.org/

Strauss, S. (2005). *The Linguistics, Neurology, and Politics of Phonics: Silent "E" Speaks Out.* Mahwah, NJ: Lawrence Erlbaum Associates, Inc.

United States Census. (2000). Retrieved November 1, 2005, from http://www.census.gov/.

United States Department of Education: Office of the Inspector General. (2006). *The Reading First Program's Grant Application Process: Final Inspection Report.* Washington, DC: U.S. Department of Education.

United States Department of Education. (2005). *Toolkit for Hispanic Families.* Washington, DC: Department of Education.

Van Manen, M. (1986). *The Tone of Teaching.* Edmonton, Canada: Scholastic.

Wheelis, A. (1973). *How People Change.* New York: Harper & Row.

Wolfe, P., Martens, P., & Meyer, R. (2003). Roots of Partnerships/Emerging Identities. Paper presented at the Annual Conference of the National Council of Teachers of English, San Francisco.

5

Restore My Language and Treat Me Justly: Indigenous Students' Rights to Their Tribal Languages

DOROTHY AGUILERA AND MARGARET D. LECOMPTE

Language preservation is critically important to American Indian, Alaska Native, and Native Hawaiian communities. School achievement and school completion rates of Native Americans are strongly linked to students' positive cultural identity (Deyhle, 1992), and especially influenced by strong support from culturally resilient families (Cleary & Peacock, 1998). Our own recent research on indigenous language immersion schools demonstrated that students in such programs outperformed their grade-level peers in English instruction programs in most content areas (Aguilera & LeCompte, 2007); we attribute this to the grounding in cultural knowledge in such programs. Research about culturally responsive pedagogy and curricula and indigenous language revitalization also indicate that effective culturally compatible education enhances both social and emotional development and academic success for indigenous students (Aguilera, 2003). In fact, students who become fluent in their native language as well as another language achieve greater cognitive flexibility (Cummins, 2000; Escamilla, 1994) and are stronger scholars than those who are monolingual. By contrast, mainstream education does not produce high academic achievement among Native American students, as proponents of culture-based education have long argued (Demmert & Towner, 2003).

These facts notwithstanding, the Indigenous Language Institute (Native Language Network, 2000) researchers predict that within 60 years only 20 of the more than 300 indigenous languages existing in the 19th century will remain. Researchers found fewer than one-third of Navajo kindergarteners were fluent in Dine' by the 1970s (Arviso & Holm 2001; Holm & Holm, 1995); however, currently the vast majority of Native American children entering schools speak variations of English dialects (i.e., American Indian English, Hawaiian Creole English, Alaskan English, and village English) as their first language which means immersion education is key to the revitalization of indigenous languages (Feldman, Stone, Wertsch & Strizich 1977; LaFortune, 1999; Leap, 1993).

Often the efforts that initially go into developing language immersion programs are enormous, particularly with the limited number of native language speakers, language materials and curriculum resources. Of critical importance in the revitalization of what has historically been an oral language tradition is whether or not written or audiotaped resources and tape archives exist in the native language for use in schools and communities. Second language acquisition by adults who can then teach the language in schools and consistent funding is critical to revitalize and sustain the few remaining indigenous languages. Interestingly, the deciding factor for predicting whether a language is endangered is not simply the number of its speakers, but the esteem granted to that language in comparison to dominant culture languages. Much of the language shift to English has been stimulated by a "mainstream" ideology that depreciates indigenous language fluency, arguing that linguistic and cultural diversity are un-American because they allegedly undermine nationality identity and unity. Native language preservationists struggle to reconcile tensions between the two ideologies, as well to prevent the global extinction of language diversity.

This chapter examines policy issues relevant to indigenous students' rights to instruction in and preservation of their ancestral languages. We begin with two examples of Native American's encounters with education, to set the stage for our critique of how Federal and state laws and policies undermine these efforts. In the second section, we describe educational policies that have impeded revitalization of indigenous languages. In the third section, we describe benefits of educational policies. Finally, we offer recommendations for policy changes to support more collaborative, interactive planning with Native Americans.

Two Illustrative Examples

Indigenous students are entitled to schooling that supports their ancestral languages and cultural identities, just as mainstream children are. Below we describe how two communities—Central Alaskan Yup'ik and Native Hawaiian—struggled to restore and sustain their languages and cultures. These examples typify events in many places where Native American families have worked to create educational systems that reflected their cultural backgrounds—including their languages.

The Hawaiian Islands: Revitalizing Traditional and Linguistic Knowledge

Native language loss in Hawai'i began in the 1890s, when an English Only law was imposed after the overthrow of the Hawaiian Monarchy by U.S. forces (Wilson & Kamanā, 2001). This law ending more than 50 years of public Hawaiian-medium education was continued after formal U.S. annexation of Hawai'i in 1898. Hawaiian language use continued in churches, newspapers, and politics in the early 1900s, although English was the language of instruction for Hawaiian children (Wilson & Kamanā, 2001). By the 1920s, the English Only law had seriously affected the Hawaiian people. Native Hawaiians instituted "foreign language" courses in Hawaiian to avert language loss. By the time of statehood in 1959, no Hawaiian speaking children were entering school, except for the tiny population on isolated Ni'ihau Island. In 1983, the 'Aha Pūnana Leo, a non-profit organization created by parents interested in restoring their Native Hawaiian language through Hawaiian-medium education, successfully persuaded the state government to suspend the English Only law. In 1986, Hawaiian was allowed once again in public and private schools.

'Aha Pūnana Leo leaders, advocating the Pūnana Leo (nest of voices) approach, opened their first preschool on Kaua'i. The "nest of voices" was designed to simulate the environment of an extended family, where adults and children exchange and preserve language, cultural knowledge and traditions. The school was unique because for the first time in 50 years, Native Hawaiian teachers who provided cultural knowledge and language skills to children through formal and informal means, were providing instruction exclusively in Hawaiian, and both Native Hawaiian and English speaking Hawaiian children attended. Using a total immersion model, the 'Aha Pūnana Leo "nest of voices" evolved into the Hawaiian medium pre-K-12 educational system. Beginning with preschools, students matriculate through followup streams of Hawaiian medium education. Presently, the system enrolls about 2022 children in 33 schools across the state, creating a unique combination of private, charter, and public schools and programs for grades pre-K-12. It includes a laboratory school system administered by a collaboration among the Department of Education, the charter schools, the Áha Pūnana Leo and the College of Hawaiian Language. Hawaiian medium education continues to evolve and its grassroots efforts become more successful and innovative, it has become more institutionalized in the public education system statewide. Its multiple partners are described thusly:

> The 'Aha Pūnana Leo was also the initial source of all curriculum materials and teacher assistance, later partnering with the Hale Kuamo'o Hawaiian language center established by the state legislature at the University of Hawai'i at Hilo. Still later Ka Haka 'Ula O Ke'elikōlani College of Hawaiian Language was established at the Hilo campus to further develop Hawaiian medium education. (W. H. Wilson, personal correspondence, January 9, 2005)

The first senior class graduated in 1999. Since that time the completion rate holds steady at 100% with about 80% of graduates attending college. Of these, most have completed postsecondary and advanced graduate degrees at the Ka Haka 'Ula O Ke'elikōlani Hawaiian Language College, University of Hawai'i-Hilo, which was the only college in the country offering a master's degree in an indigenous language in 2005 (Wilson & Kawai'ae'a, 2007).

A Yup'ik Village: Preserving Subsistence Practices and Language

For many generations, the Central Alaskan Yup'ik people, one of the largest tribes in Alaska, have practiced subsistence hunting, fishing, and berry gathering as both traditional and survival practices in isolated villages for centuries. On seasonal outings each summer families gather traditional food at the fish camps. Such family camps continue to transfer native languages, cultural practices, and intellectual knowledge from one generation to the next. Preservation of these traditions and knowledge through indigenous language immersion education is considered important by many Alaska native communities.

In the summer of 2002 teachers and administration were making plans for the dual language immersion charter school which had been instituted at the local school. Until the 1970s, Central Alaskan Yup'ik had been spoken widely among adults and children alike in this remote village. Now, children once again were learning Yup'ik in school.

Similar to the predominance of Hawaiian Creole English among Native Hawaiians, village English is typically the first language of the Central Alaska Yup'ik. Consequently, only about 25% of the school's teaching staff had sufficient bilingual ability to teach in the program (B. Williams, personal communication, November 4, 2004). Three years after the institution of No Child Left Behind (NCLB) educational reforms, the district learned they had been stripped of the bilingual education funds that had supported the district's dual immersion (Yup'ik and English) programs. As one frustrated school administrator lamented:

> Our Yup'ik language program struggles to survive amidst the English instruction promoted at all the different governmental levels . . . [even though] our immersion program was built on a 30 year effort by a group of Native Alaska parents/ teachers to preserve our indigenous language. (B. Williams, personal communication, November 4, 2004)

How long can a district maintain bilingual and immersion programs without consistent funding? These administrators' stories typify the problems encountered by native communities as they struggle with educational mandates for English instruction. Administration for the NCLB legislation fails to recognize that the benefits to indigenous students of learning through their native language are the same as they are for mainstream English speaking students in the U.S. Further, by denying this funding, NCLB impedes hiring of qualified teachers; the limited number of Yup'ik people who still are fluently bilingual and also are licensed teachers—and hence, eligible to teach under NCLB—poses a tremendous challenge to implementing a dual language immersion program. In addition, using Title VII funds to hire and provide professional development support to train fluently bilingual teachers (which means teaching English speakers to acquire Yup'ik) has not been allowed under the current administration of the NCLB legislation. Districts also are not permitted to use such funds to hire non-licensed Alaska Native consultants/staff who *are* fluent Yup'ik speakers to work with teachers to develop Yup'ik language educational materials.

Similar dilemmas over how to provide classrooms with bilingual teachers delay establishment of language immersion programs in many tribal communities. Many schools have tried to supplement the shortage of teachers with the use of ancestral language speakers from the community. Both researchers and practitioners agree that when teaching materials produced for revitalization of Native American languages are created by collaboration between native speakers and regular classroom teachers in language immersion programs, they often are richer in meaning, tradition, and authentic content substance (Aguilera & LeCompte, 2007; Barnhardt & Kawagley, 2005; McCarty & Romero, 2005). The historical meaning and authentication for the Yup'ik instructional materials could not have been provided without language support from Yup'ik speakers (J. Lipka, personal communication, 2005). However, these efforts have been undermined by current reform initiatives and the press for English fluency at the expense of ancestral languages.

Language and Cultural Oppression: U.S. Hegemony

U.S. Government Policy on Indigenous Language Rights

Historically, the principal attacks on Native American languages have come via Federal offices and agencies concerned with Indian affairs (currently the Bureau of Indian Affairs (BIA)). In 1880, these agencies established policies and orders regarding indigenous education and languages, while at the same time relocating the majority of native people into reservations.

On Native American reservations, English instruction was a policy strictly enforced by mission and government schools alike. All were required to administer instruction in the English language (Annual Report of the Commissioner of Indian Affairs, 1886). Similarly, the regulations from the Indian Office in 1880 required that:

> All instruction must be in English, except in so far as the native language of the pupils shall be a necessary medium for conveying the knowledge of English, and the conversation of and communications between the pupils and with the teacher must be, as far as practicable, in English. (p. 2)

Because it was deemed imperative that Native Americans acquire the English language as quickly as possible, the Federal government removed Indian children from their homes and families and placed them in boarding schools, arguing that they could not be "citizenized," placed on homesteads, and expected to "transact business with English speaking people" unless they lost their vernacular languages (p. 3). Although acquiring English automatically gave native people the responsibility of citizenship, it did not give them the concomitant citizenship privileges granted to Whites. Even some agents and other Federal officials in the Office of Indian Affairs understood that the policy violated natives' rights to their ancestral languages and "dealt a cruel blow to the sacred rights of the Indians" (p. 4).

Mission and boarding schools evolved with the reservation system. Some of the worst forms of assimilation and abuse occurred in these schools, including pervasive bans on speaking indigenous languages and practicing non-Christian ceremonies; burning of traditional Indian clothing, destruction of religious and cultural artifacts, and a mandate that native children must choose a Christian religion and name and adopt clothes suitable for servants and workers in Christian homes and businesses. These factors notwithstanding, resistance to imposition of English language instruction began early on, as, for example, in 1766, when Onondaga Nation leaders discouraged the headmaster of the Indian Charity School (known later as Dartmouth University) from using an assimilationist education policy (Commissioner of Indian Affairs, 1887). Resistance is even evident today, as tribal members and language activists protect and nurture their remaining language resources.

Attempts to impose English as the official language in the United States made use of the fictional existence in the United States of a primarily Anglo-Saxon "race" to create a nation where none really existed. Crawford (1992) argues that this fiction was accompanied by an argument that English should be the only language of the United States because "a nation (and presumably a nation with Anglo-English ancestry) can have only one language" (p. 396). The effect was to undermine tribal nations' sovereign rights, lands, cultural traditions, and political systems.

McCarty and Romero's (2005) research examining issues around language loss and revitalization reveals the sociocultural and emotional impact for generations on native people disserved by assimilationist education systems. Both the strictly mandated policies instituted in boarding schools and policies at the national level regarding education of indigenous and non-English speaking people directly influenced the patterns of native language loss. Requiring that students be educated in boarding schools, the failure of Indian schools to provide same-tribe teachers and role models, and the outright banning of native languages meant that entire generations grew up without adequate instruction in or exposure to their languages. As parents, members of these generations could not pass on indigenous language fluency to their children, which meant that children could not grow up learning the language of their parents and grandparents and using it daily—a critical factor in language preservation. Consequently, about one-third (47 of the 136) of Native American languages have fewer than 100 speakers (Crawford, 2004).

The causes of indigenous language loss are complex and include the legacy of colonization and genocide. Perhaps the most critical of these has been explicit Federal policies designed to obliterate Native languages and cultural traditions. These policies have had the desired effect, at least with regard to native languages. The influences of English media, technology, and schooling also have taken a toll. Further, when Native American children come to school speaking English, they tend to be labeled as "limited English proficient" (LEP) because of their use of dialects or American Indian English. This results in their placement in remedial classes or special education—placements ill suited to their abilities—and aggravates their isolation and alienation in mainstream education, coinciding with loss of traditional identities. We attribute the widespread academic failure of native students not to the students, but to assimilationist education and flawed academic assessments that have failed to provide adequate and equal educational opportunities for Native Americans. Systemic inequities have long been a source of anger and a point of resistance among Native Americans. Our stance is bolstered by research describing highly successful and culturally resilient Native Hawaiian youth exiting language immersion secondary schools with diplomas and entering higher education institutions (Wilson & Kawai'ae'a, 2007). There are many examples of native framed success stories (Demmert & Towner, 2003). When education reflects the students' linguistic and cultural identities, and indigenous intellectual knowledge and epistemologies, resistance will change to learning.

We now examine issues of sovereignty and describe Federal and state legislation that has both strengthened and impeded efforts by Native Americans to restore and sustain ancestral languages and indigenous intellectual knowledge through educational systems.

Sovereign Rights: Tribal Nations within a Nation

Sovereign rights are not well understood by public administrators, education policymakers or even state officials, yet these rights are at the "heart of tribal existence" (Ortiz, 2002, p. 477). In 1819, the Civilization Act established the Federal government's responsibility to American Indian education. The source of that government to government relationship between Congress and the tribal nations represents the foundation of sovereignty and sets the legal basis for funding educational services. Tribes, as "nations within a nation" have individually acted on sovereignty rights variously, depending on their unique cultural traditions and practices (Deloria & Lytle, 1984). Tribal leaders carry the responsibility of making sure the tribe's sovereign rights are at the cornerstone of legal negotiations and contracts with local, state, and Federal governments. Ortiz (2002) elaborates:

> [I]ssues of tribal sovereignty do matter and must be understood, because they weigh heavily in all intergovernmental relationships. . . . A great challenge lies in determining how governmental structure and program policy initiatives involve the nation's federal system with regard to tribal governance. (p. 477)

Tribal nations constantly struggle with non-Indians' misunderstandings and misrepresentations of what sovereign rights entail, particularly in regards economic, sociocultural, education, religious, and political issues and legislation and policies from other jurisdictions that invade their schools, homes, and communities and often contradict tribal practices. Masten (2001) states:

> The status of Indian Nations as a form of government is at the heart of nearly every issue that touches [American] Indian country. It is only when the general public and Congress understand that an American Indian tribe functions as a government and provides basic governmental services, that the principles of tribal governance will be recognized and protected. (p. 2)

Although, Native Hawaiians do not have a treaty with the Federal government, they have worked extensively with state and Federal governing bodies to write legislation for ancestral language and to build advocacy for getting these bills passed (W. H. Wilson, personal correspondence, December 6, 2007).

Bilingual Education Legislation and Civil Rights Laws since the 1960s

When President Johnson's "War on Poverty" and the Title VII Bilingual Education Act of 1968 were implemented, bilingual/bicultural education was virtually non-existent in tribal schools (McCarty, 1993). This legislation created opportunities for innovative programs that reflected local funds of knowledge and languages, and many Native Americans came to view Title VII and bilingual education as a viable option to restore and preserve their tribal languages. This was critical, since schools serving indigenous populations had systematically excluded local languages and cultural knowledge (McCarty, 1993; Medicine, 1982). However, inequities across Native American communities existed within the Federal administration of Title VII funds; Native Hawaiians were left out of bilingual education funding until 1989 (W. H. Wilson, personal correspondence, December 6, 2007).

Initially, five tribal communities received funds to develop bilingual education programs, and within 10 years, 70 programs were implemented in tribal school communities across the nation (McCarty, 1993). Rough Rock Demonstration School began its bilingual education project in 1966, even before the 1968 Act was passed. Rough Rock's newly tribal-elected school board, together with a Navajo board of trustees, contracted with the BIA and the Office of Economic Opportunity to operate its own school. Operated by an elected tribal governing board, this school became the first locally controlled "tribal contract" school, establishing its own Navajo Curriculum Center. The Center developed teaching and learning materials were embedded with both Dine' and mainstream values and traditions. Title VII funds also helped to create a Native American Materials Development Center in Albuquerque, which produced and disseminated hundreds of Navajo language materials during 8 years of funding. University courses were brought directly to Rough Rock to certify Navajo educators. Later, Navajo elementary teachers adapted reading strategies of the Kamehameha Early Education Program (Hawai'i) for Rough Rock students (Dick, Estell, & McCarty, 1994). In the 1970s, Lucille Watahomigie, Leanne Hinton, and the late John Rouillard began developing language training institutes for native speakers interested in sustaining their ancestral languages by acquiring the skills to develop language/culture based curricula, and writing systems. These institutes grew into the American Indian Language Development Institute (AILDI), which has resided at the University of Arizona for the past 18 years (McCarty, Watahomigie, Yamamoto, & Zepeda, 1997).

Key Legislation and Civil Rights Cases for Native Americans: 1970s–1990s

In the 1970s several landmark Federal laws shifted authority for schools serving indigenous students from the U.S. Bureau of Indian Affairs to local tribes and supported bilingual education specifically for Native American tribes. The Indian Education Act (1972) provided funds to develop Indian and Alaska Native bilingual education programs.

Two key civil rights cases also shifted the political environment such that students' legal rights to receive instruction in their ancestral and/or heritage languages and in English were recognized. In 1973, the lower courts ordered the Denver Public Schools to provide bilingual and bicultural instruction to Navajo students (Denetclarence v. Denver Board of Education). In 1974 the Supreme Court ruled in Lau v. Nichols (1974) that ELL students were not receiving an education equal to that of White students because it was not based on integrated school facilities, curricula, and teachers. Lau v. Nichols (414 U.S. 563 [1974]) is a U.S. Supreme Court decision, ruling that public schools must provide appropriate language instruction for students with limited English, to alleviate language barriers and provide equal access to the curriculum.

A short time later, Congress passed the Equal Educational Opportunity Act of 1974, which established criteria governing how schools provided more equitable instruction to non-European American students. The 1975 Indian Self-Determination and Education Assistance Act funneled money for education and other social services directly to tribal communities. This significantly changed the governance of local schools by allowing tribes to contract with the BIA to run their own local schools. No particular instructional methods or models were mandated for the teaching of non-English languages in classrooms under any of these laws; however, U.S. civil rights laws required schools to implement educational programs that offered equal opportunities for language learning among culturally and linguistically diverse children. The Federal courts and the Office of Civil Rights mandated that schools provide:

1. theoretically sound and research-based programs;
2. adequate resources for programs, including staff, training, and materials;
3. standards and procedures to evaluate programs and action plans by which to modify ineffective programs.

In 1974, the reauthorization of the Bilingual Education Act provided grants that continued earlier efforts by tribal schools and added provisions for teacher training and professional development activities emphasizing local control of schools, as well as supporting instruction in native languages and culture in regular class-rooms, rather than in the compensatory models of bilingual education (Crawford, 1992). Examples of these localized efforts include Rough Rock and Rock Point schools, where teacher education programs in the local communities were extremely successful. In a decade, the majority of certified indigenous teachers in the elementary schools were Navajo (Holm & Holm, 1995). Much of the success with bilingual education in Navajo schools can be attributed to the fact that the Navajo are the largest tribe in the U.S., and before the 1970s, they had many fluent speakers. However, the rapid shift from ancestral languages as the dominant language to English (American Indian English) as the first language has occurred with many tribes. Many Native American communities have limited resources for language revitalization including audio/videotape archives of oral language traditions, or written records of their ancestral history, language and cultural knowledge. Similar trends are seen with the increasingly fewer numbers of native speakers among Native Americans (e.g., three Tonkawa speakers).

By 1983 Title VII funding had created national systems of support for schools serving culturally and linguistically diverse student populations. These included: the National Clearinghouse for Bilingual Education (1977), regional bilingual education service centers, 16 multifunctional resource centers (MRCs), and the National Indian Bilingual Center in Arizona. Staffed with AILDI personnel, the

National Indian Board Center initially provided training and technical assistance to 85 Native American bilingual programs in 13 states to support classroom-based native language instruction; later expanding the training nationwide (McCarty, 1993). However, when the Federal government emphasized educational priorities for English language acquisition targeting language minority students, primarily immigrant populations, with reauthorization of the Bilingual Education Act in 1980, the funding shifted as well.

Native Hawaiian Activism and Resistance to Disparities in Federal Funding

Resistance to the disparities in Federal administration of Title VII funding increased as Native language activists and policy groups called for new legislation targeting restoration and maintenance of indigenous languages and cultural traditions. Arnold (2001) notes that William (Pila) Wilson drafted the wording for the Native American Language Act (1990) which grew out of the 1987 Hawaii legislature resolution that confronted the Federal policy barring use of ancestral language in territorial schools. Wilson reports:

> Although initially excluded from Native American provisions of the Bilingual Education Act, Native Hawaiians began with what has been recognized as a national model for grassroots and state level activism for indigenous language retention. In the late 1970s, they had successfully lobbied for major changes in the state's recognition of Hawaiian and support of the language. By 1983, a grassroots organization called 'Aha Pūnana Leo had established language nests opening the way for promotion of Hawaiian as a full medium of education equal to English. In 1987, Pūnana Leo developed a state legislature resolution calling for reversal of the federal policy that had earlier resulted in Hawaiian being banned as a medium of education in territorial schools. The resolution was taken to Hawai'i Senator Daniel Inouye, then head of the Senate Indian Affairs Committee, for introduction as a bill to be called the Native American Languages Act (NALA). The 'Aha Pūnana Leo then teamed up with the Native American Languages Issues Institute (NALI) and others to develop national support resulting in passage of NALA in 1990. (W. H. Wilson, personal correspondence, December 4, 2007)

The Native American Language Act of 1990 (P.L. 101-477) is a Federal law declaring that Native Americans have a right to use their own languages and that it is Federal policy to promote, preserve, and protect the development of Native American languages. States, Federal agencies, and other institutions are charged with carrying out this policy. Two years later, the NAL Act (1990) was amended with the Native American Languages Act of 1992 (P.L. 102-524) establishing funding through grants awarded to Native American tribes and organizations supporting activities for the preservation of Native American languages. The stated principles in NALA 1990 established a basis for subsequent national efforts to create distinct approaches and funding sources in Federal legislation for Native American language revitalization.

English Only Impact on Ancestral Languages

Federal policy for bilingual education began to change dramatically with the Reagan administration. First, authority over Federal funding for specific educational programs was given to the states. Funding now was sent to the individual states in "block grants" that could be distributed as the state saw fit, rather than being earmarked for individual programs. Then, on creation of the Department of Education, major cuts were made in Title VII and other educational programs serving Native Americans. The shift occurred even with the Bilingual Education Act, as reauthorized by Title VII of the Improving America's Schools Act of 1994 (P.L. 103-382), which has provisions that recognize the endangered status of Native American languages, provide flexibility to schools and tribal organizations in planning and implementing bilingual education programs, including the development and production of high-quality instructional materials for Native American students. By 1995, even with the NAL Act of 1992 and other legislation supporting ancestral language services, bilingual education funds shifted to nonnative populations in schools. Language immersion programs existed in only about 182 schools nationwide, primarily for nonNative American populations such as those from China, Russia, Portugal, France, Spain, Korea, Arabic speaking countries, and Japan (Cummins, 2000).

National Trend in English Only Legislation among States

Only Hawaii has successfully passed legislation for both English and Hawaiian as official languages. New Mexico, Oregon, and Washington in 1989, and Rhode Island in 1992, passed English Plus Resolutions, which promote English, plus other languages, particularly the preservation of ancestral and heritage languages (i.e., immigrant children's first/heritage language). Another 27 states have passed English Only legislation, but some of these were deemed unconstitutional including Alaska. A total of 25 states have active official English Only laws (Crawford, 2004).

Sovereign Rights to Native Language Revitalization and Preservation

Since the shift to transitional models of bilingual education began in the 1980s, American Indians once again have had to reclaim their sovereign right to their ancestral languages. The right of native students to their tribal languages is written in law. However, far too often, local, state, and Federal administration's failure to carry out the mandates in legislation has impeded language maintenance efforts. A clear example is the NCLB of 2001 legislation, specifically, Title VII, Parts A, B, and C and Title III subparts, A and B which include provisions for American Indian, Native Hawaiian and Alaska Native education including native language instruction (U.S. Department of Education, 2002). Title VII also provides supplemental grants to tribes, native organizations, local educational agencies, educational organizations, and others to meet the educational needs of Native American children including language, cultural, and academic programs and activities. Generally these provisions have been ignored by states in their focus on meeting other goals required under NCLB.

The NAL Act (1990) "specifically declares federal policy is to protect Native American 'rights' regarding use of native languages" (Ferrin, 1999, p. 2). According to Ferrin, these rights are to "use, practice and develop Native American Languages," (p. 3). Nonetheless, the broader and conservative policies for limiting and finally ending bilingual education funds for preserving and restoring indigenous languages in the past have also curbed the potential benefits that might have accrued in native communities from the Act. Passage of the NAL Act (1990) "reversed the federal government's previous policy of eliminating Native American languages ... [establishing] a federal policy to preserve, protect, and promote the rights and freedoms of Native Americans to use, practice, and develop Native American languages" (NIEA, Educational Facts and History, n.d.). The Native American Languages Act of 1992 provided funding through the Administration for Native Americans (ANA) for the creation of Native American language programs in tribal communities.

Legislation alone has not resulted in widespread implementation of language immersion programs. Despite the Bilingual Education Act (re-authorized by the Title VII of the 1994 Improving American Schools Act) (P.L. 103-382), and the White House Conference on Indian Education (1992), only Native Hawaiians have reinstated their language rights through legislative action at the state level. The NIEA advocates increased Federal funding for Native language immersion programs through ANA and supported Federal legislation that would amend NAL Act (1992) to provide increased support for Native American language immersion programs. Further, the majority of native communities, rural and urban alike, desire to use educational systems to restore and preserve their languages and cultural traditions. A multigenerational stream of tribal support for culturally responsive education for indigenous communities is evident, particularly education that involves language immersion programs and culturally specific education utilizing local funds of knowledge (Aguilera, 2003; Barnhardt & Kawagley, 2005; Demmert & Towner, 2003; Lipka, 2002; Yazzie, 2002).

Recent Amendment to Native American Languages Act of 1992

In spring of 2006 H.R. 4766, the Esther Martinez Native American Languages Preservation Act of 2006, was introduced by Representative Heather Wilson (New Mexico) and co-sponsored by Representative Rick Renzi (Arizona). This bill, signed into law on December 14, 2006, amends the Native American Languages Act of 1992. The NIEA reports:

[T]he bill authorizes competitive grants through the U.S. Department of Health and Human Services to establish Native American language "nests" for students under the age of seven and their families. It supports Native American language survival schools. It will help to preserve all the indigenous languages that are still being spoken, and increase the support for Native American language immersion programs to create fluent speakers, and allow tribes and pueblos to develop their own immersion programs. (National Indian Education Association, 2006)

Legislation for preservation of indigenous languages is an issue, but so is significant funding. The NIEA and ANA continue to lobby legislators to achieve the level of funding necessary to develop sufficient program resources and implement language immersion schools. When the goal is to produce fluent speakers it is counter-productive to reduce the use of native language.

Language Preservation Today

Language immersion preschools currently serve children in Ojibwe, Cree, Ute, Blackfeet, Native Hawaiian and Alaska Native communities. Summer and winter language/culture camps, after school and family education programs occur in rural and urban settings (Crow, Umatilla, Northern Cheyenne, Ojibwe, Phoenix and Milwaukee). Tribal members participate in language and culture classes that include leadership training, language teaching and certification as preservation measures. Another language immersion model developed by California tribes and adopted by North Dakota and Montana tribes, involves master/apprenticeship relationships where an adult native speaker mentors a child or youth in indigenous language and culture.

Currently, the Central Alaskan Yup'ik, Blackfeet, Ojibwe, Lakota, Cochiti Pueblo, Cherokee, Mohawk and others have established schools and streams of education— Pre-K to graduate degree programs (Navajo and Native Hawaiian) using their ancestral language as the medium of instruction, recognizing that mainstream assimilationist models of education have failed their children. An array of governing structures (private, public charter, public, laboratory) are used to accomplish key objectives: autonomy which reduces oversight by state and district authorities, often dominated by Whites; closer links among indigenous school or charter founders, teachers, and community; and, infusion of native language/cultural standards and pedagogy weighted equally with state- mandated academic standards. These are key differences between conventional mainstream public schools where native language and culture play "second fiddle" to mainstream English language curricula and the locally controlled schools and education streams from language nests to graduate degree programs established by the Navajo and Native Hawaiian.

Recommendations for Change

Maintenance of indigenous language schools and culturally responsive curricula has been possible only where Native Americans control their own schools (Aguilera, 2003; Lomawaima & McCarty, 2006). Today, the majority of Native American students attend public schools where they constitute a very small minority of the population; hence, they lack power to achieve adequate representation on the school boards which run their schools. The 185 schools and dormitories in 23 states that serve 47,000 students under the umbrella of the Bureau of Indian Affairs are more homogenous ("Summer Newsletter," 2006). One might think that these schools would hold promise for providing culturally compatible instruction and language services as mandated in NALA 1990 Sec. 104 (5) and allowed for in several areas of NCLB, e.g., Sec. 3128. This hegemonic collage of authority, funding, and organizational structures controls local reservation community school systems and makes them subject to the most profound impacts of NCLB and high stakes testing—ones that obviate *and* denigrate—proper instruction in native languages and culture.

Thus, tribes now see that control of their own schools is the only way to improve education for their children. They have begun to establish public charter, private and a combination of public, charter, and private schools which can be excluded from many, if not all, of the mandates described earlier. Much of this trend involves recognizing that tribes must gain both political autonomy and absolute control over their schools and children. Establishing their own academic programs through culturally responsive standards, curricula, and assessments constitutes reclaiming their sovereign rights to effective education. The goal is simply to blend tribal language and intellectual knowledge with mainstream content to best serve their community and children.

Native communities are as diverse as mainstream and White schools with regard to multiple perspectives on how best to educate their children, particularly when it comes to specific curricula and academic activities such as language instruction. Nonetheless, many Native Americans feel that native languages and cultural knowledge should be taught at schools. Urban schools face issues of ethnic heterogeneity in their communities making it difficult to teach specific languages particularly with fewer fluent speakers; often encouraging school districts to avoid native language instruction altogether. Above all is the disparity of esteem accorded to Indian culture and native languages in the face of the mainstream hegemony of English. Native students and their teachers struggle with this hegemonic issue daily; it has a significant detrimental effect upon their sense of ethnic identity and self-esteem.

Given the problems outlined in this chapter and the long history of hegemonic oppression of Native American language and culture, the recommendations that follow must address both long- and short-term goals. We cannot, after all, have any confidence that the U.S. government would immediately reverse the five centuries of conquest and the negative attitudes toward native peoples it actually created. However, we can begin with educational issues, move to issues of sovereignty, and hope that as tribal communities gain strength and self-confidence, they will become increasingly effective in fighting off attempts to suppress them. To that end, we offer the following recommendations:

1. Eliminate English Only requirements and Federal/state policies restricting language rights in Native American communities so that native language instruction can flourish.
2. Create exceptions to NCLB specifically tailored to tribally controlled and indigenous language-based schools. For example:
   - permit achievement testing in the traditional content areas in both native languages as well as English
   - assess annual yearly progress in both indigenous languages and English measure and count individual student gains, as well as mastery to grade-level proficiency, in assessing whether or not a school is "successful"

- eliminate the negative financial sanctions of failing to meet AYP for schools with large Native American populations
- eliminate the requirement that Native American schools failing to make AYP for 3 consecutive years be closed
- create procedures by which non-certified but highly qualified persons can be hired to support native language resource development work and teaching, both of which are vital to language restoration and preservation.
3. Provide funding for effective immersion schools and other bilingual programs that are not transitional bilingual programs. Provide funding for:
   - materials and test development in native languages
   - scholarships for individuals who wish to become certified bilingual (in native languages and English) teachers and school leaders
   - tribal colleges to organize teacher training and staff development programs for native bilingual teachers
   - the design of and research on demonstration projects
   - dissemination centers to distribute research from demonstration sites and materials development to interested tribal groups
   - lengthened funding cycles to permit more stable and consistent support for innovative native language programs.

We recognize that these recommendations simply involve making alterations in the existing laws, and do not address deeper societal problems. To that end, we make the following recommendation:

4. Create a panel of lawyers and Native American experts to review treaty rights granted to Native Americans related to language, education, and tribal autonomy, and funds still owed to tribal groups for unpaid land compensation, oil, gas, and other royalties.

Discussion Questions and Activities

1. Develop a timeline of government policies regarding Native Americans and list the five most important factors uniquely affecting them in those policies.
2. Identify and discuss at least three positive benefits of litigation/legislation to Native Americans that also were beneficial to both non-mainstream and mainstream groups.
3. Of the recommendations offered, discuss three that you would be most likely to support, if given the opportunity. What are the three most important things you would do in such a campaign?
4. Discuss your understanding of sovereignty and how this relates to educational programs in schools serving Native American communities.

References

Aguilera, D. E. (2003). Who's Defining Success: An Analysis of Competing Models of Education for American Indian and Alaskan Native Students. Doctoral Dissertation, University of Colorado-Boulder. *Dissertation Abstracts International*, 64, 3939.

——, & LeCompte, M. D. (2007). Resiliency in Native Languages: The Tale of Three Indigenous Communities' Successful Experiences with Language Immersion. [Special Issue] *Journal of American Indian Education*, 46(3), 11–37.

Arnold, R. D. (2001). To Help Assure the Survival and Continuing Vitality of Native American languages. In L. Hinton, & K. Hale (Eds.). The Green Book of Language Revitalization in Practice. San Diego, CA: Academic Press.

Arviso, M., & Holm, W. (2001). Tse'hootsooi'di Olta'gi Dine' Bizaad Bi'hoo'aah: A Navajo Immersion Program at Fort Defiance, Arizona. In L. Hinton, & K. Hale (Eds.). The Green Book of Language Revitalization in Practice. San Diego, CA: Academic Press.

Barnhardt R., & Kawagley A. O. (2005). Indigenous Knowledge Systems and Alaska Native Ways of Knowing. *Anthropology & Education Quarterly*, 36(1): 8–23.

Cleary, L. M., & Peacock, T. D. (1998). *Collected Wisdom: American Indian Education*. Boston, MA: Allyn & Bacon.

Commissioner of Indian Affairs. (1886). Annual Report to the Secretary of the Interior. Washington, DC: Government Printing Office 8375 I A 1337. Retrieved March 17, 2007, from http://ia331341. us.archive.org/2/items/annualreportofco188700nitrich/annualreportofco188700unitrichdjvu.txt.

——. (1887). XXI Annual Report to the Secretary of the Interior. Washington, DC: Government Printing Office 8222 I A. Retrieved March 17, 2007, from http://ia331326.us.archive.org/2/items/ usindianaffairs86usdorich/usindianaffairs86usdorich_djvu.txt.

Crawford, J. (1992). *Language Loyalties: A Source Book on the Official English Controversy*. Chicago, IL, and London: University of Chicago Press.

——. (2004). *Educating English learners: Language Diversity in the Classroom*, 5th edn. Los Angeles: Bilingual Educational Services, Inc.

Cummins, J. (2000). Beyond Adversarial Discourse: Searching for Common Ground in the Education of Bilingual Students. In C. J. Ovando, & P. McLaren (Eds.). *The Politics of Multiculturalism and Bilingual Education*. Boston, MA; McGraw-Hill Higher Education.

Deloria, V., & Lytle, C. M. (1984). The Nations Within: The Past and Future of American Indian Sovereignty. New York: Pantheon Books.

Demmert, W. G., Jr., & Towner, J. C. (2003). *A Review of the Research Literature on the Influences of Culturally Based Education on the Academic Performance of Native American Students*. Portland, OR: Northwest Regional Educational Laboratory.

Deyhle, D. (1992). Constructing Failure and Maintaining Cultural Identity: Navajo and Ute School Leavers. *Journal of American Indian Education*, 31(2), 24–47.

Dick, G. S., Estell, D. W., & McCarty, T. L. (1994). Saad Naakih Bee'enootihji Na'alkaa: Restructuring the Teaching of Language and Literacy in a Navajo Community School. *Journal of American Indian Education*, 33(3), 31–46.

Escamilla, K. (1994). The Sociolinguistic Environment of a Bilingual School: A Case Study Introduction. *Bilingual Research Journal*, 18(1–2), 21–47.

Holm, A., & Holm, W. (1995). Navajo Language Education: Retrospect and Prospects. *Bilingual Research Journal*, 19(1), 141–168.

Feldman, C., Stone, A., Wertsch, J. V., & Strizich, M. (1977). Standard and Non-Standard Dialect Competencies of Hawaiian Creole English Speakers. *TESOL Quarterly*, 11(1), 41–50.

Ferrin, S. (1999). Reasserting Language Rights of Native American Students in the Face of Proposition 227 and Other Language-Based Referenda. *Journal of Law and Education*, 28(1), 1–23.

LaFortune, R. (1999). *Native Languages as World Languages: A Vision for Assessing and Sharing Information about Native Languages across Grantmaking Sectors and Native Country*. Arden Hills, MN: The Grotto Foundation.

Lau v. Nichols, 414 U.S. 563 [1974].

Leap, W. L. (1993). American Indian English and Its Implications for Bilingual Education. In L. M. Cleary, & M. D. Linn (Eds.). *Linguistics for Teachers*. New York: McGraw-Hill.

Lipka, J. (2002). Schooling for Self-Determination: Research on the Effects of including Native Language and Culture in the Schools (ERIC Document Reproduction Service No. ED459989). Charleston, WV: ERIC.

Lomawaima, T., & McCarty, T. (2006) To Remain an Indian: Lessons in Democracy from a Century of Native American Education. New York: Teachers College Press, Columbia University.

Masten, A. S. (2001). Ordinary Magic: Resilience Processes in Development. *American Psychologist*, 56(3), 227–238.

McCarty, T. (1993). Federal Language Policy and American Indian Education. *Bilingual Research Journal*, 17, 13–34.

——, Watahomigie, L., Yamamoto, A., & Zepeda, O. (1997). School–Community–University Collaborations: American Indian Language Development Institute. In J. Reyhner (Ed.). *Teaching Indigenous Languages*. Flagstaff, AZ: Northern Arizona University.

——, & Romero, M. E. (2005). What Does it Mean to Lose a Language? Investigating Heritage Language Loss and Revitalization among American Indians. *Show and Tell.*

Medicine, B. (1982). Bilingual Education and Public Policy: The Cases of the American Indian. In E. Padilla (Ed.). Bilingual Education and Public Policy in the United States. *Ethnoperspectives in Bilingual Education Research*, 395–407.

Native American Languages Act, Pub. L. No. 101-477 (1990). Pub. L. No. 102–524 (1992).

Native Language Network. (2000). [Electronic version]. Newsletter of the Indigenous Language Institute. *Copy Editor*, Winter, 1–8.

National Indian Education Association (2006). Representative Heather Wilson Introduces a Bill to Amend the Native American Languages Act. Media/Education News. Retrieved September 2, 2007, from http://www.niea.org/.

——. (n.d.). History of Indian Education. Education Facts & History. Retrieved September 2, 2007, from http://www.niea.org/.

Ortiz, J. (2002). Tribal Governance and Public Administration. *Administration & Society*, 34(5), 459–481.

U.S. Department of Education, Office of Elementary and Secondary Education. (2002). *No Child Left Behind: A Desktop Reference*, Washington, D.C. Government Printing Office.

Wilson, W. H., & Kamanā, K. (2001). Mai Loko Mai O Ka 'i'ini: Proceeding from a Dream: The 'Aha Pūnana Leo Connection in Hawaiian Language Revitalization. In L. Hinton, & K. Hale (Eds.). The Green Book of Language Revitalization in Practice. San Diego, CA: Academic Press.

Wilson, W. H., & Kawai'ae'a, K. (2007). I Kumu; I Lā-Lā-: "Let There be Sources; Let There be Branches": Teacher Education in the College of Hawaiian Language. [Special Issue] *Journal of American Indian Education*, 46(3), 38–55.

Yazzie, T. (2002). Culture Deep Within Us: Culturally Appropriate Curriculum and Pedagogy in Three Navajo Teachers' Work. Doctoral Dissertation, Harvard University, Cambridge, MA. *Dissertation Abstracts International*, 63, 2122.

6

Power, Politics, and Pedagogies: Re-Imagining Students' Right to Their Own Language Through Democratic Engagement

VALERIE KINLOCH

The many debates concerning multilingual and bidialectical students (Baugh, 1983; Jordan, 1985; Kinloch, 2005b; Smitherman, 2003), particularly in the context of public education in America, reiterate the importance of examining public attitudes toward language as well as teacher dispositions, instructional approaches, and classroom teaching methods. From the Ann Arbor Black English court case (1979) to the English Only Movement (1980s) and the Oakland Ebonics debate (1996), approaches to working with linguistically diverse students—variously labeled "people of color," "poor," "working class," and "urban"—have been met with criticism and resistance. Since the 1960s, professional organizations such as the National Council of Teachers of English (NCTE), the Conference on College Composition and Communication (CCCC), and the Modern Language Association (MLA), despite diverse-exclusive histories, have made attempts to address a crisis in secondary and college-level classrooms created by "the cultural and linguistic mismatch between higher education and the nontraditional (by virtue of Color or class) students who were making their imprint upon the academic landscape for the first time in history" (Smitherman, 2003, p. 19). This mismatch resulted, in part, from the history of racism, segregation, and academic exclusion of people of color from American higher education, which in turn ignited rights' movements of the 1960s and public outcries at the assassination of Martin Luther King, Jr. in 1968.

In response to this "cultural and linguistic mismatch" (Smitherman, 2003, p. 19), officers of CCCC charged a small committee (1971) with the task of creating a policy statement on students' language rights and dialects. This proved monumental, given the political involvements of "marginalized" people in America during this period: the integration of the first Black students at Little Rock Central High School in 1957; the popularity of the Black Liberation Movement; the 1963 March on Washington for Jobs and Freedom; organized freedom rides and voter registration across Southern states; and the Montgomery bus boycott. What became the Students' Right to Their Own Language (SRTOL) resolution was presented to and passed by the Executive Committee of CCCC in 1972, and by the organization's general membership in 1974. (See the SRTOL resolution in Chapter 1.)

Proving to be controversial, SRTOL assaulted educational practices and policies that ignored linguistically, racially, and culturally diverse students whose mastery of English fell below "academic" sophistication. In addressing the dialects and language rights of students, SRTOL served as a commentary on a reality already known by many: that literacy differences among students (i.e., communicative practices and speech patterns; reading and writing competencies; teacher engagements with diverse learners) have always been associated with unequal individual and group access to economic and educational resources. This reality is marked by a number of events including Brown v. Board of Education (1954), the Civil Rights Act (1957), the Voting Rights Act (1965), Poor People's Campaign launch (1967), and the emergence of educational programs and policies such as Upward Bound, Educational Opportunity Program (EOP), and Open Admissions at City College in New York City (1970s). This reality is also marked by public reactions to SRTOL (1974).

During the height of SRTOL, many critics insisted that the resolution was an inappropriate statement because of its acceptance of non-standard Englishes and dialects in schools, and thus, should be rescinded. Others hailed the resolution as a long overdue step in supporting student-centered classrooms and promoting the language varieties of multilingual and bidialectical students. However controversial, the resolution brought attention to a larger, more universal concern associated with "the wider social legitimacy of all languages and dialects" as well as the "struggle, wherever one had a shot at being effective, to bring about mainstream recognition and acceptance of the culture, history, and language of those on the margins" (Smitherman, 2003, p. 18). This was one of the goals of SRTOL during the 1970s, a goal worth revisiting in light of the continued marginalization of linguistically diverse students in educational settings and throughout the world.

With this historical context in mind, the remainder of this essay responds to the following questions: What is the value of SRTOL? What can be learned about power, politics, and pedagogies from listening to students and enacting an "interpretive attitude" (Nino, 1996) through Democratic Engagements (Kinloch, 2005a) in educative exchanges around language differences and diversities? To address these questions, I briefly provide a working theoretical framework by which to talk about language rights and democracy in relation to the work of SRTOL. Then, I move into a brief analysis of youth perceptions of language rights by focusing on Quentin, an African American teenager and Black English speaker from New York City's Harlem who is challenged by ideas presented in SRTOL. Throughout this analysis, I argue that SRTOL, having been initiated shortly after the assassination of King, remains an important political statement in that it has situated language studies and instruction in a discourse of differences that, before 1968, was highly ignored in the work of CCCC.

Framework

The unfulfilled promise of SRTOL is best captured by Smitherman (1987), who challenges language and literacy scholars to address the work that the Students' Right Committee began in the 1970s as a way to respond to the negative attitudes and ensuing criticisms many people have toward language diversity. In her challenge, she outlines three aspects by which language and literacy scholars can employ if they are to advance the work of SRTOL: "1) reinforce the language of wider communication; 2) promote and extend the legitimacy of mother tongue languages and dialects; and 3) promote the acquisition of one or more foreign languages, preferably those spoken in the Third World" (p. 35). Taken together, these aspects point to Smitherman's belief that because the struggle for language rights has always been highly political, and because schools have never truly affirmed and accepted the mother tongue of non-mainstream English speech communities, a redefinition of the significance of SRTOL in relation to language rights, language policies, education, and power is necessary.

Jordan (1985, 1989), whose writings on language rights in general and Black English in particular articulate a message similar to Smitherman's claim. Both advocate the preservation of Black English and other non-mainstream languages and dialects in America. Acknowledging the many myths and detriments of a Standard English in terms of power and politics, silence and fear, Jordan draws attention to the need to take action against the continued relegation of Black English to a level of subordination in relation to "Standard" English. She recommends that we join forces "to cherish and protect our various, multifoliate lives against pacification, homogenization, the silence of terror, and surrender to standards that despise and disregard the sanctity of each and every human life" (1989, p. 38). In order to do this, Jordan suggests the following:

> We can begin by looking at language. Because it brings us together, as folks, because it makes known the unknown strangers we otherwise remain to each other, language is a process of translation; and a political process, taking place on the basis of who has the power to use, abuse, accept, and reject the words—the lingual messages we must attempt to transmit—to each other and/or against each other. (p. 38)

Both Jordan and Smitherman are concerned with the ways in which the proliferation of non-standard Englishes and dialects have received public resistance, and, much like the SRTOL resolution, have been met with silence and inaction. It is this continued silence that reiterates non-standardizations (i.e., Black English; non-Englishes as first languages) as subordinate to standardizations (i.e., edited American English, academic writing; mainstream practices and habits), and that delegitimizes the political histories, oppressions, struggles, and "lingual messages" (Jordan, 1989, p. 38) of groups of people whose mother tongue is other than English.

For when Smitherman (1977) asks teachers to consider: "How can I use what the kids already know to move them to what they need to know?" (p. 219), she is actively seeking to legitimize the prior knowledges, languages, cultural diversities, identities, and histories of students. She is also responding to Jordan's (1989) question: "And what is everybody going to do about it?" (p.38) in her recognition of how CCCC sought to translate the meanings of a changing national climate—heightened by the 1960s' and 1970s' civil rights movements and by the implementation of educational programs designed to address the increase of language diverse students in educational settings. Because language, according to Jordan, "brings us together" (p. 38), it is important for those invested in language studies to locate ways to accept and acknowledge as valid the "students' right to their own patterns and varieties of language" (CCC, 1974).

Lloyd (1953) claims a similar message years before CCCC became concerned with SRTOL. Insisting that students retain their mother tongue and that teachers respect students' language traditions, Lloyd recognizes the interconnections of language to identity to historical experiences. He writes:

> If we find anything that we have to change—and we do—we know that we are touching something that goes deep into [a student's] past and spreads wide in his personal life. We will seek not to dislodge one habit in favor of another but to provide alternative choices for freer social mobility. We seek to enrich, not to correct. (p. 42)

From language practices to learning habits, Lloyd is aware of the need to respect students' cultural histories. Elaborating on this point, he insists: "By respecting their traditions and the people from whom they come, we teach them to respect and hold tight to what they have as they reach for more" (p. 42). Elbow (2000) echoes Lloyd's belief "to enrich, not correct" (Lloyd, p. 42) as he, himself, seeks to dismantle the silence around and rejection of language varieties inside of writing classes. Wanting to provide his students with access to "the written language of power and prestige" (p. 323), Elbow is all too aware of the ways in which non-mainstream, non-standard Englishes are relegated to characterizations of "inferior," "subordinate," and "wrong."

In this relegation, Elbow (2000) attempts to situate the writing classroom as a site where students can openly make use of their mother tongue without the threat of abuse, assault, or rejection. Even with Elbow's teaching practices and Lloyd's insistence that teachers respect the traditions of students, the question of safety presents itself. According to Elbow: "I'm seeking safety for all languages that come naturally to the tongue, and yet I know that such language cannot be safe, and that the mother tongue cannot flourish, unless we also help our students produce final drafts that conform to the conventions of SWE" (p.329). Elbow is in search of a balance between oral (i.e., mother tongue) and written (i.e., SWE in print) forms of communication, a balance that—often taken as conformity—can be problematic for a number of reasons: "Standard" English, in speech and in writing, is already reiterative of a language and a position of power, prestige, and privilege whereas other communicative forms/tongues are already deemed non-standard and unprivileged. While Elbow seeks "safety," many others do not, thus, punishing students who use their mother tongue in the context of classrooms (i.e., discussions; group engagements; writing assignments) that are often constructed in threatening, unsafe, and conformist ways. For such reasons, a universal understanding of Black English and other languages as rule governed and as connected to particular identities, communities, struggles, and histories is necessary.

Smitherman (2000) calls attention to how Black English has contributed to the survival and world views of African American peoples: "Through song, story, folk sayings, and rich verbal interplay . . . lessons and precepts about life and survival are handed down from generation to generation" (p. 199). Similarly, Jordan (1985) claims that Black English has always been an important system of communication for Black people in her recognition that "most of the thirty-five million Afro-Americans living here depend on this language for our discovery of the world" (p. 123). Additionally, the SRTOL Committee urged those concerned with the success of multilingual students to "preserve its [the nation's] heritage of dialects" by affirming the students' "dialects of their nurture or whatever dialects in which they find their own identity and style" (CCC, 1974). In many ways, this latter message has been lost in the throes of English Only campaigns, anti-bilingual policies, and legislative mandates that seek to maintain ideals of a quickly decreasing White majority society.

The research of Smitherman (2000) and Jordan (1985) as well as the SRTOL resolution demonstrate the value of interrogating language mandates/policies by focusing on how teachers can build on the language practices and literacy acts within students' in-school and out-of-school worlds. Such scholarship, among others, provides literacy research one way by which to accept and affirm the "funds of knowledge" of linguistically diverse students in public schools, college classrooms, and in societies writ large (Moll & Gonzalez, 2001).

In a recent study of the linguistic register of Black English in an academic context, I pay attention to how "Nikki," "Maria," and "Jose," speakers of Black English and/or Spanglish, employ aspects of their home languages in classrooms to both contextualize and critique literary readings (Kinloch, 2004, 2005b). This employment, I argue, encourages students to establish "connections between race and language" (Kinloch, 2004, p. 83) in ways that maintain the relevancy of languages by working against linguistic silencing, exclusions, and oppressions. Similarly, Mahiri and Sablo (1996) analyze the writings of "Keisha" and "Troy," African American high school students, to assert that the students' poetry, raps, and songs "correspond to some of the behaviors and skills they need to develop and display in school" (p.178). Whether students are drawing on their facilities with Black English, Spanglish, or "Standard" English, their languages and writings can serve as significant texts for teachers to examine, affirm, and teach. The literacy lives of "Nikki," "Maria," "Jose," "Keisha," and "Troy," and the reality of current research, national policies, and propositions prove that the debate over students' language rights is definitely not over.

SRTOL Through Democratic Engagements

In his discussion of democracy, shared values, and deliberative character, Nino (1996) draws attention to the value of public participation in a democratic state. He posits the phrase "interpretive attitude" in regards to democratic relations in government, society, and, importantly, in education. Nino asserts:

> Democracy is a social practice, consisting of regular conduct and predict-able attitudes. These practices make up institutions that in turn are oriented

toward a certain goal or value. We cannot participate thoughtfully in the practice, nor can we understand it as intelligent observers, if we do not adopt an interpretative attitude, putting the conduct and attitude in the light of certain goals or values. (p. 9)

In relation to SRTOL, Nino's interpretive attitude speaks to the importance of re-imagining the democratic prospects of the resolution across and in direct relation to educational fairness and inclusion as well as quality educational opportunities for multilingual students. To adopt such a disposition where "the conduct and attitude [are placed] in the light of certain goals" (Nino, 1996, p. 9) requires a renewed commitment to SRTOL, honest conversations about language rights, and democratic engagements in classrooms, communities, and other places of public interest. Further, an interpretive attitude signifies a "greater consciousness of language politics, greater sensitivity to the multiple voices of students, and greater appreciation for the language and cultural background of a pluralistic society" (Scott and Kinloch, 2001, p. 710).

Articulating a move towards an interpretive attitude in terms of students' language rights and collaborative work, I posit the phrase "democratic engage-ments" (Kinloch, 2005a). I define this term as exchanges that are grounded in "interactive significations such as speech acts and code-switching, collaborative-based literacy assignments, group performances, and peer feedback students have with one another and with language as they write and share ideas" (p. 98). Such exchanges, in my opinion, encourage students to use an interpretive attitude as they come into or build on their consciousness of differences to engage in democratic and reciprocal conversations, particularly as they produce socially responsible writing (Kinloch, 2005a).

Nino's (1996) interpretive attitude parallels my idea of democratic engagements (Kinloch, 2005a) insofar as conversations, relationships, and conduct are grounded in mutual exchanges people have with one another through the negotiation of multiple, competing discourses. If, as Nino indicates, democracy is a social practice (see also Dewey, 1907), then this social practice must find its way into schools. One way for this to happen is through the affirmation of the languages of multilingual students inside and outside school contexts. At this intersection of democracy and language lies the prospects of a truth shared by countless literacy scholars: that students do, in fact, have a right to their own language, that the languages of our students are significant aspects of their identities and histories, and that this right to language has a place in academic research, power paradigms, politics, and in the pedagogies that we practice and enact in classrooms.

To further build on this intersection of democracy and language pertaining to SRTOL, I recall students who have challenged me to rethink my approaches to working in multilingual contexts. From former students Jose, Maria, and Nikki in Houston, Texas, to current students Kavon, Quentin, and Alicia in New York City, I have come to listen more closely to the diversities of human voices that insist on being heard in multiple languages, in multiple contexts. This work, as I will show by focusing on the language perceptions and practices of one student, Quentin, relates to the goals of SRTOL and has implications for related research in teaching and teacher education.

The Study

Nineteen-year old Quentin was a participant in an ongoing ethnographic research project in an urban high school and community in New York City's Harlem. Born and raised in Harlem, he attended a local high school in the area that is committed to a social justice and arts-based curriculum. The youths who attend the high school, identifying as Black/African American (54%), Latino (45%), White (2%), and Asian (1%) are either residents in the surrounding community or residents of local boroughs such as the Bronx, Brooklyn, Queens, or Staten Island. In this research project, I am examining how the language and writing practices of young people are connected to the politics of and ensuing struggles within various spaces (i.e., classrooms, home communities). By working within both the classroom space and students' community space, I am able to notice the shifts in students' dispositions towards and facilities with "literacies" in the postmodern spaces of Harlem (see Kinloch, 2007).

Throughout the classroom component of the project, spanning one and a half years, I was a participant-observer in three junior- and senior-level English Language Arts classrooms. I observed students' responses to readings, literacy activities, and with one another and their teacher, an African American female. Many of the students, including Quentin, took a quick liking to me because of shared characteristics: African American and code-switchers. Quentin became an active participant in the project because of his interest in language, "talk," and community revitalization in Harlem. He and I created a shared rhyme book, which served as our paper space to pose questions and illicit responses from one another on language, writing processes, struggles, and community. From our rhyme book as well as from videotaped community interviews, we engaged in data member checking sessions (Lincoln & Guba, 2000), shared analysis discussions, follow-up interview meetings, and post-session reflections.

Later in this chapter, I draw on my work with Quentin in relation to his language beliefs, which are, in fact, related to the value of SRTOL and to the intersections of democracy and language as framed within democratic engagements. This work stems from a series of 10 extensive survey questions generated and responded to by participants over a 3-month period. The following question guides this aspect of the project: What are youth perceptions of language rights, particularly in the contexts of schools and home communities, and what do their perceptions say about students having a right to their own language? To address this question, I focus on data collected during my engagements with Quentin.

Quentin and Language Rights

Quentin is an avid Black English speaker whose talk reflects a sophisticated combination of Black English and "Standard" English conventions. Often, we discussed issues of language rights, urban communities, and youth struggles as these things pertain to democracy. His talk captures his ongoing thinking about the ethnically diverse and situated voices he hears throughout Harlem. As Quentin sat in my university office talking with Kavon, another youth participant in the study, about community language and Black English, he turned his attention to one of the survey questions: "Have you ever heard of the terms 'Ebonics' and 'Black English?' What do they mean to you?" He eagerly read his written response to the question: "I heard the term 'Black English' for a while now and to me it's a way of how blacks communicate with one another." On this point, Quentin continued: "Black English is not always English or Proper English (not to some people) that will get you a wealthy job or anything like that, but it is how blacks understand each other in a way other ethnic groups can't." After a short pause, he shared the following sentiments:

> A lot of students, mostly blacks, do not know Standard English because of how society and communities are . . . structured. We as blacks have to understand the proper way to speak English and also have our fun times to speak freely. As for "Ebonics," well I just don't like that term.

Quentin seemed concerned about how Kavon and I understood his sentence: "We as blacks have to understand the proper way to speak English and also have our fun times to speak freely." He explained that Black English is an important language for many Black people, and while some "will not understand why we use it," we know "we have to use it because it is a part of our identity. We have to be able to speak freely, be who we are, but we need to know the other way to prove our rights." The other way is "Standard" English, or, as Quentin so characterized it, "the proper way to speak English." While Quentin identified a dichotomous relationship between Black people speaking Black English and "Standard" English, he was particularly careful to recognize the value of both languages: "Why can't we [Black people] use what's ours? I speak Black English, but that doesn't mean I can't speak anything else. Both have value and both belong to me, and I have a right to them . . . this is a democracy we live in, right?"

For Quentin, a democracy represents a space of rights, freedom, experiences, and exchanges that supports people's goals (Nino, 1996). Within this space, according to Quentin, exists "a set of policies, communities of people who diverse, lots of differences." In relation to language, Quentin viewed a democracy as all encompassing of a discourse of rights that "we all entitled to, regardless of how we look or talk." Therefore, his attention to "this is a democracy we live in, right" speaks to his belief that a democracy should respect and uphold the rights of people, and to not respect and uphold indicate unfairness, bias, and prejudice towards people who are told "you have rights, just not right now." Quentin believed that language is connected to democracy, and in this connection, "I have a right to them [Black English and "Standard" English]."

His point, "I have a right to them," relates well to another survey question: "What does the phrase 'students' right to their own language' mean to you?" Quentin replied:

This phrase to me gives students the right to their own way of language and of life, which is cool. It gives students a choice. But if we as blacks and minorities continue this way of life, how is our children of the future going to have a better education if we continue this phrase.

I asked Quentin to clarify this last point, and he said the following:

If we use this phrase "students' right to their own language" as a scapegoat instead of using it to better ourselves, our situations, and the future of our young people, then how will we really improve our status in society. When I say we I am talking about black people and all minorities.

While Quentin appreciated that SRTOL recognizes the validity of students' languages, he does not believe that teachers will readily affirm the language rights of students because "they think it's too hard to do; they see it as blacks using their language as a scapegoat, as an excuse. That's not what I do when I use it." Four months after sharing his initial response with me, I noticed a shift in Quentin's position, particularly when he noted: "I thought about the language question again. I think students would like if teachers would believe that . . . students' have rights. If I need to talk Black English in a classroom to get what I'm doing, who's to make me not use it? We need to know we have a right to our language. I like the students' right statement."

Quentin's reflexive disposition reveals the power of language to "give students a choice," "to get what I'm doing," and to live in "a democracy [that] represents a space of rights, freedom, experiences, and exchanges." He still does not understand why students would not have a right to use the language that they know as they experiment with various other language forms, including "Standard" English. Quentin concluded that institutional policies, teacher attitudes toward language-diverse students, and the culture of many schools prevent students from drawing on the expressive economies that they are familiar with (i.e., their mother tongue) because of student fear of being publicly embarrassed or chastized. He recalled how he draws on his familiarity with language and aesthetic power including variations of English, rhyme schemes, stress, breaks, and bodily signals found in popular music (i.e., hip hop, rap, R&B) and current dance moves (i.e., Harlem Shake, Chicken Noodle Soup) to learn about a discourse of rights, based in democratic engagements and framed around self-expression, movement, freedom, and performance. Powerfully, he confessed: "See, schools should help students explore the languages . . . of things they really know and that way make connections to other things they don' really know. That'll be engagement, democratic style, but that's not the case." On this point, Quentin provided a specific example by talking about how "if students have a right to their language, that's still limited 'cause the teacher determines what that right's based on. Like we always study the language Shakespeare uses and never the language Mos Def [a hip hop artist] might use." I asked him to elaborate on this latter point, and he insisted:

Mos Def puts some cool lines and structures together. Or like the language of the white writers, the ones you [Valerie] say are in the canon and not the writers who lived up in Harlem or not the writers who wrote about blacks' struggles in the Civil Rights Movement. I know many of them mixed up Black English (Kavon calls it community language or something) with standard English. But we don't study that type of thing in schools. This makes me wonder if schools believe students have a right to our own language. I don't think so.

Quentin's understanding of the phrase "students' right to their own language" is foundational in his learning to think critically about language, identity, rights, and choice. He is just as aware of the significance of such a phrase just as he is of the difficulties of many teachers to affirm the diverse languages of students in classrooms. From teaching Shakespeare in tandem with teaching Mos Def, or asking students to critique the structures of their home language in comparison with another language, teachers can employ imaginative ways to accept and affirm as valid the rights of students in classrooms, an affirmation that can then find itself inside of a larger, out-of-school context.

SRTOL and "Community Language": A Final Examination

Quentin's reference to mixing Black English with "Standard" English, or what Kavon names "community language," is elaborated on in Quentin's response to the survey question: "Is there such a thing as home/community language? If so, then what does it mean?" He replied, "There is such a thing as home and community language. Think about it: Black, Spanish, Mexican, French, White, and West Indies communities all have their own ways of life, style, and language." Before continuing with the reading of his written response, Quentin admitted that he never considered the value of community language "until this research study." He then explained that some communities have many different types of people who bring their cultural practices, traditions, and languages into their shared contexts, or locations. "All of this means," according to Quentin's written response, "that there is more than one language to learn and study. Who is to say Standard English is the best language form or is better than the rest?"

Home and community languages play an invaluable role in the literacy lives of multilingual and bidialectical students. Much like Quentin's reference to the languages of Shakespeare and Mos Def, his questioning of "Standard" English as "the best" or "better than the rest" demonstrates a concern for the legitimization of other languages, including Black English. He constantly returned to his sentiments on democracy: "I'm thinking democracy is suppose to allow people to be who they are with all the rights and freedom, so that includes freedom of their language. Maybe this is what Nino means" (see Nino, 1996). Simultaneously, Quentin is continuing to work on establishing connections among his ideas on democracy, schooling, and students' language rights. Quentin's attention to such connections speak to the ideals of SRTOL insofar as language diversity, identity, rhetorical effectiveness, and awareness of differences are concerned. And yet, he is aware that institutional structures can interfere with teachers affirming students' languages and with students demonstrating rhetorical sophistication in multiple languages, especially the language of schools, mainstream institutions, and of power constructs.

Conclusion

In my attempt to highlight the value of accepting and affirming the language rights of students, I must admit, much like Quentin, my awareness of the difficulties of this affirmation, given institutional policies and the reality of power dynamics in educational contexts and in the larger society. My argument for the legitimization of SRTOL is embedded in my own social, cultural, and political identities.

In another study (Kinloch, 2005b), I discuss that as an African American daughter to working-class Southern parents, I am familiar with utilizing both Black English and "Standard" English. My familiarity allows me to code-switch in ways that mix Black rhetorical traditions of my mother tongue with "Standard" English forms. For example, when I code-switch, often unconsciously, I explain to students the connections among language, audience, meaning, and the politics of space. We discuss relationships between race and language, language and culture, and language and history, a discussion that oftentimes leads to talk about public perceptions of "minority" languages in a "White" America. This work is important because it encourages students to demonstrate their proficiency in multiple languages—the language of their mother tongue and the language of wider communication (Smitherman, 2000). It also invites students to code-switch as meaning is created and recreated, as positions are articulated and challenged, and as debates on the legitimization of language and "minority" identities are critiqued.

However much my students or I code-switch, I am still aware of the power of language, particularly as it constructs identities, however veiled, and positions people in certain classes and categories, however falsely. Much like Quentin, I recognize the politics of institutional spaces and discourses that tend to be committed to markers of White middle- to upper-class socioeconomic values. While some students seek to imitate such values in their quest for social class mobility and success, this imitation oftentimes presents a duality between practices within primary and secondary communities of socialization (Dubois, 1903/1989; Gee, 2001). In the absence of an "interpretive attitude" (Nino, 1996) and democratic engagements (Kinloch, 2005a), the different sets of beliefs, cultural traditions, and language practices of students become relegated to a subordinate category in relation to academic codes and conventions. This last point reiterates the significance of a position statement such as SRTOL in terms of the acceptance and affirmation of students' language varieties both inside and outside schools.

Advocating for the language rights of multilingual students such as Quentin means, for example, that students would be encouraged to ask freely, "who is to say Standard English is the best language form or is better than the rest?" At the same time that students question this talk, teachers would do well to inquire into additional ways to affirm the languages of students as meaningful, which reiterates Quentin's assertion that students be invited to use their language inside of classrooms to "get what I'm doing." This point connects well to Elbow's (2000) suggestion to educators:

> If we want our students to take on the power of full mainstream literacy, we can never remove the difficulty or even identity anxiety that some of them may experience in having to move past an oral culture (not necessarily to leave it) and take on a culture of literacy. But we can substantially mitigate their anxiety by inviting them to take on *full literacy* in their oral dialect. (p. 372)

Delpit (1996) makes a similar claim when she states: "All we can do is provide students with the exposure to an alternate form, and allow them the opportunity to practice that form *in contexts that are nonthreatening, have a real purpose, and are intrinsically enjoyable*" (p. 54). Both Elbow and Delpit's claims, however controversial they seem on the surface, support Quentin's inquiries into the role of language—in a democracy—on people's engagements, "interpretive attitude" (Nino, 1996, p. 9), rights, struggles, and representations.

This last idea also connects my argument (Kinloch, 2005b) to arguments by Smitherman (2000) and Jordan (1985), which insist students be afforded opportunities to participate in literacy learning in ways that demonstrate the richness of languages in action. This can only happen, I believe, if teachers "adopt an interpretive attitude, putting the conduct and attitude in light of certain goals or values" (Nino, 1996, p. 9). This adoption could encourage teachers and researchers to re-imagine our pedagogies and practices, which are heavily embedded in political stances, as we work with linguistically diverse students inside and outside of our classrooms. Such a re-imagination could instigate a re-visitation of and re-commitment to policies that advocate for students' language rights. Or, as Quentin believes, "until we all accept other people's languages, like Black English, we'll never make strides and live in a democracy. We all have language rights." If Quentin's sentiments are true, and I believe that they are, then additional research on the interconnections among language, identity, and place is necessary in our private and public attempts to affirm the rights of linguistically diverse students.

Discussion Questions and Activities

1. How do socioeconomic status and/or geographical location influence the language practices people use? In your class, have students listen to musical selections of artists from different places. Ask them to pay attention to how artists use language to appeal to an audience. Describe the artists' language use, choices, and moves. Write a response to the lyrics by considering how language changes based on context.
2. Invite students to examine the spatial location and demographical trends of their university community juxtaposed with their home community affiliation(s). I begin by asking students to consider such questions as: How would you describe the languages you hear in school in comparison to the languages you hear in your home community? What are the similarities and differences?

Comment on the value of speaking and understanding multiple language forms across locations.

3. In what ways does the poetry of Langston Hughes combine elements from the African American rhetorical tradition? Ask students to listen to recordings of Hughes' poetry and map out various techniques he employs. Then, respond to the question: What about Hughes' poetry is musical, and what do his writings say about language and expressiveness?

[1 *Author's note*: Aspects of this ethnographic study was partially funded by Spencer Foundation and the National Council of Teachers of English. The ideas expressed here are those of the author and do not reflect the ideas of the funding organizations.]

References

Baugh, J. (1983). *Black Street Speech: Its History, Structure, and Survival.* Austin, TX: University of Texas Press.

College Composition and Communication. (1974). *Students' Right to Their Own Language.* [Special issue] *CCC,* 25(3), 1–32.

Delpit, L. (1996). *Other People's Children: Cultural Conflict in the Classroom.* New York: The New Press.

Dewey, J. (1916). *Democracy and Education.* New York: Macmillan.

——. (1907). *The School and Society.* Chicago, IL: University of Chicago Press.

DuBois, W. E. B. (1989). *The Souls of Black Folk.* New York: Bantam Books. [Original published in 1903.]

Elbow, P. (2000). *Everyone Can Write: Essays Toward a Hopeful Theory of Writing and Teaching Writing.* New York: Oxford University Press.

Gee, J. P. (2001). Literacy, Discourse, and Linguistics: Introduction and What is Literacy? In E. Cushman, E. R. Kintgen, B. M. Kroll, & M. Rose (Eds.). *Literacy: A Critical Sourcebook.* Boston, MA: Bedford/St. Martins.

Jordan, J. (1985). *On Call: Political Essays.* Boston, MA: South End Press.

——, J. (1989). *Moving Towards Home: Political Essays.* London: Virago.

Kinloch, V. (2004). June Jordan and the Linguistic Register: A Statement about Our Rights. In V. Kinloch, & M. Grebowicz (Eds.). *Still Seeking an Attitude: Critical Reflections on the Work of June Jordan.* Lanham, MD: Lexington Books.

——. (2005a). Poetry, Literacy, and Creativity: Fostering Effective Learning Strategies in an Urban Classroom. *English Education,* 37(2), 96–114.

——. (2005b). Revisiting the Promise of Students' Right to Their Own Language: Pedagogical Strategies. *CCC,* 57(1), 83–113.

——. (2007). "The White-ification of the Hood": Power, Politics, and Youth Performing Narratives of Community. *Language Arts,* 85(1), 61–68.

Lincoln, Y. S., & Guba, E. (2000). Paradigmatic Controversies, Contradictions and Emerging Confluences. In N. K. Denzin, & Y. S. Lincoln (Eds.). *Handbook of Qualitative Research,* 2nd edn. Thousand Oaks, CA, London, and New Delhi: Sage.

Lloyd, D. J. (1953). An English Composition Course Built around Linguistics. *CCC,* 4, 40–43.

Mahiri, J., & Sablo, S. (1996). Writing for Their Lives: The Non-School Literacy of California's Urban African American Youth. *Journal of Negro Education,* 65(2), 164–180.

Moll, L., & Gonzalez, N. (2001). Lessons from Research with Language-Minority Children. In E. Cushman, E. R. Kintgen, B. M. Kroll, & M. Rose (Eds.). *Literacy: A Critical Sourcebook.* Boston, MA: St. Martin's Press.

Nino, C. S. (1996). *The Constitution of Deliberative Democracy.* New Haven, CT: Yale University Press.

Scott, J. C., & Kinloch, V. (2001). Review of *Class Politics: The Movement for the Students' Right to Their Own Language,* by S. Parks. *JAC,* 21(3), 705–710.

Smitherman, G. (1977). *Talkin and Testifyin: The Language of Black America.* Detroit, MI: Wayne State University Press.

——. (1987). Toward a National Public Policy on Language. *College English*, 49: 29–36.

——. (2000). *Talkin That Talk: Language, Culture, and Education in African America*. London and New York: Routledge.

——. (2003). The Historical Struggle for Language Rights in CCCC. In G. Smitherman, & V. Villanueva (Eds.). *Language Diversity in the Classroom: From Intention to Practice*. Carbondale, IL: Southern Illinois University Press.

7

Exploring Attitudes Toward Language Differences: Implications for Teacher Education Programs

LAURIE KATZ, JERRIE COBB SCOTT, AND XENIA HADJIOANNOU

Demographers predict that children of color will constitute the statistical majority of the student population by 2035 and account for 57% by 2050 . . . It is not the changing demographic profile of the nation's school children in and of itself that is an obstacle to providing high-quality schooling for all . . . The problems are the persistent and pernicious disparities that exist in educational achievement, resources, and life chances between students of color and their White peers. (Hollins & Guzman, 2005, p. 478)

Already most school districts have experienced an increase in the diversity of their student population and a decline in the diversity of the teaching workforce. Furthermore, research has shown that schools with large numbers of students of non-mainstream language backgrounds fall victim to low standardized test results, reduced resources, and reductionist approaches to instruction. At no time has the need for diversity training for teachers been so great. Studies of language attitudes have much to contribute to our understanding of what teachers need to know and be able to do to reduce the persistent and pernicious disparities in educational achievement. Simply put, in language diverse classrooms, attitudes toward language affect what is taught, how it is taught, and how well it is taught.

In response to this need, issues related to language attitudes are being revisited not only in relation to classroom practices, but also in relation to teacher education programs. This chapter examines attitudes toward language diversity and implications for teacher education programs. The first part summarizes the major findings of the Language Knowledge and Awareness Study (LKAS) conducted by the authors of this chapter. Next, the findings are discussed relative to other studies of language attitudes. In the final section, implications for teacher preparation programs are explored.

Language Knowledge and Awareness Study

The intent of our exploratory study of language attitudes was to identify factors about language attitudes that needed to be studied in relation to how teacher education programs prepare teachers to address issues of language diversity. Consequently four broad questions were posed:

1. What are the attitudes of pre- and in-service teachers toward language differences?
2. How does language background affect sensitivity to language differences/or language attitudes?
3. How does exposure to speakers of non-dominant varieties of language affect sensitivity to language/or language attitudes?
4. What effect does training have on language attitudes?

Study Participants

The respondents who completed the Language Knowledge and Awareness Survey (LKAS) attended universities in three different locales: one in the Midwest and one in the Midsouth regions of the United States and one in Cyprus. The Midsouth and Midwest regions of the United States were of interest because of their differential status in terms of regionalisms: Midwestern dialects are generally considered the most neutral and least stigmatized of regional dialects, whereas Southern dialects are generally considered the least neutral and most highly stigmatized of regional dialects. The Cyprus situation was selected because of studies that show the Greek Cypriot dialect as a stigmatized variety of Greek and because of its high incidence of bi- and multilingual speakers, as compared to the high incidence of monolingual speakers in the United States.

The Survey

The survey used in this study was originally developed, validated, and administered between 1996 and 1997 by members of the Conference on College Composition and Communication of the National Council of Teachers of English (NCTE). The instrument was used to assess the language attitudes and concerns of NCTE members. Reliability and validity of the survey was established through a pilot study involving approximately 200 randomly selected English professionals at 2- and 4-year colleges, secondary school levels and English education majors in teacher preparation programs. For the purpose of our study, adaptations were made to the questionnaire with permission granted by NCTE. Four items were added to the original set of seven items for the purpose of eliciting responses to different approaches to teaching linguistically diverse students. Also, the survey administered in Cyprus was translated to Standard Greek, the language of instruction, to ensure that knowledge of the language would not be a barrier for any of the participants. Of course, references to Standard English and English dialects had to be changed to Standard Greek and the Greek Cypriot dialect.

The following are the 11 items on the questionnaire:

1. A student whose primary language is not the dominant variety should be taught solely in the dominant variety.
2. Students need to master Standard English for upward mobility.
3. In the home, students should be exposed to Standard English only.
4. Students who use non-standard dialects should be taught in the standard variety only.

5. There are valid reasons for using non-standard dialects.
6. There are valid reasons for using language other than the dominant language.
7. Students should learn grammar rules to improve their ability to understand and communicate concepts and information.
8. Teachers should learn and use strategies that focus on accepting language patterns and cultural differences in order to ensure that *all* students are active participants in the classroom community.
9. Teachers should use non-standard dialect patterns to help students learn the standard language and reading and writing skills.
10. Teachers should utilize the grammar and rhetorical patterns of students' home community to enhance learning in the language arts.
11. All children would benefit from having access to multicultural texts in the language arts classroom.

Data Analysis

Participants responded to the items using a four-point Likert scale, ranging from "strongly agree" to "strongly disagree." The scores were computed based on responses to nine of the 11 questions on the survey. For the purpose of data analysis, adjustments were made in the scale so that the lowest number represented the most positive response to language diversity. Thus, the lower the score for each item the more positive the responses. In this analysis, items two and seven were omitted since responses could not readily be assigned a positive or negative rating. Using the demographic information on the questionnaire, scores for respondents with different demographic profiles were computed according to (a) language background (e.g. monolingual, bilingual, or multilingual; (b) exposure to non-standard speakers (e.g. infrequent, moderate or frequent; and (c) diversity training or coursework (e.g. none, little, moderate, or concentrated. The following analyses were conducted: Correlations (relationships between factors) and ANOVAs (differences among the three universities). A Tukey post-test was used to better understand the differences identified among the three universities.

Data Set

A total of 306 questionnaires were submitted: 108 from the Midsouth group; 92 from the Midwest group; and 106 from the Cypriot group. The majority of the participants (83%) were female. Most participants (74%) were between the ages of 21 and 40. Respondents differed in their degree programs: undergraduate students (57%); master's students (43%). Of those seeking certification, 63% was seeking certification in early childhood education (pre-K third or fourth grade), and 23% were seeking certification in middle grades (fourth to ninth). The remaining 14% was certified teachers pursuing master's degrees in education.

Findings

Major findings of the study are summarized in relation to the research questions.

WHAT ARE THE ATTITUDES OF PRE- AND IN-SERVICE TEACHERS TOWARD LANGUAGE
DIFFERENCES?

The total LKAS scores from all the participants ranged from nine to 36 with a mean
score of 19.12. This mean score indicated a relatively negative attitude toward
language diversity. Two points are noted. First, responses from the Midsouth group
were the most negative (M = 20.5), while responses from the Midwest were the
least negative (17.74). Second, responses of teachers (M = 20.69) were more
negative than responses of undergraduate students (M = 18.9).

HOW DOES LANGUAGE BACKGROUND AFFECT SENSITIVITY TO LANGUAGE DIFFERENCES/
OR LANGUAGE ATTITUDES?

One of the main differences of participants in the three universities was in their
language background. The majority (61%) of participants from Cyprus were
bilingual, with 19% monolingual and 20% multilingual. The majority of the
participants in the U.S. universities were monolingual (91% Midsouth and 86%
Midwest) with fewer than 4% of Midsouth respondents and fewer than 12% of
Midwest respondents being multilingual or bilingual. The mean score to the
questionnaire for the monolinguals was 19, 19 for bilinguals and 18 for
multilinguals. Contrary to expectations, there was no statistically significant
difference in responses by language background (i.e. monolingual, bilingual, or
multilingual).

HOW DOES EXPOSURE TO SPEAKERS OF NON-DOMINANT VARIETIES OF LANGUAGE
AFFECT SENSITIVITY TO LANGUAGE/OR LANGUAGE ATTITUDES?

There was a significant correlation between the exposure the participant had to
non-English or non-Standard English speakers and the LAS score (r2 =. 259,
p < .01). In other words, the greater the exposure to speakers of non-dominant
language varieties, the more positive were the scores.

WHAT EFFECT DOES TRAINING HAVE ON LANGUAGE ATTITUDES?

Only 2.3% of respondents indicated that they had moderate and concentrated
training in diversity or multicultural courses. The remaining (97.7%) reported little
or no training in diversity or multicultural courses. There was a statistically
significant difference between scores of those who indicated little to no training
and those who indicated moderate and concentrated training in diversity and
multicultural education (r2 z .206, p < .01). In other words, the more coursework
participants had in diversity or multicultural education, the more sensitive they
were to language differences.

In sum, the exploratory study of language attitudes resulted in three conclusions.
First, overall our respondents' attitudes toward language differences were relatively
negative, a conclusion supported by other research. Second, exposure to speakers
of non-dominant language varieties positively affects language attitudes. Third,

training has a highly positive effect on language attitudes. This study implies that teacher education programs should give more attention to teacher candidates' degree of exposure to speakers of non-dominant language varieties and to the training offered to prepare teacher candidates for work in language and culturally diverse schools. The following section examines other language attitude studies for a fuller explanation of LKAS findings as well as other factors that should be considered in preparing teachers to work with language diverse students.

Findings of Other Language Attitude Studies

Sources of Negative Attitudes

Given the LKAS findings that respondents' attitudes toward language differences were relatively negative, a logical question to consider is the source of these negative attitudes. In their study of ethnic biases, Richman, et al. (1997) found that negative associations with students of color were prevalent. Based on photos, respondents rated students of color low on academic expectations, e.g. low GPA and IQ, as well as on personal qualities, e.g. less ambitious, less self-confident, and little initiative when compared to students of European descent. As far back as 1976, Williams found a similar pattern and concluded that negative stereotypes associated with non-mainstream groups accounted partially for teachers' negative attitudes toward minority languages and low expectations of students, suggesting ethnic bias as another source of negative attitudes toward speakers of non-dominant language varieties.

In their study of socialization, Smith, Moallem, and Sherrill (1997) reported that 20% of their respondents indicated they were socialized to believe in equality and retained that belief; 30% were socialized to believe in discrimination but had rejected that belief; 14% were socialized to believe in discrimination but had subsequently developed mixed views. In contrast, 12% reported they were socialized to believe in discrimination and had retained that belief. Some of the factors reported as eroding deeply entrenched, socialized beliefs in discrimination included exposure to individuals from different cultural and experiential backgrounds, education, travel, and personal experience with discrimination. Since only 12% of respondents retained their socialized beliefs in discrimination, this study suggests that changes in beliefs are possible for a large number of these respondents.

Together, these studies offer two possible sources of negative attitudes: ethnic biases and socialized beliefs in discrimination. Regarding changes in negative attitudes, it appears that two of the factors we studied, exposure and training, can influence changes in people's belief systems.

Language Background

In the LKAS study, the assumption that language background (monolingual v. bilingual v. multilingual) would have a differential effect on language attitudes was not supported. Though the Cypriot group had a high percentage of bilingual and multilingual speakers, the respondents did not show a higher level of tolerance for language differences. A similar hypothesis was refuted in a study by Richardson (2003). Richardson explained the non-differentiated responses in terms of ideological differences, indicating that "many language educators may support the ideology of English monolingualism" (p. 49). Another explanation is that learning to speak a language in school may not be accompanied by exposure to speakers of non-dominant language varieties. So, beyond language background, the factors of ideology and exposure to speakers of other languages are possible overriding factors. We turn next to the question of exposure to speakers of non-dominant language varieties.

Exposure to Non-Dominant Language Speakers

One of the LKAS findings suggested that exposure to speakers of non-dominant language varieties may be an important variable in language attitudes. Su (1997) investigated the attitudes of minority teacher candidates and found that unlike most White candidates, minority candidates came into teacher education programs with social justice goals. This makes sense since minority teacher candidates are likely to be exposed to language variations in their homes and communities. Exposure to diversity in school settings also seems to be important.

Terrill and Mark (2000) found that 52% of their teacher candidate respondents had never been in classrooms with students of color, and 75% had spent 10 hours or fewer in such classrooms. Also, though 75% percent of respondents reported interest in working in Spanish-dominant schools, when asked to indicate their choice for student teaching placements, 64% chose a White suburban school.

Similarly, respondents in Gilbert's study (1997) said they respected urban teachers. However they also thought urban students were uninterested in learning and urban schools were plagued with violence. Almost half said they absolutely would not teach in an urban school. Hardaway and Florez (1987) found that most teacher candidates in their study had limited experiences with language and culture other than their own, and few had long-term interactions with people of other races and cultures. These candidates reported that they did not feel prepared to teach students of diverse backgrounds. Together these studies raise questions about the relationship between exposure to, or respect for, language differences and teachers' willingness to work with children who are different from themselves.

In many of these studies, including the LKAS, preservice teachers were overwhelmingly White, female, and middle class. Their responses revealed little exposure to non-mainstream students and a variety of reasons for not wanting to work with them. Across the studies having to do with exposure to speakers of non-dominant language varieties, respondents had mixed views about recognizing the importance of respecting children's linguistic variation but a definite unwillingness to work with children who are culturally or linguistically different from themselves. Respect, then, does not always transfer into willingness to work with students who are culturally and linguistically different. Some expressed concerns over their lack of preparedness/training for working with students of diverse backgrounds. So, what effect does training have on the attitudes of preservice teachers?

Training

Research in this area is often approached by looking at courses that either seek to reduce prejudices or improve the effectiveness of equity pedagogy. Regarding prejudice reduction, findings range from positive to negative impacts on attitudes. Studies of equity pedagogy treat a range of ideological and pedagogical changes. All point to factors about course offerings that need to be considered by teacher education programs.

On the positive side of prejudice reduction, Nathenson-Mejia and Escamilla (2003) found positive changes in a fieldwork seminar that used children's literature. Obadiah (2000) investigated changes in perceptions about prejudice in response to a course in multiculturalism. He concluded that students' perspectives on multiculturalism broadened; their understanding of bias and cultural assumptions in teaching and learning increased; and, their ability to critique their own beliefs and assumptions about different groups of people improved.

Considering the effects of field-based v. non-field based courses, Sparks and Verner (1995) compared differential effects of four types of multicultural education course: a discipline-specific course, an integrated course that focused on generic multicultural concepts, a discipline-specific field experience, and an integrated field experience. Candidates' perceptions of multicultural knowledge increased significantly in the discipline-specific and the integrated courses, but not in the field experience courses.

On the negative side of prejudice reduction, Cockrell, Placier, Cockrell, and Middleton (1999) found that a multicultural foundations course had little impact on students' views of diversity. They concluded that teacher candidates' views of diversity are based not on training but on personal experiences, political ideologies, and beliefs about the roles of schools and teachers. Some of their resistance to multicultural education was related to a strong affinity for individualism and monoculturalism. Here again, we find evidence that ideological factors and teachers' beliefs about education may be operating.

Katz (2000) studied the impact of a bilingual education course on the attitudes and beliefs of 200 teacher candidates. He found growth in students' knowledge, but neither a change in attitudes nor a reduction in prejudice. Those already supportive of bilingualism became more articulate in their support, whereas those already skeptical rejected the research. Regardless of whether the courses treated multiculturalism or bilingual education, these studies suggest that knowledge about diversity does not necessarily translate into prejudice reduction.

In-service training for practicing teachers has been used as another way to sensitize teachers to ideological and pedagogical issues regarding language diversity. McDiarmid (1992) investigated the impact of in-service training on the stereotypic attitudes of practicing teachers. Based on responses to a questionnaire with scenarios keyed to workshop objectives, McDiarmid concluded that multicultural workshops neither reduced teachers' acceptance of stereotypes nor diminished their use of culturally inappropriate assignments. These studies reaffirm what we already know: Attitudes are difficult to change, partially because they represent deep seated feelings that have a diehard quality (Scott & Smitherman, 1985).

Teacher education courses intended to prepare teacher candidates to provide equity pedagogy in K-12 classrooms have been frequently investigated. Studies of equity pedagogy reveal some of the factors that need to be considered in relation to language attitudes and pedagogical changes. In these studies, one sees an interweaving of ideological and pedagogical issues. Cross's (2003) research points to a factor of relevance to training in equity pedagogy. Through her interviews of White teachers who had participated in a course that sought to prepare them to teach in racially and linguistically diverse classrooms, Cross found that though the teachers could recall the main points of the course, they were dismayed that they learned more about how not to put down students than how to modify their instruction to facilitate student learning. Cross concluded that training in diversity needs to allow teachers to see the relevance of equity pedagogy to their everyday teaching practices.

Equity pedagogy often treats issues related to inclusive approaches to teaching. Southerland and Gess-Newsome (1999) found that *positivistic views of knowledge and authority* interfered with the development of inclusive approaches to science. In explaining the failures of inclusive approaches, Rodríguez (1998) points to preservice teachers' resistance to both *ideological and pedagogical change.*

Clark and Medina (2000) offer a possible solution to ideological barriers to change. In their study, teacher candidates worked in self-selected reading groups where they read book-length narratives of their choice. During the course, teacher candidates began to understand multiple perspectives, contexts, and how individuals construct literacy. This enabled candidates to correct their overgeneralized views about those from cultural and experiential backgrounds different from their own and to better understand cultural conditions. Noteworthy to the prospects for ideological change is teachers' correction of their own overgeneralized conclusions.

Regarding pedagogical changes, Greenleaf, Hull, and Reilly (1994) identified two ideological barriers: a belief in the right answer and the belief that diversity is an obstacle to pupils' learning. They suggested that a group inquiry, problem-solving type process might prompt participants to reconsider their expectations for diverse students. This is in alignment with the findings of Morales (2000) who reported that most of the minority candidates she studied as they were taking a course employing a constuctivist philosophy with a developmentally appropriate framework, acquired an understanding of cultural and experiential differences and the construction of developmentally appropriate strategies for young children. They also gained confidence working with children and families different from themselves. Notice that constructivist-oriented pedagogy emphasizes problem posing as well as problem solving, asking questions as well as answering questions, and critical reflection as well as critical thinking.

There exists a strand of studies on equity pedagogy that uses an inquiry approach to effect ideological and pedagogical changes. Training that invites teachers to study the variation present in their own language (oral and written) has resulted in positive changes in attitudes toward language variation (Wilson, 2001). Teaching teachers about language variation—its naturalness, usefulness, and wide use—has produced positive results when approached in an exploratory manner that demonstrates relevance to teacher's everyday work (Wolfram 1999). Using self-reflection as a means of making implicit assumptions about language differences more explicit has also yielded positive results (Okawa 2003) and Shelton (this volume). Also, the success of critical discussions of dominant language ideology (see Bloome, Carter, Christian, Otto, & Shuart-Faris, 2005) demonstrates the effectiveness of using an exploratory approach to conversational engagement.

Capitalizing on teachers' orientation to practical information can lead to change. Interestingly enough, it appears that ideological and pedagogical changes interact in ways that make success with one yield success in the other. In other words, when teachers find success with changing pedagogical practices, they also are less resistant to changing their ideological persuasions. Or, when teachers make discoveries about their own overgeneralizations and biases, they are less resistant to modifying their instruction to address the needs of language-diverse students. What all approaches have in common is not content, but shared strategies for delivering the content: They embrace the notion of using an inquiry, as opposed to a transmission, approach to delivering content.

In sum the studies of language attitudes described in this section reveal mixed results. It is important to take note of what the research both does and does not tell us about preparing teachers to teach linguistically and culturally diverse students. It does *not* tell us:

- whether diversity content works better in field-based or non-field-based courses;
- whether diversity content should be integrated into courses or presented in diversity-specific courses;
- which types of diversity-specific course get best results: multicultural, bilingual education, or literacy courses.

Results were less mixed with regard to the delivery of course content. The research suggests that:

- resistances are found across the spectrum of course offerings;
- more attention should be given to how the content of diversity courses is delivered;
- an inquiry approach to delivering content yielded positive results more systematically than any of the other approaches;
- ideological and pedagogical changes do not operate separately but most likely have a synergistic effect on educators.

Implications for Teacher Education Programs

The research examined here has several broad implications for teacher education programs. First, teacher education programs will likely face obstacles in their attempts to change attitudes and practices, including attitudes related to low expectations, socialized discrimination, and to limited exposure to speakers of non-dominant language varieties. Second, teacher education programs can reasonably expect some benefits from efforts to change negative attitudes toward language differences, including (a) enhanced understandings of language and cultural differences, (b) improved abilities to plan differentiated instruction that considers learning styles, background knowledge, prior life experiences, and (c) increased skills in designing appropriate strategies to facilitate learning in language diverse settings. Third, there is growing evidence of effective programmatic approaches, including (a) offering teacher candidates more choices with regard to the selection of materials to study; (b) providing problem-posing and problem-solving experiences; and (c) allowing for self-discoveries and self-evaluations. These solutions fit best into a growing interest in the use of an inquiry approach to instruction in language and cultural diversity. This section addresses the inquiry approach by discussing its rationale, the development of an inquiry stance in the teaching of language diverse students, three aspects of an inquiry approach to teaching about language and cultural diversity, and inquiry-based instructional tasks that teacher educators might use to better prepare teachers to teach students of diverse language backgrounds.

Rationale for Using an Inquiry Approach

The rationale for using an inquiry approach is driven by three factors: adaptability, responsibility, and practicability. An inquiry approach can be adapted for use with courses that teacher education programs already use, whether the courses are diversity specific or have diversity units integrated into other courses. An inquiry approach allows teacher education programs to honor their responsibility to deliver a curriculum that prepares teachers to manage changes in educational systems. These changes are happening not only in relation to higher demands for account-ability, but also in relation to changes in the student population, the teaching workforce, as well as in measures taken to reduce the performance gaps between mainstream and non-mainstream students.

The inquiry approach is practical, for it allows teacher education programs to maintain their overriding commitment of bridging research to practice and linking pedagogical strategies taught in teacher education programs to those used in the schools. Via an inquiry approach, sociolinguistic research is heavily utilized to inform instruction and an alignment between inquiry practices used in teacher education programs with those in schools.

Development of an Inquiry Stance

Taking an *inquiry stance* toward diversity instruction means developing the habits of mind and heart that permeate all dimensions of pedagogical actions. The question, then, becomes—how can teacher educators help teacher candidates and practicing teachers discover their goals for treating diversity and develop an approach to language instruction that is relatively free of unfounded generalizations about perceived linguistic inadequacies?

Postman (1996) poses a highly provocative metaphorical question about the purposes of education in the *End of Education*, a book title that cleverly uses "end" ambiguously to refer to the purposes of education and the demise of public education. He uses the exclamation point and the question mark as metaphors for the purpose of education: Postman infers that what we have to fear about this current era of educational accountability is that "someone will insist on putting in an exclamation point when we are not yet finished" (p. 97). The exclamation point metaphor represents well the views that many people have about diversity, views that are based on strong ideological persuasions about language rights and on teachers' reality-based justifications for prescriptivisms. The view that teachers must help students to "talk" right in order to succeed is too often accompanied by a righteous disdain for other varieties of English and their speakers. The question mark metaphor represents open-mindedness, the willingness to admit that knowledge and information change continuously, and the view that an inquiring mind is necessary for the ongoing production of new knowledge.

Inspired by Postman's punctuation metaphor, Scott adapted the punctuation metaphor for use in a graduate course on adaptive literacy strategies. Given that the course emphasizes the use of an inquiry approach to developing adaptive literacy strategies for language diverse students, Scott began the course with this question: What kind of punctuation mark best represents your purpose for teaching language-diverse students—an exclamation point or a question mark? She then asked students to respond to a language awareness questionnaire aimed at eliciting folk perceptions of dialects and modeled after the work of Wolfram (1999). Scott (personal communications) found that those who chose the exclamation point also tended to have a high number of folk perceptions about language diversity. Conversely, those who chose the question mark as their metaphor tended to have a low number of folk perceptions about language diversity.

When the same procedures were repeated at the end of the course, most of the students chose the question mark metaphor, and again those who chose the question mark had sharply reduced folk perceptions of language variation. These results suggest that the course objective of engaging students in serious thinking about the importance of developing adaptive instruction to meet the needs of language diverse students had been attained. Scott found that this exercise had placed the students on a direct path to developing an inquiry stance for the purpose of teaching students of diverse language and cultural backgrounds.

Another important aspect of developing an inquiry stance on language diversity instruction is an appreciation for a descriptive, rather than a prescriptive, approach to language instruction. As Goodman (2003) notes, a prescriptive view of language "holds that language is either right or wrong, that through direct and isolated teaching of skills, language improves" (p. 67). In contrast, a descriptive approach to language instruction emphasizes objective descriptions that involve questioning and hypothesizing about how language works, followed by the collection and analysis of language data that leads to data-based generalizations about language— how it is structured, how forms and usages vary, and how, when and why different variants are used. In short, generalizations are made about how language works, rather than how we think it "should" work. Many researchers have emphasized the value of developing a conscious awareness of one's own attitudes toward language in the diversity training of teachers.

In her course on diversity, Okawa (2003) engages her students in a process she calls "resurfacing the roots" of language ideologies, as part of her attempt to develop a "pedagogy of language awareness." She explains that "even teachers who make language their business, the roots of language are buried deep within our personal, family, and community histories and experiences" (p. 109). Within this process, students are allowed to "write themselves into language awareness" by reconstructing their individual language histories, which are, in turn, analyzed using sociolinguistic inquiry methods. Students document their family language histories and memories of personal language acquisition and development and assess the origins of their language attitudes. The cumulative effect, she notes, is "usually a significant awakening for the students" (p. 119).

Goodman (2006) incorporates sociolinguistic methods into her descriptions of language, which she considers useful in moving away from prescriptivisms. In her class, students use firsthand language data to develop and refine their awareness of language by telling their own language stories: "the words of funny (or not so funny) incidents that we tend to laugh (or cry) about with family and close friends" (p. 146). For example, one of her students, related a story about her young child's pronunciation of "pish" for "fish." This led naturally to further data collection on language acquisition patterns, a topic already taught in the course.

The three tasks just described, Scott's metaphors for the purposes of education, Okawa's (2003) language biographies, and Goodman's (2006) language stories, can be used by teacher educators to develop an inquiry stance toward diversity education. An inquiry stance, remember, refers to habits of heart and mind that permeate all dimensions of pedagogical action, a step that prepares one to develop an inquiry orientation to instruction for language diverse students.

An Inquiry Orientation to Diversity Instruction

An inquiry orientation to diversity instruction uses strategies such as questioning, dialoguing, and reflecting. These strategies are utilized differently in an inquiry verses a transmission orientation. A transmission orientation to instruction treats questioning as a domain reserved largely for the teacher. Teachers ask the questions and students respond, usually with a view toward regurgitating information presented by the teacher. A transmission orientation to instruction tends to be highly monologic—the teacher conveys knowledge and the students receive that knowledge. In a transmission orientation to instruction, the teacher maintains authority over opening and closing the gates of change. Instruction is often geared towards directing reflective thinking processes to accord with established practices, rather than changing established practices. Questioning, dialoguing, and reflecting in inquiry-oriented instruction are far more open, student directed, and discovery driven than in transmission-oriented instruction. To paint a picture of how inquiry-oriented diversity instruction looks in teacher education courses, we provide examples of tasks associated with questioning, dialoguing, and reflecting.

A valuable approach to supporting teachers in developing a questioning orientation in their delivery of content about language diversity is helping them discover for themselves the typical types of questioning pattern that are used in the classroom and in the homes of different ethnic groups. One way to do this is by creating a sense of wonder about questioning patterns so that teachers create questions, pose problems, and solve problems related to question–answer episodes that peak their interest. To get a feel for the subtle ways that different questioning patterns can affect the classroom climate, it is useful to begin observing question–answer episodes in classrooms and in homes. Video- or audiotaped recordings of interactions in homes and schools can be conducted and then analyzed in relation to questions raised by teachers and teacher educators. Some of the elements to pay attention to about inquiry-based questioning strategies are the use of (a) learner generated questions; (b) choices about questions to explore, (c) real v. rhetorical questions, and (d) data-based generalizations about how questioning patterns can be altered to bridge the gap between home and school. (See Au (2003) for discussion of changes in participation structure in Hawaiian schools.)

Shifting the focus to dialoguing, it is sometimes difficult for students of language diverse backgrounds to use this type of talk to learn in classrooms settings. Dialoguing involves both students and teacher(s) constructing knowledge. Dialogue, as Barnes (1990) asserts, is "the means by which the assimilation and accommodation of new knowledge to the old is carried out" (p. 28). The failure to match the prior knowledge and experience that language diverse students bring to the classroom with the new knowledge to be acquired in the classroom accounts partially for the performance gaps between students of mainstream and non-mainstream group (Scott & Marcus, 2001). It is argued that since the prior knowledge and experiences of non-mainstream students are not taken into account in planning, the use of children's prior knowledge and "home-grown" language patterns to learn is hampered.

Using talk to learn is one of the purposes served by dialoguing in collaborative groups. Another dimension of talking to learn is the development of metalinguistic knowledge (i.e. the use of talk to talk about language) as a means of learning about language differences. As students talk about language, they learn the terms associated with different language constructs and develop a more conscious awareness of the meaning of the language terms. Two terms for which teachers need to develop metalinguistic knowledge are code-switching and style-shifting. Code-switching refers to the switching from patterns used in one dialect to those used in another dialect, e.g. switching from African American English to standard English. Style-shifting refers to shifting from one style (e.g. formal) to another, e.g. informal style. Having teachers in training work in collaborative groups to use exploratory talk is helpful for discovering how and why people switch codes and shift styles.

One strategy to facilitate this task involves the use of literature, such as *Flossie and the Fox* by Patricia McKissack, that demonstrates the switching of codes and the shifting of styles. From a language structure perspective, the group might consider the forms manipulated by the author to represent different ways of saying things. From a literary perspective, they might examine how the author used different codes to achieve certain stylistic effects, e.g. to present a point of view, to develop a character, to emphasize a point, to capture an attitude, to demonstrate an authoritative voice. Analyzing the language in the text requires discussants to talk about the language used and to use the language terminology appropriately, which, in turn, enhances their metalinguistic knowledge.

In an inquiry orientation to dialogue, emphasis is placed on using talk to learn and drawing on pre- and in-service teachers' experiences with language to talk about language. Regarding talking to learn, emphasis is placed on exploratory talk and student-to-student talk as it naturally occurs in collaborative learning groups, usually with minimal sanctions on language forms and use. See, for example, Adger's (1998) discussion of register shifting and the development of an authoritative stance by African American children.

Regarding the final strategy, reflection, one might focus on either personal reflections or critical reflections. Personal reflection is what teachers in training are often asked to do in order to make self-discoveries about what they have learned. For example, in Scott's metaphor activity examined previously, after having students report their response to the metaphor question and the language awareness survey, Scott asked students to compare their pre- and post-responses, reflect on their experiences in the course, and write an essay describing the differences in their responses. Looking back, the students asked themselves questions such as what did the question mark mean to me at the beginning of the course? What does it mean to me now? Introspectively, a student might ask what happened during this course to influence a change in my thinking, my feelings, or my understanding of teaching and learning in language diverse settings? What metaphor can I create to represent my purpose for teaching students of language-diverse backgrounds? Thus, through personal reflection, the teacher candidates discover something about themselves.

Reflection is also discussed in relation to critical literacy. Critical literacy gained prominence with the work of Freire who emphasized the political nature of teaching, reading, and writing. In his *Letter to North American Teachers*, Freire explains: "Clearly, those who are illiterate need to learn how to read and write. However, reading and writing words encompasses the reading of the world, that is, the critical understanding of politics in the word" (1987, pp. 212–213).

Indeed, Bloome, et al. (2005) demonstrate how one teacher helped her students manipulate their reading of the word and the world in a lesson that focused on the poem *After Winter* by Sterling Brown. They note that "Her questions are not about the content of the poem per se, or what feelings were invoked by the poem, but ones that require students to reflect on their own experiences and sociocultural histories" (2005, p. 98). They further point out that "an analysis of the poem as a coherent text to determine or construct a meaning for it is displaced by what Freire and Macedo called *reading the world*" (p. 98).

Comments by the teacher help to illuminate how a teacher educator can provide teachers in training with a model of how to read in a way that differs from the typical model of classroom literacy practices:

Hold on, hold on, hold on. Whatever it is I want you to marinate on your thoughts and then think about yourself in relationship to your comments.

A lot of you are making excellent comments but they are devoid of you as a person. It's very easy to make generalizations about people or about other people when you're able to take yourself out of it. But when you put yourself back into your statements, put yourself in relationship to your comments you're making, and then see if the comment still works. (p. 99)

This type of reading gives rise to transformative acts at the personal, classroom, and even societal level. What students are doing, argues Bloome and his colleagues, "is acting on the world by interrogating it, re-presenting it, and problematizing it. The tension, therefore, is between accepting the world as given (including one's place within it) and acting on it to change" (p. 93).

It is useful, we maintain, for teacher educators to learn how to engage practicing and developing teachers in critical inquiry type conversations without having vicious arguments with no resolve. A good starting point is with demonstrating how teachers can silence their students, as was done by Goodman (2006) when she used the poem *Rayford's Song* by Inanda to show how teachers can silence students. In this poem, a student asks to sing the song "Swing Low, Sweet Chariot" during music class. The teacher corrects the students' non-standard language, instead of taking the opportunity to help the student make personal and cultural connections to the poem or to explore its aesthetic value. Poems like *Rayford's Song* can also be used to open critical inquiry conversations about the social status of language. Some teacher educators have also reported using language policy documents, such as the Students' Right to their Own Language resolution to engage students in critical reflection on issues such as language rights. (See, for example, Kinloch's chapter in this volume. See also Geneva Smitherman's (2003) critical analysis of language policies and practices, which can be used in teacher education courses to engage teachers in a variety of critical literacy tasks.)

We are suggesting that critical literacy tasks in language can be used to engage students in critical reflection on the use of text to interrogate, re-present and problematize the world, using topics such as language and power, identity, privilege, and dominance. A critical starting point is with opening up conversations about language and power. We have identified a couple of different types of text that teacher educators can use to engage students in conversations on topics that are typically addressed in critical literacy. The central point is that reflection is an inquiry-based instructional strategy that, along with questioning and dialoguing, can be used to help teachers develop an inquiry orientation to teaching students of diverse language and cultural backgrounds.

At the outset, we stated that one of our main intents for conducting a pilot study on the language attitudes of pre- and in-service teachers was to identify factors about language attitudes that warranted further study, especially for the purpose of maximizing the impact that instruction in teacher education programs have on teacher candidates. The LKAS research, the description of a body of research that looked at language attitudes in teacher preparation courses, and the suggested pedagogical strategies treated here might well be thought of metaphorically as a series of questions marks. What are our purposes for engaging in diversity instruction for teachers? What if teacher educators were to choose the question mark as their metaphor for the purpose of diversity instruction? What if teacher educators incorporated an inquiry-based system for delivering some of the diversity content in their courses? If teacher educators could imagine different ways to change the system for delivering diversity content, chances are we would select more inquiry-based strategies for diversity instruction.

Quite possibly we have been concentrating primarily on the content of diversity courses in teacher education programs and giving too little attention to whether the content is delivered as exclamation points—as though teacher educators have the answers and can transmit their answers to developing and practicing teachers. Quite possibly, teacher educators may set up diversity instruction for resistance. Preparing and practicing teachers also have answers that sometimes differ from ours. Instead of simply taking in the information and acting on it, they defend their answers. This is good if their views are aligned with ours, but obviously bad if their answers run counter to their instructors.

More importantly, we have suggested that more attention needs to be given to how to help developing and practicing teachers develop an inquiry stance that clearly articulates the purposes for teaching language minority students and that helps develop an appreciation for descriptive, rather than prescriptive approaches to studying language variation, be it the acquisition and development of varied linguistic forms and language functions, varied ideological persuasions, or exposure to different types of pedagogical method. All in all, we should be ever mindful of a provocative statement that occurs in the letter of Paulo Freire to North American teachers:

> Therefore, any teacher who rigidly adheres to the routines set forth in teaching material manuals is exercising *authority* in a way that inhibits the freedom of students, the freedom they need to exercise critical intelligence through which they appropriate the subject matter. Such a teacher is neither free nor able to help students become creative, curious people. (p. 214)

Discussion Questions and Activities

1. Respond to the items on the Language Knowledge and Awareness Survey. Identify three items that reflect your experiences with language attitudes or teaching practices. Engage at least three people in a discussion of problems and solutions related to your experiences.
2. In the article, punctuation marks were used as metaphors for the purpose of education in language diverse settings. The question mark was presented as the ideal metaphor for inquiry-based teaching. Create your own metaphor for the purpose of educating students of language diverse backgrounds. Ask a colleague to give you feedback on the value of your metaphor for communicating important issues that teachers need to consider in their teaching.
3. Design an instructional strategy that makes use of inquiry-based instructional strategies. Be sure to describe the procedures for implementing your instructional strategy. Try to implement the strategy with your students and record your

observations about the effectiveness of your strategy. Ask a colleague to implement the strategy and give you feedback on its usefulness.
4. Consider the implications presented in this article for teacher education programs. In a reflective essay, explain the possible effects on teaching that might evolve if teacher education programs were to reform courses in ways suggested in this paper.

References

Adger, C. (1998). Register Shifting with Dialect Resources in Instructional Discourse. In M. Holye, & C. T. Adger (Eds.). *Kids Talk: Strategic Language Use in Later Childhood.* New York: Oxford University Press.

Au, K. H. (2003). Multicultural Factors and the Effective Instruction of Students of Diverse Backgrounds. In A. E. Farstrup, & S.J. Samuels (Eds.). *What Research Has to Say about Reading Instruction.* Newark, NY: International Reading Association.

Barnes, J. (1990). Oral Language and Learning. In S. Hynds, & L. Rubin (Eds.). *Perspectives on Talk & Learning.* Urbana, IL: National Council of Teachers of English.

Bloome, D., Carter, S.P., Christian, B.M., Otto, S., & Shuart-Faris, N. (2005). *Discourse Analysis and the Study of Classroom Language and Literacy Events: A Microethnographic Perspective.* Mahwah, NJ: Lawrence Erlbaum Associates, Inc.

Cross, B. (2003). Learning and Unlearning Racism: Transferring Teacher Education to Classroom Practices. *Theory into Practice*, 42(3), 203–209.

Clark, C., & Medina, C. (2000). How Reading and Writing Literacy Narratives Affect Preservice Teachers' Understanding of Literacy, Pedagogy, and Multiculturalism. *Journal of Teacher Education*, 57(1), 63–76.

Cockrell, K. S., Placier, P. L., Cockrell, D. H., & Middleton, J. N. (1999). Coming to Terms with "Diversity" and "Multiculturalism" in Teacher Education: Learning about Our Students, Changing Our Practices. *Teacher and Teacher Education*, 15(4), 351–366.

Filmore, L. W. (2005). When Learning a Second Language Means Losing the First. *The New Immigration: An Interdisciplinary Reader*, 302–306.

Freire, P. (1987). Letter to North-American teachers. In I. Shor (Ed.). *Freire for the Classroom: A Sourcebook for Liberatory Teaching.* Portsmouth, NH: Heinemann Educational Books.

———, & Macedo, D. P. *Reading the Word and the World.* Westport, CT: Praeger/Greenwood.

Gilbert, S. L. (1997). The "Four Commonplaces of Teaching": Prospective Teachers' Beliefs about Teaching in Urban Schools. *The Urban Review*, 29(2), 81–96.

Goodman, D. (2006). Language Study in Teacher Education: Exploring the Language in Language Arts. *Language Arts*, 48(2), 145–156.

Goodman, Y. (2003). *Valuing Language Study: Inquiry into Language for Elementary and Middle Schools.* Urbana, IL: National Council of Teachers of English.

Greenleaf, C., Hull, G., & Reilly, B. (1994). Learning from Our Diverse Students: Helping Teachers Rethink Problematic Teaching and Learning Situations. *Teaching and Teacher Education*, 10(5), 521–541.

Hardaway, N. L. & Florez, V. (1987). Diversity in the Classroom: Are Our Teachers Prepared? *Teacher Education & Practice*, 4(1), 25–30.

Hollins, E., & Guzman, M. (2005). Research on Preparing Teachers for Diverse Populations. In M. Cochran-Smith, & K. Zeichner (Eds.). *Studying Teacher Education: The Report of the Aera Panel on Research and Teacher Education.* Mahwah, NJ: Lawrence Erlbaum Associates, Inc. (for the American Educational Research Association).

Katz, S. R. (2000). Promoting Bilingualism in the Era of Unz: Making Sense of the Gap between Research, Policy, and Practice in Teacher Education. *Multicultural Education*, 8(1), 2–7.

McDiarmid, G. W. (1992). What to Do about Difference? A Study of Multicultural Education for Teacher Trainees in Los Angeles Unified School District. *Journal of Teacher Education*, 43(2), 83–93.

Morales, R. (2000). Effects of Teacher Preparation Experiences and Students' Perceptions Related Developmentally and Culturally Appropriate Practices. *Action in Teacher Education*, 22(2), 67–75.

Nathenson-Mejia, S., & Escamilla, K. (2003). Connecting with Laqtino Children: Bridging Cultural Gaps with Children's Literature. *Bilingual Research Journal*, 27(1), 101–116.

Obadiah, J. E. (2000). Mediating Boundaries of Race, Class, and Professional Authority as a Critical Multiculturalist. *Teachers and College Record*, 102(6), 1035–1960.

Okawa, G. Y. (2003). "Resurfacing Toots": Developing a Pedagogy of Language Awareness from Two Views. In G. Smitherman, & V. Villanueva (Eds.). *Language Diversity in the Classroom: From Intention to Practice*. Carbondale, IL: Southern Illinois University Press.

Postman, N. (1996). *The End of Education: Redefining the Value of School*. New York: Vantage Books.

Richardson, E. (2003). Race, Class(es), Gender, and Age: The Making of Knowledge about Language Diversity. In G. Smitherman, & V. Villanueva (Eds.). *Language Diversity in the Classroom: From Intention to Practice*. Carbondale, IL: Southern Illinois University Press.

Richman, C. L., Bovelsky, S., Kroovand, N., Vacca, J., & West, T. (1997). Racisms 102: The Classroom. *Journal of Black Psychology*, 23(4), 378–387.

Rodríguez, A. J. (1998). Strategies for Counterresistance: Toward Sociotransformative Constructivism and Learning to Teach Science for Diversity and Understanding. *Journal of Research in Science Teaching*, 35(6), 589–622.

Rodríguez, C. (2006). Language and Participation. *California Law Review*, 94, 687.

Scott, J. C., & Marcus, C. (2001). Emergent Literacy: Home–School Connections. In J. Harris, A. Kamhi, & K. Pollock (Eds.). *Literacy in African American Communities*. Mahwah, NJ: Lawrence Erlbaum Associates, Inc.

——, & Smitherman, G. (1985). Language Attitudes and Self-Fulfilling Prophecies in the Elementary School. In S. Greenbaum (Ed.). *The English Language Today*. Oxford: Pergamon.

Smith, R., Moallem, M., & Sherrill, D. (1997). How Preservice Teachers Think about Cultural Diversity: A Deeper Look at Factors which Influence their Beliefs towards Equality. *Educational Foundations*, 11(2), 41–61.

Smitherman, G. (2003). The Historical Struggle for Language Rights in CCCC. In G. Smitherman, & V. Villanueva (Eds.). *Language Diversity in the Classroom: From Intention to Practice*. Carbondale, IL: Southern Illinois University Press.

Southerland, S. A., & Gess-Newsome, J. (1999). Preservice Teachers' Views of Inclusive Science Teaching as Shaped by Images of Teaching, Learning, and Lnowing. *Science Education*, 83(2), 131–150.

Sparks, W. G., III, & Verner, M. E. (1995). Intervention Strategies in Multicultural Education: A Comparison of Preservice Models. *Physical Educator*, 52(4), 170–186.

Su, Z. (1997). Teaching as a Profession and a Career: Minority Candidates' Perspectives. *Teaching and Teacher Education*, 13(3), 325–341.

Terrill, M. & Mark, D. L. H. (2000). Preservice Teachers' Expectations for Schools with Children of Color and Second-Language Learners. *Journal of Teacher Education*, 51(2), 149–155.

Williams, F. (1970). Psychological Correlates of Speech Characteristics: On Sounding Disadvantaged. *Journal of Speech and Hearing Research*, 13, 472– 488.

Wilson, M. (2001). The Changing Discourse of Language Study. *English Journal*, 90(4), 31–36.

Wolfram, W. (1999). Repercussions from the Oakland Ebonics Controversy: The Critical Role of Dialect Awareness Programs. In C. Adger, D. Christian, & O. Taylor (Eds.). *Making the Connection: Language and Academic Achievement among African American Students*. Washington, DC: Center for Applied Linguistics.

Xu, H. (2000). Preservice Teachers Integrate Understandings of Diversity into Literacy Instruction: An Adaptation of the Abc's Model. *Journal of Teacher Education*, 51(2), 135–142.

8

Positionality: Using Self-Discovery to Enhance Pre-Service Teachers' Understanding of Language Differences

NANCY RANKIE SHELTON

I was born in a small town in upstate New York and lived in that region for the first 19 years of my life. I was taught from a very early age that the grammatical structure of my oral language was a reflection of my intellectual ability—I was corrected often and was required to speak what my parents considered to be Standard English. "*May* I go outside?" was the required alternative to the colloquial "*Can* I," and verb tenses were expected to be in perfect agreement with the subject. No "got" for "have" and "ain't" was countered with the childhood rhyme: "Don't say ain't, your mother will faint, and your father will fall in a bucket of paint." When my family traveled, we would comment on the variations of American English and even teasingly mimic the New York City and Boston accents. I understood my dialect as being superior—those "others" were wrong.

Self-Discoveries about Positionality and Students' Rights to Language

Language is learned in a social context, and the various social roles we participate in help shape our social identities. These identities, shaped by our discourse patterns, "position" us within a discourse community and enable us to act out our social roles. As our interactions with others expand our discourse patterns, we intuitively understand and internalize the cultural and political context within which we communicate, thus increasing our communicative competence as we become selective participants in the process of communication (Schieffelin & Ochs, 1986). In so doing, we "position" ourselves socially and linguistically, depending upon our role in the social group or interaction. This "positionality" is so intuitive that many people do not consciously realize they are participants in multiple discourse communities. By becoming conscious of this process in myself, I began to understand the value of language diversity in others.

In 1976 I moved away from my family and my roots, relocating in St. Petersburg Beach, Florida. Listening to the various speech patterns became a game of sorts. Being that there were so many people from all over the United States either visiting or permanently relocating to this city, oral language became our identifier. While I once thought I was alone in my feelings of superiority in my language, I discovered that most of my new friends held that same belief—each of us thought our language was the "real" American English, the best one. We would joke and tease each other about differences in our speech patterns. The stress my family had put on precise oral language loosened, and I reshaped my oral language patterns to resemble the language of the people with whom I socialized. And though I had not formally studied language variations at that point in my life, I came to realize that each of us has different speech patterns which are greatly influenced by where we live and with whom we associate.

Although perceptive, this early realization failed to appreciate the breadth and depth of the social implications associated with the stigma attached to non-standard dialect speakers. It wasn't until I moved to North Central Florida and started associating with people of diverse racial backgrounds and nationalities that I discovered the overwhelmingly negative impact of the widely held stereotypes against the language variations of "others" in our society. This once playful game was revealed to have an ugly underbelly. Different wasn't just different. Oral language variations were used as markers of social acceptance, perceived intelligence, and workplace exclusion. This was no longer a case of joyful mimicking but a powerful mechanism of oppression.

In the north central region of Florida a number of variations of Southern dialects are spoken. The city to which I relocated has a major university drawing residents from across the nation and the world. It was in this area of the country that I began my career as an elementary school teacher. I worked in a school where the language diversity of the students was viewed with contempt and indignation; many teachers often complained about their students' home language and made frequent comments about their belief that students' inability to learn the material required was related to their "limited" language. And though these teachers certainly had diverse backgrounds and used a variety of American English, they seemed to be much like I was back in 1976: they believed their discourse patterns were far superior to those of their students.

This belief did not stop at enhancing the believers' sense of superiority. Instead, I witnessed it being waged as a powerful and wide-ranging weapon against children who spoke disrespected variations of American English. In the schools where I taught and witnessed prejudicial behavior towards language minority students, the offended students were overwhelmingly African American students who spoke in one of the Southern dialects. These same students were disproportionately identified as having serious academic weaknesses and were referred for special education.

According to Preston (1996), the Southern dialect in its various versions is widely recognized but also widely perceived as the most "incorrect" American English dialect. The deficit view of language, related to the teachers' perceptions of the students' families, greatly influenced the teachers' expectations for the students' academic potential: they were "lacking" and unable to "keep up" with the curriculum. Teachers frequently interrupted oral language interactions to "correct" students' accents, vocabulary, and syntax. The constant corrections led to hesitations and alienation of the students. Short-answer responses were used to avoid language "problems." Casual conversations between teachers and students who spoke using non-standard dialects rarely took place, and many of my peers used a skill and drill approach to teaching grammar.

A common strategy used to this effect was a school-wide practice of pulling two sentences a day (when possible from the students we taught) for daily oral language (DOL) exercises. The "incorrect" grammar was written on the blackboard and the class would "correct" the language forms used by our students. In this environment, language minority students were almost always perceived as less capable learners who needed correction and special services to support their academic development. Much research has confirmed that teachers' perceptions and expectations of their students have a profound affect on student performance (Benard, 1995; Crozier, 2005; Radcliffe, Caverly, Peterson, & Emmonds, 2004), and it was clear to me that the teachers, although seemingly well-meaning, were actually hindering their students' language learning.

Approaches to Changing Teacher Attitudes

Resistance to multicultural education is well documented (Sleeter & Grant, 1994; Tatum, 1992). As the student population in our schools becomes increasingly diverse and the teaching force remains predominantly White, middle class, and female, the need to be culturally sensitive becomes increasingly important (Ladson-Billings, 1994). These changing demographics require teachers to develop an understanding of and empathy for culturally diverse students (McAllister & Irvine, 2002).

As a classroom teacher, I had little power to change the school culture outside my own classroom, but as a teacher educator my sphere of influence has the potential to be much greater. However, various approaches to changing teacher attitudes toward language differences have been tried, and many yield very limited positive affects. Because of my experience as a classroom teacher, one of my primary concerns in any of my courses with preservice teachers is to try to bring an awareness of subconscious biases toward others based on language differences. Knowing that teaching about language variation has been met with much resistance from preservice teachers (Major & Perreault, 2004), my primary goal is not necessarily to change any of my students' beliefs, but to make sure that they give conscious thought to:

1. their own perceptions of people who speak variations of American English;
2. how perceptions become biases and influence teachers' expectations of students' abilities;
3. how lower expectations for student achievement often translates to lower performance for that student.

In taking this approach, I hope to challenge my students from a theoretical perspective that is not perceived as my attempt to change them. I seek instead to enable my students to become responsible for their actions by confronting their ethical obligations that all professional educators uphold: to create an environment where *all* students have an opportunity to succeed.

Evolution of the Language Positionality Project

Since 2000, I have used the National Council of Teachers of English (NCTE) Students' Right to Their Own Language (SRTOL) resolution and the Conference on College Composition and Communication's (CCC, 1974) explanation of adoption of the resolution as required reading in my education courses at both the graduate and undergraduate level in Florida, Georgia, South Carolina, Maryland and Washington. My students read the document and the explanation of the adoption, and I facilitate both small and large group discussions on the concepts explained in these documents. During the discussions, I share my experiences teaching language minority elementary students and the successes these students attained in reading and writing. After the discussions and lectures, the preservice teachers compose an essay that explains their position on the inclusion of diverse dialects in the elementary classroom.

My graduate students respond positively to this approach—they are often in-service teachers who easily recognize the language diversity around them. Most challenge their previous practice, and come to understand the importance of including culturally and linguistically diverse teaching methodologies in their own practice. They often express relief and are happy to embrace a theoretical stance that allows them to accept their students' language. By way of contrast, my undergraduate students' reaction to the assignment was predominantly negative— they held strongly to their belief that home dialects have no place in the classroom.Unsatisfied with my undergraduate students' lack of "understanding of how language works in their own lives and in the lives of their students" (Valdes, et al. 2005, p. 127) and their resistance to SRTOL, I turned to other professionals who share my goal of helping preservice teachers understand this complex issue. Based on feedback from colleagues on the NCTE Language Commission, I decided to implement a new strategy. Before thinking about language diversity in others, my students would examine their own oral language. It was my hope that by examining their own interactions, students would become aware of the diversity and changing nature of their language according to the communicative situation at hand. I also anticipated that a focused examination of the patterns of their own language would help them begin to understand the intricate relationship between language, culture and power. In what follows, I describe the revised assignments and discuss how they impacted undergraduate preservice teachers as they grappled with the complex issues surrounding language diversity. Although this description refers to an implementation by only one teacher educator, I believe that the experiences, realizations, and learning described can provide valuable insight and direction to the process of helping all preservice teachers examine their bias against non-standard dialects.

Revised Assignment

The assignment has evolved into a five-part project that spans over several weeks. Table 8.1 provides an overview of the assignment outline given to the students. The assignment begins with students defining dialect in order for me to assess their

TABLE 8.1 Overview of the Positionality Project

Project Phase	Activities
Phase 1: Foundational knowledge	Students defining dialect
Phase 2: Data collection segment	Students record three conversations from their own lives
Phase 3: Data analysis segment	Students analyze the conversation recorded in Phase 2
Phase 4: Essay writing	Students write in response to the question: "How do you say what you say when you are in multiple environments?"
Phase 5: Studying the SRTOL documents	Students read, discuss and respond to the documents. Guiding principle: step back from own language use and evaluate language diversity from a teacher's perspective

knowledge base and prior experience with language diversity. The students are required to capture three conversations in which they participate.

My experience has taught me that to be successful in this endeavor, students need to be supported through the use of explicit examples, in-class practice recording conversations without using audio-recording devices, and guidance in learning how to transcribe recorded conversations.

When the data collection is complete, analyzing the conversations begins. During this phase of the project, I frequently share writing samples of elementary student and audiotapes of elementary students' oral language so that my preservice teachers can see and hear examples of effective communication with speakers of various dialects. Concurrent with the lectures on elementary student language development, in class and over time, the students analyze their conversations based on the following:

- *Content:* Who controls the content of each conversation, how do topics change, are there clear senders and receivers of information?
- *Turns:* How long are speakers' turns, how do turns change?
- *Sentence grammar:* Are complete sentences needed to express meaning, do speakers use *accurate* noun/verb agreement, and how does sentence grammar change across conversations?
- *Slang, colloquial, jargon:* What evidence of use is there, are the incidents noted spread across conversations?

As the typescripts of the recorded conversations are analyzed in class, the students are asked to be conscious of their oral language the following week, attending specifically to the constructs we discussed in class that week.

After the students have a chance to deconstruct their own conversations, they write an essay that describes their findings and addresses the question: How do you say what you say when you are in multiple environments? In their discussion, the students are expected to support their interpretations with data from their recorded conversations.

In the revised project, it is only after the students have carefully examined their own language that we turn to the NCTE documents. The students read, discuss and respond. They are asked to step back from their own language use and evaluate language diversity from a teacher's perspective. This 3-week process intentionally follows the examination of the students own language and is designed to help them understand that elementary "students are not cognitively or linguistically deficient just because they have not mastered a particular set of literacy practice to which they have not been exposed" (Valdes, et al., 2005, p. 145).

Following is a description of my approach, "positionality in language: the search for identity."

Part One: Assessment

Pre-assessment of students' knowledge: In class written response to the question: What is dialect? Give examples.

Activity: In this assignment, you will examine your own positionalities in language communities. It is designed to help you identify and reflect on the language forms you use in a variety of environments (e.g. dinner conversations, job interview, chat with friends). The question posed is this: how do you say what you say when you are in multiple environments?

Part Two: Recording Conversations

1. Record three conversations that involve you and at least one other participant.
2. Each conversation must last for at least five minutes.
3. Capture conversations via tape-recording or taking explicit notes immediately after the conversation. In your transcription, include the context of the conversation as well as the roles of the participants. Avoid any identifying information such as names of participants as well as the contexts for the conversations. Be sure to record exactly how the participants speak such as choice of words, sentence phrasing and structure, vocal emphasis, and voice inflections. In your transcriptions, record the intonation, exaggeration of terms/words, exact sentence structure and other features of language.

Choose your conversations from three different interactions with, for example, your friends, other students, family members/relatives, team members, co-workers, supervisors, persons who are both older than you AND familiar, person who are both older than you AND a stranger. The contexts for these conversations include: your home/neighborhood, clubs, parties, religious environments, community/employment, schools, Bring your transcriptions to class to discuss. The first transcript is due on ___ and the second two are due on ___.

Part Three: Analyzing Transcripts

Bring your notes and transcriptions to class. In small groups, you will analyze the conversations according to guidelines that will be discussed in class.

Part Four: Describing Findings

Write an essay that describes your findings. Remember the purpose of this activity is for you to examine your own positionalities in language; to examine what's going on when using language, to recognize how language is privileged or not, and how language is used in diverse spaces. Return to your overarching question: how do you say what you say when you are in multiple environments?

Part Five: Analyzing Students' Rights to Language

Access the Students' Right to Their Own Language (SRTOL) document at www.ncte.org. Read the resolution, the reaffirmation of the resolution, and the background information that supports the resolution. Come to class prepared to discuss your perspective: Do students have the right to their own language? After class discussion, you will write an essay that articulates your position.

Students' Responses

What is shared in the following are data collected from two groups of students to illustrate the powerful effect of the five-part project.

Foundational Knowledge

In order to assess prior knowledge of my students' understanding of dialects, I asked each student to explain his/her current understanding of dialect. The students responded in writing and were given as much time as needed to answer the question. A breakdown of the 38 students' responses is provided with examples to help the reader understand the overall knowledge base of the students: Three answers could not be categorized because of vagueness ("The way information is relayed. How you say it"). One student confused dialect with foreign language ("Dialect is a set of words that is considered a language in cultures. Ex. English, Spanish").

Two students defined dialect as a foreign accent ("Dialect—form of speaking, having an accent but speaking the same language. Example: A man from Paris asks for the bathroom, but it sounds different with an accent").Two students provided a definition for "dialogue" ("Dialect is a conversation in writing between two or more people. For example, 'Hi George,' called Fred, 'How are you Fred? Long time no see.'). Sixteen students identified dialect as a regional accent (only phonological) ("Dialect is the articulation, sound and accent that one has when he/she speaks. An example of dialect is a southern drawl"). Four students identified phonological and lexical difference in language ("Dialect is different ways of speaking depending on where you live. Ex. Bald-a-more v. Balt-a-more and pop v. soda"). Ten students provided varying levels of correct understanding of dialect, from general ("Dialect can vary from place to place. Dialect is how people talk") to much more detailed responses leaving no doubt about the student's understanding ("The way someone speaks that is influenced by their culture, for example the pronunciation of words, phrasing, word order"). As can be noted in these data, only 26% of the students in my combined classes could correctly define "dialect" when they entered the course. The remaining students had either partial or incorrect knowledge.

Discovering Variations in One's Own Language

As explained previously, the students were asked to record and analyze naturally occurring conversations from their own lives. Subsequently, the students wrote an essay reflecting on the finding of this analysis. In these essays, students over-whelmingly focused on issues of power. In class discussions, they had expressed surprise at the dynamics of the power relationships played out so clearly in their transcripts. Often the students made comments like Katie's: "I know I talk to my parents differently than I talk to my friends, but I didn't know how different! My mother controlled the whole conversation I had with her." In the essays the students used data to explain their conclusions, offering elaborated examples: "She had a whole paragraph while I could only get out two vocal cues" and "I lack the ability to complete a sentence. I held back on speaking my thoughts" were typical obser-vations made by students.

Students noted other conditions besides power relations that cause them to speak in incomplete sentences. These included high levels of comfort and common background between participants in the conversation, and interjections used to prompt a conversant to continue speaking and/or affirm a comment. Although they knew this was true in their conversations before this project, many were surprised at the level of informality in their language when interacting with peers.

The students also commented on how familiarity and comfort contribute to the content of their conversations: "When I get uncomfortable I try to lighten it up with a joke to take the attention off me." Many articulated their disappointment in their oral language proficiency, commenting that they "sound stupid" or often "have nothing to say."

Regardless of their findings, all the students expressed gratitude for the opportunity the project gave them to examine their language in a way that they had ever done before, regardless of what they found. The students' essays indicated that they took the assignment seriously and had thoughtfully examined both the positive and the negative conclusions they drew about the social positions revealed in their language. Excerpts from Nicky's poignant conclusion capture the importance of this work:

> In writing this language position paper, there are several revelations about myself that came to the surface. I am a quiet person, but not because I have nothing to say. I have plenty to say, it's just I worry about how people are

going to interpret what I say. . . . It's hard to really know if I will be accepted for who I am. Who I am is a person with many disguises or roles. I put these roles together to make myself feel better about who I am . . . I am insecure as a person, and I am insecure as a writer.

Reading and Responding to SRTOL

At the very beginning of this 3-week section of the project, the students were instructed to read SRTOL independently before class met and to come to class prepared to discuss the content of the document. In class, the students first worked together in small groups to share their personal reactions to the article and then, as a small group, compose one sentence encapsulating the most important message of the document. The examples that follow indicate that the preservice teachers understood that the authors of SRTOL express concern for teachers' acceptance of diverse speakers:

Teachers should be accepting of different dialects, and not push their students toward the standard dialect, so that students are not limited in expressing themselves through writing. As teachers we need to *focus* on the meaning instead of Standard English by using the students' own dialects. (emphasis in original)

Teachers should be *aware, accepting,* and *embracing* of different cultures and dialects that are present in all classrooms so a students' learning is meaningful for them. (emphasis in original)

These statements served as grounding for the class discussion and were excellent support for the students' learning: they understood the message that exclusion of dialects often equates to exclusion of individuals and that individual teachers can and do set the tone for language inclusion and exclusion in a classroom setting.

The final phase of the language positionality project asked students to write an essay that summarized their understanding of SRTOL and positioned themselves within the larger debate regarding the place dialect has within an elementary classroom. Four major themes emerged from these essays:

1. Preservice teachers developed an understanding of the importance of studying language diversity.
2. Preservice teachers understood the importance of allowing elementary students the right to their own language.
3. Preservice teachers developed an understanding of the tension between theory and practice.
4. Students' final essays indicated that more explicit attention to teaching methods is needed.

PRESERVICE TEACHERS DEVELOPED AN UNDERSTANDING OF THE IMPORTANCE OF
STUDYING LANGUAGE DIVERSITY

In past teaching experiences, when students read SRTOL without examining their own discourse patterns, they were sometimes resentful of being assigned SRTOL as a reading assignment and were resistant to the ideas therein proposed. In spite of my efforts to explain and share examples where non-standard dialects were used effectively for teaching and learning in elementary classrooms, my students would often express a lack of interest in learning about language diversity. In group discussions they would ask, "Why do we have to waste our time talking about this?" and state, "It isn't our job to teach Ebonics." It was common for students to recommend dropping the assignment when they submitted student course evaluations.

In contrast, adding the examination of their own oral language patterns to the course content had an overwhelmingly positive affect on my students' understanding of the importance of studying language diversity. All the students, regardless of their final position on the issues surrounding allowing students the right to their own language, understood the importance of including this in the course content. The following excerpt is taken from one of the student's essays and is a typical comment that articulates the importance of the issue:

> This article [SRTOL] is very important to us as teachers. We are going to be in situations where we have students in our classrooms that will not speak EAE [edited American English] or in a dialect like mine. My first reaction to a student who speaks "poor English" is to correct them. When the students at my placement in Baltimore City say "They is," I immediately say, "They are." So this article was very informative to me.

Not only did the students understand that EAE is not likely to be spoken by their students, they understood, because of their examination of their recorded conversations, that they do not speak EAE themselves. This is an important step in understanding others, for in the past, my students have held closely to the belief that they speak "correctly" and dialect speakers are the "other". Because of this realization, they find importance in studying issues of language diversity. Furthermore, at the conclusion of the semester when students are given the opportunity to anonymously evaluate the course, none of the students recommended dropping this project from the course. In fact, 15 of the 38 students took the initiative to comment positively on this assignment in their course evaluations.

PRESERVICE TEACHERS UNDERSTOOD THE IMPORTANCE OF ALLOWING ELEMENTARY
STUDENTS THE RIGHT TO THEIR OWN LANGUAGE

Helping my preservice teachers recognize their resistance to allowing students the right to their own language was the singular motivation for me in redesigning this assignment. Not only did an examination of their own interaction patterns positively affect my students' understanding of the importance of studying language diversity, it also helped them become determined to be teachers who will accept language diversity in their own classrooms. Overall, the responses from the students who participated in the revised project were remarkably different from responses of previous students who did not examine their own language before evaluating their beliefs regarding the need to "promote classroom practices to expose students to the variety of dialects that comprise our multiregional, multiethnic, and multicultural society" (SRTOL, 1974).

Thirty-six of the students came to understand the need for accepting language diversity and were able to articulate that learning in their essays. The excerpt that follows illustrates learning that occurred in the students as a result of the language positionality project being combined with reading:

> When I attended school, I remember spending a lot of time on grammar skills and writing skills. I especially remember my teacher stressing the improper use of double negatives. This is imbedded in my brain along with the dire need to correctly spell and pronounce each and every word spoken and written. To this day, I am a stickler for finding errors in writing and for editing other people's work. From this background I have had a really difficult time accepting the use of dialect in the classroom. I was especially irritated by the character's use of dialect in stories presented to students who speak in dialect. I felt like this was just an invitation to allow them to continue speaking what I believed was non-standard English.
>
> After reading the article, "Students' Right to Their Own Language" I realize that there is no one dominant language and that this myth was placed on our society by people of power who were intolerant to any other language but their own. The most important thing that I learned from reading this article is that accepting a person's dialect which is a part of their culture is the same as accepting that person's culture. Therefore, it is most important as a teacher to embrace diversity in dialect among students in the classroom rather than try to reduce its use. With the ever-growing diverse population, it will become inevitably necessary for teachers to have an understanding of the variety of language and be able to represent this variety to students.

The students were able to recognize that their own experiences with language are not necessarily examples of how we can best help our students learn. They came to understand that "Standard English" is by and large a myth, and that when teachers try to eliminate language variation they are also trying to eliminate cultural identity.

Only two of the 38 students involved in this project held fast to their original position that EAE should be *demanded* and forms of dialect should not be accepted for any written assignment, but those students did not come to their conclusions without examining the importance of the issue. As one student wrote:

> We, as teachers, must know how to approach this problem [whether or not a main dialect should be imposed in the educational setting] and how to handle it. We have to learn why students speak the way they do and understand that

it is because of their upbringing. We must learn how to correctly communicate with the students and recognize the impact of society on young people. We should learn what the rest of the world thinks about dialects so that we can better prepare our students. Some teachers believe that everyone should speak in the same "professional" dialect (or at least learn it) while others believe that different dialects are okay, acceptable, and should be allowed in the school setting. We as teachers have to decide where on that spectrum we stand and why we feel that way. I believe that all people have a right to their own culture, which includes the way they speak. I do, however, believe that there should be one dialect for writing.

Although the two students found no room for flexibility in written language, they came to understand that accepting diversity in oral language is appropriate.

PRESERVICE TEACHERS DEVELOPED AN UNDERSTANDING OF THE TENSION BETWEEN THEORY AND PRACTICE

As is often the case with preservice teachers who are studying theory in the university classroom while simultaneously completing placements in elementary schools, my students felt a strong disconnect between what they were learning in class and what they were witnessing in their placements. Although a few (four of the 38) students were working with teachers who accepted variations of American English in oral interaction and even used children's literature written in a variety of dialects, most of the students were placed with teachers who demanded conformity to some version of what the teacher considered to be "Standard English." Many students felt torn between what they were learning and the current climate surrounding language diversity issues. This caused my students to at first doubt the practicality of teaching an inclusive curriculum, and then frustration over the challenges they face in a system that knowingly puts some students at a disadvantage. These tensions are articulated well by one of the students:

> The writers point to the thought that those who are in control are the ones who perpetuate the idea that there is only one correct way to speak English and thus put others who grew up learning a different dialect at a great disadvantage when it comes to advancing in the world. . . . Of course the problem is not that different dialects are incomprehensible. Most people can understand the majority or at least some of what others of different dialects are saying. However, strict grammarians will not allow such talk and style to permeate writing. When it comes to standardized tests it really has an effect because they are so language biased it definitely hinders anyone outside of the used dialect. . . . But what can be done about the standardized test issue? Can you write the test in multiple dialects so that it makes sense to everyone? Once again, this is realistically unfeasible, and not really necessary. Really the importance of standardized tests should be reduced as a tool for placement in higher education but still be used to help see where students are in terms of language and for follow-up in said area.

Since my students in previous classes had rarely been able to critically view the school as a whole or classroom teachers they were placed with, I believe that it was the examination of their own language that enabled this important change both in their attitude toward non-standard dialects and toward established practices.

In retrospect, I can see that in the initial approach that simply required students to read the NCTE documents was interpreted as forcibly pushing a point of view on the preservice teachers that attempted to invalidate many long-held, deeply ingrained beliefs about language. In the revised project, however, the introspective scrutiny of their own language allowed preservice teachers to see how the "common wisdom" they held failed to effectively describe even their own linguistic behavior. This, I believe, cultivated in them the readiness to consider the ideas proposed by the SRTOL documents. Thus, the change in attitudes and beliefs was not imposed on the preservice teachers but rather offered them an opportunity to become aware of their subconscious biases.

STUDENTS' FINAL ESSAYS INDICATED THAT MORE EXPLICIT ATTENTION TO TEACHING
METHODS IS NEEDED

Although the combined assignments were effective in helping preservice teachers theoretically understand the need to accommodate language diversity, and even celebrate it, many students were left uneasy about how to teach in ways that actualize this goal. Although the course included several methods embedded during the project that include translating phrases; using diverse literature that enables explicit study of language variations (for example, Patricia McKissock, Langston Hughes, and Marguerite Henry); analyzing oral and written elementary student samples; instruction on how to teach writing; participation in a writers' workshop; and inclusion of poetry reading and writing, many students expressed the need for more methodological recommendations. For example, one student wrote:

> One thing I wondered about when reading this article is how to teach students, if at all, about the "standard", without implying that is it better. On the one hand, I think I should tell my students that they need to learn how to speak the "standard" way because it will be expected in certain situations. In addition, I would be honest and say that, unfortunately, many teachers, and many employers are biased and expect them to speak "proper" English. On the other hand, I know that it is important to teach children that any dialect they speak should be acceptable, but it would seem unfair to not inform them about prejudices they may face in the future. So, how do I explain this without perpetuating the current system?

As teacher educators struggle to prioritize the vast amount of knowledge preservice teachers need, we must find a way to include not only a theoretical understanding of language variation, but practical methods for teaching. Since completing this formal project, I have added more explicit instruction of linguistically responsive teaching methods, and recommend the readers of this chapter do the same.

This language positionality project enables students to realize that they don't speak what they would consider "correct English" all the time. They have learned to communicate appropriately within a specific communicative situation as a result of social knowledge that is acquired through experience. Because of the variation in the college students' linguistic behaviors, the students come to understand that different linguistic communities have different social roles that govern seemingly similar communicative situations, and non-standard dialect speakers also differentiate their language according to the affordances of the communicative situation within which they are interacting. Communicative competence is not solely a privilege of speakers of the standard, yet American classrooms are governed by social norms of linguistic behavior unfamiliar to many students. Teachers often assume that all students know these rules and we often penalize any transgressions. This project helps teachers confront the realities of language variation and affords them the opportunity to position themselves theoretically before they are placed in a school culture where they may well be socialized to see difference as deficit, thereby lowering expectations for students whose dialect is marginalized by schools.

Discussion Questions and Activities

1. Think about your perceptions of people with non-mainstream varieties of English. Have your perceptions changed over time? Where the changes positive or negative? To what do you contribute the changes?
2. Remember your experiences with teachers who have low expectations of students. What role do you think language played in low expectations?
3. Think about your experiences in teacher education programs. How were teacher expectations treated? To what extent were you exposed to language differences as an attributing factor? How did your training affect your classroom practices?
4. On your own, tape record a conversation of students, then analyze the conversation using the guidelines presented in the article—content, turn taking, grammar, story. Then discuss your discoveries with a colleague.
   [*Author's note*: Special thanks are extended to Geneva Smitherman and Valerie Kinloch for their support in designing the activities.]

References

Benard, B. (1995). Fostering Resiliency in Urban Schools. In B. Williams (Ed.). *Closing the Achievement Gap: A Vision to Guide Change in Beliefs and Practice*. Alexandria, VA: Association for Supervision and Curriculum Development.

Conference on College Composition and Communication (1974). Vol. XXV. Retrieved March 17, 2007, from http://www.ncte.org/library/files/About_NCTE/Overview/NewSRTOL.pdf?source=gs.

Crozier, G. (2005). There's a War against Our Children: Black Educational Underachievement Revisited. *British Journal of Sociology of Education*, 26, 585–598.

Ladson-Billings, G. (1994). *The Dreamkeepers: Successful Teachers of African American Children*. San Francisco: Jossey-Bass.

Major, E. M., & Perreault, G. (2004). Preparing Teachers for Social Consciousness: Issues of Engagement and Resistance. *Teacher Education and Practice*, 17, 255–278.

McAllister, G., & Irvine, J. J. (2002). The Role of Empathy in Teaching Culturally Diverse Students: A Qualitative Study of Teacher's Beliefs. *Journal of Teacher Education*, 53, 433–443.

NCTE. (n.d.). The National Council of Teacher's of English SRTOL documents retrieved March 17, 2007, from http://www.ncte.org/about/over/positions/ category /lang/107502.htm?source=gs.

Preston, D. R. (1996). Where the Worst English is Spoken. In E. Schneider (Ed.). *Focus on the USA*. Amsterdam: John Benjamins.

Radcliffe, R., Caverly, D., Peterson, C., & Emmonds, M. (2004). Improving Textbook Reading in a Middle School Science Classroom. *Reading Improvement*, 41, 145 –156.

Sleeter, C., & Grant, C. A. (1994). *Making Choices for Multicultural Education*. New York: Merrill/ Macmillan Publishing Company.

Schieffelin, B. B., & Ochs, E. (Eds.) (1986). *Language Socialization across Cultures*. Cambridge: Cambridge University Press.

Students' Right to Their Own Language. (1974). Conference on College Composition and Communication. Vol. XXV. Retrieved March 17, 2007, from http://www.ncte.org/library/files/ about_NCTE/Overview/NewSRTOL.pdf?source=gs.

Tatum, B. D. (1992). Talking about Race, Learning about Racism: An Application of Racial Identity Development Theory in the Classroom. *Harvard Educational Review*, 62(1), 1–24.

Valdes, G., Bunch, G., Snow, C., Lee, C., & Matos, L. (2005). Enhancing the Development of Students' Language(s). In L. Darling-Hammond, & J. Bransford (Eds.). *Preparing Teachers for a Changing World: What Teachers Should Learn and be Able to Do*. San Francisco: Jossey-Bass.

9

Beyond the Silence: Instructional Approaches and Students' Attitudes

DAVID E. KIRKLAND AND AUSTIN JACKSON

The image in Figure 9.1 was produced by Lamar, a 10-year-old male who attends a small junior high school, quietly tucked away in the center of a large Midwestern city. The students in Lamar's class were part of a research project that we conducted on code- switching pedagogies, particularly the contrastive analysis (CA) approach to language instruction, an approach modeled after the one used in Oakland at the time of the 1996 Ebonics controversy. Before and after receiving CA instruction, the students were asked to respond to instruction by depicting their views of African American Language (AAL) and Academic English (AE).

Lamar picked up a smooth-tipped black pen, grabbed a blank sheet of white paper, and began to scribble his view of AAL with rude and insightful magic against the blank white slate. When Lamar was done waving his ink-filled wand, he unveiled his portrait of an older woman, "Big Momma," conversing with a younger woman who is depicted pushing a stroller:

> Big Momma: Oh, chile, this baby ugly.
> Young Mother: Big momma my baby ain't ugly.
> Big Momma: Ain't ain't a word.
> Young Mother: If ain't ain't a word why did you use it?
> Big Momma: I'm from the South that all I know.

Lamar's illustration is insightful because it brings attention to a variety of critical linguistic concerns for which both traditional and progressive instructional approaches to language fail to address. The two women are at once engaged in a complex conversation about AAL, ironically speaking AAL in their critique of it. From their brief exchange, at least three rather conflicting assumptions about AAL and the identity politics of language are revealed:

1. AAL is a legitimate medium of expression for certain people only (e.g., I'm from the South).
2. Despite its legitimacy and sociolinguistic value in certain contexts, AAL is not seen as socially or intellectually valuable even in the familiar context of family and must be suppressed or corrected (e.g., "Ain't ain't a word").
3. Finally, in spite of its effective communicative use (the two individuals are holding a mutually intelligible, meaningful conversation), AAL has to be justified when used (e.g., "I'm from the South that all I know").

Figure 9.1 A 10-year-old's View of Ebonics

By illustrating the complexities of AAL use, Lamar's drawing, along with other responses that we later analyze, exposes enduring and, we think, threatening assumptions about AAL and its speakers, assumptions that endorse institutional racism and further the academic failures of Black students. As critical scholars of language, the assumptions that surface in Lamar's drawing invite us to rethink the politics of identity inherent in any given linguistic situation and the various power relations that mediate dangerous and discriminatory language teaching practices.

Given the complexities of African Americans' language use and its relationship to identity and power, this chapter revisits the central language issue in education that Lisa Delpit (1988) raised 20 years ago with regard to educating other people's children. That is, how can language education best serve "our children"? Commenting on the failure of progressive language pedagogies, we argue that even the most progressive and radical language instructional approaches, like the ones suggested by Delpit and others (Delpit & Dowdy, 2002), are problematic when they fail to consider the matrix of language, identity, and power. Even those teachers of language who are committed to critical and democratic approaches to language instruction, such as social and linguistic equality, run the risk of reifying unfair assumptions about marginalized languages and their speakers (Alim, 2005).

Second, we describe the research methods that allowed us to uncover students' perceptions that further illustrate potentially negative effects that instruction can have on students' attitudes toward AAL and its speakers. In the final section, we demonstrate the value of moving towards a critical instructional framework for addressing the subtleties of language, identity and power. This last section includes recommendations for rethinking language instruction from a critical perspective.

Failures of Progressive Language Pedagogies

The history of language instruction and the African American child has been one of contestation and negotiation (Baugh, 1999; Smith, 1998). Even after the groundbreaking 1972/1974 Students' Right to Their Own Language resolution and the 1974 Lau v. Nichols decision, the tendencies of language classrooms have been to embrace wholesale a generic brand of American English (AE). Under dominant instructional and ideological framework of AE, mainstream White students flourish in their literacy education: learning what amounted to their language, about their language, and through their language about themselves and their world in a context that was by design made meaningful to them (Halliday, 1975). Where did this put the Black child who never learned about her language and whose words and ideas were an immediate reflection of a distant, disdainful world, enchanted by its own disregarded linguistic regularities and governed by its own ignored sociolinguistic rules (Rickford & Rickford, 2000; Smitherman, 1977, 1999; Smitherman & Villanueva, 2003).

To address this question, many Black scholars have advocated approaches to language instruction that does more than reinforce the dominance of AE and the linguistic inferiority of AAL. Over 70 years ago, Carter G. Woodson (1933/1990) observed that:

> In the study of language in school pupils were made to scoff at the Negro dialect as some peculiar possession of the Negro which they should despise rather than directed to study the background of this language ... in short to understand their own linguistic history, which is certainly more important for them than the study of French Phonetics or Historical Spanish Grammar. (p. 19)

For Woodson, language instruction, especially for Black children, needed to attend to and educate against negative assumptions about AAL that are proliferated in American society. Without knowledge concerning the historical validity of AAL, students, according to Woodson, would "despise" AAL. The learned hatred of AAL has been, perhaps, most harmful to Black children (Rickford & Rickford, 2000). Jones (2004) explains, "One of the main reasons African-American youngsters do poorly in school is because of language differences between black and white children." (p. 1).

Given the complex yet enduring relationship between language and identity, Black students, through language instruction, though certainly not language instruction alone, come to despise, not only their language, but also themselves. In recognizing the dangers of making AAL subsidiary to AE, Woodson points to a key tension in the current emphasis on teaching Black children to "code-switch": to teach Black children to code-switch without affirming their cultural and linguistic heritages, without teaching White children to code-switch too, and without explicitly dealing with the politics inherent in both language and identity, the code-switching that is the intended outcome of the CA approach can be as dangerous as traditional, explicitly hegemonic approaches to teaching language.

In the mid-1960s, Beryl Bailey sought practical and pedagogically innovative applications for AAL in classroom instruction. Working with Black pre-freshman at Tougaloo College in Mississippi, Bailey (1968) analyzed the speech and writing of 100 students. The students consistently and systematically used language patterns directly traceable to AAL, which according to Smitherman (1999), "had been unaffected by the piecemeal corrections and irrelevant drills of language arts classrooms" (p. 160). Similar to Woodson's argument that the history of AAL should be taught to Black children explicitly in language classrooms, Bailey maintained that *teachers* needed to recognize that Black students' language patterns are not linguistics errors but part of a language system that is structured, rule governed, and "only partially similar to that of standard English" (p. 24). Bailey notes:

> These observations may appear to some as no more than a rehashing or recataloging of well known facts of language usage, not only in the writing of Negro students in Mississippi, but throughout the country. It is my contention that like effects do not necessarily spring from like causes . . . . Recognition of this fact should and must lead to a revision of our classroom techniques. (pp. 23–24)

Although they wrote from different places in terms of time, space, and relative audience, Bailey and Woodson essentially came to a similar conclusion. Bailey maintained that teachers needed to be educated about AAL in order to make sound pedagogical decisions. Woodson maintained that teachers needed to place an emphasis on a kind of language instruction that would demystify negative assumptions about AAL. What is important here is that neither Bailey nor Woodson viewed AAL as an intermediary to AE, but as a social and historical entity of profound value in its own right.

More than two decades ago, the judge in the 1979 "Black English Case" acknowledged the sentiment carried out in Bailey's and Woodson's work. In the case, a group of African American parents successfully sued the Ann Arbor School District for placing their children in special education classes solely on the basis of linguistic difference. The presiding judge over the case, Judge Charles W. Joiner, determined that teachers' prejudices against African American students were due more to linguistic "differences" (i.e. the presence or absence of AAL linguistic features) than to developmental ones.

Judge Joiner ruled that the Ann Arbor School District unjustly used language as the sole barometer for placing African American students, who possessed equal or above academic aptitude as their White counterparts, in classes reserved for students with developmental concerns. As Joiner put it:

> [I]t is a straightforward effort to require the court to intervene on the children's behalf to require the defendant School District Board to take appropriate action to teach them to read in the standard English of the school, the commercial world, the arts, science and professions. . . . It is an action to keep another generation from becoming functionally illiterate. (in Smitherman, 1999, p. 132)

In addition to finding the Ann Arbor School District and its teachers guilty of violating the students' civil rights, as outlined in the language provision of the 1974 Equal Educational Opportunity Act, Judge Joiner, reminiscent of what Woodson (1933/1990) and Bailey (1968) had advocated, recommended that *teachers* undergo training to learn the dynamics of AAL grammar and discourse style. Judge Joiner's objective for his recommendation was to help prevent what he called linguistic discrimination by making teachers aware of AAL's legitimacy and, therefore, combat teachers' negative perceptions of AAL. Formal training in AAL grammar (syntax, semantics, phonology, and pragmatics) would help teachers develop respect for AAL as another and equally viable systematic and robust means of interpersonal communication. However, the ultimate objective of AAL training for teachers, from Joiner's perspective, was to help Black students become proficient in AE.

One can logically assume that Joiner was not interested in having teachers teach the history of AAL, show its social and historical importance in their classrooms, or demonstrate its effective rhetorical use. Nonetheless, Joiner's ruling was profoundly radical at the time. However, by merely requiring training for teachers in AAL and by not mandating that teachers teach students the history of AAL, its legitimacy, and possible application in their classrooms and in their students' lives, Joiner's ruling laid the groundwork for very questionable language pedagogies, as depicted in Figure 9.2. In this figure, African American students (**S**) code-switch vertically, either going up to AE or spiraling down to AAL, an approach that represents asymmetrical relations of power with regards to code-switching.

A more recent example comes from the "Ebonics controversy" in Oakland, CA. Similar to the King ruling, the 1996 Oakland resolution, too, seemed radical at the time. But as John Rickford (1999) sorely reminds us, the Oakland resolution was anything but radical. According to Rickford, Oakland proposed to use contrastive analysis techniques associated with California's "proficiency in Standard English for speakers of Black language" or "Standard English proficiency" [SEP] program. These techniques clearly explained the technical (not social or historical) differences between vernacular and Standard English, and directed students towards proficiency in Standard English through discrimination, identification and translation drills and other exercises.

Well before Oakland set out to employ contrastive analysis instructional programs, architects of language reform, while celebrating its benefits, were quiet about CA's inability to change in any positive way negative views that students held

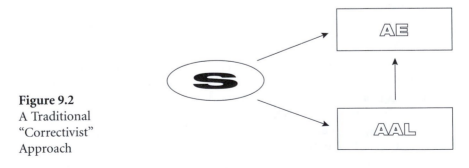

Figure 9.2
A Traditional "Correctivist" Approach

toward AAL (Vaughn-Cooke, 1999). Prior to the 1996 Oakland resolution, the CA approach had been widely discussed in the research literature. After the 1996 Oakland resolution, the CA approach was resurrected. A number of researchers (Anderson-Janniere, 2001; Smith, 2001) revisited the possibility of using CA to bridge the achievement gap between African American students, other "linguistically diverse" students, and their White counterparts. Researchers and practitioners saw CA as an instructional approach that teachers could use to help African American students learn and perhaps master AE in order to enhance their school destinies and ultimately their economies (Palacas, 2004).

Research literature on the effects of CA, perhaps tainted by the politics of the Oakland controversy, described mixed results for CA approaches. However, the most declarative reports that surfaced pre-Oakland suggested that some African American students actually increased AE reading and writing proficiency due to CA. Hanni Taylor's (1989, 1991) studies illustrate how CA significantly reduced the frequency of AAL features appearing in students' writing composition. Kelli Harris-Wright's (1999) bidialectal contrastive curriculum in DeKalb County, Georgia, was shown to increase reading scores.

While there is evidence suggesting that CA can be an effective instructional approach, we maintain that without addressing the social, cultural, and political complexities of language, identity, and power, CA approaches are yet limited, as negative attitudes about AAL and its speakers may persist. Thus, CA instructional approaches leave unchecked the pervasive assumptions that require some students to alter their language and identities in the first place. By using AAL simply as a "scaffold" (up) to AE, CA approaches reinforce the asymmetrical positioning between the two languages—relegating AAL, as well as the people who speak it, to an inferior social status. Figure 9.3 depicts the assymmetrical positioning between the two languages. In the figure, "S" represents student, "OW" represents official word, and "UW" represents unofficial word. The model, while encouraging codeswitching, teaching from the point of the native language, keeps in place the vertical relationship criticized in correctivist approaches to language instruction. As such, the two approaches to language instruction are essentially the same despite having different names.

Smitherman's critique of bidialectalism is consistent with our critique of codeswitching pedagogies like CA. Smitherman's critique highlights the need for a more critical evaluation of language and language instruction. As Smitherman (1999)

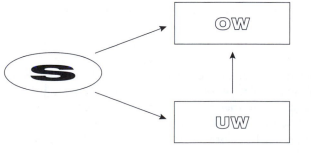

Figure 9.3
An Actual Contrastive Analysis Model

observes, the underlying assumption was that even if all dialects are equal, some are more equal than others. Blacks, then, would have to learn White English although Whites would not have to learn Black English. Thus, the term "bidialecticism" was a misnomer, which obfuscated the racism and acts of discrimination, which created the social and environmental conditions of Blacks, scholars, in effect, blamed the victims for their failure to conform to White linguistic (and/or cognitive) standards. Through this kind of academic discourse in the Black Power era, racism was reproduced in another form. As White linguist James Sledd (1969) argued, bidialecticism was, at bottom, the "linguistics of white supremacy" (p. 80).

By not focusing on and even avoiding the relationships between language and identity, language and society, and language and power, CA instructional approaches leave unbridled widely held racist assumptions that undermine language and literacy learning. As presented, research on CA programs—beyond mere "inclusion" in classrooms—offer little towards altering the conception of AAL as deficient speech possibly of deficient people. In spite of the seeming success of these programs, people, Black people included, have held firmly to the idea that AAL is to be despised (Baugh, 1999; Delpit, 2002; Wolfram, 2004). Such negative conclusions, complemented by uncritical, potentially precarious pedagogies, simply cover up and confuse sociolinguistic realities that call for teachers to address the politics of language, identity, and power. Given the increasing failure of Black students in both school and society, we believe that a critical approach to language instruction is no longer an option but an imperative.

Studying Language, Identity, and Power

This chapter reports on a study, where we examined the various critical-linguistic complexities that, for us, shed new light on CA instruction. We briefly describe our research methods now.

Notes on Research Methods

Our study was conducted as part of a mixed methods research project at Malcolm X Academy in Detroit, MI. The larger project, which spanned approximately 3 years, explored critical literacy and examined the educational effects of CA instruction on 16 students, enrolled in Malcolm X's "My Brother's Keeper" (MBK) male mentoring program. Our research question asked, do code-switching pedagogies, instructional approaches like CA, improve students' attitudes toward AAL?

In order to assess students' attitudes, we designed an experiment that used illustrations (pre and post) and developed a CA curriculum based on the one used in Oakland (see Rickford, 1999). Conceptually, the CA approach adopted by Oakland "valued" the primary languages of students and used students' primary languages to strengthen students' proficiency in AE. The architects of the curriculum used in Oakland hoped to create a situation of linguistic respect and tolerance around various ways of speaking by embracing students' primary languages.

To test these beliefs, we asked students to create drawings to illustrate their attitudes toward Ebonics before and after they received instruction through the CA language program that we created for them. Students were instructed in the CA program for approximately 9 months. Each lesson in the CA program that we created employed AAL as a scaffold to AE. In this way, the CA curriculum could be seen as an intervention that would increase students' proficiency in AE. Also important to us was whether or not it would affect students' attitudes toward language, particularly AAL. Daily lessons followed the translation approach modeled after the CA language lessons used in Oakland (Rickford, 1999). It should be noted that the students in the MBK program were early adolescent and adolescent (10–14 years of age) African American males, who all used AAL as a primary language.

As researchers, our interactions with the young men relied mostly on our interests in understanding the young men's language and literacy development. Initially, our purpose was to explore how the program influenced the young men's critical and academic literacy development. During the course of the program, we observed the young men engaging in practices that countered our expectations and made us question their attitudes about AAL and its speakers. Based on our observations, we felt that our initial research focus was incomplete because the young men's attitudes influenced how they learned language and literacy. The influence of their attitudes, in turn, surprisingly served to shape how language and literacy was practiced among everyone in the program.

Because critical and academic literacy development was clearly our focus toward the beginning of this study, at times it was difficult to take rigorous, objective, and descriptive notes on student attitudes. We gradually resolved this dilemma once we recognized that it would be necessary to enter the field without pre-fixed expectations. Thus, we began to regularly revise and challenge our notions of what was happening in the classroom with regards to the young men's attitudes about AAL and identity. We also began to rely heavily on the students to make sense of how their illustrations represented their attitudes toward AAL, their ideas about AAL and its speakers, and their understandings of AAL's relationship to AE.

In order to make sense of students' attitudes toward AAL, we also documented the young men's responses, rigorously compiling four types of information that were based on observations of and interactions with the young men. These included: video- recordings, fieldnotes, interview transcripts, and field artifacts (i.e., illustrations, students' work, program plans, textbooks, etc.). By assembling a wide range of data sources, we were able to more clearly understand the meanings that the students were making of language and identity and the politics inherent in both. That is, multiple types of information revealed multiple aspects of the relationship between language instruction and the young men's attitudes toward language. From here, we interpreted what this information meant to us with respect to language, identity, and development.

We interpreted information using themes loosely outlined by Fairclough (1995). Our interpretation examined the following aspects of language:

- relationships between language and identity
- relationships between shared understandings, beliefs, and values and the cultural production of associated language practices
- the relationship between students' bodies and their symbolic representations of gender, race, and sexuality (as represented by language and vice versa)
- issues of power and positionality, which, according to Fairclough, influences all these linguistic relationships.

We coded data into three major categories:

1. language and identity
2. language and society
3. language and power.

Although we use these categories for analytical purposes, we hold that each category is constitutive of the other. That is, the relationship between language and identity does not exist apart from the relationship between language and society and language and power. They all intersect complexly. Also, for analytical reasons, we defined language as an "utterance" (Bakhtin, 1981) or form of expression that allows individuals to communicate with other individuals and in the process make sense of experience and nature in her or his larger social universe. Since the predominant view of AAL is generally negative (Kirkland, Jackson, & Smitherman, 2001), we felt defining how we viewed language would be helpful in disrupting AE privilege found in standard definitions of English.

Observations

The students who we observed retained and sometimes reinforced negative attitudes about AAL. In spite of CA language instruction, they were never truly able to resolve the critical-linguistic relationships of language and identity, language and society, and language and power during the course of the CA program. The students were, however, implicitly struggling with relationships between AAL and AE and the various and very different ways the languages constituted their identities. Although it was never explicitly dealt with in class, we noticed that students were struggling with how the languages positioned them in the world and how their use of either language positioned others with respect to social context. Interestingly, they were not learning, implicitly or explicitly, about the politics of positioning— that is, language and power—in the classroom. Nonetheless, they were dealing with these tensions almost daily as they struggled to find value in AAL.

As illustrated in Lamar's picture in Figure 9.1, students were learning through language about themselves and about language and its complex relationship to power. For example, in learning about language (i.e., how to code-switch), the students were also learning how linguistic forms and structures get affixed to meanings and contexts, about who can use particular linguistic forms and structures, and about the social implications of their use. The CA approach to language instruction did little to account for these complexities. Although students

Figure 9.4 Kel's Illustration of Code-switching

were engaging AE in pedagogical allegiance to AAL, they were learning AE, nonetheless, which was privileged over AAL even in a CA instructional approach. The students were learning AE and about AE, as opposed to AAL, even though AAL was used to support the students' AE learning. For example, Kel, one of the older students in the program at age 12, illustrates a portrait in Figure 9.4 that reveals an asymmetrical relationship between AE and AAL.

Figure 9.4 depicts a speaker of AE alongside a speaker of AAL. The AE speaker is dressed in a suit and a tie, and his demeanor is poised and calm. An aura of success pervades the character and an air of accomplishment is artistically woven into the image. Kel depicts his AAL speaking character not so elegantly. The AAL speaker demonstrates a street aura and criminal characteristics. The character spouts profanity, as if such words were integral to the AAL lexicon.

Two things are apparent from Kel's illustration. First, it seems as though Kel has gained, not unproblematically, a terse understanding of issues of language appropriateness and the value of specific language forms used in specific social contexts (Fairclough, 2002). Based on Kel's illustration, AE is needed to live in the greater social establishment (the official world), and AAL reduces an individual to the streets, somewhere perched along the margins of the greater social establishment (the unofficial world). His illustration is careful at creating the appropriate situation for the appropriate language type. Hence, he has not superimposed AE on his unofficial world. By the same token, he has not superimposed AAL into his official world.

Second, Kel's illustration highlight social issues that relate to language and identity. He adorns his AE speaking character with the special privileges related to carrying out official business (e.g. handling a briefcase). This suggests that Kel has made a connection between who is able to work and who is not based solely on linguistic practices. This does not mean that the character who spoke AAL did not work. Rather, based on the illustration, such speakers do not work in official spaces. Further, it is telling that the character who spoke AAL was illustrated "working" in the unofficial world, tagged as dope dealers or some other criminal type.

Kel's illustration demonstrates that just as language defines identities (e.g., a business person as opposed to a criminal), language also defines social existences. Hence attitudes about language speak back to selves and societies and are yet condemned to the political constraints from which they have been forged. And yet, the very words that emanate from our minds are in competition with other such words and ways of delivering them. Assumptions about languages are never neutral, but carry political imbrications, hotly contested due to the ideological and social impulses of people and their interests. Hence, a language is seen as valuable when the dominant group defines it as valuable. Logically, a language looses value when wielded by people who lack the power to assign value.

Many CA approaches blindly assume equality between languages and symmetry between the official world (OW) and unofficial world (UW) (see Figure 9.5). In the CA model we used, our students ever felt their inequality, feeling forced to straddle between unlike social worlds depending on a given rhetorical situation. According to Kel: "If I want to get a good job and be something in life, I gotta learn to talk White [which, based on his illustration is code for AE]." For us, Kel's statement suggested that the social, historical, and political forces that shape language are important aspects in language learning. However, in most CA approaches like the one used in Oakland, these forces are either ignored or dismissed. Yet the contexts of language use are never politically innocent and, therefore, can never be seen as entirely neutral sites.

By not considering the social, historical, and political aspects of language and linguistic contexts, CA approaches may inadvertently reinforce existing asymmetrical relationships among the official and unofficial worlds and the languages needed to access them. However, being critical of CA instructional approaches, we view students' words and worlds not as separate entities but as entities mutually constitutive of one another. The words and worlds of students are dynamic constructs, engaged through constant and unconscious (Richardson, 2003) shifting of languages and subjectivities. Such shifting, beyond mere code-switching, unconsciously takes into account the social, historical, and political milieu that shapes language, the individual, and the society, as depicted in Figure 9.6. Learning as a process happens in the midst of the mutual and complicated interplay between contexts. Hence, one learns language for school not just in school and practices language for home not just at home.

To reconceptualize language with respect to students' attitudes, a critical approach to language instruction needs to account for the various critical-linguistic

Figure 9.5
Theoretical Model
for Contrastive
Analysis

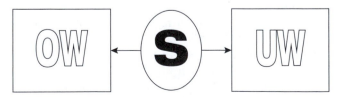

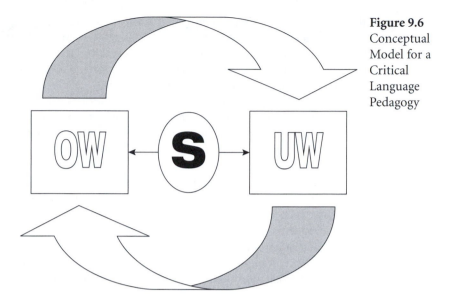

Figure 9.6 Conceptual Model for a Critical Language Pedagogy

relationships that exist among language, identity, society, and power. Such relationships constantly influence, shape, and reconfigure students' perceptions of language, themselves, their social universe, and their own possibilities for action.

Language and Identity

A significant amount has been written on the relationship between language and identity (Fairclough, 2002; Gilyard, 1991; Rickford & Rickford, 2000). This work argues that language is necessarily tied to one's identity development and, at least linguistically, constitutes one's identity itself. For Rickford and Rickford, language is "a symbol of identity" (p. 222), and "For many African Americans, the identity function of Spoken Soul [i.e. AAL] is paramount" (p. 223). It is plausible, then, that uncritical language pedagogies work to impair or "eradicate " the identity development of students from non-White backgrounds. Gilyard (1991) suggests that "to successfully challenge current practices that justify eradicationist attempts aimed against African-American identity and the language variety in which that identity is most clearly realized is a worthwhile place to begin" (p. 165). Hence, we begin to dissect the relationship between language and identity here.

Advocates of CA recognize the connection between language, the individual, and collective identity. Dismissing or vilifying a student's language then is tantamount to dismissing and vilifying the student her- or himself—as well as the discourse community to which the student belongs. Given this, the CA approach fails to offer a way to add to students' linguistic repertoire without creating a situation that reduces or even denigrates non-elite students and their home language (Cazden, 1999).

There is an implicit assumption that including AAL in language instruction leads to positive linguistic results (Rickford, 1999), but our study and other studies suggest that inclusion alone is not enough to challenge racist attitudes (Baugh, 1999, 2000). In fact, introduced uncritically, evidence from this study suggests that CA can actually increase students' negative perceptions about their language. Figure 9.7 illustrates a theme which characterizes our students' attitudes toward themselves and their language even after CA intervention.

The literature on the success of CA typically does not account for the attitudes students hold toward their language, nor does it offer a way to help students foster positive views of language. Our study found that even after CA instruction with overt attention given to AAL grammar and discourse style, sometimes using elements of African American popular culture such as rap and hip hop, students still associated AAL with the base, superficial, and stereotypical elements of African American culture. For example, many student illustrations demonstrated associations between AAL speakers and violence, drugs, or other criminal activities. Additionally, quite a few students' interpolated views of themselves (or who they saw as themselves) into their drawings. For instance, Ian—a student who came to class often dressed in Polo, Nike, or other name brand items, wore earrings in both ears and had a brimming Afro hairstyle—drew the character in Figure 9.7, which bore a striking resemblance to him.

Figure 9.7 Stereotypical Image of Students' Attitude Towards AAL?

We found it alarming that the students' illustrations of AAL speakers were often of gangbangers and members of notorious national crime syndicates like Crips and Bloods. However, we found it more alarming that the images shared striking resemblances to the students themselves—their clothing and their language styles. At the same time, seeing the students and the images makes one wonder how these are affected by the celebration of guns, profanity, and malt liquor bottles manifested in the hands of children. Why does Ian, an honor roll student who professes to love hip hop, sketches an autolinguistic portrait that reflects negative reaction to African American culture? To resolve this question for ourselves, we conclude that any pedagogy professing to use African American students' language must address the forces that allowed Ian to draw a disparaging portrait of himself.

Language and Society

As much as it reflects the identities of individuals, language too is a primary artifact, reflecting certain qualities and characteristics of a society (Cole, 1998; Vygotsky, 2006). As Asa Hilliard (2003) so powerfully reminds us: "Language is rooted in and is an aspect of culture" (p. 89). Hence, the perceptions that one makes of languages are indeed socially manufactured. We are not born despising our language, but through our day-to-day interactions and continual participation within the American social activity system (school, work, media, etc.), we learn to despise AAL. Smitherman and van Dijk (1988) help us to understand the relationship between language and society. According to these authors: "Ethnic attitudes in general, and prejudice in particular, are not individual aberrations, or pathological exceptions, but structurally rooted, shared cognitions" (p. 22).

At the societal level, language attitudes, if not language itself, works to manufacture what Smitherman and van Dijk (1988) call *symbolic racism*. For them:

> [S]ymbolic racism allows for subtlety, indirectness, and implication. It may, paradoxically, be expressed by the unsaid, or be conveyed by apparent 'tolerance' and egalitarian liberalism. Whereas the racial slur, the graffiti, or the old movie may be blatantly racist, many other present-day types of talk may communicate racism in a more veiled way. Speakers of such discourse may go to great lengths to dissimulate the deeper, underlying beliefs, social models, opinions, goals, values, interests, that is, ideologies, concerning ethnic minority groups in society. (p. 18)

It is within this heated atmosphere that so many of us, too many of our students, are learning, perhaps have already learned, to despise AAL and its speakers. Further: "The media in our information societies play the crucial role in presenting such dominant ideologies, if only by the failure to present alternative interpretations or counter-ideologies" (Smitherman & van Dijk, 1988, p. 22). As mentioned earlier, CA approaches are not immune to the gravity of these social forces, as they do little to challenge "symbolic racism." Hence, they fail to either "present alternative interpretations or counter-ideologies" or address the influences, such as media, family, friends, and educational institutions that manufacture linguistic racism today.

For example, Isaac, another student in the program, pinpoints some of the historic and institutional influences that gave birth to AAL:

> *Isaac*: [Raises hand] In slavery . . . I think they weren't well educated, and nowadays people just look at it like something we say. But [in actuality] because, uh, African Americans in slavery weren't educated so that's all they knew.
>
> *Teacher*: So are you saying that Ebonics is the language of people who are not educated?
>
> *Isaac*: Our ancestors were in slavery; they weren't educated, so they had . . . this is all they know. But later on in life, *people on the street*, they just . . . they just say it. *People on the street don't think anything wrong with it.*
>
> *Teacher*: Is anything wrong with it [AAL]?
>
> *Isaac*: . . . *yeah* . . .

Isaac's comments illustrate a double consciousness of sorts. He acknowledges AAL as the default language of enslaved Africans who "weren't well educated," that made the language a legitimate form of communication. At the same time, he recognizes something inherently wrong not only with AAL, but with its speakers who live "on the street." The statement Isaac seems to be making is that, while AAL was necessary during slavery, Black people today have no excuse for failing to master AE. In fact, it could be said that Isaac sees a cause-and-effect relationship between a decision to use AAL ("people on the street don't think anything wrong with it") and their socioeconomic condition as being "people on the street." When pressed to explain what was "wrong" with AAL, Isaac, also one of the more vocal students in the classroom, gave a vague "yeah" and trailed off.

Isaac's example more clearly highlights the relationship between language and society. While language in some ways is an emblem of the self, it is in other and perhaps more complex ways, a statement of the other (recall Kel's illustration). For Isaac, African Americans used AAL to negotiate slavery. However, since the other (slavery as opposed to African Americans) no longer exists, he argues that AAL is necessary only if one desires to participate in a sort of "uneducated" street/slave culture.

The attention that Isaac pays to the social role of languages is glaring. Although CA approaches, on the surface, do a fairly good job at addressing a social problem, they do not address the social origin of the problem. Further, the social histories of language and the conclusions about these histories are generally made for students when they arrive to classrooms. In order to enhance their learning of language, students need opportunities to revise these conclusions by learning how languages evolve in history and behave in society.

Language and Power

Perhaps the most important critical-linguistic issue to be discussed here involves language and its relationship to power. As Norman Fairclough (1995) reminds us: "It is an age in which the production and reproduction of the social order depend increasingly upon practices and processes of a broadly cultural nature. Part of this development is an enhanced role for language in the exercise of power" (p. 219). Further, negative attitudes towards AAL and its speakers are perpetuated through linguistic methods of manufacturing consent, rather than by "force." Negative attitudes, working in the interests of the dominant group, are sustained through self-regulating practices rather than imposition, passed on through the implicit renderings of language rather than overt expression. For Fairclough, "the issue of language and power in education is just a part of the more general social problematic of language and power" (p. 219). Hence, the instructional methods that schools embrace, especially those that emphasize the importance of AE over all other linguistic forms, function to empower the linguistic elite over the linguistically oppressed.

A revised conception of CA should include overt discussions of power, hegemony, and ideological control through discussions of language (Fairclough, 1995, 2002; Gilyard, 2001). It is only then that students (and teachers) will be able to realize that the true obstacle to language learning lies not in students' "home" language, but in discrimination and a largely uninformed, intolerant national sentiment that sees AE as the only acceptable means of "intelligent" communication. From a critical perspective, language pedagogy should provide students with understandings of the power relations inherent in language and identity so that students can develop the critical ability needed to make sound linguistic choices related to their own empowerment and not simply the maintenance of someone else's power.

If students are given a choice to value AAL, they are also given a choice to value themselves and other languages. By choosing to value AAL, students would be simultaneously choosing the "discourses [that] have been the major means by which people of African descent in the American colonies and subsequent republic have asserted their collective humanity in the face of an enduring white supremacy and tried to persuade, cajole, and gain acceptance for ideas relative to black survival and black liberation" (Gilyard, 2001, p. 1). When inserted into the public sphere through slave narratives, pulpit oratory, civil rights polemics or Black nationalist propaganda, AAL has served as the primary tool for achieving Black sociopolitical empowerment in times when racism made access to mainstream institutions of political power unavailable. In short, AAL has served as a language for positive action for Black people and natural evolution of American and African languages. It is both empowering and powerful.

Conclusion

As we seek more effective approaches to language instruction, educators must see and help their students see AAL as an asset as opposed to a liability—a language not only on par with AE but a language to be learned for its unique value. By cultivating a lack of understanding of AAL, which ultimately impedes the language development of Black children, teachers of language make endemic "linguistic parochialism and prejudice" (Gilyard, 1999, p. 17). This tendency toward discrimination adversely affects the linguistically oppressed and their languages. To more effectively approach language instruction, teachers must not only explicitly teach AE. Teachers must also be explicit about the political nature of language to offset assumptions about neutrality in language use. So when using language, it is important that students know that they are engaging in a political act, especially in their choice to code-switch, to accommodate one language over another.

Workers in language and literacy studies have sought to facilitate such choices through CA approaches. Such approaches, in theory, use students' home language as a scaffold to build "Standard" or Academic English proficiency, making students self-conscious of both discourses, helping them match the "appropriate" discourse to the "appropriate" rhetorical situation. With both AAL and AE in their linguistic repertoire, Black students, it is assumed, will have the rhetorical dexterity to apply AE in situations that warrant the discourse. Conversely, AAL is deemed "appropriate" only for the playground, the home, or the street.

Few scholars of AAL and literacy have questioned this pedagogical model, but, among those that have, Gilyard (2001) argues that programs like CA "that emphasize the eradication of AAVE or . . . that merely focus on getting students to translate from AAVE to Standard English" will not work. Gilyard explains: "Merely turning classrooms into translation seminars avoids the education in critical perspective, especially about issues such as language. . . . Merely pushing a doctrine of 'translation for success in the mainstream' ignores some of the realities of American racism" (pp. 209–210). By advocating a critical language pedagogy that affirms AAL, we seek to improve students' attitudes about AAL and themselves by preserving students' culture and heritage, by making language classrooms safe places in which all students can master new words and traverse new worlds.

Language instruction, then, "must not go beyond providing a resource for people to use in making their own decisions—it must scrupulously avoid setting out blueprints for emancipatory practice" (Fairclough, 1995, p. 218). Indeed, language educators are already well aware that "the success (or failure) of particular teaching methods has more to do with the cultural and political factors involved than with any particular pedagogical formula" (Moore, 1996, p. 34). With all this in mind, we resist the impulse to outline a "critical language lesson plan." This notwithstanding, there are a few points with which we wish to leave you:

1. Language instruction must address critical-linguistic issues related to the proliferation of racism and Black student failure.
2. Language instruction must consider the significance of all sociolinguistic forms and give students rich opportunities to investigate, accommodate and critique such forms.
3. Language instruction must address negative assumption about languages and their speakers.

4. Finally, all students regardless of race or ethnicity must receive language instruction that offsets the assumptions that perpetuate linguistic discrimination.

Discussion Questions and Activities

1. How will your students depict different varieties of English? Give or have students select language samples from two different varieties of English. Ask them to construct cartoons featuring two persons expressing their feelings about the language varieties.
2. Assign students to read a book that has dialogue writen in a dialect other than Standard English. Based on the language presented in the text, ask students to describe the speaker based on their speech. Discuss the images of the person that the author might have wanted to create through language.
3. Read a scholarly discussion of language differences. Elicit students' responses to the author's discussion, either in writing or in a class discussion.

References

Alim, H. S. (2005). Critical Language Awareness in the United States: Revisiting Issues and Revising Pedagogies in a Resegregated Society. *Educational Researcher*, 34(7), 24–31.

Anderson-Janniere, I. (2001). Teaching Students of Diverse Language Backgrounds. In C. Crawford (Ed.). *Ebonics and Language Education of African Ancestry Students*. New York: Sankofa World Publishers.

Bailey, B. L. (1968). Some Aspects of the Impact of Linguistics on Language Teaching in Disadvantaged Communities. In A. L. Davis (Ed.). *On the Dialects of Children*. Champaign/Urbana, IL: National Council of Teachers of English.

Bakhtin, M. M. (1981). *The Dialogic Imagination: Four Essays by M. M. Bakhtin*. In M. Holquist (Ed.). Austin, TX: University of Texas Press.

Baugh, J. (1999). *Out of the Mouths of Slaves: African American Language and Educational Malpractice*. Austin, TX: University of Texas Press.

——. (2000). *Beyond Ebonics: Linguistic Pride and Racial Prejudice*. New York: Oxford University Press.

Cazden, C. (1999). The Language of African American Students in Classroom Discourse. In D. C. Temple Adger, & O. Taylor (Eds.). *Making the Connection: Language and Academic Achievement among African American Students*. Urbana, IL: National Council of Teachers of English.

Cole, M. (1998). *Cultural Psychology: A Once and Future Discipline*. Cambridge, MA: Belknap Press.

Delpit, L. (1988). The Silenced Dialogue: Power and Pedagogy in Educating Other People's Children. *Harvard Educational Review*, 58(3), 280–298.

——. (2002). No Kinda Sense. In L. Delpit, & J. K. Dowdy (Eds.). *The Skin that We Speak: Thoughts on Language and Culture in the Classroom*. New York: The New Press.

——, & Dowdy, J. K. (Eds.) (2002). *The Skin that We Speak: Thoughts on Language and Culture in the Classroom*. New York: The New Press.

Fairclough, N. (1995). *Critical Discourse Analysis: The Critical Study of Language*. London: Longman.

——. (2002). *Language and Power*. Addison-Wesley-Longman.

Gilyard, K. (1991). *Voices of the Self: A Study of Language Competence*. Detroit, MI: Wayne State University Press.

——. (1999). African American Contribution to Composition Studies. *College Composition and Communication*, 50(4), 626–644.

——. (2001). It Ain't Hard to Tell: Distinguishing Fact from Fallacy in the Ebonics Controversy. In C. Crawford (Ed.). *Ebonics and Language Education of African Ancestry Students*. New York: Sankofa World Publishers.

Halliday, M. A. K. (1975). Anti-Languages. *UEA Papers in Linguistics*, 15–45.

Harris-Wright, K. (1999). Enhancing Bidialecticalism in Urban African American Students. In D. C. Carolyn Temple Adger, & O. Taylor (Eds.). *Making the Connection: Language and Academic Achievement among African American Students*. Urbana. IL: National Council of Teachers of English.

Hilliard, III, A. G. (2003). No Mystery: Closing the Achievement Gap. In T. Perry, C. Steele, & A. G. Hilliard III (Eds.). *Young, Gifted, and Black: Promoting High Achievement among African-American Students*. Boston, MA: Beacon Press.

Jones, S. (2004). Living Poverty and Literacy Learning: Sanctioning Topics of Students' Lives. *Language Arts*, 81(6), 461–469.

Kirkland, D., Jackson, A., & Smitherman, G. (2001). Leroy, Big D, and Big Daddy Speakin Ebonics on the Internet. *American Language Review*, 22–26.

Moore, R. (1996). Between a Rock and a Hard Place: African Americans and Standard English [electronic version]. (ERIC Document Reproduction Service No. ED 402 593).

Palacas, A. L. (2004). Write about Ebonics: A Composition Course at the University of Akron. *Journal of Teaching Writing*, 21(1), 97–122.

Richardson, E. (2003). African American Female Literacies. In *African American literacies*. New York: Routledge.

Rickford, J. R. (1999). Language Diversity and Academic Achievement in the Educaiton of African American Students: An Overview of the Issues. In D. C. Carolyn Temple Adger, & O. Taylor (Eds.). *Making the Connection: Language and Academic Achievement among African American Students*. Urbana, IL: National Council of Teacher of English.

——, & Rickford, R. J. (2000). *Spoken Soul: The Story of Black English*. New York: John Wiley & Sons, Inc.

Sledd, J. (1969). Bidialectalism: The Linguistics of White Supremacy. *English Journal*, 58(9), 1307–1315.

Smith, E. (2001). Ebonics and Bilingual Education of the African American Child. In C. Crawford (Ed.). *Ebonics and Language Education of African Ancestory Students*. New York: Sankofa World Publishers.

Smith, H. L. (1998). Literacy and Instruction in African American Communities: Shall We Overcome? In B. Perez (Ed.). *Sociocultural Contexts of Language and Literacy*. Mahwah, NJ: Lawrence Erlbaum Associates, Inc.

Smitherman, G. (1977). *Talkin and Testifyin: The Language of Black America*. Detroit, MI: Wayne State University Press.

——. (1999). *Talkin that Talk*. New York: Routledge.

——, & van Dijk, T. A. (1988). *Discourse and Discrimination*. Detroit, MI: Wayne State University Press.

——, & Villanueva, V. (Eds.) (2003). *Language Diversity in the Classroom: From Intention to Practice*. Carbondale, IL: Southern Illinois University Press.

Taylor, H. (1989). *Standard English, Black English and Bidialectism: A Controversy*. New York: Peter Lang.

——. (1991). Ambivalence toward Black English: Some Tentative Solutions. *Writing Instructor*, 10(3), 121–135.

Vaughn-Cooke, F. (1999). Lessons Learned from the Ebonics Controversy and Implications for Language Assessment. In D. C. Carolyn Temple Adger, & O. Taylor (Eds.). *Making the Connection: Language and Academic Achievement among African American Students*. Urbana, IL: National Council of Teachers of English.

Vygotsky, L. S. (2006). *Mind in Society: Development of Higher Psychological Processes*, 1st edn. Cambridge, MA: Harvard University Press.

Wolfram, W. (2004). Social Varieties of English. In E. Finegan, & J. R. Rickford (Eds.). *Language in the USA: Themes for the Twenty-First Century*. Cambridge: Cambridge University Press.

Woodson, C. G. (1933/1990). *The Miseducation of the Negro*. Nashville, TN: Winston-Derek Publishers, Inc.

III
TOWARD A PEDAGOGY
OF SUCCESS IN CLASSROOMS

10

"We Have Our Own Language as Well as the Languages We Bring": Constructing Opportunities for Learning Through a Language of the Classroom

BETH V. YEAGER AND JUDITH L. GREEN

In our Tower community, we have our own language as well as the languages we bring from outside (like Spanish and English) which helped us make our own language. . . These words are all part of the common Tower community language and if someone new were to come in, we would have to explain how we got them and what they mean. We also would tell them that we got this language by reports, information, investigations, and what we do and learn in our Tower community. (Arturo, excerpt of community essay, 1994–1995) (bilingual policy)

But sometimes it's hard to know the things the people in the community talk about when one of us leaves. Like me, when I went to Mexico and came back, it was hard for me to catch up with the class, but when I caught up by listening and observing the class community, I was happy and kind of interested in all the new things I learned. (Juan, excerpt of community essay, 1999–2000) (English Only policy)

Today we live in a fluid and mobile world. Our schools are no longer *becoming* more linguistically and culturally diverse. Rather, in many places in this country, schools are linguistically, culturally and socially complex spaces with as many as 18 languages spoken in a single school. Having children who speak more than one language is ordinary, as is having a class with multiple languages spoken by students with culturally diverse backgrounds. The new level of complexity that this brings to the work of teachers and their students means that the question is not which language to use, but rather how to construct an explicit and purposeful language that builds on the multiple languages *in* the classroom, while creating a *common community* and *language for learning of* the classroom.

In this chapter, we unfold how Beth and Sabrina, two bilingual teachers, who were teacher researchers and themselves second language learners of Spanish, created opportunities for learning that honored the complex and multiple linguistic resources of students (sometimes three languages spoken in their classrooms). Additionally, we provide ways of understanding how Beth's (1999) and Sabrina's

(1999) role of teacher as ethnographer became an important resource for their work in developing what Arturo argued was a language of the classroom as they constructed opportunities for learning with students (Tuyay, Jennings, & Dixon, 1999). We draw on what was learned by taking an ethnographic perspective on everyday classroom life to uncover what occurred first in the fifth grade class taught by Arturo and Juan's teacher, Beth, and then contrasting this with what unfolded in Sabrina's third grade class. In doing so, we seek to make visible a common set of principles for language as social and cultural resource that others may draw on as they seek ways of creating linguistically and culturally rich communities with their students.

An Ethnographic Perspective as a Resource: What Teachers and Students Know and Theorize

To frame how an ethnographic approach became an important resource for Beth and Sabrina, we first present their voices as teacher researchers to complement those of Juan and Arturo, and to uncover how we (Beth and Judith, co-authors of this chapter, and Sabrina), and others, can connect research and practice, and can see ways that teachers *theorize practice* as they work with linguistically diverse students in the small moments of classroom life.

> *Beth*: Classroom research is not separate from the act of teaching for me, but rather central to understanding teaching and learning relationships in the context of what happens for students in my classroom. My challenge as a teacher and a researcher has been to find a lens through which I could look at and talk about what was being accomplished in everyday life in my classroom: how it was being accomplished, what difference what I said or did with students made in what opportunities for learning were available to my linguistically diverse students and how it made a difference; what students were doing and learning, with whom, when, where, how, for what purposes, and with what potential consequences.

> Grounding practice in theory has always been important to me. A view of classrooms as cultures-in-the-making, in which members (students, teachers, families, others) construct locally situated patterned ways of being, knowing and doing through their actions and interactions made sense to me as a teacher. Taking an ethnographic perspective over time in my classroom enabled me to do systematically, and gave me a language for talking about, what already made sense to me as a teacher. It enabled me—and my students—to examine life in the classroom over time and to engage with multiple layers of data in a reflexive and responsive process (I look at the data I gather, ask questions of the data, analyze and raise new questions).

> Taking up an ethnographic perspective on life in our classroom brought a heightened sense of paying attention for me and for my students, like Arturo and Juan, that was different from the ways in which we had paid attention

before. It gave us a language for making sense of, interpreting, talking about and making visible what we knew and understood about reading and interpreting the texts of our class. (Yeager, 2006)

Sabrina echoed Beth's, Arturo's and Juan's understanding of the importance of an ethnographic perspective in writing about her own work with her bilingual students in her third grade class (Tuyay, 1999, p. 17):

> Because I value process as evidence of learning, I sought ways to articulate what I was seeing in my classroom from an alternative perspective. Viewing my classroom as a culture provided me with a lens to begin to understand how knowledge is socially constructed in and through the interactions of members of a group . . . to share some of my own understandings (which are continuously in the process of being shaped and refined) about what was happening in our classroom and about the relationships between literate practices and opportunities for learning.

The perspective on teacher as ethnographer and the lens that it afforded Beth and Sabrina for understanding life in their classrooms and constructing opportunities for learning for their linguistically diverse students grew out of their common experiences co-researching with Judith, Carol Dixon, and other ethnographers. Together, this community of teacher ethnographers, university ethnographers, and in some instances, student ethnographers developed the Santa Barbara Classroom Discourse Group, in collaboration with others in the South Coast Writing Project (SCWriP) (Tuyay, 1999; Tuyay, et al., 1995; Yeager, 1999; Yeager, Floriani, & Green, 1998). All members of this ongoing research community (1990 to the present) have learned from this collaborative work new ways of understanding and talking about the complex, moment by moment, and dynamic patterns of life in classrooms and their consequences for all members, students and teachers alike (for example, Brandts, 1999; Craviotto, Herás, & Espíndola, 1999; Jennings, 1998; Rex & McEachen, 1999).

We begin our exploration of how theory guided our ethnographic perspective by returning to Juan and Arturo, both of whom became student ethnographers in Beth's fifth grade class. In their community essays, essays written at the end of the school year on what it meant to be a member of their particular fifth grade classroom communities, Arturo and Juan each make claims about the ways in which life in classrooms shapes and is shaped by the discursive and social interactions. They argue that outsiders to their classes (Arturo), or students returning after a period of time (Juan), need to understand how ways of knowing, being and doing are talked-into-being over time in relationship to particular events and activity at the group as well as individual level. The arguments that Arturo and Juan make about the interdependent nature of learning and development echo conceptual arguments in sociocultural theory. For example, Souza Lima (1995) argues:

> We have two dimensions of development [and by implication, learning]: one that resides in the individual and the other in the collectivity. Both are interdependent and create each other. Historically created possibilities of cultural development are themselves transformed by the processes through which individuals acquire the cultural tools that are or become available in their context. (Souza Lima, 1995, pp. 447–448)

In other words, Arturo and Juan, at age 10, like Beth and Sabrina, understand the constructed, local and situated nature of the developing text(s) of the classroom. They also understand how they, as members of the class, are afforded particular opportunities for learning, which in turn, shape personal or individual knowledge of content, practices, and processes required within the group. In our research community, we call these consequential progressions (Putney, et al., 2000).

In the sections that follow, we make visible why Arturo and Juan claim that the challenge of understanding language and actions in these diverse settings involves more than knowing which language students and teachers speak, what types of curriculum exist, and what skills students need. We will continue to tie the understandings that Juan, Arturo, Sabrina, and Beth inscribe with current theories about classrooms as cultures and learning as a collective and individual, interdependent process. In this way, we make visible how everyday knowledge and practices of students and the professional knowledge of these teachers constitute sociocultural theory that is consistent with perspectives on the study of language, discourse in use, and knowledge construction. Drawing on this view of theory–practice relationships, we construct a *theoretical perspective* on the *language of the classroom* that teachers can use to construct their own principles of practice for exploring language as resource, not barrier, in the classroom (for example, Frank, Dixon, & Green, 1999; Green, Dixon, & Zaharlick, 2003).

Initiating Community in Beth's Fifth Grade Bilingual Class

From Individual Entry to Formulating a Language in the Classroom

As Arturo and Juan argued earlier, life in classrooms, including what is "talked-into-being" as a common language of the classroom, is constituted in the discursive work that members of the group do together, and requires teachers and students alike to continually shift how they are reading and interpreting the developing texts being constructed. What is constructed as "class" and ways of being, knowing and doing in that class, occurs over time in and through small moments of actions and interactions that are both explicit and implicit. How students are greeted when they first enter the classroom on the first day of school, or how they know where to sit and with whom, are examples of small moments that are both visible and often invisible, that students must learn to read and interpret in order to know what to do, how to position themselves within the group, who they can be, which language(s) to use in particular contexts, what to do, what to display, and what to know. The small moments that occur over time and events, particularly when taken cumulatively, have potential important consequences for the kinds of opportunities for learning what it means to be a student (or mathematician, reader, writer, historian, scientist, member of a group, and so forth) that are available and to whom they are available.

In his essay, Juan shares the consequences for students who do not have Immediate access to those moments as they are "talked-into-being" as part of a developing, dynamic classroom culture. He describes his exit from the classroom for several months to Mexico and how "it's hard to know the things the people in the community talk about when one of us leaves." At the same time, he makes visible the ways in which small moments of discourse and action can be seen as texts that become observable and available to be read by members, if members learn how to read them. He argues that by observing his community in action and listening to "the people in the community talk," he is able to meet the challenge of understanding and figuring out the new ways of knowing, being and doing required at this point in time in the class to which he has returned. Juan, who had an opportunity in the beginning of the year to learn how to observe as an ethnographer, reflects arguments made by Erickson and Shultz (1981), who view people as contexts for each other and people's actions as texts to be read and interpreted.

The idea that people are texts for each other has become a key part of our ethnographic perspective for understanding how Beth (and others) initiate and construct a series of *public texts* with students in and through discourse and actions. Our unfolding of these processes of text construction will show how she formulated (began to talk into being) a set of norms and expectations, roles and relationships, and rights and obligations for members of the group that framed the individual–collective relationships. In so doing, we make visible the discursive work of teacher and students across the initiating events and subevents of the first day in this classroom (8:10 am–12:15 pm). Through this process, we identify ways Beth initiated with students a range of practices and principles for talking and acting a language of the classroom into being that became resource for their dynamic, evolving and locally situated "community."

Table 10.1 represents a map of the unfolding sequences of activity, constructed from video records of the first two events of the morning (8:10–10:45). In this table, the work of students and teachers is represented as actions, using the present continuous form of the verb (verb + ing).

As can be seen in Table 10.1, the chains of action/work (Bloome, Carter, Christian, & Otto, 2005) led us to identify ways in which the teacher, with students, drew on two languages (English and Spanish), shifting between the two languages to both languages as a common resource for the collective as well as for individuals-in-the-collective (Souza Lima, 1995) from the first moments of class. For example, there was a common (representative) pattern of entry and greeting. As a student arrived in the classroom door, Beth greeted him/her in either Spanish or English. If a parent came to the door with the student, the parent was also greeted in Spanish or English. The teacher's choice of language of greeting indicated her prior knowledge of the student's (and parent's) language background and her observations of parent–student and student–student interactions as they entered

TABLE 10.1 Mapping Two Events of the First Day of Class: Onset of "Group"

Time	Actions	Language	IS	Sub-event	Event	Creating Opportunities for Collective and Individual Activity Within Collective
8:10	– St/P **arriving** in the classroom	**Span/Eng**	T–I			– seeing and "reading" what other participants are doing
	– St/P **meeting** teacher	**Eng/Span**	I–TG			– re-establishing contact with friends
	– T **greeting** St/P	**Span/Eng**				– meeting new people
	– St/P **responding** to T	**Eng/Span**		ENTERING THE TOWER		– listening to English or Spanish to be spoken
	– T **orienting** students to get name card and choose place to sit	**Span/Eng**				– speaking English or Spanish
	– St **choosing** where to sit		I–I			– meeting new people
	– St **decorating** name square	**Span/Eng**			O	– getting acquainted with others
(45')	– St **talking** to classmates sitting at table group	**Eng/Span**			N S	– choosing language to interact with others
	– T, TA, ST **talking** to St at table groups	**Span/Eng**			E	– interacting with individuals at table groups
	– St **talking** to T, TA and St T	**Eng/Span**			T	– responding to student initiations
8:55	– T **introducing** chime as a sign	**Eng/Span**	WC		O	– creating signals for focusing when not in whole group
				COMMUNITY	F	
	– T **welcoming** participants	**Eng/Span**	St–WC			– greeting students as whole group for first time
	– T **celebrating** the languages of the Tower	**Span/Eng**				– re-situating self within large group

INITIATING TOWER

(40') Community: Spanish and English   **Span/Eng**

– T **explaining** way of using Spanish and English in the classroom   Eng/Span

– T **introducing** adult members to students   Eng/Span

– T **introducing** ethnography as community practice   Span/Eng

– T **talking** about basic routines: drinking water, signing up for lunch, bathroom, recess, etc.   **Eng/Span**

– T **exploring** students' knowledge about Tower Community and introducing Tower as community with own traditions   **Eng/Span**

– T **presenting** multiple physical spaces of Tower classroom, discussing possibilities of use   Eng/Span

Span/Eng

COMMUNITY

C – getting support from adults and classmates
O – helping ST learn her job partner
M – becoming ethnographer
M – knowing local community ways of leaving
U –
N – establishing norms being established for the group
I – becoming a Tower Community member
T – exploring own knowledge and experience in constructing Tower Community in 96/97
Y – defining uses and exploring multiple spaces

– speaking language of choice

– orienting members to physical environment

Key: **IS** = interactional space; **T–I** = teacher–individual student; **I–TG** = teacher–table group; **I–I** = individual–individual; **St–WC** = student–whole class the Tower. At the end of the greeting, the teacher used one of the languages to reorient the student to a table with namecards on it, just beyond the door, and asked her/him to select their name and then select a seat at a table group. Students were also asked to decorate their namecard in any way that they chose to represent themselves to the others at the table and in the class. These varying uses of language become texts to be seen, read and interpreted by students already in the room.

At the table group, students were able to talk with those at the table in their language of choice or to work silently, creating further opportunities for exploring their own language use in the classroom. The students also interacted with the teacher assistant (bilingual) and student teacher (English dominant), as these actors walked around the room greeting students at tables. Although the student teacher was English dominant, Beth encouraged her to use whatever Spanish she knew, implicitly signaling to the students that everyone in the room would try to speak the language of his/her interactional partner. Ethnographic evidence reveals that the namecard moved with the student to new table seats on subsequent days as the teacher regrouped students to create table groups with Spanish dominant, English dominant and bilingual speakers, who supported opportunities for learning for table group members who spoke only one language.

At the same time, students could see books on shelves (in two languages and representing multiple genres and disciplines), posters in two languages, and other graphic and visual resources that constituted part of the evolving classroom "texts" (Bloome & Egan-Robertson, 1993) that were available to be read as potential material resource for what it would mean to be a student in this classroom. In this way the teacher created opportunities in these opening moments for students to see, hear and interpret how the two (or more) languages were valued ways of communicating and signaled the potential for their use in subsequent academic work.

Reformulating Community: From Small Group and Individual Work to Collective Activity

What happened next marked a distinct shift in activity, which served to reorient students from table group and individual work within the table group to a whole group activity with a common floor. As indicated in the actions column in Table 10.1, the teacher initiated this shift by using a chime as a signal for changing focus at 8:55. She then began to use a metadiscourse about practice (talk about the actions and language use), in and through two language(s) that we view as a public text (Kelly, Crawford, & Green, 2001) available to be read by members. In this case, through using two languages (English and Spanish) herself, she made explicitly visible aspects of classroom life by: (a) explaining the value of having two languages (English and Spanish); (b) explaining how she would use two languages in the classroom; (c) introducing adult members (including researchers) and their (adults and students) roles as ethnographers; and (d) defining basic routines related to instrumental dimensions of classroom life.

As shown in Table 10.1, the teacher explicitly referred to the Tower as a "community" with "traditions" and a history that extended beyond that which was being constructed with students in the moment. In subsequent actions, in which the teacher invited students to share knowledge they had about the Tower community, the teacher again reoriented students to a change in interaction space, providing them with opportunities to shift roles from audience for the teacher's developing text, to participant in the construction of a common text. This shift signaled to students that the teacher was aware that many had prior knowledge that they brought to the Tower class. The shift in participation structure (Erickson, 1982) also made visible how their knowledge would become a potential material resource for the group, since they were accepted in the language which they offered as part of the developing text and since they were invited to participate in constructing that text.

When we examined the first two subevents, Entering the Tower and Initiating the Tower Community, in Table 10.1, we were able to see ways in which the teacher shaped with students, individually and then collectively, a range of physical configurations that were possible in the Tower—for example, table groups, whole group with a common floor. Her practice of changing the physical spaces for interaction in the classroom supported different types of interaction among students and between teacher and students. By orienting and (re)orienting students to ways of constructing and being in different interactional spaces, the teacher developed a discourse of practices for routines necessary for the community to accomplish different types of work together and/or individually. In asking them what they knew about the Tower community, therefore, she invited students to create intertextual ties (Bloome & Egan-Robertson, 1993) between background knowledge and current actions needed to participate in the group. Each of these actions drew on English and Spanish to create a developing text that was available to all students and to create the discourse practices and referential system that initiated, what Arturo called "our own language of the classroom."

Across the events and subevents of the morning, each action served as "initiating moments" of practices that began to shape what counted as ways of doing, saying and knowing in the Tower community. Beth did this by creating, what we refer to as *a metadiscourse about key organizing practices*, and a referential system for how to name these practices. As she engaged in this process, she also made visible three important aspects of this language system. First, she retrospectively named the practices in which they had just engaged (for example, the chime is a signal for orienting to the group). Second, she framed how a practice looked and what it sounded like in action. And, third, she provided an explicit rationale for engaging in and using the practice (e.g., this is what mathematicians do; this is what members of the class do; this is what students or adults do in different situations). In this way, she helped students initiate a set of norms and expectations, with their roles and relationships, for different events within the class, which were important for constructing a common community, or what we call a culture-in-the-making.

Together these events served to construct with the students a range of actions that were possible in this space, which would eventually become part of *a repertoire for action*, defining what counted as "class" in the Tower in this year. Understanding the ways in which teacher discourse and actions served to initiate and develop with students this range of actions enabled us (and the students) to build an under-standing of the ways in which languages entered into classroom life and became a resource for constructing life. Understanding how this occurred ultimately led to the construction of a new interpretation of Arturo's claim that to understand the language of the classroom, an outsider needs to understand *how* this language and system of use was created, in and through the actions of the developing collective.

In order to understand *how* these patterns of action became material resources for academic as well as social and instrumental work (Christie, 1995), we turn to another event occurring on the first day of class, the "Watermelon Project." By examining the chains of actions in this event, we unfold how academic study was talked into being. As part of the discussion of this developing event, we describe how the practices and actions identified in the first events of the morning became resources that the teacher reformulated, modified, and expanded to create new practices, shaping what counted as the study of mathematics in this class.

Reformulating Language as Resource for Academic Study

The Watermelon Project

We briefly visit the watermelon project, a 4-day investigation that served to initiate academic study on the first day of class. We use this project to show how the pattern of organizing what occurred in the classroom across multiple spaces, of the development of the individual–collective relationship, and of multiple language use continued in this new context. We make visible how these patterns were refo-rmulated and initiated a new set of actions required by students to successfully investigate watermelons as mathematicians.

The watermelon project was initiated by the teacher as she discursively described, in two languages, having watermelons in the class on the first day as part of the "Tower community tradition." In particular, she stated that getting "*to investigate mathematically the watermelons*" was part of this tradition. In this way, the teacher not only signaled to students that watermelons were a tradition but that academic study as mathematicians was also part of that tradition (*y vamos a llegar a ser/matemáticos/con nuestras sandias* [we're going to become mathematicians with our watermelons]).

The actual mathematical study using watermelons on this first day of the project was formulated and reformulated in and through a subsequent series of subevents in the morning (Brilliant-Mills, 1993). These subevents, while not investigated in depth here, included: preparing notebooks (math logs), developing a question to investigate (e.g., how much did Ms. Yeager pay for the watermelons assigned to each table group?), making an individual/personal "guess" about the cost of the watermelon, defining ways to approach the problem (for example, determining weight, price per pound), refining estimates (making a table group estimate), gathering data as a table group (including accessing multiple sources, revising estimates of weight and cost, and reporting findings, in English and Spanish, for placement on a collective data chart). Students were able to contrast their estimated answers with "actual" weight and cost of each watermelon when they were given those additional data after lunch.

The initiation of the content of mathematics began with the discussion of questions about watermelons in a whole group configuration that also included the earlier pattern of inviting individuals to share their thinking and under-standings in the public space, using their language of choice, thus contributing to the construction of the developing text about questions. This chain of actions also foreshadowed ways of engaging in inquiry that were being developed. In using a pattern of whole group focus and inviting individuals to contribute ideas (questions, in this case), Beth afforded students an opportunity to expand their understanding of this practice and how a common practice would be used in flexible or variable ways across events and discipline areas in future academic study. In both instances of this practice, however, Beth invited students to use their historical understandings to accomplish a new task, showing that she valued personal knowledge as a material resource for academic work and for constructing a collective text.

This pattern of talking about practice (*metadiscourse about practice*), providing a rationale for engaging in practices in particular ways, and doing so in a whole group configuration while inviting individuals to share their thinking and ideas in the public space continued across all subevents. In addition, as part of the teacher's metadiscourse, she *named* students *as* mathematicians doing important work, while foreshadowing the ways in which what was formulated as practice on this first day would become important as resource in future inquiries.

Ethnographic evidence shows that Beth also drew on other patterns of participant structures formulated earlier. Students were afforded opportunities to move from the whole group configuration to small group interactional spaces in order to engage in the practices that were reformulated in the collective. In addition, the teacher and other adult actors moved from table to table, engaging with individuals, and with table groups. Students were then asked to reorient to the whole group in order to revise the collective text being constructed.

Thus students were afforded opportunities to access the mathematical investigation and its content in multiple spaces, both public and private. At the same time, Beth *proposed and acknowledged that differences existed* among members in terms of language and knowledge and actions, while *building on these differences* to indicate that all, including herself, would grow in their capacity to do this work, both individually and collectively. In this way, she made visible the interdependence of collective development and the development of individuals within the collective as well as the importance of the common language and practices being formulated to what would constitute that interdependent relationship over time.

Formulating and Reformulating Patterns of Practice across Days

By unfolding much of the first morning of class, we made visible the ways in which Beth drew on language as resource to initiate and formulate, to "talk-into-being," practices that would potentially become part of students' repertoire of action for knowing, being and doing in this classroom. To become part of a repertoire of actions, to become *patterns* of practice or *principles* of practice, however, processes and practices must be repeated, constantly formulated and reformulated over time, both proposed to and recognized by the collective and, potentially, by individuals-in-the-collective.

In the following brief analysis, we make visible patterns of practice that were formulated and reformulated across the first three weeks of school in this classroom.

As Table 10.2 shows, practices formulated on the first day of class (FP) were sometimes repeated every day across the first three weeks of school as part of an ongoing process. But sometimes new things were introduced and/or Beth reformulated with students *how* a practice would be used in new ways in new contexts. For instance, observing (in row 1 in Table 10.2) as mathematicians on the first day was reformulated on subsequent days as observing as artists in order to paint a self-portrait, observing as ethnographers in order to study the actions of people, and observing as writers, all types of observing, but in different ways for different purposes. In each case, Beth discursively formulated the practice and named it as part of the common language of the classroom and then reformulated it with students in each of the new contexts. Building a repertoire for actions in the first moments, then, is not just a tool but an ongoing way to reformulate practice as resource for future academic study.

Because Juan began the year in the Tower classroom, he was both present when practices were formulated across the first three weeks of school *and* had available ways of observing and reading the evolving classroom texts as an ethnographer. This was important when he left for three months, because practices were both reformulated and introduced while he was gone. The evolving classroom texts and the language of the classroom changed in and through the moment-to-moment interactions. Because Juan had a way of *paying attention* to and observing what was occurring in his classroom community when he returned, and to what people were doing and saying, he was able to "*catch up*" and to continue to learn. Juan's interpretation of what he needed to do to re-enter the evolving classroom community makes visible that it is important that teachers not assume that students know what to do or how to be on entering or re-entering the classroom community after an absence. *Reformulating* practice(s) (reshaping, making visible the new ways practices may look or sound in the new context) in explicit ways for individuals-in-the-collective as well as for the collective becomes important as a way of affording students opportunities for successfully accessing, reading and interpreting the evolving classroom text, both academic and instrumental (Morine-Dershimer, 2006).

Reformulating Language As Resource: Writing Planet Stories in Sabrina's Class

When we looked at Beth's class, we focused on the ways in which she drew on language as resource to formulate and reformulate a language *of* the class, in and through, as Arturo claimed, discourse and actions, or what "we do." The language and practices that were initiated and reformulated across the first three weeks of school can be seen as having been made available to the group or collective across

TABLE 10.2 Range of Actions and Practices Observed in First Three Weeks of School, 1996–1997

Actions	9-9	9-10	9-11	9-12	9-13	9-16	9-17	9-18	9-19	9-20	9-23	9-24	9-25	9-26	9-27
Observing	FP	x				RP	x				x			RP	x
Using two languages	FP	x	x	x	x	x	x	x	x	x	x	x	x	x	x
Writing in language of choice	FP	RP	x	x		x		x	x	x	x	x	x		
Introducing and defining roles	FP	x	x			x	x				x			x	
Collecting data	FP	RP	x				x	x	x		x	x		x	x
Interpreting data	FP		x				x		x					x	x
Comparing/contrasting data	FP		x	x			x		x	x		x		x	
Visually representing data		FP	RP	RP		x	x	x	x				x	x	
Reading data (e.g., graphs)			FP				x	x	x					x	
Working in pairs	FP	x													
Working in groups	FP	x	x	x		x	x	x	x	x	x	x	x	x	x
Explaining/Practicing new processes	FP	x	x	x		x	x				x			x	
Thinking and writing about process			FP			x								x	
Defining terms	FP	x	x	x		x	x					x	x	x	
Asking questions	FP	x	x				RP			x	x	x	x	x	x
Reporting to class	FP	x		RP			RP		x	x		x	x	x	RP
Participating as member of audience	FP	x	FP	x			x		x			x	x	x	x
Identifying patterns			FP				x		x						
Making generalizations														FP	
"Writing to think"	FP	x		x		x					x				
Recording in learning logs (math and social science)	FP	x	x	x			x	x	x	x	x	x	x	x	x
Revising thinking	FP		x					x					x	x	
Defining what things mean	FP	x	x				x							x	
Negotiating group answer	FP	x	x	x			x	x				x			

continued

TABLE 10.2 Continued

Actions	9-9	9-10	9-11	9-12	9-13	9-16	9-17	9-18	9-19	9-20	9-23	9-24	9-25	9-26	9-27
Writing in a writer's notebook	PP			FP		x	x		x		x	x		x	
Recording and responding in literature logs	PP					FP	x			x	x	x	x		x
Constructing artifacts				FP											
"Brainstorming"			FP								x			RP	x
"Note taking"										FP	x			RP	
"Note making"															
Supporting ideas with evidence	FP		x		x				x				x		x
Writing from evidence		FP										x			
Formulating theory															
Using chronology									FP			RP			
Sharing opinions and ideas	FP	x	x	x	x					x	x	x	x	x	x

Key: FP = formulating new practice; RP = reformulating a practice when used in a new way (e.g., observing as artists in order to do a self-portrait; PP = potential practice (foreshadowing a practice that may be introduced in future; e.g. having literature logs on table on first day and indicating that they will be introduced and used on future days multiple interactional spaces (for instance, whole group, table group, teacher and individual). But both teachers and students know that simply because something is made available does not always mean that it is actually "available" in the same way, as a readable and accessible text, to all individuals-*in*-the-collective. By reconfiguring the group and reorienting members to multiple interactional spaces and participant structures, teachers afford students different ways of entering, accessing and taking up potential resources. But, even when this occurs, much discursive work may be required to help students to access and take up opportunities *to* learn (Tuyay, et al., 1995). We draw on one small moment in Sabrina's third grade bilingual class to again make visible the interdependent relationship between collective and individual-in-the-collective development. This time we focus on how, through small interactional moments, Sabrina, *with* students, drew on language(s) to reformulate opportunities for learning in ways that could potentially impact how particular individuals took up those opportunities (Tuyay, 1999).

Ethnographic evidence shows that Sabrina, like Beth in her fifth grade class, had formulated and reformulated ways of knowing, being, and doing in her class since the first days of the school year. She had formulated over time norms and expectations for participating in class, including the use of two languages, for engaging in and with academic content, and for engaging in literate practices in order to compose pieces of writing (Tuyay, et al., 1995).

The particular event presented here, in which students wrote what they defined as "realistic fiction" planet stories, unfolded across two days as part of an integrated science/language arts study of the solar system in which Sabrina and her students had been engaged for over a month. The planet story event began when a student brought in a book about extraterrestrials and asked that Sabrina read it to the group. After listening to the story, another student proposed that the group write their own stories about the planets and extraterrestrials. This idea was accepted by Sabrina and the other students in the group, reflective of the particular norms and expectations for participating and *contributing to the public texts* that had been formulated and reformulated over time in this class.

The next day, the third graders worked in small group interaction spaces as part of the writing workshop, during which they selected co-authors, brainstormed, generated and recorded ideas, and began drafting stories. All of these literate practices had been formulated and reformulated over time and so were familiar to the students. As part of the workshop, Sabrina then brought students together in a whole group space, reorienting them to the classroom collective in and through a class discussion, in order to help students understand more about realistic fiction, the writing process, and norms and expectations for participation in this class, and to construct a collective text that would be available to the group (inviting students to share their prewriting ideas with the class).

As shown in columns 1 and 2 of Table 10.3, in and through this group discussion, Sabrina and students co-constructed multiple potential opportunities for learning ways to share ideas, talk about, and write stories with others as co-authors in a bilingual context. The practices that were formulated and reformulated in and through this group discussion (e.g., writing stories means having and sharing ideas)

TABLE 10.3 Opportunities For Learning During Whole-class Discussion

Learning About Realistic Fiction	Learning About the Writing Process	Learning About Norms and Expectations for Class Participation
Realistic fiction (e.g., a planet story) includes both fantasy and reality	• Writing stories means having and sharing ideas	• Use of two languages (Spanish and English) is encouraged and accepted
Fantasy	• Writing stories takes time	• Conversations are not always teacher directed
• People can use spaceships to get to space	• Authors need to communicate clearly with their audience	• Joining the conversation doesn't require raising one's hand
• People can crashland on planets	• Talking is a valuable part of the composing process	• Clarification or explanation of ideas may be necessary
• People can live on planets	• Co-authors need to talk about their writing	• It's okay to share information and ideas with others
Reality	• Stories may include information from multiple sources	• Students in this class may be viewed as experts
• There are different planets in the solar system	• This is a particular genre of writing that includes both fact and fiction	• It's okay to question an author's/expert's ideas
• Planets are different sizes	• It's okay to question an author's writing	• Students may express their opinions
• Distance from the sun affects planet's temperature	• Writers may need to work in different locations	• Students have choices
• Rockets and planes face different directions		• It's okay to interrupt the teacher
• Height of rocket needs to be considered if story is to be realistic		• Humor is accepted

became a part of a dynamic and evolving *public text*, constituted in and through a language of the class. This text, in turn, became potentially available to be read and interpreted—and taken up as resource—by members of the group. As teachers know, understanding how students understand and take up potential opportunities for learning, what counts as and becomes a resource on which students can draw, is not necessarily possible to see in the moment. For this reason, we unfold one small interactional moment that occurred *following* the group discussion as students worked in small groups to draft their stories.

We focus on a group composed of three boys, Roberto, José Luis, and Beto. José Luis and Roberto spoke Spanish and English, while Beto spoke only Spanish. Table 10.4 represents a segment of transcript from their work. In this segment, Roberto and José Luis began, in English, to plan how they would draft their story. After overhearing the first part of their interaction, Sabrina joined the conversation.

As Roberto and José Luis began their conversation, it was clear, as the boys planned to write *five lines in English and five lines in Spanish*, that they understood that one of the norms for group discussion was the use of two languages (column 1). They also understood that co-authors needed to talk about their writing. In other words, they were taking up what had become available to them in the collective discussion as opportunities for learning what it meant to work together on a story. However, the two boys were talking only with each other and only in English, even though they were aware that Beto, also part of their group, spoke only Spanish. Sabrina writes that it became apparent to her (1999, p. 18) that the boys had interpreted available opportunities for learning in ways that, because Beto may not have been able to contribute his ideas, were potentially excluding one member of their group (see also Tuyay, et al., 1995). What she overheard led her to join the conversation in order to help reshape what counted as language use in this group.

As seen in Table 10.4, Sabrina framed her contributions to the conversation in the form of questions, in Spanish. This discursive choice served to make her comments available to all members of the group, to signal to the boys that, although Sabrina had heard the boys speaking English and spoke English herself, she purposely *chose* to use Spanish in this moment, and, to signal, as well, that they were *invited to contribute their ideas* in response to the questions about what was possible and not possible in the group as it was being constructed by its members. She also positioned herself as a writer through the way in which she framed one of her questions (*Si yo estoy escribiendo un cuento* . . . [If I am writing a story . . .]), thus making visible that norms and expectations for what it meant to use language, to share ideas, and to write a story with co-authors, applied to her as well.

Finally, Sabrina ended her participation in this small moment of interaction by asking José Luis what he could do to solve the problem, thus affording him a potential opportunity to co-construct a solution with her. José then moved closer to Beto and began speaking Spanish and translating what Roberto (who was more fluent in English) was saying in English so that Beto could better understand what was happening. In and through her discursive choices, *with* the students, in this brief moment of interaction, Sabrina reformulated the opportunities, available to the group through the whole class discussion, for learning what it meant to

TABLE 10.4 Reformulating Opportunities for Learning in Small Moments of Interaction: Planet Story-writing Project

Potential Opportunities for Learning Constructed in Whole Class Discussion	Planet Story Small Group Student Discourse	Planet Story Small Group Student Actions	Planet Story Small Group Teacher Discourse	Planet Story Small Group Teacher Actions	Reformulating Opportunities for Learning During Small Group Time
• Use of two languages is encouraged and accepted • Talking is a valuable part of the composing process • Co-authors need to talk about their writing	R: Let's write. Let's write five things in English . . . and then in Spanish JL: And five things in . . . R: In Spanish JL: We're gonna write five things in English . . . and five things in Spanish	[Looks at Beto] [Talks to teacher]			
			Beto, entiendes lo que están haciendo ellos? [Beto, do you understand what they are doing?]	[Working with pair of girls at another table]	
• Joining the conversation doesn't require raising one's hand • Writing stories means having and sharing ideas	Linda: They don't even let him write, I bet	[Roberto looks up at Linda briefly and then			

JL: No les está diciendo ideas. No más estás jugando. [*He is not saying ideas. He's only playing.*] [resumes writing]

Cómo puede decir ideas si no sabe lo que está escribiendo? Es posible? [*How can he tell you ideas if he doesn't know what you are writing? Is that possible?*]

In order to contribute ideas, one must understand the language being spoken/written

[Moves to end of table next to Beto]

JL: Nope

Si yo estoy escribiendo un cuento con Christina, y estames hablando en inglés, tú puedes darnos ideas? [*If I am writing a story with Christina and we are speaking in English, can you give us ideas?*]

JL: Yeah

Si no sabes inglés? [*If you don't know English?*]

JL: No

TABLE 10.4 Continued

Potential Opportunities for Learning Constructed in Whole Class Discussion	Planet Story Small Group Student Discourse	Planet Story Small Group Student actions	Planet story Small group Teacher Discourse	Planet Story Small Group Teacher Actions	Reformulating Opportunities for Learning During Small Group Time
			Entonces, qúe puedes hacer tú? [*Then, what can you do?*]		
		[Roberto looks up from paper]			
		[JL moves closer to Beto. Puts paper he and R were writing on in center of work space. Speaks in Spanish and begins to translate what R was saying in English			Students have a responsibility to help one another understand the task at hand
		Consequence: Beto does all the illustrations of the group's stories			It is okay to participate in different ways

co-author a story in a group using two languages as resource. As shown in column 6, *using two* languages and *talking with co-authors about their composing and writing* now also meant taking responsibility, as members and co-authors, for whether all members of the group could, in fact, do that. That Beto ultimately understood the story and was willing to contribute his ideas following this interaction, is evidenced not in the moment, but by the fact that he eventually did all of the illustrating for the group. Thus, what it meant to *contribute* to the group story was also reformulated (members can contribute in different ways—column 6) and then taken up in particular ways by individuals-in-the-collective.

José Luis' and Beto's actions make visible how Sabrina, using language(s) in and of the class as resource, reformulated opportunities for learning what it meant to know and do in particular ways in this context of co-authoring a story using two languages. The discourse and actions of Sabrina and the boys also make visible the ways in which a small moment of interaction had important consequences for how students could access opportunities for learning content and practice. As Sabrina has argued: "This evidence suggests we cannot assume that simply providing an event for learning will be sufficient. Teachers play an important role in facilitating how students interact with the information presented, and, in so doing, providing an opportunity for learning, not merely an event" (Tuyay, 1999, pp. 19–20).

Developing Principles of Practice

While the analyses and descriptions in this chapter have been of two bilingual, English/Spanish classes, teachers and students today participate in complex worlds in which multiple languages may be spoken in their classrooms. While Beth is a second language learner of Spanish, she also had students in her classroom (both her bilingual classes and later her English Only classes) on different occasions whose heritage languages were Vietnamese, Portuguese, Hebrew, and Arabic, as well as Spanish, among others. The same was often the case for Sabrina. Both teachers found that their principles of practice, grounded in a view of language as resource, not barrier, and developed in and through their ethnographic work, continued to guide their discursive and instructional decisions as they, with their students, constructed a common language of the class while drawing on the multiple languages *in* the classroom as resource.

Rather than attempting to identify *"best" practices* in their approach to affording equitable and accessible opportunities for learning to their linguistically diverse students, what became important to Beth and Sabrina was making visible the often invisible *principles* that guided the ways in which they took up and shaped patterns of practice and a language *of* the class with their students. By making visible the *principles of practice* that underlay and guided their discourse and actions, they were able to draw on those principles in flexible ways to meet the locally situated and changing needs of students in each of their classes across multiple years.

To conclude this chapter, we offer a series of ethnographic questions that readers can take up and ask themselves as a way of developing and/or making visible their own principles of practice. We hope the principles they construct or uncover will guide them in shaping a classroom culture-in-the-making in which the multiple languages they and their students "*bring from outside*" serve as resource for constructing their "*own language*" of the classroom. In turn, we hope that the language of the classroom that teachers and their students co-construct will serve as resource for constructing equitable opportunities for learning rich academic content and practice for and with those linguistically diverse students.

Discussion Questions and Activities

When you (and your students) explore your own classroom, take some time to observe and/or ask yourself questions, such as:

1. What can you do and say in this classroom? When? Where? With whom? How? Under what conditions? For what purposes? With what potential consequences and/or outcomes for yourself and others?
2. What questions can I ask myself about my students and content when planning the curriculum? When and how will I use a metadiscourse about practice?
3. Do I and/or my students have a language of the discipline? Do I and/or my students understand the rationale for why we are doing a particular practice? What rationale is available to me and to each student in a language that she/he can understand? (And if I don't speak a particular language, what can I draw on to make the rationale available?)
4. If I view language(s) as resource, then what do I need to know, ask, and do in order to "talk this view into being" with my students? What would I hope our evolving classroom text and practices for constructing these texts would look and sound like from the first moments of the first day of class, and to whom will they be accessible.

References

Bloome, D., & Egan-Robertson, A. (1993). The Social Construction of Intertextuality in Classroom Reading and Writing Lessons. *Reading Research Quarterly*, 28(4), 305–333.
——, Carter, S., Christian, B., & Otto, S. (2005). *Discourse Analysis & the Study of Classroom Language & Literacy Events: A Microethnographic Perspective*. Mahwah, NJ: Lawrence Erlbaum Associates, Inc.
Brandts, L. (1999). Are Pullout Programs Sabotaging Classroom Community in our Elementary Schools? *Primary Voices K-6*, 7(3), 9–16.
Brilliant-Mills, H. (1993). Becoming a Mathematician: Building a Situated Definition of Mathematics. *Linguistics and Education*, 5(3 & 4), 301–334.
Christie, F. (1995). Pedagogic Discourse in the Primary School. *Linguistics and Education*, 7(3), 221–242.
Craviotto, E., Herás, A. I., & Espíndola, J. (1999). Cultures of the Fourth-Grade Bilingual Classroom. *Primary Voices K-6*, 7(3), 25–36.
Dixon, C., de la Cruz, E., Green, J., Lin, L., & Brandts, L. (1992). (Santa Barbara Classroom Discourse Group.) Do You See what We See? The Referential and Intertextual Nature of Classroom Life. *Journal of Classroom Interaction*, 27(2), 29–36.
Erickson, F. (1982). Taught Cognitive Learning in its Immediate Environments: A Neglected Topic in the Anthropology of Education. *Anthropology & Education Quarterly*, 13(2), 149–180.

——, & Shultz, J. (1981). When is a Context? Some Issues and Methods in the Analysis of Social Competence. In J. L. Green and C. Wallat (Eds.). *Ethnography and Language in Educational Settings*. Norwood, NJ: Ablex.

Frank, C., Dixon, C., & Green, J. (1999). Classrooms as Cultures: Understanding the Constructed Nature of Life in Classrooms. *Primary Voices K-6*, 7(3), 4–8.

Green, J., Dixon, C., Lin, L., Floriani, A., & Bradley, M. (1992). (Santa Barbara Classroom Discourse Group.) Constructing Literacy in Classrooms: Literate Action as Social Accomplishment. In H. Marshall (Ed.). *Redefining Student Learning: Roots of Educational Change*. Norwood, NJ: Ablex.

——, ——, & Zaharlick, A. (2003). Ethnography as a Logic of Inquiry. In J. Flood, S. B. Heath, & D. Lapp (Eds.). *The Handbook for Research in the English Language Arts*. Mahwah, NJ: Lawrence Erlbaum Associates, Inc.

Jennings, L. B. (1998). Reading the World of the Classroom through Ethnographic Eyes. *The California Reader*, 31(4), 11–15.

Kelly, G., Crawford, T., & Green, J. (2001). Common Task and Uncommon Knowledge: Dissenting Voices in the Discursive Construction of Physics across Small Laboratory Groups. *Linguistics and Education. Special Issue on Language and Cognition*, 12(2), 135–252.

Morine-Dershimer, G. (2006). Classroom Management and Classroom Discourse. In C. Evertson, & C. S. Weinstein (Eds.). *Handbook of Classroom Management*. Mahwah, NJ: Lawrence Erlbaum Associates, Inc.

Putney, L., Green, J., Dixon, C., Durán, R., & Yeager, B. (1999). Consequential Progressions: Exploring Collective–Individual Development in a Bilingual Classroom. In P. Smagorinsky, & C. Lee (Eds.). *Constructing Meaning through Collaborative Inquiry: Vygotskian Perspectives on Literacy Research*. Cambridge: Cambridge University Press.

Rex, L., & McEachen, D. (1999). "If Anything is Odd, Inappropriate, Confusing, or Boring, It's Probably Important": The Emergence of Inclusive Academic Literacy through English Classroom Discussion Practices. *Research in the Teaching of English*, 65–127.

Souza Lima, E. (1995). Culture Revisited: Vygotsky's Ideas in Brazil. *Anthropology & Education Quarterly*, 26(4), 443–457.

Tuyay, S., Floriani, A., Yeager, B., Dixon, C., & Green, J. (1995). Constructing an Integrated, Inquiry-Oriented Approach in Classrooms: A Cross-Case Analysis of Social, Literate, and Academic Practice. *Journal of Classroom Interaction*, 30(2), 1–15.

Tuyay, S., Jennings, L., & Dixon, C. (1999). Classroom Discourse and Opportunities to Learn: An Ethnographic Study of Knowledge Construction in a Bilingual Third Grade Classroom. *Discourse Processes*, 19(1), 75–110.

Tuyay, S. (1999). Exploring the Relationships between Literate Practices and Opportunities for Learning. *Primary Voices K-6*, 7(3), 17–24.

Yeager, B. (1999). Constructing a Community of Inquirers. *Primary Voices K-6*, 7(3), 37–52.

——. (2006). Teacher as Researcher/Researcher as Teacher: Multiple Angles of Vision for Studying Learning in the Context of Teaching. *Language Arts Journal of Michigan*, 22(1), 26–33.

——, Floriani, A., & Green, J. (1998). Learning to See Learning in the Classroom: Developing an Ethnographic Perspective. In D. Bloome & A. Egan-Robertson (Eds.). *Students as Inquirers of Language and Culture in their Classrooms*. Cresskill, NJ: Hampton Press.

11

"Taylor Cat is Black": Code-Switch to Add Standard English to Students' Linguistic Repertoires

REBECCA S. WHEELER

We have slept through the alarm. Nearly 30 years ago, the children's mothers spoke and Judge Joiner responded. From Ann Arbor's Green Road housing project, mothers called out that schools were failing to educate their young. Unprepared to understand the language of their African American students, teachers disparaged children, suspended them, diagnosed kids as learning disabled, and banished them to speech pathology remediation labs. For talking while Black, children suffered teachers' disdain and low, low expectations. After years of such treatment, the children were at risk of functional illiteracy. In the "Black English Case," Martin Luther King Junior Elementary School Children v. Ann Arbor School District Board, Judge Joiner said it had to stop. He ordered the school to "take appropriate action to overcome linguistic barriers" that vernacular speaking children suffer in mainstream speaking classrooms (Labov, 1995, p. 46). That was 1979.

Today, teachers are still at a loss of how to reach African American students, how to help students' springboard to mainstream American literacy while respecting the language and culture of the children entrusted to them.

Here's a classroom snapshot:

Student: Mrs. Swords, why you be teachin' math in the afternoon?
Teacher: Why do I what?
Student: Why you be teachin' math in the afternoon?
Teacher: Why do I WHAT?
Student: Why you *be teachin' math* in the afternoon?
Teacher: We don't say, "why you *be* teaching math in the afternoon . . ." We
    say, "why *are* you teaching math in the afternoon?"
Student: Oh, OK.

But the next day the child would begin again: "I be walking my dog on weekends." And Swords would reply, "You WHAT?" It was always the same. She would attempt to "correct" the child's "error," but it was clear that no learning was taking place.

Like many teachers, my collaborator, Rachel Swords, began her career in an urban elementary school by correcting every sentence she deemed incorrect. However, she noticed as time went on that her students were asking fewer and fewer questions. She would call for questions and her students would begin: "Mrs. Swords, why you be . . . is you? Ain't you? Never mind." The students knew she was going to correct them. They tried to ask the question in the form the school wanted, but they didn't know how. Rather than risk being corrected, students became silent. After Swords realized why the questions had stopped, she tried another approach. When a child asked "Mrs. Swords, why you be teachin' math after lunch?" she would repeat their question in Mainstream American English ("Why do I teach math after lunch?") and then answer it, also in the same language variety. While this method didn't embarrass the children or hinder their questioning, the children's language did not change. Even though Swords consistently corrected their speech and writing, her students still did not learn the Standard English (SE) forms.

Rachel was perhaps notable in that she did not disdain her students or think less of their intelligence and potential. Not all students are so fortunate. Surely not the students from the Black English Case, and surely not Tamisha. Joni, an urban second grade teacher, was concerned when she discovered that Tamisha could neither read nor write, even at first grade level. She went to the child's first grade teacher to see what had happened. The teacher replied, "Why you can't do *anything* with that child. Did you hear how she talks??!!!" Joni persisted, "What *did* you do with Tamisha?" "I put her in the corner with a coloring book," the first grade teacher explained. Two, three beats passed as Joni processed what this implied. "All year?" Joni asked, incredulously. "Yes," the teacher replied. "The corner. With a coloring book."

Concern with the vernacular dialects our children bring to school has been longstanding. Heath (1983) noted that school desegregation in the 1960s brought out these issues. "Academic questions about how children talk when they come to school and what educators should know and do about oral and written language sounded in practical pleas of teachers who asked: 'What do I do in my classroom on Monday morning?'" (p. 1).

Now, more than three decades later, student language is an ever increasing issue. Christenbury (2000, p. 202) has observed that "[o]ne of the most controversial—and difficult—issues for English teachers is their responsibility to students who speak what is considered 'non-standard' English, English that violates the usage rules we often mistakenly call 'grammar'". English teachers routinely equate Standard English with "grammar," as if other language varieties and styles lack grammar, the systematic and rule-governed backbone of language. Nothing could be further from the truth. Indeed, when traditional approaches assess student language as "error filled," they misdiagnose student writing performance. The child who speaks in a vernacular dialect is not making language errors. Instead, she or he is speaking correctly in the language of the home discourse community. Teachers can build on their students' existing linguistic knowledge to help students learn Standard English, to help students code-switch—choose the language variety *appropriate* to the time, place, audience and communicative purpose. In doing so, we honor linguistic and cultural diversity, all the while fostering students' mastery of the language of wider communication, the de facto lingua franca of the United States.

The motivation for this chapter lies in our desire to bring the insights of 20th-century linguistics to bear on the achievement gap, the "devastating rates at which schools fail African American students" (Rickford, 1999, p. 22). Rickford asserts, "the evidence that schools are failing massive numbers of African students with existing methods is so overwhelming that it would be counterproductive and offensive to continue using them uncritically" (p. 3). Accordingly, this chapter offers insights and strategies which enable teachers to (1) accurately assess African American student writing performance and (2) successfully foster Standard English mastery among African American students who speak and write in a English vernacular. After exploring how traditional language arts methods fail many African American students, relevant key notions from applied linguistics are outlined offering a new vantage on language (from correction to contrast) in the classroom. This approach is illustrated by describing how students discover plural and possessive patterns across everyday English and Standard English. Finally, research is outlined showing that code-switching works and details ways to address language varieties in the reading and writing classroom.

Traditional Language Arts Methods Fail Many African American Students

When an urban teacher tells minority dialect students that their language is wrong and error filled, when she seeks to eradicate vernacular language and culture, not only does she remove the link of relevance, but she assails the child's family and home community. As Smitherman observed: "When you lambaste the home language that kids bring to school, you ain just dissin dem, you talking bout they mommas!" (as cited in Richardson, 2002, p. 677).

In *A Teacher's Introduction to African American English: What a Writing Teacher Should Know*, Redd and Webb (2005) quote William Labov describing the damaging effects traditional correctionist methods have on students: "Research suggests that a teacher's attitude toward a student's speech is 'the most powerful single factor' in determining a teacher's expectations for that student" (Labov, 1995, p. 49; see also Godley, et al., 2006). Indeed, in Michigan's Black English Case, the court found that teachers' "negative attitudes toward the children's language [AAE] led to negative expectations of the children which turned into self-fulfilling prophecies" (Smitherman as cited in Redd &Webb, 2005, p. 44). Moreover, Christenbury (2000, p. 203) observes, "telling or teaching students that their language is *wrong* or *bad* is not only damaging, but *false*." Doing so presupposes that only one language form is "correct" in structure and that form is "good" in all contexts.

The question of why African American students struggle revolves around a thicket of issues concerning poverty, distribution of goods and resources, adequacy of school facilities, the training of teachers in urban schools, language and culture, and ethnic and linguistic bias in standardized tests, just to name a few factors. While all of these issues need to be addressed, my work focuses on approaches to language and culture in the dialectally diverse classroom.

To begin with, we know that many urban African American children speak a language variety—African American English (AAE)—often not valued by school and the broader society (Wolfram & Schilling-Estes, 2006). While some educational researchers have found that dialect difference does not interfere with reading acquisition (Goodman & Goodman, 2000), others have increasingly demonstrated that "dialect is a source of reading interference" for speakers of AAE. Thus, Steffensen, Reynolds, McClure, and Guthrie (1982, p. 296) showed that the syntax of AAE verb phrases resulted in African American students losing information regarding time structure of events in a Standard English reading passage. And in an experiment on vernacular speakers' acquisition of consonant clusters, Labov and Baker (n.d., p. 15) found that "variability in speech is responsible in part for difficulties in decoding" Standard English.

Similarly, in 2004, researchers studying reading abilities in African American children, K-second grade, reported that the degree to which children are familiar with school English has strong positive correlation with the child's ability to read Standard English texts. That is, the greater the child's familiarity with school English, the better their reading achievement, and the lower their familiarity with school English, the lower their reading achievement (Charity, Scarborough, & Griffin, 2004). Thus, while merely speaking a vernacular dialect does not in itself interfere with learning to read Standard English, the child familiar only with their vernacular does suffer in early reading acquisition.

Beyond linguistic structure, cultural conflict lies at the heart of why our schools fail African Americans. Thus, in Harlem, the child's "cultural system . . . opposed the values of the school system, which was seen as the particular possession and expression of the dominant white society" (Labov, 1995, p. 42; see also Godley, et al., 2006). Further, as teachers absorb "widespread, destructive myths about language variation" (Wolfram, 1999, p. 78), their cultural vantage turns to pedagogical damage. In other words, whether Black or White, a teacher is likely to consider a child speaking African American Vernacular English as slower, less able, and less intelligent than the child who speaks Standard English (Labov, 1995). Such *dialect prejudice* reduces teacher expectations for the child's abilities (Baugh, 2000). As teacher expectations are reduced, so potential child performance is diminished (Delpit & Dowdy, 2002; Nieto, 2000). No wonder that under these conditions, "the longer African American inner city kids stay in school, the worse they do" (Rickford, 1996, p. 1).

If we are going to succeed in meeting African American students' educational needs, we must first understand what is going so wrong in the language arts classroom. Teachers envision a single "right way" to construct a sentence (Birch, 2001). Given examples such as "I have two sister and two brother," "Christopher family moved to Spain," and "Last year, he watch all the shows," teachers often assess error in Standard English believing that the child does not know how to show plurality, possession, or tense. Teachers see the student as "leaving off," "forgetting," or struggling with "-eds" and "s", and they correct student writing. This approach seeks to eradicate the child's community language variety.

In my workshops around the country with teachers K-14, I always start by showing a sample student essay or two, illustrating the style of grammar we've been discussing. I ask participants: "Is this grammar familiar to you?" Teachers moan.

Heads nod. I ask teachers, "So, what do you do?" Over the past 10 years, I've asked this question to more than 1000 teachers. To a person, they respond in unison: "We correct the paper." Teachers talk about the *right* way to show possession, plurality and so forth. They red pen that paper, and the next paper, over and over again.

Then I ask: "Is it working? Do students learn the Standard English you're trying to teach?" This time, a sea of heads shakes from side to side. Teachers report: "They just keep using the same bad grammar." And so, teachers invest a huge amount of time correcting—a huge drain on teacher resources and energy—without the desired student payoff in learning. Indeed, it is not surprising that attempts to "correct" children's language do not produce change in their performance. As Gilyard (1991) shares in his account of his life as a Black child in the American educational system, "generations of Black English speakers have been subjected to 'correction' programs that haven't worked" (p. 114). Redd and Webb (2005) affirm: "We cannot expect correcting students' speech to improve their speaking or reading or writing" (p. 79). And experts from applied linguistics also attest that while "various strategies can be useful for learning Standard English equivalents . . . [o]ne that does not work is correcting vernacular features" (Wolfram, Adger, & Christian, 1999, p. 122).

So, the very approach teachers have tended to take—correcting student language—is the very approach that doesn't work! Dialectologists point out that for over 30 years, linguists have known that correction fails to teach Standard English to minority dialect speakers: Indeed, language researcher Anne Piestrup "found that vernacular speakers who were corrected when they used vernacular features actually used more, not fewer vernacular features over time" (Adger, Wolfram, & Christian, 2007, p. 109).

Thus the traditional approach attempts to correct, repress, eradicate, or subtract student language which differs from the standard written target. But once we recognize that language comes in different varieties and styles and that each is systematic, and rule governed, a different classroom response to language becomes possible (Redd & Webb, 2005; Smitherman, 1981; Sweetland, Rickford & Sweetland 2004; Wheeler, 2005; Wheeler & Swords, 2006).

Instead of seeking to correct or eradicate styles of language, we may *add* language varieties to the child's linguistic toolbox, bringing a pluralistic vantage to language in the classroom. This approach maintains the language of the student's home community, and also adds mainstream American English, a linguistic tool needed for access to our broader society.

Key Notions from Applied Linguistics

A cluster of notions from applied linguistics are central to our work with language varieties in the classroom: *dialect, language variety, style,* and *language transfer.* Three insights about language underlie all these terms:

1. Language is structured.
2. Language varies by circumstance of use.
3. Difference is *distinct from* deficiency.

A *dialect* is "variety of the language associated with a particular regional or social group" (Wolfram & Schilling-Estes, 2006, p. 391). Since everyone is associated with a particular regional or social group, everyone speaks a dialect. Also known as *language varieties*, dialects vary in structure (sound, vocabulary, grammar and social conventions for structuring conversations) on the basis of speaker "age, socio-economic status (SES), gender, ethnic group membership, and geographic region" (Adger, et al., 2007, p. 31). This means that so-called "standard" English is a dialect of English. Contrary to popular understanding, "'[d]ialect' does not mean a marginal, archaic, rustic, or degraded mode of speech" (Pullum, 1999, p. 44).

While variation in language structure is always present, a different kind of variation lies in the public's *attitudes* toward language. "Standard" English is often called "good" English while "non-Standard" English is considered "bad." Not based on linguistic grounds, these judgments are sociopolitical in nature. Thus, what we call the *standard* is the language variety "associated with middle-class, educated, native speakers of the region" (Wolfram & Schilling-Estes, 2006, p. 315). People regard this variety as good because they regard its speakers as meritorious, a judgment having nothing to do with an inherent structural superiority of "Standard" English.

Vernaculars (AKA non-standard varieties) are those "varieties of a language which are not classified as standard dialects" (Wolfram & Schilling-Estes, 2006, p. 14). They contain socially stigmatized features such as the so-called English double negative ("I ain't got none") or irregular verb forms ("I seen it"). Just as the public holds standard varieties in high regard because of their high regard for their speakers, the public holds vernaculars in low regard and typically views its speakers with disregard. The judgment of inferiority is sociopolitical and has nothing to do with any structural inadequacy of vernacular dialects.

"Standard" English is a misnomer, implying that only one standard exists. Yet, we can readily identify a range of standards, from formal Standard English (written Standard English of grammar books, reference works, and the most established mainstream authors), informal Standard English (a spoken variety defined by the absence of socially stigmatized structures), as well as regional standards (the accepted dialect of English in a particular region).

Language transfer, a concept coming to us from second language acquisition studies, lets us understand how a student who writes "My goldfish name is Scaley" is not making mistakes in Standard English. More than 50 years ago, in Linguistics across Cultures, ESL specialist Robert Lado (1957) explained that the patterns of people's first language (sound, word endings, and grammar) will transfer into how they talk and write in a second language. A conversation I heard recently at a Chinese takeout illustrates this. A customer had asked the woman behind the counter, "Ma'am, could I please have two forks, two plates, and two napkins?" to which the Chinese owner replied, "Yes sir, two fork, two plate, and two napkin." Since Chinese shows plurality by number words and sentence context, that grammar pattern transferred into the woman's English exchange with her customer.

Language transfer also applies when we are talking about a person learning to speak or write in a second dialect. So, when an African American student writes or says "I have two dog and two cat," we see the grammar of community language transfer into school expression. In such examples, we hear the grammar echoes of the student's home language variety.

These basic linguistic facts (i.e., that all language and dialects are structured, that features of a first dialect transfer in as students learn Standard English as a second dialect (SESD)) provide teachers the tools to positively transform their language arts classroom, and succeed in teaching Standard English with African American vernacular speakers.

A New Vantage on Language in the Classroom: From Correction to Contrast

Swords comments on her own transition from the traditional to the linguistically informed approach. She had noticed that home speech patterns transferred into many of her students' writings. As a correctionist, she would explain what "we do and do not say". For example, when a student wrote, "the three friend went for a walk," she initially responded by correcting her student's grammar and explaining that '-s' goes on the end of plural nouns. But after learning about code-switching and contrastive analysis in Wheeler's class on language varieties in American Schools in the master's in teaching (MAT) program, she turned to a linguistically informed approach.

The first notion students need is that variation is natural—in life, and in language. We approach this by exploring how we choose clothing to fit the setting; Swords asks students what kind of clothes they wear to school. Since Rachel's school has a strict dress code, the students typically name the school uniform—collared shirts, slacks, and belts. She then asks students what they like to wear on the weekends. Students typically respond "jeans, tee shirts, sweatpants, and swimsuits." Extending the discussion, Rachel brainstorms with the class on other places or events that they might attend where more formal clothing is expected. The students respond, "church, weddings, and graduations." Then, they decide that informal clothing is more appropriate for playing basketball, watching TV, and going to the pool.

Talking about how we vary our clothing according to the context sets the stage for students to explore how their language varies by context. In Swords' class, students explain that "yes, sir" and "excuse me" are formal and that "yo, wa's up?" and "he ain' nobody" are more informal. As students thought back on earlier class discussions, Rachel recorded the following on the board for group discussion:

> Student 1: Yo, Mz. Swords! Dat junk be *tight*!
> Student 2: McKinzie! You ain sposed ta talk t' Mrs. Swords dat way.
> Student 1: OK. Mrs. Swords. Dat stuff be *cool*!

Clearly, students come to school already having a good grasp of language *style* (the variation language shows in levels of formality), within their own variety, here, AAE. In this way, Rachel's students were able to use their own prior knowledge to define formal and informal language.

Students Discover Plural Patterns Across Everyday and Standard English

Rachel then leads the students to apply their understanding about shifts in style to the grammar of sentences. Using chart paper, she creates two columns of sentences drawn from her students' own writing, the left column shows the everyday English ("I have two dog") that many children speak and the right column shows the same sentences translated into Standard English ("I have two dogs"). She labels the SE examples as "formal English" and the everyday examples as "informal English." That year, the class began with plural patterns, because Swords knew that students would immediately see the difference between the formal and informal usage.

In the beginning of the year, students, following the dominant language ideology of our society, may exclaim "Oh, that's wrong. All the ones on that side (informal) are wrong and the ones on the other side (formal) are right" (Godley, et. al., 2006). To address the students' confusion, just remind them that we all vary our style (both clothing and language) setting by setting. Swords offers her own style shifts as example. At home, she tells the students, she might say: "I'm fixin' to go the store—ya'll need anything?" However, she wouldn't say to her fellow Virginia teachers "I'm fixin' to make copies—ya'll need any?" She knows this language variety is not appropriate at school. Instead, she might say, "I'm going to make some copies; do you need any?" So, Rachel talks to the students about how she changes her language setting by setting. She told them that when she makes these language choices, she is *code-switching*.

To *code-switch* is to choose the pattern of language appropriate to the context. To support children in learning how to code-switch between informal and formal language patterns, we use a classroom technique called *contrastive analysis* (Rickford, Sweetland, & Rickford, 2004;Schierloh, 1991; Taylor, 1991; Wheeler, 2005; Wheeler & Swords, 2006). In contrastive analysis, the teacher leads students in discovery learning as they explore how the grammar of their everyday English compares and contrasts with the grammar of school English. Commanding explicitly and consciously the differences between them, students then code-switch to choose the variety appropriate to the setting. In this way, we apply Marzano's #1 most successful strategy—comparison and contrast—to grammar (Marzano, Pickering, & Pollock, 2001).

Of course, the contrasts of formal/informal (or home/school) are over-simplifications of the different ways that language is patterned by variety and style, but the key point we want to convey was one of contrast—that different language patterns are appropriate to different contexts. *Formal/informal* is a user-friendly way to get that notion across with students, teachers, administrators and the lay public.

Moving back to the chart, Swords leads her class in contrastive analysis. She asks students if they understand what each sentence means and if, "I have two dog," has the same meaning as "I have two dogs." Again, the class will agree they do so, she asks: "Ok, so the informal and the formal sentences have the same meaning. What differences do you see between the two columns?"

Since the class had previously talked about nouns and pronouns, the children are easily able to articulate responses. One child explained: "In this one [the formal form], the noun has an '-s' on it." Swords asked: "What does that mean? What is the '-s' doing there?" They said: "It's making it more than one." The class talked about how the '-s' makes it "more than one." She then explains that this is the way we show "more than one" in formal language (see Table 11.1). To help guide children, Rachel creates a heading—"How to show 'more than one'"—for the contrastive patterns they were discovering. Under the formal column, following the children's observation, Swords wrote "-s."

Then, the class looked at the informal example to explore its patterns. Reminding the children that the examples had the same meaning, Swords asks how the informal sentence shows us that the number is more than one. One child said: "You know it's more than one because it has the number 'two' in it." So Rachel wrote in the column on informal examples "number words," and commented that "number words show there's more than one." Then the class looked at "Taylor likes cat." There's nothing in that sentence that tells you it's more than one cat. The children explained: "You have to look at the whole paragraph." So Swords wrote, "other words in the paragraph," and commented "other words in the paragraph show there's more than one." Next the class looked at "All the boy are here today." Rachel asked: "What tells you there is more than one boy?" One child replied: "The other words in the sentence—'all'." So, she wrote on the chart, "Other words in the sentence." Actually, the child elaborated his understanding, "Mrs. Swords, it say 'all.' You can't have part of a boy. If part of a boy come then all of the boy come. There got to be more than one boy." Rachel amplified that common knowledge is another way we know we mean more than one. She wrote "common knowledge" on the chart. In this way, the children explored and named the contrasts in grammatical patterning between formal and informal language. The plural chart (along with charts for possessive, showing past time, and subject/verb agreement) stay up on the classroom walls for easy reference during the editing process in children's writers' workshop time.

Table **11.1** Discovering the Rules for Plural Patterns Across Language Varieties

Informal English	Formal English
I have two dog	I have two dogs
Taylor likes cat	Taylor likes cats
All the boy . . .	All the boys . . .
"How to show more than one":	
Number words	
Other words in paragraph	
Other words in sentence	
Common knowledge	

Students Discover Possessive Patterns Across Language Varieties

Swords soon based another lesson around students comparing and contrasting sentences with formal and informal possessive structures (see Table 11.2). To lead this discovery, Swords wrote the term "possessive" on the board, and asked if the students knew what it meant. As needed, she explains that possession means "someone owns something" and provides several examples.

Students looked closely at the underlined words on the chart and worked in small groups to find ways to describe how each language variety expresses ownership. When the entire class reconvened, students shared their responses and constructed a rule for using possessive patterns in the two language varieties. Students reported that in informal English, we show possession by the pattern *owner + owned* ("the boy coat"). However, inside formal English, we show possession by a different pattern: *owner + 's + owned* ("the boy's coat"). Once students confirmed that this rule covered all the data at hand, they looked for and made up additional examples. Through these instructional strategies, teachers can lead students to discover the grammatical rules of each language variety.

TABLE 11.2 Discovering the Rules for Possessive Patterns Across Language Varieties

Informal English	Formal English
Taylor cat is black	Taylor's cat is black
The boy coat is torn	The boy's coat is torn
A giraffe neck is long	A giraffe's neck is long
Did you see the teacher pen?	Did you see the teacher's pen?
_____	_____
_____	_____
_____	_____

What is the rule for using possessive patterns in informal English?
What is the rule for using possessive patterns in formal English?

Directions: Write three more informal and three more formal sentences that include possessive patterns. Then answer the questions.

Research Shows that Code-Switching Works

Research shows that code-switching is highly successful in teaching Standard English to vernacular speakers. In Chicago, Taylor (1991) studied student performance across two kinds of college writing classroom. With one group, she used the traditional English department techniques and, in the other, she led her students in explicit grammar discovery, contrasting the grammatical patterns of AAE and SE. The control group, using the correctionist model, showed an 8.5% *increase* in African American features in their writing after 11 weeks, but the experimental group, using *contrastive analysis*, showed a remarkable 59.3% *decrease* in African American vernacular features. Taylor (1991, p. 150) observed that students had been neither "aware of their dialect" nor of "grammatical black English features that interfere in their writing." By contrasting the language varieties, students were able to learn the detailed differences between the two, thereby limiting the AAE features transferring into their Standard English expression

Parallel results come from a New York study of African American elementary students. Educational psychologists Howard Fogel and Linnea Ehri (2000) analyzed whether traditional approaches or contrastive ones were more successful in teaching African American children Standard English. While students in the traditional groups showed *no improvement*, students learning through contrastive analysis nearly *doubled* in their ability to produce Standard English forms.

The same kind of approach was also implemented by teachers in DeKalb County, Georgia, who helped young speakers of minority dialects explicitly contrast their mother tongue with the standard. Thus, when a fifth grader answered a question with a double negative ("not no more"), the teacher prompted the student to "code-switch," to which the student replied, "not any more." This program has been designated a "center of excellence" by the National Council of Teachers of English. The bidialectal approach is further affirmed by Sweetland's research on sociolinguistic approaches to teaching writing in African American classrooms. Her results from a study of 13 intact upper elementary classes (188 students, nine teachers) in the Midwest indicate that "in classrooms where dialect awareness lessons and Contrastive Analysis were used, students developed significantly more positive writing self-confidence over the course of ten weeks" than students who continued in traditional classroom approaches (Sweetland, 2006, p. 148).

Finally, results from Rachel Swords' third grade classroom attest strongly to the effectiveness of contrastive analysis and code-switching, not only in fostering Standard English mastery, but in supporting increased student performance across the board. From 1997–2000, under traditional language arts methods, Swords' Black students languished 30 points under in achievement compared to her White students. In 2001, her first year implementing code-switching, Swords *eliminated the achievement gap* in her classroom between Black and White students: With code-switching, Swords' Black students equaled or outperformed her White students on all NCLB tests. These results have held constant in each subsequent year. In 2006, with a class of 19 students (three White, two Hispanic, one Native American, one Asian, 12 Black), her overall class pass rate was 100% for reading, 100% for math, 94% for science and 94% for social studies—one White student failed science and social studies. Thus, in 2006, 100% of Rachel's Black students passed 100% of the yearend NCLB tests. Further affirmation comes from the scores of other teachers at her grade level. Of the other teachers on Rachel's team, three have adopted a code-switching approach, and one has not. The three adopting teachers' classes scored 83%, 85% and 87% on NCLB tests of writing while the teacher not adopting code-switching continues to struggle. Overall, her class failed in writing; only 65% passed writing. Clearly, contrastive analysis holds great promise in fostering Standard English mastery in our schools (Rickford, 1999; Rickford, Sweetland, & Rickford, 2004; Sweetland, 2006; Wheeler & Swords, 2006).

Language Varieties in Reading and Writing

Swords' interest in contrastive analysis as a literary tool is reflected in her literary selections. She begins with *Flossie and the Fox* by Patricia McKissack (1986). In this story, Flossie speaks in everyday English patterns while the fox speaks in a Standard dialect. This book quickly became a favorite among her students, who chose it for every student-selected read-aloud. At the third reading, children spontaneously joined in as a chorus call of a favorite line: "Shucks! You aine no fox. You a rabbit, all the time trying to fool me." Kids were *engaged* with this reading.

After contrasting several different grammatical patterns and reading literature reflecting differing language varieties, students implement their new linguistic know-how within their own writing. When the task is to produce formal English, Rachel makes editing into a game as she gives each student a colored highlighter to use during editing. After students have completed the substantive content of their reports, in the endgame, during the editing process, children highlight their successes in matching the patterns of Standard English. If students find a sentence in informal patterns, they change it to formal English, and then highlight. Students are enthusiastic about noting their grammar successes.

By the same token, as children construct story narrative, they choose a range of language styles to build character. Characters wouldn't seem very human or real if they talked like an encyclopedia. So, to create characters with voice, students use the Everyday cadences of the regional or social group they're trying to evoke. During one class discussion, Swords invited students to explore how different characters use different speech patterns for effect. Several children mentioned, *Flossie and the Fox*. Then, the class discussed how the different voices of Flossie and the fox made the book more interesting. Following the discussion, the class created dialogue for a story they were writing together about a teacher and a giant cockroach. When Swords asked who would speak in what language style, the students decided the teacher would speak informal English while the cockroach would use formal speech. After completing several lines of the story, Swords asked the students to think about the characters their own stories and decide the speech style each would use. Some had each character speak with formal English, others chose each informal, while other students mixed it up with both formal and informal dialogue.

Swords has observed tremendous growth in her students' command of language. Prior to teaching code-switching, students simply guessed what language form was expected. One student explained: "It's because you don't know how to say it and you're just wondering how you're suppose to say it." Now that Swords uses comparison and contrast to teach grammar, her students are becoming clear about the differences between formal and informal language and when to use each style.

David's work is a good example. He wrote Rachel a series of stories about Spy Mouse, a school detective. In "Spy Mouse and the Broken Globe," the mouse spoke informally ("I won't do nothin' to you"). Rachel, circulating around the class during writing time, asked David about the informal language in his story. David was clear: "Why Mrs. Swords, *I* know the difference between formal and informal English, but Spy Mouse doesn't." Indeed, David's author's note used formal English patterns

("My name is David. I am in the third grade. I like math and science"). In this way, David was able to independently articulate the reasons for his language choices, an impressive accomplishment for any student, let alone an urban third grader.

So, through code-switching and contrastive analysis, students come to understand that just as one tool doesn't suit all jobs, neither does one language variety suit all communication tasks. Indeed, a well-stocked linguistic toolbox offers a diverse range of language forms to the mature speaker and writer. We *add* Standard English to our children's repertoires.

However, the issue of who learns what language is deeply political, rooted in the social and cultural structure of our society (Nieto, 2000; Wolfram & Schilling-Estes, 2006). It can be a very damaging human experience for an AAE speaking child to learn mainstream American English while the teacher dismisses AAE as broken and error filled.

With contrastive analysis and code-switching, we move to break the cycle. Exercising their analytic eye, the teacher and all students, Black, White, Asian, Native American, Hispanic, alike, engage in critical thinking as they discover and analyze the patterns of diverse language varieties. In doing so, we take steps to unbind the "widespread, destructive myths about language variation" that underlie the dialect prejudice so rampant in our nation (Wolfram, 1999, p. 78).

Techniques of contrastive analysis also offer students tangible help in interpreting standardized test questions. Students come to understand that when the test asks whether a sentence is "correct" or "incorrect," it is asking for the patterns of the mainstream written language. This helps students know to choose the Standard English answers on test questions. Indeed, as Rickford (1999) observes, "teaching methods which DO take vernacular dialects into account in teaching the standard work better than those which DO NOT" (p. 1).

Conclusion

In Ann Arbor, 30 years ago, Judge Joiner decided: "[N]o child should be deprived of equal educational opportunity because of the failure of an educational agency to take appropriate action to overcome linguistic barriers" (Labov, 1995, p. 46). We have slept through the alarm. African American children still suffer educational failure. The question remains: *How do* we take "appropriate action to overcome linguistic barriers?"

We know the answer. We have known it for more than 30 years. The barriers that interfere with African American children mastering Standard English lie primarily not within the children themselves, but within the assumptions, beliefs and pedagogy of the U.S. educational system. From the deficit perspective of children "making mistakes" in Standard English, our schools have failed long and hard scaffold the new literacy knowledge we're trying to teach. We know the answer.

Linguistics offers us insights and research-based strategies for teaching Standard English with minority dialect students. When students write My goldfish name is Scaley or Ellen Goodman essay say it all, linguistically informed teachers recognize the grammar rules of everyday English. We then build on students' existing knowledge (community English grammar) to add new knowledge (Standard

English). Our strategies, contrastive analysis and code-switching, employ the scientific method, skills of critical thinking, and the #1 most successful teaching strategy—comparison and contrast—as applied to discovery learning of grammar (Marzano, et al., 2001).

We have said we want to teach our children the language of wider communication, Standard English. Which approach shall we take? The traditional approach that can inadvertently silence children or the research-based, linguistic approach—contrastive analysis and code-switching—an approach that affirms the children's voices and succeeds, fostering Standard English mastery? The choice is ours and all of our futures depend on it.

Discussion Questions and Activities

1. Is your current approach to grammar working?
   a What works? Why?
   b What doesn't work? Why?
2. Is all language linguistically equal? What does it mean for a style of speech or writing to be "linguistically equal" to another?
3. Is all language socially equal? What correspondence do you see between prestige of a given social group and prestige of their language? Give specific examples.
4. With your peers, generate a list of settings where
   a the most formal registers of Standard English would be wildly inappropriate
   b the vernacular patterns of community speech would be highly appropriate.
5. Choose a setting (the mall, the beach, a formal dance, and so forth). Draw a picture illustrating how a person or people would dress, stand, and behave in that setting. In your picture, draw a balloon illustrating the style of language you might expect them to use in that setting.
   [*Authors' note*: This chapter is a revision of Wheeler, R. S., & Swords, R. (2004). Codeswitching: Tools of language and culture transform the dialectally diverse classroom. *Language Arts*, 81(6), 470–480.]

References

Adger, C. T., Wolfram, W., & Christian, D. (2007). *Dialects in Schools and Communities*. Mahwah, NJ: Lawrence Erlbaum Associates, Inc.

Baugh, J. (2000). *Beyond Ebonics: Linguistic Pride and Racial Prejudice*. New York: Oxford University Press.

Birch, B. (2001). Grammar Standards: It's All in Your Attitude. *Language Arts*, 78, 535–542.

Charity, A. H., Scarborough, H. S., & Griffin, D. M. (2004). Familiarity with School English in African American Children and its Relation to Early Reading Achievement. *Child Development*, 75(5), 1340–1356.

Christenbury, L. (2000). *Making the Journey: Being and Becoming a Teacher of English Language Arts*, 2nd edn. Portsmouth, NH: Boynton/Cook Heinemann.

Delpit, L., & Dowdy, J. (2002). *The Skin that We Speak: Thoughts on Language and Culture in the Classroom*. New York: The New Press.

Fogel, H., & Ehri, L. (2000). Teaching Elementary Students who Speak Black English Vernacular to Write in Standard English: Effects of Dialect transformation Practice. *Contemporary Educational Psychology*, 25, 212–35.

Gilyard, K. (1991). *Voices of the Self: A Study of Language Competence.* Detroit, MI: Wayne State University Press.

Godley, A., Sweetland, J., Wheeler, R. S., Minnicci, A., & Carpenter, B. (2006). Preparing Teachers for the Dialectally Diverse Classroom. *Educational Researcher*, 35(8), 30–37.

Goodman, Y., & Goodman, D. (2000). I Hate 'Postrophe s: Issues of Dialect and Reading Proficiency. In J. Peyton (Ed.). *Language in Action: New Studies of Language in Society.* Cresskill, NJ: Hampton Press.

Heath, S. B. (1983). *Ways with Words: Language, Life, and Work in Communities and Classrooms.* Cambridge: Cambridge University Press.

Labov, W. (1995). Can Reading Failure be Reversed? A Linguistic Approach to the Question. In V. Gadsen, & D. Wagner (Eds.). *Literacy among African- American Youth.* Cresskill, NJ: Hampton Press.

——, & Baker, B. (n.d.). *Linguistic Component, African American Literacy and Culture Project.* Retrieved August 13, 2007, from the William Labov website: http://www.ling.upenn.edu/~wlabov/FinalReport.html.

Lado, R. (1957). *Linguistics across Cultures.* Ann Arbor, MI: University of Michigan Press.

Marzano, R., Pickering, D., & Pollock, J. (2001). *Classroom Instruction that Works: Research-Based Strategies for Increasing Student Achievement.* Alexandria, VA: Association for Supervision and Curriculum Development.

McKissack, P. (1986). *Flossie & the Fox.* New York: Dial Press.

McWhorter, J. (1998). *The Word on the Street: Debunking the Myth of Pure Standard English.* New York: Plenum Press.

Nieto, S. (2000). *Affirming Diversity: The Sociopolitical Context of Multicultural Education*, 3rd edn. New York: Longman.

Piestrup, A. M. (1973). *Black Dialect Interference and Accommodations of Reading Instruction in First Grade.* Berkeley, CA: University of California, Language and Behavior Research Lab. (Monograph 4, ED119113.)

Pullum, G. (1999). African American Vernacular English is not Standard English with Mistakes. In R. S. Wheeler (Ed.). *The Workings of Language: From Prescriptions to Perspectives.* Westport, CT: Praeger.

Redd, T. M., & Webb K. (2005). *Teacher's Introduction to African American English: What a Writing Teacher Should Know.* Urbana, IL: NCTE.

Richardson, E. (2002). "To Protect and Serve": African American Female Literacies. *College Composition and Communication*, 53, 675–704.

Rickford, J. R. (1996). *The Oakland Ebonics Decision: Commendable Attack on the Problem.* Original text of the article printed in the *San José Mercury News*, December 26, 1996. Retrieved August 13, 2007, from http://www.stanford.edu/~rickford/ebonics/SJMN-OpEd.html.

——. (1999). Language Diversity and Academic Achievement in the Education of African American Students: An Overview of the Issues. In C. Adger, D. Christian, & O. Taylor (Eds.). *Making the Connection: Language and Academic Achievement among African American Students.* Washington, DC: Center for Applied Linguistics.

——, Sweetland, J., & Rickford, A. E. (2004). African American English and Other Vernaculars in Education: A Topic-Coded Bibliography. *Journal of English Linguistics*, 32, 230–320.

Schierloh, J. M. (1991).Teaching Standard English Usage: A Dialect-Based Approach. *Adult Learning*, 2, 20–22.

Smitherman, G. (1981). "What go round come round": King in Perspective. In G. Smitherman (Ed.). *Talkin that Talk: Language, Culture and Education in African America.* New York: Routledge.

Steffensen, M., Reynolds, R., McClure, E., & Guthrie, L. (1982). Black English Vernacular and Reading Comprehension: A Close Study of Third, Sixth, and Ninth Graders. *Journal of Reading Behavior*, 3, 285–298.

Sweetland, J. (2006). Teaching Writing in the African American Classroom: A Sociolinguistic Approach. Unpublished doctoral dissertation, Stanford University.

Taylor, H. U. (1991). *Standard English, Black English, and Bidialectalism: A Controversy.* New York: Peter Lang.

Wheeler, R. S. (2005). Code-Switch to Teach Standard English. Teaching English in the World. *English Journal*, 94(5), 108–112.

——, & Swords, R. (2006). *Code-Switching: Teaching Standard English in Urban Classrooms*. Urbana, IL: NCTE.

Wolfram, W. (1999). Repercussions from the Oakland Ebonics Controversy—the critical Role of Dialect Awareness Programs. In C. T. Adger, D. Christian, & O. Taylor (Eds.). *Making the Connection: Language and Academic Achievement among African American Students*. McHenry, IL:Delta Systems.

——, Adger, C. and Christian, D. (1999). *Dialects in the Schools and Communities*. Mahwah, NJ: Lawrence Erlbaum Associates, Inc.

——, & Schilling-Estes, N. (2006). *American English*, 2nd edn. Oxford: Blackwell.

12
There's No "1" Way to Tell a Story

LAURIE KATZ AND TEMPII CHAMPION

Four-year-old Reggie stands next to his teacher in front of his fellow classmates who are sitting on the floor in a half-circle. He starts telling the following story:

> *Reggie*: Three little bears, one little bear made he house with brick, what's dey called?
> *C* (another child): Three little pigs.
> *Reggie*: Da house, Da house.
> *Teacher*: Ok, go ahead so he went to the house.
> *Reggie*: An' dey made a house an' one little bear was sticks, an' one, an' one little an' one
> *Teacher*: Um, um.
> *Reggie*: I don't know da other house.
> *Teacher*: Something about the other house you want to tell us?
> *Reggie*: It's . . .
> *Teacher*: Is that it?
> *Reggie*: Yes.
> *Teacher*: Thank you Reggie.

Reggie's story appears to be a retelling of the *Three Little Pigs*, a well-known classic American folktale. How will Reggie's teacher evaluate his oral telling of this story? Will the teacher decide that Reggie has difficulty sequencing the story? Will the teacher decide that he has the wrong characters in his story? Will the teacher find his story coherent with an opening and an ending? These are typical questions posed by teachers when they listen to a young child tell a story.

Many published written and oral versions of this story exist. Examples include *The Three Little Pigs* by Steven Kellogg, *The Three Little Pigs* by Barry Moser, *Three Little Pigs and the Big Bad Wolf*, by Glen Rounds, *The Three Little Pigs* by David Wiesner, *The True Story of the Three Little Pigs* by Jon Scieszka and finally an oral version of *Three Little Pigs* by Eshu Bumpus. All are different versions of the same story. These differences may include the title, characters, and language, but the plot or "storyline" is basically the same.

Even though there may be acceptable published versions of the same story, typically, teachers evaluate all children's narratives using one standard format. This format emphasizes the basic parts of a story, beginning, middle, end, and includes story elements of characters, setting, events, plot/problem solution and theme. Many of these formats are based on adaptations of story grammar and primarily help Caucasian children from middle- to upper-middle-class families. Typically, these children use specific narrative structures in their homes that are consistent with the narrative structures used in school programs (Heath, 1983). However, literacy scholars have noted that story grammar and other narrative analyses that use stage theories oversimplify the complexity of how children from diverse linguistic backgrounds learn to use narratives in a range of social contexts (i.e. home, school, community). Unfortunately, children who don't follow a standard format may be perceived as deficient in their development and perhaps at risk for needing remedial or special education services.

Learning a standard format helps children become more successful in responding to standardized tests, since these tests tend to evaluate story comprehension on the basis of recognition of story elements and story parts. Even so, when evaluating children's narratives we argue for multiple formats that will consider the wide variety of young children's narrative styles and structures (Bloome, Champion, Katz, Morton, & Muldrow, 2001) they bring into the classroom from their homes and communities. This chapter will first discuss the importance of oral literacy as part of children's literacy development. Second, research from three studies of the ways children tell stories will demonstrate how following only one type of analysis may not identify positive linguistic features in children's narratives and therefore be misleading. Finally, we suggest strategies for integrating the use of young children's own narrative structures and styles into standards-based teaching for oral language development.

Oral Literacy

Learning how to communicate orally provides an important foundation for reading and writing (Ohio Office of Early Childhood Education, 2004). Children's use of words, phrases and sentences, their sensitivity to the sound system of words, and their understanding of word meanings influence their beginning attempts to read and write. The early development of oral communication skills is often assessed through oral stories. Children tell stories not in isolation but through interactions with their peers and adults in their lives who help them make sense of their world. Their stories consist of narratives that form chronologies of past or ongoing events abstracted from real or imagined experiences. From research grounded in sociolinguistic ethnography (Gumperz, 1986) and related approaches to the study of language as a social and cultural phenomenon (Rowe, 1994; Schieffelin & Ochs, 1986; Street, 1993), children's stories include narratives that contain the social and cultural practices of the groups to which they belong, that is, their families, schools and other community groups. These experiences are not inherently packaged as stories with beginnings, middles, and ends, neither do their experiences necessarily provide coherent relationships between events. Rather, stories transform experiences into events and impose boundaries, a chronology, and a set of coherent relationships onto experiences (Solsken & Bloome, 1992). From this perspective, storytelling is important to oral language development because it serves as a mechanism for transforming experiences into an orderly sequence of meaningful events.

The National Council of Teachers of English (NCTE) and the International Reading Association (IRA) address the importance of diversity in oral literacy through four of their 12 English language arts standards that address oral literacy (Ohio Center for Curriculum and Assessment, 2002). These standards are:

- *Standard 4: Communicate Effectively with a Variety of Audiences and for Different Purposes.* Children are expected to learn how to adjust their spoken and visual language for different audiences. They should be able to use certain words, phrases and sentences with their peers and others words, phrases and sentences for communicating with adults and other audiences.
- *Standard 9: Teachers Should Help Children Develop an Understanding of and Respect for Diversity in Language Use.* Children's stories reflect their identities, experiences, places, as well as people who are important in their lives. When their diverse stories are respected and validated, children feel and act like active members of the school culture.
- *Standard 10: Teachers Should Help Children Use Their First Language to Develop Competency in English Language Arts.* English language learners (ELLs) whose first language is not English come to school like other children, speaking the language spoken within their families and communities. According to Cummins (2000), the best way for children to learn is for them to use their first language to develop competency in the English language arts curriculum.
- *Standard 12: Teachers Need to Help Students Use Spoken, Written and Visual Language to Accomplish Their Own Purposes.* Children's communicative purposes are varied: They communicate what they've learned, their desires, their feelings, and other types of information orally, through their gestures as well as through their writings. Teachers, therefore, need to help students understand how to use language to accomplish different purposes.

These standards not only demonstrate the importance of oral language development but also clarify the need for teachers to take into account children's cultural and social practices in the development of oral literacy (Champion, Katz, Muldrow, & Dail, 1999).

In the following discussion, we illustrate how different narrative patterns are highlighted and interpreted when implementing particular narrative analyses of African American and Haitian children from three different research studies, the Storytelling Project, the Afterschool Study, and the Haitian Study. The children from these studies were born in the United States and between the ages of 4 and 10 when the narratives were collected. All three studies found that children have a wide repertoire of narrative styles and structures. To demonstrate the variations in the narratives, descriptions of children's narrative patterns will be presented in two parts. The first part will present variations in children's narrative structures and styles, while the second part describes how the children's narratives reflect children's social patterns for creating their identities and other relationships.

Variations in Narrative Patterns

One of the standard formats used in classrooms to analyze children's narratives is adaptations of the evaluative or high point analysis. The evaluative analysis has been developed by Peterson and McCabe (1983) and McCabe and Peterson (1991) based on Labov's work of a fully formed narrative with African American children (1972) (see Table 12.1). Labov describes a fully formed narrative as consisting of: an abstract (a summation of the story), orientation (setting and characters), a complicating action (the backbone of the series of events leading up to the climax), an evaluation (tells the listener why the story is being told), a resolution (follows the result of the problem or climax), and coda (signals the narrative is finished). The evaluative analysis consists of seven narrative structures. The first structure follows Labov's classic structure of a fully formed narrative where a child is able to develop a topic or theme. The other six structures are developed by Peterson and McCabe (ending at highpoint, leapfrogging, chronological, two-event narratives, disorientated, and miscellaneous). One of the concerns with an evaluative analysis format is that children's narrative development is perceived as hierarchical following a linear pattern with stages only occurring at specific ages.

In the Afterschool Study, Champion (2003) examined the narratives of 15 African American children from 6 to 10 years old using the evaluative analysis. The following narrative is from an 8-year-old African American female. She is

TABLE 12.1 Evaluative Analysis

Structures	Description
1 Classic – developed by Labov (1972)	Speaker provides "a complete narrative (which) begins with an orientation, proceeds to the complicating action, is suspended at the focus of the evaluation before the resolution, concludes with resolution, and returns the listener to the present with the coda" (p. 369)
2 Ending at highpoint	Speaker presents a series of events leading up to the complicating action. The highpoint is reached, but there is no resolution
3 Leapfrogging	Speaker jumps from one event to another
4 Chronological	Speaker provides a list of events that have occurred without an evaluative mode
5 Two event narratives (McCabe & Peterson, 1991)	Speaker uses a few sentences that are difficult to analyze. Narrator may provide two successive events, and then go over and over them, often providing "extensive orientation and evaluation about these two events" (p. 45)
6 Disoriented	Speaker is either confused or disoriented about the action described in the narrative and therefore is not understood by the listener
7 Miscellaneous	Speaker provides narratives that do not fit any of the preceding patterns

Source. Adapted from Labov, 1972; McCabe and Peterson, 1991; Peterson and McCabe, 1983.

responding to the prompt "Tell me a time when you were scared." The analysis of this narrative highlights the problems with evaluating the leapfrogging structure produced by many African American children according to only this type of analysis. The leapfrogging structure is a format in which children jump from one event to another unsystematically:

Scared

01	C. When when when it's dark in my room on Halloween
02	C. 'cause my my cousin
03	C. I was sleepin'
04	C. My cousin he he cut all da lights off
05	C. I wasn' asleep
06	C. but my cousin he cut all da lights off
07	C. an' I started to scream
08	C. an' my cousin he kep' laughin'
09	C. an' my mother she tol' my cousin's mother
10	C. an' my cousin got in trouble
11	C. an' den another time when we went trick or treatin' on Halloween night
12	C. I got a big bag o' candy
13	C. an' den my cousin he had he was like um one o' my cousins was ninja
14	C. an' he had dis sword dis fake sword
15	C. an' my other cousin he was um Freddy Krueger and he had dese claws
16	C. an' I was scared 'cause he was I was scared
17	C. an' las' night I had dream dat me
18	C. me an' you know Tierra?
19	C. me an' Tierra, she came over my house
20	C. me an' Tierra was playin' outside in da dark in da middle o' da night
21	C. an' an' Freddy Krueger came and kep' chasin' us
22	C. an' all my cousin we kep' runnin' da store
23	C. I had a dream 'bout dat

In this narrative, the child does not follow a linear structure of one event with a beginning, middle, and an end. Instead, she talks about three events that are thematically related to the prompt. Lines 01 to 03 are an orientation (setting and characters) of the first event. The time was Halloween night, the place was a room. The characters were the narrator and her cousin. The complicating action begins in line 04 and ends in line 07. The result is presented in line 10. Line 11 begins the next event about trick and treating on Halloween. The orientation is in lines 11 to 15 that situate the characters (narrator and her cousins) in this event. In line 16, there is a reaction that she got scared. The third event is a dream which begins in line 17. The orientation is in lines 17 to 20. The characters in the event are the narrator and Tierra. The time was at night and the place was outside. The complicating action begins in line 21 and ends in line 22.

According to the evaluative analysis (McCabe & Peterson, 1991) the child has parts of a fully formed narrative such as the orientation, character development and complicating action. However, the leapfrogging structure is considered one of the more primitive forms of a child's narrative common in children who are 4 years old and starting to decrease around the age of 4½ years. Since the leapfrogging pattern is found in the narrative of this 8-year old girl, she may be considered deficient or missing the requisite psychological and/or linguistic skills for reading and writing. Accordingly, one might ignore the rich, qualitative nature of how she develops the setting, characters and the complicating action.

The example from the Afterschool Project demonstrates the difficulties of only following a linear pattern. The following findings in the Haitian Study (Colinet, Champion, & McCabe, 2004) demonstrate that only highlighting linguistic features from cultural patterns may also be misinterpreted. In the Haitian Study, personal narratives of Haitian American children between the ages of 7 and 8 were analyzed. One of the analyses used was the African analysis, which takes into consideration three stylistic features that have been identified in African oral literature (Okpewho, 1992). The first stylistic feature is "repetition" of a phrase, line, or passage, often using a singsong voice. The second feature is parallelism when "the same words or phrases are used but simply transposed in consecutive lines" (Okpewho, 1992, p. 78). With parallelism the change is not in the positions of words within the structure but in the sense or meanings assigned to them (p. 79). The third feature is detailing, which is adapted from Okpewho's (1992) "piling and association." Detailing is defined as piling one descriptive detail on top of another so that the whole performance builds up to a climax.

The narrative "Worms!" by a 7-year-old girl (Colinet, Champion, & McCabe 2004), when analyzed in Africanist analysis, demonstrates that her narrative is rich in repetition, parallelism, and detailing about the many places the worms were found. This narrative was elicited using an interviewing technique developed by Peterson and McCabe (1983) where the interviewer narrated a brief narrative of her own experience and then asked the child whether anything like that had ever happened to him/her:

Worms!

1   Once the crossing guard
2   —you know the crossing guard?
3   (He) lets the stop sign for the bus.
4   The bus has it too.
5   Once he said, "Watch out for the worm!"
6   And there was no worm.
7   Once, you know when it was pouring yesterday,
8   There was so many worms I kept on screaming for real.
9   So, it can get washed off.
10   But I like, "Ewww"
11   There was so many worms.
12   There was a worm on front of me.

13   There was a worm right there [gestures].
14   There was worm right here.
15   There was a hundred worm.
16   And when the kids came out,
17   they said, "I never saw a hundred worm before."
18   It was a lot of worms.
19   When they dig up the ground,
20   I don't know where those worms come from
21   But the worm don't come from that ground.
22   And it maybe come from somewhere else.
23   It was on floor.
24   It was on the street.
25   It was on the street where,
26   Oh my goodness,
27   I was like "Eww, eww, eww, eww, eww, eww!"
28   Once this boy, he said, "There was it was this worm that it was it was it could have."
29   It's not a worm.
30   It evolve into, um yeah.
31   And oh this is pink.
32   This is pink.
33   Pink is my favorite color.
34   And my friend, and he said never saw that once there was so many worms.
35   And there was worms on the street.
36   And there was worm everywhere.
37   There was worms right there, right there, and right there.

Examples of repetition include the use of phrases with the word "worms" in 10 out of 18 lines. Some of these phrases with worms are duplicated in different parts of the narratives such as in lines 8 and 11 "so many worms." Examples of parallelism include "There was no worm" (in line 6) with all the many different places that there *were* worms (lines 12, 13, and 14). Her description of the many different locations of the worms is also an example of her detailing. She not only explains where the worms are but provides gestures (line 13) along with her verbal description to emphasize their location. Included in her detailing are the ways she quantifies the amount of worms; for example, "so many worms" (lines 8 and 11); "a hundred worm" (lines 15 and 17).

If this narrative were evaluated according to the evaluative analysis, one might interpret the duplication of phrases consisting of the word "worms" as part of two-event narratives because the child provides the same events about worms several times; thus it may appear that the child is talking about only two separate events. Referring to Table 12.1, one sees that the structure of "two-event narratives" would be associated with early stages of narrative development, thereby concealing the richness of the narrative.

The narratives "Scared" and "Worms" demonstrate the complex nature of narratives produced by young children that can be discovered when using analyses that go beyond typical structural analyses. If the evaluative analysis is used, these narratives would be evaluated on the low end of the continuum and would be taken as evidence that these children were language *delayed* or *deficient* in their abilities to produce a well-formed narrative. For example, in the previous examples the narrative "Scared" would be classified as leapfrogging and "Worms" would be classified as two-event narratives; both are considered lower level structures. Teachers using only a structural analysis are apt to ignore the strengths children bring to their narratives and focus solely on correcting the "missing components" from the child's narrative. These *missing* components may actually be present in the narrative, as demonstrated in "Scared," but do not show up in a linear fashion due to the child's inclusion of three separate events instead of the development of one event. Alternate analyses, such as the Africanist analysis, use cultural meanings to guide interpretation of the narratives. These cultural interpretations are representative of the children's family or community experiences and are indicative of the identities that children bring to their narratives. The next section expands the notion of rich narratives by evaluating the content of children's narratives that reflect on their own identities.

Narratives as Social Patterns for Creating Identity and Relationships

Young children socially construct their narratives by adopting, adapting and transforming the narrative styles, structures and content available to them. In so doing, children begin positioning themselves in their worlds by organizing themselves in relationships to the people who are important to them. These processes of adaptation and adoption are borrowed from anthropological studies of cross-cultural contact and culture change (Street, 1993). Examples from the Storytelling Study are presented to demonstrate how children personalize their narratives in a manner that reveals aspects of their social identities and relationships.

The Storytelling Study was part of a larger project that examined young children's written and spoken narrative development in preschool and kindergarten classrooms over a 4-year period. This study involved a 4-year-old preschool classroom located in a community center in a predominantly African American, low socioeconomic urban community within the southeast region of the United States. The classroom had approximately 20 children who were predominantly of African American descent and one full-time lead teacher and various part-time assistant teachers throughout the day. Data collection consisted of oral and written narratives of stories told by the children or from their handmade books. These narratives were captured via audio/videotapes, fieldnotes and interviews with the teachers and children as well as from their own writing.

In the Storytelling Project, the children "experimented" with narrative style, structure, and content, to create social relationships, affiliations (e.g. with their family and peer group), and social identities. These social relationships and identities were conceptualized in three domains: family, themselves (e.g., gendered identities) and people in the classroom (teachers and classmates). The children's identities were analyzed according to (a) how the children positioned themselves and were positioned in relationship to others, (b) the activities they conducted, and (c) the locations of their activities.

Children's adaptation of narratives included various hybridizations and transformations of extant narratives. Sources for these narratives included formal and informal instructional contexts, family contexts, and others. Likewise children's adoption of narratives included their imitation and reproduction of narratives in the ways they experienced them (e.g., they might attempt to tell *Goldilocks and the Three Bears* in the same way they were told the story).

The adaptation or adoption of storytelling practices is a component of children's attempts to help personalize their narratives to accomplish various social goals. For example, the performance-based structure helped children establish group membership with other students. In this structure, the speaker's narratives are socially constructed between him/herself (the storyteller) and the audience. According to Bauman (1986), narratives exist in the event in which they are "performed." Bauman links the analysis of narratives from solely a literary task to a sociolinguistic and ethnographic task (Bloome, et al., 2001). Another type of a social goal was identified around children's expressions of their morals in their storytelling. In a moral-centered structure, the speaker embeds a lesson to be learned by the listener/audience.

Malik, 4 years old, tells the following narrative of "Goldilocks and the three bears." In his narrative, we highlight how he personalizes a "previously heard story" by his positioning within this narrative.

Goldilocks and the Three Bears
01   This is the new three bears
02   Um Goldilocks and the three bears
03   [Unintelligible]
04   And Goldilocks ate all they food
05   And went upstairs
06   Den she went in the daddy bed
07   It was too big
08   She went in the mommy bed
09   She was jumping on it
10   And den she went in the baby bed
11   She said it was just right
12   And den God come and said what you
13   Doing in somebody's house
14   And den the three little bears
15   And dey say somebody been eatin something
16   And somebody been eatin all our food
17   Den day say somebody been sittin in our chair
18   Somebody been in my bed
19   Somebody been jumpin on my bed

20   And there she is

21   That's the end

In this narrative, Malik adapted his narrative to his audience. He was aware that the children had heard the traditional version of *Goldilocks and Three Bears* many times. In line 01 he starts his story by stating that his story is the "new" story. Lines 05 to 11 seem to be representative of the traditional version or a version he has already heard as he describes how Goldilocks tries out the different beds of the three bears. In lines 12 and 13 he provides his own "twist" to the story by including "God" and dialogue shared from God. Malik's inclusion of his own aspects of the story could be examples of his storytelling structure and style as performance based and moral centered. By talking about God, Malik is giving a message that Goldilocks has done something wrong by entering someone else's house and using other people's property. Furthermore, his story is performance based in that inserting "God" into his narrative could be interpreted as a strategy to gain the children's attention.

This section demonstrates both how children personalize their narratives by using performance-based and moral-centered structures, as well as how they positioned themselves within their narratives. Moral-centered and performative narratives appear to have links to the African American and possibly West African culture. Our data indicated that African American children produce a wide repertoire of narrative styles, structures, and content that are made available to them through their homes, communities, and schools. In doing so, they construct their social identities and relationships. Our findings are not necessarily specific to African American children. There are culturally specific aspects of narratives that vary across cultures (Gutierrez-Clellen & Quinn, 1993; Scollon, 1988) but that have applicability for reframing how children's narratives and narrative development might be approached. Further, these three studies demonstrated that when a particular narrative style is used to evaluate children's narratives, this structure may invalidate children's identities as well as hinder their literacy learning. Thus, it's important to value narrative structures that children bring to school as well as develop other structures within school.

Integrating Language Variation Within the Standards

This section offers suggestions from the research strategies of the Storytelling Project for integrating children's language variations within the curriculum to promote young children's (pre-K-third grade) oral development. Although research strategies from all three studies are applicable for this section, the Storytelling Project was selected because that study was ongoing and conducted in a classroom setting. The research strategies are provided under the respective English arts standards 4, 9, 10, and 12 as noted previously.

Standard 12: Teachers Need to Help Students Use Spoken, Written and Visual Language to Accomplish their Own Purposes

The research team (i.e. classroom teachers, university faculty and students) implemented procedures in the Storytelling Project to involve children in presenting their own experiences and creations using multiple languages through storytelling. This procedure began with one of the members of the research team telling or reading a story from a variety of genres (e.g. folktales, modern children's stories, personal stories) while the children were gathered in a rug area. All stories were either traditional African American or African stories or personal stories created by the members of the team. The selection of the stories was based on the cultural interests of the children since the stories were to be used as prompts for the children's own storytelling. *Next,* the children volunteered to tell a story by standing up (next to the "adult" who read or told the first story) in front of the other children. *Third,* the children went to a table area where they wrote and drew stories in their handmade author books. The author books consisted of pages of white scrapbook paper with a colored paper cover. During this time, the adults circulated among the students, dating the children's pages and writing each child's dictated story in standard orthography. The final procedure involved the children returning to the rug area where they volunteered to "read" or tell a story from their author books.

Standard 4: Communicate Effectively with a Variety of Audiences and for Different Purposes

The format of the Storytelling Project and its ongoing implementation gave children pleasurable opportunities to practice their oral skills in a place where they felt secure. In this context children were *not forced* to tell a story; rather they volunteered because they wanted to be part of the classroom activities. While many children enjoyed the opportunity to "perform" in front of their peers, others were hesitant to get up and tell a story. Some children got up and were silent or said one or two words with lots of prompting from the teacher. These children often were provided with time to think about what they were going to share before they actually told their story. This move assisted them in organizing their story. Others began their story but needed assistance to continue. Often, prompts were helpful to expand their oral narratives, including the following: "What happened next?" or "Then, what did the (character) do?" Although most of the children who spoke little at the beginning, shared longer narratives in later weeks, others needed more specific interventions.

The example of Max from the Storytelling Project demonstrates how setting a context for storytelling in combination with teacher strategies can assist with children at all developmental levels. Max, 4 years old, was identified as developmentally delayed and received services for speech and language and cognition. He had a pleasant personality and enjoyed playing with trucks and dinosaurs. He exhibited little social interaction with the other children. He rarely engaged in classroom activities and would often cry if teachers tried to engage him in these activities. Max was always in the general education classroom when the storytelling project was conducted. At the beginning of October, he was described as having little speech with most of his verbalizations being unintelligible.

For the first five weeks of the storytelling project, Max did not join in or tell an oral story. Several weeks into the project, the researchers observed some nonverbal clues that indicated a possible interest in telling a story. So, members of the research team began to work directly with Max to tell a story. For example, when he provided eye contact or smiled at the student telling the story, a member of the research team would ask Max if he wanted to tell a story. When he nodded yes, he was instructed to raise his hand, an action modeled by a teacher. A teacher then physically took Max's hand and raised it or raised her hand so Max would copy the action. When Max raised his hand, he was permitted to stand in front of the class to tell his story. Each time he stood up in front of the class he would close his eyes or place his hands over his eyes but say nothing. All the children would wait patiently for Max, but he would continue to say nothing. Nevertheless, he was given verbal positive reinforcement for each attempt. Toward the end of November, Max verbalized his first words. He pointed to his drawing and said, "That Daddy." His verbalizations became a public statement that he could engage in the activity like the other children. All the adults and children recognized Max's accomplishment and cheered for him!

The consistency of the storytelling event and the participation structures of the event were important for Max in addressing Standard 4. He needed time to learn the rules of the storytelling event; for example, what it meant to tell a story, volunteer a response, and model the storytelling activities from his teachers and typically developing peers.

Standard 9: Teachers Should Help Children Develop an Understanding of and Respect for Diversity in Language Use

and

Standard 10: Teachers Should Help Children Use Their First Language to Develop Competency in English Language Arts

Children of varying developmental levels and cultural, socioeconomic, and ethnic backgrounds socially constructed their stories based on their own experiences (real or pretend) in the presence of other children and adults. Within this context, meaningful relationships began to develop between the children and teachers as the teachers better understood the meanings of the children's narratives. In other words, the teachers were learning about the children's "funds of knowledge" or their families sociocultural histories and cultural resources (Gonzalez, Moll, & Amanti, 2005). Such knowledge was gained in part through the teachers' contacts with the children's families. For example, during the Storytelling Project family members were invited (a) into the classroom to tell or read their own stories and (b) to authors' parties where the children shared with their family one of their stories that were made into a "published book." In these ways, the teachers began to identify the social practices (e.g., locations, activities, and social relationships) of their children's everyday lives, thus providing them with opportunities to validate the children's backgrounds including linguistic variations. Since the children in this study were speakers of African American English (AAE), we validated the children's use of AAE and did not correct to Standard English. It was important to allow the children to use their first dialect to express their narratives. The children, in turn, developed an understanding of and respect for diversity in language use as they shared stories that reflected their own identities.

Conclusion

This chapter addresses different narrative structures and styles African American and Haitian children bring to the classrooms. For many of these students what they brought to their classrooms was often very different from the narrative structures typically described for use in schools. To ignore these narratives meant not valuing their identities and their relationships with their peers, families and community. To misunderstand these narratives had negative implications regarding their status as students. Several of the English Language Arts standards allow teachers to incorporate children's linguistic and storytelling variations in meaningful ways that reflect each child's own unique experiences and identities.

Discussion Questions and Activities

1. Why is it important to consider variation in narrative structures when evaluating children's language skills?
2. How can teachers help children with language delays learn narrative structures?
3. What are the implications of the standard narrative techniques for helping children from culturally and linguistically diverse groups draw upon their own cultural experiences to produce better narratives?
4. How does oral narration help prepare children for later literacy learning?

References

Bauman, R. A. (1986). *Story, Performance, and Event: Contextual Studies of Oral Narrative.* Cambridge: Cambridge University Press.

Bloome, D., Champion, T., Katz, L., Morton, M. B., & Muldrow R. (2001). Spoken and Written Narrative Development: African American Preschoolers as Storytellers and Storymakers. In J. L. Harris, A. G. Kamhi, & K. E. Pollock (Eds.). *Literacy in African American Communities.* Mahwah, NJ: Lawrence Erlbaum Associates. Inc.

Bumpus, E. (2004). *Lion in Love.* Belchertown, MA: Shoestring Studios. (CD)

Champion, T. B. (2003). *Understanding Storytelling Among African American Children: A Journey from Africa to America.* Mahwah, NJ: Lawrence Erlbaum Associates, Inc.

——, Katz, L., Muldrow, R., & Dail, R. (1999). Storytelling and Storymaking in an Urban Preschool Classroom: Building Bridges from Home to School Culture. *Topics in Language Disorders,* 19(3), 52–67.

Colinet, Y., Champion, T., & McCabe, A. (2004). The Whole World Could Hear: The Structure of Haitian American Children's Narratives. *Journal of Child Language,* 22(4), 381–400.

Cummins, J. (2000). *Language, Power, and Pedagogy: Bilingual Children in the Crossfire.* Clevedon: Multingual Matters.

Gonzalez, N. C., Moll L. C., & Amanti, C. (2005). *Funds of Knowledge: Theorizing Practices in Households, Communities, and Classrooms.* Mahwah, NJ: Lawrence Erlbaum Associates, Inc.

Gumperz, J. (1986). *Discourse Strategies.* New York: Cambridge University Press.

Gutierrez-Clellen, V. F., & Quinn, R. (1993). Assessing Narratives of Children from Diverse Cultural/Linguistic Groups. *Language, Speech, and Hearing Services in Schools,* 24, 2–9.

Heath, S. (1983). *Ways with Words.* Cambridge: Cambridge University Press.

Kellog, S. (1997). *The Three Little Pigs.* New York: Morrow Junior Books.

Labov, W. (1972). *Language of the Inner City.* Philadelphia, PA: University of Pennsylvania Press.

McCabe, A., & Peterson, C. (1991). Parental Styles of Narrative Elicitation. In A. McCabe, & C. Peterson (Eds.). *Developing Narrative Structure.* Hillsdale, NJ: Lawrence Erlbaum Associates, Inc.

Moser, B. (2001). *The Three Little Pigs.* Boston, MA: Little, Brown, & Company.

Ohio Center for Curriculum and Assessment. (2002). *Academic Content Standards K-12 English Language Arts.* Columbus, OH: Ohio Department of Education.

Ohio Office of Early Childhood Education. (2004). *Early Learning Content Standards.* Columbus, OH: Ohio Department of Education.

Okpewho, I. (1992). *African Oral Literature: Backgrounds, Character, and Continuity.* Bloomington, IN: Indiana University Press.

Peterson, C., & McCabe, A. (1983). *Developmental Psycholinguistics: Three Ways of Looking at a Child's Narrative.* New York: Plenum Press.

Rounds, G. (1992). *Three Little Pigs and the Big Bad Wolf.* New York: Holiday House.

Rowe, D. (1994). *Preschoolers as Authors: Literacy Learning in the Social World of the Classroom.* Cresskill, NJ: Hampton Press.

Schieffelin, B. B., & Ochs, E. (Eds) (1986). *Language Socialization across Cultures.* Cambridge: Cambridge University Press.

Scieszka, J. (1999). *The True Story of the Three Little Pigs.* New York: Penguin Putnam Books for Young Readers.

Scollon, R. (1988). Storytelling, Reading, and the Micropolitics of Literacy. In J. E. Readence, & R. S. Baldwin (Eds.). *Dialogues in Literacy Research: Thirty Seventh Yearbook of the National Reading Conference.* Chicago, IL: National Reading Conference.

Solsken, J., & Bloome, D. (1992). Beyond Postructuralism: Story and Narrative in the Study of Literacy in the Everyday World. Paper presented at the meeting of the American Educational Research Association.

Street, B. (1993). The New Literacy Studies: Guest Editorial. *Journal of Research in Reading,* 16(2), 81–97.

Wiesner, D. (2001). *The Three Little Pigs.* New York: Clarion Books.

13

Culturally Responsive Read-Alouds in First Grade: Drawing Upon Children's Languages and Cultures to Facilitate Literary and Social Understandings

JEANE COPENHAVER-JOHNSON, JOY BOWMAN, AND
ANGELA JOHNSON RIETSCHLIN

In attending deeply to children and trying to empathize with them, as in studying other cultures, one is constantly reminded that these beloved strangers are behaving in ways that are only intelligible if their world is recognized as differently structured, laid out according to different landmarks. Much of the time, we are busy trying to talk children out of their perceptions, giving them the correct answers, the ones that are widely shared and fit neatly into familiar systems of interpretation. (Bateson, 1994, p. 56)

Many teachers consider read-alouds a critical component of the literacy and social curriculum in their classrooms, and we find increasing evidence that teachers have begun integrating culturally conscious literature into their classroom libraries in an effort to enact culturally responsive and/or critical pedagogy (e.g., Lehr & Thompson, 2000; Leland, et al., 2003; MacPhee, 1997). After the "multicultural literature" is chosen for reading, however, a critical process for promoting responsiveness is too often overlooked. Teachers, who are disproportionately White, tend to read to and with children in ways that fail to acknowledge the depth of diversity in worldviews, attentiveness, and discourses (Bateson, 1994). If the NCTE resolution, "On the Students' Right to Their Own Language" (SRTOL), is to be followed, one feature of read-alouds worth examining is the degree to which the *talk* encouraged between children and teachers actually taps into the discourse styles familiar to children and validates the worldviews they, as children and as members of diverse communities, hold. In this chapter, we describe how a study of culturally diverse first graders' responses to classroom read-alouds helped us identify principles that might guide other teachers' choices as they work to create culturally responsive read aloud settings for young children.

Our Own Preparation as Teachers

We are two first grade teachers (Joy and Angela, who taught for several years in the same urban elementary school) and a university-based teacher educator and former classroom teacher (Jeane) with a shared interest in fostering culturally responsive read-aloud environments for young children. As White teachers we did not always, however, recognize the ethnocentrism of many common literacy practices. During our teacher preparation, we participated in student teaching experiences in which our ability to exhibit "classroom management" was highly valued, so we elicited children's comments and questions during read-alouds but controlled the volume, duration, and perhaps most importantly the focus of children's talk. Comments not immediately recognizable as "relevant" were redirected. We are not proud of this history.

Research on the relationships between culture and response was emerging during the years we completed our programs, so advice we received about reading aloud to children naturally included general directives such as those identified by Fisher, Flood, Lapp, and Frey (2004). These researchers found the practices of 120 "expert" teachers in grades three through eight included to read fluently and with expression, to preview books, to establish clear purposes for read-alouds, to stop and question students about the text, and to connect texts to students' reading, writing, and interests. From our perspectives, reading aloud felt like a skill every new teacher would learn with minimal preparation. Only later did we consider how students' experiences and cultures differed from our own and how we had privileged our own ways of reading and responding as we facilitated read-alouds. Therefore, we began to interrogate assumptions about read-alouds. Currently, a body of work is emerging in which *students' characteristics* and cultures become significant considerations in how to best engage children in the literary read-aloud experience (Copenhaver, 2001a; Hefflin, 2002; Sipe, 2003). It is this scholarship, and our own research on students' responses to read-alouds, that help us better integrate the tenets of the SRTOL resolution into work with young children.

Read-Alouds and Students' Right to Their Own Languages

Read-alouds serve powerful literacy and literary functions (Feitelson, Kita, & Goldstein, 1986; Sipe, 2000a; Teale, 1984). Common pedagogical advice for teachers on "effective" read-aloud practices, however, can often reify discourse styles more commonly found among White, middle-class teachers. Willis and Harris (2003) explain that cross-cultural literacy research can result in a "normalizing and universalizing of the 'American' literacy experience that presumes histories and levels of commonality among multiple groups in our society" (p. 293). General directives about conducting effective read-alouds sometimes inadvertently reinforce normative expectations about classroom discourse simply because so few explicitly problematize dominant classroom participant structures or question the role of culture in shaping response.

Researchers of the interactive read-aloud recognize the significance of students' active participation in read-alouds (Barrentine, 1996; Oyler & Barry, 1996; Sipe, 2000a; Smolkin & Donovan, 2003; Sychterz, 2002), and their work is beginning to attend to the varied discourse styles of children and the typical participant structures employed by teachers in read-aloud conversations. Sipe (2003), for instance, complicates the notion of a single read-aloud style; his description of an urban teacher's storytelling-style and read-alouds demonstrates the bridging of children's home and school discourses and encourages teachers and researchers to consider ways read-alouds might become culturally responsive.

We found ourselves questioning the assumption of an expert methodology in which *teachers* identify the salient questions and vocabulary in advance of reading texts with children (for example, Beck & McKeown, 2001; Conrad, Gong, Sipp, & Wright, 2004). In this work, we examine what lessons a more child-centered approach to read-alouds might offer teachers interested in culturally responsive instruction. Hickman (1992) notes: "The responses children offer without being asked are the foundation for the understandings and insights we hope to help them develop" (p. 193). Finding ways to elicit, learn from, and validate these child-initiated responses has been an important part of culturally responsive read-alouds in the classrooms we will describe.

The Research Context

We conducted a 3-year study of read-alouds in Joy and Angela's two urban first grade classrooms. Our initial research question, "How do children in culturally diverse primary grade classrooms express inquiry during free response read-aloud conversations?" focused our attention on *child-initiated* talk during read-alouds. In the subset of our work described here, we focus on how the teachers created read-aloud environments that permitted this kind of participation from students with different backgrounds, discourse styles, and personalities.

Joy and Angela's students (new students each year, for a total of three classes per teacher—or 105 students in all during the larger study) participated in this work with us. Children self-identified as Black, White, and bi-racial; approximately 80% of the building's students were identified as "economically disadvantaged" by the state. Approximately one-fourth of the students used Black English vernacular, and three- fourths spoke a dialect common to the former Appalachian population who relocated to the area within the last two generations.

Jeane served as a participant observer (Spradley, 1980), joining the classrooms approximately twice a week, observing read-alouds, and occasionally conducting read-alouds. All three of us collected fieldnotes and transcribed audiorecorded read-alouds (125 complete read-aloud observations in all). We paid particular attention to (1) children's different ways of demonstrating engagement with text and (2) changes Joy and Angela made, over time, to foster children's oral, physical, and written responses to free-response read-alouds.

Teachers and outside researchers can offer "different and complementary" contributions to research (Cazden, 2003, p. 47). Joy and Angela offered insights about children's lives that helped make their responses more comprehensible, sharing the kind of insights that Cazden asserts are "gleaned from hours of living together" (p. 47). Studies in which the teachers themselves actively participate in collecting and analyzing data (e.g., Kemmis & McTaggart, 2005; Rogers & Mosley, 2006) can offer a richer, and perhaps more critical, context for the study of practice. We feel our analysis is more trustworthy because of this collaboration.

We analyzed our data in several ways, borrowing from the methods of grounded theory (Strauss & Corbin, 1990); we read and reread transcripts of the read-aloud conversations, categorized conversational episodes by the ways children expressed inquiry, coded the topics of children's curiosities, and then looked to the teachers' behaviors to see the practices employed in the most conversation-rich transcripts. In the following section, we discuss these practices—and the larger principles related to community and ethnocentrism that we believe drove these practices and encouraged children's participation.

Reading Aloud with Linguistically and Culturally Diverse Groups of Children: Principles and Practices to Facilitate Response

Joy and Angela helped elicit active student participation in read-alouds by validating the discourse styles, cultural interests, and experiences upon which children drew as they interpreted literature. Particular elements of facilitative pedagogy positioned students' own languages as tools for furthering literary and social understandings. The following principles guided their practices: (1) Developing a sense of community and (2) Revising ethnocentric notions of relevance. These principles will be explained with examples from practice to convey how the principles were enacted in these classrooms.

Principle One: Develop a Sense of Community

The first principle is a commitment to classroom community and respect. Without trust, children fail to take the risks necessary to respond freely to literature (Rosenblatt, 1938/95), and community has long been recognized as a key principle of culturally responsive instruction (Ladson-Billings, 1994), helping teachers better understand students' lives and fostering the trust that encourages children to explore genuine curiosities. Angela and Joy commented that they wanted children to express the issues on their minds and to feel that it was acceptable to talk about what might otherwise be considered "taboo" topics like racism, family conflict, poverty, or religion. Heath (1982) reported how little "'real' exchange of information, feeling, or imagination" (p. 107) occurs in urban classrooms because children are not understood by teachers. Feeling *invited* to talk is prerequisite to using one's language to express, learn, and rethink ideas.

PRACTICE ONE: VALIDATE CHILDREN'S STORIES, CONNECTIONS, COMMENTS

Joy and Angela showed authentic interest in stories that bubbled up from children's lives as they responded to read-alouds, even when children's stories represented values and life situations very different from those of the teachers. It is common, of course, for teachers in cross-cultural settings to find students' experiences and connections different from their own (Copenhaver, 2001b; Henkin, 1998; Jones, 2004). Topics such as religion, violence, incarceration, or bullying may be overlooked or invalidated when children mention them during read-alouds. However, these topics, sometimes perceived as irrelevant or controversial, can provide important supports for understanding literature and building community. In Joy's and Angela's classes, children regularly used their knowledge of parental jail and court time, being relocated due to unpaid rental bills, and drunkenness to make sense of (and to critique) stories. When reading *The Leaving Morning* (Johnson, 1992), several children reflected on separations from loved ones (the book has a moving/goodbye theme) by telling about parental fighting, police arresting their parents, and fears that noncustodial parents would be unable to find them after moving out. Their experiences informed their predictions and influenced empathy toward characters. We do not suggest that the potentially sensitive connections children made characterize their cultures or families; rather, we single out these connections because they are realities in *many* children's lives but may be significantly less familiar to many teachers.

We noted children's interest in religion as an important means of interpreting and understanding picturebooks. In a discussion of *Jazzy Miz Mozetta* (Roberts, 2004) in Angela's class, for instance, children began debating the validity of stories from the Bible. After reading about the "fat moon," Aiden and James discussed how the moon was "God's Eye," which Aiden contended was "evil." Terrance, James, Shaina, and Wade vigorously debated the authority and authorship of the Bible, and, after a pause, James commented, "I still don't trust them people that, um . . . write the book [The Bible]."

The temptation for some teachers might have been to hush the children's talk here (and later, when they employ *The Passion of the Christ* as another intertextual connection) because of its focus on religion or because the focus was not clearly related to the story. However, if children believe the moon foreshadows something bad because they believe the Bible, a book some of them hold in high authority, suggests an evil moon, this interpretation is likely to guide their expectations for the story—their predictive analysis, their assumptions about the main character's choice to go dancing, and so on. The difference of perspectives offered in a literature conversation can contribute to analytical considerations of text (for example, authorship authority or the "rightness" of certain intertextual comparisons). Children frequently attended Sunday School, and when Angela visited one of their places of worship, she heard many similar literary connections made by attendees. Children easily employed faith-based knowledge in analysis, and Angela chose to allow children to negotiate their faith-based conversations as they interpreted and discussed books together.

Children also regularly used knowledge of violence as a means to understand stories. During a reading of *The Story of Ruby Bridges* (Coles, 1995), for example, children reading with Jeane conveyed fury at the way Ruby was treated by the mob outside of the school she was integrating:

Travis: They're being bad to her.
Joshua: If she was my sister, I'd beat them.
Jeane: So if she were your sister, you'd beat them? [To be sure I heard correctly—he nods.]
Lee: I'd protect her.
Darrell: I'd take my dad's shot gun, if that was my sister, and they were going to kill her, and I'd be like, "If you guys really want to kill my sister, you got to go through me, and that means you're going to get dead."
Lee: If I was her brother, I would ask her, let's pray for her.

Darrell's comments here convey passion for the story and protectiveness toward Ruby's character. One might argue that his imagining Ruby as his own sister represents a highly aesthetic response to the story—evidence of significant engagement. Although we encouraged children to share their different perspectives and talk one another through them—and we shared our own candid responses to stories, too—we found it oppressive to tell students that their responses were not "appropriate." While Darrell's reaction was different than Joy's or Angela's, it was also different from Lee's, other students', and Jeane's responses. Encouraged to talk through his reactions, rather than being marginalized, Darrell heard many ways of perceiving and experiencing this story. We facilitated the process Rosenblatt (1969) describes: "In the light of what he brings to the transaction, the reader arrives at a tentative interpretation *and then tests it by further study of the text or by comparison with others' interpretations of it*" (p. 45, emphasis added). In this example, we did revisit the text to see if, indeed, the text or illustrations conveyed that the angry mob wanted to kill Ruby. Decisions about how to respond when children's responses differ from our own (or differ from what we consider to be socially just interpretations) are not easy (Pataray-Ching & Kavanaugh-Anderson, 1998), but teachers hold power when they silence or include these comments in the larger conversations (Harris, Trezise, & Winser, 2004; Jones, 2004) for the logic guiding children's responses comes from genuine experience.

PRACTICE TWO: EXPECT AND INVITE ALTERNATIVE PARTICIPANT STRUCTURES

The teachers' choice to value a range of response modes during read-aloud appeared to be community developing since children responded to stories in diverse ways. Teachers encouraged call-and-response, permitted call-outs to stories, and came to understand the significance of physical movement as children responded. Joy and Angela deliberately resisted a highly IRE (teacher Initiates, students Respond, teacher Evaluates) participant structure (Mehan, 1979), instead encouraging children to talk to each other and to share responses naturally.

One of the most popular books read during our study was *Nappy Hair* (Herron, 1997). This title, the source of much controversy (hooks, 2004; Lester, 1999), was a child-requested favorite in both classrooms each year. We agonized somewhat over using this text, reading it only in response to student requests. As Lester (1999) acknowledges, the rhythm, the call-and-response, and the topical focus make this book popular with children. Joy and Angela often paired it with other books that celebrate hair (e.g., hooks, 1999; Tarpley, 1998). Response to these books often included touching the books, touching each other's hair, and singing with call-and-response language. The use of an IRE participant structure would have likely disrupted the experience of these texts.

During one reading of *Nappy Hair*, Jeane had involved children in Joy's class in a modified call-and-response read-aloud when Casey interrupted:

Casey: Mrs. Copenhaven [sic], you sound like a different girl talking like that.
Jeane: I sound like a different girl talking like that? What makes me sound different?

Brent: You're saying it different.

Jeane: I'm saying it the way she writes it. She writes it the way her [Herron's] family told stories. Her family talked differently than I do, so they say things like, "Don't cha know?" and things that I probably wouldn't say. But I *like* the way her family sounds.

Brent: That's why you're saying it like that.

Casey: I like it.

Children paid special attention to dialectical differences in these books, even if they did not *name* them as dialect and were intrigued by dialects other than their own. They paid similar attention to the linguistic playfulness in books with regional dialects (e.g., Lowell, 2001) and repeated, enthusiastically, lines that were rich with inflection, engaging in what we call the "directive response" whereby children insist on directing the ways they will participate in the story.

Children engaged in immediate responses to stories—often *calling out* at the moment of insight. Sometimes these responses questioned the text (or the author, or the teacher's rendering of the story, or the illustrations), and sometimes the responses actively tried to point out an observation about the text. Joy and Angela integrated these in-the-moment responses into conversations because children's insights prompted new literary considerations. For example, during a reading of hooks' (2002) *Be Boy Buzz*, in Joy's class, children commented on how "funny" they thought the book sounded—responding to lines such as "All bliss boy. All fine beat. All beau boy," (unpaged) with comments like, "That don't make *no* sense! That don't make no sense!" and laughter. They then discussed *why* the text yielded such amusement; it did not conform to their expectations for "story." Children's called-out responses to *Be Boy Buzz* provided evidence of what Sipe and McGuire (2006) have called "literary critical resistance" (p. 9) to the text, in which children raise critical questions about the structure or logic of a text—response experiences critical to the development of literary understanding.

PRACTICE THREE: WELCOME CHILDREN'S RACE-FOCUSED TALK

Since we value critical literacy, we helped children recognize, name, and feel a sense of agency around inequity. Leland, et al. (2003) describe critical literacy as focused on "helping readers understand how they and other people are positioned by particular texts and particular social practices" (p. 14), and children openly questioned how they were positioned and identified by others because of race. Children compared arm colors, discussed whether characters in books were Black, White, or mixed (the terms of children's preference), and analyzed how race influenced literary *and* here-and-now worlds. This exchange occurred during a reading of *The Other Side* (Woodson, 2001):

Brent: Oooh. The girl in the blue dress looks like she's white. She's gonna be in trouble.

Casey: She's tan, white, and brown.

Thomas: She might be mixed. When I was a little baby, I was mixed.

Brent: I'm not mixed. My mom said I'm not mixed. Some people think I am, though.

Children recognized that the racial identification of the girl in the blue dress would influence her role in the story and how other characters would respond to her. Similar questions were often asked about the tan skin of individuals in the angry mob in *The Story of Ruby Bridges* (Coles, 1995) or the ethnicity of the racist man in *White Socks Only* (Coleman, 1996) whose reddish skin children failed to associate immediately with Whiteness but whose power they *did* associate with Whiteness. Notably, children also discussed how Whiteness might affect their own privileges. Casey noted that she and Bethany (both White) would be able to drink from the White drinking fountain portrayed in *Martin's Big Words* (Rappaport, 2001), and the children discussed how unfair that situation would be—where some of them could enjoy privileges denied to others of them.

Conversations where children identified the capital Whiteness conveys (see Copenhaver-Johnson, 2006) were followed with discussions about contemporary racism. Joy and Angela trusted children to challenge one another, and children did so—not in ways that created social isolation or confrontation but in ways that created the kind of "threat" Fecho (2001) references as essential in critical inquiry classrooms. In spite of—or because of—this sense of threat, children were trusted to hypothesize, make difficult observations, and ask critical questions of each other.

When reading *'Twas the Night B'fore Christmas* (Rosales, 1996), some children in Angela's class challenged the realness of the Black Santa who appears in this version of the story. Ilona claimed that the Santa in the text did not "look like Santa Claus," and Wade agreed, after which Shaina and Chantel, two African American girls, defended the authenticity of the Santa in the book (see also Copenhaver-Johnson, Bowman, & Johnson, 2007). Shaina asserted, "We got something to say about this!" At this point, four girls approached Angela and held the book, pointing out how the Santa of the book carried toys, had a bag, and referenced a paper (list) just like "real" Santa. Together, Shaina and Chantel methodically compared White Santa to the Black Santa of the text and to the "real" Santa of children's holiday traditions, challenging their classmates to consider his realness.

In read-aloud discussions such as these, children talked about issues adults might find controversial and freely shared many facts about their lives. As soon as children entered these classrooms, they were treated as competent members of communities that valued discussions and differences of perspective.

Principle Two: Revise Ethnocentric Notions of Relevance

Barrentine (1996) says of the interactive read-aloud, "after you have planned the read-aloud event, be prepared to relinquish your plans" (p. 42). Teachers—particularly teachers in cross-cultural contexts—are likely to encounter students whose curiosities about books are not quite what their teachers anticipated and may not quickly be able to identify the relevance of the insights children share.

PRACTICE ONE: ASSUME THE LOGIC OF THE CHILD'S RESPONSE

When children made oral contributions to read-aloud conversations, both Joy and Angela consciously *assumed* connections between the literature and the point being made by the child. These assumptions generally were validated if teachers patiently sought clearer understandings of the points children were posing. White, adult teachers may not be sensitive to the connections children are making and might be impatient—expecting the relevance of the child's connection to be immediate.

For example, in some classrooms, children are asked to make comments that are clearly connected to the story. We have even observed posters in classrooms on which children are "reminded" to consider whether their comments are related to stories. Although we acknowledge the risk inherent in conversations that "bridge" (Newkirk & McLure, 1992) so widely that conversations fail to focus on the substance of the texts—a criticism of watered-down reader response approaches— we also recognize that many teachers may not be able to immediately understand the significance of a child's connection (Lehr & Thompson, 2000).

Sipe (2000b), for instance, describes a child's intertextual connection to the show "Married With Children" during a reading of *Fly Away Home* (Bunting, 1991)—a connection that was not immediately clear to the teacher but which represented "spectacular interpretive effect" (p. 81). Since the popular cultures to which children are exposed may vary considerably from those familiar to their teachers, the logic guiding children's literary understandings may require more faith on the teacher's part to understand. A student's first (and perhaps hard-to-understand) response is a prerequisite for deeper analysis of literature.

Angela was puzzled when girls in her class connected *White Socks Only* (Coleman, 1996), a story about racial prejudice, discrimination, and a community's courage, with lighthearted David Shannon's *No, David!* (Shannon, 1998) series. As Angela read *White Socks Only*, Rosalind commented, "This remind me of *No, David*." When questioned further about her connection, Rosalind elaborated, "Cause he bad, she bad," and soon Angela recognized (with the help of Chantel chiming in, "Cause [of] when David was like, 'Come back here, David!'") that the children had noticed that in both stories—one playful and one highly serious— the protagonist disobeys authority by leaving the home at an inappropriate time. David had made repeated appearances in children's independent and shared writing. The connections Rosalind and Chantel made were apt ones—comparisons of plot and theme—and were not ones Angela would have made or voiced as she responded to Coleman's book. We repeatedly noted, in our analysis, children analyzing stories in ways that were not clearly understandable (to the teachers) when children initiated their conversational turns but which ultimately demonstrated children's thoughtful insights—children connecting to television programs, episodes at the morning bus stop, and other books. When teachers patiently listened, the comments' relevance became clear.

PRACTICE TWO: GIVE THE CHILDREN TIME TO VOICE THEIR RESPONSES

Read-alouds with diverse groups of children take time. For Joy and Angela, protecting read-aloud time was essential to protecting the community developed in the classrooms. Read-alouds were the one time of day where children were all together—focused on a single experience, and even in very close seating proximity—building "common knowledge" (Edwards & Mercer, 1987) and the common experiences that foster community. Teachers, particularly those working cross-culturally, need *time* to discern the meaning behind children's remarks. Picturebook read-alouds often took 45 minutes in these classrooms.

Clearly, interactive read-alouds do require more time than more teacher-directed read-alouds (Barrentine, 1996; Copenhaver, 2001b), especially in classrooms with linguistic and cultural diversity. Because these classrooms were marked by changes in participant structure, whereby students were encouraged to address one another rather than just the teacher (Rosenblatt, 1938/95), the teachers exhibited less control over the duration of conversational turns, the number of turns taken, and the breadth of topics explored in discussions. The teachers still participated and were the official timekeepers of read-alouds, but they purposefully attempted to include as many children's oral contributions as possible while maintaining the momentum of stories.

In other classrooms, teachers are often forced to read aloud stories rapidly, in small segments of time. Such rushing can result in the silencing of children whose narrative styles are unfamiliar to their teachers or children who immediately call out their responses to literature. Irvine (1990) notes the strong potential for African American children, in particular, to be misunderstood when their ways of accessing the "floor" for talk violate teachers' expectations. In a summary of research by Kochman and Hanna, Irvine notes: "Teachers find black students impolite, aggressive, and boisterous when they cut off another student or fail to restrain themselves so that every student can have a turn to talk" (p. 29).

Children can and in these classrooms do learn to negotiate different ways of responding. Children learned that Thomas would "call out" responses to stories, but Kelly would speak only after raising her hand. We noted the *children* openly discussing these differences, hearing them register good-humored warnings that some children were "talking too much" or that they all needed to listen closely to hear softly spoken children's remarks. Negotiating these different understandings about participant structures was not simple, but helping children voice their responses *during* the story was paramount for facilitating literary understanding (Sipe, 2000b). Children found their comments important enough to speak often, to interrupt a reading to ask an immediate question, and to hold on to conversational turns. Their efforts to talk provided evidence of the profound desire to be heard and to participate in collaborative meaning making. Teachers will find it difficult to honor the principles we describe here without enacting a practice that protects read-aloud time.

Conclusion

Honoring Students' Right to Their Own Language

Cazden (2003) references systemic inequalities in schools by which *some* students receive lesser opportunities for successful learning and engagement. "The total picture," she explains, "of these all-too-common structures of inequalities suggests that they may be the default option, how the educational system works unless special effort is made to change it" (p. 38). We believe read-alouds is one way to facilitate cultural responsiveness in classrooms. If students' languages and lives support literary understandings, and if read-aloud responses are mediated through children's language, it only makes sense that teachers have an obligation to see if traditional means of reading aloud (e.g, teacher centric, preplanned questions, limited time and modes of response) facilitate the involvement of *all* students. If certain children are routinely left out of conversations, it is likely time to consider children's languages and experiences as *supports* for literacy rather than as interference.

Discussion Questions and Activities

1. Visit a classroom where read-aloud occurs regularly, and observe a whole-class read-aloud. Make notes on what you see and hear. Where does the reading take place? In what ways do children get access to the conversational "floor" to make contributions? When and why are some children redirected? In this classroom, infer the hidden curriculum.
2. Take a look at the classroom library. Are the children in this school represented by the texts available in the classroom?
3. Tape record yourself reading aloud to a whole class and then, later, with a small group (three or four students). What happens as you read aloud? What do you notice about your *own* practice? To what extent might these practices be the result of your own elementary school socialization? What changes do you observe as the group size changes?
4. What possible complications do you imagine might occur for teachers who try to enact the principles (and related practices) described in this chapter? Share your concerns with a classmate, and see if you can identify two or three strategies to help ameliorate the problems you're anticipating.

References

Barrentine, S. B. (1996). Engaging with Reading through Interactive Read-Alouds. *The Reading Teacher*, 50, 36–43.

Bateson, M. C. (1994). *Peripheral Visions: Learning Along the Way*. New York: HarperCollins.

Beck, I. L., & McKeown, M G. (2001). Text Talk: Capturing the Benefits of Read-Aloud Experiences for Young Children. *The Reading Teacher*, 55, 10–20.

Cazden, C. B. (2003). Teacher and Student Attitudes on Racial Issues: The Complementarity of Practitioner Research and Outsider Research. In S. Greene, & D. Abt-Perkins (Eds.). *Making Research Visible: Literacy Research for Cultural Understanding*. New York: Teachers College Press.

Conrad, N. K., Gong, Y., Sipp, L., & Wright, L. (2004). Using Text Talk as a Gateway to Culturally Responsive Teaching. *Early Childhood Education Journal*, 31, 187–192.

Copenhaver, J. F. (2001a). Listening to Their Voices Connect Literary and Cultural Understandings: Responses to Small Group Read-Alouds of *Malcolm X: A Fire Burning Brightly*. *The New Advocate*, 14, 343–359.

——. (2001b). Running Out of Time: Rushed Read-Alouds in a Primary Classroom. *Language Arts*, 79, 148–158.

Copenhaver-Johnson, J. F. (2006). Talking to Children about Race: The Importance of Inviting Difficult Conversations. *Childhood Education*, 83, 12–22.

——, Bowman, J. T., & Johnson, A. C. (2007). Santa Stories: Children's Inquiry about Race during Picturebook Read-Alouds. *Language Arts*, 84, 234–244.

Edwards, D., & Mercer, N. (1987). *Common Knowledge: The Development of Understanding in the Classroom*. London: Routledge.

Fecho, B. (2001). "Why are You Doing This?": Acknowledging and Transcending Threat in a Critical Inquiry Classroom. *Research in the Teaching of English*, 36, 9–37.

Feitelson, D., Kita, B., & Goldstein, Z. (1986). Effects of Listening to Stories on First Graders' Comprehension and Use of Language. *Research in the Teaching of English*, 20, 339–356.

Fisher, D., Flood, J., Lapp, D., & Frey, N. (2004). Interactive Read-Alouds: Is there a Common Set of Implementation Practices? *The Reading Teacher*, 58, 8–17.

Harris, P., Trezise, J., & Winser, W. N. (2004). Where is the Story?: Reflections on Literacy Research and Practices in the Early School Years. *Research in the Teaching of English*, 38, 250–261.

Heath, S. B. (1982). Questioning at Home and at School: A Comparative Study. In G. Spindler (Ed.). *Doing the Ethnography of Schooling: Educational anthropology in Action*. New York: Rinehart & Winston.

Hefflin, B. R. (2002). Learning to Develop a Culturally Relevant Pedagogy: A Lesson about Cornrowed Lives. *The Urban Review*, 34, 231–250.

Henkin, R. (1998). *Who's Invited to Share? Using Literacy to Teach for Equity and Social Justice*. Portsmouth, NH: Heinemann.

Hickman, J. (1992). What Comes Naturally: Growth and Change in Children's Free Response to Literature. In C. Temple, & P. Collins (Eds.). *Stories and Readers: New Perspectives on Literature in the Elementary Classroom*. Norwood, MA: Christopher Gordon.

hooks, b. (2004). Keynote Address: Convention Kick-Off Session. Presentation at the National Council of Teachers of English Annual Meeting, Indianapolis, IN.

Irvine, J. J. (1990). *Black Students and School Failure: Policies, Practices, and Prescriptions*. New York: Praeger.

Jones, S. (2004). Living in Poverty and Literacy Learning: Sanctioning the Topics of Students' Lives. *Language Arts*, 81, 461–469.

Kemmis, S., & McTaggart, R. (2005). Participatory Action Research: Communicative Action and the Public Sphere. In N. K. Denzin, & Y. S. Lincoln (Eds.). *The Sage Handbook of Qualitative Research*, 3rd edn. Thousand Oaks, CA: Sage.

Ladson-Billings, G. (1994). *The Dreamkeepers: Successful Teachers of African American Children*. San Francisco: Jossey-Bass.

Lehr, S., & Thompson, D. L. (2000). The Dynamic Nature of Response: Children Reading and responding to *Maniac Magee* and *The Friendship*. *The Reading Teacher*, 53, 480–493.

Leland, C. H., Harste, J. C., Davis, A., Haas, C., McDaniel, K., Parsons, M., & Strawmyer, M. (2003). "It Made Me Hurt Inside": Exploring Tough Social Issues through Critical Literacy. *Journal of Reading Education*, 28(2), 7–15.

Lester, N. A. (1999). Roots that Go Beyond Big Hair and a Bad Hair Day: *Nappy Hair* Pieces. *Children's Literature in Education*, 30, 171–183.

MacPhee, J. S. (1997). "That's not Fair!": A White Teacher Reports on White First Graders' Responses to Multicultural Literature. *Language Arts*, 74, 33–40.

Mehan, H. (1979). *Learning Lessons: Social Organization in the Classroom*. Cambridge, MA: Harvard University Press.

Newkirk, T., & McLure, P. (1992). *Listening in: Children Talking about Books (and other Things)*. Portsmouth, NH: Heinemann.

Oyler, C., & Barry, A. (1996). Intertextual Connections in Read-Alouds of Information Books. *Language Arts*, 73, 324–329.

Pataray-Ching, J., & Kavanaugh-Anderson, D. C. (1998). When Children Pose Inquiry Questions that Disagree with Society's Beliefs. *Educational Forum*, 63(1), 73–78.

Rogers, R., & Mosley, M. (2006). Racial Literacy in a Second-Grade Classroom: Critical Race Theory, Whiteness Studies, and Literacy Research. *Reading Research Quarterly*, 41, 462–495.

Rosenblatt, L. M. (1938/1995). *Literature as Exploration*, 5th edn. New York: MLA.

——. (1969). Towards a Transactional Theory of Reading. *Journal of Reading Behavior*, 1, 31–49.

Sipe, L. R. (2000a). The Construction of Literary Understanding by First and Second Graders in Oral Response to Picture Storybook Read-Alouds. *Reading Research Quarterly*, 35, 252–275.

——. (2000b). "Those Two Gingerbread Boys could be Brothers": How Children Use Intertextual Connections during Storybook Read-Alouds. *Children's Literature in Education*, 31, 73–90.

——. (2003). It's a Matter of Style: One Teacher's Storybook Reading in an Urban Kindergarten. *The New Advocate*, 16, 161–170.

—— & McGuire, C. E. (2006). Young Children's Resistance to Stories. *The Reading Teacher*, 60, 6–13.

Sisti, E. (Executive Producer), & Gibson, M. (Director). (2004). *The Passion of the Christ* [Motion picture]. United States: Icon Productions.

Smolkin, L. B., & Donovan, C. A. (2003). Supporting Comprehension Acquisition for Emerging and Struggling Readers: The Interactive Information Book Read-Aloud. *Exceptionality*, 11(1), 25–38.

Spradley, J. P. (1980). *Participant Observation*. New York: Holt, Rinehart, & Winston.

Strauss, A., & Corbin, J. (1990). *Basics of Qualitative Research: Grounded Theory Procedures and Techniques*. Newbury Park, CA: Sage.

Sychterz, T. (2002). Rethinking Childhood Innocence. *The New Advocate*, 15, 183–195.

Teale, W. H. (1984). Reading to Young Children: Its Significance for Literacy Development. In H. Goelman, A. Oberg, & F. Smith (Eds.). *Awakening to Literacy*. Portsmouth, NH: Heinemann Educational Books.

Willis, A. I., & Harris, V. J. (2003). Afterword. In A. I. Willis, G. E. Garcia, R. Barrera, & V. J. Harris (Eds.). *Multicultural Issues in Literacy Research and Practice*. Mahwah, NJ: Lawrence Erlbaum Associates, Inc.

Children's Books Cited

Bunting, E. (1991). *Fly Away Home*. New York: Clarion.

Coleman, E. (1996). *White Socks Only*. Morton Grove, IL: Albert Whitman & Company.

Coles, R. (1995). *The Story of Ruby Bridges*. New York: Scholastic.

Herron, C. (1997). *Nappy Hair*. New York: Alfred A. Knopf.

hooks, b. (1999). *Happy to be Nappy*. New York: Hyperion.

——. (2002). *Be Boy Buzz*. New York: Hyperion.

Johnson, A. (1992). *The Leaving Morning*. New York: Orchard Books.

Lowell, S. (2001). *Dusty Locks and the Three Bears*. New York: Henry Hold.

Rappaport, D. (2001). *Martin's Big Words: The Life of Dr. Martin Luther King, Jr.* New York: Scholastic.

Roberts, B. C. (2004). Jazzy Miz Mozetta. New York: Farrar Straus Giroux.

Rosales, M. (1996). *'Twas the Night B'fore Christmas*. New York: Scholastic.

Shannon, D. (1998). *No, David!* New York: Scholastic.

Tarpley, N.A. (1998). *I Love My Hair!* Boston: Little, Brown, & Company.

Woodson, J. (2001). *The Other Side*. New York: G. P. Putnam's Sons.

14

Developing Culturally Responsive Teacher Practitioners Through Multicultural Literature

TAMARA L. JETTON, EMMA SAVAGE-DAVIS, AND MARIANNE BAKER

As our school districts and society at large grow more diverse, teachers face the daunting challenge of meeting the needs of students from diverse social, economic, and cultural backgrounds. Like many teacher education programs, our middle education program in a MidAtlantic state consists predominately of bright, young, White, middle- to upper-middle-class women. Many of our students come from large, diverse cities; however, few of them have had many experiences with diversity. They either attended private schools or were tracked into public school classrooms with predominately White classmates. We understand the difficulties that many of these future teachers face as they gain employment in schools and classrooms that are quite different from those that they attended.

It is for this reason that our middle education teacher certification program at a MidAtlantic university focuses on issues of diversity and cultural awareness in addition to the courses preservice teachers take in their academic domains. As their university instructors for courses in literacy and multicultural education, we encourage our teacher practitioners to consider the many challenges middle school students face in and out of school. We provide our teachers with field experiences in the diverse environment of one of our local school district middle schools. The sixth through eighth grade students who attend this middle school represented a very diverse population. The number of ethnic minorities increased from 27% to 34% in just 3 years, according to reports of the state's Department of Education (Virginia Department of Education, 2000). The Hispanic/Latino population increased from 12% to 18%, a 63% growth during a 3-year period. According to the local city school statistics, 875 students spoke 36 different languages and were from 43 different countries (Mellott, 2002). Sixty four percent of those students spoke Spanish as their native language. These demographics demanded that teachers working in the area be well prepared to engage students from linguistically and culturally diverse backgrounds in meaningful and productive learning.

As teacher educators, our challenge was to help our teacher practitioners develop a positive and multidimensional understanding of cultural diversity and gain knowledge of pedagogy that they can use to encourage their future students to understand how various cultural groups use language to convey their unique experiences. Through the coursework that we provided, these teacher practitioners explored their own histories and the histories of others in gaining a more positive and multidimensional understanding of different cultural groups. These teachers discussed ways to prepare students from diverse cultural backgrounds who may be oppressed by the dominant culture because of their race, ethnicity, gender, class, language, religion, ability, or age (Gollnick & Chinn, 2002). We also engaged our teacher practitioners in discussions of quality multicultural literature that celebrates a multidimensional understanding of culture. Through the literature, we showed our teacher practitioners how they could use discussion and writing to explore the linguistic variability among diverse cultural groups. This chapter focuses on one particular project designed by the first and second author that focused on the use of multicultural literature to guide discussion and writing.

Multicultural literature richly portrays the history, customs, values, and language of many diverse cultural groups. Students can learn to understand and appreciate the literary heritages of people from diverse backgrounds (Norton, 1990; Sims, 1982). For example, when students read multicultural literature, they can develop a heightened sensitivity to diversity issues and extend their knowledge of other cultures and expose their future students to differences and similarities between their culture and that of other groups. They can also begin to understand how people of different cultures use language to communicate their experiences and feelings.

Background Information

Despite encouragement by experts to use multicultural literature to increase awareness of diversity issues, many schools and teacher education programs still offer students literature authored primarily by White men (Holmes, Powell, Holmes, & Witt, 2007). Furthermore, just using multicultural literature does not mean that teachers are practicing multicultural pedagogy (Cook & Amatucci, 2006). Teacher preparation programs and schools need to link multicultural literature with effective pedagogy that focuses on culturally responsive teaching (Cook & Amatucci, 2006). Gay defines culturally responsive pedagogy as "using the cultural knowledge, prior experiences, frames of reference, and performance styles of ethnically diverse students to make learning encounters more relevant to and effective for them"(Gay, 2000, p. 29). We believe that teachers of culturally responsive classrooms encourage students to use reading, discussion, and writing to engage in multicultural literature.

Characteristics of Responsive Classrooms

Reading High Quality Multicultural Literature

In designing culturally responsive pedagogy that encourages students to examine how other cultures use language to communicate experience, teachers must incorporate a variety of quality multicultural literature into their language arts curriculum (Jetton & Savage-Davis, 2005). Wells (1986) suggests that because students often find it easier to assimilate new meanings when they are presented within the structure of a story, teacher practitioners can begin to develop new meanings and conceptualizations of what diversity means through literature. Stories about other cultures can increase teachers' sensitivity to and knowledge about those who are different from themselves and help them realize that although people have many differences, they also share many similarities. Incorporating multicultural literature into the curriculum can not only expand teachers' awareness of different cultures, but also decrease negative stereotypes of individuals from other cultures (Litchner & Johnson, 1973). By reading multicultural literature, teachers begin to understand their own cultural heritages as well as those of others (Rasinski & Padak, 1990), allowing them to view the world from multiple perspectives. When the world is viewed from more than one perspective, readers' views of others are broadened, and they gain insight into their own behavior (Banks, 1989). Of course, realizing these potential benefits depends largely on the type of multicultural literature that is used.

Several sources provide excellent suggestions for evaluating the quality of multicultural literature (Fox & Short 2003; Harris, 1997; Henderson & May, 2005). The criteria for selecting high-quality multicultural literature involve three areas: literary quality, accuracy, and authenticity. Regarding literary quality, one should consider literature that has well-developed plots and characters, genuine and complex character dialogue, and illustrations that enhance the text quality. Regarding accuracy, special attention should be given to fictional works that examine the historical trends in the roles of minority groups in America and that are historically accurate with no omissions or distortions, accurate portrayal of women, the elderly, the family, heroines and heroes according to their cultural group, and cultural values. Authenticity refers to seven important characteristics:

1. strong, independent characters not in need of a White authority figure
2. settings in the United States, so readers can understand the nature of cultural diversity in the U.S.
3. the legacy of several minority groups
4. the absence of loaded words that have derogatory overtones and negative or inaccurate stereotypes
5. genuine representation of the lifestyles of characters who exhibit authentic and realistic behaviors
6. some minority characters as leaders and problem solvers
7. authors and illustrators who deal with cultural group accurately and respectfully.

Quality multicultural literature does not merely focus on the issue of diversity but displays characters as individuals who express an array of attitudes and actions as they participate in the events of the story (Nilsen & Donelson, 2001). Through reading multicultural literature, students gain an understanding of how the authors use language to share these diverse experiences through both their powerful descriptions and realistic dialogue.

Discussion

Just as the reading of multicultural literature helps students gain an appreciation for the depth and richness of language used by the authors of diverse cultures, students can also use their own language within the language arts classroom to talk about their own experiences and how those experiences are the same or different from the characters in the literature. Teachers should encourage their students to use their own spoken language to communicate their views of diverse topics presented in the literature. Cooperative learning groups is one of the staples for encouraging students' use of their natural language to communicate. Cooperative groups consist of a heterogeneous group of students who have a common task or goal in order to accomplish a project or product (Farris, 2005; Slavin, 1996). Through cooperative learning groups, students use language to discuss their understandings and as a tool of solidarity, thereby unifying students from different backgrounds who share the common human experiences that the characters encounter (Godina & McCoy, 2000). Cooperative learning groups have been found to have consistent positive effects on learning among culturally diverse students (Slavin, 1996). By sharing their diverse perspectives through discussion, students become more accepting of diverse thoughts, emotions, and beliefs.

By participating in discussions, students engage in a shared culture in which participants are encouraged to be responsive to others and attentive to diverse opinions (Mannheim & Tedlock, 1995; Bridges 1979). That is, through discussions "cultures are produced, reproduced, and revised in dialogues among their members" (Mannheim & Tedlock, 1995, p.2). Discussion cannot occur when the cultural context causes members to believe that they cannot speak openly and express their opinions because their views are not valued. Furthermore, discussion will not be optimal if group members perceive one individual as the authority (Bridges, 1979). Rather group members should be equal participants in the activities, with teachers acting as facilitators.

Writing

Writing is another way in which students can use their own language in diverse and interesting ways. By writing about people from many cultural backgrounds, students can experiment with the tone, styles, sentence structures, vocabulary, and diction that people of diverse cultures use to communicate their experiences. Students can also use their own style and diction to communicate through many different genres of writing, including poetry, short stories, diaries, and autobiographies. As Maxine Hairston (1997) points out, students are "our greatest multicultural resource, one that is authentic, rich, and truly diverse. Every student begins class with a picture of the world in his or her mind that is constructed out of his or her cultural background and unique and complex experience" (p. 672). Through writing, students can articulate experiences through their own cultural lens. They can play with language as they write, experimenting with syntactical patterns, exploring word connotations, and understanding the dynamic nature of writing that changes according to various purposes and audiences.

Multicultural Literature Project

We designed a project in our middle education program that incorporated the reading, discussion, and writing about multicultural literature to not only help our teacher practitioners develop an appreciation for cultural diversity, but also to help them understand how they can use literature, discussion, and writing with their future middle school students. Through the curriculum that we designed as teacher educators, we wanted to use a culturally responsive pedagogical framework in which teacher practitioners used their natural oral and written language to express their views of the world and unique experiences. We provided developing teacher practitioners with an environment conducive for discussing and writing about such issues as race, ethnicity, and social status. Through discussions and writing activities, they were encouraged to explore the experiences and conflicts that individuals face as they encounter difficult and challenging life experiences. In this chapter, we will focus on how the project addressed, (a) reading high-quality multicultural literature, (b) creating comfort zones for discussion, and (c) writing as a response to multicultural literature.

Reading High-Quality Adolescent Literature

The first step in the process of designing our curriculum to increase an understanding of cultural diversity and how the author uses language to portray different cultural orientations was to select quality adolescent multicultural literature that presented an array of diversity issues. We determined the quality of literature according to the criteria for high quality multicultural literature previously described. We also analyzed the books according to the characteristics for quality adolescent literature suggested by Nilsen and Donelson (2001).

Nilsen and Donelson (2001) suggest that good-quality adolescent literature has seven characteristics. First, the author must write through the eyes of an adolescent. Second, the adolescents in the literature have the power and freedom to take credit for their own accomplishments and come to terms with their own problems. In quality adolescent literature, the adolescents, who are the protagonists, take the opportunity to look more honestly at themselves and the relationships that they have with others. Third, literature for adolescents must be fast paced to mimic the way in which adolescents are participating with media that includes the internet and MTV. Stories that keep a good pace, while still providing vivid images and complex themes, appeal to adolescents. Fourth, adolescent literature encompasses a variety of genres, themes, and subjects that range from short stories to biographies to historical fiction to fantasy and science fiction to realistic fiction.

Fifth, adolescent literature must include stories about characters from a variety of ethnic and cultural groups. Sixth, adolescent literature involves characters who make worthy accomplishments in the face of challenges, pessimism, and life-defeating events. The stories are often satisfying because adolescent characters face challenges, but they learn from them and change in the process. Seventh, quality adolescent literature focuses on emotions that are seen as critical and important to adolescents such as sex roles, understanding the changes in one's body, and preparing for sex, marriage, and occupations.

We began our search for literature from a wide array of adolescent multicultural literature, but we narrowed our list to eight novels that have quality stories that represent an array of diversity issues that our developing teacher practitioners would face as they began their practicum courses in the local schools and as they enter their own classrooms as practicing teachers. Also, the eight books selected were popular among students who attend the middle schools in which these teacher candidates would complete their practicum and student teaching requirements. To more fully understand the procedures and responses to the multicultural literature discussed that follow, it is useful here to briefly describe the books selected:

- *Tulip Touch* by Anne Fine (1999) recounts a story of two girls from two very different backgrounds who become friends. Natalie, who comes from a family with both parents and a little brother, experiences life very differently from Tulip, who lives with a neglectful mother and an alcoholic father.
- *My Louisiana Sky* by Kimberly Willis Holt (2000) is concerned with an adolescent, Tiger Ann Parker, who comes to terms with the shame she feels about her mentally challenged parents.
- *Necessary Roughness* by Maria G. Lee (1998) is about a young adolescent boy, Chan Jung Kim, who moves to a tiny Minnesotan town where he doesn't fit in because of his Korean heritage.
- In *Maniac Magee* by Jerry Spinelli (1990), the main character, Jeffrey Lionel (Maniac) deals with homelessness and confronts racism in a small town. He tries to lessen tensions between rival factions on the tough side of town.
- *The Devil's Arithmetic* by Jan Yolen (1990) deals with diversity of religion as a young Jewish girl, Hannah Stern, is transported to a Nazi death camp.
- *Dangerous Skies* by Suzanne Fisher Staples (1998) focuses on the issue of racial diversity with the story of two friends, Buck Smith, the son of a White farmer, and Tunes Smith, an African American girl, who discovers the body of one of the farm's managers.
- *While No One Was Watching* by Jane Leslie Conly (2000) concerns three neglected children from a working-class urban neighborhood who must cope with life when their guardian aunt disappears, and they are left to take care of themselves.
- *The Skin I'm In* by Sharon G. Flake (2000) details the life of a 13-year-old African American girl, Maleeka, who has low self-esteem because of the taunts she receives about her dark complexion.

We introduced these novels to our teacher candidates by explaining that the objective was to expose them to quality adolescent literature that portrays unique characters who face many challenges throughout the events of the novel. They chose one of the aforementioned books by picking a number out of a basket. This selection strategy forced them to confront diversity issues occurring in public schools that they may have wanted to avoid.

Creating Comfort Zones for Discussion

We wanted to create an environment in which the teacher candidates could comfortably use their natural language to discuss the diversity themes that emerged from their novels. By examining these themes in peer discussion and class presentations, they were free to use their own language to share experiences that, in turn, would begin to break down the notions that multicultural literature only offers superficial insights into issues of diversity. We grouped teachers according to their respective novel choices into groups of three to four people and asked them to discuss their own views and interpretation of the literature by referring to the ideas and comments they had written as they read the novels. Each group also planned a presentation of their novel for the whole class by crafting a synopsis of their novel and reaching a consensus about the important issues of diversity evoked by the novel.

The peer groups' discussions of the issues of diversity in the novels were important in two ways. It was the first chance for these developing teacher practitioners who read the same book to discuss their thoughts, feelings, and beliefs about the characters and the diversity issues they faced. Also, they were confronted with the similarities and differences in their own beliefs about diversity and those of their peer group members. Peer discussion provided a decentralized context in which group members verbalized their own ideas and views, decided on the topics, elicited each others' contributions, and, importantly, negotiated the participatory rules for themselves (Almasi, O'Flahavan, & Arya, 2001).

Many times during the discussion, class members conflicted over their views about particular issues. This conflict caused the practitioners to reconsider their own textual interpretations and restructure them as they heard contrasting views of others (Almasi, 1994). For example, while discussing *Maniac Magee*, members of the class had very different views about the importance of the diversity issues in the book. Some group members believed that Maniac's homelessness was the central issue of the book, while others focused more on the racial issues between the two sides of the town.

The class presentations created an environment in which these practitioners could convey their group members' thoughts, feelings, and beliefs about diversity to the larger audience. As each group presented the novel, the audience began to see the wider range of diversity issues that authors have used to center plots, develop themes and illustrate characters. They also began to understand that multicultural literature, like the Eurocentric literature that they had studied in school, conveys powerful and compelling stories that enable the reader to enter and experience another world.

The novels became so compelling that several class members chose to read the novels of other groups. Ericka, who originally read *Maniac Magee*, read *Devil's Arithmetic* after hearing the group presentation. She wanted to learn more about the Holocaust by reading *Devil's Arithmetic* in which a character lives through the experience. After the group presentation, Teresa chose to read *Skin I'm In* because Maleeka, the main character, reminded her of a friend. By reading the book, she hoped to gain a deeper understanding of her friend's feelings. Ericka and Teresa illustrate that when students are given the opportunity to use their own language through class presentations of various diversity issues, a comfort zone is created that enables students to become deeply engaged in learning.

Writing as a Response to Multicultural Literature

As part of our culturally responsive pedagogy, we encouraged the group to read their books and freely respond through writing by noting their own important and interesting ideas. Thus, the teachers could use their own language to convey their thoughts about the issues, characters, themes, conflicts, and outcomes of the novel. By relating to the characters, they could initially examine issues of diversity from a somewhat detached perspective as one of the characters in the novel. Then slowly they could begin to examine how their own experiences and views of these issues transpired in their own lives. Group members wrote about their empathy for the characters who faced discrimination. They also expressed that it was easier for them to begin or build on their thinking, feelings and beliefs about various diversity issues through the conflicts that the characters dealt with in the novels. Subsequently, they conveyed their thoughts, emotions, and attitudes about diversity issues that have occurred in their own lives.

Emily, who read *Necessary Roughness*, wrote about the issue of ethnic prejudice by expressing outrage over the narrow mindedness of the people who chanted derogatory words while Chan, the main character, was on the football field. She was disappointed by the physical abuse that he suffered in the locker room just because he was different. By first confronting the conflicts of the character, Emily was then able to address these same issues in her own life. She wrote about her experiences with the same narrow-minded attitudes encountered when she moved from a small town to a large city. Emily felt that her perspectives on life and school were different from the other students. In her small school, everyone knew each other and grew up having similar values and experiences. Now that she was in a larger city, no one seemed to care. According to her perspective, she was ostracized by the popular group and relegated to the "nobody group." She felt confused and upset about her circumstances because she felt as if she had no control. She became quiet and withdrawn, and her academic performance declined. With the support of her family, she was able to make the adjustment in time. This experience made her more sensitive to Chan's plight in the novel. She was able to feel an affinity for Chan and the discrimination he experienced as he moved to the new town.

Kara also used writing to express her disgust with the poverty that the characters faced in *While No One was Watching*. She wrote that she hated what poverty does to people and how the government structure doesn't help individuals with their situation. She, then, began to write about her own life, growing up poor in the Philippines. She expressed that no matter how hard people work and struggle, society makes it impossible for individuals to escape the binds of poverty.

Putting Reading, Writing, and Discussion Together

As the course instructors, we incorporated peer discussion and writing into the course in one other significant way. We believe that culturally sensitive/responsive pedagogy involves using one's own language to communicate experiences, but it also involves listening to others express their unique views through discussion and reading others' written expressions of their life knowledge. We incorporated the "tandem story" (Jetton & Savage-Davis, 2005) in our curriculum to encourage these developing teachers to listen to others' views of the novels and to read to discover how other colleagues crafted outcomes to these stories. A tandem story is one in which several authors collaboratively compose a story in sections. One writer drafts the first section, followed by the second and third writers until all group members believe the ending is complete.

We began the process of introducing them to tandem story writing by asking each person to revise the original ending of the novel they had read by writing an ending that would reflect their own decisions about how they would resolve the conflicts that arose in the novels. They constructed and revised their own endings without consulting other group members. We encouraged each person to write the outcome in his or her own voice and language.

Rebecca crafted a different ending for *Tulip Touch* by providing a happier ending in which Tulip is saved from her self-destructive behaviors. Rebecca viewed Tulip as incapable of having enough agency to overcome the obstacles that she faced without the help of someone else. This outcome was in stark contrast to the author's ambiguous ending in which the reader doesn't really know what happened to Tulip. Rebecca still believed that some issues of diversity were still too difficult to overcome, so the heroine in her ending takes a subservient position as someone who needs to be saved by someone, rather than someone who possesses the power to save herself.

Laura chose not to change the ending of *Devil's Arithmetic*, because she believed that the history in the novel was too powerful to change. Instead, she extended the ending by adding a conversation between Hannah and Aunt Eva, so Hannah could convey more deeply the personal sacrifices that she endured for her aunt. In contrast to Rebecca, Laura saw Hannah, the heroine, as having the power within herself to remedy the misperceptions that existed between herself and Aunt Eva. Laura's rewritten ending transcended the character stereotype of "helpless teen in need of assistance" that exists in some literature. Rather, she constructed a strong, independent character who took action to solve her own problems.

After each person had written or amended her own ending, the group was instructed to engage in more critically conscious dialogue about the issues in the novels and understand how others might portray these issues according to their own experiences and knowledge. We grouped together those who had read the same book and written their own ending. We asked them to keep their own endings in mind as they constructed a group "tandem ending" to the book in which they tried to hold true to their own values about how the book should end, but they also had to understand other group members' values and reach an acceptable compromise as to how the outcome of the story would be constructed.

We reminded them of how tandem stories worked. As they constructed their "tandem endings," we asked them to provide a group rationale that included justification for the changes they made. As they began the task, individuals took turns on email, constructing the ending and trying to create a seamless story. For some of them, this was a difficult task because they had to face the decisions of other group members that did not coincide with their own values or beliefs. Rachel, for example, changed the ending of *Maniac Magee* by enabling Maniac to find a home with the couple in the story who couldn't have children. Like Rebecca, Rachel placed Maniac in a submissive position as someone who needed help from others to solve his problems of homelessness. Other group members, however, disagreed. They believed that Maniac should take responsibility for his situation and succeed in life, despite his difficulties. They believed that it was more fitting of Maniac's character to succeed in spite of the obstacles he faced. They finished their story with a more positive ending than the one presented by the author. They wrote:

> So, Maniac started running and he kept running right out of town. No one saw him after that day, but you always hear the schoolgirls jumping rope and chanting:
>
> Ma-niac, Ma-niac, He's so cool
> Ma-niac, Ma-niac, Don't go to school
> Runs all night, Runs all right
> Ma-niac, Ma-niac, Kissed a bull!
> The legend of Maniac Magee will live on forever in Two Mills.

By examining their rationales for making certain changes, we found that the teachers believed that other powerful themes should take precedence over the diversity issues. For example, the group that wrote the tandem ending for *Dangerous Skies* focused on how friendship can transcend racial differences by having the characters look beyond color and other physical traits and look inside each other to find a deeper friendship. In their ending, Tunes was acquitted, and her name was cleared. The rest of the community came to the realization that Jumbo was guilty and had set Tunes up from the start. Thus, Buck and Tunes remained friends without having to worry about what everyone in the community thought. By creating this tandem ending, this group wanted to achieve a more positive ending without losing the realism of the racial issues in the original story. They ended the story with Tunes freed from all charges, but she still had to come to terms with her feelings for Buck:

> It took a while for Tunes to come around and forgive me. . . . She was upset that I had been too blind to see that no one would believe her word against Jumbo's. The truth was that it took Travis, a White man, to convince the court of Tunes' innocence. The experience has taught me that we live in a world that is not always just, but I have made it a point to try to change that scary reality. The first step, friendship. Tunes and I proved to the world that there are no colors when it comes to friendship.

As illustrated by this example, the group decided that it was up to a White man to "save the day." Thus, the story loses some of its realism, as opposed to gaining the hard edge of reality, and it maintains the stereotype that people of minority ethnic groups must be saved by a White authority figure. Despite this event, the group wanted to present the characters as seeing beyond color and looking toward friendship; characters who needed to work together to eliminate the feelings left by the acts of discrimination that were evident in the novel.

Another group that wrote a tandem ending for Necessary Roughness chose to emphasize the theme of family as much more precious than any problems that occurred due to cultural diversity. Thus, Young, Chan's sister, did not die. Rather her survival brought the family closer together:

> As I was about to kick the field goal, I heard the single note screaming from a flute. I turned around and looked into the bleachers, and there were Abogee, O-Ma, and Young sitting in the first row waving Minors' banners. At that moment I knew that things would be O.K. because everything that was important to me was right there. As the ball made it through the goal posts, the game ended with the cheers of my family ringing in my ears.

As the project came to a close, we wanted these teacher practitioners to be aware that they can utilize similar pedagogy with their own sixth through eighth grade students. We closed our tandem story activity with a discussion about how they can encourage middle school students to examine the language of other cultures through multicultural literature. We emphasized that they can provide their future middle school students with choices of quality multicultural literature and encourage them to use oral and written language through discussion and writing to express their views of the characters and themes within the literature. By using discussion and writing as the basis for exploring diversity, the teacher practitioners will also encourage their future middle school students to employ the valuable learning strategies that these activities help them develop.

As our society and public school classrooms grow more diverse, teachers must become culturally responsive educators. We hope that as part of their pedagogical stance, they will find multicultural literature to be a tool for understanding how language is used by diverse cultures to construct compelling stories of characters who face life's conflicts and challenges in many ways.

Discussion Questions and Activities

1. Examine the books that you use in your classroom by determining whether your books include quality multicultural literature as stipulated by the criteria in this chapter.
2. Design three discussion tasks in which students use their own language to express their views of the topics represented in a quality multicultural book.
3. Design three writing tasks in which students have the opportunity to use their own language through writing to share their views of topics represented in a quality multicultural book.

4. How can the ideas represented in this article be used to promote students' use of their own language through electronic journaling, emailing, and text messaging?

References

Almasi, J. F. (1994). The Nature of Fourth Graders' Sociocognitive Conflicts in Peer-Led and Teacher-Led Discussions of Literature. *Reading Research Quarterly*, 29, 304–306.

——, O'Flahavan, J. F., & Arya, P. (2001). A Comparative Analysis of Students and Teacher Development in More and Less Proficient Discussions of Literature. *Reading Research Quarterly*, 36, 96–120.

Banks, J. A. (1989). Integrating the Curriculum with Ethnic Content. In J. A. Banks, & C. A. McGee (Eds.). *Multicultural Education: Issues and Perspectives*. Boston, MA: Allyn & Bacon.

Bridges, D. (1979). *Education, Democracy, and Discussion*. Windsor: National Foundation for Educational Research.

Conly, J. L. (2000). *While No One was Watching*. New York: HarperCollins Children's Books.

Cook, L. S., & Amatucci, K. B. (2006). A High School English Teacher's Developing Multicultural Pedagogy. *English Education*, 38, 220–244.

Farris, P. J. (2005). *Language Arts: Process, Product, and Assessment*, 4th edn. Long Grove, IL: Waveland Press, Inc.

Fine, A. (1999). *The Tulip Touch*. New York: Laurel Leaf Library.

Flake, S. G. (2000). *The Skin I'm In*. New York: Jump at the Sun.

Fox, D. L., & Short, K. G. (2003). *Stories Matter: The Complexity of Cultural Authenticity in Children's Literature*. Urbana, IL: National Council of Teachers of English.

Gay, G. (2000). *Culturally Responsive Teaching: Theory, Research, and Practice*. New York: Teachers College Press.

Gollnick, D. M., & Chinn, P. C. (2002). *Multicultural Education in a Pluralistic Society*, 6th edn. Upper Saddle River, NJ: Merrill Prentice-Hall.

Godina, H., & McCoy, R. (2000). Emic and Etic Perspectives on Chicana and Chicano Multicultural Literature. *Journal of Adolescent and Adult Literacy*, 44, 172–179.

Hairston, M. (1997). Diversity, Idealogy, and Teaching Writing. In V. Villanueva, Jr. (Ed.). *Cross Talk in Comp Theory: A Reader*. Urbana, IL: National Council of Teachers of English.

Harris, V. J. (Ed.) (1997). *Using Multicultural Literature in the K-8 Classroom*. Norwood, MA: Christopher Gordon.

Henderson, D. L., & May, J. P. (Eds.) (2005). *Exploring Culturally Diverse Literature for Children and Adolescents: Learning to Listen in New Ways*. Boston, MA: Allyn & Bacon.

Holmes, K., Powell, S., Holmes, S., & Witt, E. (2007). Readers and Book Characters: Does Race Matter? *Journal of Educational Research*, 100, 276–282.

Holt, K. W. (2000). *My Louisiana Sky*. New York: Yearling Books.

Jetton, T. L., & Savage-Davis, E. (2005). Preservice Teachers Develop an Understanding of Diversity Issues through Multicultural Literature. *Multicultural Perspectives*, 7, 30–38.

Lee, M. (1998). *Necessary Roughness*. New York: HarperCollins Children's Books.

Litchner, J. H., & Johnson, D. (1973). Changes in Attitudes toward Negroes by White Elementary Students after the Use of Multiethnic Readers. *Journal of Educational Psychology*, 65, 295–299.

Mannheim, B., & Tedlock D. (1995). Introduction. In D. Tedlock, & B. Mannheim (Eds.). *The Dialogic Emergence of Culture*. Urbana, IL: University of Illinois Press.

Mellott, J. (2002). City Ranks Second in Virginia for ESL Percentage. *The Daily News Record*, 13–14.

Nilsen, A. P., & Donelson, K. L. (2001). *Literature for Today's Young Adults*, 6th edn. New York: Longman.

Norton, D. E. (1990). Teaching Multicultural Literature in the Reading Curriculum. *The Reading Teacher*, 44, 28–41.

Rasinski, T. V., & Padak, N. D. (1990). Multicultural Learning Through Children's Literature. *Language Arts*, 67, 576–580.

Sims, R. B. (1982). *Shadow and Substance*. Urbana, IL: National Council of Teachers of English.

Slavin, R. E. (1996). Research for the Future: Research on Cooperative Learning and Achievement: What we Know, What we Need to Know. *Contemporary Educational Psychology*, 21, 43–69.

Spinelli, J. (1990). *Maniac Magee*. Boston: Little, Brown, & Company.

Staples, S. F. (1998). *Dangerous Skies*. New York: Harper Trophy.

Virginia Department of Education (2000). Fall 2000 Membership by School Division. Retrieved April 11, 2002, from the Virginia Department of Education website: http://www.pen.k12.va.us/VDOE/dbpubs/Fall_Membership/.

Wells, G. (1986). *The Meaning-Makers: Children Learning Language and Using Language to Learn*. Portsmouth, NH: Heinemann.

Yolen, J. (1990). *The Devil's Arithmetic*. New York: Puffin Books.

15

Educating the Whole Child: English Language Learners in a Middle School

MARI HANEDA

This chapter considers the issue of children's rights to their own languages with respect to school-aged English language learners (ELLs). A central issue to be addressed is that of equitable education for ELLs in grade-level classes in which several different first languages are represented and the medium of instruction is English. I begin the chapter by describing what has been considered to be key for the education of ELLs and proceed to discuss some problematic issues identified in the literature. I then provide an example of one middle school teacher who has attempted to create a supportive community for ELLs in her grade seven social studies class. I conclude the chapter by considering implications of this example for practice.

The Education of English Language Learners

When considering the education of English language learners in our schools, it needs to be emphasized that they are, first and foremost, children like any others. And, as Dewey (1956) reminds us, education involves the whole child, and is concerned to help children to form the fundamental dispositions that will enable them to become socially responsible and productive members of society and to find fulfilling ways of developing and using their talents in their individual lives. Also important is to recognize that the development of the whole child occurs within the overall context of the system of relationships with the others with whom the child interacts. Thus, Rogoff (1995), for example, proposes that, in addition to focusing on the child as an individual, one must attend also to his or her interpersonal relationships with family members, peers and teachers, and also to his or her relationships with the wider society, as these are mediated by the school and community and by the artifacts that are employed in everyday activities. As she emphasizes, while it is convenient when studying or planning children's learning and development to focus on either the individual, the interpersonal or the societal, it must be remembered that these analytic perspectives are all simultaneously relevant. In sum, as with their native English speaking peers, the education of ELLs needs to be concerned with the whole child in the context of the complex systems of relationships in which their learning and development takes place.

However, while there is a growing body of research on the education of ELLs, there has been a tendency in much of it to treat the individual student as the basic unit of analysis (Hawkins, 2004) with a skewed focus on cognitive-linguistic aspects of language development at the expense of the role of language in students' social and emotional development (e.g., Carlisle, Beeman, Davis, & Spharim, 1999; Reese, Garnier, Gallimore, & Goldberg, 2000). Focusing on the role of English in enabling ELLs to achieve success at school, research has identified a number of dimensions that are considered to be key: linguistic, cognitive, academic, and social/emotional. Nevertheless, while research has addressed the first three dimensions, it has tended to ignore the fourth, despite the fact that, in our daily lives, all activities are inherently social and affect laden (John-Steiner & Tatter, 1983). For example, consider a child helping her/his mother to carry out a household task. Undertaken together, such an activity is necessarily social and is likely to be mediated by linguistic and nonverbal communication and to involve emotion (for example, the child's desire to help and the mother's appreciation) as well as cognition (for example, the child's understanding how to carry out a given task). The responsibility of the school, then, is to ensure that all these dimensions are included in an integrated way in the range of school activities, as they are in everyday life outside school.

At the same time, however, schooling differs from everyday life in that children are required to participate in a different kind of community from that of their family unit and to learn the use of academic language, namely, the register and genres associated with curricular content in the different disciplines. Thus, Cummins (1981) distinguishes the academic English requisite for school success, "cognitive academic language proficiency" (CALP), from "basic interpersonal communication skills" (BICS). Vygotsky (1987) similarly distinguishes "scientific concepts" from "everyday concepts." Likewise, Halliday, a linguist, contrasts the "synoptic" mode of language with its "dynamic" use in everyday situations:

> All learning—whether learning language, learning through language, or learning about language—involves learning to understand things in more than one way. In a written culture, in which education is part of life, children learn to construe their experience in two complementary modes: the dynamic mode of the everyday commonsense grammar and the synoptic mode of the elaborated written grammar (Halliday, 1993, p. 112).

Nevertheless, in this formulation it is clear that learning English in school is not just about mastering language form but learning how to construe and construct experiences using a wider repertoire of language resources, and it is ultimately about learning to live in a new culture.

Given the importance of academic language for school success, however, scholars have explored how to help ELLs and language minority students to bridge the gap between the two modes of language use and knowing: the synoptic (academic) and dynamic (everyday). For example, Gonzalez, Moll, & Amanti (2005) argue for the active incorporation of students' households' "funds of knowledge" into the curriculum. In so doing, language minority students (in this case working-class Mexican American students) can develop academic language, building on their existing community-based knowledge and linguistic and cultural resources. Another example is Gutiérrez and her colleagues' work (Gutiérrez, 2002; Gutiérrez, Baquedano-Lopez, & Tejeda, 1999) also with bilingual Spanish–English students. What is highlighted in their work is the importance of creating a discursive space in the classroom where students' everyday and academic language, both in Spanish and English, are actively recruited. This hybrid space, in which everyday registers are intermingled with the academic register, is shown to enable students to make personal connections between their life worlds and the curricular content. This bridging between the two modes of language use is also central to Tharp and his colleagues' (2000) work at the Center for Research on Education, Diversity, and Excellence (CREDE), which is set out in terms of the *Standards for Effective Pedagogy*. These standards represent research-based guidelines for effective instruction for all students, in particular language minority students at risk of academic failure:

1. Facilitate learning through joint productive activity in which teachers and students work together to create a product or an idea.
2. Develop language and literacy across the curriculum—competence in the genres of language and literacy of the academic disciplines through extended reading, writing, and speaking activities.
3. Contexualize instruction in the experiences and skills of students' homes and communities so that ELLs can make meaningful connections between the curricula content and their existing knowledge and life experiences.
4. Teach complex skills through challenging activities that require the application of content knowledge to achieve an academic goal, with clear outcomes in mind and systematic feedback on performance.
5. Teach dialogically, using planned, goal-directed instructional conversation between teacher and students, particularly in small groups.

The picture of classroom practice that emerges from these standards is that of a community of learners who are academically engaged, tackling linguistically and cognitively challenging tasks in a supportive environment.

Factors Hindering Effective Instruction for English Language Learners

Descriptive studies have shown that the features of effective pedagogy for ELLs delineated in the previous section are rarely fully realized in practice, and a variety of factors have been identified as preventing effective instruction from taking place (Rumberger & Gandara, 2004). One factor is the limited extent to which grade-level teachers with ELLs in their classrooms have knowledge about effective ways of teaching these students. A national survey revealed that the majority of general education teachers who had ELL students in their classes had little or no training with respect to the teaching of ELLs (NCES (National Center for Educational Statistics), 2002). Furthermore, it is frequently the least experienced teachers who are assigned to classes containing a large number of ELLs. Another major factor, particularly at the secondary level, is the tracking system. It has been reported that secondary ELLs, who tend to be placed in low-track classes, are fed with a steady diet of unchallenging tasks with diluted curricular content on the assumption that their less than complete command of English is an index of their academic ability (Haneda, in press). Further, ELLs tend to be placed in low-track classes by default, and once this placement is made, it is difficult for ELLs to move to more advanced tracks (Reeves, 2004). Not surprisingly, therefore, Callahan's (2005) study confirmed the detrimental effect of the tracking system on ELLs' overall academic achievement. Another contributing factor may be the ethos of the school, particularly the ideology of "color blindness" (in this case blindness to the degree of students' English language proficiency and to their linguistic and cultural diversity) that permeates some schools (Reeves, 2004). Under this ideology, teachers would feel obliged to treat every student in the same manner without differentiated instruction. This often results in blinding them to the need to make extra efforts to connect the curricular content with ELLs' linguistic and cultural backgrounds and to focus explicitly on language and literacy, which, by contrast, are at the heart of the CREDE standards set out earlier.

Equalizing Learning Opportunities for English Language Learners

In attempting to meet the needs of ELLs, teachers may receive appropriate support or find themselves working under specific institutional constraints. They may work in schools that ban or endorse the tracking system, encourage or discourage differentiated instruction, and offer or do not offer ongoing professional development with respect to the teaching of linguistically and culturally diverse students. Given these external factors, it is important to consider individual teachers' practices in conjunction with the institutional structures that support or discourage particular types of practices. In this section, drawing on my research, I wish to focus on the classroom practices of Ms. Kristen Bennett, a social studies teacher in a middle school, as an example of how one teacher has attempted to equalize learning opportunities for ELLs in her grade-level class. I will first introduce Ms. Bennett, the school, and her students and then discuss the specifics of her classroom practices.

Kristen Bennett has taught social studies at the middle school level for over 10 years, and has a strong reputation as a competent and caring teacher. Currently, she teaches grade seven social studies in a suburban school district in a U.S. Midwestern city, located in a middle class neighborhood. Highland Middle School (HMS), where Ms. Bennett has worked for the past 6 years, has a good academic standing and the student body comprises 602 students, of whom 67 % are White, 17% Asian and Pacific Islander, 6% Black/non-Hispanic, 4% Hispanic, and 6% multiracial. Ten percent of the students are designated "limited English proficient." Because of the presence of a prominent Japanese automobile plant in a nearby city, schools in this district, including HMS, have a high proportion of Japanese ELLs. More recent newcomers to the district and HMS are Mexican ELLs. Since the district does not endorse ability grouping (except for gifted classes in some subjects), ELLs, regardless of their English proficiency level, spend one period per day in an ESL class and attend grade-level classes for the rest of the day.

Consequently, teachers have incoming ELLs with a wide range of English language proficiency in their classes. In other words, ELLs, including those with little English competency, attend mainstream grade-level classes from their first day of school, a common practice among other suburban school districts near HMS.

Being keenly aware that ELLs, particularly beginners, were "getting lost" in her regular social studies classes, Ms. Bennett wanted to provide them with tailored instruction. While pursuing her master's degree in global education, she further explored this issue—meeting the needs of ELLs through differentiated instruction. She not only took a TESOL course but also carried out a research project as an independent study, exploring what it was like to be a student in a completely new language and culture. In order to gain firsthand experience of being a student with virtually no proficiency in the language of instruction, she spent 8 days attending the local Japanese school, where her Japanese ELLs study school subjects in Japanese on Saturdays. She also talked with Japanese parents about their feelings about American public schools and took Japanese mothers on a field trip around the city. Building on the insights gained through her cross-cultural experiences and her graduate studies, she felt that she could offer ELLs more appropriate instruction. So, 2 years ago, despite the district policy against grouping students, she approached her principal with a proposal to offer a grade seven social studies class designed specifically for ELLs, in order that she could better meet their needs. With the principal's support, Ms. Bennett created and taught the class for the first time in the academic year of 2005–2006; the class consisted mainly of ELLs with all levels of English language proficiency (the majority being Japanese ELLs) and also included a few native English speakers. While Ms. Bennett does not call this special class "sheltered," I am using the term, "sheltered instruction" to describe her class, because it shares common features with a sheltered class in that efforts are made to make grade-level academic content more accessible for ELLs through various instructional strategies (Echevarria, Vogt, & Short, 2004). Although, in the literature, "sheltered" classes usually consist solely of ELLs, I am using this term more broadly here.

My observation of Ms. Bennett's sheltered grade seven social studies class, to which she refers as "my third period class," started in her second year of implementation, with a different mixture of students. In 2006–2007, the class consisted of 13 ELLs (five Japanese, five Mexican, one Chinese, one Sudanese, one French), whose overall English proficiency ranged from beginner to intermediate level, and nine native English speakers, mostly Caucasian students from the local area and two ethnic minority students. These Caucasian students were those whom Ms. Bennett felt would benefit from the slower pace of the sheltered class for a variety of reasons (for example, not functioning well in regular classes). At the outset of my observation in October 2006, I was struck by the students' high level of engagement in learning the curricular content and the collegial atmosphere among them, which is very different from the dismal portraits of many sheltered classes presented in the literature (Valdes, 2001). There was also a great deal of discussion about various curricular-related topics in whole class settings. In fact, when one of my colleagues accompanied me to observe Ms. Bennett's sheltered and regular classes, he could not tell which one was "sheltered." My observation then came to focus on what contributed to creating the positive classroom ethos that made high intellectual engagement possible for her students. In the next section, I first describe the way in which Ms. Bennett approaches the teaching of her sheltered social studies and then the strategies that I observed her use.

Ms. Bennett's Approach to Teaching

In an interview, Ms. Bennett stated that, for all her social studies classes, she started with the state curriculum standards for each unit and considered how best to meet them by grouping the standards and thinking about appropriate activities for them. She ensured that she included all the content standards for all her classes. What differentiated her regular classes from the sheltered one was the inclusion of additional enrichment activities designed to go beyond the standards, a faster pace of classroom interaction, the nature of warm-up activities at the beginning of each lesson, and the types of project assigned. For example, in regular classes, the warm-up activity was for students to write in their journals a paragraph-length response to a written prompt related to the lesson (for example "In your opinion, how were the pyramids of ancient Egypt constructed?"), whereas in the sheltered class, students did a vocabulary activity in which they looked up one key word related to the lesson content. In terms of assessment, the unit test was written in such a way that language would not hinder ELL students' comprehension (e.g., rephrasing the questions she posed). Ms. Bennett added that she included more time for discussion in the sheltered class, since the students tended to ask many more questions than those in the regular class; in particular, they liked to explore cultural differences.

During the course of the observations that I carried out in Ms. Bennett's sheltered and regular classes, I gradually came to understand the ways in which she managed to maintain her high standards for academic performance in the sheltered class. The instructional strategies that she utilized can be summarized as follows:

1. slowing the pace of the lesson with more wait time
2. calling on all ELLs in each lesson and giving them sufficient time to respond
3. repeating and rephrasing key information
4. giving answers in both speech and writing
5. setting aside more time to deal with clarification questions raised by the students
6. using visual aids to promote comprehension
7. respecting students' use of their first languages
8. having students work in heterogeneous groups (i.e., ELLs with English-proficient students).

The first five strategies are identical to those recommended by scholars for making the curriculum content accessible for ELLs (Echevarria, Vogt, & Short, 2004). However, it should be noted that not all these strategies occurred in any particular lesson, but rather across lessons within a curriculum unit. In order to illustrate how

Ms. Bennett used some of these strategies in practice, I present one lesson from the beginning of her Egyptian unit. While no lesson can be said to be representative, this particular lesson includes frequently occurring features of Ms. Bennett's classroom practices.

Lesson from the Egyptian Unit

Just before the bell rings, the students start to walk into the classroom, greeted by Ms. Bennett at the door. They retrieve their "vocabulary boxes" from the front of the classroom and start working on today's key word, 'disaster,' which is written on the whiteboard at the front. Some are looking up the word in the glossary of their history textbooks, and others, such as Japanese ELLs, are busily looking it up using their electronic bilingual dictionaries. As they check the meaning of the word, three languages —English, Japanese, and Spanish—are heard as the students talk with one another. They are writing down the word on the front of an index card and the definition of the key word on the back. Several minutes into the lesson, Ms. Bennett asks what the word "disaster" means. Jim volunteers, "Something that causes harm or problems." She writes down the answer on the whiteboard and then asks what kind of pictures they drew for a disaster. Jeff responds, "tornado" and Taro, a Japanese ELL, says, "tsunami." Chris, a Chinese ELL, jokingly chimes in, "a man-eating monster!" Ms. Bennett tells the students that she selected this word in relation to the Nile River. She asks them whether it would be a disaster if the Nile River flooded, to which many say yes. Some students mention Hurricane Katrina and the disaster it left. Ms. Bennett says that they are partially right because, in most cases, the flooding of a river does cause disaster, but she draws their attention to the fact that the flooding of the Nile River had certain benefits. She explains that when the Nile River flooded, it left silt, which made the soil rich. Some students ask her to explain what silt is, to which she complies. She then asks whether it was a disaster when the Nile River flooded in ancient Egypt. The majority of students say "no." However, one of the ELLs, Paul, from France, loudly says, "Yes." In response, Ms. Bennett again explains that the reason ancient Egyptians liked the flood was because it left brown silt, which is great for growing crops in. This is followed by a brief explanation of what silt is and how it makes the soil fertile. José, a Mexican ELL, asks whether the flood destroyed people's houses, which would be a disaster. Acknowledging the question, Ms. Bennett answers that Egyptians built their houses away from the bank of the river. In the background, one student asks for clarification of the meaning of the word "bank," to which Ms. Bennett quickly responds. José is still puzzled and asks the same question from a different angle, "How about people?" With a nod to José, Ms. Bennett briskly walks to the back of the room, sifts through students' work, and walks back to the middle of the classroom with a miniature model of ancient Egypt in her hand. Pointing to this model and looking directly at José, she explains that Egyptians built their houses on higher places away from the river (gesturing and emphasizing AWAY) so that the flood would not affect their homes. Jeff then asks, "Wouldn't it ruin their crops, though?" Complimenting Jeff for asking a good question, Ms. Bennett explains that ancient Egyptians were able to predict when the flood was coming because they had a calendar; they took advantage of the flood rather than having it cause a disaster in the region. Following that, the class compares planting and harvesting seasons in Ohio and ancient Egypt. She reviews the names of the months and seasons very quickly, nominating ELLs to answer. She draws a chart of the planning and harvesting seasons on the whiteboard. She then asks what the farmers in Ohio do during the winter season. Several ELLs, José, Chris, and Paul, volunteer answers: "They fix machines," "They take care of their animals, and " "they sell animals." She explains that Egyptians were the same as farmers in Ohio, because their pharaoh said, "You guys have to do something during the flood season." She asks the students again whether the flooding of the Nile River was a disaster; all students say "no" this time.

The class then proceeds to do preview questions on the Egyptian unit that they started the day before (approximately 25 minutes being spent on this activity). The students are working from their handouts at their seats, and Ms. Bennett is displaying the questions on the overhead projector. The class goes through the remaining questions together. She nominates the students one by one, including all the ELLs, to read and answer questions. The preview questions deal with topics such as what a pyramid is, what is inside it, why/how bodies were mummified, how ancient Egyptians used the Nile River, and who were some famous Egyptian pharaohs. Lively exchanges between the teacher and the students and between the students continue throughout this activity. When the students give vague answers, Ms. Bennett pushes them to be more specific. Some Mexican beginner-level ELLs are seen to respond to a question by pointing to a picture or an object in the classroom or in the textbook; this is accepted as a legitimate answer. Further, Maria, a Mexican ELL who is intermediate English proficient, is seen to translate Ms. Bennett's questions and explanations into Spanish for two beginner-level Mexican ELLs who are sitting near her. Similarly, Keiko, a Japanese ELL who is also intermediate English proficient, is observed to translate for a beginner-level Japanese ELL sitting behind her.

As the last activity for the day, Ms. Bennett tells the students to come up to the front of the room, to examine pictures related to ancient Egypt that she has spread out on the floor, to write one question that they really want to ask on a sticky note, and place their note on the target picture. She announces that she will pick the five best questions for the whole class to consider. The students enthusiastically engage in this activity. There is a great deal of talk among the students about the pictures. Again, three languages —English, Japanese, and Spanish—are simultaneously heard during this activity, as some of the ELLs discuss possible questions in groups who speak the same first language. After about 10 minutes, Ms. Bennett collects all the pictures, quickly goes through the questions written by the students, and selects five questions. She reads out the five chosen questions and writes them on the whiteboard at the front. She also tells the class that these questions are their homework and they need to be writing them down, too. The selected questions are:

1. What is hieroglyphics?
2. Who were some of the Egyptian gods? (Name three.)

3. What is mummification?
4. Which pyramid in Egypt is biggest?
5. Who was Rameses?

Ms. Bennett wraps up her lesson by reminding the students that they need to find answers for all these questions that night. Taro asks whether he can use the internet as a resource to find answers, to which Ms. Bennett responds positively.

Analysis of the Lesson

In order to illustrate the way in which Ms. Bennett created a classroom community highly engaged in learning the curricular content, I examine the presented lesson in the light of dimensions that are identified in the second language research literature as key for ELLs to achieve success at school: linguistic, cognitive, academic, and social/emotional.

With respect to the cognitive and academic dimensions, the discussion of the flooding of the Nile River can be considered as an example of moving toward what Vygotsky (1987) terms "scientific concepts," in the sense that discipline-specific knowledge is constructed in conjunction with the associated linguistic forms. After introducing the academic lexical item "disaster," Ms. Bennett addresses a commonly held assumption that flooding causes disaster (everyday concept). Then she provides counter-evidence that, in ancient Egypt, flooding was an annual blessing because it left silt, which made the soil fertile; it enriched the soil—a condition desirable for farming. In the process, she introduces other academic vocabulary, "silt" and "fertile," explaining their meanings. José, the Mexican ELL, is not convinced that the flood was beneficial for ancient Egyptians and asks about the disastrous effects of flooding on people's houses and humans. Since José does not fully understand Ms. Bennett's first response, she appeals to a visual aid, a paper model of ancient Egypt. By showing where houses were built in relation to the Nile River on the model, she explains how Egyptian people prevented the flood from becoming a disaster. Then, Jeff, a native English speaking student, poses a further question about ruined crops. Here, the discussion centers on how ancient Egyptians used a calendar to predict when flooding would occur and thus built the cycle of flooding into their economy. In these ways the students are introduced to "scientific concepts" and the associated academic language; and by encouraging the students to ask questions Ms. Bennett tries to ensure that the discussion is also cognitively challenging for them. Evidence of this is seen in students' collaboration on formulating questions in the last activity. It is also worth noting that both ELLs and native English speaking students contribute to the ongoing discussion.

The importance that Ms. Bennett attaches to the social/emotional dimension can be seen in her efforts to create a positive classroom community in a number of different features of the present lesson. First, ELLs' first languages are respected, which sends a strong message to the students that their language resources are valued. ELLs are observed to draw on their first languages freely where appropriate: providing translation for peers when necessary and discussing the definition of the key word and curricular-related matters with peers. The validation of their first languages is important because it also validates who these students are, bilingual students with rich linguistic and cultural repertoires, as opposed to students with "limited English proficiency." Second, Ms. Bennett attentively responds to students' questions and comments, respecting their points of view; this applies equally to ELLs and native English speaking students in the class. She is not dismissive of students' questions, but attempts to build on them. Third, in her willing uptake of the students' questions, Ms. Bennett tends to repeat or rephrase key curricular information, as is seen in the discussion of the flooding of the Nile River; she also frequently provides answers in both speech and writing. Both these strategies are responsive to some ELLs' anxiety about not being able to follow the class. Fourth, the fact that the students frequently volunteer answers is evidence that Ms. Bennett has succeeded in creating a supportive environment in which they feel comfortable enough to voice their opinions in public. Furthermore, all ELLs were nominated at least once in a given lesson; being able to participate in each lesson helps ELLs feel that they are legitimate members of the classroom community. Fifth, as is exemplified in the last activity, questions generated by the students are highly valued, which reinforces a positive social environment.

In terms of the linguistic dimension, the reinforcement of key information through repetition and rephrasing as well as the provision of answers in both speech and writing not only make the curricular content accessible to ELLs but also provide an abundance of what Krashen (1985) calls "comprehensible input," which is considered to be critical for second language learning. While there is little explicit focus on grammar, as in an ESL class, there is an emphasis on academic vocabulary (e.g., silt, fertile, disaster, mummification, Pharaoh, hieroglyphics).

Finally, I focus on the inclusion of native English speakers in this social studies class. These students, whom Ms. Bennett described as "not doing well in mainstream classes," are actively involved in all activities (e.g., volunteering answers and helping ELLs) with renewed confidence. For example, Dean, who Ms. Bennett described as 'non-functioning' in his mainstream social studies class, is observed to respond to his teacher's questions, to give help to ELLs with English, and to converse about curricular topics with others. Ms. Bennett thought Dean became more engaged in his learning when he found that he could help his classmates with the English language.

Analysis of Ms. Bennett's Classroom Practices

I started this chapter by emphasizing the need to see ELLs, like all others, as students whose education needs to be concerned with the whole child. This is very much the concern of Tharp and his colleagues in proposing the *Standards for Effective Pedagogy* for all students, particularly those at risk of educational failure. I wish now to review Ms. Bennett's practices in the light of the standards proposed by CREDE. Because these standards are concerned with sustained classroom practices, I will include my observations from other lessons in my analysis, as well as the one presented earlier.

The first standard, *Joint Productive Activity*, was clearly enacted in the last activity of the preceding lesson, in which the students discussed the pictures of ancient Egypt and generated their own questions. In this case, the jointly created product was the five questions selected by the teacher at the end of the lesson, which then became the students' homework, requiring them to do research. Another example of this standard is the use of the students' "vocabulary boxes" in the review of each curricular unit (e.g., Egypt, Mesopotamia); Ms. Bennett would select some vocabulary boxes and use them for the unit review in the whole class for the benefit of all students.

The second standard, *Language and Literacy Development*, was nurtured in almost all instructional activities. As shown in the presented lesson, there was extended discussion between the teacher and the students in the whole class setting, in which a great deal of "comprehensible input" was generated. Important language functions, such as eliciting information, questioning, restating, probing, were used by both the teacher and the students. Also, as noted earlier, there was an explicit focus on subject matter vocabulary. Also emphasized in many lessons was the whole class read-aloud. Unlike in her regular class, in which she let her students take turns to read paragraphs, Ms. Bennett read one or two paragraphs at a time, enunciating words very clearly, and then either asked for a volunteer or nominated a student to read the same passage. After each paragraph, Ms. Bennett clarified key words or information before moving to the next paragraph (for example, "What are nomads?"). After repeating this procedure several times to complete a subsection of the history textbook, the class usually proceeded to answer questions about key information on a worksheet. On some occasions, Ms. Bennett asked her students to skim a subsection of their textbook for specific key information (underlining or extracting it) or requested they read a story related to a particular topic, followed by a discussion. In different units, she also included readers' theater, in which all the students became involved in acting out a play set in the region and period that they were studying, for which she provided a script on the over-head projector for everyone to follow. In this way, the students were exposed to a variety of reading experiences in the class.

The third standard, *Contextualization,* which is the establishment of meaningful connections between curricular content and students' experiences and skills, was also frequently observed. For example, in the discussion of the flood, Ms. Bennett tapped into a popular belief about the flood disaster connection (everyday concept), drawing on the students' existing knowledge. Building on that, she explained that flooding was a blessing in the case of ancient Egyptians. Although this "everyday concept" of flooding as a disaster was probably part of the "funds of knowledge" of the students' communities, she utilized their more general cultural knowledge to help them construct a more "scientific concept" that was independent of the often harmful consequences of flooding. In addition, the use of student-generated questions in the last activity can be seen as another attempt to make instruction meaningful and relevant for the students. Another important strategy she frequently used was the establishment of intertextual connections between the units. The students were frequently reminded of what they had learned in preceding units and asked to connect the previously learned information with what they were currently learning. This intertextuality was built into each unit test, which became longer as the semester progressed because the previously learned information was also included in the new test.

The fourth standard, *Cognitively Challenging Activities*, involves the use of complex tasks that require the application or use of content knowledge to achieve an academic goal. As noted earlier, Ms. Bennett aligned her activities with the state curriculum standards for each unit; these activities were often taken from *History Alive* and presented in a way that was cognitively challenging. She had her students in the sheltered class engage in the same activities as in the regular class, but with additional support. One example of such an activity was where the students were asked to imagine themselves to be archeologists who were uncovering artifacts in the subcontinent of India. Seven stations were set up around the classroom, at which various artifacts were displayed. Working in heterogeneous groups (ELLs with native English speakers), the students were directed to visit each station, examine the artifacts, and try to figure out what they were. Next, they were to use the textbook to find the archeologists' inferences about the function of these artifacts and then compare them with their own guesses. Finally, following this group activity, there was a whole class discussion to wrap it up and the assignment of homework that related to this activity, in which they would reinforce what they learned by writing about it.

As explained earlier, the fifth standard, *Instructional Conversation*, is a planned, goal-directed conversation between a teacher and a small group of students. This did occur, but not very frequently. When it occurred, it was in relation to a group activity, in which Ms. Bennett circulated and spent time with each group, answering questions and providing assistance where needed. In addition, the whole class discussion was dialogic, as the students' frequently voiced opinions that were taken up and built upon.

Implications for Practice

Examining Ms. Bennett's classroom practices in some detail shows that, even in an English-medium instructional environment, it is possible to respect and honor students' bilingual resources in such a way as to enable them to feel validated and accepted for who they are (Cummins, 2006). Supporting Ms. Bennett's intention to create a learning community, I would suggest, was her commitment to equity and advocacy so that all her students, regardless of their proficiency in English or current academic performance, had a fair chance at learning the curriculum content and gaining confidence in their academic abilities. She strove to teach the whole child in terms of all the dimensions important for meaningful teaching and learning: linguistic, cognitive, academic, and social/emotional. She demonstrated her commitment, not only through differentiated instruction, grouping of her students, and the use of various sheltered instructional strategies, but also through her caring attitude; she was aware of her students' lives outside school and used this knowledge as a basis for interacting with them. It is remarkable that Ms. Bennett was able to enact so many of the strategies and principles recommended for sheltered instruction and equitable education without formal training in such pedagogy. This is encouraging in the light of the rapid demographic change that is taking place in the United States. In 1992, only 15 % of U.S. teachers had one or more ELLs in their classrooms, but the figure had increased to 43% by 2002 (McCardle & Chhaba, 2006). Thus, teaching ELLs in mainstream classes is a challenge that faces an increasing number of teachers in the United States.

However, for a number of reasons, Ms. Bennett's example cannot be treated as a model appropriate under all circumstances for all subject teachers whose classes include ELLs. First, Ms. Bennett is exceptionally committed to equity and has constantly strives to improve her teaching in order to meet the needs of ELLs. For example, she put herself through intercultural training to better understand what her ELLs are experiencing at school, resulting in what Ladson-Billings (2002) called cultural competence. Second, other teachers may be working with very different groups of ELLs (e.g., with respect to their level of English proficiency, SES status, prior schooling,) and in very different sociopolitical settings (e.g., implementation of a tracking system, banning of bilingual education). Nevertheless, what her example does teach us is that providing high-quality education for ELLs is not simply a matter of teachers' mastering various techniques involved in sheltered instruction, as has been interpreted by some schools and school districts across the country (e.g., Langman, 2003). Rather, enacting equitable education requires schools and teachers to develop a democratic vision of education for all students, including ELLs, which includes sheltered instructional techniques to help make the curriculum content comprehensible for ELLs.

Ms. Bennett's way of attempting to equalize learning opportunities for ELLs also raises some questions that require further consideration, particularly in relation to tracking. Recall that the school district in which she works does not endorse tracking of students. Consequently, schools in the district, including HMS, are detracked. Rubin and Noguera (2004) describe detracking as an attempt to group students heterogeneously "as a means of ensuring that all students, regardless of their race, class background or their academic ability, have meaningful access to high quality curriculum, teachers, and material resources" (p. 93). However, detracking at the school level leaves many issues unresolved at the classroom level, leaving the responsibility for meeting the needs of diverse students in the hands of individual teachers, as Ms Bennett had become aware. As her example shows, one of the ways to achieve this is through differentiated instruction, tailored to the needs of different students. However, such differentiated instruction needs to be considered as a purely temporary scaffolding, with the assumption that, over time, all students are capable of mastering the registers as well as the content of the different school subjects. Furthermore, as Ms. Bennett's practices made clear, differentiated instruction needs to encompass all aspects of teaching: planning the unit and activities, selecting appropriate projects/assignments and assessments, and modifying patterns of classroom interaction. However, because ELLs in middle and secondary school take classes in many school subjects taught by multiple teachers, the provision of quality education in detracked classes requires the commitment of the whole school to make it work.

Ms. Bennett's example is suggestive of at least two strategies that schools can employ in ensuring quality instruction for ELLs in detracked classes. First, although tracking has been associated with negative consequences for language minority students (Oakes & Lipton, 2003), a temporary provision of sheltered instruction in different school subjects appears to be one of the effective ways to help ELLs successfully transition into mainstream grade-level classes. Such classes should be characterized by high academic rigor and high support, as opposed to the ESL "ghetto" characterized by low expectation and reduced content instruction, a ghetto from which ELLs cannot escape (Valdes, 2001). Second, as shown by numerous studies (e.g., Lucas, Henze, & Donato, 1990; Oakes & Lipton, 2003), in order to realize the vision of equitable education for all students, the entire school staff needs to be involved in achieving this shared goal. Such reform requires a strong, distributed leadership by the principal in order to promote interdepartmental collaboration. This, in turn, needs to be supported by the school district personnel. Just like students, educators also work in the web of human relations. The kind of change described earlier requires a commitment to a shared vision of educational equity not only at the level of educational policy but also at that of the school community.

Discussion Questions and Activities

1. Consider what kind of differentiated instruction might be needed to meet the needs of the ELL students that you know of. In what ways could you ascertain what these needs are?
2. Imagine you were in a twelfth grade science classroom in China, and you were not familiar with the language. What types of social and academic challenge might you incur? What could the teacher do to make your experience more productive and pleasant?
3. Create one unit of study that would benefit all learning styles and needs, especially those of ELLs. Your unit should include key vocabulary and concepts, visuals, hands-on activities, cooperative learning experiences, teacher led instruction, interactive student discussion questions, opportunities for reading and writing and an assessment piece.
4. As a way of further understanding your ELL students' second language development, design an action research project that you might carry out in your classes.

References

Callahan, R. (2005). Tracking and High School English Learners: Limiting Opportunities to Learn. *American Educational Research Journal*, 42, 305–328.

Carlisle, J., Beeman, M., Davis, L., & Spharim, G. (1999). Relationship of Metalinguistic Capabilities and Reading Achievement for Children who are Becoming Bilingual. *Applied Psycholinguistics*, 20, 459–478.

Cummins, J. (1981). Age on Arrival and Immigrant Second Language Learning in Canada. A Reassessment. *Applied Linguistics*, 2, 132–149.

——. (2006). Identity Texts: The Imaginative Construction of Self through Multiliteracies Pedagogy. In O. Garcia, T. Shutnabb-Kangas, & M. E. Torres-Guzman (Eds.). *Imagining Multilingual Schools: Languages in Education and Glocalization.* Clevedon: Multilingual Matters.

Dewey, J. (1956). *The School and Society & the Child and the Curriculum.* Chicago, IL: University of Chicago Press.

Echevarria, J., Vogt, M. E., & Short, D. (2004). *Making Content Comprehensible for English Learners: The SIOP Model,* 3rd edn. Boston, MA: Allyn & Bacon.

Gonzalez, N. C., Moll, L. C., & Amanti, C. (2005). *Funds of Knowledge: Theorizing Practices in Households, Communties, and Classrooms.* Mahwah, NJ: Lawrence Erlbaum Associates, Inc.

Gutiérrez, K. (2002). Studying Cultural Practices in Urban Learning Communities. *Human Development,* 45(4), 312–321.

——, Baquedano-Lopez, P., & Tejeda, C. (1999). Rethinking Diversity: Hybridity and Hybrid Language Practices in the Third Space. *Mind, Culture, & Activity: An International Journal,* 6, 286–303.

Halliday, M. A. K. (1993). Toward a Language-Based Theory of Learning. *Linguistics and Education,* 5, 93–116.

Haneda, M. (2008). Contexts for Learning: English Language Learners in a U.S. Middle School. *The International Journal of Bilingual Education and Bilingualism* 11(1): 75–94.

Hawkins, M. (2004). Researching English Language Development and Literacy in Schools. *Educational Researcher,* 33, 14–25.

John-Steiner, V., & Tatter, P. (1983). An Interactionist Model of Language Development. In B. Bain (Ed.). *The Sociogenesis of Language and Human Conduct.* New York: Plenum Press.

Krashen, S. (1985). *The Input Hypothesis: Issues and Implications.* New York: Longman.

Ladson-Billings, G. (2002). *Crossing Over to Canaan: The Journey of New Teachers in Diverse Settings.* San Francisco: Jossey-Bass.

Langman, J. (2003). The Effects of ESL-Trained Content Area Teachers: Reducing Middle School Students into Incidental Learners. *Prospect,* 18, 14–26.

Lucas, T., Henze, R., & Donato, R. (1990). Promoting the Success of Latino Language Minority Students: An Exploratory Study of Six High Schools. *Harvard Educational Review,* 60, 310–340.

McCardle, P., & Chhaba, V. (2006). Commentary. *Elementary School Journal,* 107, 239–248.

National Center for Educational Statistics. (2002). *Schools and Staffing Survey, 1999–2000: Overview of the Data for Public, Private, Public Charter, and Bureau of Indian Affairs Elementary and Secondary Schools.* (NCES Publication No. 2002-313). Washington, DC: U.S. Department of Education, National Center for Educational Statistics.

Oakes, J., & Lipton, M. (2003). *Teaching to Change the World,* 2nd edn. Boston, MA: McGraw-Hill.

Reese, L., Garnier, H., Gallimore, R., & Goldberg, C. (2000). Longitudinal Analysis of the Antecedents of Emergent Spanish Literacy and Middle School English Reading Achievement of Spanish-Speaking Students. *American Educational Research Journal,* 37, 633–662.

Reeves, J. (2004). "Like Everyone Else": Equalizing Educational Opportunities for English Language Learners. *TESOL Quarterly,* 38, 43–66.

Rogoff, B. (1995). Observing Sociocultural Activity on Three Planes: Participatory Appropriation, Guided Participation, and Apprenticeship. In J. V. Wertch, Del Río, P., & Alvarez, A. (Eds.). *Sociocultural Studies of Mind.* New York: Cambridge University Press, pp. 139–164.

Rubin, B. C., & Noguera, P. A. (2004). Tracking Detracking: Sorting Through the Dilemmas and Possibilities of Detracking in Practice. *Equity and Excellence in Education,* 37, 92–101.

Rumberger, R., & Gandara, P. (2004). Seeking Equity in the Education of California's English Learners. *Teachers College Record,* 106(10), 2032–2056.

Tharp, R. G., Estrada, P., Dalton, S. S., & Yamauchi, L. (2000). *Teaching Transformed: Achieving Excellence, Fairness, Inclusion, and Harmony.* Boulder, CO: Westview Press.

Valdes, G. (2001). *Learning and Not Learning English: Latino Students in American Schools.* New York: Teachers College Press.

Vygotsky, L. S. (1987). Thinking and Speech. (N. Minick, Trans.). In R. W. Rieber, & A. S. Carton (Eds.). *The Collected Works of L. S. Vygotsky, Volume 1: Problems of General Psychology.* New York: Plenum Press.

16

New Chinese Immigrant Students' Literacy Development: From Heritage Language to Bilingualism

DANLING FU

Over the past two decades the number of English language learners (ELLs) in the United States over the age of 5 has grown from 23 million to 47 million, or by 103% (U.S. Census Bureau, 2003). This means that in the United States, about one out of every five students (20%) resides in a home in which a language other than English is spoken. By the year 2030, this number is expected to double to roughly 40% of all students. U.S. Congress's recent passage of a bill making English the national language reflects American dominant society's anxiety or fear of this rapidly growing and ever diverse population and of the possibility that English's dominant status will be overtaken by a minority language such as Spanish. However, whether English becomes the national language or not, children who immigrate to the United States and those born to recent immigrants from non-English speaking countries continue to live in the "borderlands" (Anzaldua, 1987) where two languages and two cultures come together. Such settings offer numerous opportunities to transition between languages and cultures, for immigrants find that they need to be able to move fluidly from one group or situation to another without significant misunderstanding or loss of identity.

The fact that over half of the world's population is bilingual (Kohnert, 2004) suggests that bilingualism not only helps serve transitional needs, but that becoming at least partially bilingual is not as overwhelmingly difficult or potentially confusing as one might suspect. Further, the fact that the acquisition of a second language has historically been a mark of erudition among the educated elite suggests that, at some level, bilingualism is a socially and culturally desired goal. Despite this, in the United States, bilingualism represents, at best, a necessary but mostly transitional state which cannot be counted among the socially and academically privileged. The political push for "English Only" in the United States obliterates many opportunities for nonnative English speaking students. It not only affects most new immigrants at a personal level, but also serves to place them at a distinct linguistic and cultural disadvantage by determining the nature of the educational programs that serve their children in American schools across the nation (Fu & Matoush, 2006).

For new immigrant children, opportunities for educational success, economic advancement, and sense of self worth as an "American" must be weighed against keeping open lines of communication with one's immediate or extended family, neighbors, and cultural affiliates. Because the majority of immigrant children come from low-income families, most have little choice but to adopt English as their language of preference if they hope to flourish in this country. Further, although first generation immigrant children may find themselves serving as bilingual translators for their parents, neither they nor their children are apt to be afforded the opportunities to further develop their native language skills beyond those required by domestic situations, and so a shift to monolingual English within the first three generations is prevalent (Anderson, 2004; Tse, 2001). Under the pressure of *No Child Left Behind*, the demand for new immigrant students to pass the same standardized tests as their native English speaking peers pushes these students into English monolingual status, resulting in rapid loss of their primary language. Some have argued that these losses are simply the price immigrant families must pay for choosing to live in the United States. However, many believe this high price is not paid by immigrants alone. The negative consequence of language loss and the benefits of preserving heritage languages have far reaching implications for the individual and larger U.S. society alike (Tse, 2001).

In this chapter, I begin with a brief review of perspectives on the benefits of bilingualism, followed by a discussion of discoveries I made in a study of how new immigrant students moved from first language toward Chinese–English bilingualism. Specifically, I present discoveries made from the use of students' first language to help them learn about America, followed by descriptions of my observations about processes involved in becoming bilingual. Grounded with this study, suggestions for teaching ELLs are provided at the end of the chapter.

Perspectives on the Benefits of Bilingualism

A growing body of empirical evidence indicates both cognitive abilities and scholastic achievement are positively associated with bilingualism. Fernandez and Nielsen (1986) provided evidence from national longitudinal data that, among Hispanic and European American high school students, proficiency in both English and parental native languages were positively related to academic achievement. Matute-Bianchi (1986) found in an ethnographic study of Mexican-American children that advanced bilingual skills were related to a strong Mexican identity and that fully bilingual young Mexican-Americans tended to perform better in school than those who lacked proficient bilingual skills. She concluded that proficiency in the native language allows young people to gain greater access to the emotional and normative supports of the ethnic group.

In a study of Chinese immigrant children in New York City's Chinatown, Sung (1987) found that bilingual students had higher student retention rates, more graduates, and higher self-esteem. Other researchers have found that language maintenance bilingual programs (maintaining students' native language while learning English), as opposed to transitional bilingual programs (students will shift to learn only in English once their English reaches certain proficiency) helped students learn the language of the dominant society effectively (Cazden & Snow, 1990; Cummins, 1981). Tse's study (2001) suggested that bilingual students of Hispanic/Latino heritage were better readers in English and had higher academic aspirations than those who were Hispanic/Latino but monolingual in either English or Spanish. This indicates that those who develop their heritage language and know English will do better in school than those who leave the heritage language behind. All these studies suggest that bilinguals have an advantage because they have more than one way of thinking about a given concept, making them more "divergent" thinkers and more effective problem solvers (Tse, 2001).

Using First Language to Learn about America

In this section, I present information from my study of how new immigrant students continued to develop their first language literacy in a bilingual program in a New York City's Chinatown middle school (grades six to eight). Eighty-five percent of the student population in this school is from China; 34.5% of whom were recent arrivals (less than 3 years). All the recently arrived immigrant students in this school, no matter their grade placement, were required to take Chinese language arts (CLA)/social studies, a bilingual program specifically designed for newcomers with limited English proficiency. They were also required to take ESL classes daily along with math, science, and other subjects required by the middle school curriculum. My study focused on the CLA/social studies class where students studied American history, government, New York City, and current events in their first language, Chinese. My background as a first-generation Chinese immigrant and my high proficiency in both English and Chinese gave me both advantage and insight in this study.

Most of the new Chinese immigrant students in this middle school were able to read and write in Chinese, though not necessary at their grade level. Following Krashen's "gradual exist" (1991) theory on bilingual education, the CLA/social studies program was designed to use the students' first language to build the content knowledge these newcomers needed for both their schooling at middle school level and their transition into the American society. These new immigrant Chinese students resided in the Chinatown community, where they were deeply immersed in their ethnic culture and used Chinese for their daily activities such as shopping, dining out, seeing doctors, and engaging in any social and commercial services. After discovering these new immigrant students had so little knowledge about the United States, its history, or the society as a whole, the school administrators decided to integrate the Chinese language arts program with American studies, a class named CLA/Social studies.

The social studies content in CLA covered a wide range of American history topics, such as Native Americans, Columbus's discovery of the "New World", the Revolutionary and Civil Wars, slavery, immigrants, Western expansion, World War II, the American government. The students read fiction and nonfiction textbooks in Chinese, along with supplementary children's literature in English that were added later due to lack of books written in Chinese on the topics of America. In the class, the students discussed events in groups, collaborated on inquiry projects. They were required to complete two or three pieces of writing weekly to demonstrate their learning.

Reading, writing, and discussion of the American society were constantly linked to the students' own life experiences and their knowledge of their own home country and culture. The following excerpt is from a group discussion that was recorded in Chinese (all translations from Chinese to English are mine) after the class studied the Vietnam War:

Boy 1: Except for the current war in Afghanistan, the Americans fought all the other wars to help others. For instance, they joined WWII to help the Europeans, fought in the Korean War to help the South Koreans; and in Vietnam War they helped the south regime in Vietnam and then helped Kuwait fight against Iraq in Gulf War. Only in this Afghanistan war, it is for American's own revenge after the September 11 terrorist attack.
[Several students agree with him.]
Boy 2: Americans love to help others, that is, to keep them as a world superpower. Now, we are suffering, and look what the Arabs did to us in New York.
Girl 1: [softly] I think the American fought all the wars for themselves. In WWII, they joined the war only after the Pearl Harbor attack. They fought the Korean and Vietnam wars to prevent Communism from gaining power in the world. That is also for their own ideology. Then they fought Gulf War for the oil supply.
Girl 2: In China, we call America the imperialist, because they go to other countries to fight . . .
Boy 3: [cutting in] You can't say that about the WWII and the war in Afghanistan now. They are the wars for justice, to fight against German Nazis and to fight the Muslin [sic] Terrorists.
Girl 2: My great uncle died in the Korean War. My grandpa told me that he was killed by Americans.
Girl 3: But my great aunt told me American helped us fight against Japanese during WWII. The Japanese killed a lot of Chinese in China.
Girl 1: [trying to pull the group back to the Vietnam War] How about the Vietnam War? The American people were against this war themselves.
Boy 3: But nobody is against our war in Afghanistan. We hate those terrorists and want to kill them all. They kill so many here in our city. And it is hard to find jobs now.
Boy 1: Yea, the first time, America was invaded like this and suffered by the outsiders' attack on its own land. Of course, we have to fight back.

The bell rang, ending the discussion or the discussion would have continued. It was impressive to hear the connections the students made from one war to another and their confidence in expressing their opinions. Although students didn't discuss the Vietnam War extensively, they certainly knew a lot about wars and why the American fought those wars. From their family stories, they also knew a great deal about wars in which the Chinese was the enemy of Americans, and in which the Chinese and Americans were friends.

It is interesting to notice how they shifted their positions when they talked about different wars. For example, when they talked about the current war in Afghanistan, they felt more personally connected by referring to it as "our war" and their uses of phrases such as "WE have to fight back."

In the CLA class, learning of American history and making connections with what they knew gave them a sense of being part of the nation and helped them become interested in current government and political events in this country. During election time, they voiced their opinions about Republicans and Democrats, and debated about which parties that supported immigrants, social service, and labor unions. They paid special attention to the AIDS epidemic in Africa, terrorist bombings and fighting in the Middle East, and other global current events.

One of the major discoveries of my study was that actively engaging in reading, writing, and talking about historical and current events in their native language prepared these students to function as literate citizens in this new world and fostered their new identities in becoming Chinese-Americans. Through the development of this kind of thinking and their broad interest and knowledge in their first language, these students were preparing not only for their education in America, but also their present and future lives in this democratic world. Had the students not been allowed to use their first language to study content knowledge, they would not have been able to read, write, and talk about such sophisticated topics, thereby delaying their intellectual development, and leaving them significantly behind their peers.

The students enjoyed comparing/contrasting their learning of America with their knowledge of China and their own experiences. For instance, while studying immigration in the 1920s, students were able to compare experiences of the new immigrants to the experiences of the Pilgrims, as well as to the experiences of oppressed groups in American history; e.g., Native Americans, African slaves, and new immigrants. These comparisons led them to comparisons of the experiences of the early Chinese immigrants with their own experiences. The following excerpt of a student's work about his people in Chinatown was produced while studying immigrants in the United States:

New York is like a land filled with gold, which magically attracts immigrants for centuries. Our Fuzhounese [people from Fuzhou City] is among those. ...[M]ost of them were smuggled into this country. They risked their lives to come here, and paid a big fee to the smugglers. Their relatives loaned all the money ...[they] needed for coming here. ... [They] can't disappoint them and [they] have to work hard to pay them back. That is why some Fuzhounese have to do something illegal, because they need money badly. That is how our Fuzhounese got the bad reputation. But actually we Fuzhounese are the hardest workers. We are working hard to change the bad impression the people have on us. I am glad I am a Fuzhounese, because we are the hardest workers among all immigrants. I am determined to study hard and have a good future. I want to gain a good reputation for Fuzhounese and not let others continue to look down upon us Fuzhounese. I want every one to know we, Fuzhounese, are the strongest of all.

This student expressed strong feelings about being discriminated against in the Chinatown community where, as the most recent newcomers, they were trodden to the bottom ranks of the Chinatown society. His writing not only helps one understand his people, but also leads one to admire his solidarity and determination.

Encouraging comparisons in the CLA class between American and China often led to heated discussions between the two cultures. During the study of American history they compared American's colonial time with China's imperial period; American's slavery with China's feudal system. Also, they contrasted democratic and communist governments. Interestingly, many of the students were puzzled about why treatments of World War II failed to mention Japan's invasion of China, which lasted 8 years. Consequently, these students became critical of the history books. One student wrote:

The history book we read in China had a big chunk of information about the Japanese invasion to China, killing people, burning houses, bombing bridges, and torturing women and children. But the history book here on World War II didn't mention anything about that. That made me realize we can't simply trust books. Our teachers said history is written by people, so people can write the way they want. I used to think a history book recorded the true facts.

Thus, a third important discovery of my research was that discussing and questioning history books not only helped students understand the American society and their home country better, but it also encouraged them to become more critical of what they read. This was a huge leap for these students, as their training in the Chinese culture had taught not to question books or authorities.

The new immigrant students faced many challenges in their new lives in the new world. The loss of their past identity and everything familiar was hurtful enough, yet they also encountered daily discrimination, alienation, humiliation and confusion at school and within their communities (Fu, 2003). Writing in their first language provided a way for them to express their thoughts, vent their emotions, forge new identities, and understand their new positions and relationships with others around them. From the following excerpt written by a seventh grader on Chinese New Year, much can be learned about the "ethic spirit" of new immigrants:

Chinese New Year is the biggest and most significant holiday in China. The whole nation celebrates it wholeheartedly, and every corner smells the holiday joy and excitement. . . .

On New Year's Eve, the whole nation would start the celebration in China. . . . All the family members will get together. . . . While eating the New Year's dinner, we talk, laugh, eat the most delicious food, and enjoy more concerts and musicals on TV. That is the best and happiest time of the year.

Having Chinese New Year in America is very different. On New Year's Eve, nothing happened, no family, no concert and no delicious food. Dad and Mom have to work, and only me and my brother are at home. . . . We wait and wait, till 10:00 at night. They still didn't come home. . . . I miss my family in China, the joy, and excitement at the New Year's celebration. I feel so lost. It says "Holidays are the time when people usually get most homesick." . . . I want to cry, but I can't. . . . If the parents see me cry, they would be very sad. They work so hard, and I can't add more pain to them. When they come home, we will act like what we would do in China. We would prepare a big delicious meal for the family. . . . My parents got home at nearly midnight. We had our New Year's dinner together. We talked, laughed, and enjoyed our time together till 2:00 in the morning. Though the food was not as delicious or didn't have the variety as we would have in China, we had a good time, and that still was the most significant time of the year for us.

Chinese New Year's celebration in China and in America is indeed very different, but in my heart, it is the same. It is always the beginning of the year, and on that day, I will always set the new goals and new resolutions for the new year. On each New Year's Day, I want to walk into the new year as a new person.

This piece painted a vivid picture of a new person emerging through his words and thinking. I was impressed with the maturity revealed in this piece. I shared this piece with other monolingual, English speaking teachers. They were surprised, as this student had showed very limited literacy skills in his English writing. The teachers envied me, as I was able to read these students' Chinese writing and gain much insight of the new immigrant students through their own words. From their writing, I learned that these children all had vivid memories of their lives in China. Their families live harder lives, but one can see in this example their quiet determination, the strong unity of the family, and the beautiful love among the family members. My fourth discovery was that as students find ways to adapt to their new world, their new lives help students build new personalities, new characters, and new identities.

The maturity and strength of these students raised serious questions about what counts as success. How can we measure the maturity and positive attitude our new immigrant students display when coping with their hardship and transitions to their new lives in this country? Is there a standardized test for this kind of growth? I felt so fortunate to be able to translate and read Chinese and to understand these students' competency levels. I also felt that these students were also fortunate to be allowed to learn and to express themselves in their native language in this school, which in turn, enabled them to learn as much as their English speaking peers, to express themselves, and to display their true literacy abilities.

On Becoming Bilingual

In this CLA/social studies class, the immigrant students started with reading, writing, and speaking in Chinese. As they gradually developed higher levels of proficiency in the use of English patterns and vocabulary in their ESL class and other classes, the students began to include English words and phrases in their Chinese-dominant writing or speaking. This behavior is linguistically defined as code-switching. Code-switching between two languages is "a natural consequence of a situation of intense daily contact" (Callahan, 2004, p. 121). Living in the "borderlands" (Anzaldua, 1987) between two languages and two cultures, immigrant children naturally mix two languages in their oral and written communication. Some people view language-mixing as a sign of limited English proficiency and describe it as a borrowing strategy that is conveniently used when the speaker does not know the words of the second language or how to translate words and concepts of a second language. This is a likely explanation when students are required to write in English, as they do not have enough English vocabulary to express themselves, causing them to insert the words from their native language into the English text (see Figure 16.1). I view this practice as a necessary transitional stage: The students use the linguistic funds of knowledge they possess to express their ideas as fully as possible. It is similar to children's use of invented spelling in writing. Before they know how to spell the words they need to express themselves: they go through a transitional phrase, using their phonetic knowledge to spell the words.

Based on analysis of the data in my study of new immigrant students who were allowed to use their heritage language at will, a different explanation is needed to illustrate the mixing of forms from different languages. The English language

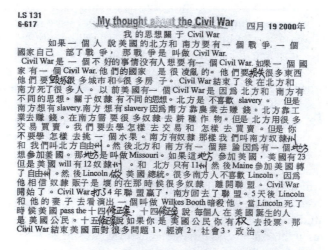

Figure 16.1 Learning About the American Civil War Written in Mixed Language

learners in my study began early to mix English words in their native language-dominant texts (see Figures 16.2 and 16.3). The mixing of English with Chinese dominant language patterns seems to signal the beginning point on a continuum of patterns of f becoming bilingual.

Looking closely at the types of English word or phrase that students tended to insert in their Chinese writing, I found evidence of the tendency to insert English words for the names of people, places, and special terminology such as "the Whig Party," "Yankees," and "the Gettysburg address," and concepts like "spring fever," "flea market," and "yard sale" or general terms that have no comparable terms in the Chinese language such as "uncle" for all male relatives, "aunt" all female relatives, "party," and "shopping." The translations of those words or phrases into Chinese would distort some the original meaning or flavor of the English words. From this perspective, code-switching reflects rather sophisticated bilingual understanding pertaining to each language, but can also lead to insight concerning the importance of word choice and the special nuances of a language and culturally based meanings.

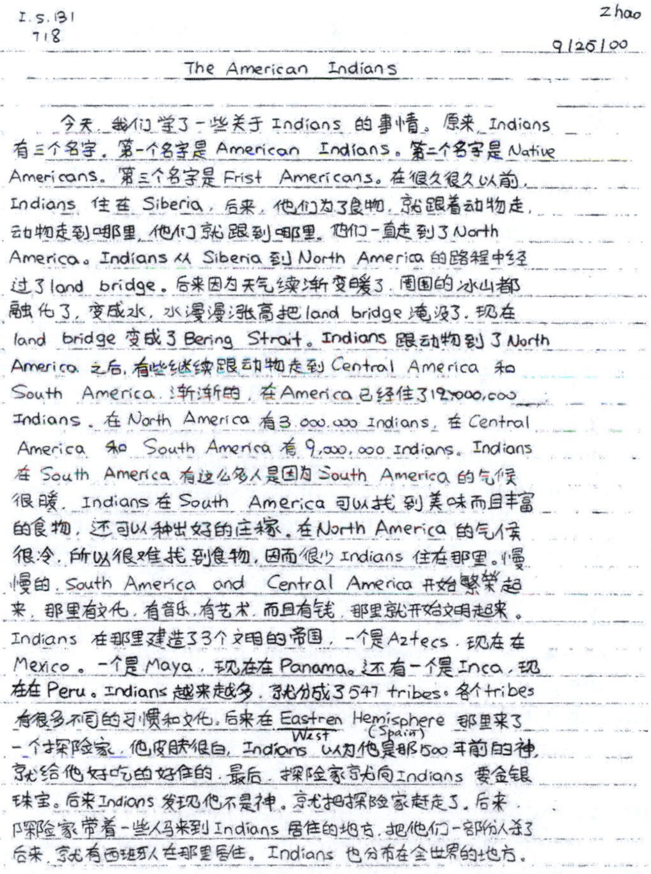
I.S.131
718

Zhao

9/25/00

The American Indians

今天，我们学了一些关于 Indians 的事情。原来 Indians 有三个名字。第一个名字是 American Indians。第二个名字是 Native Americans。第三个名字是 Frist Americans。在很久很久以前，Indians 住在 Siberia，后来，他们为了食物，就跟着动物走，动物走到哪里，他们就跟到哪里。他们一直走到了 North America。Indians 从 Siberia 到 North America 的路程中经过了 land bridge。后来因为天气续渐变暖了，周围的冰山都融化了，变成水，水漫漫涨高把 land bridge 淹没了。现在 land bridge 变成了 Bering Strait。Indians 跟动物到了 North America 之后，有些继续跟动物走到 Central America 和 South America。渐渐的，在 America 已经住了12,000,000 Indians。在 North America 有3.000.000 Indians，在 Central America 和 South America 有 9,000,000 Indians。Indians 在 South America 有这么多人是因为 South America 的气候很暖。Indians 在 South America 可以找到美味而且丰富的食物，还可以种出好的庄稼。在 North America 的气候很冷，所以很难找到食物，因而很少 Indians 住在那里。慢慢的，South America and Central America 开始繁荣起来，那里有文化，有音乐，有艺术，而且有钱，那里就开始文明起来。Indians 在那里建造了3个文明的帝国，一个是 Aztecs，现在在 Mexico。一个是 Maya，现在在 Panama。还有一个是 Inca，现在在 Peru。Indians 越来越多，就分成了547 tribes。各个 tribes 有很多不同的习惯和文化。后来在 Eastren (West) Hemisphere (Spain) 那里来了一个探险家，他皮肤很白，Indians 以为他是那500年前的神，就给他好吃的好住的，最后，探险家就向 Indians 要金银珠宝。后来 Indians 发现他不是神。就把探险家赶走了。后来探险家带着一些人马来到 Indians 居住的地方，把他们一部份人杀了后来，就有西班牙人在那里居住。Indians 也分布在全世界的地方。

Figure 16.2 Learning About Native Americans in Bilingual/SS Classes

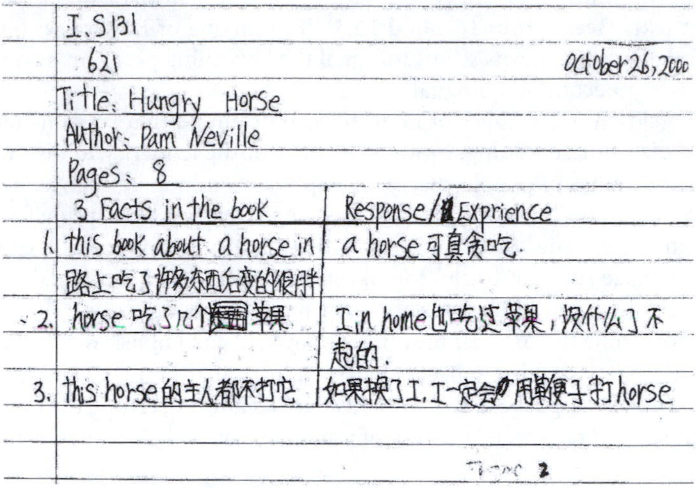
I.S131
621 October 26, 2000
Title: Hungry Horse
Author: Pam Neville
Pages: 8

3 Facts in the book	Response/Exprience
1. this book about a horse in 路上吃了许多东西后变的很胖	a horse 可真贪吃.
2. horse 吃了几个苹果	I in home 也吃过苹果，没什么了不起的.
3. this horse 的主人都不打它	如果换了I, I一定会用鞭子打horse

Figure 16.3 Double Entry Reading Response Written in Mixed Language

Looking at this type of code-switching among their English language learners (ELLs) as bilingual practice, rather than a linguistic deficit, both bilingual and ESL teachers in the New York City's Chinatown middle school accepted their students' choice of language usages. The freedom to choose enabled all students to participate in class discussion and writing. It also made it possible for students to focus on the content and ideas of their communication, rather than language conventions. As a result, students fully displayed their potential as learners in their schooling by drawing on their language strengths rather than being constrained by their limited English proficiency. I noticed that before being able to express themselves in complete English sentences, the beginner ELLs were able to use some English phrases and words in the context of their native language writing—an effective way to practice what they had learned. Importantly, though, a picture began to emerge about the patterns of language mixing or code-switching that occurred.

Given a choice of languages to use, students varied in their choice of language and degrees of language mixing. I found the following patterns:

1. Chinese only
2. Chinese with a few English words and phrases mixed in
3. English with Chinese words here and there
4. interlanguage writing: i.e. English words in Chinese syntax
5. close-to-conventional English patterns (see Figure 16.4).

These appeared as the stages of writing development pertaining the students' progress in their English language learning. These patterns are similar to those found when people learn to speak English in a second language. They have to speak their first language before they can express themselves in English. Later, they mix

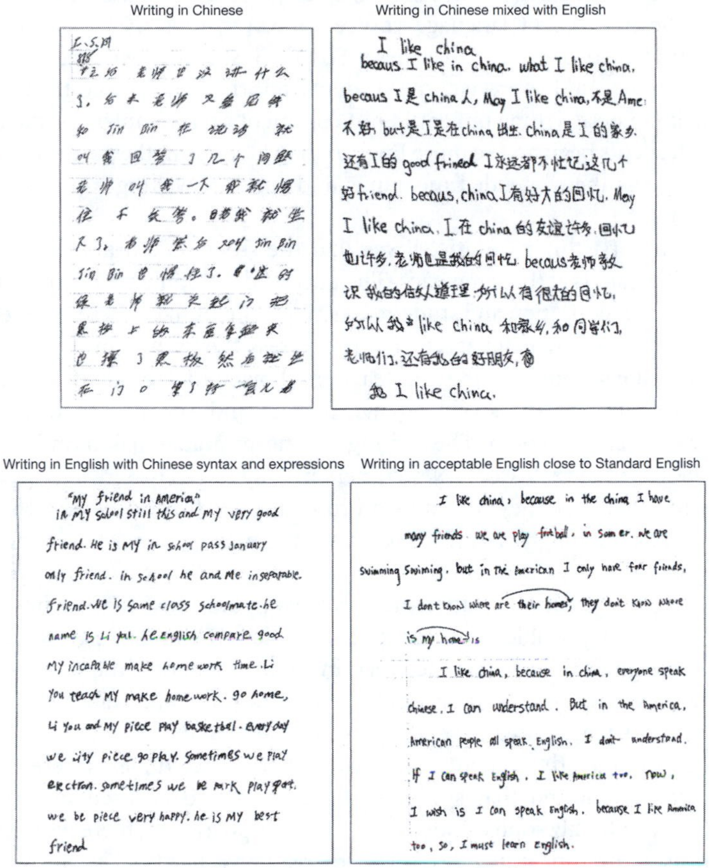

Figure 16.4 The Four Stages of ELLs' Writing Development

a few English words in their speech. After they study English intensively for a while, they speak English mixed with some native language words. Gradually, they try to speak English, but still think in their first language, making their speech sound very foreign, as in Chinese-English. With much practice in English listening and speaking English, their speech patterns move toward English norms of conventional Standard English. This gradual development toward English norms occurs most rapidly when learners never stop speaking, and intentionally try to use English as much as possible in their speech.

In the ESL and CLA/social studies classes at this Chinatown middle school, the students develop their writing skills in the same way people develop their English speaking ability. They never stop writing (starting with writing in their native language). Once they learn some English: either individual words, phrases or some simple sentences, they are encouraged to utilize them in their writing. The teachers in this school are used to reading their students' writing in different language styles, and have learned to look through the structure to get to the meanings.

Not only in CLA classes, but also in their ESL class, the ELLs in this middle school are given the freedom of language choice. However, most ESL teachers in the school cannot read or write in Chinese. For their students' writing in Chinese, they at first only could appreciate the students' effort. They showed their admiration of their Chinese writing but could not comment on the content or the quality. When the students begin to use more English than Chinese in their writing, teachers are able to guess their intended meanings and conduct writing conferences with them.

One of the first things I noticed was that the students did not develop their English writing skills at the same pace. The pace of development depended heavily on their previous education and students' writing abilities in Chinese. To encourage students to choose any language forms to express themselves in writing, at the beginning of the school year, the ESL teachers showed their students examples of writing with different styles of language mixing and encouraged them to use English whenever they could. The writing was never graded based on how much English they used in their work. Newcomers usually began by writing in Chinese. One or 2 months later, they would begin inserting English words and phrases in their writing, a seemingly natural process for them since they were immersed in English learning every day.

In the CLA class, although the students usually did most writing in Chinese, they also took any possible opportunity to practice writing in English. They did their CLA assignments, such as the work in their notebooks, the posters on the walls, the papers they turned in, and their classroom publications, in mixed English-Chinese languages.

When I examined the students' portfolios where selected pieces were arranged chronologically, I found that students chose the language used in writing to communicate in highly sophisticated ways. In their portfolios, there were a variety of writing samples, including responses to readings, personal narratives, essay presentations, summaries of reading, and charts and graphs. They were written with varying degrees of language mixture, as shown in Figure 16.4. Interestingly, the most recent pieces were not written in English, and those written in English were usually short and simple. The lengthy pieces that presented more complicated ideas, tended to be written in Chinese. I began to realize that it was the topic or the complexity of the content that influenced students' choices about the language to use in their writing. This shows that these students were able to use language freely as the tool to express themselves and they knew what language they needed for what topics and how they would like to present themselves as writers. I concluded that neither the type of assignment nor the level of English mastery determined the degree or the language and type of language-mixing that occurred. Rather, the content and ideas presented in writing determined its form and style. As thinkers and writers, students in the CLA classes were given the kind of freedom to make rhetorical choices that other students usually do not have when they are learning to write in a new language. Those choices were determined not so much by levels of English or Chinese proficiency but by rhetorical decisions related to the message to be presented and how best to present the message, with regard to how the writer wanted to position themselves.

The writing of these students showed that when we value their language choice to express themselves and when they perceive our emphasis is truly on what they say (i.e. mean) rather than merely how they say it, they will attend to the content and ideas in their writing, rather than attending solely to correct usage of the new language they are learning. In fact, when the students choose a language based on how they feel, they are able to express themselves quite adroitly. And that is a very promising sign, suggesting their tendency to focus more on the deep structure of their writing than writing purely for the sake of demonstrating the new language skills they have learned: a goal for all writers.

I conducted further analyses to compare the ELLs who were given the freedom in use of language forms in writing compared to those who were not given this kind of freedom. Tracing the writing development of 44 first year ELL in two ESL classes (22 in each) for a whole year, I found 70% of the students (including students with weak first language literacy) in the class where they were given language freedom were able to produce writing in close-to-conventional English by spring (in terms of grammar, spelling and vocabulary), 7 months into the school year; whereas only 20% (mostly with strong first language literacy) of the students in the class where they were only required to write in English were able to produce work in close-to-conventional English by spring. What might count partially for this gap is the students' freedom in language usage, as they had less fear of writing and more opportunities to practice using language(s) in meaningful contexts. They had learned and improved their language skills through frequent writing practice. When they were allowed to travel back and forth between languages, no matter how complicated the topics they had to write on, they could freely and confidently demonstrate their best ability as thinkers through words. I also found that the group with freedom showed a greater interest in writing than the group without the freedom. They were willing to try different genres and wrote more and longer with much better quality. This is obvious because the group with language freedom could rely on their strengths (whatever they could do better) to compose and the group without this freedom could only compose with limited skills. Actually, the ELLs' freedom to choose the language to use developed their English skills at a much faster rate than those who were only allowed to compose in English.

Suggestions

In the 21st century, our world is becoming more globally interdependent. As a nation of immigrants, we should view new immigrants as an asset rather than as liability. We should also value what they bring with them, including their languages, cultures, and ethnic spirit, as resources (human capitals) rather than barriers to learning or threat to society. Meeting this goal begins with school, where we should practice this value by educating our children with a vision and capacity for globalization—mutual economic and political dependence among nations in today's world.

My study on the literacy and writing development of the new immigrant students in a New York City's Chinatown middle school suggests that in order to help ELLs' overall literacy development, teachers who work with ELLs should:

- Encourage, guide, and support them in their efforts to read and write in their native language because reading and writing are deep structure activities that involve thinking.
- Promote biliteracy by planning literacy programs across the subject areas such as bilingual, social studies and ESL, and promote the view of writing development as bilingual thinking.
- Help students to fully express their thoughts and emotion by allowing them to code switch. Writing must be acquired within the context of students' current "funds of knowledge" (Moll, 2001) if it is to be understood as a tool for thoughtful communication.
- Value students' selection of language patterns to use in writing, allowing these choices based on the complexity of the writing topics, the depth and fluency of what the writers want to say with their writing, and their need to develop understandings via language play.
- Help them recognize the advantages of biliteracy. As they learn to value each language for its unique characteristics, teachers can help them recognize the values of word choice and voice.
- Stress thinking, content, and ideas in writing, and encourage students to move back and forth between languages so they have a good chance to develop into critical thinkers, thoughtful writers, and proficient users of Standard English.

It is easy to lose a language, but it takes time and effort to become bilingual and biliterate. Being bilingual and biliterate are useful skills for individuals and invaluable human resources for American society at large.

Discussion Questions and Activities

1. What is the role of ELLs' native language in learning English language skills and other subject areas?
2. How should teachers help ELLs at the secondary level to choose interesting books that are not too linguistically sophisticated?
3. How can teachers assess the speaking, reading, and writing in language that they do not understand?
4. What kinds of accommodations should teachers make to facilitate communication with parents who have not yet learned English?

References

Anderson, R. (2004). First Language Loss in Spanish-Speaking Children: Patterns of Loss and Implication for Clinic Practice. In B. A. Goldstein (Ed.). *Bilingual Language Development and Disorders in Spanish-English Speakers*. Baltimore, MD: Paul H. Brooks Publishing Co.
Anzaldua G. (1987). *Borderlands/La Frontera: The New Mestiza*. San Francisco: Aunt Lute Books.

Callahan, L. (2004). *Spanish/English Codeswitching in a Written Corpus*. Amsterdam: John Benjamins.

Cazden, C., & Snow, C. (1990). English Plus: Issues in Bilingual Education. *Annual American Academics, Politics, and Social Science*, 508, 9–11.

Cummins, J. (1981). Four Misconceptions about Language Proficiency in Bilingual Education. *NABE*, 5, 31–45.

Fernandez, R. M., & Nielsen, F. (1986). Bilingualism and Hispanic Scholastic Achievement: Some Baseline Results. *Social Science Research*, 15, 43–70.

Fu, D. (2003). *An Island of English: Teaching ESL in Chinatown*. Portsmouth, NH: Heinemann.

———, & Matoush, M. (2006). Writing Development and Biliteracy. In P. Matsuda, C. Ortmeier-Hooper, & X. You (Eds.). *The Politics of Second Language Writing*. West Lafayette, IN: Parlor Press.

Kohnert, K. (2004). Processing Skills in Early Sequential Bilinguals. In B. A. Goldstein (Ed.). *Bilingual Language Development and Disorders in Spanish-English Speakers*. Baltimore, MD: Paul H. Brooks Publishing Co.

Krashen, S. (1991). *Bilingual Education: A Focus on Current Research*. Washington, DC: National Clearinghouse for Bilingual Education.

Matute-Bianchi, M. (1986). Ethnic Identities and Patterns of School Success and Failure among Mexican-Descent and Japanese-American students in a California High School: An Ethnographic Analysis. *American Journal of Education*, 95, 233–255.

Moll, L. C. (2001). The Diversity of Schooling: A Cultural-Historical Approach. In M. Reyes, & J. H. Halcon (Eds.). *The Best for Our Children: Critical Perspectives on Literacy for Latino Students*. New York: Teachers College Press.

Sung, B. (1987). *The Adjustment Experience of Chinese Immigrant Children in New York City*. Staten Island, NY: Center of Migration Studies.

Tse, L (2001). *Why Don't They Learn English? Separating Fact from Fallacy in the U.S. Language Debate*. New York: Teachers College Press.

U.S. Census Bureau (2003). *Profile of the Foreign-Born Population in the United States, 2003*. Retrieved December 28, 2003, from http://www.census.gov/population/www/socdemo/foreign/foreign/foreign03html.

17
High Stakes Testing and the Social Languages of Literature and Literate Achievement in Urban Classrooms

DOROTHEA ANAGNOSTOPOULOS

This chapter examines the consequences of high stakes testing for students' engagement with literature in urban classrooms. The study of literature has long occupied a central position in the secondary English curriculum. Although the purposes of literature studies have long been contested, understanding literary texts remains central to our notions of literate achievement. In particular, substantively engaging students with literary texts is critical to developing students' social imaginations. Over the past two decades sociocultural literacy research has illuminated the complex social, cultural, and political processes through which students construct meaning with and through literary texts as they navigate the social worlds represented in such texts and interrogate and construct their own social, moral and political stances towards these worlds (Knoeller, 1998; Langer, 1995, 1987; Schultz & Fecho, 2000; Wortham, 2001). Research that draws on Bakhtin's (1981, 1986) literacy and linguistic theory has further documented the importance of students appropriating the social languages, or verbal-ideological belief systems and worldviews, available within literary texts and within students' own social worlds (Hicks, 1996; Lensmire, 1994; Nystrand, 1997; Nystrand & Gamoran 1991).

With the intensification of high stakes testing policies questions of how such policies shape students' engagement with literary texts have become increasingly significant. Understanding the consequences of high stakes testing in urban classrooms is especially urgent. Proponents argue that high stakes testing will most benefit the low- income students of color who attend urban schools by holding the schools accountable for ensuring that these students meet "world class" learning standards. While recent research presents conflicting findings on the effects of high stakes testing on students' performance on standardized assessments (Fuller, Wright, Gesicki, & Kang, 2007), the nearly singular emphasis on outcomes has obscured critical questions about how high stakes testing shapes students' engagement with the social, moral, and political issues that lie at the center of literary texts and literature studies.

I explore these questions in this chapter by examining how a high stakes testing policy shaped the ways in which students in an urban high school classroom engaged with the issues of race and racism in the novel, *To Kill a Mockingbird*.

Drawing from a 3-year research study I conducted with colleagues in several urban high schools, I use a Bakhtinian perspective to delineate the discursive processes through which the test authorized an "academic" reading of the novel that both neutralized racial conflicts in the novel and marginalized students' own attempts to grapple with these conflicts in the novel and in their own lives. I conclude the chapter by identifying dialogic assessment practices that can counter the standardization imposed by high stakes testing and foster students' literate achievement.

High Stakes Testing and the Standardization of Social Languages: A Bakhtinian Perspective

A Bakhtinian perspective is premised on the understanding of language as socially saturated. In contrast to formalistic linguistic theories that depict language as a system of abstract grammatical categories, Bakhtin (1981, 1986) emphasized the social and ideological nature of language. Rather than being unitary, he argued that all national languages are continually being stratified into multiple languages that reflect and contribute to the differentiation of society according to age, professions, institutional positions, and other types of difference. Each social language is a verbal-ideological and social belief system that provides people with "specific points of view on the world, forms of conceptualizing the world in words, specific world views, each characterized by its own objects, meanings and value"(Bakhtin 1981, p. 300). As a result of this linguistic and social stratification, there are no "neutral" words or forms; language at all times is shot through with the tastes, meanings and intentions of a range of social groups.

Given the essentially ideological nature of language, social groups vie for power, in part, through attempts to codify or resist particular ways of producing and reading texts. Powerful groups seek to impose standard linguistic forms onto speech and writing and authoritative readings onto texts and readers. In response, subordinate groups seek to resist and subvert such actions through infecting, inflecting, and supplanting the social languages of powerful groups with their own languages and meanings. This struggle between centrifugal and centripetal forces, respectively, is both ongoing and generative of literary and social heteroglossia.

Studies that draw on Bakhtin's theory of language and literature document how students construct meaning through appropriating the social languages of "others," both within and outside of literary texts, as they engage with literature and develop literacy skills (Hicks, 1996; Knoeller, 1998; Lensmire, 1994; Nystrand, 1997; Schultz & Fecho, 2000). These dialogic processes are essential to understanding novels, in particular. Novels, according to Bakhtin (1981), are "heteroglot;" they are planes on which the social languages that co-exist in a particular sociohistorical moment interact, variously compete with, supplement, or inflect one another. Because of this heteroglossia, novels cannot be understood as having a single, readily decoded meaning. Instead, understanding a novel involves navigating, engaging, and making sense of the multiple social languages that co-exist within it. Because readers are, themselves, members of various social groups situated in a particular sociohistorical moment, these navigations further involve students assessing and inflecting the social languages in a novel with and against the meanings and intentions at play in their own social worlds. In short, making meaning of novels is a complex interplay between text and context, between the social languages that essentially structure the worlds inhabited by the author and those inhabited by the reader.

From a Bakhtinian perspective, high stakes testing of students' understanding of literature both reflects and constitutes the ongoing contestation between forces of standardization and the realities of linguistic, cultural, and ideological diversity that characterize urban classrooms. Indeed, high stakes testing has been an integral tool in national and international efforts to rescale relationships between the global, national and local in ways that shift control over teaching and learning away from the local and to higher levels through the use of nationally normed tests and the imposition of "world class" standards (Robertson, 2002).

At the same time, a Bakhtinian perspective also helps to illuminate the ways in which teachers and students resist as well as succumb to such standardization. According to Bakhtin, "alongside verbal-ideological centralization and unification, the uninterrupted processes of decentralization and disunification go forward" (Bakhtin, 1981, p. 272). Understanding the consequences that high stakes testing holds for students' interaction with and understanding of literature and of their own social worlds thus involves specifying the practices through which linguistic and social diversity disrupt and challenge the standardization such testing seeks to impose. Illuminating this dialectical relationship helps to point the way to more dialogic practices that can honor the social languages and identities students (and teachers) bring to the classroom and facilitate students' critical co-construction of new understandings with and through these languages.

Testing and the Standardization of Classroom Talk about Literature

In this section, I present an episode of classroom talk drawn from a longitudinal, qualitative study I conducted with my colleagues that examined the implementation of an accountability agenda in the Chicago Public Schools (CPS) from 1995 to 2000. The CPS is the third largest school district in the U.S., enrolling roughly 430,000 students, the vast majority of whom come from low-income families and are classified as racial minorities. In the late 1990s, the district was at the forefront of the national test-based accountability movement. During this period, district officials used state law to enact an accountability agenda that used multiple tests to measure, intervene in and sanction student and school performance. As part of this agenda, the CPS established district-wide standards and assessments for each core academic subject at the ninth and tenth grade. In 1997, the district adopted a revised version of the Chicago Academic Standards (CAS) for all grade levels, produced programs of study for ninth and tenth grade academic courses that specified core content, skills, and processes to be taught each semester, and began piloting the Chicago Academic Standards Exam (CASE) in the high schools. The district intended to use CASE results as another criterion for placing schools on probation and for determining students' promotion from tenth to eleventh grade.

The CASE tested students' knowledge of the texts and skills identified in the Program of Study. It had two parts, a multiple-choice section that contained questions about literary terms and devices, and a constructed response essay that included three short-answer questions that students developed into a three- to five-paragraph essay in response to a final question about the semester's core work.

The core works were texts that the district mandated all ninth and tenth graders read each semester. Significantly, the core works for tenth grade English, which included Chief Joseph's surrender speech, selections from The Biography of Frederick Douglas, and Lorraine Hansberry's A Raisin in the Sun, dealt explicitly with issues of racial prejudice and oppression in American society. The core text for the second semester during which I draw the observations for this chapter was the novel, To Kill a Mockingbird. This novel tells the story of two White children, Scout and her brother, Jem, coming of age in the Jim Crow South. Narrated by the adult Scout, the novel has several plotlines that involve Scout and Jem encountering and learning to empathize with characters who, because of their race, class, gender, or personal histories, were ostracized by the White townsfolk. One of the central plotlines revolves around the trial of Tom Robinson, a Black man falsely accused of raping Mayella Ewell, a poor White woman. Scout's father, Atticus, serves as Tom's lawyer. Several of the novel's plotlines intersect and are resolved through the story of Tom's trial, imprisonment and eventual death at the hands of prison guards.

The classroom episode that I analyze here came from my observations of Mr. Jones' class in Colson High School. (All names of schools, teachers and students are pseudonyms.) Colson served a racially, ethnically and linguistically diverse group of students. The district classified 90% of Colson's students as racial and ethnic minorities, 30% as English language learners, and 80% as low income (Chicago Public Schools, 2000). In 1996, the district placed Colson under district intervention for having fewer than 15% of students scoring at national norms on the reading portion of the Test of Achievement and Proficiency (TAP), a nationally normed, standardized test. Colson remained on probation through the 1999–2000 school year.

Mr. Jones had taught at Colson for 5 years, and, like most of the school's English teachers, was White. Mr. Jones's class was racially and ethnically diverse, 74% of the students were African American, 10% were White, and 16% were Latino. For this part of the larger study, I interviewed Mr. Jones twice and observed one section of his tenth grade English class six times in 1998–1999 as Mr. Jones taught the novel To Kill a Mockingbird. During each observation, I constructed descriptive notes of all classroom activities that identified the time of each activity, the materials used, and the classroom arrangements. I audiotaped all whole class talk and transcribed the tapes for analysis. I analyzed interview and classroom data using critical discourse analysis (Fairclough, 1992) to identify the discursive processes through which the CASE entered into and shaped classroom talk about To Kill a Mockingbird. I attended to how Mr. Jones' explicit references to the CASE positioned particular elements and content of the novel and students' statements about it as important or irrelevant. I also analyzed the talk to identify the voices from the novel, the classroom and the larger social world that Mr. Jones and his students voiced, and to identify how the CASE legitimized or marginalized these voices. (For a complete description of the research design and method, see Anagnostopoulos, 2003.)

High Stakes Testing and the Monologic Classroom

The Chicago Academic Standards for grade ten English language arts that dealt with literary texts were quite comprehensive. The standards required students to "construct and extend meaning from" texts; to "analyze and evaluate literary texts" by drawing on author biographies and by making connections among literary texts; to "analyze" "style and literary form and their effects upon the reader"; and to "illustrate" how literary texts reflect 'the cultures, literary periods and ideas that shaped them' (Chicago Public Schools, 1998, pp. 64–66). Taken together these standards reflected a dialogic view of reading centered on the interaction of student, text and context.

The scoring rubric the district provided teachers to grade the CASE response essays, however, positioned students as minimally skilled and uncritical readers. In order to pass the test students had only to demonstrate an "accurate but limited" understanding of the text; "use information from the text to make simplistic interpretations;" make "limited connections to contexts," and "generalize without illustrating key ideas" (Chicago Public Schools, 1999). The scoring rubric defined reading as text reproduction. According to the criteria, "good readers" cited details from a text, but did not use these details to make sense of core ideas or issues.

The CASE operated in Mr. Jones' classrooms (and in other classrooms that my colleagues and I observed) to reinforce monologic instruction focused on students remembering key details and authorized interpretations of the novel (Anagnostopoulos, 2005). Mr. Jones characterized his instructional goals as "covering the novel" so that his students were prepared for the CASE. Both tasks and talk about the novel centered primarily on questions in the study guide that he and Ms. O'Reilly, the special education teacher assigned to his classroom, had created. Ms. O'Reilly and Mr. Jones devoted the majority of class time to leading students through the study guide while students graded each other's worksheets.

In the following episode of classroom talk about the novel, Ms. O'Reilly stood at the front of the classroom, students sat in rows facing her, and Mr. Jones sat at the back of the classroom maintaining class records. Ms. O'Reilly led the class through the study guide. This particular episode centered on the following question from this guide: Why does Jem knock the top off her flowers? The question displays the definition of reading as text reproduction also embedded in the structure of classroom tasks and talk. As with the other questions on the study guide, Mr. Jones and Ms. O'Reilly identified the pages on which the students could locate the answer to the question, signaling that a correct answer was one that remained close to the text and that meaning inhered within the text. Mickey, an African American girl, and Jessica, a White girl, who were among the most participatory students in the class, responded to the question as follows:

Mickey: She said . . . Atticus was no better than Tom Robinson . . . that he's
    a nigger lover.
Jessica: But he is a nigger lover. That's what it says in the book.
Mickey: I don't mean, I don't mean, I don't mean nothing personal
O'Reilly: Wait.
Jessica: But they say it in the book.
Jones: Raise your hands.

In this exchange, Mickey and Jessica violated the structural and substantive norms of classroom talk about the novel. They responded to each other rather than to the teacher, disrupting the dominant pattern of recitation discourse. More substantively, they also initiated explicit talk about race and racism in the novel. Although, like other teachers in the larger study, both Ms. O'Reilly and Mr. Jones did talk explicitly about these issues, their talk was overwhelmingly teacher centered and teacher controlled. Here, Mickey and Jessica asserted control over talk about racism. Although Ms. O'Reilly and Mr. Jones tried to reassert their control over the talk, demanding that the girls "wait" and "raise (their) hands," Mickey and Jessica ignored the demands and continued:

Mickey: I don't mean to be rude or nothing, but I don't like, you know, "nigger
    lover" because nobody's really a nigger. Nobody's a nigger.
Jessica: I know.
Mickey: So, if you want to say it's from the book that he does like black people
    or African Americans, don't say he's a nigger. I was just quoting from the
    book. I wasn't saying he's a nigger.
Jessica: I was quoting from the book too.
Mickey: No, you said he is a nigger.
O'Reilly: Okay. What did you mean?
Jessica: I was saying is that Scout asked Atticus if he was.
Mickey: And what does Atticus say?
Jessica: He says, yes I do.

Mickey and Jessica's exchange here reveals the interplay of the social languages in the novel and in the classroom and the contest between centripetal and centrifugal forces. Within this exchange, the girls grappled with the meaning of the racial slur, "nigger lover," both as it was used by characters in the novel and as they used it in their own classroom. In the novel, the racist White characters used the epithet to isolate and condemn Atticus, the novels' White protagonist, and his defense of an African American man. As Jessica noted, in another part of the novel Atticus attempted to inflect the slur with an anti-racist stance by embracing it. Each girl, in this episode, appropriated the different social languages of race in the novel. Mickey voiced the racist White characters in her initial response to the study guide question, while Jessica appropriated Atticus's use of the epithet. The girls began to articulate their own stances towards racism as they appropriated these competing social languages of race from the novel and navigated the languages of race in their classroom.

Significantly, both girls justified their stances by drawing on the discourse of textual reproduction. Each asserted that she was "quoting from the book" thus claiming legitimacy for her own voicing of the racial slur. At the same time, the girls inflected this epithet and the social languages of race available in the novel with their own meanings, intentions and identities. In their exchange, then, we can see the interplay of the standardization of classroom talk about literature imposed by the test-focused instruction and the countervailing forces of literary and social heteroglossia. The girls challenged the monologic discourse of classroom tasks and talk to engage with, at least momentarily, the dialogism of the novel and of class-room discourse. They inflected the discourse of textual reproduction, both disrupt-ing it and claiming it for their own, to navigate the competing social languages at play in the novel and in their classroom.

Mr. Jones ultimately ended the girls' exchange nine turns later by announcing that the class needed to "move on" to prepare for the CASE. As we see in the following, the test became a tool to silence the girls' nascent exploration of the social languages of race in the novel and their meaning in their classroom:

> This is a childish argument and I'll tell, Ok . . . we're going to be talking about it in the section of this book that is about the trailer trash, the white trash. It's going to be an actual thing called "white trash." . . . Don't worry about it. I'm not going to worry about it. . . . We've got to move on. We've got two and a half weeks. . . . But, May 24, and 26, we got to break for the CASE. We don't have time to argue about stuff like this.

Mickey and Jessica's exchange exposed the political and ideological dimensions of reading literature in the era of test-based accountability. Mr. Jones shut down the exchange by (re)defining "academic" reading as a neutral process aimed at identifying and reproducing a definitive authorial message. In contrast to the girls' attempts to construct their own stances towards race and racism by navigating the novel's social languages, Mr. Jones took up an ostensibly objective position as an "academic" reader, asserting that, as a White man, he would not take offense to the term "white trash" in the novel. Mr. Jones thus opposed his "academic" stance to Mickey's response, ultimately de-legitimizing it. Mr. Jones' reference to the CASE finally relegated the girls' efforts to grapple with issues of racism as "childish" and irrelevant to the main purpose of the talk, preparing for the CASE.

Reflective Pedagogy and Dialogic Assessment

This episode from Mr. Jones' class illuminates how high stakes testing can marginalize students' engagement with the social issues that lie at the heart of literary texts and of students' own social worlds. The test affected a standardization of classroom talk as it reinforced monologic practices. At the same time, the episode also shows that such standardization is never entirely achieved, especially in urban classrooms that enroll an ethnically, culturally and linguistically diverse group of students. As Mickey and Jessica challenged each other to examine their stances towards racism the girls began to construct a dialogic space in which they could engage with and through their racial differences.

Such dialogic spaces are critical to developing students' abilities to engage independently and successfully on challenging literary tasks (Applebee, Langer, Nystrand, & Gamoran, 2003). Rather than imposing standardized assessments that reduce reading to text reproduction, fostering dialogic spaces in urban classrooms requires a reflective pedagogy that envisions assessment as sites of inquiry and learning for both students and teachers, revealing what students can do and yielding information for teachers about how to restructure instruction. Such assessments:

1. allow for students' understandings of literary texts to evolve, change and deepen over time and encourage students to develop insight into this evolution;
2. encourage students to explore their own and others' interpretations of literary texts using disciplinary conventions, that is literary terms and rules of analysis, as well as drawing on knowledge and experiences that exist beyond such conventions;
3. engage students in relating ideas across texts;
4. foster students' capacities to critically interrogate their own and others' stances towards the social, political and moral issues represented in literary texts and present in students' lives.

In short, assessments of students' literary understanding should, over time and as a set of inquiry-based practices, allow students to exhibit and develop their social imaginations.

At the most basic level, dialogic assessments of students' literary achievement should be centered on open-ended responses to extended literary texts that allow students to construct their own interpretations of literary texts. Such responses should also encourage students to make connections across multiple texts, to engage in disciplinary conversations and to grapple with key social, moral and political issues. As this study suggests, however, order for such assessments to re-envision assessment as inquiry, they must be integrated into a broader set of dialogic practices. When monologic practices are reinforced by standardized assessments, as they were in the study presented here, teachers tend to re-contextualize dialogic assessments, reducing and narrowing their dialogic potential to valorize textual reproduction rather than meaning making and critique. Open-ended, extended responses to literary texts must, therefore, be accompanied by dialogic instructional practices that in addition to discussions include practices such as think-alouds in which teachers and students explore their responses to literary texts together to co-construct interpretations (Ivey, 2003; Wilhelm, 1999) and collaborative group work in which students explore multiple perspectives to open-ended questions or scenarios to reach some common shared understanding (Johannessen, 2003; Marshall, Smagorinsky, & Smith, 1995; Sperling, 1996).

Other types of dialogic assessment value and encourage student collaboration. Dialogue journals can be used as a type of formative assessment, allowing the teacher and the students a window into how students are envisioning a particular literary text or set of literary texts over time, and helping teachers to track and support students' emergent capacities for examining and extending their own and each other's interpretations and perspectives. In addition, assessments that allow students to represent their understandings of literary texts through different modalities, such as dance, painting and music, can provide students the opportunities not only to explore multiple forms of representation but also to engage in new forms of intertextual conversations that can deepen students' understanding of how meaning gets constructed in and through texts, as well as provide students the opportunities to explore key social issues through multiple lenses (Smagorinsky & O'Donnell-Allen, 1998). As the stakes attached to large-scale, standardized assessments of literacy continue to intensify, such dialogic assessment practices become increasingly important. They counter the narrow definitions of literate achievement endorsed by standardized assessments, valuing, instead, a range of literacy practices and fostering students' social as well as literary imaginations.

Conclusion

The classroom talk I presented here raises fundamental questions obscured by the prevailing discourse of "effects" and "outcomes" that dominates current debate and research on high stakes testing policies. In particular, it prompts us to ask what we mean by "literate achievement?" What kinds of literate practices do we value and what kinds do we devalue in this age of test-based accountability? What kinds of opportunities are being made available for our young people, particularly those who attend urban high schools, to grapple deliberatively and critically with key moral, social and political issues of our time?

As the stakes of testing policies intensify, particularly for students who attend urban schools and who have historically been disadvantaged by and in our nation's public schools, we need to engage these questions more directly and more urgently. Standardized tests fail to capture the complex cognitive, social and cultural processes that are central to meaningful literate achievement. Thus, they tell us little about students' abilities to engage in the social worlds of literary texts or to construct their own stances in relation to these worlds and to the contemporary social worlds in which students live. In short, standardized tests tell us little about and may even inhibit students' development of a social imagination that is essential not only to a substantive understanding of literature but also to the deliberation on pressing social conflicts and the construction of social, moral and political stances towards them. Countering this standardization will require fostering the multiple social languages that co-exist and that often come into conflict in our nation's urban classrooms to make possible new understandings that can enable our young people to have honest and meaningful dialogue about the social conflicts that characterize our times.

Discussion Questions and Activities

1. The author uses the terms "monologic" and "dialogic" in this chapter. What do those terms mean and how do they relate to students' language? How do they relate to students' engagement with and understanding of literature?
2. The author argues that high stakes testing limits students' opportunities to think carefully about critical social issues, such as racism, because such testing tends to support simplistic readings of literary texts. Examine how high stakes testing affects the ways teachers teach literature in a local school. What kinds of literary texts are being read? Why? What is the focus of classroom talk about the texts? When and why do teachers and students talk about the tests? How does this shape the ways in which they talk about the literary texts they read?
3. The author argues for the use of "dialogic assessments" in contrast to standardized testing. What are the characteristics of "dialogic assessments?" Design a dialogic assessment to assess students' literary understanding.
4. Think of a novel you were taught in school or one that you recently taught. What social, moral and political questions did the novel raise? How did your teachers engage you with these questions? How did you engage your students with these questions? Which questions were not raised or were silenced? How did this shape your own or your students' understanding of the novel?

References

Anagnostopoulos, D. (2003). Testing and Student Engagement with Literature in Urban Classrooms: A Multilayered Perspective. *Research in the Teaching of English*, 38, 177–212.

———. (2005). Testing, Tests and Classroom Texts. *Journal of Curriculum Studies*, *37*, 35–63.

Applebee, A. N., Langer, J. A., Nystrand, M., & Gamoran, A. (2003). Discussion-Based Approaches to Developing Understanding: Classroom Instruction and Student Performance in Middle and High School English. *American Education Research Journal*, *40*, (3) 685–730.

Bakhtin, M. M. (1981). *The Dialogic Imagination: Four Essays by M. M. Bakhtin*. In M. Holquist (Ed.). Austin, TX: University of Texas Press.

———. (1986). *Speech Genres and Other Late Essays* (C. Emerson & M. Holquist, Eds.; V. W. McGee, Trans.). Austin, TX: University of Texas Press.

Chicago Public Schools. (1998). *Chicago Academic Standards Examinations: Constructed Response Scoring Rubric/Answer Keys*.

Chicago Public Schools. (1999). *CASE English II Sample Exam*.

Chicago Public Schools. (2000). Chicago Public Schools website. Retrieved September 23, 2002 from http://www.cps.k12.il.us.

Fairclough, N. (1992). *Discourse and Social Change*. Cambridge: Polity Press.

Fuller, B., Wright, J., Gesicki, K., & Kang, E. (2007). Gauging Growth: How to Judge No Child Left Behind? *Educational Researcher*, 36, 268–278.

Hicks, D. (1996). Contextual Inquiries. In D. Hicks (Ed.). *Discourse, Learning and Schooling*. New York: Cambridge University Press.

Ivey, G. (2003). "The Teacher Makes it More Explainable" and Other Reasons to Read Aloud in the Intermediate Grades. *The Reading Teacher*, 56, 812–814.

Johannessen, L. R. (2003). Strategies for Initiative in Authentic Discussion. *English Journal*, 93, 73–79.

Knoeller, C. (1998). *Voicing Ourselves: Whose Words We Use when We Talk about Books*. Albany, NY: State University of New York Press.

Langer, J. A. (1987). A Sociocognitive Perspective on Literacy. In J. A. Langer (Ed.). *Language, Literacy, and Culture: Issues of Society and Schooling*. Norwood, NJ: Ablex.

———. (1995). *Envisioning Literature: Literary Understanding and Literature Instruction.* New York: Teachers College Press.

Lensmire, T. J. (1994). *When Children Write: Critical Revisions of the Writing Workshop.* New York: Teachers College Press.

Marshall, J., Smagorinsky, P., & Smith, M. W. (1995). *The Language of Interpretation: Patterns of Discourse in Discussions of Literature.* Urbana, IL: National Council of Teachers of English.

Nystrand, M. (1997). *Opening Dialogue: Understanding the Dynamics of Language and Learning in the English Classroom.* New York: Teachers College Press.

———, & Gamoran, A. (1991). Instructional Discourse, Student Engagement, and Literature Achievement. *Research in the Teaching of English,* 25, 261–290.

Robertson, S. L. (2002). *The Politics of Re-Territorialisation: Space, Scale and Teachers as a Professional Class.* London: Institutions for Educational Policy Studies.

Schultz, K., & Fecho, B. (2000). Society's Child: SocialXContext and Writing Development. *Educational Psychologist,* 35, 51–62.

Smagorinsky, P., & O'Donnell-Allen, C. (1998). Reading as Mediated and Mediating Action: Composing Meaning for Literature through Multimedia Interpretive Texts. *Reading Research Quarterly,* 33, 198–226.

Sperling, M. (1996). Revisiting the Writing–Speaking Connection: Challenges for Research on Writing and Writing Instruction. *Review of Educational Research,* 66, 53–86.

Wilhelm, J. (1999). Think-Alouds Boost Reading Comprehension. *Instructor,* 111, 26–28.

Wortham, S. (2001). Teachers and Students as Novelists: Ethical Positioning in Literature Discussions. *Journal of Adolescent and Adult Literacy,* 45, 126–137.

IV
GLOBAL PERSPECTIVES
ON LANGUAGE DIVERSITY
AND LEARNING

18

Possibilities for Non-Standard Dialects in American Classrooms: Lessons from a Greek Cypriot Class

XENIA HADJIOANNOU

Current policy trends in the U.S. claim that monolingualism is the norm, and view non-standard dialects as a threat to academic success. This chapter presents an example from the diglossic Greek Cypriot community, which suggests that U.S. policies may be misguided. The investigation of interactions in a sixth grade Greek Cypriot classroom revealed discursive patterns which indicated that both the teachers and the students competently code-switched between Standard Greek and their native Greek Cypriot dialect. Also, the findings suggest that the students were aware of their code-switching practices and felt competent in both dialects but carried some native stereotypes regarding their home dialect:

> Every day in class I always speak in Standard Greek, but only when I want to say something about the lesson, express an idea or give an answer. When I talk to my teacher to ask something, and when my classmates and I discuss subjects besides class, I speak in the Cypriot Dialect. I think I do the same when we work in groups. . . . I do not really [consciously] think when I have to speak Cypriot or Standard Greek. It just happens to me on its own.

In this excerpt, a 12-year-old Greek Cypriot girl reflects on how she uses Standard Greek (SG) and the Greek Cypriot dialect (GCD), the two main language varieties present in the Greek Cypriot community, in her daily interactions. The phenomenon she so eloquently describes is *diglossia*. Ferguson (1959) defines diglossia as the situation where in addition to the primary dialects of a language (L variety), there exists a "divergent, highly codified," superposed variety that is taught in school and is used for writing and formal communications (H variety).

The overwhelming trend that currently characterizes American society in general and educational legislation in particular is one that rejects diglossia as undesirable and even harmful and proposes monolingualism as not only the norm but also as a vitally important goal. This, however, is not a global trend and the experience of various societies around the world is that diglossic situations are not only common but can actually play a crucial role in promoting children's literacy learning and expanding children's communicative abilities.

Cyprus provides an interesting example of a community that has created important inroads for the functional use of a non-standard language variety in school. In this chapter, I analyze the presence of the GCD in a Greek Cypriot class-room and examine its function in the interactions of the classroom community. Although the findings of this study are tied to the idiosyncratic circumstances of the Greek Cypriot community, they can have valuable implications for U.S. education as they can provide important insight into how non-standard varieties can find legitimate and functional roles in the classroom and support students' learning.

Linguistic Circumstances of the Greek Cypriot Community

The native language of Greek Cypriots is a regional dialect of Greek known as the Greek Cypriot dialect (GCD). The official language in Greek Cypriot schools, however, is Standard Greek (SG). The GCD differs from Standard Greek in several aspects of syntax, vocabulary, and phonology (Arvaniti, 2002; Karyolemou, 2000a). It is essentially an oral dialect and much like the non-standard U.S. dialects, it does not have a standardized system of writing. When the need arises it is phonetically coded, conventionally using the Greek alphabet and SG orthographic rules (Arvaniti, 2002).

The linguistic situation of the Greek Cypriot community can be described as involving classic diglossia as it entails two related varieties that are distinguished into a high (H) and a low (L) variety based on the criteria of *acquisition* and of *differentiated use* (Tsiplakou, 2003): The GCD is the L variety since it is learned through the natural acquisition manner of native languages, whereas SG is the native language of virtually no Cypriot (Arvaniti, 2002). Rather, it is systematically taught and learned through the educational system (Moschonas, 1996). As far as the differentiated use criterion is concerned, whereas the GCD is the main variety used in oral interactions, SG is the principal mode of written communication and is used in formal interaction contexts. Interestingly, however, Greek Cypriots use the GCD not only in the familiar contexts of family and friends but also in areas where H varieties are typically used, such as in public affairs and professional con-versations (Karyolemou, 2000b).

Karyolemou (2000a) reports that Greek Cypriots have conflicting feelings toward the two varieties of their linguistic repertoire. Although they feel an emotional connection to the GCD and on occasion take measures to preserve it, they view the SG as a finer, more eloquent and superior variety. As Moschonas (1996) mentions: "SG has the prestige of the codified language ('the beautiful/ correct Greek')" but it feels artificial. However, the GCD is regarded with a compilation of both positive and negative descriptions: "[I]t is 'the language of the illiterate'—'peasant talk,' 'inferior,' 'incomplete,' 'without grammar' but also a language that is 'familiar,' 'unpretentious,' 'natural'" (n.p.).

In Greek Cypriot schools, SG is fundamentally the only variety present on the written-language level, as all the books available are written in SG. According to Charalambopoulos (1990), even textbooks designed to be relevant to the lives and the socio-cultural experiences of Greek Cypriots do not appear to also take into account the linguistic particularities of the Greek Cypriot community. Even in such publications, the GCD is only marginally present (Hadjioannou, 2006). On the oral language level, things in Greek Cypriot schools are more complex. The Ministry of Education and Culture repeatedly issues express instructions and directives urging educators to refrain from using the GCD in class and to discourage its use by the students both orally and in writing (Hadjioannou, 2006). As Karyolemou (2000a) notes, the use of the GCD in the classroom is discouraged and stigmatized. However, she continues:

> [I]n reality, the presence of the GCD is intense, not only because it is the natural variety that students bring with them to school and which they continue to use throughout their school lives, but also because the educators themselves are dialect speakers. Therefore, the teachers, often unconsciously, insert dialect elements in the process of learning, thus reinforcing their students' dialect practices. (n.p.)

Dialect in the United States

Diglossia describes the experience of not only Greek Cypriots but also of numerous linguistic communities both around the world and within the United States. In the U.S. the phenomenon is encountered in communities where Standard American English is used along with one or more local language varieties, such as Ebonics or the White Southern dialects. In addition, based on Fishman's (1969) extended definition, diglossia also describes the experience of immigrant groups who use their native languages for their daily interactions but switch to English when communicating in formal contexts.

Although a multitude of languages and language varieties are used in the U.S., and despite linguistic evidence that all dialects have grammatical rules and are equally expressive, cognitively powerful and able to support abstract ideas, the myth of the inferiority of non-standard dialects is still quite prevalent (Lindfors, 1987; Wolfram, 1990). Some Americans look at other languages as unnecessary and dangerous to national unity and consider non-standard varieties of English as lazy, slang, defective, "broken" and inadequately expressive (Gupta, 1999). Standard American English is frequently viewed as the only desirable mode of linguistic expression, and educational reform ventures that have emerged from this outlook invariably banish other languages and non-standard dialects from American classrooms. The "English Only" movement that is currently sweeping the nation argues that monolingualism is the norm and that it is the only avenue for achieving high-quality education and for developing a powerful and effective workforce. Manifestations of this view can be traced in the effective "outlawing" of bilingual education in California with the 1998 passage of California's Proposition 227 (Grisham, 2000), as well as in the intense controversy that erupted when the Oakland Unified School District Board of Education passed a resolution that recognized Ebonics as a legitimate language variety (Gupta, 1999).

Beyond its substantial grip on social attitudes and political decision making, the view of non-standard dialects as inferior is also present on the school level. In a study of 156 preservice teachers, Townsend and Harper (1997) found that two-thirds of the participants had significant misconceptions about the nature of non-standard dialects and the abilities of their speakers. Adger (1994) reports that African American dialect speakers are disproportionately referred to special education services precisely because of their dialect. According to Adger, this trend stems from teachers' negative stereotypes against non-standard dialects, from the fact that non-standard varieties conflict with education's language ideals, and from the bias inherent in the instruments used to assess students' language development. In general, the use of non-standard varieties in school contexts is often strongly discouraged. As Delpit (1997) and Gupta (1999) note, children's use of a non-standard dialect tends to be constantly corrected, to the degree that children often prefer to remain quiet rather than risk being "wrong."

A Closer Look at the GCD in the Classroom

Given that non-standard dialect speakers typically encounter a very unfriendly environment in educational settings, the fact that the GCD is reportedly extensively present in Greek Cypriot classrooms is quite notable. In my study of the use of GCD in the classroom, I sought to examine this rather uncharacteristic presence. The setting of this examination was a sixth grade classroom in a rural Greek Cypriot elementary school where I had worked as a teacher the year preceding data collection. All 15 student participants (eight female and seven male) were Greek Cypriot and had grown up in the area. For the purposes of this study, two data sources were used: video and audio recordings of two classroom sessions and the reflective essays written by eight students on the issue of dialect. The research focused on the following questions: (1) To what extent was the GCD used in the two classroom sessions analyzed? (2) If the GCD was used, when was it encountered? Was there a relationship between the purposes of the speakers and the use or avoidance of the dialect? (3) What were the participating students' thoughts regarding the GCD and their linguistic behavior?

The first session recorded involved a 45-minute whole-class discussion on a short Standard Greek story (Zacharias Papantoniou's *The Department Manager*), which I read aloud to the class (henceforth, literature discussion). The classroom teacher was present for approximately 5 minutes of this session. The second session was a 25-minute conversation between the students and me about my graduate studies and the students' feelings regarding their imminent elementary school graduation (henceforth: free discussion). The two recorded sessions were transcribed verbatim and were examined using two lines of analysis: (a) the transcripts were coded as to the presence of the GCD and (b) the transcripts were analyzed as per the purposes each one of the participants' utterances appeared to be pursuing (as proposed by Lindfors, 1999; also by Sinclair & Coulthard, 1975.) Finally, the findings of the two analyses were combined to explore the relationship between the speakers' purposes and the use of the GCD.

The reflective essays were given as a voluntary assignment 1 week after the recordings. Without any relevant preparation, the eight participating students used a 40-minute writing period to express their thoughts on the GCD and to reflect on their linguistic behavior. The essays were analyzed using open content coding.

The Presence of the GCD in the Two Discussions

To determine whether the GCD was indeed present in the classroom, I divided the classroom transcripts into utterances (as per Bakhtin's (1986) definition) and determined the presence of GCD elements. An utterance was coded as *dialect* when it contained at least one element that is not acceptable in SD, but is in accordance with the GCD rules. For example, in the utterance: /*epiame* kala tin *alli* fora kiria/ ("*Did we* do well *last* time, madam?"), the verb /*epiame*/ is correct in terms of the GCD but unacceptable in SG.

Figures 18.1 and 18.2 present the results of the dialect coding of the two transcripts. The figures indicate that the GCD was used quite frequently in both discussions: 34% of the total utterances in the literature discussion and 55% in the free discussion. Beyond verifying the presence of the GCD, a comparison of Figures 18. and 18.2 raises a number of interesting questions regarding the causes of the remarkable rise in the frequency of the GCD in the free discussion. What is even more interesting is the fact that the sharp rise of the GCD in the free discussion is due solely to a dramatic difference in the speech of the students. Whereas the presence of the GCD in my (teacher researcher) utterances is roughly the same in both transcripts, the students' speech goes from 23% in the literature discussion to 55% in the free discussion.

These results seem to suggest that something in the nature of the free discussion led the students to use the GCD more extensively. This discrepancy may be related to the students' conceptions of the language behavior expectations associated with their student roles and to their understanding of the nature and the functions of the two discussions. The essays (to be reviewed in detail later) made clear that the students believed that, in class, they should speak SG, especially during formal lesson time. The literature discussion was clearly structured like a lesson: a teacher held a book, read a portion of a literary text from it, asked questions, read the rest of the text and then asked more questions. This set up possibly gave the students a sense of "Oh, yeah! We know the routine …" and so they slipped into the linguistic practices associated with classroom literature discussions. Case in point: Immediately after the completion of each read-aloud event, without being asked to do so, the students started summarizing the text.

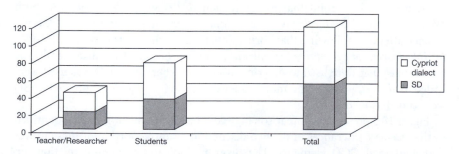

Figure 18.1 Presence of the GCD in the Literature Discussion

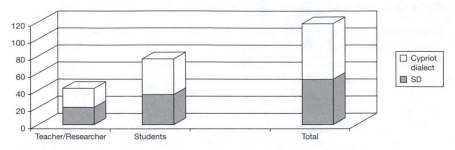

Figure 18.2 Presence of the GCD in the Free Discussion

The free discussion, by way of contrast, was different. Instead of having a lesson structure with books, the students sat in a circle with me and were invited to talk about an issue that was current and relevant to them: their impending graduation from elementary school. And even beyond that, they were able to steer the conversation toward an issue that clearly interested them: Why did I leave their school and what was I doing in the United States? It seems then that, as the conversation involved a less formal issue, the students chose to use a more informal language and therefore their speech was characterized by a higher frequency of dialect use.

The analyses of the transcripts showed that the GCD was definitely present in this classroom. The distinct difference in the students' GCD use between the two discussions suggests a pattern in code choice. Participant purposes (discourse moves) are a particularly useful tool when considering the choices speakers make regarding their linguistic behavior. Therefore, I reexamined the transcripts, exploring the possible relationship between the purposes of the speakers and the use of the GCD. In pursuing this inquiry, a two-phase analysis procedure was followed: (1) the classroom transcripts were repeatedly scrutinized, seeking to surmise the discursive purposes pursued through each one of the participants' utterances (move analysis); and (2) the results of the move analysis were viewed in combination with the presence of the GCD.

In the move analysis phase, the examination of the transcripts yielded a list of nineteen overlapping discourse moves (see Table 18.1). For example, the student utterance "Maybe he did that to bring them *better* water" was coded as both *Wondering* S6 and as *Offering possible explanation or interpretation* S8, whereas the teacher utterance following that "Bring *better* water where?" was coded as *Asking for information or prompting for elaboration or clarification* T3. Subsequently, the move codes that were used to describe utterances where the GCD was used were coded as *dialect*, whereas the move codes describing utterances expressed in SD were coded as *no dialect*.

Figure 18.3 presents a comparison between the total number of moves identified in the teachers' utterances in the two discussions and the portion of these moves that contained GCD elements. The diagram indicates a definite relationship between the teachers' purposes and the presence the GCD. The GCD was pervasive

TABLE 18.1 Types of Discourse Move According to Purpose

Student moves	Teacher moves
S1: Initiating subject or adding new dimension	T1: Initiating subject or adding new dimension
S2: Making decisions and moral judgments based on reality or text-based or hypothetical situations	T2: Expressing personal opinion and feelings
S3: Seeking information or asking for clarification	T3: Asking for information or prompting for elaboration or clarification
S4: Giving information	T4: Giving information and explanations/ clarifying
S5: Predicting	T5: Repeating/summarizing aiming to enhancement of understanding
S6: Wondering	T6: Wondering
S7: Joking	T7: Joking
S8: Offering possible explanation or interpretation	T8: Classroom management
S9: Assisting the speaker's expression, i.e. offering word options when the speaker is staggering on a word	T9: Assisting the speaker's expression, i.e. offering word options when the speaker is staggering on a word
S10: Agreeing or disagreeing with previous statements	

when the teachers were expressing their personal feelings and opinion, holding the dramatic percentage of 100%. Furthermore, the GCD was also preferred when the teachers attempted to initiate a subject or add a new dimension to the discussion (77%); where they repeated or summarized themes of the discussion (71%); and when they offered a lighthearted comment (60%). It is also noticeable that in the case of some other moves, the classroom teacher and I were less inclined to use the GCD. The most striking example of this is the complete absence of the GCD in utterances where the teacher tried to restore order in the classroom (0%).

These observations suggest that the classroom teacher and I allowed elements of the GCD in our speech when we were being more personal and informal (for example, expression of feelings, joking), or when we were trying to stimulate students' attention or make an punchy comment that would be remembered by the students (for example, initiating new discussion subject, summarizing ideas). By the same token, we *excluded* the GCD when we felt the need to assert our authority, take charge of the conversation, and call the students to order.

The results of the corresponding analysis of the students' moves are presented in Figure 18.4. The diagram reveals that GCD elements are entirely absent from

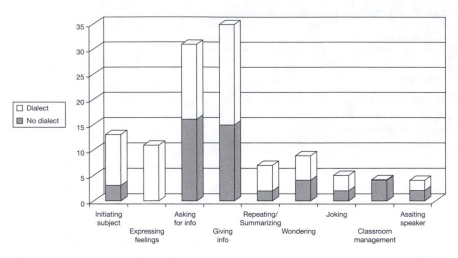

Figure 18.3 Presence of the GCD in the Teachers' Discourse Moves

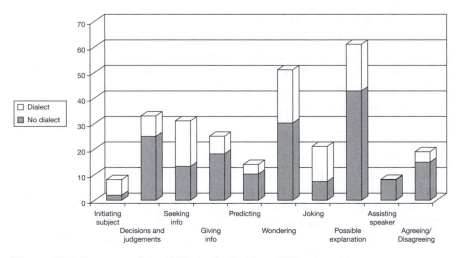

Figure 18.4 Presence of the GCD in the Students' Discourse Moves

utterances where the students attempt to assist a speaker's expression (0%), and relatively rare in instances where they express agreement or disagreement with another speaker (21%), make decisions or judgments (24%), impart information (28%), or make predictions (29%). Conversely, the students were more willing to use the GCD dialect when initiating a new conversation subject (75%), when joking (67%), when seeking information or clarification (58%) and when wondering (41%).

An overview of Figure 18.4 suggests the presence of a pattern in the students' choices regarding the use of the GCD. Engagement in acts that are labeled as "school work," seemed to make them more conscious of their role as students and compelled them to produce what they considered proper student language; that is language consistent with SG. Conversely, the instances of more overt use of the GCD coincide with moves that require a leap from the traditional student role. The initiation–response–evaluation patterns characterizing traditional classroom interactions (Mehan, 1979) do not allow discursive space for students to engage in speech acts entailing imposition (Lindfors, 1999). Moves such as initiating conversation topics, wondering, and asking for information or clarification place the speaker in a leadership role within the interaction, and invite the other participants to forgo their own discursive agendas and partake in the agenda set by the speaker. As Lindfors notes, such speech acts are more likely to be hazarded in more familiar and secure environments; the exact types of discursive environments where L varieties are used in diglossic communities. The same is true of joking, as engaging in such a move in a formal environment can be quite perilous.

Students' Perspectives Regarding the CGD

In their reflective essays, the students indicated an awareness of their diglossic circumstances: They all claimed that they speak SD in class and GCD in their everyday communications. In addition, they all appeared to be cognizant that they code-switch between the GCD and SG according to the circumstances of each interaction. They claimed that the switch happens "automatically" and they offered explanations about this change in linguistic variety. As a student noted:

> In the classroom we all speak Standard Greek, whereas during recess or at home I speak with my friends and my brothers in Cypriot. I do not have any difficulty in speaking in either one of the two languages and I do not really think about it when I use each one. This happens by itself. It depends on how I am used to speaking in each place.

The students' assertion that they speak SG in class is to a degree verified by the results of the analysis of the two audiotaped discussions where only a total of 10 utterances could be described as "purely Cypriot." All the other utterances had a primarily SG syntactical structure but were "sprinkled" by elements of the GCD.

Interestingly, even though the students recognized that when they spoke in class "a couple of Cypriot words may slip in," they were not aware of how extensively present the GCD truly was in their classroom speech. In a fairly typical type of statement, one of the students asserted: "Everybody in my class speaks and writes in SD." This belief may stem from the students' confidence in their ability to appropriately shape their linguistic behavior to classroom expectations. This confidence allows them to not be self-conscious about their code choices and to therefore not pay much attention to the degree the GCD finds its way in classroom interactions. After all, their teachers not only accepted the students' language as produced, but they also used the GCD in their own speech.

At the same time, however, the student essays include evaluative descriptions that reveal negative stereotypes toward the GCD. Despite some statements of pride for their native tongue, the students often suggested that the GCD is less developed and less expressive than SG and seemed to think that using SG in class is a matter of inevitability rather than a social convention. According to their reasoning, the GCD cannot be used in school simply because it does not provide the speaker with the necessary expressive tools for communicating her/his thoughts in discussions of educational nature: "The Cypriot language is beautiful but you can only discuss everyday subjects with it."

Surprisingly, some students claimed that one of the reasons why they do not use the GCD in formal in-class communication is that they are not really fluent in the GCD. The following is indicative of this view: "If I wanted to say what I need to say in class using all Cypriot words, I think I would have a really hard time because I do not know all the words, whereas I know all the Greek words."

Similar unexpected findings were reported by Tsiplakou (2003), whose teenage informants claimed to know SG better than the GCD. At a first glance, the young Greek Cypriots' assertion that they are not as competent in their native tongue as they are in another idiom sounds absurd. However, their logic becomes clearer when it is considered in conjunction with another claim widely present in the student essays: that they do not speak the *authentic* GCD. In their essays, the students maintain that "[the GCD] is spoken nowadays only by the old people in small villages and in [folk] plays on TV." Such statements reveal that the students equate the GCD with "village Cypriot" (Arvaniti, 2002) which is spoken by older individuals. Failing to recognize the dynamic sociocultural processes that shape and reshape languages and impel them to evolve, the students also fail to recognize that their own mother tongue (*Urban Cypriot*, Arvaniti, 2002) is as much a part of the GCD continuum as the village Cypriot. Therefore, they believe that in their everyday communications they use a sort of *mild* version of the GCD.

The difference between the "heavy," "authentic" Cypriot and the "urban Cypriot" (Arvaniti, 2002) spoken by the students was used to articulate further negative stereotypes regarding the use of the GCD:

> I am sure that if somebody spoke real Cypriot in class, or even when we play, it would stand out, and some would make fun of them. The ones that speak only "heavy" Cypriot and cannot speak in SG are people that never went to school and so we should not make fun of them.

The quotes just examined are quite revealing of the existence of negative assumptions regarding dialect speakers, even in a culture where code-switching across dialects is widely accepted. People who only speak village Cypriot and cannot code-switch appropriately are made fun of and are perceived to be uneducated and unsophisticated. Interestingly, however, in all the essays, the stigma was not so much attached to the use of the GCD per se but to the inability to code-switch according to the expectations framing different communication instances.

At this point, it is important to note that the students did not appear to perceive their linguistic heritage as a deficiency, and stated that being GCD speakers is a very important part of who they are. They described the GCD as a beautiful language which should be respected, spoken, and passed on to subsequent generations.

Implications for U.S. Educational Practice

The issue of non-standard dialects is an urgent one in American education. The proponents of the "English Only" or rather the "Standard English only" movement in the United States contend that non-standard dialects inhibit students' academic learning and demand that all students use Standard English all the time. However, this contention is missing a vital part of what we know about effective language communication: that even monolingual people do not speak the same way in all communication instances (see Shelton's chapter in this publication). A major part of an individual's communicative competence is the ability to shape her/his verbal and nonverbal behavior in ways that better serve the speaker's discursive purposes (Lindfors, 1987). Complying with the social expectations of which language register or variety is to be used at any given communicative situation is part of that ability. As Giesbers, Kroon, and Liebrand (1989, p. 251) note, "code switching is in fact an indication of a very well developed structural as well as pragmatic language proficiency."

The case of the Greek Cypriot class under study suggests that the woes of the "Standard English only" proponents regarding the dangers of non-standard dialect use are unfounded. Allowing the presence of a non-standard dialect in this classroom did not render the students unable to use the standard when the situation demanded it: All students spoke in SG, particularly when expressing moves associated with their formal student roles; all students wrote in impeccable SG when authoring their essays; all students indicated positive attitudes toward the standard; and all students felt competent in both their mother tongue (urban Cypriot) and the standard.

The analysis of the two classroom discussions indicates that the participants know very well how to shape their linguistic behavior in accordance with the social expectations associated with the functions they mean to express. Contrary to the contentions of Standard English only proponents who assert that speaking a non-standard dialect disrupts the acquisition of the standard, the study participants bounce back and forth between SG and the GCD with elegance, weaving an interesting exchange of ideas, never causing breaches in the conversation or awkward moments because of the use of inappropriate language forms. If teachers and students were to be allowed to use their home dialects in the classroom, similar communication patterns are not hard to imagine in U.S. schools.

The study participants' code-switching competency was also demonstrated through the patterns identified in their code-switching: the GCD was consistently used in moves that are more intimate or intended to be noticed (for example, joking, wondering, summarizing). This is not surprising, as individuals tend to default to their mother tongue in their more relaxed and relationship-building conversations (Blom & Gumperz, 1972; Myers-Scotton, 2002). The possible implications of this inference for American education are indeed significant. Researchers of classroom environments stress the importance of a relaxed and intimate classroom atmosphere in fostering student engagement and student learning (Anderson, O'Flahavan, & Guthrie, 1996; Raider-Roth, 2005; Seabrook, 1991). These findings suggest that providing legitimate spaces for home dialects in American classrooms may play a crucial role in facilitating the development of such classroom environments.

In addition, the use of the home dialect in utterances intended to be noticed can also hold significant value in the teaching and learning that takes place in American classrooms: In a sea of utterances spoken in the formal standard dialect, the listeners surely are more inclined to pay attention to and better understand and remember an utterance spoken in their mother dialect.

The student moves associated with frequent use of the GCD are characterized by intimacy. Notably, these same moves are also closely associated with the kind of thinking and talking we want our students to engage in when we are trying to cultivate authentic, dialogic interactions in our classrooms (Hadjioannou, 2003). Just imagine how this class's interactions would look if we were to remove the high GCD moves: wondering, asking for information and clarification, initiating conversation topics and joking. The students would be stuck answering questions, with no independent, critical thinking of their own. Given this, one can only wonder about the limitations placed on the quality of class interactions in U.S. classrooms where non-standard dialects are disallowed.

Furthermore, the literature on diglossia suggests that the rejection of the students' home dialect by school can be the source of a series of problems. One such problem, which has frequently been identified in U.S. minority youth, is that dialect speaking students face a confusing array of mixed signals: What is praised in the home is a cause for scolding and ridicule in school and vice versa. Furthermore, by adopting the linguistic behavior promoted by school, the children "risk losing an awareness of themselves and of the world in which they live" and their social and linguistic identity is put in jeopardy (Rosenberg, 1989, p. 79).

This study indicates that competence in a non-standard dialect and in the standard are not mutually exclusive. The study participants appear to have adequate exposure to both variants of Greek to be fluent in both. Through their participation in the Greek Cypriot linguistic community they seem to acquire enough knowledge to not only understand and use both dialects, but to also make appropriate choices of which dialect to use in different situations. The same could be true of American children of diverse linguistic backgrounds, provided that they have abundant opportunities to truly engage with both their home dialect and the standard.

Overall, schooling may be more effective if aimed at the development of the student's competency in both their home dialect and the standard. As Van de Craen and Humblet (1989) write, school "should contribute maximally to the development of all aspects of language proficiency, in a stimulating linguistic environment" (p. 26). After all, the more language variation individuals are able to master, the more competent they become in their communications. From this perspective, the role of the school, whether in Cyprus or the U.S., is not simply to be accepting of non-standard dialects, or to merely help the students learn how to speak the standard. Its major responsibility is to help children develop effective strategies for using the appropriate dialect in different situations. As in the case of the Cypriot class under study, this goal can be pursued through indirect and natural ways, such as modeling by the teacher and encouraging the children to participate in real discussions, where they will have the chance to experience language at work and create their own patterns of communication.

However, as many theorists posit, beyond the implicit ways of language use, schools should also provide instances of explicit dialect study and conversations regarding the social aspects of language and code switching (Adger, 1997; Andrews-Beck, 1997; Delpit, 1988; Erickson, 1997; Smitherman, 1999; Wolfram 1990; Wolfram & Christian, 1989). Regrettably, such explorations are not part of the curriculum in Cyprus, since the presence of the GCD in classrooms is not officially condoned. It is therefore not surprising that, despite their significant metalinguistic awareness, the Greek Cypriot students studied held some significant misconceptions regarding the nature, the quality and the expressiveness of the GCD. Similar misconceptions are frequently expressed in the U.S. not only by students but also by the general public as well as by teachers and policymakers. A good start in addressing such erroneous beliefs is the initiation of discussions about the grammaticalness, the expressiveness and validity of all dialects (Lindfors, 1987; Wolfram 1990; Wolfram & Christian, 1989).

Comparative examination of dialects can also assist in better understanding the syntax, the grammar and the phonology of both the standard and non-standard dialects (Adger, 1997; Harris-Wright, 1999; Smitherman, 1999). Equally important can be conversations that explicitly examine the sociolinguistic factors that determine which language variety is appropriate for different communicative circumstances (Wolfram & Christian, 1989). Such conversations can assist U.S. minority students in recognizing the code demands of various types of communication and in appreciating the importance of being fluent in both their mother tongues and in the standard. Intertwined with issues of language is the "culture of power," which, according to Delpit (1988) entails the rules, the patterns and the styles of interaction that are valued in the wider social context. Delpit argues that teaching all students the implicit and explicit rules of power is an essential prerequisite of equity education.

Conclusion

In sum, then, the increased push for Standard English only education in the U.S. asserts that monolingualism is not only the norm but also a significant prerequisite of academic success. In spite of resolutions defending students' right to their own language, non-standard dialects are viewed as imperfect language codes that interfere with students' school learning and should therefore be banished from classrooms and replaced with the standard. This study indicates that bidialectism can have a productive and functional place in the classroom. Instead of alienating and disenfranchising dialect speaking students by rejecting their mother tongue and stigmatizing its use in school, this case study provides a useful example of how the simultaneous presence of a standard and a non-standard dialect in the classroom can culminate in nurturing students who are comfortable with their linguistic identities, who are fluent in both dialects and who successfully code-switch between two dialects in pursuing their communication objectives. In other words, this study shows that monolingualism is not the norm and it does not have to be an objective of American education. Instead, it indicates that a healthier attitude toward diglossia can help in fostering student academic success as well as in honoring the linguistic diversity of American society.

Discussion Questions and Activities

1. In groups of three, plan, act out through improvisation, and record two different conversations. Each conversation must involve two participants, be 2–3 minutes long, and have a sense of completeness. The conversations must differ in two or more of the following dimensions: participants (who they are, relationship between them), subject, purpose of the conversation, medium (face to face, telephone), and location.

   Review your recorded conversations trying to identify differences in the two conversations in terms of:

   • language: vocabulary, syntax, grammar, use of non-standard dialects, length of sentences;
   • turn taking: length of utterances, interruptions;
   • other aspects.

   Try to explain the differences you observed. Share your conversations, your observations, and your explanations with the class.
2. Record and transcribe two naturally occurring conversations to which you have legitimate access. Each conversation must involve two to three participants and be 2–3 minutes long. The conversations must differ in two or more of the following dimensions: participants (who they are, relationship between them), subject, purpose of the conversation, medium (face to face, telephone), location.

   Bring your transcripts to class. In groups of three, review your recorded conversations trying to identify differences in the two conversations in terms of:

   • language: vocabulary, syntax, grammar, use of non-standard dialects, length of sentences;
   • turn taking: length of utterances, interruptions;
   • other aspects

   Try to explain the differences you observed. Share your conversations, your observations and your explanations with the class
3. In the 2005 motion picture *Crash* by writer/director Paul Haggis, a Caucasian actor (Tony Danza) approaches the African American director (Terence Howard) of his TV show to complain that an African American fellow actor delivers some of his lines in Standard English instead of Black English. He concludes his complaint with the following: "I mean, 'cause all I'm saying is it's not his character. Eddie's supposed to be the smart one, not Jamal, right?" Discuss the implications of this statement.

4. How can teachers who do not speak the home dialects of their students succeed in the recommendations proposed in this chapter?

References

Adger, C. (1994). *Enhancing the Delivery of Services to Black Special Education Students from Non-Standard English Backgrounds*. Final Report. ERIC Document Reproduction Service No. ED370377.

——. (1997). *Dialect Education: Not Only for Oakland. ERIC Digest*, 20(2). Retrieved January 2, 2006, from http://www.cal.org/ericcll/News/9703Dialect.html.

Andrews-Beck, C. (1997). What Can Teachers Learn from the Ebonics Controversy? *Ohio Reading Teacher*, 31(2), 58–59.

Anderson, E., O'Flahavan, J., & Guthrie, J. (1996). The Influence of Embedded Word Study Instruction, Social Context and Motivation of Children's Independent Reading and Writing: A Case Study of Three First Graders. *National Reading Center. Reading Research Report* No. 95.

Arvaniti, A. (2002). Dimorphy, Diglossia and the emergence of Cypriot Standard Greek [in Greek]. *Recherches en Linguistique Grecque*, I, 75–78. Paris: L' Harmattan.

Bakhtin, M. (1986). *Speech Genres and other Late Essays*. Austin, TX: University of Texas Press.

Blom, J., & Gumperz, J. (1972). Social Meaning in Linguistic Structures: Code. In J. Gumperz, & D. Hymes (Eds.). *Switching in Northern Norway. Directions in Sociolinguistics: The Ethnography of Communication*. New York: Holt, Rinehart, & Winston.

Delpit, L. (1988). The Silenced Dialogue: Power and Pedagogy in Educating Other People's Children. *Harvard Educational Review*, 58(3), 280–98.

——. (1997). Ebonics and Culturally Responsive Instruction: What Should Teachers Do? Rethinking Schools. *Online*, 12(1). Retrieved January 2, 2006, from www.rethinkingschools.org.

Erickson, F. (1997). Culture in Society and in Educational Practices. In J. Banks, & C. McGee (Eds.). *Multicultural Education: Issues and Perspectives*. Boston, MA: Allyn & Bacon.

Ferguson, C. (1959). Diglossia. *Word*, 15(2), 325–340.

Fishman, J. (1969). National Languages and Languages of Wider Communication in the Developing Nations. *Anthropological Linguistics*, 11, 111–135.

Giesbers, H., Kroon, S, & Liebrand, R. (1989). Language in the Classroom: The Amsterdam and Groningen Projects. In J. Chesire, V. Edwards, H. Munstermann, & B. Weltens (Eds.). *Dialect and Education*. Philadelphia, PA: Multilingual Matters Ltd.

Grisham, D. (2000). Class Size Reduction: Learning from the California Experience. *Reading Online*, 4(5). Retrieved January 2, 2006, from www.readingonline.org.

Gupta, A. (1999). What's Up with Ebonics, Y'all? *Reading Online*. Retrieved January 2, 2006, from www.readingonline.org.

Hadjioannou, X. (2003). *An Exploration of Authentic Discussion in the Booktalks of a Fifth Grade Class*. Doctoral dissertation, Gainesville, FL: University of Florida.

——. (2006). Linguistic Variation in Greek Cypriot Elementary Education. In W. Wiater, & G. Videsott (Eds.). *School Systems in Multilingual Regions of Europe*. Frankfurt-am-Main: Peter Lang.

Harris-Wright, K. (1999). Enhancing Bidialectism in Rrban African American Students. In D. Adger, D. Christian, & O. Taylor (Eds.). *Making the Connection: Language and Academic Achievement among African American Students*. Washington, DC: Center of Applied Linguistics.

Καρυολαίμου (Karyolemou), M. (2000a). Η ελληνική γλώσσα στην Κύπρο. *Ηλεκτρονικός Εγκυκλοπαιδικός Οδηγός για τη Γλώσσα*. Retrieved January 2, 2006, from www.komvos. edu.gr.

——. (2000b). Κυπριακή πραγματικότητα και κοινωνιογλωσσική *περιγραφή . Μελέτες για την ελληνική γλώσσα* (Πρακτικά της 20ής Ετήσιας Συνάντησης του Τομέα Γλωσσολογίας, Α.Π.Θ., 23–25 Απριλίου 1999), 203–214, σελ. 206–207.

Lindfors, J. (1987). *Children's Language and Learnin*, 2nd edn. Boston, MA: Allyn & Bacon.

——. (1999). *Children's Inquiry: Using Language to Make Sense of the World*. New York: Teachers College Press.

Mehan, H. (1979). *Learning Lessons: Social Organization in the Classroom.* Cambridge, MA: Harvard University Press.

Μοσχονάς (Moschonas), Σ. (1996). Η γλωσσική διμορφία σιην Κυπρο. *"Ισχυρές" και "ασθενείς" γλώσσες στην Ευρωπαϊκή Ένωση: Όψεις του γλωσσικού ηγεμονισμού* (Πρακτικά Ημερίδας, Θεσσαλονίκη Απρίλιος 1996), 121–127. Θεσσαλονίκη: Κέντρο Ελληνικής Γλώσσας, σελ. 123–124.

Myers-Scotton, C. (2002). Frequency and Intention in (Un)marked Choices in Code-Switching: "This is a 24-Hour Country." *International Journal of Bilingualism*, 6(2), 205–219.

Raider-Roth, M. (2005). *Trusting What You Know: The High Stakes of Classroom Relationships.* San Francisco: Jossey-Bass.

Rosenberg, P. (1989). Dialect and Education in West Germany. In J. Chesire, V. Edwards, H. Munstermann, & B. Weltens (Eds.). *Dialect and Education.* Clevedon, PA: Multilingual Matters Ltd.

Seabrook, G. (1991). A Teacher Learns in the Context of a Social Studies Workshop. *Harvard Educational Review*, 61(4), 475–485.

Sinclair, J. M., & Coulthard, R. M. (1975). *Towards an Analysis of Discourse: The English Used by Teachers and Pupils.* Oxford: Oxford University Press.

Smitherman, G. (1999). Language Policies and Classroom Practices. In D. Adger, D. Christian, & O. Taylor (Eds.). *Making the Connection: Language and Academic Achievement among African American Students.* Washington, DC: Center of Applied Linguistics.

Townsend, J., & Harper, C. (1997). What Future Teachers Know and Don't Know about Language Diversity. *The Professional Educator*, 20(1), 35–44.

Τσιπλάκου(Tsiplakou), Σ. (2003). Στάσεις απέναντι στη γλώσσα και γλώσσική αλλαγή: Μια αφίδρομη σχέση; *Πρακτικά 6^{ov} Διεθνές Συνέδριου Ελληνικης Γλωσσολογίας.* Retrieved January 2, 2006, from www.philology.uoc.gr/conferences/6thICGL/ebook/.

Van de Craen, P., & Humblet, I. (1989). Dialect and Education in Belgium. In J. Chesire, V. Edwards, H. Munstermann, & B. Weltens (Eds.). *Dialect and Education.* Clevedon, PA: Multilingual Matters Ltd.

Wolfram, W. (1990). Incorporating Dialect Study into the Language Arts Class. *ERIC Digest.* ERIC Document Reproduction Service No. ED318231.

———., & Christian, D. (1989). *Dialects and Education: Issues and Answers.* Englewood Cliffs, NJ: Prentice-Hall/Regents.

Χαραλαμπόπουλος (Charalambopoulos), A. (1990). Γλωσσική διδασκαλία: η περίπτωση της Κύπρου. *Γλώσσα 22*, 69–94.

19
The Writing on the Wall: Graffiti and Other Community School Practices in Brazil

ANA CHRISTINA DASILVA IDDINGS

This chapter examines the processes by which a decaying urban area in São Paulo, Brazil was transformed into a vibrant community/school through the creation of sociocultural spaces where the right of expression has been made sovereign. Projeto Aprendiz (Project Apprentice), as it is called, was created in 1997 by Gilberto Dimenstein, a renowned journalist with a vision to end dualisms between school and community and to instill social investment (citizenship) among the residents of a deprecated area punctuated by violence, educational inequities, and social contradictions materialized by the lavish homes and the many favelas (slums) co-existing alongside one another in the same street block.

The ideas that guide Aprendiz are fundamentally based on sociocultural theoretical perspectives (Lave & Wenger, 1991) that view learning as participation in the social practices of a community, consider the interrelationships between learning and identity, emphasize the unity of individual and context, and focus on processes of change, rather than on learning outcomes with individuals as agents of social change. In addition, Paulo Freire's (1970) pedagogical approaches are utilized and expanded, promoting the empowerment of individuals through purposeful engagement in dialogue and through the recognition and preservation of their respective modes of expression and cultural histories.

In light of these theoretical and methodological assumptions, the practical goal of the project is to create opportunities for members of the communities to participate together in unique learning experiences. Even though the content of these experiences correspond to traditional school curricula, the activities students participate in are integrally embedded in their lived experiences within the community. Through this project a neighborhood newspaper, a radio station, a restaurant, an internet café, an urban art studio, a bookstore, and various other community spaces were all re-created, re-organized, and operated by members of the community. All were transformed into "classrooms" of sorts, thus serving as vehicles for social reintegration of individuals in the community.

It is important to note that Aprendiz does not aim to serve the poor. It does not aim to acculturate socioeconomic or ethnic minorities into dominant paradigms or doctrines, neither does it aim to prepare individuals to 'exit' the community. Instead, participants of the community/school Aprendiz are neighborhood residents who are simultaneously beneficiaries and benefactors of the community, extinguishing the class disparities between "self" and "other" through their engagement in sociocultural practices. For example, participants of Aprendiz transformed a sullied beco (no outlet street), often used as a site where drug dealings took place, into an open-air gallery where skilled and colorful graffiti art (learned at one of Aprendiz's urban art workshops) is now displayed (see Figures 19.1 and 19.2).

Figure 19.1 No Outlet Street "Beco" (Before)

Figure 19.2
No Outlet Street
"Beco" (After)

The members of the community/school Aprendiz are individuals of various ages and diverse socioeconomic, racial, ethnic and linguistic backgrounds. In addition, the project is multigenerational with respect to both age groups and time in the community. Old-time members and newcomers participate together in the practices of the community, and over time old-timers become instructors of the various classes and workshops offered in the various spaces for learning. In this chapter, I will describe the actual practices of community/school Aprendiz, demonstrate how the engagement in these practices contributed to extraordinary transformations of the community and of individuals' identities, and discuss the projects' possible implications for the education of linguistic minority students in the United States. However, before turning to the descriptions of Aprendiz's activities, I provide a brief explanation of the theoretical foundations and pedagogical approaches in which this project is rooted.

From Practice to Theory: Theorizing Aprendiz

Although *Projeto Aprendiz* has its basis on *practice* (i.e. what people actually do, the tools they use, the ways they interact, how they share the labor and generate and utilize resources), the application of a theoretical frame may provide a useful lens for understanding the transformational potential of the project. At the risk of oversimplifying complex theoretical concepts, I highlight four key principles aligned with sociocultural paradigms that underlie the practices of community/ school *Aprendiz*.

Principle 1: Learning as Participation in the Social Practices of a Community

From this perspective, learning occurs as a process of apprenticeship where newcomers fulfill various peripheral roles alongside more experienced or competent members in community practice. This principle reflects the essence of Lave and Wenger's (1991) theory of legitimate peripheral participation. That is, as individuals belong to multiple and overlapping communities of practice constituted by members' mutual engagement in joint enterprises, they hold diverse participatory roles. The social relations they entail offer newcomers distinct insights into the nature of the community of practice and opportunities to acquire the knowledge and skills necessary for full participation in the practices of the community.

Principle 2: Interrelationships Between Learning and Identity

Participation in community practice results in the acquisition of new identities in addition to new knowledge and skills. This principle is closely related to the first and also issues from Lave and Wenger's (1991) monograph. The theory of legitimate peripheral participation accentuates the intrinsic relationship among social relations, learning, and identity. Lave and Wenger state: "Learning implies becoming a different person with respect to the possibilities enabled by systems of relations. To ignore this aspect of learning is to overlook the fact that learning involves the construction of identities" (p. 53).

Principle 3: Unity of Individual and Context

Incommensurable with traditional theories of knowledge construction that retain dualist distinctions between mind and world, sociocultural theory set out to resolve

Cartesian splits in psychology by focusing on the dialectical interrelationships between thought and the material world, mind and body, individual and society. In this respect, this theory tries to demonstrate (through both theory and practice) the inextricable relationship between mind and activity as well as the inseparability of mind/activity from the historical, cultural, and social contexts in which it is embedded (Leont'ev, 2002).

Principle 4: Human Agency and Social Change

Central to sociocultural approaches to understanding the human mind and activity is the concept of change. Here this concept is closely related to individual's *agency*, or the power to act on (not merely react to) their material and social worlds, and thus to transform and provoke change. That is, individuals' will and purposes to exercise autonomy and to affirm themselves as social actors create possibilities for change. In turn, as society changes, these social actors engage in shifting practices and are faced with finding solutions to new problems, thus developing new consciousness in response to social transformations.

Note that many important theoretical assumptions related to sociocultural theory have been left out in the interest of time and space. Keeping the foregrounded theoretical principles in mind, I now provide a glimpse into the pedagogical approaches that permeate the practices of *Aprendiz*.

The Pedagogy of Opportunities for Authentic Expression

Aprendiz's methodological approaches reflect Paulo Freire's critical pedagogy perspective as it applies to the concept of empowerment of oppressed populations and their communities through the purposeful use of dialogue. Freire viewed the concept of *dialogism* as central to human interactions. For him, dialogue is a tool for liberation and transformation of reality, and, without it, there can be no true education. The main implications of his research lie in the fact that literacy education can provide the knowledge, dispositions, and skills for the redistribution of power and income among the oppressed masses. He revolutionized the traditional views of teaching literacy claiming that to be literate meant to be able to *read the world*, not just the *word*. Thus, following Freire, literacy is not merely a series of skills to be taught, but rather a social condition which empowers individuals. That is, by learning to read and write, individuals are more able to participate in the textual community in which we live. Later, David Olson (1994) further explained:

> We must acknowledge the fact that any society is organized around a body of beliefs, sometimes expressed in textual form, access to which is a source of power and prestige. In a bureaucratic society the issues of law, religion, politics, science and literature make up this privileged domain, and access to, and participation in, those domains define a particular form of literacy [. . .]. Literacy from this perspective is the competence required for participation in these privileged domains. (Olson, 1994, p. 274)

Another important element of Paulo Freire's (1970) methodology is the fact that it views the development of oral communication as a means of achieving competency in reading and writing. Therefore, through dialogue that utilizes the student's authentic language (representing their sense of self), the teacher is able to help students to know that they know. In this way, students' strong cultural and personal histories are utilized as a resource to facilitate their understandings of the world around them. In his chapter on the "Banking Concept of Education" in *Pedagogy of the Oppressed* (Freire, 1970), Paulo Freire pointed out the essentially monological nature of traditional teacher–student relationships and explains that in these educational settings, the students are often seen as a container to be filled by the teacher—the sole holder of information. That is, topics of study are generated by the teacher, and the fact of whether they are relevant or even pertinent to the experiences of the students is secondary. In this way, "education becomes an act of depositing, in which the students are depositories and the teacher is the depositor" (Freire, 1970, p. 208)—hence the banking concept. In this model, the students receive, memorize, and repeat information given by the teacher. The creative process and the process of inquiry are completely removed from learning and from instruction.

Freire argues that the banking concept of education is another way by which the dominant class imposes power and subordinates others to learn their values and realities however far remote from the students' reality they may be. He explains further that this model of instruction perpetuates the oppressed/oppressor relationships by severely limiting the students' creative powers and by failing to develop students' critical consciousness. This process serves the interests of the oppressors who do not aim to change the status quo. As Freire explains, "Projecting an absolute ignorance onto others, a characteristic of the ideology of oppression, negates education and knowledge as a process" (p. 237). For the author, the solution to this issue lies not in the integration of cultural minorities into this structure of oppression, but on the transformation of this structure so that they can become beings for themselves. This is done by means of dialogical relations and problem-posing education. This approach breaks the vertical patterns characteristic of the banking concept and fosters authentic learning by enabling students to engage in meaningful cognitive activities that not only permit but also encourage critical thinking about social, political and economic contradictions. Problem-posing education is liberating in nature, as it empowers students to take action against the oppressive elements of reality.

In his *Pedagogy of the Oppressed* (1970), Freire presents a pedagogy that must be forged with, not for, the oppressed (whether individuals or peoples) in the incessant struggle to regain their humanity. For the oppressed to change their reality, they must first analyze that reality in order to understand its causes, and then work together to transform, rather than adapt to, that reality. This transformation can be materialized through praxis, reflection and action, and then further reflection on that action, in order to transform the world.

Another concept that is crucial to understand in the study of Freire's pedagogy is the generative theme. To derive the program content of education, we must turn to the reality that mediates men and their perception of that reality. The themes of a particular epoch are the concrete representations of the complexity of ideas, concepts, hopes, doubts, values, and challenges in dialectical interaction with their opposites, striving toward plenitude and man's full humanization. These themes both contain and are contained in what Freire calls limit situations, beyond which the unperceived practical solutions to the situation lie. Also, these themes are termed *generative* because they contain the possibility of unfolding again and again into many themes, which in their turn call for new tasks to be fulfilled. Freire considers the fundamental theme of our epoch to be that of domination, which implies its opposite, the theme of liberation, as the objective to be achieved. In the dialogical, problem-posing method of education, the student must find his own generative themes, and the task of the dialogic teacher is to re-present these themes as problems.

Freire's approaches are remarkably substantiated in the practices of *Aprendiz*. The project provides many opportunities in the way spaces, vehicles, and tools for community members to engage in purposeful dialogue, reflection, and action, to generate themes of study, and to express themselves authentically through written and oral communication, arts, crafts, graffiti, music, and many other media. Some of these practices are described in the following sections.

Community Practices

The Newspaper and the Radio Station

The community/school *Aprendiz* began with the creation of a newspaper and website (www.aprendiz.org.br) designed to disseminate information about education and to promote citizenship in a particular neighborhood of São Paulo (Vila Madalena) marked by social contradictions (coincidentally, the very area where I grew up in Brazil). In time, the newspaper became an important vehicle for the reinsertion of marginalized youth into community affairs. It provided individuals with a keen awareness about the political, economic, and educational issues faced by the community; elicited action, and created affordances for participants and readers to understand their world and to deal with their own realities in productive ways. The newspaper staff combines professionals of various fields related to education and members of the community, many of whom learned to read and write through their engagement in the practices of creating text.

To fulfill the need to reach out to a larger public and disseminate information to non-readers, a radio station was created. The station is predominantly run by young members of the community (mainly adolescents) and provides them with yet another vehicle for self-expression. Through their broadcastings, individuals are able to voice their opinions, invite new dialogues, and engage in reflective activities. In a more practical sense, the station also serves as a vehicle for community members to advertise their services, launch partnerships with the public and private sectors, establish networks with other non-governmental organizations (NGOs), and scout for needed resources. Through donations and selling of advertisement space, both the newspaper and the radio station generate sufficient income for their own financial sustainability and for the sponsorship of new apprenticeship programs.

It is worth noting that although the fully equipped offices of the newspaper and the radio station are situated in an area where crime and violence were once prevalent, their doors and windows now remain open during the day in an inviting gesture (see Figure 19.3).

The Café

In addition to being a sophisticated gastronomic space, the Café is also a center for the intellectual life of the community, providing many opportunities for its members to engage in informal conversations and/or organized debates, to display and sell their art, to read their poetry, to play games, and to navigate the internet. Decorative tiles, hand painted by community members, line the interior walls of the Café forming a glossy quilt, reminding the guests that they are an integral part of the community (see Figure 19.4). Cooking classes are available to children and adults on a regular basis. In these classes, members of the *Aprendiz* learn not only how to prepare meals, but through their participation in these very contextualized experiences, they also learn how to read, write, count, measure, as well as various other skills, which in more traditional settings are reserved for highly inauthentic "lesson" situations. Many of the "graduates" have become chefs in the Café as well as in other restaurants in the city.

The Café is also a site for intergenerational teaching/learning about the internet. There, teen members of the community are often seen side by side their elders, teaching them how to type and how to access practical information, entertainment, and news. Remarkably, the use of the equipment is free of charge and has not been vandalized nor stolen since the opening of the Café in 2001. The Café generates much of *Aprendiz*'s revenue, although not everyone is asked to pay for their meals.

Figure 19.3 The Office of the Newspaper and Radio Station

Figure 19.4 The Café Wall

The Graffiti

While most communities view the practice of graffiti as a menace to society, *Aprendiz* finds their community embellished by the presence of brightly colored walls with intricate drawings and vivid public messages (see Figure 19.5). In an audacious initiative, *Aprendiz* led an organized movement to provide graffiti artists with the proper space to create art and to express their voices. The movement was highly successful: Graffiti has now been sanctioned by public authorities to be displayed in various designated areas of the city. In fact, during the commemorative activities of São Paulo's 450th anniversary, 150 graffiti artists were commissioned to apply their unique painted language in the public spaces of the major avenues of the city.

Moreover, workshops designed to teach graffiti techniques to layman are a popular activity at the *Aprendiz* Urban Art Studio. Many well-known artists spend much of their time collaborating with newcomers to the art form, creating elaborate murals that intentionally interfere with the otherwise dull urban landscape. In this way, multimodal forms of literacy are engaged and skills related to geometry, proportion, and general graphic arts principles are developed. Curiously, the murals are usually signed by the artists and no graffiti is placed over another unless by permission of the authors. Also of note is the fact that many new and well-established artists have been given contracts by multinational corporations such as Nike, Adidas, and others, and have received large sums of money for the right to use the authors' graffiti designs on fashion t-shirts.

Figure 19.5 The Graffiti

The Workshops

Confirming that learning is ubiquitous (i.e., not confined to the walls of classrooms), at the *Aprendiz* Plaza, learning/teaching take place in the open air (see Figure 19.6). Picnic tables and wide benches make up "classrooms" where many workshops come alive. It is largely through these experiences that children learn the fundamental competencies of the general school curriculum as they participate in a variety of generative thematic activities, in the Freirian sense. For example, historical events are questioned, discussed, re-enacted through puppet plays (using puppets created by the participants in the puppetry workshops), and reflected upon; the geography of the national rivers is learned in story telling workshops that recount folk tales of the Amazon.

The workshops are numerous and varied, consisting of candle making, mosaics, dance, sports, arts, and many others. In addition to providing students with basic curricular competencies, these ongoing events aim to develop different perspectives, convictions, knowledge, and citizenship for members of the community. More than 15,000 people of many different age groups, educational levels, races, ethnicities, and social classes have by now participated in long- and short-term workshops and events.

Aprendiz has grown beyond its community and now incorporates many different partnerships and projects. Many decaying areas of São Paulo have been revitalized by some facet of *Aprendiz*. For example, in many parts of the city horrific levels of social inequalities are reified by tall brick walls that separate the rich from the poor. Participants of *Project Cem Muros* (*Project Without Walls*), a spinoff from *Aprendiz*, brings down these walls and replaces them with colorful community-made mosaic illustrating peaceful themes—a hopeful sight. *Aprendiz* has been recently recognized by UNESCO as a world model for educating urban youth. Not only the community as a whole has been extraordinarily changed by the advent of the project, but through the engagement in the social practices described here (and others not mentioned), the identities of individuals are also transformed. In the next section, I relay the story of one particular individual, whom I had the opportunity to interview.

Figure 19.6
The Classrooms
in the Open Air

Sophie's Story

Sophie (pseudonym), a 21-year-old Afro-Brazilian woman, is one of the pioneering members of *Aprendiz*. Like many who live in São Paulo, Sophie was born and raised in the streets. For as long as she could remember, survival from one day to the next was her main intent. Typical of children who call the streets their home, Sophie had gotten used to the inclemency of concrete and wet days, the pervasive violence, and the sexual assaults. Although she lived in constant fear, she had not lost hope of someday being able to change her course and to tell her story to more sheltered populations whom she thought had become numbed by their everyday routines and viewed street dwellers as a nuisance that must be ignored.

Along the years, Sophie formed a "family" in the streets. She had street "brothers," "sisters," and a "father," Arnaldo (pseudonym), whom she considered her "savior." He had taken and kept her out of crime, alcohol, and drugs. He took care of her when at the age of 16 she became pregnant (by an unknown man) with her first child. She described Arnaldo as a kind and educated man who was relegated to the streets because of an alcohol addiction. According to Sophie, Arnaldo had been a father figure to more than 100 children in the streets. They lived in the neighborhood streets where *Aprendiz* was founded.

While preparing a special report on street dwellers, Gilberto Dimenstein (Founder of *Aprendiz*) came to know Arnaldo, who, in turn, introduced Sophie to him. In this way, Sophie was finally able to begin telling her story. Gilberto was then inspired to create the neighborhood newspaper so that Sophie and others could share their stories and perspectives, express their opinions, and become known as integral members of the community. Through working in the newspaper office, Sophie learned to read and write and was able to reflect on her life experiences and provoke change. At the time of the interview, Sophie was living in an apartment in the neighborhood and was starting her own family with a husband, her daughter, a new baby on the way, and a dog by the name of *Cheiode [pulgas]* (or, in translation, *full of [fleas]*). She is the author of four plays about her life in the streets and has sold the rights to her story to a British filmmaker. Of course, not all members of *Aprendiz* have gone through such remarkable transformations. However, by keeping the right of expression sovereign, the project clearly imparts a sense of confidence and hope onto those who had previously been invisible and whose voices had otherwise been muffled or ignored.

Implications for Educating Linguistic Minority Students in the United States

As a teacher in an American university, I (the author) frequently detail the practices of *Aprendiz* as described in this chapter in my teacher preparation courses, as my students often ask me what sociocultural theory or critical pedagogy *looks like* in practice. In truth, without vivid illustrations, even the most astute teachers-to-be in my college classes have at times exhibited difficulties comprehending truly democratic educational practices where hierarchies are minimized, where learning is pervasive, and where, potentially, the languages of every individual form the voice of a community.

More than an exuberant practical portrait of theoretical principles, this example from Brazil will hopefully remind us of the creative energy that is generated from the promise of liberation through tenable rights of self-expression. Evoking Freire once again, this fundamental right is secured by creating opportunities for individuals to voice their opinions and histories and to engage in community reflection and action, ebullient transformations. Then, true education becomes a real possibility.

I offer this example, for I am concerned that in the United States, we seem to be moving in a radically different direction—one of domination. Recent educational reforms and legislative acts at the national, state, and local school board levels have grossly limited freedom of expression for both students and teachers. For example, the English Only movement (initiated in California with Proposition 227 and proliferated across the country), prohibits students who come from linguistic backgrounds other than English from speaking their own language in school. In addition, the No Child Left Behind Act of 2001 has greatly limited opportunities for self-expression in U. S. classrooms by promoting rigidly prescribed curricula and by focusing on educational standardization.

Such policies function to prioritize the voices of dominant populations, to prevent possibilities for equitable education and, ultimately, according to Freirian perspectives, to confine the human spirit.

Conclusion

In closing, it is my hope that the example illuminated here provides inspiration to fuel the idealism of those who continue to see hopeful possibilities for reclaiming the role of education (and schools) as a vehicle for democracy and equality. Without considering ways to counteract the stratifying effects on society of pedagogies based on domination, the potential of individuals will remain under-estimated and our educational future as a nation may be seriously compromised.

Discussion Questions and Activities

1. What are some of the lessons that can be learned from the *Aprendiz* project in Brazil that may help improve learning practices in U.S. schools?
2. What are the advantages/disadvantages of conceptualizations of school and community as unity?
3. How might some of the community practices discussed in this chapter (e.g. graffiti art) be interpreted as forms of literacy?
4. How do recent educational policies in the United States (e.g. English Only movement) affect the development of multiple forms of self-expression for language minority students?

References

Freire, P. (1970). *Pedagogy of the Oppressed*. New York: Herder & Herder.
Lave, J., & Wenger. E. (1991). *Situated Learning: Legitimate Peripheral Participation*. New York: Cambridge University Press.

Leont'ev, D. (2002). Activity Theory Approach: Vygotsky in the Present. In D.
Robbins, & A. Stetskenko, *Voices within Vygotsky's Non-Classical Psychology. Past, Present, Future.* New York: Nova Science Publishers, Inc.
Olson, D. (1994). *The World on Paper.* New York: Cambridge University Press.
Vygotsky, L. S. (1978). *Mind in Society.* Cambridge, MA: Harvard University Press.

20

The Social Construction of Literacy in a Mexican Community: Coming Soon to Your School?[1]

PATRICK H. SMITH, LUZ A. MURILLO, AND ROBERT T. JIMÉNEZ

As we wrote this chapter, the U.S. government approved plans to build a 700-mile-long wall along our southern border with Mexico. Despite disapproval by people living in close proximity in the states on both sides of the border, illustrated by the billboard shown in Figure 20.1, Congress and President Bush have decided that a wall between the two countries is needed to prevent immigrants from Mexico and other countries from entering the U.S. illegally.

Never mind the obvious—that cheap immigrant labor remains a major source of U.S. wealth and that companies continue to attract and employ undocumented workers because they profit from it (Akers Chacón & Davis, 2006), or that recent attempts at border control have actually lengthened the average period of time that undocumented workers from Mexico stay in the U.S. (Durand & Massey, 2004). Physical barriers like the proposed border wall may eventually reduce the number of undocumented immigrants in the U.S., but they will not keep out migrants' languages and literacies, in the form of letters, advertisements, and especially digitally transmitted messages in the form of email, chat, text messages sent by immigrants in the U.S. and their families in Mexico (de Luna, 2006).

More importantly, building walls won't help educate the millions of Mexican-origin children currently attending U.S. schools. In addition to approximately one million Mexican-born minors in the U.S. without authorization (Tuirán, 2006), many others are U.S. citizens and legal residents. Even if all new immigrants were kept out, the number of U.S.-born Mexican origin children is significant and deserving of education. Because students have a right to their languages and because we see a critical opportunity to redress the historic and ongoing miseducation of Mexican-origin children in U.S. schools, we have framed our discussion in the form of a question: Will Mexican literacies be coming soon to a school near you? In a sense, of course, they already have, embodied in the students in classrooms in New York, Chicago, North Carolina, Los Angeles, Nashville, and countless other U.S. school systems. The larger question, then, is what will educators make of this opportunity? Will we continue to shut out and ignore these forms and practices of literacy, or will we make the effort to understand them as legitimate and powerful ways of using written language that, with careful attention, schools can harness to improve literacy instruction for all learners?

Figure 20.1 "No Berlin Wall in Texas" (Courtesy of Mercedes O. Torres)

This chapter is written in the belief that *puentes*, linguistic and cultural bridges, rather than walls, are needed to help schools do the best possible job of educating Mexican-origin children. By focusing on the literacy practices of San Andrés Cholula, a central Mexican community from which many young people migrate to the U.S., our purpose is to inform U.S. educators about how literacy is viewed and treated in Mexican families and schools in a specific region. Specifically, we hope to help build bridges between literacy policy and practice in Mexico and between research findings and practice.

The chapter is organized as follows: In the following section, we explain why Mexican literacies are important for educators in the U.S. Next we provide a brief overview of recent research, showing that more research is needed from rural and urbanizing areas. We then describe our study, beginning with the context of our study as a site of great linguistic and cultural diversity. We list the key theories on which we based our work, as well as our methods of data collection and analysis. We consider our findings based on what we know from other studies of Mexican literacy. We conclude with policy and practice implications for U.S. literacy educators working with Mexican learners.

Why Mexican Literacies Matter for U.S. Schools

U.S. schools are attended by increasing numbers of students from home language backgrounds other than English (Perie, Griggs, & Donahue, 2005), a trend that is permanently changing the country's student population. Because the teaching force continues to be composed mainly of White, middle-class educators and monolingual speakers of English, relatively few teachers share the linguistic, education, and cultural backgrounds of these learners. This is not simply a case of mismatch, however, between the backgrounds of learners and those who teach them. Because U.S. schools have not participated in the worldwide movement to "internationalize" curriculum (Pinar, 2006), U.S. curricula typically assume that English language learners will assimilate to U.S. education practices. According to Stromquist (2002):

> As the migration of people accelerates, the South is coming to the North. This makes it necessary to understand the dynamics of both regions. Educators in the North . . . need to learn the background of students, their cultural norms, their cognitive patterns, and the nature of their school systems of origin, and to determine how the North must adjust to new pressing conditions rather than demand full assimilation. (p.90)

The "South," in this case, is primarily Mexican, as Mexican-origin learners are the largest group of English language learners in U.S. schools and the fastest growing group in many school systems. As a group, Mexican-origin children are poorly served by current approaches to literacy instruction.[2] Academic achievement for Mexican-origin students is disproportionately low and a lack of specific kinds of literacy is at the core of this problem (Perie, Griggs, & Donahue, 2005). Mexican-origin students experience disproportionately high dropout rates in the U.S. (Smith, 2004; Valenzuela, 2005). Problems learning basic content area information result in losses in economic productivity (Muñoz Cruz, 2002), not to mention the freedoms and dignity afforded by individual human capital. Mexican learners are characterized by linguistic and cultural diversities that pose a tremendous challenge to U.S. educators. Effective solutions to the persistent problem of low literacy among Mexican learners in U.S. schools await findings from research that considers the nature of their literacy experiences in Mexico.

Research on Mexican Literacies

A primary motivation for our research has been to contribute to knowledge about Mexican literacies. Important lines of research have recently developed in the areas of emergent literacy, language arts, and ethnographic studies have added to our understanding of adult and family literacies. As a result, we now know that Mexican children from diverse backgrounds begin school with a range of rich literacy experiences and that schools in Mexico tend to marginalize the experiences of children perceived as linguistically and culturally different.

A widespread finding concerning writing instruction is the strong emphasis on "form" over "meaning" (Carrasco Altamirano, 2003; De la Garza & Ruiz Ávila, 1994; Ferreiro, 1999). Writing in school tends to be controlled rather strictly for spelling, correct placement of diacritics and punctuation, and handwriting, and students' texts typically consist of isolated words and sentences (Vargas, 2001) copied from the board or dictated by the teacher. This concern for form suggests that Mexican elementary schools seldom encourage students to "author" their own texts or to write for meaningful, contextualized purposes (Weiss, 2000). Peredo Merlo (2005) claims that expressive writing is not taught until students reach high school and even college. These findings suggest that many Mexican elementary and middle school students are not learning to use written language in ways typically valued in higher education and in some U.S. schools.

A third major research finding is that, despite a national concern that Mexicans are not reading enough, literacy instruction generally emphasizes writing over reading. Since the institution of the *Libro de Texto Gratuito* [Free National Textbook program] in 1959, the dominant and often the sole source of reading material in public school classrooms has been a series of graded readers produced and distributed by the national government. Analysis of the activity book that accompanies the current first grade textbook, for example, shows 89 activities dedicated to writing and 55 to reading (Vargas, 2001).

The relatively high cost of books in Mexico and the inaccessibility of children's literature in particular also contribute to a paucity of reading material in Mexican classrooms. The government's *Libros del Rincón* program aims to increase children's access to books by commissioning and publishing authentic, age-appropriate literature for distribution in small classroom collections of approximately 20 books per grade level. According to teachers, however, rural schools seldom receive sufficient numbers of the promised books. According to educational researchers, specific training for teachers on how to use classroom libraries has also been lacking (Acevedo, 2004).

These findings come primarily from studies done in and around Mexico City, and much less research has been done in *la provincia*, the rural and semi-rural regions outside Mexico City (Kalman, 2003). There is a particular need for research in the areas of family and community literacies (Secretaría de Educación Pública, 2001). Because a great deal of recent Mexican migration to the U.S. originates in rural sending communities in central and southern states such as Puebla, Tlaxcala, Oaxaca, Veracruz and Chiapas, greater knowledge about literacy practices in these regions is especially relevant for U.S. schools.

The Study

Overview of a Study of Literacy in a Central Mexican Community

This section summarizes findings from a 4-year qualitative study of school, family, and community literacies in a small city in the state of Puebla. From a preliminary study conducted in first and fourth grade classrooms in two local private schools (Jiménez, Smith, & Martínez-León, 2003), we expanded our focus to literacy instruction in two public elementary schools in the same community. In addition to interviews with teachers and administrators, we conducted multiple home visits and informal and taped interviews with students, families, and community members. Data were collected by us and our students at the Universidad de las Américas, Puebla. In addition to master's theses on topics including first graders'

English/Spanish biliteracy development; fathers' roles in children's literacy development; and the literacy practices of migrant families, students documented literacy practices in the municipal library, parks, and other public spaces; the uses of literacy in a home-based pizzeria; and a case study of biliteracy development in Nahuatl and Spanish (see Smith & Holzrichter, 2005). Occasionally, student projects were based in nearby communities, including teacher research with Spanish/English bilinguals in an elite bilingual kindergarten in the capital city of Puebla (Kimbrough, 2003), and projects on transnational literacies eventually led us to collect data in the U.S. and Canada (de Luna, 2006; Sullivan, 2006). Thus, the findings reported in this chapter come from domains of family, school, and community literacies in San Andrés Cholula. Collectively, they offer a rare view of literacy as developed and practiced by members of a single community with a rich indigenous past and present and characterized by rapid urbanization and transnationalism.

Context of the Study

Since 2002 we have been studying the uses of written language in San Andrés Cholula, a city of about 60,000 located 2 hours east of Mexico City and bordering the capital of the state of Puebla. We know this community well because we have lived and studied here. Patrick Smith lived and taught here from 1991 to 1996 and from 2000 to 2006, and Luz Murillo did so from 2003 to 2006. Robert Jiménez graduated from the local university and did his student teaching at one of our participating schools in the late 1970s, returning as a Fulbright scholar in 2002. We have also gotten to know Cholula schools as parents because all our children have studied there at one time or another.

Cholula is a special place in many ways. Archeologists believe that it is the longest continuously occupied site in Mexico. Speakers of various indigenous languages have been living here for at least 2000 years and over time they constructed a series of pyramids—each new pyramid atop the older ones—with the largest base of any pyramid in the world. In Nahuatl (locally referred to as *Mexicano*), the word for pyramid is *tlachihualteptl* [mountain made by people]. One of the most important religious centers in Mesoamerica, Cholula was a multilingual city-state (López Austin & López Luján, 2003), with a tradition of receiving rulers from far away polities who came to be blessed by the priests of Quetzalcoatl, a deity of knowledge and learning (Bernal García, 2006).

Like contemporary Mexico, the story of Cholula is also one of survival and of resistance and adaptation to new ways from outside. In the first years of the Spanish conquest, Hernán Cortés and his troops massacred some 6000 *Cholultecas*, supposedly out of fear that they were plotting against him. The invaders and their indigenous allies burned the local temples and with them probably many *códices*, the sacred books in which the Indians recorded their ideas about history, religion, and science. They forced the *Cholultecas* to adopt the Catholic religion and to build atop the indigenous shrines the many churches that continue to mark the local landscape today.

As indigenous people did across central Mexico, the *Cholultecas* transformed the Spaniards' religion to make it their own. They did this by keeping their own gods under the new names of Spanish saints and virgins, and by continuing their own social organization in *barrios* around the neighborhood church. Nearly 500 years after the conquest, these Mesoamerican practices are still part of everyday life for many residents of Cholula. *Maize, nopales,* and other native foods, the practice of bargaining and exchanging for goods and services, and the ways people live in extended families around the patriarchal home all remind us that Mesoamerican aspects of Mexican culture are simultaneously ancient—much older than U.S. culture—and contemporary. One of the most vivid examples of the syncretism of Spanish and indigenous cultures is the *Virgen de los Remedios* church, shown in Figure 20.2. Built atop the pyramid by Indian labor in the 17th century, this church is the site of Catholic ceremonies as well as recreations of indigenous harvest and solstice celebrations.

Like other Mexican communities, Cholula is also a place in transition. It has become nearly impossible to make a living solely through agriculture, and the jobs that are most available, such as brick making and construction, are poorly paid. School teachers—among the most highly paid employees in the community—make about U.S.$500 a month. Although approximately three-quarters of the townspeople we surveyed own their own homes, usually built on small inherited parcels, other basic necessities such as clothing, gasoline, and non-local foods cost about the same as in the U.S. Due to the increasing disparity between income and expenses, more and more Cholultecans are moving to large cities and to the U.S. to find work.

Most of these migrants work for part of each year in the New York/New Jersey area, Chicago, Los Angeles, or North Carolina (Smith, 2006). They come home to visit when they can, often for religious festivals, weddings, and other family celebrations. Some migrants end up staying in the U.S. but nearly all of the people we have talked to dream of saving enough money to build a home or a business and return to live in Mexico.

In the meantime, many also send *remesas* [remittances] home to their families. In addition to covering basic necessities such as healthcare and school-related expenses (uniforms, school fees, and supplies), we know many families who use

Figure 20.2
The Virgen de los Remedios Church Atop the Tlachihualteptl Pyramid (Courtesy of Patrick H. Smith)

Figure 20.3
List of Contributors
(Courtesy of
Patrick H. Smith)

these funds to pay for community obligations associated with membership in the *cargo* system. An example of this can be seen in Figure 20.3, a sign we found posted on the door of a church in the nearby town of Calpan announcing contributions to the church made in pesos and a much greater number of contributions made in dollars.

Theoretical Framework

Key theoretical supports underlying our study include viewing texts, literacy events, and literacy practices as a guide to data collection and analysis (Barton, 2007). Specifically, we drew on Barton's distinction between the "authoring" and "scribal" functions of writing for thinking about the texts and practices we observed. With Freire and Macedo (1987), we thought about the differences between understandings of reading as (1) a strict act of decoding the ideas of others and (2) a broader understanding aimed at (re)interpreting written language in the context of the reader's knowledge and experience. Other key ideas included Bourdieu's (1991) notion of forms of language as social capital, an idea we extended to written language. We also read the works of scholars exploring children's before-school experiences with literacy (Ferreiro, 1999), which gave us insights into how children's literate identities may be different and broader than the practices observed in school. We also read and discussed concepts by Latin American scholars, importantly Kalman (2003) and Rockwell's (2005) notions of *disponibilidad, acceso y apropiación*, the availability, access, and appropriation of texts by users.

How We Learned About Literacies in Cholula

Our findings are based mainly on qualitative data in the form of observations, interviews, and documents produced by case study children and their families, as well as educators and community members. Observation protocols and interview formats were developed and modified according to the specific research questions posed in each study. Data collection instruments were developed in situ, including a socioeconomic and linguistic survey of 150 families whose children attended two of the participating schools; an inventory of home texts and literacy practices; and forms for recording information about the labor and education histories of case study students and their families. The second author gathered the bulk of the community and household data and student researchers, and graduate research assistants frequently accompanied us as a means of gaining experience before they collected data independently.

At the request of participating teachers, we also developed and conducted writing activities that we believed to be novel for students and teachers alike. These lessons typically began with group reading of a story, followed by discussion and a reader response activity. Students respond to these stories in several ways. First graders in the two public school classrooms drew pictures illustrating their understanding of the story. In one classroom, we asked students to write any questions they wanted to ask of the characters in the story. Another group of first graders was asked to retell the story in their own words. After an oral reading and discussion of the Nahua legend *Tlakwatsin* [The Possum] (Flores Farfán, 1999), fourth graders worked in small groups to write and illustrate a sequel to the story. We collected these texts and other student work in order to better understand the literacy proficiencies of the case study students relative to their classmates, but also to gain a sense of the students' ability to undertake novel writing tasks, that is, tasks that were intentionally different from those we observed the students regularly practicing in school but, we believe, similar to writing tasks expected of students in U.S. classrooms.

Analysis

Following the constant comparative method described by Bogdan and Biklen (2003), frequent discussion and contextualization of data were basic features of our analysis. In addition to the courses in literacy research methods and applied linguistics research design taught by the authors and in which student researchers were enrolled, we met several times each month, often weekly, to share and discuss the data we had collected. We used these opportunities to compare field notes, transcriptions of interviews, and photographs featuring case study classrooms and participating students and families, as well as our impressions of reading materials and instructional techniques employed in first and fourth grade classrooms. These discussions also led to further reading on topics including transnational migration, masculinity and gender roles, and continuities of Mesoamerican indigenous cultures. In turn, our collective reading provided new perspectives on the data being considered. This collective analysis was greatly enriched by the perspectives of Spanish/English bilinguals schooled in Puebla and other regions of Mexico, as well as the U.S., Canada, and Colombia. They allowed us to think about our data from up close and far away at the same time (Anderson-Levitt, 2004).

Results

Regarding school-based literacies, what we learned from our classroom observations is generally consistent with previous descriptions of the focus on form over content in literacy instruction in Mexican primary schools (Peredo Merlo, 2005; Weiss, 2000). Across first and fourth grade classrooms in two very modest public schools, a semi-private alternative school with a mixed economic class population, and a first grade class in a prestigious bilingual school, we found that student writing was closely controlled for form and generally limited to individual words, phrases, and short sentences. Reproducing pages of *planas*, the repetitive copying of individual letters, syllables, and words, was an important part of the initial literacy instruction that we observed, and continued through first grade and into the second grade.

Older learners seldom had the opportunity to do extended writing and when they did it was often in the form of copying or summarizing texts provided by the teacher or the textbook. Our observations in a fourth grade social studies classroom give a sense of how such texts are produced. From the *Libro de texto Gratuito de Ciencias Sociales*, the teacher copied onto the whiteboard two paragraphs of text about the Maderista movement concerning the origins of the Mexican Revolution, with certain names and terms ("Francisco Madero", "*antireeleccionista*" [opposed to re-election] highlighted in a different color marker. The students' task was to copy this lengthy text from the board into their *libretas* [notebooks], complete with the sections which had been underscored by the teacher. This exercise, including the teacher's writing on the board and students copying the text into their notebooks, took the greater part of a 50-minute class period.

We also found numerous examples of the practice of copying texts as homework assignments. Figure 20.4 depicts a type of commercially produced text known locally as *láminas* or *biografías*, which can be purchased at *papelerías* [stationery stores] for the equivalent of between 5 and 10 U.S. cents.

Typically, students copy these phrases into homework assignments, often pasting the image on the reverse side of the *lamina* onto their papers, as in Figure 20.4, a biography of the last Aztec emperor, Cuauhtémoc. Such assignments were among the few examples of student produced texts we found displayed on classroom walls. Interestingly, we observed little discussion of their content, and teachers' comments were generally restricted to the aesthetic qualities of the reproduction, focusing on students' handwriting and spelling. It is important to note that these school-based practices contrast sharply with the national

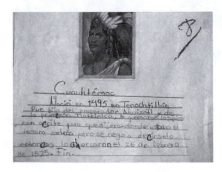

Figure 20.4 Example of a Lamina About the Life of Cuauhtémoc (In the Public Domain)

curriculum's recent emphasis on communication in oral and written language development (Secretaría de Educación Pública, 2001).

Regarding family and community literacies, we found a wide range of home literacy practices. When asked about the texts present in their homes, families usually showed us school-based forms first, including textbooks, student notebooks, homework assignments, and encyclopedias purchased on payment plans. We learned that parents, including those with limited formal schooling, go to considerable lengths to provide their children with access to school-based forms at home. For example, the mother of a first grader showed us a chart she had created to help her son learn the letters of the alphabet. Like approximately half the parents we interviewed, this woman was forced to leave school before finishing primary school in order to work and help support her family, a limitation that nevertheless motivated her to support her children's education.

Most homes also contained a diverse range of non-school forms of literacy, including calendars, religious texts, recipes, and family records of banking and healthcare. We found that families produced and used texts connected to the *cargo* system and to Cholula's indigenous roots. These included commercially printed and publicly displayed posters and invitations to religious ceremonies, as well as handwritten lists naming the heads of the families who collaborated to sponsor such events. Among the most spectacular texts we observed were *arcos*, such as the example in Figure 20.5. These large flowered arches are composed of both

Figure 20.5 An Arch at the Entrance of the Main Plaza in San Andrés Cholula (Courtesy of Patrick H. Smith)

Mesoamerican (pictorial) and European (alphabetic) designs, and are displayed at the entrances of churches and *barrios* (neighborhoods) to welcome the Virgin Maria and San Andrés and other patron saints.

From the *floristas*, the contemporary artisans commissioned to create the arches, we learned that although plastic and cloth flowers are now sometimes used, the most elaborate and expensive arches continue to feature natural flowers, as in the days of the *xochimanque* (flower artisans) before the Spanish invasion (Jiménez & Smith, 2008).

Other texts found in Cholula homes point to families' participation in the transnational migration circuit, including remittance forms, birth certificates, voter registration cards, drivers licenses, and other forms of identification needed to claim the dollars sent electronically from the U.S., and records of the bank accounts into which these funds are deposited. Publicly displayed texts also reflect the extent to which the local economy is increasingly transnational. Figure 20.6 depicts a *lona* [a canvas sign] we found hanging outside a small store, advertising the speedy and safe delivery of packages to and from Chicago and New York. Such services are advertised in a variety of formats, including posters that incorporate handwritten text with computerized forms such as digital photographs and elements from "Clip Art."

Finally, our study also hints at the rapid emergence of digital literacy practices in Cholula. Only one of the primary schools that we observed has the financial resources to offer computer instruction, though access to the internet is quite limited by U.S. standards. The costs of buying a computer and of installing/maintaining internet connections (approximately U.S.$30 per month) make connectivity from the home a rarity in this community. Yet, young people are acquiring digital forms of literacy in other ways, typically at one of the many *cafés internet* (cybercafés) around town. For 10 pesos (about U.S.$1) an hour, students visit cybercafés to use the internet to research, type up, and print out homework assignments. Teenagers tell us that parents are more apt to give them money to pay to use cybercafés if the trip involves homework. However, they also tell us about staying longer in order to use the internet for personal reasons not related to

Figure 20.6
"Import and Export Mariana" (Courtesy of Patrick H. Smith)

homework, including chat, email, and gaming. Because computer technologies are relatively new to many in this community, we are still learning how these encounters influence what children are able to do with written language. Tracing the flows and influences of online communication and other digital forms of literacy is thus a compelling line of inquiry, particularly among transnationals who are developing identities that are not solely based on geography and who may have, by virtue of the remittances sent by relatives working in the U.S., greater access to computer technologies at home.

The relative availability of cell phones (the cheapest at about U.S.$35 with 300 minutes of credit) also means that children in public schools, whether they own their own phones or not, are now learning about digital practices such as text messaging. We interviewed several fathers in the Chicago area who had sent text message about family expenses to their wives in San Andrés. As the Federal government moves to make computer technology available across large numbers of public school classrooms for the first time, beginning with fifth and sixth grades in Mexico City (Secretaría de Educación Pública, 2006), we wonder whether teachers will attempt to appropriate children's digital funds of knowledge for the purpose of developing these new forms of literacy in school contexts.

Conclusion

Implications: Bridges from Policy and Research to Practice

In this concluding section, we offer suggestions for how U.S. teachers can use these findings in working with Mexican-origin learners. It is important to remember, of course, that Mexico's cultural and linguistic diversity make it impossible to generalize from our study of one community's literacy practices area to the ways that written language is used in other parts of the country. Certainly there are regions where international migration is even more established than in Cholula and other places from which few people migrate. There are also communities where people generally regard themselves as more European than indigenous in their origins and habits (Farr, 2006). For this reason, we believe that our findings may be especially relevant for educators and schools working with Mexican learners from the central and southern states of Puebla, Mexico, Tlaxcala, Hidalgo, and Oaxaca. Because Mexico's national curriculum continues to be highly centralized, we believe that the school-based findings reported here are probably similar to the ways literacy is used, taught, and perceived across schools in a larger number of states. With these caveats in mind, we invite educators to consider the following implications for bridging research, policy, and practice in literacy instruction with Mexican learners.

With regard to teacher training, we found that teachers in Cholula hold varying degrees of knowledge of alternative approaches to literacy instruction, with recently trained teachers reportedly more comfortable with content-oriented instruction but feeling limited in their ability to initiate meaningful changes. As barriers to new ways of teaching literacy, teachers mentioned the centralized curriculum, a shortage of reading materials other than the *Libro Gratuito*, as well as their own school experiences and, especially, parents' beliefs about the importance of form. Our findings also suggest that, in contrast to U.S. schools in which "working class children receive a reduced and intellectually inferior curriculum compared with their wealthier peers, as part and parcel of the stratification of schooling" (Moll, 2005, p. 276), approaches to literacy education in Mexico are relatively homogenous for children in both wealthy and poor schools.

Based on our findings, we hope that U.S. teachers will avoid assuming that students from middle-class backgrounds have had different literacy experiences in school than children from working-class backgrounds. Instead, we would ask teachers to look carefully at the schooled literacy experiences of the Mexican learners in their classrooms. Specifically, teachers would do well to understand that students schooled in Mexico have likely been directed to concentrate primarily on the form of their writing rather than on the expression and development of their own ideas in writing.

Similarly, although Mexican-educated students may excel at oral and choral reading in Spanish (a strength that will not be evident in English Only classrooms), fewer students will have had experience with being asked to interpret and critique what they read. Thus, difficulty with such assignments should not be interpreted as a sign of low literacy, but rather as a logical consequence of the form of literacy instruction they have received before coming to U.S. schools. Rather than attempting to "replace" these forms of knowledge about reading and writing with the knowledge that is valued in U.S. schools, we believe that teachers and students will be more successful by acknowledging these differences and by attempting to build on what the students already know how to do well.

Despite national and local complaints that Mexicans are not much interested in reading and writing, our analysis of locally produced texts and practices showed that Cholutecans are continuously involved in the production and interpretation of written texts. Many, however, do not consider these to be legitimate forms of reading and writing or worthy of consideration in schools. Because school-based definitions of language and literacy are so strongly present in discourses about written language, a paradox emerges in which Cholutecans denigrate the forms of language that they themselves produce and use on a daily basis. These attitudes were certainly present in the Mexican homes and schools we worked in, and we have also found them expressed by Mexicans living in the U.S. Stigmatizing the language of learners is always destructive, but the effects of linguistic discrimination is potentially even more harmful for Mexican students studying in U.S. schools, as they perceive their status as non-legitimate speakers of two languages, English and Spanish (Beckstead & Toribio, 2003).

We recommend that U.S. teachers support the rights of Mexican students to their own language(s) by using home and community texts as points of departure for literacy instruction. One place to begin is by reading Cohen and Estrada's (2002) book, *De Cómo los Mexicanos Conquistaron Nueva York*, which is full of texts produced by transnationals from Izucar de Matamoros, Atlixco, Cholula, and other Mexican communities living in the New York City area. Perhaps the best source of such materials is to ask students to record Spanish and bilingual texts from their neighborhoods using digital cameras. These texts can then be analyzed in class by asking students to think about the authors of such texts, as well as their purposes, intended audience, and the effectiveness of the messages they convey.

Finally, although we believe that the literacies of Mexican learners and their families have much to offer those schools that have learned to see their value, gaining access to them can be easier said than done. Outreach efforts aimed at bringing Mexican parents and families into closer contact with teachers and schools is difficult when parents have not had the experience of being consulted by their children's teachers. Furthermore, the fact that so many immigrant parents are working multiple jobs means that traditional outreach efforts such as open house nights and parent–teacher conferences may be less effective. In such cases, teachers will need to be creative in order to learn more about the ways that literacy is present and used in the homes of their students. Having children take digital photographs of the texts present in their homes is a fine way to do this, but, in our experience, there is no better way to understand family literacies than for teachers to visit some homes and see and hear about the texts for themselves.

Discussion Questions and Activities

1. According to the authors, knowledge of Mesoamerican forms of writing is not widely promoted in Mexican schools. They argue that some forms, however, are in almost daily use and that these can serve as the focus for valuable literacy lessons for Mexican-origin and other students. Select the forms you think will be most recognizable to your students (the Mexican flag, images on Mexican currency, Mexico City metro icons, etc.). Then, ask your students to write about them. What do they know about these images? What are their theories about the indigenous cultures that produced them? What emotions or memories do these evoke in student writers?

2. The authors show that Mexican forms of literacy are appearing in locally prepared advertisements and other texts in U.S. communities as widespread as Chicago, Nashville, and the New York City area. Using a digital camera, look for similar examples in your community. How do they compare to those described in this chapter?

3. A central idea of this chapter is that Mexican-origin children living on both sides of the border are growing up in homes with rich and diverse language and literacy practices. To observe this diversity from a child's perspective, ask students to bring in examples or photographs of texts from their homes, or take a digital camera with you to a home visit with the family. Such texts can serve as focal points for questions, including how the forms and practices observed in Mexican-origin homes in the U.S. compare to those described in this chapter.

Notes

1   The research described in this chapter was supported by funding from the Mexican Consejo Nacional de Ciencia y Tecnología, the U.S.-Mexico Fulbright Commission, the Office for Research and Graduate Studies at the Universidad de las Américas, Puebla, and the Center for the Americas at Vanderbilt University.

2   This is not to suggest that current approaches to literacy instruction in Mexican schools serve all learners well. Indeed, there are many critiques (see Ferreiro, 1999; Pellicer & Vernon, 2004; Weiss, 2000), but our purpose here is to describe practices rather than critique them.

References

Acevedo, M. (2004). *Los Libros, Esos Desconocidos en las Escuelas.* Primer Congreso Nacional de Lectura y Escritura. Durango, Durango, Mexico, May 2004. Retrieved December 27, 2006, from http://www.paginadigital.com. ar/articulos/2004/2004terc/educacion/e1034177-4pl.asp.

Akers Chacón, J., & Davis, M. (2006). *No One is Illegal: Fighting Racism and State Violence on the U.S.–Mexico Border.* Chicago, IL: Haymarket Books.

Anderson-Levitt, K. (2004). Reading Lessons in Guinea, France, and the United States: Local Meanings or Global Culture? *Comparative Education Review,* 48(3). Retrieved March 19, 2007. from http://www.journals.uchicago.edu/. CER/journal/issues/v48n3/480301/480301.web.pdf

Barton, D. (2007). *Literacy. An Introduction to the Ecology of Written Language,* 2nd edn. Oxford: Blackwell.

Beckstead, K., & Toribio, A. J. (2003). Minority Perspectives on Language: Mexican and Mexican-American Adolescents' Attitudes toward Spanish and English. In A. Roca, & M. C. Colombi (Eds.). *Mi Lengua: Spanish as a Heritage Language in the United States.* Washington, DC: Georgetown University Press.

Bernal García, M. E. (2006). Tu Agua, Tu Cerro, Tu Flor: Orígenes y Metamorfosis Conceptuales del Alteptel de Cholula, Siglos XII y XVI. In F. Fernández Christlieb, & A. J. García Zambrano (Eds.). *Territorialidad y Paisaje en el Alteptel del Siglo XVI.* Mexico, DF: Fondo de Cultura Económica.

Bogdan, R., & Biklen, S. K. (2003). *Qualitative Research for Education: An Introduction to Theory and Methods,* 4th edn. Boston, MA: Allyn & Bacon.

Bourdieu, P. (1991). *Language and Symbolic Power.* Cambridge: Polity Press.

Carrasco Altamirano, A. (2003). La Escuela Puede Enseñar Estrategias de Lectura y Promover su Regular Empleo. *Revista Mexicana de Investigación Educativa,* 8(17), 129–142.

Cohen, S., & Estrada, J. (2002). *De cómo los Mexicanos Conquistaron Nueva York.* Mexico, DF: Colibrí.

De la Garza, Y., & Ruiz Ávila, D. (1994). La Producción del Texto Escrito en el Sexto Año de Primaria. In L. E. Galván, M. Lamoneda, M. E. Vargas, & B. Calvo (Eds.). *Memorias del Primer Simposio de Educación.* Mexico, DF: Centro de Investigaciones y Estudios Superiores en Antropología Social.

de Luna, M. (2006). *Prácticas de Lectoescritura en Familias Inmigrantes Mexicanas en Canadá: El Papel de las Familias como Mediador en el Ejercicio de las Prácticas de Lectoescritura en el Hogar.* Unpublished MA thesis, Universidad de las Américas, Puebla, Mexico.

Durand, J., & Massey, D. S. (Eds.) (2004). *Crossing the Border: Research from the Mexican Migration Project.* New York: Russell Sage Foundation.

Farr, M. (2006). *Rancheros in Chicagoacán: Language and Identity in a Transnational Community.* Austin, TX: University of Texas Press.

Ferreiro, E. (1999). *Cultura Escrita y Educación: Conversaciones con Emilia Ferreiro.* Mexico, DF: Fondo de Cultura Económica.

Flores Farfán, J. A. (1999). *Tlakwatsin/El Tlacuache.* Mexico, DF: Centro de Investigaciones e Estudios Superiores en Antropología Social.

Freire, P., & Macedo, D. (1987). *Literacy. Reading the Word and the World.* Westport, CT: Bergin & Garvey.

Jiménez, R. T., & Smith, P. H. (2008). Mesoamerican Literacies: Indigenous Writing Systems and Contemporary Possibilities. *Reading Research Quarterly,* 43(1): 28–46.

——, Smith, P. H., & Martínez-León, N. (2003). Freedom and Form: The Language and Literacy Practices of Two Mexican Schools. *Reading Research Quarterly,* 38(4), 488–508.

Kalman, J. (2003). El Acceso a la Cultura Escrita: La Participación Social y la Apropiación de Conocimientos en Eventos Cotidianos de Lectura y Escritura. *Revista Mexicana de Investigación Educativa,* 8(17), 37–66.

Kimbrough, J. (2003). *Literacy Learning and Instruction in a Mexican Bilingual School.* Unpublished MA thesis, Universidad de las Américas, Puebla, Mexico. Retrieved March 23, 2007, from http://catarina.udlap.mx:9090/u_dl_a/tales/documentos /mla/kimbrough_n_jz/index.html.

318 · Patrick H. Smith, Luz A. Murillo, and Robert T. Jiménez

López Austin, A., & López Luján, L. (2003). *El Pasado Indígena*. Mexico, DF: Colegio de México/Fondo de Cultura Económica.

Moll, L. C. (2005). Reflections and Possibilities. In N. González, L. C. Moll, C., & C. Amanti. (Eds.). *Funds of Knowledge: Theorizing Practices in Households, Communities, and Classrooms*. Mahwah, NJ: Lawrence Erlbaum.

Muñoz Cruz, H. (Ed.) (2002). *Rumbo a la Interculturalidad en Educación*. Mexico, DF: Universidad Autónoma Metropolitana.

Pellicer, A., & Vernon, S. A. (Eds.) (2004). *Aprender y Enseñar la Lengua Escrita en el Aula*. Mexico, DF: SM de Ediciones.

Peredo Merlo, M. A. (2005). *Lectura y Vida Cotidiana: Por qué y Para qué Leen los Adultos*. Mexico, DF: Paidos Educador.

Perie, M., Griggs, W. S., & Donahue, P. L. (2005). *The Nation's Report Card: Reading 2005* (NCES 2006–451). U.S. Department of Education, Institute of Education Sciences, National Center for Education Statistics. Washington, D.C. Retrieved April 5, 2006, from http://nces.ed.gov/nations reportcard/pdf/main2005/2006451.pdf.

Pinar, W. F. (2006). Internationalism in Curriculum Studies. *Pedagogies: An International Journal*, 1(1), 35–42.

Rockwell. E. (2005). La Apropiación, un Proceso entre Muchos que Ocurren en Ámbitos escolares. *Memoria, Conocimiento y Utopia. Anuario de la Sociedad Mexicana de la Historia de la Educación, 1*. Mexico: Pomares.

Secretaría de Educación Pública. (2001). *Programa Nacional de Lectura*. Mexico: Secretaría de Educación Pública. Retrieved February 28, 2007, from http://lectura.ILCE.edu.mx/documentos/pnl/html/pnl/html.

——. (2006). *Programa Enciclomedia*. Retrieved February 28, 2007, from http://www.sep.gob.mx/wb2/sep/sep__Programa_Enciclomedia.

Smith, P. H., & Holzrichter, A. (Eds.) (2005). *Working Papers in Applied Linguistics/Cuadernos de Trabajo en Lingüística Aplicada, 1*. Universidad de las Américas, Puebla, Mexico.

Smith, R. C. (2004). Imaginando los Futuros Educativos de los Mexicanos en Nueva York. In R. C. Cortina, & M. Gendreau (Eds.). *Poblanos en Nueva York: Migración Rural, Educación y Bienestar*. Puebla, Mexico: Universidad Iberoamericana.

——. (2006). *Mexican New York: Transnational Lives of New Immigrants*. Berkeley, CA: University of California Press.

Stromquist, N. P. (2002). Globalization, the I, and the Other. *Current Issues in Comparative Education*, 4(2), 87–94. Retrieved March 19, 2007, fromhttp://www.tc.columbia.edu/cice/articles/nps142.htm.

Sullivan, T. (2006). *Transnational Family Literacy Practices: Three Case Studies in Central Mexico*. Unpublished MA thesis, Universidad de las Américas, Puebla, Mexico. Retrieved March 23, 2007, from http://catarina.udlap.mx:9090/u_dl_a/tales/navegacion/carrera_mla.html.

Tuirán, R. (2006). La Reforma Migratoria Pendiente. *Migraciones Internacionales*, 3(4), 161–174.

Valenzuela, A. (2005). *Leaving Children Behind: How "Texas-Style" Accountability Fails Latino Youth*. New York: State University of New York Press.

Vargas, M. A. (2001). Actividades de Producción Oral y Escrita en Libros de Texto de Español: Aproximaciones a un Análisis de Dos Libros Destinados a Primer Grado de Primaria. *Revista Mexicana de Investigación Educativa*, 6(12), 249–261. Retrieved December 27, 2006, from http://www.comie.org. mx/rmie/num12/12investTem3.pdf.

Weiss, E. (2000). La Enseñanza de las Competencias Básicas. In J. Ezpeleta, & E. Weiss (Eds.). *Cambiar la Escuela Rural: Evaluación Cualitativa del Programa para Abatir el Rezago Educativo*. Mexico, DF: Centro de Investigación y de Estudios Avanzados del Instituto Politécnico Nacional.

21

Multilingualism in Classrooms: The Paritetic School System of the Ladin Valleys in South Tyrol (Italy)

GERDA VIDESOTT

The *paritetic* school system is an effective multilingual *best practice* model that has developed in the Ladin Valleys of South Tyrol, located in the Alps in the North of Italy, on the border to Austria and Switzerland. It was conceived in order to accommodate the needs of the Ladin population (see Videsott, 2005a, for a definition of Ladin), which is a minority group that lives close to other ethnic groups—primarily Germans and Italians—and therefore has to adapt to a multilingual reality (see Belardi 1995; Richebuono 1991; Taibon 2005; Verra 2000).

Ladin people speak a language that derives from Latin (Videsott, 2005b) and is spoken by approximately 4.37% of the total population of South Tyrol in comparison to 26.47% of Italians and 69.15% Germans, who form the majority. The reason for this is that prior to World War I, South Tyrol was part of the Austrian Empire. For historical reasons, South Tyrol is an autonomous area, which means that there are special rights to protect their minority groups, especially in relation to their language.

Because Ladin is spoken by only a small group of people, there is a need for the Ladin people to learn languages other than their mother tongue in order to survive outside the boundaries of their territory (Balboni, 1997; Calliari 1991). Therefore, in 1948, the *paritetic* school system was introduced in the Ladin Valleys of South Tyrol. The decision to institute this particular school model was politically and socially motivated. If the whole school system were to be concentrated only on the Ladin language, problems would arise when the Ladin people leave their valleys due to the fact that outside their territory they would have to speak a language other than Ladin.

In the *paritetic* school model, two languages, German and Italian, are used for instruction in equal ways, as the adjective *paritetic* derives from the Latin *pari* which means "equal." An immersion approach is practiced with these two languages: German and Italian are used for teaching all subjects. Ladin, by way of contrast, is used as a "supporting language" for explaining issues and can be used all the time. Furthermore, Ladin is taught as a subject of its own for 2 hours per week. A few years ago English was also introduced as a subject in school. The aim of this school model is not only to make sure that the number of hours of instruction in German and Italian is the same, but also that the students will reach the same levels of language competence in all three languages: Ladin, Italian, and German.

Structure of the *Paritetic* School System

Basically the *paritetic* school model is founded on the Italian school system (see Figure 21.1). It is interesting to note that there exist in South Tyrol two completely different systems concerning the linguistic typology of the school. The Italian school system is governed by a centralistic policy, but through the *autonomy status* the juridical bases were put in place to ensure the establishment of norms for South

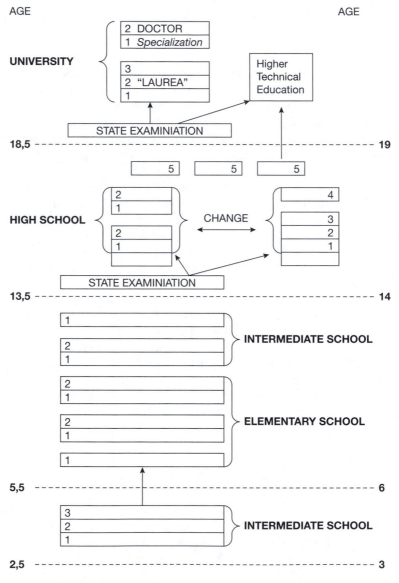

Figure 21.1 The Paritetic School System

Tyrol. In the First Autonomy Statute of 1848, the instruction of the mother tongue was sanctioned. That means that the language used in Italian schools is Italian. In South Tyrol, there is also a special regulation referring to the German school, put in place to accommodate the German people so that their situation is reversed in relation to the Italian school model: German is used instead of Italian (Seberich 2000; Wiater & Videsott 2006).

For the Ladin people, the *paritetic* school model was instituted (Crazzolara 1972; Ellecosta 1972; Irsara 1980; Verra 1989, 2003, 2004; Vittur 1977, 1988, 1990, 1994, 2000). Article 87 refers especially to the instruction of the Ladin people, stating that Ladin should be a subject, but not an instructional language. This changed with the Second Autonomy Statute (1972) under Article 19, which states that "the Ladin language should be used in the kindergarten and should be taught in the elementary schools of the Ladin Valleys." From then on Ladin could be used at every school level in order to support the instruction. In these schools, the instruction in the subjects is prescribed to take place in Italian and in German, each language having an equal number of hours. How this could be put into practice would be decided later through further rules and norms of actuation (see Rifesser 1992, 1999, 2000a, 2000b, 2005, 2006).

Kindergarten

In the kindergarten, there exists a natural situation of multilingualism. The language used most is Ladin, but this can differ in different kindergarten sections. The overall rule is that the children may use their own mother tongue if they wish to. So every kindergarten teacher in the Ladin valleys has to know three languages: Ladin, German, and Italian. The children are mixed together in classes without a single mother language. The majority of the children grow up bilingual in language-mixed families. For example, a child could speak Ladin to her mother and Italian to her father.

In kindergarten, some experimental projects have been developed that require equal competence in all three languages. The idea is to teach languages in a playful way. Children perform theatre plays in different languages. For example in the project "Snow White", the character Snow White speaks German and the prince speaks Italian. The seven dwarfs speak Ladin. Children also sing songs and listen to stories told in all three languages. Often they play games to aid in learning vocabulary: Everybody has to produce words in the different languages, such as in picture-naming games.

The teachers report that, in multilingual education projects, the children improve their use of different languages. They also noted two unexpected positive collateral effects. Noting that these playful exercises involved every single child, teachers felt that even the very shy children became more talkative when playing with the languages. Another positive effect is that the teachers were able to notice very early if the children were experiencing pronunciation problems.

Elementary School

At the elementary school level, multilingual education is further introduced in a more systematic way (Rifesser 1999). Italian and German are taught an equal number of hours and divided between the subjects. The subdivisions are flexible, allowing individual teachers to decide which languages to use and with which subjects. The result is different configurations. Students might have 1 week or a half-week of instruction in German and the other in Italian. Another arrangement is that one subject is taught the whole year in one language and the following year in the other language. The choice could be to arrange the language instruction by topics, with, for example, the history of Italy taught in Italian, the history of South Tyrol in German, and the history of the Ladin valleys in Ladin. The only subjects that are taught in all three languages are religion and music.

Intermediate School and High School

The situation is different at intermediate and high school levels. Here the language depends on the subject. Normally the humanistic subjects are taught in Italian and the scientific subjects in German. Music education can be taught in either German or Italian. Religion can be taught in all three languages, as occurs in elementary school. For 2 hours per week, Ladin is taught as a subject and can be used for instructional support, even though its use decreases with higher level education (see Table 21.1).

English is taught at the high school level, and for several years, it has been taught at the intermediate level as well. This arrangement began as an experimental project in some schools. English was an optional course that could be attended after school and in the course of time it became part of the curriculum. Now English is introduced in the elementary school, though this remains an idea in progress, rather than a policy (Ellecosta, 2002) (see Table 21.2).

University

The teachers of the *paritetic* school are instructed in a special program. The university curriculum for the Ladin people reflects the *paritetic* school model of the Ladin valleys. Preservice teachers must attend half of the courses in the Italian section, half in the German section, and about 20% in the Ladin section, with some courses in English. The aim of this university degree is to prepare teachers to work well in the multilingual school model.

Some multilingual projects have been started in the last few years at the *paritetic* schools. One example is the *European language portfolio*. It is a project started by the European Union. The project is a kind of "diary" of the language competences of the students. A second program is the *integrated didactics program* (Cathomas & Carigiet, 2006) that has been in progress for approximately 3 years. The program dedicates 1 or 2 hours per week to a comparative study of the languages. In this *integrated didactics program*, the languages are compared at different levels. At the simplest level, pupils learn words. For example, they learn that the English word "sun" means the same as the Ladin word "sorëdl," the German word

TABLE 21.1 Example of a 2-Week Lesson Table

Week 1: German

	Monday	Tuesday	Wednesday	Thursday	Friday	Saturday
1st hour	Math	German	Math	Religion	German	German
2nd hour	Ladin	Math	Physical Ed	Math	German	German
Break						
3rd hour	Ladin	Science	German	German	Math	Music
4th hour	Religion	German	Science	German	Science	Arts
Lunch						
5th hour				German		
6th hour				Arts		

Week 2: Italian

	Monday	Tuesday	Wednesday	Thursday	Friday	Saturday
1st hour	Italian	Italian	Math	Religion	German	German
2nd hour	Italian	Science	Physical Ed	Math	Italian	Italian
Break						
3rd hour	Math	Math	Italian	Ladin	Math	Music
4th hour	Religion	Italian	Italian	Ladin	Science	Arts
Lunch						
5th hour				Italian		
6th hour				Arts		

"Sonne," and the Italian word "sole." As the work progresses and the children improve, they start to compare entire sentences.

Teachers have noted that this metalinguistic thinking facilitates the sensitiveness in the dealing with individual languages. They observed that the students could more easily distinguish and keep apart the different languages, improving language proficiency.

There exist quite a large number of publications, school books and working material to support the lessons at the *paritetic* school that have been developed specifically for use in the *paritetic* school. It should also be noted that students with handicaps are integrated into the normal school classes, and they are also taught in all the languages with the help of special teachers.

Evaluation

The decision to introduce this multilingual school model did not happen without some resistance. At the beginning, some Ladin people were against it, because they

TABLE 21.2 Distribution of Languages at Intermediate School 3

	German	Italian	Ladin	English
1st class	German, History, Math Science, Social Education and Economics, Chemistry		Italian, Music Arts, Geography Physical Ed	
Hrs per week	*16*	*16*	*2*	*2*
2nd class	German, History, Math Science, Social Education and Economics, Chemistry		Italian, Music Arts, Geography Physical Ed	
Hrs per week	*15*	*17*	*2*	*2*
3rd class	German, History, Math Science, Social Education and Economics, Chemistry		Italian, Music Arts, Geography Physical Ed	
Hrs per week	*16*	*16*	*2*	*2*

Source. Rifesser, 2006

were pragmatically opinioned and believed that it would be better to learn a language that their children did not know rather than to learn something that they already know. Nowadays the majority of the people who have attended the *paritetic* school system are in favour of it, although occasionally there are some who think that it would be better to have learned one language perfectly than learning several languages at an intermediary level. This belief might also result from an ancient European nationalistic mentality, where perfect competence in one language seemed to be a more important aim of language instruction than the ability to communicate as in other countries (e.g., Canada). Another potential problem is that some children could be stressed by instruction in multiple languages being taught at the same time. But, for practical purposes, in today's global world, knowing more languages becomes quite important, particularly for the Ladins, the majority of whom work in the tourist sector. For them, multilingualism is a necessity for every day life (Frabboni 2002; Hilpold 2000; Höglinger 1980; Holtzmann 2000; *Lesestudie Südtirol Kurzfassungen,* 1994).

An important consideration at this point is that there is an asymmetric prestige relationship among the languages. Pragmatic languages and languages used in the economy are seen as more important to teach in class than the mother tongue or the languages spoken by the immigrants, who are not taken into consideration at all. Any immigrants are assimilated, and they have to adapt—or at least that is the situation we experience now. However, this may change as the number of immigrants increase.

Statistical Data: Results of the Bilingualism Exam

In South Tyrol, there exists the so-called *exam of bi- or trilinguism,* which is the same for everyone, regardless of their heritage language group. This exam has to be passed in two or three languages. As shown in Figure 21.2, the success rate of the Ladin people is 63.4%, while the pass rate of Germans is 27.35% and that of the Italian 16.9%(Figure 21.2). Ladin people rarely reach a perfect score in all languages, but they normally reach a good level in both German and Italian. In contrast, Germans and Italians reach a perfect level in their mother tongue, but the level of the other languages is low in comparison to the Ladins.

Conclusion

In keeping with the intent of this book, the *paritetic* school model could be considered as a model that respects the mother language of students, but that also tries to satisfy the needs of a particular situation, thereby incorporating the aim of building a bridge between languages and cultures. This school model is a particular teaching practice of languages that starts very early in life and could be considered as an advantage for the individual child, according to neurolinguistic research that shows the plasticity of the brain that makes it easier for children to learn languages during the early childhood years.

Last, but not least, having the instruments to communicate in more than one way should be always seen as a richness: It amplifies a person's horizons because every language one learns to speak implicitly provides another point of view in comprehending the world. As Wittgenstein puts it, "the limits of my language are the limits of my world" (Wittgenstein, 2000, p. 67).

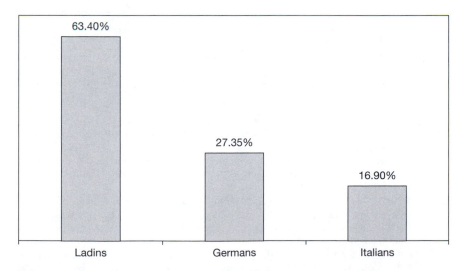

Figure 21.2 Results of the Examination of Bi-/Trilingualism in South Tyrol

Discussion Questions and Assignments

1. As mentioned earlier, one way to teach in the *paritetic* school model is to choose the language on the basis of the different topics, such as the history of Italy is taught in Italian, the history of South Tyrol in German, and the history of the Ladin valleys in Ladin. Try to make similar language assignments for the history of the United States of America tied in with historical events, for example, the history of the colonization of Texas could be taught in French and Spanish.

2. Reflect on the definition of language:

   - What does "monolingual" and "bilingual, and multilingual" mean?
   - Regarding different levels of language competence, is language competence similar in all domains and situations? For example, if a manager can comprehend a written scientific text about economics in German does it mean that he can also fluently speak the German slang of Berlin? What level of competence is needed in order for you to say that this manager knows German?
   - When should an individual be considered bilingual or multilingual?

3. Active and passive language learning could be fun: Search on the web for a common song in a language other than English. Try to find the text in the original language and the translation into English. Try to sing it in the original version!

4. Translate the language of a common movie on DVD of an animated film into another language. Watch the movie and try to understand. You can help yourself by putting in the English subtitles.

Notes

1. These data emerge from the last census (2001): From the total of the population of South Tyrol (428.691), the Ladin people are 18,736 in number (v. 296,461 Germans and 113,494 Italians) (cf. ASTAT Landesinstitut für Statistik, 2004). These data are biased, however, because this statistical record does not take immigrants' languages into account.
2. With Decree No. 670 (August 31) it became constitutional law.
3. These data refer to the success rate of the exam of *bi-/trilingualism* during the period 1978–1990 (career B). Thereafter, for privacy reasons, the mother language need not be declared any more.

References

ASTAT Landesinstitut für Statistik (2004). Autonome Provinz Bozen-Südtirol. Retrieved January 15, 2006, from http://www.provinz.bz.it/astat/.

Balboni, P. (1997). Ladino–Italian Bilingual Programs in Italy. In J. Cummins, & D. Corson (Eds.). *Encyclopedia of Language and Education. Vol. 5 Bilingual education..* Dordrecht/Boston, MA/London: Kluwer.

Belardi, W. (1995). *Breve Storia della Lingua e della Letteratura Ladina.* San Martin de Tor: Istitut Cultural Ladin "Micurà de Rü".

Calliari, F. (1991). *La Minoranza Ladino-Dolomitica. Costituzione, Statuto d'Autonomia, Leggi Regionali e Provinciali.* Rimini: Maggioli.

Cathomas, R., & Carigiet, W. (2006). Auf dem Wege zu einer integralen (mehr-) Sprachendidaktik. In W. Wiater, & G. Videsott (Eds.). *Schule in mehrsprachigen Regionen [School Systems in Multilingual Regions of Europe].* Vienna: Peter Lang.

Crazzolara, E. (1972). *25 Agn Scola Mesata*. St.Ulrich: Union Maestri Ladins.

Egger, K., & Lardschneider, M. (2001). *Dreisprachig werden in Gröden*. Bozen: Ladinisches Pädagogisches Institut.

Ellecosta, L. (1972). *Les Scoles dla Val Badia 1958–1972*. Vienna: Urtijëi.

———. (2002). *English Knowledge. Studio Docimologico e Comparativo. Bewertungstest der Englischkenntnisse nach dreijährigem Schulversuch*. Vienna: Intendënza Scoles Ladines.

Frabboni, F. (2002). *La Parola Saporita*. Milano: F. Angeli.

Hilpold, F. (2000). TIMSS-Studie in der Region Trentino Südtirol, Bozen. In A. E. Beaton, I. V. S. Mullis, M. O. Martin, E. J. Gonzalez, D. L. Kelly, & T. A. Smith (Eds.). *IEA's Third International Mathematics and Science Study (TIMSS)*. Chestnut Hill, MA: TIMSS International Study Center, Boston College.

Höglinger, E. (1980). Interferenzen des Ladinischen und des Italienischen in das Deutsch von Grödner Schülern. *Ladinia IV*, 287–302.

Holtzmann, R. (2000). *Mehrsprachigkeit und Sprachkompetenz in den ladinischen Tälern Südtirols. Eine ethno- und soziolinguistische Darstellung*. Mannheim: Peter Lang.

Irsara, A. (1980). Die gesetzlichen Bestimmungen zum paritätischen Unterricht an den Schulen der ladinischen Ortschaften Südtirols. *Ladinia IV*, 277–285.

Lesestudie Südtirol Kurzfassungen. (1994). Bozen: Institut Pedagogich Ladin.

Richebuono, B. (1991). *Picia Storia di Ladins della Dolomites*. San Martin de Tor: Istitut Cultural Ladin "Micurà de Rü".

Rifesser, T. (1992). Die Schulordnung an den Schulen der zwei ladinischen Täler der Provinz Bozen. *Europa Ethnica*, 2, 75–89.

———. (1999). Alphabetisierung und Mehrsprachigkeit in den Schulen Ladiniens. In *Mehrsprachigkeit und Schule*. Bozen: Europäische Akademie.

———. (2000a). Esperienze di Bilinguismo Precoce nella Scuola Ladina. *Bambini Bilingui . . . Non è un Sogno*, 73–83.

———. (2000b). L'Apprendimento Linguistico in Ambito Ladino. *Palermo: Skanderbeg 3000*, 93–106.

———. (2005). Die ladinische Schule in Südtirol—Gegenwart und Zukunftsperspektiven. In *Die Ladine—eine Minderheit in der Minderheit*. Vienna: Neuer Wissenschaftlicher Verlag.

———. (2006). Das ladinische Schulmodell im Vergleich zum deutschen und italienischen in Südtirol. In W. Wiater, & G. Videsott (Eds.). *Schule in mehrsprachigen Regionen [School Systems in Multilingual Regions of Europe]*. Vienna: Peter Lang.

Seberich, R. (2000). *Südtiroler Schulgeschichte*. Bozen: Raetia.

Taibon, M. (2005). Informaziuns sön la Realté Ladina. Retrieved January 10, 2006, from http://www.gfbv.it/ladin/dossier/ladin/ladinia.html.

Verra, R. (1989). La Lingua e la Cultura Ladina nella Scuola in Val Gardena ed in Val Badia. *Mondo Ladino XIII*, 49–58.

———. (Ed.) (2000). *La Minoranza Ladina*. Bolzano: Istitut Pedagogich Ladin/Intendënza Ladina.

———. (2003). *Plurilinguismo e Scuola Ladina*. Bolzano: Intendenza Scolastica Ladina.

———. (2004). *Ladinisch–Paritätisch–Mehrsprachig. Aspekte der Mehrsprachigkeit in der ladinischen Schule*. Bozen: Ladinisches Schulamt.

Videsott, G. (2005a). El Ladì. In M. D. Burdeus, & J. Verdegal (Eds.). Europa Parla (I). Llengües Romàniques Minoritzades d'Europa. *Anuari de l'Agrupació Borrianenca de cultura*, 16, 209–220.

———. (2005b). Analisi Statistica della Scuola dell'Infanzia delle Valli Ladine in Alto Adige con Particolare Riguardo alla Pluralità Linguistica [Statistische Analyse der ladinischen Kindergärten in Südtirol mit besonderer Berücksichtigung der Mehrsprachigkeit]. In A. Augscholl (Ed.). *Der pädagogische Auftrag von Kindergarten und Grundschule*. Frankfurt/Berlin/Bern/Brussels/New York/Oxford/Vienna: Peter Lang.

Vittur, F. (1977). La Scuola delle Valli Ladine nella Provincia di Bolzano. *Mondo Ladino*, 1-A, 15–20.

———. (1988). *Vire cun Plö Lingac. Publicaziun dada Fora in Gaujun di 40 Agn dla Scola cun Plö Lingac dles Valades Ladines*. Balsan: Istitut Pedagogich Ladin.

———. (1988). *La Lingua Ladina nella Scuola Elementare delle Valli Ladine della Provincia di Bolzano [The Ladin Language in Primary Education in the Ladin Valleys of the Province of Bolzano]*. Leeuwarden: Peter Lang.

——. (1990). *Nrescida sön la Scola de Oblianza de Gherdëina y Badia*. Balsan: Istitut Pedagogich Ladin.

——. (1994). *Ein Leben, eine Schule. Zur Geschichte der Schule in den ladinischen Ortschaften*. Bozen: Institut Pedagogich Ladin.

——. (2000). Die ladinische Schule im Südtirol. *2000 Jahre Ladinien 40/1985*, 30–35.

Wiater, W., & Videsott, G. (2006). *Schule in mehrsprachigen Regionen Europas [School Systems in Multilingual Regions of Europe]*. Frankfurt/Berlin/Bern/ Brussels/New York/Oxford/Vienna: Peter Lang.

Wittgenstein, L. (2000). Tractatus Logico-Philosophicus. In *Ludwig Wittgenstein Werkausgabe in 8 Bänden*. Frankfurt-am-Main: Suhrkamp.

Links for further information

Free University of Bolzano (Bozen): www.unibz.it
History of Ladins (Ladin, German, and Italian): www.vejin.com
Information on Ladins (in Italian): www.noeles.net
Istitut Pedagogich Ladin: www.istitut.pedagogich.it
Ladin Culture–Autonomous Province Bolzano-Bozen: www.provinz.bz.it/intendenza ladina
Official Website of the Dolomite Ladins: www.ladinia.net

22

Educational Policies and Practices in Post-Apartheid South Africa: The Case for Indigenous African Languages

NKONKO M. KAMWANGAMALU

South Africa is known to the rest of the world mostly for its now defunct, divide-and-rule apartheid system, on the basis of which the country was ruled from 1948 to 1994 and whose legacy is likely to haunt the country for years to come. In academic circles around the world, however, South Africa is also known for something else, namely its liberal language policy, a policy which Bamgbose (2003), perhaps writing too soon, says "will considerably reduce the problem of exclusion of the masses, since nine African languages will be available to different segments of the population for participation in the national system" (pp. 51–52).

Indeed, the final draft of the Constitution of the new South Africa, which was adopted on May 8, 1996, makes several references to language. Language is singled out in the Constitution because language was aptly used by previous governments, particularly the apartheid government, as an instrument of social and political control and domination of the country's majority Black population. But after the demise of apartheid and the subsequent birth of democracy in South Africa in 1994, the country adopted a multilingual language policy giving official recognition to 11 languages including English and Afrikaans and nine indigenous African languages: Ndebele, Pedi, Sotho, Swati, Tsonga, Tswana, Xhosa, Zulu, and Venda. This policy had one key objective: to redress the imbalances of the past by promoting the use of previously marginalized languages, for example the indigenous African languages, in higher domains such as education, the media, government, and administration.

A little over a decade since South Africa liberated itself from apartheid in 1994, it seems that not much progress has been made as yet in attempts to implement the new language policy. On the contrary, and in spite of South Africa's constitutional commitment to multilingualism, language practices in virtually all of the country's institutions point to what Fishman (2006a) in "English Only: Its Ghosts, Myths and Dangers" has termed the *unum ideal*. That is, rather than promote pluralism, which is what the policy was designed for in the first place, there is now a drift towards unilingualism in English in public services with concomitant marginalization and freezing of opportunities for functional development of the indigenous African languages.

In this chapter, I report on language-in-education practices in South Africa against the background of the country's new language policy, and on the challenges facing the policy and the consequences of language policy failure especially for the indigenous African languages and the majority of their speakers. The chapter is divided into three sections. In the first section, I offer a sketch of South Africa's social history and related past language policies to provide the background against which the new language policy was developed and enshrined in the country's constitution. Such a background is necessary because, as Cooper (1989) explains, "to understand the impetus for any given instance of language planning, one must understand the general social context in which it is embedded and the history which produced that context" (pp. 177, 182). In the second section, I discuss some of the factors that, in my view, interact in complex ways to prevent the implementation of the new language policy. These include the legacy of past (apartheid) language policies, the escape clauses in the new language policy, the economic value and status of English as a global language, and emergent Black elite closure in the post-apartheid polity.

In the third section, I discuss the way forward for the new language policy. I argue that for the policy to succeed, it must be revised with a view not only to questioning what it means for indigenous African languages to be official languages, but also and more importantly, what it takes to give these languages a real cachet in the broader socioeconomic context. I make this argument against the background of current theories of the economics of language, also known as language economics and some of the consequences of language policy failure for the indigenous African languages and those who speak them.

South Africa's Social History and Language Policies

The social history of South Africa indicates that over the past 350 years the country has experienced four major ideologies in language policy, with each ideology impacting the whole society as well as societal language use. The four ideologies include *Dutchification* (1652–1795), *Anglicization* (1795–1948), *Afrikanerization* (1948–1994), and *Democratization* (1994–present) (Kamwangamalu, 2003).

Dutchification refers to the imposition of the Dutch language in all higher domains such as the administration, education, trade, etc. by the Dutch officials of the "Dutch East India Company" who were the first Europeans to colonize South Africa. During the century and a half (1652–1795) of Dutch occupation of the country, only knowledge of Dutch served as a catalyst for access to resources and employment in the civil service. The ideology of Dutchification of what was then called the Cape Colony, now Cape Town, came to an end in 1795 when the territory fell under British control. With the territory now in their hands, British authorities imposed English as the official language of the colony, hence the next phase, *Anglicization.*

The policy of Anglicization (1795–1803; 1806–1948) "sought to replace Dutch by English in all spheres of public life" (Davenport, 1991, p. 40). Anglicization required knowledge of English for access to whatever resources were available in the colony. The policy of Anglicization ended effectively in 1948 when the Afrikaners came into power and swiftly replaced it with what I call *Afrikanerization.*

The change from Anglicization to *Afrikanerization* (1948–1994) saw the Afrikaans language, an offspring of Dutch, increase its power dramatically and take center stage in the administration of the state. Knowledge of Afrikaans became a requirement for entry into the civil service, much as was that of Dutch and English in the eras of Dutchification and Anglicization, respectively. Webb and Kriel (2000) remark that the apartheid state invested heavily both politically and financially in the development of Afrikaans and often praised the language as a gift from God.

In 1953 the apartheid government adopted a controversial language policy, commonly known as the *Bantu Education Act.* This was an effort to further "Afrikanerize" South African society with a policy that sought to (a) promote Afrikaans and reduce the influence of English in Black schools; (b) impose in these schools the use of both Afrikaans and English on an equal basis as media of instruction; and (c) extend mother tongue education in African languages from grade four to grade eight (Kamwangamalu, 1997). According to Alexander (1989), Black pupils resisted mother tongue education because they perceived it as a dead-end, a barrier to more advanced learning, a lure to self-destruction and a trap designed by the apartheid government to ensure that Black pupils did not acquire sufficient command of the high-status languages (English and Afrikaans), for it would enable them to compete with their White counterparts for well-paying jobs and prestigious career options.

Black pupils' resistance to the Bantu Education Act and the apartheid government's determination to impose it led to the bloody Soweto uprising of June 16, 1976, in which several pupils lost their lives. The aftermath of the Soweto uprisings saw Afrikaans emerge, in the minds of Black South Africans, as the language of oppression, and English as the language of advancement and liberation from apartheid. Unfortunately, however, the indigenous African languages became identified as inferior and unsuitable for use in the educational system. In other words, the Soweto uprisings reinforced Black people's hatred towards Afrikaans; boosted the status of an already powerful language, English, over both Afrikaans and African languages in Black schools and in Black communities at large; and led Black South Africans to associate education in their own languages with inferior education.

It is ironic that one of the most controversial policies of the apartheid era, the Bantu Education Act, had a totally opposite effect to that desired. Despite the fact that in most former British colonies English is often viewed as an interloper imposed from outside and thus politically suspect (Silva, 1998), English emerged in South Africa completely untainted from its colonial history (Smit, 1998), as Afrikaans shielded English from this stigma (Silva, 1998). From the time of the Bantu Education Act until the birth of a democratic South Africa in 1994, English has never looked back. Rather, the language has become far more hegemonic than any other in the land (Webb & Kriel, 2000). It is against this background that one must understand issues of language education policies and practices as well as the development of the new language policy in the post-apartheid state, a policy that brought about *the ideology of language democratization.*

The new language democratization policy (1994) accords official status to 11 languages including English and Afrikaans and nine African languages. The policy itself is stipulated as follows in South Africa's 1996 Constitution:

> The official languages of the Republic (of South Africa) are Sepedi, Sesotho, Setswana, siSwati, Tshivenda, Xitsonga, Afrikaans, English, isiNdebele, isiXhosa and isiZulu. (Constitution of the Republic of South Africa, 1996, Chapter 1, Section 6(1))

Concerning the promotion of African languages, which is the primary goal of the new language policy, the Constitution states that "recognizing the historically diminished use and status of the indigenous languages of our people, the state must take practical and positive measures to elevate the status and advance the use of these languages" (Chapter 1, Section 6(2)). In Section 6(2), a related clause states that "all official languages must enjoy parity of esteem and must be treated equitably." Also, in Chapter 1, Section 6(5a), the Constitution makes provision for the establishment of a pan-South African language board with the responsibility to, inter alia, "promote and create conditions for the development and use of these (African) and other languages."

Theoretically, the new language policy reflects *internationalization* and *pluralism*, two of the four ideologies (including assimilation and vernacularization) in language planning. As explained by Cobarrubias (1983), internationalization refers to the adoption of a non-indigenous language, for example English, as an official language. By the same token, pluralism is the official recognition of more than one language, such as English, Afrikaans and the other nine African languages. Internationalization corresponds more or less to what Schmidt (1998) calls a "centralist policy," that is, a policy that ensures the hegemony of one ethnolinguistic group and rationalizes the exclusion of other languages from public domains such as education. In this case, however, the centralist policy does not specify whether the selected dominant language is endoglossic (i.e. language internal to the state), or exoglossic (i.e. language external to the state). In Cobarrubias's framework, however, internationalization refers to the choice of an exoglossic language, usually a former colonial language, as the official language of the state.

Cobarrubias (1983) describes the other two ideologies, assimilation and vernacularization, as follows. Assimilation is the belief that everyone, regardless of origin, must learn the politically and economically dominant language of the society. Vernacularization refers to the restoration and adoption of an indigenous language as an official language. As will be demonstrated later, in South Africa assimilation towards English is becoming increasingly evident, albeit unofficially, in current language practices in most of the country's institutions. Although vernacularization has been implemented successfully elsewhere in the world, e.g., Amharic in Ethiopia, Somali in Somalia, Hebrew in Israel, Malay in Malaysia, and, to a limited extent, Swahili in Tanzania, in South Africa this ideology has apparently been avoided to prevent potential language-related, interethnic conflicts among

South Africa's Black population. With this theoretical background in mind, I will now examine briefly how South Africa's new policy has fared in practice.

Factors Preventing Policy Implementation

This discussion will focus on language-in-educational practices, with passing comments on language practices in other higher domains, especially the media and the government and administration. I argue that the policy has failed to achieve the objective for which it was designed, namely, to promote the use of the indigenous African languages in these and related higher domains.

Language Practices in Education

It is worth noting that in the apartheid era, education-related language debates were concerned with the territorial struggle between English and Afrikaans and with questions about how much English or Afrikaans should be used, where, and why. The Bantu Education Act referred to earlier was a by-product of this struggle. When apartheid ended in 1994, the struggle between English and Afrikaans shifted toward promoting the status of the indigenous African languages. In reality, however, the historical struggle between English and Afrikaans has continued unabashed, and has moved, covertly of course, from the question of how much English or Afrikaans should be used and where to the question of how much territory should English take from Afrikaans.

As evidence of the shift, consider changes in the medium of instruction at South African colleges and universities in 1994 and in 2004.

Table 22.1 shows that with post-apartheid educational reforms came a merger of some of South Africa's colleges and universities, reducing the number of these institutions from 36 in 1994 to 22 in 2004. Note that in 1994 there were five monolingual Afrikaans-medium universities, now there is none. Previously Afrikaans-medium universities have been required to transform themselves into bilingual universities to accommodate Black students' demand for English-medium

TABLE 22.1 Medium of Instruction at Higher Education Institutions

Type	Afrikaans	English	Bilingual	Total
Medium of instruction in 1994				
Universities	5	13	3	**21**
Technikons	0	8	7	**15**
Total	5	21	10	**36**
Medium of instruction in 2004				
Universities	0	7	4	**11**
Universities of technology	0	5	0	**5**
Comprehensive universities	0	3	3	**6**
Total	0	15	7	**22**

Source. Du Plessis, 2006, pp. 100–101

education. Also, although the 2002 Ministry of Education's *Language policy for Higher Education* recognizes English and Afrikaans as the only languages of instruction in higher education, it rejects the continuation of monolingual Afrikaans-medium institutions (paragraph 15.4.3). Yet, as Du Plessis (2006) notes pointedly, the *National Plan for Higher Education in South Africa* states, in no uncertain term, that universities in contemporary South Africa can be neither Black nor White, neither English nor Afrikaans speaking, but only "unabashedly and unashamedly South African universities" (Department of Education, 2001, p. 82).

In spite of this, Universities in South Africa use either English or Afrikaans as the medium of instruction, with English having far more territory than Afrikaans. The languages that have no comparable territory in education are those for which the new language policy was designed—the indigenous African languages. Concerning these languages, all that the *Language Policy for Higher Education* says is that it "envisage[s] a program for the development of other South African languages as languages of instruction at this level" (paragraph 15.2). It follows that African languages, despite their status as official languages, remain marginalized in education and are confined as the medium of instruction to the first 3 years of primary education in Black schools, much as they were in the apartheid era.

Language Practices in Higher Domains

With respect to language practices in other higher domains, such as the media and the government and administration, research shows that, here, too, English reigns supreme. English is used in South Africa's media more than any other official languages. Table 22.2 shows the distribution of program types and languages by television channels.

Notice that English is the only language that is used across the three channels. Moreover, in a survey of language use on South African television for the month of May 1998, Kamwangamalu (1998) found that of the 378 hours shared by the 11 official languages per month, English took up 348 hours or 91% of the total airtime, followed by Afrikaans with 21 hours or 5.66%, and all the nine African languages with only nine hours, or an average of 1 hour per language per week. English not only has an entire TV channel to itself but it also takes the lion's share of airtime on the other state TV channels.

Similar conclusions obtain with regard to language practices in the domain of government and administration, where English has become the de facto lingua franca. For instance, Pandor (1995) reports that in 1994, 87% of the speeches made

TABLE 22.2 SABC Television

Channel	Character	Languages
SABC 1	Aspirant, youthful	Nguni, English
SABC 2	Family focused	Sotho, English, Afrikaans
SABC 3	Cosmopolitan, spirited	English

Source. South African Broadcasting Corporation, 2005

in parliament were in English; fewer than 5% were in Afrikaans and the remaining 8% were in the nine African languages. In other words, the nine African languages had less than 1% each. In a more recent survey, Hibbert (2001) found that the percentage of speeches made in English in parliament had actually increased to 97%, while those in Afrikaans had decreased from 5 to 3%. As for the indigenous African languages, they are no longer used in the public discourse, save at election times, when politicians seek to win votes from their constituencies.

To sum up, language practices in South Africa show that the country makes use of English more than other official languages. But why English? Why not Afrikaans or the African languages which, in the main, were the intended target of the new language policy? I suggest that there are factors, some of them internal and others external to the new language policy, which interact in complex ways to turn the tides in favor of English. One of these factors, namely past apartheid policies and especially the Bantu Education Act, has already been discussed. It must be pointed out, however, that the legacy of that policy continues to impact negatively on language policy and practices in South Africa and represents, in my view, the most serious challenge facing the new language. Three other factors are treated here, namely the escape clauses in the new language policy, the status of English as a global language, and emergent Black elite closure.

Escape Clauses in the new Language Policy

Clauses 1 and 2 of the Constitution govern language use in education, government and administration. Since Public Broadcasting is an independent body, the policies it formulates are not dictated by the Constitution. Regarding education, clause 1 of the constitution states:

> Everyone has the right to receive education in the official language or languages of their choice in public educational institutions *where that education is reasonably practicable.* (Constitution of South Africa, 1996, Chapter 2, Section 29(2)), emphasis added)

Regarding government and administration, clause 2 of the Constitution states:

> (2) The national government and provincial governments may use *any particular official languages* for the purposes of government, taking into account usage, practicality, expense, regional circumstances and the balance of the needs and preferences of the population as a whole or in the province concerned; but the national government and each provincial government must use at *least two official languages.* (Constitution of South Africa, 1996, chapter 1, Section 6, 3(a), emphasis added)

The policy statement for media (www.sabc.co.za/home.asp (2005)) is as follows:

> SABC (South African Broadcasting Corporation) is committed to treating all the official languages equitably. . . . The term equitable treatment means just, fair and reasonable—*not necessarily equal*—treatment. (emphasis added)

Concerning language practices in education, about 95% of schools in South Africa use English as the medium of instruction. By offering tuition in English, schools abide by the Constitution, for they not only do what they believe is practicable, but also that which parents want for their children, namely, English-medium education. The laissez-faire approach, which is implicit in the education-related language clause, has led to an increased demand for English, even within the Afrikaans speaking community.

With regard to language use in government and administration, English again dominates over other official languages. Since the Constitution does not specify which official languages should be used in which provinces or by the national government, both provincial and national governments have tacitly opted for the status quo: They use English and Afrikaans as the languages of administration, much as was the case in the apartheid era. Also, the negative attitudes of government officials towards indigenous African languages, as already alluded to, have contributed to the further marginalization of these languages. Due to the stigma of the Bantu Education policy and the socioeconomic benefits associated with English, those who speak an indigenous African language in the legislature are perceived as uneducated, while those who speak English are invariably perceived as well informed and better educated.

Concerning language use in the medium of television, South African Broadcasting Corporation (SABC) states that it is committed to treating all the official languages equitably. There is, however, a caveat. For SABC, "the term equitable treatment means just, fair and reasonable—not necessarily equal—treatment." It is therefore not surprising that SABC does not feature all the official languages in its recent allocation of languages per channel, as shown in Table 22.2.

The Hegemony of English

The literature offers two theories to account for the spread of English around the world: the *Anglo-American conspiracy theory* and the *global grassroots theory*. Christian Mair (1999) explains that the key argument advanced by adherents of the conspiracy theory, among them Robert Phillipson and Alastair Pennycook, is that the spread of English has been engineered by powerful British and American interests through systematic and often semi-secret language policies. The grassroots theory of the spread of English comes primarily from a collection of essays titled *Post-Imperial English*, edited by Fishman, Conrad, and Rubal-Lopez (1996). This collection is based on empirical investigations of English in 20 different settings, including the European Union, Nigeria, Sudan, and Cuba. The main argument of the book is that the spread of English in the world today is not the product of British and American conspiracy. Rather, the language spreads for many different reasons, chief among them is that individuals opt for English rather than alternative languages. Along these lines, Ager (2001) acknowledges that international organizations often have a language policy and that global corporations frequently standardize one form of communication, and in many cases they require the use of English. Ager's view, which I am inclined to share against the backdrop of the language situation in South Africa, is that, historical factors aside, currently the motivation for individuals and communities to choose English is basically economic and pragmatic.

Whichever theory one espouses, the fact remains that in the context of South Africa, use of English is spreading like wildfire, particularly in urban Black communities, where it has infiltrated the family domain. I would believe that in South Africa, the hegemony of English over local languages stems from what Schiffman (1996) has called the country's linguistic culture, as well as what Lionel Wee (2003) in his discussion of Singapore has termed "linguistic instrumentalism." Linguistic instrumentalism refers to a view of language that justifies its existence in a community in terms of its usefulness in achieving specific utilitarian goals, such as access to economic development or social mobility. I will return to the question of the relationship between indigenous African languages and the economy in the last section of this paper.

Emergent Black Elite Closure

Another factor in the choice of English is elite closure. Scotton (1990) defines elite closure as a strategy by which those persons in power maintain their powers and privileges via language choices. She describes elite closure as "a tactic of boundary maintenance that involves institutionalizing the linguistic patterns of the elite, either through official policy or informally established usage norms in order to limit access to socio-economic mobility and political power to people who possess the requisite linguistic patterns." (p. 25). In this regard, Naregal (2001) explains how British colonial education in Western India served the development of an English-educated elite and fixed the vernacular in a secondary position vis-à-vis English. (See also Hock in this volume.) Likewise, Pool (1990) asserts that "language regimes with inaccessible foreign official languages, which the general public is neither invited nor expected to learn, operate to bring about and maintain elitist political regimes, where powerful parents pass their exclusive privileges to their children" (p. 244).

Evidence of such language regimes is of at least two kinds, policy and attitudinal, that can readily be found in South Africa, much as it can elsewhere in the African continent. The policy type is exemplified by the escape clauses that are embedded in South Africa's multilingual language policy. The covert negative attitudes that the elite themselves have towards the indigenous African languages exemplify the attitudinal type. These attitudes betray the elite's two-facedness in assigning official status to indigenous languages, while suggesting equal status to English and Afrikaans. However, it is easy to see through the policy which confers official status to indigenous languages, as the policy has what Schiffman (1996) has termed a *false front*. That is, the policy publicly and constitutionally promotes multilingualism but it conceals the reality that in practice, and if language practices in the higher domains are any indication, only English remains the sole medium through which the emergent ruling Black elite exerts control over the country's economy and political system.

Taking into account language policy and practices, on the one hand, and the factors that govern these practices, on the other, it is clear, as Fishman (2004) remarks with respect to immigrant languages in the United States, that in South Africa indigenous African languages remain exposed to the Darwinian law of the linguistic jungle, according to which the strong survive and, in competition with the strong, the weak die off.

The question that arises at this juncture is this: How do we ensure that weak languages, in this case economically minority indigenous African languages in South Africa, do not succumb to the law of the linguistic jungle? I address this question in the next section. I will explore ways in which South Africa's multilingual language policy can be revised so that the indigenous African languages become, like English and Afrikaans, the tools for access to economic resources and for upward social mobility.

The Way Forward for the New Language Policy

Indigenous African Languages and the Economy

In this section, I discuss the relationship between these languages and the economy, drawing on current theories of language economics. I argue that for indigenous languages of South Africa to survive, especially in urban Black communities, they need to be given a share of the market value that their sister official languages, here Afrikaans and English in particular, have in the South African linguistic marketplace.

The literature increasingly recognizes the importance of the relationship between language and the economy in the success or failure of language policies (Grin 2006; Kamwangamalu, 2004; Nettle and Romaine, 2000; Paulston, 1988; Walsh, 2006; Wright, 1994). Paulston (1988) observes that language planning efforts are most likely to be successful if they are supported by economic advantage or similar social incentives for the minority groups. Likewise, Nettle and Romaine (2000) remark that "true development of a political, economic, or social nature cannot take place, however, unless there is also development of a linguistic nature" (p. 172). Nettle and Romaine's remarks are in tune with recent developments in the field of language economics, a field of study that focuses on the theoretical and empirical analyses of the ways in which linguistic and economic variables influence one another (Vaillancourt & Grin, 2000). To paraphrase Sue Wright (1994), a recognition of the very richness of language as a social phenomenon lies at the heart of the economics of language. Issues raised in language economics that are of special relevance to this chapter are:

- the relevance of language as an element, in the acquisition of which individual actors may have a good reason to invest
- language teaching as a social investment, yielding net benefits (market related or not)
- economic implications, i.e., costs and benefits of language policies, whether these costs and benefits are market related or not.

Within the framework of language economics, linguistic products such as language, language varieties, utterances, and accents are seen not only as goods or commodities to which the market assigns a value (Coulmas, 1992), but also as human capital. The acquisition of human capital is a source of economic advantage and influences the socioeconomic status of individuals (Vaillancourt & Grin, 2000). The term "market" refers to the social context in which linguistic products are used. On a given linguistic market, some products are valued more highly than others. The market value of a linguistic product such as a language, says Coulmas (1992), is determined in relation to other languages in the planetary economy. It is an index of the functional appreciation of the language by the relevant community (Strauss, 1996). Against this background, I propose that the problem that the indigenous African languages are facing in the post-apartheid state is an economic or marketing one in that unlike English and Afrikaans, the knowledge of African languages does not pay off in the linguistic marketplace.

Viewing the development of African languages as a marketing problem entails "developing the right *product* backed by the right *promotion* and put in the right *place* at the right *price*" (Cooper, 1989, p. 72). Concerning the *product*, Cooper says that language planners must recognize, identify, or design products that the potential consumer will find attractive. The second construct, *promotion*, refers to efforts to induce potential users to adopt a language, whether adoption is viewed as awareness, positive evaluation, proficiency, or usage (Cooper, 1989). The third construct, *place*, refers to the provision of adequate channels of distribution and response. A person motivated to buy a product must know where to find it. Cooper views the last construct, *price*, as the key to determining the product's appeals to the consumers (Cooper, 1989).

In South Africa, two of the four conditions proposed by Cooper for successful language marketing, namely, the *product* and the *place*, can readily be identified: the indigenous languages as the *product* and the *place* as where these languages are spoken. For instance, Zulu is the demographically dominant language in the province of Kwazulu-Natal; whereas Xhosa has a similar status in the Cape. Therefore, the issue of marketing indigenous African languages in South Africa hinges not so much on the *product* or the *place*, but rather on the *promotion* and *price* of these languages in the linguistic marketplace. For African languages to become appealing in the linguistic marketplace, they must be assigned an economic value. This entails meeting at least three conditions.

First, there is the need to vest the indigenous official languages, each in their respective geographical areas, with some of the privileges, prestige, power and material gains that have for so long been associated only with English and Afrikaans (Kamwangamalu, 1997, p. 249). Second, in order to promote functional mass literacy and thus empower the masses with the skills they need for access to resources, African languages should be used gradually throughout the entire educational systems. Third, a certified (i.e. school-acquired) knowledge of the indigenous African languages should become one of the criteria for access to employment, much as is currently the case for English and Afrikaans.

Meeting the three conditions does not necessarily entail removing English and Afrikaans or diminishing their status in education (or other higher domains). It simply means creating conditions under which the indigenous languages can play a meaningful role at least in the local linguistic marketplace. The approach I am advocating here for language policy revision in South Africa is akin to what Gibson Ferguson (2006) has called a policy of *complementarity*, involving both an enhanced role for local languages and democratization of access to English. A language policy that does not have economic advantages, especially for indigenous languages in a country such as South Africa where language has been used as an instrument of control and discrimination, is doomed to failure.

The literature provides ample evidence that language planning and policy activities succeed if they lead to desirable outcomes. With respect to *Basquecization* activities intended to promote acquisition planning for the Basque language in Spain, Fishman explains that these Basquecization activities were successful because participation in them yielded certification at various levels of competence, entitling their bearers to qualify for promotions, raises, job tenure, and other perquisites of success in the workplace (Fishman, 2006a). Like Fishman, Edwards (2004) asserts that although language is part of our cultural capital, its market value is variable. She points to the case of Welsh and Maori, noting that official status of these languages has generated a range of employment prospects for minority language speakers in education, the media, and government. Likewise, Ferguson (2006) provides a comparative study of Welsh and Breton, showing that the revival of Welsh and the continuing decline of Breton are mostly due to different sociopolitical and economic factors.

For South Africa, the research we cite in this chapter suggests that unless the new language policy is revised in the ways already suggested, the official status of the indigenous African languages will continue to be what Tariq Rahman (2001) in his discussion of language policy in Pakistan describes as only a symbolic move in the power game. Raising the status of the indigenous African languages to equal that of English and Afrikaans is a symbolic move in the power game because, as Schiffman (1996) points out, egalitarianism in language policy does not result necessarily in equal outcomes.

Consequences of Language Policy Failure

Another way to move forward with South African languages is by avoiding the consequences of language policy failures. The one consequence that I will focus on here is language shift from the indigenous African languages to English especially in urban Black communities as a result of the language dominance of English. Over a quarter of a century ago, Dell Hymes (1980) writes in a foreword to Gillian Sankoff's book, *The Social Life of Language*: "A new world that had thousands of distinct languages in 1492 is now dominated by English, French, Portuguese, and Spanish over most of its terrain" (p. ix). Today, that new world is almost exclusively dominated by one language, English. This dominance of English (and other world languages) over minority languages has created ideal conditions for the demise of minority languages. In this regard, Skutnabb-Kangas (2000) and others have expressed concern about the possibility of the disappearance of at least half of the world's 6000 or so languages by the middle of this century. Most of these language deaths are likely to take place in post-colonial settings, where various factors, such as the lack of resources and of community and institutional support mitigate against indigenous language maintenance.

In the context of South Africa, the alarm about language death has already been sounded, as is evident from the demise of South African and Indian languages such as Hindi, Marathi, Telugu, Tamil, whose speakers are now monolingual in English. It is feared that the process of language shift and death that took place in the South African Indian communities and before them in the Khoisan communities is now taking place again, this time in the urban Black communities and to some extent in the White, middle-class, Afrikaans speaking communities. That language shift is taking place at an accelerated rate in these communities is born out both in the press, as can be inferred from the following extract, taken from the *Sunday Times*, a South African local newspaper:

> South Africa has eleven official languages, but many could soon face extinction . . . (*Sowetan Sunday World*, August 5, 2001). From the remotest Khoi language of the Kgalakgadi to the pre-eminent Nguni isiZulu tongue in KwaZulu Natal, the African languages all face a common, domineering force—English (*Daily News*, December 6, 2000), [which] is spreading like the mynah bird. (*Sunday Times*, August 4, 2002)

A similar concern is found in two recent studies one each by de Klerk (2000) and Bowerman (2000). Both studies show that communication among the younger generations takes place almost exclusively in English, and that this is more so especially among the wealthier and more privileged members of the indigenous language communities.

Ralph Fasold (1984) remarks that when a speech community begins to choose a new language in domains formerly reserved for the old one, it may be a sign that language shift is in progress. In spite of the noted shift to English, Le Page and Tabouret-Keller (1985) remind us that languages, in this case, indigenous African languages, remain a marker of individual or group identity. The question is, as Sankoff (1980) puts it, under what circumstances the identity function becomes inverted in such a way that a particular group becomes alienated from its own language and begins to regard it as inferior to some other language. Sankoff explains that these tend to be circumstances in which access to a particular language works to create and maintain real differences in power and wealth.

Conclusion

Sankoff's (1980) point takes me back to the core argument of this chapter, namely, that if South Africa's new language policy is to achieve its initial goal of promoting the indigenous African languages, then the policy must be revised so that these languages become associated with at least some of the perquisites and material gains that are currently associated with English and Afrikaans. Unless the indigenous African languages are perceived to facilitate access to the wider society and economic advancement, the attraction to English and opposition to the African languages will continue to be overwhelming, despite South Africa's constitutional commitment to what Fishman (2006b) calls the *pluribus ideal.*

Discussion Questions and Assignments

1. Explain in what ways a language policy of the apartheid era, such as the Bantu Education Act, impacts the development and promotion of the indigenous African languages in the education system in post-apartheid South Africa.
2. Two theories, the *Anglo-American conspiracy theory* and the *global grassroots theory*, have been proposed to account for the spread of English around the world. Discuss the merit of each.
3. This chapter claims that for the indigenous African languages to survive in an era of globalization, they must be associated with economic advantages. Do you agree or disagree with this claim and why? Can you think of other variables that would ensure the maintenance of economically minority languages in a multilingual society such as South Africa?
4. (a) Is multilingualism a curse, a blessing, neither, or both? (b) Do you agree or disagree with the following statement and why? "True development of a political, economic, or social nature cannot take place, however, unless there is also development of a linguistic nature" (Nettle and Romaine, 2000, p. 172).

References

Ager, D. (2001). *Motivation in Language Planning and Language Policy.* Clevedon: Multilingual Matters.

Alexander, N. (1989). *Language Policy and National Unity in South Africa/Azania.* Cape Town: Buchu Books.

Bamgbose, A. (2003). A Recurring Decimal: English in Language Policy and Planning. *World Englishes,* 22(4), 419–431.

Bowerman, S. A. (2000). Linguistic Imperialism in South Africa: The Unassailable Position of English. Unpublished MA dissertation, University of Cape Town.

Cobarrubias, J. (1983). Ethical Issues in Status Planning. In J. Cobarrubias, & J. A. Fishman (Eds.). *Progress in Language Planning.* The Hague: Mouton de Gruyter.

Constitution of [the Republic of] South Africa. (1996). Pretoria: Government Printer.

Cooper, R. L. (1989). *Language Planning and Social Change.* Cambridge: Cambridge University Press.

Coulmas, F. (1992) *Language and the Economy.* Oxford: Blackwell.

Davenport, T. R. H. (1991). *South Africa: A Modern History,* 4th edn. London: Macmillan.

De Klerk, V. (2000). Language Shift in Grahamstown: A Case Study of Selected Xhosa Speakers. *International Journal of the Sociology of Language,* 146, 87–110.

Department of Education. (2001). National Plan for Higher Education in South Africa. Retrieved from http://education.pwv.gov.za/DoE_Sites /Hi. . .National%20Plan%20-%20Final%20Draft.htm.

Du Plessis, T. (2006). From Monolingual to Bilingual Higher Education: The Repositioning of Historically Africaans-Medium Universities in South Africa. *Language Policy,* 5(1), 87–113.

Edwards, V. (2004). *Multilingualism in the English-Speaking World.* Malden, MA: Blackwell.

Fasold, R. (1984). *The Sociolinguistics of Society.* Oxford: Blackwell.

Ferguson, G. (2006) *Language Planning in Education.* Edinburgh: Edinburgh University Press.

Fishman, J. A. (2006a). *Do Not Leave Your Language Alone. The Hidden Status Agendas within Corpus Planning in Language Policy.* Mahwah, NJ: Lawrence Erlbaum Associates, Inc.

——. (2006b). 'English-Only': Its Ghosts, Myths, and Dangers. In N. Hornberger, & M. Putz (Eds.). *Language Loyalty, Language Planning and Language Revitalization: Recent Writings and Reflections from Joshua A. Fishman.* Clevedon: Multilingual Matters.

——. (2004). Language Maintenance, Language Shift, and Reversing Language Shift. In T. Bhatia, & W. Ritchie (Eds.). *The Handbook of Bilingualism*. New York: Blackwell.

——, Conrad, A. W., & Rubal-Lopez, A. (Eds.) (1996). *Post Imperial English: Status Change in Former British and American Colonies, 1940–1990*. Berlin and New York: Mouton de Gruyter.

Grin, F. (2006). Economic Considerations in Language Policy. In T. Ricento (Ed.). *An Introduction to Language Policy: Theory and Method*. Malden, MA: Blackwell.

Hibbert, L. (2001). Changing Language Practices in Parliament in South Africa. Eighth International Association of World Englishes (IAWE). University of Potchefstroom, South Africa, November 29–December 1.

Hymes, D. (1980). Foreword. In G. Sankoff, *The Social Life of Language*. Philadelphia, PA: University of Pennsylvania Press.

Kamwangamalu, N. M. (2004). Language Policy/Language Economics Interface and Mother Tongue Education in Post-Apartheid South Africa. In N. M. Kamwangamalu (Ed.). *Language Problems and Language Planning, Special Issue: South Africa*, 28(2), 131–146.

——. (2003). Social Change and Language Shift: South Africa. *Annual Review of Applied Linguistics*, 23, 225–242.

——. (Ed.) (1998). *Aspects of Multilingualism in Post-Apartheid South Africa: A Special Issue of Multilingua*, 17(2–3).

——. (1997). Multilingualism and Education Policy in Post-Apartheid South Africa. *Language Problems and Language Planning*, 21(3), 234–253.

Le Page, R., & Tabouret-Keller, A. (1985) *Acts of Identity: Creole-Based Approaches to Ethnicity and Language*. Cambridge: Cambridge University Press.

Mair, C. (1999) The Continuing Spread of English: Anglo-American Conspiracy or Global Grassroots Movement? Paper presented at the third biennial MAVEN (Major Varieites of English) Conference. University of Lincolnshire and Humberside. Lincoln, September 9–11.

Ministry of Education. (2002). Language Policy for Higher Education. Retrieved from http://education.pwv.gov.za/content/documents/67.pdf.

Naregal, V. (2001). *Language Politics, Elites, and the Public Sphere: Western India Under Colonialism*. New Delhi: Orient Longman.

Nettle, D., & Romaine, S. (2000). *Vanishing Voices: The Extinction of the World's Languages*. Oxford: Oxford University Press.

Pandor, N. (1995). Constitutional Multilingualism: Problems, Possibilities, Practicalities. Proceedings of the Southern African Applied Linguistics Association Conference, 15, 57–74.

Paulston, C. B. (1988) *International Handbook of Bilingualism and Bilingual Education*. New York: Greenwood Press.

Pool, J. (1990). Language, Political Development, and Regimes. In B. Weinstein (Ed.). *Language Policy and Political Development*. Norwood, NJ: Ablex.

Rahman, T. (2001). Language-Learning and Power: A Theoretical Approach. *International Journal of the Sociology of Language*, 152, 53–74.

Sankoff, G. (1980). *The Social Life of Language*. Philadelphia, PA: University of Pennsylvania Press.

Schiffman, H. F. (1996). *Linguistic Culture and Language Policy*. London: Routledge.

Schmidt, R.J. (1998) The Politics of Language in Canada and the United States: Explaining the Differences. In T. Ricento, & B. Burnaby (Eds.). *Language and Politics in the United States and Canada*. Mahwah, NJ: Lawrence Erlbaum Associates, Inc.

Scotton, C. M. (1990). Elite Closure as Boundary Maintenance. In B. Weinstein (Ed.). *Language Policy and Political Development*. Norwood, NJ: Ablex.

Silva, P. (1998). South African English: Oppressor or Liberator? In H. Linquist, S. Klintborg, M. Levin, & M. Estling (Eds.). *The Major Varieties of English: Papers from MAVEN 97*, 69–77. Vaxjo: Vaxjo University Press.

Skutnabb-Kangas, T. (2000). *Linguistic Genocide in Education—or Worldwide Diversity and Human Rights?* Mahwah, NJ: Lawrence Erbaum Associates, Inc.

Smit, U. (1998). South African English Lexemes for South Africans—A Case in Point for a Developing Multicultural Standard of English. In H. Linquist, S. Klintborg, M. Levin, & M. Estling (Eds.). *The Major Varieties of English: Papers from MAVEN 97*, 79–92. Vaxjo: Vaxjo University Press.

South African Broadcasting Corporation. Retrieved from www.sbac.co.za/home.asp.

Strauss, G. (1996). The Economics of Language: Diversity and Development in an Information Economy. *The Economics of Language. Language Report* 5(2), 2–27.

Sunday Times. (2002). Johannesburg, South Africa, August 4.

Vaillancourt, F., & Grin, F. (2000). The Choice of a Language of Instruction: The Economic Aspects. Distance Learning Course on Language Instruction in Basic Education. Washington, DC: World Bank Institute.

Walsh, J. (2006). Language and Socio-Economic Development: Towards a Theoretical Framework. *Language Problems and Language Planning,* 30(2), 127–148.

Webb, V., & Kriel, M. (2000). Afrikaans and Afrikaner Nationalism. *International Journal of the Sociology of Language, Special Issue on Language and Ethnicity in the New South Africa,* 144, 19–49.

Wee, L. (2003). Linguistic Instrumentalism in Singapore. *Journal of Multilingual and Multicultural Development,* 24(3), 211–224.

Wright, S. (1994). The Contribution of Sociolinguistics. *Current Issues in Language and Society,* 1, 1–6.

23

Meaningful Early Literacy Learning Experiences: Lessons from South Africa

CAROLE BLOCH

After the end of apartheid rule in South Africa in 1994, major problems and challenges in educational delivery and achievement were acknowledged. To address these, significant conceptual work, policy changes and some practical initiatives were initiated in both non-formal and formal education domains. One of the focal areas was, and indeed remains, literacy. In particular, there was increased recognition of the urgent need to improve early/emergent literacy teaching. In this chapter, I provide the reader a sense of the significant language and literacy related challenges we face on the African continent and of the progress that has been made in South Africa for early literacy development and learning since the end of apartheid. First, I discuss some of the more significant contextual and theoretical issues influencing literacy development in Africa. In the second part of the chapter, I describe some of the research and practical interventions for early literacy that have been initiated in the post-apartheid years by the multilingual research and education organization where I work, the project for the Study of Alternative Education in South Africa (PRAESA).

Understanding Literacy Issues in Africa

Literacy is described as a problem for Africa, like the rest of the world (Triebel, 2001). It has been widely acknowledged that, despite decades of literacy campaigns by UNESCO and others as well as efforts such as Education for All (EFA) Triebel (2001) attempts to ensure that what is often referred to as the "spread of literacy" in Africa have failed (p. 19). A popular belief exists that Africa is an "oral" continent and that literacy, though necessary, is somehow alien to the continent: "Africa needs oracy more than any other community in the world" (Zirimu & Bukenya, 1986, p. 99, cited in Bamgbose, 2000, p. 3). However, Jung and Ouane (2001) point to the fact that "writing as a psychological and sociohistorical practice has been invented in only a few societies," but "borrowed and adapted" in many others and that, for development policy, it is critical we understand "the mechanisms of literacy transfer from one culture to another" (pp. 320–321). With the rediscovery of the Timbuktu manuscripts in Mali we are presented with unfolding documentation of the rich and varied African literacy practices that formed part of social, political and economic life in the Sahel region from the 12th century to the 16th century. This provides evidence "that it never was true that African civilizations relied on oral traditions" (Dijan, 2004, p. 10). But colonial and apartheid policies ensured a deep rupture of "transfer" to other parts of Africa, particularly subSaharan Africa, which in some ways, despite "modernization," has continued to deepen through the post-colonial language and literacy policies of many countries. This understanding is my point of departure for deliberating on early literacy development in Africa.

Language Medium and Beliefs about Literacy

Besides poverty, two intrinsically related issues have affected and continue to affect movements to integrate reading and writing into daily life in many parts of Africa. One is language, a deeply complex and political issue (Bamgbose, 2000, p. 2). The insidious consequences of being under colonialism and after independence in many cases is that most people have been taught to read and write in unfamiliar, ex-colonial languages (rather than their own mother tongues). These realities are often not faced head on, and literacy is discussed and dealt with as if it were separate and unconnected to the languages of instruction. Yet, in most African countries, "subtractive" school language policies have serious implications for literacy learning. Young children are forced to either "sink or swim" as they start learning through English, French, or Portuguese from the first day of primary school, or at best, they have had to "switch" to the ex-colonial language after 3 years of mother tongue education.

The other issue relates to people's everyday beliefs about literacy, and the effectiveness of the pedagogical approaches that arise from particular views. Two major theoretical positions occupy the paradigmatic space that determines how literacy is viewed (Edelsky, 1991). Brian Street (1984) terms these "autonomous" and "ideological" models of literacy. The more widely entrenched "autonomous" model is the hegemonic model in Africa today—it involves us in talk about "spreading literacy" like a force of good, or "eradicating illiteracy" as if it was a disease (Wagner, 2000, p. 4) or even "breaking the back of illiteracy" as if it were an evil (Asmal, 2001, p. 3).

From an autonomous model perspective, literacy is understood to be unconnected to any specific context. People can only use literacy once they have been taught the component technical skills. The assumption is that literacy by itself has transformative powers over people's lives—such as enhancing the cognitive skills of poor people and improving their chances of getting work irrespective of the social and economic conditions that gave rise to their particular situation (Street, 2003, p. 1). In terms of early literacy learning, the various methods that tend to be broadly called behaviourist, skills-based or phonics methods fall under this model.

The "ideological" model, in contrast, sees literacy as social and cultural in nature and forming part of people's daily life practices (Barton, 1994; Heath, 1983; Street 1984). People have multiple literacies rather than any one single literacy, and these are always "varying according to time and space, but also contested in relations of power" (Street, 2003, p. 1). Skills are learned as you use them to do something personally meaningful and/or economically useful. The focus is on what people *do with* literacy from particular political and ideological and economic positions (Barton & Hamilton, 2000, p. 7) rather than on what literacy can do for people.

Emergent literacy or whole language perspectives are ones that see young children constructing their own literacy in personally useful and meaningful ways as part of developmental, personal, social, and cultural learning processes (Goodman, 1986; Hall, 1987; Holdaway, 1979; Taylor, 1983).There is much synergy and overlap between such early childhood literacy conceptualizations and views of literacy as social and cultural practice. It is the conceptions of literacy that fall under the social and cultural ideological model that have recently begun influencing discussion and practice in African development programmes and education for adults and children, in both formal and non-formal situations (Bloch, 2002b; Jung & Ouane, 2001, p. 320–335; Wagner, 2000).

Environments for Literacy

If we accept that literacy forms part of people's daily social and cultural practices, the nature of the environments that people find themselves in contribute hugely to the development of literate behaviour and habits. The kinds of environments that the majority of African children grow up in are "print scarce." in their mother tongues or other familiar African languages (Bloch, 2005b, p.13). Particularly in rural areas, but even in peri-urban and urban settings, print that might be abundant tends to be in English or another ex-colonial language. Yet it is in print that the power and status functions of language are clearest. This is simply but profoundly illustrated by an analysis of the genres of public signage where African languages are *always* used. For instance, in the Western Cape Province of South Africa, where English, Afrikaans and Xhosa are spoken, Xhosa is always on signs with negative messages such as "no dumping," "no jobs," or "danger." Conversely, packaging of goods, "junk mail,", advertisements (apart from phenomena such as HIV/AIDS), newspapers and magazines are mainly in English and Afrikaans, the languages of high status Learning to read and write is greatly facilitated in situations where the language in print form is valued, used, and displayed (Ngugi 1994, p. 17) and forms part of regular sociocultural activities. Denny Taylor (1983) explains this disconnect between language and literacy:

> [T]he question emerges of whether we can seriously expect children who have never experienced or have limited experience of reading and writing as complex cultural activities to successfully learn to read and write from the narrowly defined pedagogical practices of our schools. Can we teach children on an individual level of intrapersonal processes what they have never experienced on a social level as interpersonal processes of functional unity in their everyday lives? (pp. 90–91)

For us in Africa, this is a sobering question. Globalization and present economic policies force African societies to compete for limited resources in a shrinking world. It is therefore correct and necessary that we argue and struggle for the growth and rooting of literacy practices across Africa (Bamgbose, 2000, p. 3). Yet we can see how the rapid imposition of Universal Primary Education (UPE) in Africa, carried out through anti-pedagogical language policies, has been in many ways a misguided, generally ignorant and often a brutal extension of "schooled literacy" across vastly diverse social and cultural terrains. The effects of such "modern education," as Margaret Mead (1943, p. 627, cited in Taylor, 1983, p. 79) already warned in 1943, is to deepen the "discontinuities" in the lives of many people.

In Africa, societal intellectual output suffers the scars left by the dulling of the creative impetus of many teachers and children. This is extraordinarily difficult to address, in no small part because of what Ngugi wa Thiong'o (1994) has called the "colonised mind" and Neville Alexander (2002, p. 119) has termed a "static maintenance syndrome" where people keep their languages alive largely for oral, home, and community functions but see no point in trying to develop and modernize them for high-status, often print-related functions. Furthermore, although Africa has a rich oral literature tradition, slavish interpretations of restricted pedagogy, taught in languages that neither teachers or children knew well, served to blind us to the greatest strength of African education—the wisdoms and potentials of oral stories both at personal and systemic levels for building bridges to literacy (Bloch, 2005a, pp. 69–70).

The widespread perception has been that on school entry at age 6 or 7 would be the right time for children to be taught how to read and write by teachers trained to impart the basics—sets of mechanical and phonic skills that had to be delivered from simple to complex and from part to whole. Essentially, this amounted in the first few years of school to large doses of "instructional nonsense" (Edelsky, 1991, p. 69)—consisting of phonics instruction, letter formation, and handwriting practice. In this rigid framework, which has fetishized "formal learning" as the real work of school, the importance of imagination, play, and stories for young children has been sorely neglected.

There has been no space to recognise that orality, rather than being inferior to literacy, has its own "rich store" of orature—rhymes, riddles, and stories (Ngugi, 1994, p. 23) and at an individual level, provides "powerful and effective mental strategies" (Egan, 1987, p. 181). A particularly detrimental part of this situation has been the ongoing but somehow silent collusion by the educational establishment with publishers away from developing a written African children's literature, and towards accepting the primacy of textbooks, often full of "nothing to read" for beginning literacy.

Decontextualized methods can be more or less successful for children from literate, print-rich (Hudelson, 1994, cited in Baker,1996) home backgrounds who experience reading and writing, usually in mother tongue as part of "normal" everyday life. These children "naturally" imbibe knowledge about the various cultural uses and values literacy has for families and friends (Taylor, 1983). Somehow, they just get to know conventions of print (Clay, 1991, pp. 141–154) and understand its importance. This knowledge forms the sturdy scaffold—often invisible to the teacher—for the formal exercises in class. However, the many African language speaking children who have orally oriented sociocultural realities are in very different positions. Often their first experience with written language is at school. Faced with repetitive and senseless exercises, they have little if any chance of catching a glimpse of a storybook or any other sensible text in a language they know. Under such conditions, it is not surprising that many children do not learn to read and write. The research and practical interventions discussed below came into existence because of PRAESA's intention to try out alternative, holistic approaches to literacy teaching and learning.

Lessons Learned from Research and Practical Interventions

In 1994, as the new government took office, a period of policy and curriculum reform began, which offered conceptual and actual space for intensified research, debate, and action. (For an analysis and description of educational struggle work prior to 1994, see Christie, 1991.) In order for the indigenous African languages to be given equal status to English and Afrikaans, 11 official languages were proclaimed and a Language in Education Policy (LiEP) was promulgated in 1997. These initiatives followed the constitutional obligation to (a) recognize our cultural diversity as a valuable asset, (b) promote multilingualism, (c) enhance the development of African languages, and (d) encourage respect for all languages used in the country. The LiEP supports and promotes "additive approaches to bilingualism" providing extremely positive opportunities for improvement. However, implementation of the LiEP has been extremely slow. Its policies were not developed in synchrony with the outcomes-based education curriculum, called Curriculum 2005, that was adopted in 1996. A period of struggle followed that involved language activists working to convince national and provincial departments of education that language policy implementation and curriculum change are intimately related and that in a multilingual society like South Africa, teacher trainers and teachers need to understand mother tongue teaching as well as bilingualism and biliteracy.

In 1995 PRAESA conducted research on a select number of preschool and grade one previously "White" and "colored" multilingual schools in Cape Town. Staff in such schools had not received training for multilingual classroom teaching. They had problems with the now legitimate "influx" of African language speaking children, seeking a better education than that which the townships could provide. Teachers who had been accustomed to "homogeneous" groups of children were not prepared for the linguistic and cultural mix that they found themselves facing in the classroom each morning. Information gathered from classroom observations and interviews with teachers confirmed our suspicion that many teachers were in desperate need of support and training in such areas as first and second language teaching methods, strategies for teaching emergent literacyin multilingual classrooms, and the management of diversity in appropriate and sensitive ways.

The research also indicated an urgent need to provide information for parents and teachers about the new Language in Education Policy, i.e. the benefits of mother tongue and bilingual education. Apartheid education had left many parents and teachers with the impression that mother tongue education was the same thing as Bantu education. Given the deeply oblique complexities of language, their initial tendency was to blame schooling problems on mother tongue education, an understandable but nonetheless incorrect view. The challenge we were, and still are dealing with is one of working out how to move from the existing situation where the ex-colonial languages dominate to one where the indigenous languages of Africa become dominant (Alexander & Bloch, 2004, p. 5). But at the same time, the situation was not then, and is not now, one of using *either* the African languages (mother tongues) *or* English but both mother tongue *and* English, an additive bilingualism, or mother tongue-based bilingual approach.

Mother tongue experimental studies have been carried out in several African countries (Akinnaso, 1993; Bamgbose, 2000). Most of these countries concentrated on programs that teach through the mother tongue only for the first 3 years of primary school. An important exception is Akinnaso's (1993) 6-year Ife project in Nigeria. From a pedagogical perspective, mother tongue teaching for the first 3 years of schooling is less than ideal, for research indicates that the skills required in an additional language for academic learning take on average 5 or more years to develop (Ramirez, 1992). Despite these limitations, the research shows that the learning of other languages is not hindered by the use of mother tongue and represents significant steps in what are often difficult conditions, where the political leadership in effect favors schooling for all in the ex-colonial language, which can ever only serve the interest of small elite. In South Africa, we have a history of additive bilingual education to learn from, first during the 19th century for Dutch speaking children and later for English and Afrikaans speakers (Heugh, 2002). PRAESA's Battswood Biliteracy Project, the Free Reading in Schools Project, and the Culture of Reading Project, which I discuss next, have all been attempts both to deepen our knowledge of additive bilingual education and to create models that can be learnt from and adapted to suit various contexts.

The Battswood Biliteracy Project (1998–2003)

In 1998 PRAESA initiated a development research project with the intention of raising the status of Xhosa by using it as a co-teaching medium alongside English in an ex-"colored" English-medium school. During the 6 years of work in the Battswood Biliteracy Project, we followed a mixed class of Xhosa and "English" speaking children in grades one through six. (Most of these "English" speaking children were, in fact, brought up at home bilingually in Afrikaans and English.) We used Xhosa as one of the languages of teaching for initial reading and writing, alongside English, which was the official teaching medium of the school and also introduced Xhosa as an additional language to the "English" speaking children In this way, we challenged the "normal" situation in mixed language classrooms, where Xhosa speaking children are taught to read and write only in English.

One approach was to nurture and support a Xhosa speaking teacher, Ntombizanele Nkence (known by all as Teacher Ntombi), to team teach with the resident English speaking teacher. We wanted to find out how children from relatively "print-scarce" homes would respond to emergent literacy approaches which allowed them to risk expressing themselves by communicating in writing both Xhosa and English. At the time, and even now, most children in orthodox classes are still only able to copy words and sentences by the end of the third grade because there is little or no emphasis on communication and meaning making through writing.

We challenged the following existing notions and classroom practices about initial reading and writing methods:

- Having some mother tongue teaching means less English learning—therefore keep the mother tongue out of the classroom.
- Children need to be taught through structured phonics-based methods because meaningful reading and writing can only come after the prerequisite technical skills have been set in place.
- Children become confused if they learn to read and write simultaneously in their mother tongue and an additional language. Thus, rather start with English literacy from grade 1 and don't "burden" them with the phonics and syntax of two languages.
- Children should be introduced to a second language orally followed by writing, therefore do only oral communication until children know some of the language.

The project gave rise to several insights, which I now summarize. (See Bloch & Alexander, 2003, for a more detailed analysis.)

We learned how to use an emergent literacy approach to motivate children, most of whom came from "low-literacy" homes, to read and write for personally meaningful reasons. We found that critical steps included:

- creating a print-rich environment in Xhosa, English, and Afrikaans
- hunting for Xhosa and English (and Afrikaans) stories to create a classroom library (still a rarity in most classrooms across subSaharan Africa) and making our own reading materials
- creating daily time for the teachers to read stories to the children in both Xhosa and English and for the children to explore books alone and with friends
- introducing interactive writing (Robinson, et al., 1990) as a way to stimulate (a) writing in both languages, (b) risk taking, the use of invented spellings, and (c) one-to-one nurturing (Bloch, 2002a).

We also learned how Teacher Ntombi's own orientation to literacy and learning shifted as she took on the responsibility of communicating with the children in writing. They wrote to one another in journals over 5 years. During this time, she learned to write thoughtfully back to what each child was saying to her and came to realize how important this was as she experienced positive reinforcement from the children's initiatives and responses to her (Bloch & Alexander, 2003). As they grew to trust her, many children shared their concerns and asked for advice about their lives. They constantly showed that they loved and appreciated her, and this showed how nurturing and meaningful interaction can assist learning. The writing process also encouraged Teacher Ntombi to work on technical aspects of her own writing, such as legibility, and using correct spelling and punctuation. Because of the relatively few close engagements with print that "our" children are exposed to, we felt that every opportunity to demonstrate conventional spelling was significant.

Ntombi also had to be assertive about being a Xhosa writing role model with some children who tended to want to use English. Although there were a few children who thought English was "better" than Xhosa, she never forced them into using a particular language, but did try to persuade those who were resistant by consistently answering or initiating in Xhosa.

We learned how difficult but also important it is to involve parents and caregivers in reading with the children. Although most parents came to be supportive about their children learning to read and write in two languages, our attempts to bring them into the classroom to share stories and read were largely unimpressive. We knew that we were expecting a lot, as most Xhosa speaking families lived very far from the school and would have had to struggle to find the taxi or train fare (apart from the fact that those of them who worked, had little, if any, spare time). However, we came to realize that starting small *is* significant—and that even if only one adult decides to participate, this relationship should be nurtured.

We experienced firsthand that if we wanted children to become readers in their mother tongue, they would have to have access to appropriate reading materials. Because we needed storybooks in Xhosa, we discovered how frustrating it can be to not have enough to read. The books that did exist were mainly translations from Europe, Britain and the USA, many of which contained problems with the quality of translation into Xhosa. Several stories had mistakes that we feared would "confirm" in the minds of skeptics that Xhosa could not be used in the same way as English. Arising out of our wish to give the children at Battswood opportunities to learn to read in authentic ways as well as resolve the problem that only particular types of text were available in English (Bloch & Alexander, 2003), we created and printed a trilingual year calendar in English, Afrikaans, and Xhosa to use in schools. In 1999 we produced a PRAESA Year 2000 trilingual diary for teachers (in Xhosa, Afrikaans, and English) to encourage them to value and use any or all of the three main languages of the Western Cape.

By the time the children reached the end of grade six, we had amassed documentation to illustrate that children were becoming confident and enthusiastic readers and writers of both Xhosa and English. Most were able to read and write equally in two languages, although some preferred using either one or the other language (Bloch, 2005b). The children's work showed that the development of English competence was not harmed, despite the fact that they had, unlike most African language speaking children in ex-White or colored schools, experienced a significant proportion of their teaching through Xhosa.

The Free Reading in Schools Project (2001–2004)

We knew from our own experience and from research how vital story reading is for learning and creativity; however, for some time we hesitated to "push" the storybook line, cautioned by research which argued against imposing a middle-class mode of literacy learning onto immigrant and working-class children. Instead, they promoted valuing and supporting the diversity of literacy practices in the homes of children from different cultural backgrounds (Gregory 1996; Heath, 1983). In our prior experience at Battswood, however, we had witnessed the children's enthusiasm for stories and reading in both languages. They seemed not to be view our approach as an imposition but as a welcomed extension. This, together with Krashen's (1993) research into free voluntary reading and Elley's (1991) work on the significance of free reading on first and second language learning helped us decide that this was one of the various roots of literacy (Goodman, 1984) and that African children should also have the option to read for enjoyment.

We thus conceptualized the Free Reading in Schools project (FRISC). The intention of the FRISC project was threefold: (a) to introduce and demonstrate regular reading for enjoyment in appropriate ways, mainly but not only in the mother tongue, (b) to describe its impact, and (c) to support teachers in an ongoing manner. Its actualization coincided with the Western Cape Education Department's literacy strategy for 2002–2008 that was launched in 2003 which included the compulsory introduction of a "literacy half hour" in all schools and the supplying of "100 books" over time to all primary school classrooms. Thus the FRISC provided an opportunity for PRAESA to influence the nature of the literacy half hour and to make suggestions to teachers about how to use their "100 books." Our main findings were simple. The children we observed and interacted with, loved being read to and reading for themselves in their mother tongues and in English, not least because of the sense engendered by the nurturing, non-threatening relationships that developed from regular sessions with the story reader–researcher.

We confirmed that there is not nearly enough appropriate reading material in Xhosa for regular free reading. Moreover, some teachers were unable to commit themselves to being regular reading role models. Although they expressed themselves otherwise, their *actions* suggested that they did not believe in the significance of reading for meaning and enjoyment as part of the literacy learning process. This convinced us that the teachers' own conceptions of literacy are embedded deeply within their personal language and literacy biographies, as suggested by Busch (2006). If a teacher does not know and appreciate how it feels to "get lost in a book," it is extremely difficult, even unlikely, that they are able to pass on a passion for reading to others. Jerome Bruner (1966) brings us close to the crux of the matter in his discussion of what it means to be an effective role model:

> It is not so much that the teacher provides a model to *imitate*.
> Rather it is that the teacher can become a part of the student's
> internal dialogue—somebody whose respect he [sic] wants,
> someone whose standards he wishes to make his own. (p. 124)

A challenge across Africa continues to be how to provide the kinds of interactive, "effective competence" model for teachers and family members in large enough numbers.

The Culture of Reading Project

Accepting and promoting approaches to early literacy learning that support the repositioning of stories from the periphery to the center implies that if there is not enough to read, something has to be done. A classic "chicken and egg" situation has existed in South Africa with publishers claiming there is no market for children's reading materials in African languages. Yet there can be no demand unless the benefits and joy of reading are demonstrated. The cross-disciplinary cycle of collusion (unwillingly or willingly) over time to keep children's literature "supplementary" to basic textbook production for literacy development has to be broken.

Referring to Senegal, Fagerberg-Diallo (2001) discusses the significance of the "convergence of contexts" (p. 155) for helping to root literacy as a regular community practice among a group of "new literates" and others in Pulaar, a Senegalese local language with a recent written tradition. One context was "imposed by the outside" where a national or international development project created conditions in which people needed to read to be part of the economic process. A second was "internal," created by the new readers themselves who became activists for getting others to learn to read and write the local language so as to use it in important community functions. The third context was "promoted" in the sense that during the process, good books were developed and effective teacher training was undertaken: "Very simply, the more books there are, the more that people read; and the more that they read, the more they want to continue to learn" (Fagerberg-Diallo, 2001, p. 156).

Fagerberg-Diallo also makes the point that it was in fact humor that inspired people to read the books that have been published in Pulaar since the 1990s. She quotes the following statement by an editor who read one of the most popular novels when it was still a manuscript, called *Ndikkiri Joom Moolo*:

> I would sit on the sidewalk reading from Ndikkiri. With each page I could barely keep from laughing out loud as I sat alone in the street. Each time this would happen to me, I would get up and look around to make sure no-one had noticed me, fearing that someone would think I was crazy. The next day I would entertain my friends with stories from Ndikkiri while we drank tea together. In the end, all of my friends who were literate in Pulaar could hardly wait for this book to be published. (Fagerberg-Diallo, 2001, p. 164)

We have been mindful of the fact that though such demonstrations are inspiring, getting good books into the hands of people is not enough. Those of us working in literacy education have all heard anecdotal evidence from many sources about books that gather dust "in the principal's office," "the storeroom," or "in the teacher's cupboard." I recently experienced this myself in a Namibian school, when I went with a group of education officials to visit and we offered a set of new mother tongue story books to a principal who was introducing us to a class of children whose teacher was absent. The children were sitting at bare desks, with nothing to do. We suggested giving the books to them to read. The principal refused this offer, telling us that the books needed to first be catalogued. We were then shown to the "library," a storeroom, where the books were laid to rest, on a dusty shelf, next to other piles of dusty textbooks. Equally important challenges thus, are those of ensuring effective book distribution (Wagner, 2000, p. 8) and training or orienting teachers and others towards reading and writing (Bloch, 2005a, p. 77).

PRAESA is now one of a number of pioneering projects that are taking place in the interests of culture of reading development. The development of a "culture of reading" has increasingly become accepted as desirable and necessary in South African society, although it is often still assumed that reading mainly happens in English and only when children have learned to read.

Our aim has been to contribute to establishing and consolidating a culture of reading, initially by using the three languages of the Western Cape: English, Afrikaans, and Xhosa, so that we would begin to have a body of high-quality and inspiring mother tongue texts at all levels. We reasoned that collaborative ventures with publishers could encourage them to undertake the responsibility of taking risks to publish more books in African languages. Since 2003 PRAESA has published and co-published 48 publications in at least three languages for children aged from 2 to 18.

Several insights and related challenges have revealed themselves. One is that there is a great need to nurture talent. Given that reading for enjoyment is not part of many people's past or present reality, it is not surprising that there is a dearth of African literary artists with the necessary and relevant experience to write and illustrate children's stories. This domain, small as it is, is dominated by White, middle-class people like me. The relevance of children's literature for laying the intellectual foundations of African language development has to be made increasingly apparent to potential and existing African literary artists if reading and writing once again is to be rooted in modern African society. Hence, the importance of providing opportunities for developing these talents through, for example, writers and illustrators workshops is readily apparent.

Another crucial aspect is the promotion of translation as a tool for development. Through the efforts of "culture of reading" projects, space has been created for discussing the nature of South Africa, and more widely, African children's literature. PRAESA has also begun to explore how the "'disruptive' and reconstructive potential of translation as a social practice" (Alexander, 2005, p. 6) can be used, not only to increase the stock of books available in different languages, but also to build a sense of common identity among children from differing language and cultural backgrounds. It is for this reason that in 2004 we initiated the Stories across Africa Project as a logical progression of PRAESA's work to further create by cross-fertilization on a pan-African scale a common core of literature for children, which will be used in all of the regions of Africa. The regional teams that we have set up in north, east, west, Central and Southern Africa are collecting and translating stories that will be illustrated and published in three anthologies for children of all ages. The kinds of cultural interpretations and negotiations that arise when translation decisions are made collectively in a project such as this one mean that translation and interpretation are the archetypal forms of what we now call intercultural communication. Translation is the graphical counterpart of the oral process by which peoples have since time immemorial through interaction in countless different modalities mutually influenced and, thus, "developed" one another (Alexander, 2005, p. 7).

The production of multilingual reading materials thus becomes part of an authentic process to address the intricate work of bridging the "apparently unbridgeable rupture" between tradition and modernity in subSaharan Africa (Alexander, 2005). It involves, among other things, the reinterpretation and realignment of indigenous ideas and visual forms with those from a long tradition of European and British children's print literature that already occupies a patch, albeit a tiny one, of South African and African cultural life.

One of the challenges we face in situations of scarcity is that every effort seems to be only a "drop in the ocean," but at the same time a precious one. There is a tendency to try to achieve all things with each bit of material produced. However, we have to achieve a balance between allowing for free creative expression and making appropriate decisions that reflect considered values, positive role models, and balanced perspectives for gender, age, rural–urban setting, disability, health, religion, and so on. This is not just to be politically correct. Rather, it is a recognition that if we are to offer ways for all children to discover the joy of reading and come to experience it as personally meaningful and satisfying way, then children must be able to find something of themselves in the text. It is when stories, including both their written and visual texts, are able to reach children at an affective level, "in a warm emotional context" (Frost, Wortham, & Reifel, 2005) that they wield their magic and power.

Conclusion

There are signs that significant shifts are taking place in the literacy domain in South Africa, and in other parts of Africa. The main one, from my perspective, is that the notion of reading for enjoyment has come to be accepted in educational institutions as an important aspect of learning to read. This is a real conceptual breakthrough, even though it is going to take time and conviction to be widespread and for teachers to understand how children actually learn to read by reading and to write by writing (Smith, 1978).

In South Africa, we have definitely reached a turning point in terms of what we are looking at—this is reflected in documents such as the Western Cape Education Department (WCED) *Literacy and Numeracy Strategy 2006–2016*, which claims a constructivist perspective on learning and includes teacher support and development, changes in classroom practice, a focus on preschool/early childhood, advocacy, family and community literacy, materials provision as well as a Language-in-Education Transformation Plan that promotes mother tongue based bilingual education (WCED, 2006).

Yet practically, we know that despite the catalytic function of initiatives such as the ones described here, isolated programs are not able to become more than pockets of innovation, unless the current mode of mass education undergoes major changes. The obsessive use of standardized tests to ensure high standards of "basic literacy" across educational systems in many parts of the world, including South Africa, contradicts the information I and many others have gathered over the last decade. Referring to what she titles the "backwash of high stakes assessment", in the north, Tessa Granger (2004) says:

> Classroom practice has arguably become visibly shaped by assessment criteria leading to an instrumental approach to literacy teaching, and impacting upon teachers' understandings of the nature of literacy development. A surface approach to literacy is likely to profile forms and features of text at the expense of meaning and purpose, so that from a child's perspective, naming and knowing may appear to be given precedence over using and understanding language in meaningful contexts. (p.3)

Apart from anything else, in South African and other African settings with the enormous economic and cultural extremes that exist between urban and rural contexts, we have to question the wisdom of emphasising "performance indicators" that base themselves on "international standards" in a climate where we are trying to inspire and motivate teachers and children. The vast majority live under appalling conditions characterised by poverty, ill health and brutality. Schools are *still* horribly overcrowded and ill resourced, and teachers are *still* poorly or under trained. It would take the concerted intervention of many magicians to meet these standards now. The struggle thus remains one of continuing to push for appropriate pedagogical understandings and strategies for mother tongue-based bilingual education in a climate where there is a body of "more or less" mutual rhetoric and discourse.

Discussion Questions and Activities

1. In the chapter, I argue the importance of a child's mother tongue and of story reading for literacy learning. What are your views on this in the light of your early memories about written language learning: What was your experience of language at home and school? What access to storybooks did you have in the language/s you spoke and who read to you?
2. The significance of role models for literacy is stressed in the chapter. Can you think of any person/s who were your role models for reading and writing? What did they do and in which way/s did they influence you?
3. In the chapter, I describe and promote the view of literacy as social practice. What reasons do you have for reading and writing in your daily life, and which language/s you use? What environments and pedagogical measures encourage children to learn to read and write at the same time as they are learning the requisite skills?

358 · Carole Bloch

References

Akinnaso, F. N. (1993). Policy and Experiment in Mother Tongue Literacy in Nigeria. *International Review of Education*, 43(1), 255–285.

Alexander, N. (2005). The Potential Role of Translation as Social Practice for the Intellectualization of African Languages. Keynote address delivered at the XVII World Congress of the International Federation of Translators, Tampere, Finland, August 4–7.

———. (2002). Linguistic Rights, Language Planning and Democracy in Post-Apartheid South Africa. In S. J. Baker (Ed.). *Language Policy: Lessons from Global Models*. Monterey, CA: Monterey Institute of International Studies.

———., & Bloch, C. (2004). *Feeling at Home with Literacy in the Mother Tongue*. Keynote address to the 29th International Board on Books for Young People (IBBY), Cape Town, September 5–8.

Asmal, K. (2001). READ Education Trust Readathon Launch Speech. South African Government Information. Retrieved from www.info.gov.za/speeches/2001/010806945a1006.htm.

Baker, C. (1996). *Foundations of Bilingual Education and Bilingualism*, 2nd edn. Clevedon/Philadelphia/Adelaide: Multilingual Matters.

Bamgbose, A. (2000). *Language and Exclusion: The Consequences of Language Policies in Africa*. Münster/Hamburg/London: LIT Verlag.

Barton, D. (1994). *Literacy. An Introduction to the Ecology of Written Language*. Malden, MA: Blackwell.

———, & Hamilton, M. (2000). Literacy Practices. In D. Barton, M. Hamilton, & R. Ivanic (Eds.). Situated Literacies. Reading and Writing in Context. London and New York: Routledge.

Bloch, C. (2005a). Building Bridges between Oral and Written Language: Facilitating Reading Opportunities for Children in Africa. In N. Alexander (Ed.). *Mother Tongue Based Bilingual Education in Southern Africa. The Dynamics of Implementation*. Frankfurt-am-Main/Cape Town: Multilingualism Network.

———. (2005b). Enabling Effective Literacy Learning in Multilingual South African Early Childhood Classrooms. PRAESA Occasional Papers, No.16.

———. (2002a). A Case Study of Xhosa and English Biliteracy in the Foundation Phase Versus English as a Medium of Destruction. In K. Heugh (Ed.). *Perspectives in Education, Special Issue: Many Languages in Education*, 20.

———. (2002b). Concepts of Early Childhood Development (ECD), Literacy Learning and Materials Development in Multilingual Settings. PRAESA Occasional Papers, No. 8.

———, & Alexander, N. (2003). Aluta Continua: The Relevance of the Continua of Biliteracy to South African Multilingual Schools. In N. Hornberger (Ed.). *Continua of Biliteracy: An Ecological Framework for Educational Policy, Research, and Practice in Multilingual Settings*. Clevedon: Multilingual Matters.

Bruner, J. (1966). *Toward a Theory of Instruction*. Cambridge, MA: Cambridge University Press.

Busch, B. (2006). *Sprachen leben. Biographische Zugänge in Forschung und Bildung*. Klagenfurt: Drava.

Christie, P. (1991). *The Right to Learn: The Struggle for Education in South Africa*. Johannesburg: SACHED/Ravan.

Clay M. M. (1991). *Becoming Literate. The Construction of Inner Control*. Portsmouth, NH: Heinemann.

Dijan, J.-M. (2004). Mali: The Fabulous Past of Africa. *Le Monde Diplomatique*, August.

Edelsky, C. (1991). *With Literacy and Justice for All*. London: Falmer Press.

Egan, K. (1987). Literacy and the Oral Foundations of Education. *Harvard Educational Review*, 57(4), 445–472.

Elley, W. (1991). Acquiring Literacy in a Second Language: The Effects of Book-Based Programs. *Language Learning*, 41, 375–411.

Fagerberg-Diallo, S. (2001). Constructive Interdependence: The Response of a Senegalese Community to the Question of Why Become Literate. In D. R. Olsen, & N. Torrance (Eds.). *The Making of Literate Societies*. Oxford: Blackwell.

Frost, J. L., Wortham, S. C., & Reifel, S. (2005). *Play and Child Development*. Upper Saddle River, NJ, and Columbus, OH: Pearson/Merrill Prentice-Hall.

Goodman, K. (1986). *What's Whole in Whole Language?* Portsmouth, NH: Heinemann.

Goodman, Y. (1984). The Development of Initial Literacy. In H. Goelman, A. Oberg, & F. Smith (Eds.). *Awakening to Literacy*. Portsmouth, NH: Heinemann.

Granger, T. (2004). Introduction: Travelling across the Terrain. In T. Granger (Ed.). *The Routledge Falmer Reader in Language and Literacy.* London and New York: Routledge Falmer/Taylor & Francis Group.

Gregory, E. (1996). *Making Sense of a New World: Learning to Read in a Second Language.* London: Paul Chapman.

Hall, N. (1987). *The Emergence of Literacy.* London: Hodder & Stoughton.

Heath, S.B. (1983). *Ways With Words: Language, Life and Work in Communities and Classrooms.* Cambridge: Cambridge University Press.

Heugh, K. (2002). Revisiting Bilingual Education in and for South Africa. PRAESA Occasional Paper, No. 9.

Holdaway, D. (1979). *The Foundations of Literacy.* Sydney: Ashton Scholastic.

Jung, I., & Ouane, A. (2001). Literacy and Social Development: Policy and Implementation. In D. R. Olsen, & N. Torrance (Eds.). *The Making of Literate Societies.* Oxford: Blackwell.

Krashen, S. (1993). *The Power of Reading.* Englewood, CO: Libraries Unlimited, Inc.

Ngugi Wa Thiong'o. (1994). *Decolonizing the Mind: The Politics of Language in African Literature.* London/Portsmouth, NH: James Currey Ltd/Heinemann.

Ramirez, J. D. (1992). Executive Summary. *Bilingual Research Journal,* 16(1&2), 1–62.

Robinson, A., Crawford, L., & Hall, N. (1990). *One Day You Will No All about Me.* Cambridge: Mary Glasgow Publications.

Smith, F. (1978). *Reading.* Cambridge: Cambridge University Press.

Street, B. (1984). *Literacy in Theory and Practice* Cambridge: Cambridge University Press.

——. (1995). *Social Literacies.* London: Longman.

——. (2003). What's "New" in New Literacy Studies? Critical Approaches to Literacy in Theory and Practice. *Current Issues in Comparative Education,* 5(2), 77.

Taylor, D. (1983). *Family Literacy: Young Children Learning to Read and Write.* London: Heinemann.

Triebel, A. (2001). The Roles of Literacy Practices in the Activities and Institutions of Developed and Developing Countries. In D. R. Olsen, & N.Torrance (eds) *The Making of Literate Societies.* Oxford: Blackwell.

Wagner, D. (2000). *UNESCO World Education Forum Education for All 2000 Assessment Thematic Studies Literacy and Adult Education.* Paris: UNESCO.

Western Cape Education Department (WCED). (2004). Media statement, May 25.

24
India's Multilingualism: Paradigm and Paradox

ZARINA MANAWWAR HOCK

In 1972, NCTE's Conference on College Composition and Communication passed a landmark resolution, "The Students' Right to Their Own Language" (*SRTOL*), specific to language education in the United States. Revisiting this resolution in the twenty-first century inevitably brings its relevance into global focus. Interestingly, I find that many of the imperatives expressed in the document resonate with India's official policy on language rights, with one major difference—the United States, being essentially a monolingual society, addresses *dialect* difference in *SRTOL*: "A nation proud of its diverse heritage and its cultural and racial variety will preserve its heritage of dialects. We affirm strongly that teachers must have the experiences and training that will enable them to respect diversity and uphold the right of students to their own language" (CCCC, 1974). If one were to substitute "languages" for "dialects" this statement could comfortably fit into the Indian Constitution, which was put into place in 1950, two-and- a-half years after India won independence from Britain. But comparisons can be dangerously facile, and one must look at India and her language situation more as a study in contrasts, which nevertheless can be insightful. Globalization in the twenty-first century makes such reflection essential.

India, which occupies a large part of the Indian subcontinent, is more akin to Europe in that her people are richly varied in religions, languages, dialects, ethnicities, and physical features. With a known history that goes back several millennia BCE, language attitudes and loyalties to ethnicity, religion, and caste are deep-rooted and intertwined. India's diversity has been called both her strength and her weakness. Never is this clearer than in the matter of language, which, as South Asia scholar Harold Schiffman says, "unites the well-known diversity-within-unity paradox that India is famous for" (Schiffman, 1996, p.156). Given the complexity and the abundance of literature on the subject, I have decided to confine this chapter to just a few "meditations" on the multilingual character of the Indian paradigm.

Going to School in India: Three Stories

Rajeshwari, Mahendra, and I were all born and educated in India in the decade in which India won freedom from British colonial rule and became an independent nation. We all have advanced degrees and have found satisfying careers in the

United States. Our individual language-related schooling was, however, completely different.

A Very Proper Convent Education

A group of schoolgirls stands in a semi-circle in the school hall. Impeccably dressed in the school uniform—blue jumpers (called "tunics"), white blouses and ties, and navy blazers adorned with the school crest and its Latin motto. They're singing "Bonnie Charlie" in supposedly Scots dialect accompanied by Sister Mary Cecil on the piano and Sister Ancilla conducting. The music examiner sits at a table and listens carefully, taking notes. At the end, he announces that the students have passed with flying colors. He'll leave his comments with the music teacher. He does have a small suggestion, he says good-naturedly: "Better loved" should be pronounced "Better looved" in Scots. What's strange about this story? For one thing, the students are almost all brown skinned and Indian (a few are Anglo-Indian). For another, I am one of those brown schoolgirls and this is Lucknow, India. The examiner is a teacher of music sent overseas by Trinity College, Cambridge, England, to tour British schools spread out through the British Commonwealth and to grade the students by standards set by Cambridge University.

For many urban families in India, the convent school in particular, though remote in many ways from Indian culture, was the school of choice for girls. British rule in India brought with it the British educational system, and the missionaries who came to India were largely responsible for setting up a genre of school similar to the British "public schools," which were in fact private schools available by and large to the privileged.

Although government-run "vernacular schools" (as they were called) were also an option, and many families who were strongly nationalist sent their children to such schools to be educated in their native language, my parents chose to send me to a convent. Ours was run by Irish nuns. The language of instruction was English, and Hindi, our native language, was taught only as a subject.

To graduate high school, we took examinations that were sent out from Cambridge University, England, which earned us the Overseas Certificate Examination of Cambridge. We "sat for" our exams in December and received our results in February of the following year. Needless to say, waiting for the results in an era before computers, easy phone connections, and faxes was excruciating.

We memorized poems about fluttering golden daffodils (unknown in our part of the world) and Grecian urns and sang not only of Bonnie Prince Charlie but of Killarney. And the most favored children's books were—and still are for children from these schools—by Enid Blyton. As young adults and beyond, our love affair with P. G. Wodehouse never ceased. "If the British taught us their literature to colonise our minds," says Shashi Tharoor, writer and a former representative of the United Nations, "it was only natural that Indians would enjoy a writer who used language as Wodehouse did — playing with its rich storehouse of classical precedents, mockingly subverting the very canons colonialism had taught us we were supposed to venerate" (Tharoor, 2002, p. 9). We absorbed copious amounts about the British Commonwealth, but we also learned Indian history and geography; and — after the British left—classical Indian dance. Thankfully, such English-medium schools have since become far more Indian in culture and content, and the exams are no longer administered by Cambridge University.

The children who went to such schools were from all religious groups found in India—Hindu, Muslim, Christian, Sikh, Jewish, Parsi, Jain, and the common culture that was fostered was of an English-speaking group who were able to communicate across ethnic boundaries, retaining their essential ethnicity and religious heritage but acquiring an English veneer as well. Our Irish Convent, like all such schools, recognized the many religious and cultural holidays that India enthusiastically observes—Holi, Diwaali, Eid, Guru Nanak's birthday, Christmas, Easter, and others. At our convent, we had the added bonus of St. Patrick's Day, which we celebrated with poetry and song.

In my part of north India, the regional language of the state was Hindi-Urdu. I will not go into the distinctions between Hindi and Urdu beyond saying that they are essentially one language, with two different identities and scripts. "The languages share a virtually identical grammar and also possess a very large body of common vocabulary" (Bhatia & Koul, 2000, p. ix). Urdu draws on Arabic and Persian (hence Muslim culture); and Hindi draws on Sanskrit (hence Hindu culture). "Hindi" refers to the language spoken by a large percentage of Indians; "Hindu" refers to the dominant religion of India. Although approximately 80 percent of Indians are Hindu, their mother tongue is not necessarily Hindi. In my area, many preferred a happy mix of Hindi and Urdu, calling this language "Hindustani" (a term, favored by Mahatma Gandhi, that means "derived from Hindustan [another name for India]"). I mention this here because my parents spoke and wrote Urdu, whereas I grew up with Hindi in the classroom and Urdu at home (along with English). The city I was born in, Lucknow, was admired throughout the country for its Urdu-speaking culture and its language leisurely threaded with Persian conventions of grace and elegance. But a vibrant Hindi-speaking culture and literature existed as well.

At home we were bilingual, speaking Hindustani and English interchangeably. Although they strongly supported our English education, our parents were adamant about the correct use of our native language, which we spoke frequently and fluently with family and friends and the wider community. No affectations about not speaking our mother tongue were tolerated.

My education prepared me and those with like education to communicate confidently and very well in English. This has proved enormously valuable both in India and in the United States, where it has opened many cultural and professional doors. Certainly, my grounding in English privileged me as Senior Editor at the National Council of Teachers of English and allowed me to write and speak with assurance about language and style for this professional organization. Though the language of my intellectual expression is English, I remain natively bilingual. Often at night when falling asleep, the language of thought, before I enter the world of dreams, is Hindustani.

Beating the Odds

The English way is not the only way to acquire an education in India. While I was studying in the convent, Mahendra was going to school in another part of the same state, approximately 180 miles to the west, in a small town called Hathras, small not so much in population, as in resources and worldview. Essentially, his upbringing was shaped by rural India. Unlike the United States, in India the differences between rural and urban are qualitatively vast. This was particularly so at the time that Mahendra was growing up, in immediately post-British India.

Mahendra had few educational choices in his hometown, and there were no English-medium schools. Home-schooled by his mother in Hindi at primary level, he entered the local school at 5th grade. The language of the home was a regional dialect of Hindi called Braj Bhasa, and the language of school was standard Hindi. Mahendra, like many Indians, grew up bi-dialectal, making the switch to standard Hindi easily enough. Though English was not spoken in his household, his father, being a teacher with a college education, was familiar with the language and taught his son his numerals in English. That is the only contact Mahendra had with English at that age. On his first day in school, the children were asked to write their numerals. Mahendra didn't speak or read English, but he sure could write his numbers in English. He was roundly slapped by his teacher for writing in this alien language. At secondary level, Mahendra studied both English and Sanskrit as subjects, and in grades 11 and 12 used English in his math and science classes. He recalls that actual facility in English was not essential to these subjects.

His family, whom Mahendra describes as fairly typical of his hometown, did not have the resources for expensive higher education. As in many rural families, whatever money was available was invested in education for the men folk, so Mahendra had the option to go to a small, inexpensive university not far away. He complied, but his dream was to study at Roorkee, the finest college of engineering in India at that time (and still rated top-notch). The costs being prohibitive, coming up with the necessary funds posed a challenge. Mahendra was never one to think small. With neither money nor the background in English that prestige schools like Roorkee catered to, he qualified for that engineering school and completed his degree with financial support from his uncle. He became the first person to go to engineering college from his hometown. But he was far from satisfied. After Roorkee, Mahendra qualified for a prestigious position in the competitive Indian Railway Service. This again was an enormous achievement for someone who came from a rural background. Taking a leave of absence from his job, he pursued a PhD in the United States and ultimately resigned from the Indian Railway Service to become an academic at a U.S. university.

Now, as Preston Wade Professor of Engineering at Virginia Tech, he looks back at the trajectory of his education and admits that for him the path was never easy. He doesn't doubt that Roorkee would have been easier had he studied in an English-medium school. Privileged students from English-medium schools were most readily admitted to that prestigious institution. Despite the scales being tipped against him, Mahendra never felt threatened by his limitations with the language;

the emphasis on technology and engineering allowed him to achieve enormous success without too much dependence on English.

It's been a challenging road from Hathras to Blacksburg. As someone who undertakes research, publishes, teaches, and brings in grants from the National Science Foundation, Mahendra has traveled successfully through the Indian and American systems. He recalls his struggle with the definite and indefinite article in English while writing his dissertation at the University of Illinois. Giving up, he randomly sprinkled "a," "the," and "zero article" before the nouns in his text and hoped for the best. He wryly admits that he still hasn't mastered the use of the article. In the grand scheme of his life, though, it matters little; and if I know Mahendra, he will meet this challenge as he has all the others.

A Richly Multilingual Education

In the city of Amravati, some 455 miles southwest of Lucknow, in a state whose language was Marathi, Rajeshwari was also going to school in the early years of India's independence. Of the three of us featured in these narratives, Rajeshwari had the schooling that was the most atypical and extraordinary. Her parents, both professionals, were profoundly influenced by the surge of nationalism sweeping the country, joining Mahatma Gandhi's powerful yet peaceful civil disobedience effort known as the "Quit India" movement. Pride in their native language(s) was inextricably linked to their pride in nationhood and to their identity. Rajeshwari's attorney father brought his native Hindi to the home culture, and her mother, an officer in the Education Department, spoke Marathi as her first language. No one in the family was monolingual. In fact, two dialects of Hindi were also spoken at home, as in Mahendra's case.

The household consisted not only of Rajeshwari and her siblings but children of the extended family as well, fifteen all told. Although Rajeshwari's parents had both attended English schools, unlike most Indians with this background, they decided to offer their children several educational choices. Since Amravati was a leading center of education, there was no shortage of schools to select from. The culture of the city supported educational endeavor. So, each of the fifteen children, when the time was ripe, was asked to select a school according to the language preferred for the medium of instruction—English, Hindi, or Marathi. Rajeshwari chose the Marathi school. "Since we were growing up in a multilingual household, it was quite natural for us to discuss the choice of school with our parents," she says. She didn't study English until 6th grade. Her sister chose an English-medium school; others in the household chose the Hindi school. Homework in the household happened in three different languages, with the older children overseeing the work of the younger ones.

Rajeshwari's parents believed that a grounding in Indian languages was a grounding in Indian culture. They were also convinced that any language well-learned would prepare you for any other language, and the children were all required to take proficiency exams in the languages other than the one they had chosen to be schooled in.

The language in college for Rajeshwari was also Marathi, though philosophy and logic were taught in English; and her major was Sanskrit. For her first PhD (in India), her instruction and studies were in Marathi and Sanskrit. Her first teaching appointment was in a college in Bombay, and at that time all Bombay colleges required English as the medium of instruction. Rajeshwari, with her solid language training, was capable of meeting that requirement. Her second PhD was at the University of Illinois. By then, using English was hardly a challenge.

Rajeshwari has never doubted the unflinching faith of her parents in multilingualism and in the value of learning one's native languages. Today, she looks back with gratitude at the preparation and confidence her parents gave her. Her language education enabled her to get to where she is today—writer, scholar, and professor of religious studies and linguistics at the University of Illinois (Urbana-Champaign). She writes poetry in Marathi, Hindi, and Sanskrit. She is now beginning to write poetry in English. And poetry, as we know, is a powerful expression of language.

These sketches of language schooling are instantiations of the Indian educational system, pointing to the "wide spectrum of linguistic and cultural variation in everyday life [that] denotes the over-arcing [sic] reality of the subcontinent" (Khubchandani, 2005, p. 5). Not that multilingualism is unknown in other countries. Canada, Switzerland, Russia, Belgium, and the Tyrol region of Northern Italy (see Gerda Videsott in this collection) offer other paradigms of language diversity in education. And even in an essentially monolingual society such as the United States, we see plenty of evidence of multilingual, bilingual, and bidialectal speakers. Perhaps what is different in India is that the *educational system*—assuming you have access to it—so naturally allows its students to travel down various language highways.

For better or for worse, India has demonstrated what Nobel Laureate and economist Amartya Sen describes as "the inclusiveness of pluralist toleration" (Sen, 2005, p. 34). We have evidence that even as far back as the 6th century BCE the Indian emperor Ashoka, in promoting his edicts, insisted that they be communicated in the languages of his many peoples. (Mallikarjun, 2004, para. 1).

India, then, is a land where multiple language situations coexist. For those who do have access to education (and there are many who don't), some may enjoy the benefit of an English education; others will be privileged to choose among several languages for their schooling; still others may have limited access and must jump over the barriers of language.

There is *no monolingual road* to education. And while not all the stories are stories of success, it is hard *not* to believe in the *normalness* of multilingualism.

Constitutional Privilege and Other Safeguards: Dreams and Reality

When India became independent of British rule in 1947, she established herself as a sovereign democratic republic, with a constitution that was mindful of the multicultural, multiethnic, and multilingual character of her peoples. The right to one's language and access to education in one's mother tongue, therefore, receive much attention. "Given the great diversity of India, some assurance was needed in its uniting under a democratic government that the rights of all peoples would be protected. . . . the Constitution of India provides explicit guarantees for protecting the interests of minorities" (Groff, 2003, pp. 5-6). These constitutional safeguards served an important function—to recognize and protect India's diversity, but not to slice the language onion too fine and thus to split the country apart. The ideal was to create language "policies that follow[ed] the logic of language ecology, which recognizes ethnic, cultural and linguistic pluralism as resource for nation-building" (Bhatt, 2005, p. 1). Unfortunately, as with many ideals, these too were tarnished in the implementation, as the examples below illustrate.

Official Languages, Ensuing Discontents

To affirm and maintain India's multilingual culture, the framers of the constitution recognized 14 official languages (now amended to 22), which were listed in the famous Eighth Schedule of the constitution. These official languages, generally affiliated with different regions or states, were "to be used for all or any of the official purposes of that State" (Government of India, 1949, Article 345). Hindi was declared the official language of the Indian Union. And English was deemed an additional official language, serving as a "link language" for a period of fifteen years particularly for non-Hindi speaking areas (Government of India, 1949, Article 343).

Hindi was also the regional language in several states. Since it was spoken by a comparatively large percentage (currently estimated at approximately 40 percent), the decision seemed logical at the time. But language loyalties, which send their roots deep into a culture, often run counter to logic.

The decision to make Hindi the *only* official language of the Indian Union once the fifteen-year period was over caused an uproar among non-Hindi speakers, particularly in South India, where speakers of Tamil, an ancient language with a classical tradition, objected vehemently to the hegemony that Hindi would impose. These protests erupted volcanically fifteen years later when the "expiration date" for English drew near. The demonstrations against Hindi—the marches, strikes, boycotts, and even suicide-immolations—will forever be reminders of the deep and emotional role that language plays in India (Guha, 2005). The nation was polarized between non-Hindi speakers who defiantly clung to English as the language of wider communication, and militant Hindi nationalists who arrogantly insisted on imposing their preferred variety of Hindi, bureaucratic and awkwardly Sanskritized, on all the states in the Union. Eventually, a compromise was reached, and English was firmly ensconced as an official link language in the Indian Union, coexisting with Hindi.

The framers of the constitution had dreamed of a simpler solution to linguistic diversity and language rights than was possible to achieve in a complex linguistic culture. The reality on the ground had clearly proved to be different.

"Minority" Languages

In other ways, too, the constitution's attempt to simplify India's linguistic complexity were well-intentioned but misguided. As mentioned, fourteen languages had been originally listed in the constitution; they represented the dominant regional cultures, accounting for approximately 96 per cent of the country's population (Bhatt, 2005, p. 5). This still left unnamed over a hundred languages of indigenous populations (referred to as "tribal"), along with several other viable languages that were clustered under the umbrella of one or another language recognized in the Eighth Schedule of the Indian constitution. To use an Indian concept, a language caste system was created separating the languages that had a "great tradition" (Srivastava, 1989, p. 20) codified in their literatures and their other writings from those whose literatures were primarily oral.

It is important to emphasize that despite omission from the Eighth Schedule, tribal-language communities were by no means ignored by the constitution. In fact, the constitution guarantees the protection of minority languages, emphasizing the right of minorities to receive an education in their mother tongue (Groff, 2003, pp. 5-6). And yet despite the intent, educators and scholars point to the disconnect between intention and implementation, particularly in the case of mother-tongue education. For the most part, qualified teachers are not available, students suffer from low self-esteem and are unmotivated to learn, and textbooks in the particular languages are lacking or culturally irrelevant (Gautam, 2003; Nambissan, 2000). Many linguists predict that the failure to adequately support the languages of tribal communities in India will lead to the extinction of these languages.

Indians, never a people to be less than voluble, have contested these educational inequities, and sixty years after the constitution was adopted, the debates continue. Language planners recognize that "given the functionally unequal status of minority languages relative to the dominant regional languages, language planning for minority languages becomes critical for their survival" (Bhatt & Mahboob, 2008, p. 133) as does consistent implementation.

The Three-Language Formula

Aside from the constitution, the ongoing efforts to negotiate India's language complexity have come through language policies, recommendations, and directives. The best-known attempt at equity is the Three-Language Formula, which requires —for all students—"the study of a modern Indian language, preferably one of the Southern languages, apart from Hindi and English in the Hindi speaking states, and of Hindi along with the regional language and English in the non-Hindi speaking states" (Government of India, 1968, p.3). Once again, like many official-policy attempts, this one must be commended for its support of language rights even as one acknowledges its considerable failure. Although "the Three Language Formula has neither been implemented in letter and spirit nor has it led to the effects its proponents thought that it would" (Mallikarjun, 2001, Introduction), it does demonstrate the government's commitment to multilingual education. At the very least, it can be viewed as "a negotiated outcome, a middle way between unfettered diversity and monolingualism" (Schiffman, 1996, p. 172).

To sum up, India's language complexities will continue to challenge her people. Justly characterized by Amartya Sen as an argumentative democracy, India will continue to debate and define language issues—through legislation and education commissions, as well as through public discourse. *Language matters* in India. Enormously. "In South Asia [in this case India] ... one's position within society, especially within the complex caste system, has traditionally been intimately tied up with language. ... Religious affiliation, too, is often linked to language" (Hock & Joseph, 1996, p. 394). And yet, remarkably, in a land where language pride can turn to arrogance and where resentment against another language group can cause a riot, "linguistic accommodation" ultimately prevails (Bhatia & Ritchie, 2004, p. 795). Language rights are continually negotiated—officially and unofficially, personally and politically—and the price of maintaining equity in multilingualism is continuous vigilance.

Inevitably, a comparison with the world's other large democracy is in order. Where the United States does not name any official language in its constitution, India has devoted considerable space both to specify its languages and to protect minorities' language rights. Each has had its problems. U.S. policy "is (or at least used to be characterized as) superficially tolerant of linguistic diversity, and ... does not explicitly enshrine English or any other language as *primus inter pares* [first among equals]. Yet attempts to stretch this 'tolerance' policy are met with increasing intolerance" (Schiffman, 1996, p. 279). In India, it is laudable that the Indian constitution has guaranteed language rights to its multilingual people and also that the Union (Federal) government continues to issue language policies and directives relative to individual language rights and mother tongue education, as well as to multilingual education for every student. It is less than laudable that the goals are only partially realized.

The languages most endangered in both countries are the languages of disempowered groups. In India, despite constitutional safeguards and governmental directives, the pressure to assimilate and to compete within the system has resulted in the ultimate irony, as Anvita Abbi, scholar of endangered Indian languages, points out: "The speakers of the so-called minor languages themselves do not wish to educate their children in their respective mother tongues" (Abbi, 2004, p.4). In the United States and in India, the link between power and privileged languages is all too apparent. Native American languages in the United States face the same risk of erosion and extinction as do the languages of marginalized groups in India.

The Empire Strikes Back or The Most Peculiar Case of English

India is a land long accustomed to foreign invaders and visitors, who began to appear no later than the first millennium BCE; diverse groups of settlers have usually assimilated (though Alexander the Great did call it quits), bringing their cultures and languages to mingle with those of the Subcontinent. In the early 1600s, it was Britain's turn (along with the French and the Portuguese). English traders arrived under the banner of the British East India Company. Along with their appetite for trade and spices, they brought their language too. This language began to play an increasing role in India as the East India Company became more and more entangled in Indian politics and government. In 1858, the

British government formally took control of India from the Company after an unsuccessful uprising by the Indians against their occupiers in 1857.

And thus was born the British Raj. India became the Jewel in the Crown of the British Empire, and Queen Victoria was proclaimed Empress of India.

The Language of the Raj

English, as in all of the British Empire, became the language of administration, of the courts, and for many, of education. In India, it joined the ranks of the many languages that had currency, rapidly becoming a prestige language.

The spread of the conqueror's language was given further impetus by "Macaulay's Minute on Indian Education" written in 1835 by a colonial representative of Britain, Thomas Babington Macaulay. In this document, rife with the prejudices of Empire, Macaulay sets forth his recommended language policy for colonial India thus:

> We must at present do our best to form a class who may be interpreters between us and the millions whom we govern; a class of persons Indian in blood and colour, but English in tastes, in opinions, in morals and in intellect. (Macaulay, 1835, p. 30)

Imperial approval of Macaulay's Minute laid the foundation for English education in India, although vernacular schools continued to function and to offer opportunities to those unwilling (for nationalistic reasons) or unable (for financial reasons) to acquire an English education. (And along the way, "Macaulay's Children" became a term used pejoratively to describe those Indians with an English education who were completely cut off from Indian culture and their native language.)

Here to Stay?

When India achieved independence from Britain, the Indian constitution, as mentioned earlier, proposed to retain English "for a period of fifteen years from the commencement of this Constitution" (Government of India, 1949, Article 343). It is now more than a half century since that declaration, and, instead of completing its anticipated years of service to the country and discreetly departing, English remains, acquiring a local habitation if not a new name.

English, which was carried as the conqueror's tool to the far reaches of the British Empire, became a powerful instrument for colonized countries during their struggle for freedom and long after. Braj Kachru, leading scholar of Indian English and proponent of "World Englishes" argues for the evolution of an Indian English whose lexicon, phonology, and syntax are visibly influenced by the context of Indian languages and cultures. He also points to the absorption of rhetorical styles from Sanskrit into Indian English. "English is no longer a foreign language in the sense in which this term is normally understood in literature. . . . What dictates norms . . . of English in India is an Indian 'grammar of culture'" (Kachru, 1992, p. 343).

In literature, fiction writers had begun to demonstrate this Indianization of English as early as the 1930s. Novelist Raja Rao in the foreword to his 1938 novel, *Kanthapura*, illuminates the process of literary writing in English:

> One has to convey in a language that is not one's own the spirit that is one's own. One has to convey the various shades and omissions of a certain thought-movement that looks maltreated in an alien language. I use the word 'alien', yet English is not really an alien language to us. It is the language of our intellectual make-up, like Sanskrit or Persian was before, but not of our emotional make-up. We are all instinctively bilingual, many of us writing in our own language and in English. We cannot write like the English. We should not. We cannot write only as Indians. We have grown to look at the large world as part of us. (Rao, 1963/1938, p.vii.)

Kachru emphasizes that this transformation of English into the "other tongue (a second or foreign language)" is a worldwide phenomenon (Kachru, 1992, p. 3). In fact, Nigerian writer Chinua Achebe's comments on African English lend further credence to this proposition: "What I . . . see is a new voice coming out of Africa, speaking of African experience in a world-wide language. So my answer to the question, *Can an African ever learn English well enough to be able to use it effectively in creative writing?* is certainly yes. If on the other hand you ask: *Can he ever learn to use it like a native speaker?* I should say, I hope not" (Achebe, 1994, p. 433). New varieties of English have evolved in Asia and Africa, with "their own linguistic and cultural ecologies or sociocultural contexts" and with their own identities producing rich literatures as well (Kachru, 1990, p. 12). Indian English thus is one of many varieties of "World Englishes," to use Kachru's well-known term.

Despite these credible arguments, not everyone would agree that the credentials of English can ever be authentically Indian. Among them is Probal Dasgupta, who says "English is 'not one of us,' but an important presence that one must be polite to ; and *Auntie* is the way we [Indians] express our politeness . . .; so the term 'Auntie Tongue' best expresses what English is to users in India" (Dasgupta, 1993, p. 201). In his view, English will always be unconnected to the cultural core of India, a "metropolitan" language, suitable only for technology, commerce, and external purposes.

Regardless of whether one argues for the Auntie Tongue, the Other Tongue, or in some cases the Mother Tongue, no one contests the fact that English in India is there to stay. Like many cultural encounters on the Subcontinent, this one too, has resulted in assimilation, offering some fascinating insights into how the best-laid plans of language managers (Thomas Babington Macaulay for one; the framers of the constitution for another) often get derailed.

The Story of Hinglish

Bilingualism is a natural phenomenon in any multicultural society, and India is no exception. Though reported as widely prevalent between Indian languages, Indian dialects, and between English and the Indian languages, it is difficult to get an accurate reading on the percentage of bilingualism in India because of the ambiguous and often murky distinctions between language and dialect. What we do know for sure is that "Multiple languages and multiple language identities are defining features of Indian and South Asian bilingualism" (Bhatia & Ritchie, 2004, p. 795).

As mentioned earlier, in my bilingual family English and Hindi-Urdu were used interchangeably. At school, we used English in the classroom and on the playground. But for many domestic situations English was inadequate—in the marketplace, in interacting with family and friends who didn't go to English schools, and in worship. In many social situations we would frequently switch between languages without thinking. My family, who were Christian, worshipped in a church where the Church of England's Book of Common Prayer was translated into Urdu and rendered in Roman script. (Christmas carols were sung in Urdu in church, and at our Christmas party they were cheerfully sung in English by friends who were mostly non-Christian, but who were more familiar with the English than the Urdu versions.)

Having lived away from India for several decades I'm struck with the escalation of bilingualism each time I return. I'll limit myself here just to code switching, a highly visible and often entertaining aspect of bilingualism. More and more in their daily interactions, Indians code switch—unconsciously and seamlessly— between dialects and between languages and in situations where we wouldn't have considered it appropriate when I was growing up.

Examples are readily available from Bollywood films, television talk shows, radio programs, billboards, advertisements in magazines, blogs, and in e-mail conversations. It is not just a matter of dropping an English content word into a Hindi sentence or vice versa (we've all been there and done that in my generation), but it is extensive switching in syntax as well, as in the following examples:

- From a recent Bollywood film: "TEA ESTATE *vali* DEAL *ko* FINAL *karne ke liye vo ayega* TODAY." (He'll come today to make the tea estate deal final.)
- An ad for hair coloring called Streax: "*Mera Streax baalon ko karta* COLOUR *bhi* CARE *bhi.*" (My Streax [a brand of hair coloring as well as the streaks in one's hair], colors my hair and cares for it.)
- From the Web: "BEING *bachpan ka dost* I CAN *bilkul* TRUST HIM." (Being [my] childhood friend I can totally trust him.)
- Bollywood film title: "*Jub* (When) WE MET."
- From a conversation about a recipe: "FIRST I CHOPPED THE ONIONS *khoob chhota chhota* AND FRIED THEM. THEN I PUT THE PIECES OF MEAT AND *bhoono*ED THEM WELL. AFTER THE MEAT IS *bhoono*FIED THEN THE *masalas* GO IN." (First I chopped the onions into very small, small pieces and fried them well. Then I put the pieces of meat and browned them well. After the meat has been browned [or "brownified"], then the spices go in.) [To *bhoono* is "to fry." Here it is used with the English verb suffixes -*ed* and –*fy.* In the first sentence "small, small" is used to suggest very small pieces. Duplication is used as an intensifier in Hindi and commonly transfers into Indian English.]

- From a matrimonial ad (Marriages are still mostly arranged in India, and parents advertise in matrimonial columns of newspapers and now on the Internet): "WANTED: BEAUTIFUL CONVENT-EDUCATED BRIDE, *kundli aavashyak*." (Horoscope essential.) [The layers of cultural intermixing in this ad —the medium and the message—are a wonderful commentary on the paradox of India.]

This kind of code switching is not likely to appear in formal written texts, but like Spanglish in the United States, it has become common in informal contexts. In formal speeches in India, speakers may each speak in a different language at one presentation but are not likely to code switch extensively. The same may be said of the many Indian writers, bilinguals (at the very least), who write brilliantly, profoundly, and creatively in English. Though their content is richly Indian in texture and imagery, in symbol and metaphor; and though their vocabulary, rhetorical style, and context all draw on the languages of the Subcontinent, one is not likely to see the kind of code switching illustrated above. Their code switching is most likely used to capture dialogue, to create a feel for India, or to have fun with the language.

In the United States, teachers need not wring their hands in despair over their students' use of Spanglish, a normal condition of language contact. Nor need they look on code switching between dialects as wrong or improper use of language. As Rebecca Wheeler and Rachel Swords have shown in their recent book (2006), code switching between African American English and standard English in urban classrooms can be used to empower students to use two dialects, depending on context. (See also Wheeler in this volume.) The Ebonics controversy in 1996 showed us only too well how little understood bidialectalism is and how unfortunate it is that the attempts to connect home and school dialects through primary education in the home language can be so easily misread.

"Code mixing and code switching are natural phenomena in the life of a bilingual and thus all pervasive in India. No one language is viewed as suitable for all communicative occasions" say Bhatia and Ritchie (2004, p. 796). Bilingualism is not seen as a deficit. Rather, bilinguals perform "a balancing act with the languages at their disposal" (Bhatia & Ritchie, p. 797). Although language policies are culture specific as Schiffman emphasizes (1996, p. 279), knowing how other cultures handle these language crossings could be of value to U.S. educators.

From Elitism to Equity

English in India has from the beginning been perceived as an elite language even though there have always been Indians who have chosen their regional language or Hindi as a statement of identity and national pride, particularly during the Indian Freedom Movement but also in post-independent India. English shows no intention of departing, no matter what the agenda of the language nationalists announces. Unlike the Indian languages, it is unattached to any region and serves as a pan-Indian medium, especially for those states that have resented and rejected heavy-handed attempts to enforce Hindi as a national language.

"English may be a minority language in terms of the number of its speakers; however, in terms of economic power and desirability, it has more appeal than the most widely spoken language, Hindi" (Bhatia & Ritchie, 2004, p. 802). Over the decades, the demand for English education has never been fully met, and access to the language has been denied to a vast majority simply because it is not afford-able. Now, in a dramatic twist in India's language history, the National Knowledge Commission of the Government of India in 2006 recommends that the teaching of English, along with a child's mother tongue, begin at the primary stage. The Commission believes that "English and Indian languages should be treated at par," and emphasizes "teaching/learning both languages with equal care" (Government of India, 2006, p. 1).

If India can indeed achieve the imperative set forth by the Knowledge Commission, "to make the best possible school education available to *all sections of society* [emphasis added]" (p.1), English will have truly traveled a long way, becoming not just the language of a privileged few, but one of the many languages that *every student* acquires proficiently on his or her educational journey. It will no longer be a "piece of real estate" (Dasgupta, 1993, p. 203) owned by a small segment of Indian society.

In observing the evolution of English in India, then, one might say that the process gets curiouser and curiouser, but productively so. Talking about World Englishes, Kachru points out that "the English language is now the most sought after medium for initiating and accelerating global bilingualism and multi-lingualism," bringing "hybridity and pluralism" to the language (Kachru, 2006, p. 449). The same can be said for English in India.

English no longer belongs to the colonizer; it is too intricately woven into the linguistic fabric of India, threaded through with India's other languages. Despite this, the language never will and never can replace the other Indian languages. Those who fear this do not understand India's multilingual culture (and India has her share of the fearful). "Values about language and its preservation and tradition are shared throughout the Indic area," says Schiffman, and "India's linguistic diversity is, in fact, a *product* of the culture" (1996, p. 172). I am not alone in the belief that those who learn English will continue to keep their own languages and literatures as well.

If anything, the obverse of English-Only prevails in India. It is the land of English Plus. Those in the United States who want to impose English-Only legislation do not understand that the language of power (or access) does not need to be protected with constitutional armor. It is the dialects and languages of those on the margins that need to be protected and supported.

Conclusion

Over three decades ago "The Students' Right to Their Own Language" recognized and upheld the validity of dialect difference in American English. That document, reaffirmed by the National Council of Teachers of English in 2003, is even more relevant in the twenty-first century (NCTE, 2003, Position Statement) at a time when changing demographics and global interchanges insist on our honoring not only the dialects but the many languages that students bring to U.S. classrooms.

Multilingual cultures in different countries choose different ways to support the rights of their diverse populations. The Indian paradigm is just one of many. Perhaps, as Bhatia and Ritchie suggest, "South Asian bilingualism in general and Indian bilingualism in particular [can] provide an excellent, realistic, contemporary and multicultural window on the phenomenon of bilingualism" (Bhatia & Ritchie, 2004, p. 804), helping us to read better the issue of language rights in the United States. The world's largest democracies, one monolingual and the other multilingual, can learn as much from their differences as they can from their commitments to the language rights of their peoples.

Discussion Questions and Activities

1. In India, language and identity are deeply connected. How do the dynamics of language and identity play out in a multicultural but essentially monolingual society such as the United States?
2. The essay claims that the language of power needs no support from legislation to maintain itself. What arguments can you offer to suggest this is either true or untrue in the United States?
3. The value of knowing more than one language and/or one dialect is generally recognized by scholars and researchers. How can India's multilingualism offer a window to teachers in the United States? Alternatively, if you think it is irrelevant to the US context, can you suggest why?
4. Using specific examples, show how perceptions about language and dialect affect the status of a language in a given society.

References

Abbi, A. (2004, May). *Vanishing Diversities and Submerging Identities.* Paper presented at a meeting, Dialogue on Language Diversity, Sustainability and Peace, Barcelona, Spain.
Achebe, C. (1975). *The African Writer and the English Language.* Reprinted in P. Williams & Laura Chrisman (Eds.), *Colonial Discourse and Post-Colonial Theory: A Reader* (1994). New York: Columbia University Press.
Bhatia,T. K. & Koul, A. (2000). *Colloquial Urdu: The Complete Course for Beginners.* The Colloquial Series. London: Routledge.
Bhatia, T. K. & Ritchie, W.C. (2004). Bilingualism in South Asia. In T.K. Bhatia & W.C. Ritchie (Eds.), *The Handbook of Bilingualism.* Malden, MA: Blackwell Publishing.
Bhatt, R. M. (2005, November). *Language Policies and Pedagogical Practices in South Asia.* Paper presented at lecture series, World Language Policies and Pedagogical Practices, University of Wisconsin, Madison.
Bhatt, R.M. & Mahboob, A. (2008). The Minority Languages and Their Status. In B. B. Kachru & S.N. Sridhar (Eds.), *Language in South Asia.* Cambridge: Cambridge University Press.
Conference on College Composition and Communication. (1974). *Students' Right to Their Own Language.* Retrieved May 2007 from http://www.ncte.org/library/files/About_NCTE/Overview/NewSRTOL.pdf.
Dasgupta, P. (1993). *The Otherness of English: India's Auntie Tongue Syndrome.* Language and Development Series. New Delhi: Sage Publications.
Gautam, V. (2003). Education of Tribal Children in India and the Issue of Medium of Instruction: A

Janshala Experience. UN/Governmental Janshala Programme. Retrieved 2007 from www.sil.org/asia/ldc/parallel_papers/vinoba_gautam.pdf.

Government of India. (1949). *Constitution of India.* Retrieved April 2007 from http://www.constitution.org/cons/india/const.html.

Government of India, National Knowledge Commission. (2006). *Report of the Working Group on Language.* Retrieved May 2007 from http://knowledgecommission.gov.in/.

Government of India (1968) *National Policy on Education.* Retrieved June 2007 from http://www.education.nic.in/NatPol.asp.

Groff, C. (2003). *Status and Acquisition Planning and Linguistic Minorities in India.* University of Pennsylvania's Graduate School of Education. Retrieved April 2007 from http://www.sil.org/asia/ldc/parallel_papers/cynthia_groff.pdf.

Guha, R. (2005, January 16). Hindi against India. *The Hindu.* Retrieved May 2007 from http://www.hindu.com/mag/2005/01/16/stories/2005011600260300.htm.

Hock, H. H. & Joseph, B. (1996). *Language History, Language Change, and Language Relationship: An Introduction to Historical and Comparative Linguistics.* Berlin: Mouton de Gruyter.

Kachru, B. B. (1990). *The Alchemy of English: The Spread, Functions, and Models of Non-Native Englishes.* Urbana, IL: University of Illinois Press.

Kachru, B. B. (1992). Introduction: The Other Side of English and the 1990s. In B.B. Kachru (Ed.), *The Other Tongue: English Across Cultures.* 2nd ed. Urbana, IL: University of Illinois Press.

Kachru, B. B. (2006). World Englishes and Culture Wars. In B.B. Kachru, Y. Kachru, & C. Nelson (Eds.), *The Handbook of World Englishes.* Malden, MA: Blackwell Publishing.

Khubchandani, L.M. (2005). Language Rights in Plural Society: Community Versus the State. *South Asian Language Review,* XV: 1, 1-14.

Macaulay, T.B. (1835, February). *Minute on Indian Education.* Retrieved May 2007 from http://www.geocities.com/bororissa/mac.html.

Mallikarjun, B. (2001, August). Language(s) in the School Curriculum: Challenges of the New Millenium. *Language in India,* 1: 4. Retrieved May 2007 from www.languageinindia.com/junjulaug2001/school.html.

Mallikarjun, B. (2004, February). Language Rights and Education in India. *Language in India, 4.* Retrieved May 2007 from http://www.languageinindia.com/feb2004/lucknowpaper.html.

Nambissan, G. B. (2000, September). Dealing with Deprivation. *Seminar, No. 493.* Redesigning Curricula: A Symposium on Working a Framework for School Education. Retrieved May 2007 from http://www.india-seminar.com/2000/493.htm.

National Council of Teachers of English. (2003). Position Statement. *On Affirming the CCCC "Students' Right to Their Own Language."* Retrieved June 2007 from http://www.ncte.org/about/over/positions/category/div/114918.htm.

Rao, R. (1963). *Kanthapura.* Bombay: Oxford University Press. (Originally published 1938.)

Schiffman, H. F. (1996). *Linguistic Culture and Language Policy.* London: Routledge.

Sen, A. (2005) *The Argumentative Indian: Essays on Indian History, Culture and Identity.* New York: Farrar, Straus and Giroux.

Srivastava, R.N. (1989). Perspectives on Language Shift in Multilingual Settings. *International Journal of the Sociology of Language,* 75, 9-26.

Tharoor, S. (2002, February 17). Wodehousian Magic. *The Hindu.* Retrieved May 2007 from http://www.thehindujobs.com/thehindu/mag/2002/02/17/stories/2002021700150300.htm.

Wheeler, R. & Swords, R. (2006). *Code-Switching: Teaching Standard English in Urban Classrooms.* Urbana, IL: National Council of Teachers of English.

Afterword: Reflections on Language Policies and Pedagogical Practices

JACQUELINE JONES ROYSTER, JERRIE COBB SCOTT,

AND DOLORES Y. STRAKER

Affirming Students' Right to Their Own Language: Bridging Language Policies and Pedagogical Practices treats language policies and pedagogical practices in the context of the Students' Right to Their Own Language Resolution (SRTOL) that was passed by the National Council of Teachers of English to address pedagogical problems associated with failures to take language variation into account in teaching. The SRTOL resolution was first passed in 1974, a time when intolerances gave way to noteworthy actions of the civil rights movement geared toward correcting past injustices. The time seemed ripe, then, for addressing the intolerance of language differences and solving some of the pedagogical injustices experienced by speakers of non-mainstream dialects of English. In 2003, a time when concerns over injustices in the teaching of English language learners were growing, the National Council of Teachers of English reaffirmed the Students' Rights to Their Own Language (SRTOL) resolution. By that time, conversations about language rights had broadened to include both minority dialects and minority language rights. As the title of this book suggests, it is the SRTOL resolution's call for affirming students' right to their own language that frames the diverse perspectives on language policies and pedagogical practices presented in this book.

A theme that resonates throughout the book is that substantive changes in language policies and pedagogical practices rest on a shared commitment to changing values. Parts I and II demonstrate that, while language policies have shifted in relation to the various sociopolitical contexts, there is little evidence of fundamental changes in the underlying cultural and social values that would redirect language policies towards seriously defending minority dialects and languages. The pedagogical chapters in Parts II and III suggest that, while pedagogical practices have changed in response to shifts in language policies, there is, again, little evidence of fundamental changes in values that would affirm the right of minority dialect/languages to function as resources in classrooms.

Part IV of the book places the issue of language policy and pedagogy in the global context. The chapters in Part IV make it clear that English has continued to maintain its status as a world language, but the world is changing. There is little evidence, however, of fundamental changes in values relevant to the shifting geopolitical landscapes or the shifting perceptions of dominance in the global community. The authors of Part IV remind readers that some of the internalized values of U.S. citizens, educators, and policymakers may be at odds with the realities of changing global views about language rights and pedagogical practices.

Reflecting on the types of changes suggested throughout the book, we view *Affirming Students' Right to Their Own Language: Bridging Language Policies and Pedagogical Practices* as a clarion call for a recasting of the values that inform language policies and pedagogical actions in the United States. Towards that end, the book attempts to unpack some of the complexities of language policies and pedagogical choices, as well as increase our commitment to actually doing what needs to and can be done to improve learning in our increasingly language diverse classrooms. In what follows, we reflect on recurring themes of the book that relate first to values and language policies and second to values and pedagogical practices. We turn finally to reflect on global issues with a view toward pinpointing the implications of this book for future directions for language policies and pedagogical practices in the U.S.

Fundamental Values and Language Policies in the United States

Parts I and II of *Affirming Students Right to Their Own Language* provide a glimpse of the interplay between social problems and legislated-litigated language policies. The chapters in the first and second parts of the book help readers to pinpoint and chart the trajectories of moments in time when social problems have elicited responses that have been sensitive to minority language rights and the maintenance of heritage languages and dialects. Simultaneously, these chapters pinpoint times, however, when such sentiments have shifted, illustrating that the conditions for shifting sentiments are fairly predictable. The critical focus on recounting the historical development of language polices, coupled with the expert wisdom of highly acclaimed scholars, permits this volume to highlight rather remarkably the extent to which addressing language rights has been ensnared in a repetitive cycle of tolerance and intolerance. The pendulum of actions and impacts—whether enabling or stultifying—swings.

Fishman and Fishman's (2000) description of three major types of language defense—*permissive, active*, and *proactive*—captures some of the running themes that occur in Parts I and II. In the United States, permissive and active language defense are the terms that best characterize the discussions. *Permissive language defense*, according to Fishman and Fishman, seeks to "foster a 'permissive' stance on the part of the majority authorities" (2000, p. 25). Key characteristics of a permissive stance are that (a) it carries no obligation for regulatory agents to act on behalf of disadvantaged or endangered languages; (b) it requests those in authority to abstain from particular types of oppositional or deleterious action waged against minority languages and their speakers; and (c) it prepares the grounds for future support but does not provide such support. As Fishman and Fishman note: "If language defense (and therefore, a more multilingual/multicultural society and polity) is really considered to be in the public interest (rather than merely a private hobby or even a private passion), then it too cannot merely be permissively tolerated" (2000, p. 25).

Different aspects of permissive language defense are treated by the authors in Parts I and II. A recurring theme is that the permissive language defense policies that have been prevalent in language-based legislation and litigation in the U.S. have largely failed to consider the need to protect minority language rights. For example, in the interview with Christina M. Rodríguez, she cites Meyer v. Nebraska as an example of "negative liberties," for the ruling in this case maintained parents' rights to elect the culture they pass on to their children. Fishman and Fishman describe negative liberties as hands-off governmental policies, noting specifically that in the Meyer v. Nebraska case, neither the court ruling nor the precedent that it set led to any governmental requirements or explicit support for the use of languages other than English for instructional purposes.

John Baugh and Aaron Welborn assert that opportunities to defend minority language rights have been missed time and time again. For example, the famous Brown v. Board case might have addressed language rights, along with other civil rights, but it did not. The infamous No Child Left Behind legislation could have addressed the issue of minority dialect/language rights, but it did not. In response to the question of benefits or significant policy changes that evolved from the case of Martin Luther King Junior Elementary School Children et al. v. Ann Arbor School District Board, Geneva Smitherman acknowledged that this was a landmark case, the first ever to deal with the rights of dialect speakers. Smitherman also implied that neither the King case nor the Oakland Ebonics debates brought about significant changes in language policies, though they prepared the ground for supporting changes in pedagogical decisions. Smitherman's interview prompts one to ask what types of language rights are protected in legislated-litigated actions.

Widely discussed in the first two parts of this volume are rulings that protect students' right to the language of others, not to their own language. What is protected is minority students' right to learn English or standard American English as the language of wider communication. In the interest of unpacking the terms of negotiation in legislation and litigated actions, we hasten to add Rodríguez's clarifying explanation. The legislation and litigation are geared toward protecting equal opportunities to learn, rather than equal opportunities to learn through one's heritage language. The closest that we come to protections of language rights is with what Rodríguez calls "transitional" language policies that are used for instrumental purposes. Some states provide non-English translations for such instrumental purposes as voting, safety, and security. Acknowledging these practices leads to another aspect of permissive language defense policies: the absence of constitutional protections for language rights.

Joel Spring points out that language rights are not treated in the United States Constitution, although language rights are treated in every modern constitution written since World War II. The Freedom of Speech provision of the Bill of Rights is the only reference to language rights in the U.S. Constitution. Even so, as Fishman and Fishman (2000) note, "the freedom of speech provision of the Bill of Rights does not assist those who would like to foster non-English languages in the USA, but . . . it does prohibit the most obvious legislation against such use" (p. 25).

Public discourse related to proposing a constitutional amendment on language rights is found most often in relation to the English Only Movement. As noted in this volume and elsewhere, from a language defense perspective, the English Only Movement is rather peculiar in that it is not geared towards protecting endangered languages. Instead, it attempts to protect English, a dominant, non-threatened, world language, when, in fact, it is English or Standard English that is in reality best protected by legislation and litigation. Clearly, most of the legislated-litigated language policies discussed here reaffirm students' right to learn English, or in the case of dialect speakers, to learn Standard English. The peculiar nature of the English Only Movement raises the question of why English Only advocates would direct their efforts toward proposing a constitutional amendment to protect and preserve English even though the evidence overwhelmingly suggests that English is already well positioned and well protected through legislation and litigation. Do we need a constitutional amendment to protect English? From what does English need to be protected?

Our reflections moved us to speculate that in this situation, English is being protected, not from language endangerment or loss, but from losing its dominant status as a world language and the power and privileges that come with such dominance. Notably, then, Joel Spring brings a fresh idea to the discussion of language defense when he suggests that what is needed in the United States is a constitutional amendment to protect languages that are actually threatened and endangered. Certainly, if there were a movement to protect threatened and endangered languages, it would be a move, in the terms of Fishman and Fishman, towards a more active defense of endangered languages and dialects.

A second recurring theme in Parts I and II is that *active language defense* has been largely symbolic with little sustained efforts to prevent the loss of indigenous languages. According to Fishman and Fishman, active language defense may be characterized as therapeutic in nature. It is "undertaken when danger is not only recognized but when ameliorative steps are implemented to counteract language endangerment" (2000, p. 25). Fishman and Fishman go on to note that "while pacifying the aggrieved language community, remedial steps are frequently too late and do too little to restore disadvantaged languages or the language rights of its speakers" (p. 26). The exception to this general rule is that endangered languages can be restored when actions are very carefully channeled in concert with community language preservation efforts, including ensuring that overt action is taken to transmit the language to the young and to increase the use of the language by community as well as governmental and schooling agents.

In this volume, chapters by Dorothy Aguilera and Marguerite LeCompte and Richard Meyer address the issue of active language defense, although they do not use the term "language defense." Aguilera and LeCompte call for an end to permissive, symbolic language defense policies for indigenous Native American languages and the beginning of more active language defense policies. In keeping with Fishman and Fishman's (2000) views of exceptional conditions for language restoration, Aguilera and LeCompte call for a more active agenda that involves setting in motion requirements for ensuring cooperative planning with indigenous communities and encouraging overt actions for transmitting and using indigenous languages in this country, including Hawaii and Alaska. With more of a pedagogical slant, Meyer argues that the existing language policy framework impedes the educational growth of students from minority language backgrounds. Such impediments can be halted, argues Meyer, with active language defense mechanism that offset the negative portraits now being painted of "can't-do" minority language students with more accurate "can-do" portraits.

With regard to *proactive language defense*, the third type of defense discussed by Fishman and Fishman (2000), this type of language defense is said to be preventive in nature, largely undertaken when "demographically and functionally minoritized languages show early signs of trouble" (Fishman & Fishman, 2000, p. 25). In other words, steps are taken to preserve the language before it has reached stages of severe difficulty. However, Fishman and Fishman admit that:

> Cases of long-term successful defense of threatened languages are few and far between and it is time to run the risk of erring on the side of caution (i.e., of somewhat burdening the strong rather than the weak) so as not to suffer further attrition in the ethnocultural and ethnolinguistic community. (2000, p. 25)

Since a preventive defense of minority languages is almost non-existent in the United States or elsewhere, it is not surprising that preventive language defense is also not a prevalent theme in this volume, though it does surface occasionally. The closest we have come to preventive language defense in the United States was in the 1840s when immigrant Germans sought legislation to prevent the loss of German by making it an official language of instruction, as discussed in Chapter 1 by Scott, Straker, and Katz. Quite likely however, new opportunities for preventive language defense are upon us, as new immigrant populations are entering the country with languages that are inevitably situated in the United States as demographically minoritized languages. In the future, these languages could eventually be considered as threatened within the U.S. environment. As a precaution, we note that for those seriously interested in living up to the new world order of multiple languages and their variant forms as the global norm for modern peoples, now is the time to consider and develop preventive language defense actions with respect to the languages of newly emerging immigrants and language pedagogy in U.S. classrooms.

Making more evident the opportunities to develop preventive language defense actions, this volume pushes readers to ask with a more critical view what cultural values about language are being consistently conveyed here in the United States. As explained in Parts I and II of this book, language policies in the United States have consistently and persistently placed a high value on being viewed as a monolingual society, despite the equally persistent historical and ongoing evidence that the U.S. is indeed a multilingual society. In a world, therefore, in which migration patterns are shifting for a variety of reasons in many societies, including our own, it is important to ask whether the great value placed on a monolingual identity in this country is actually warranted.

A fundamental value of the SRTOL resolution is that a nation proud of its diverse heritage (as we in the United States proclaim that we are) will preserve its multilectal (various dialects) and multilingual (various languages) heritage (a heritage that inescapably carries within it cultural and racial variety). What we know, then, is that no matter the high esteem held for the public persona of a nation that has warmly welcomed many peoples, this image of inclusion is distorted by the high esteem held for preserving the nation's monolingual identity. What this book shows is that in reality, the United States has been, is now, and will likely continue to be a multilingual nation. We are culturally and racially diverse, with a deeply embedded ethos that claims justice for all. At no time have such realities been more salient as defining imperatives for the nation in the global context than today. What we can also see in this collection, therefore, is that in various ways moving from permissive to active language policies, and ultimately to the more dynamically engaged preventive language defense approaches will take fundamental changes in values. Core to the change required is a move from the ways in which dominant language policies and pedagogical practices ascribe to a monolingual identity as a unifying force and to a multilingual identity as a divisive force.

Fundamental Values and Pedagogical Practices

The pedagogical chapters of Part II and all chapters in Part III of *Affirming Students' Right to Their Own Language: Bridging Language Policies and Pedagogical Practices* focus on the practice dimension of language rights—how pedagogical practices have been influenced by language policies and how teaching practices can be changed to yield more effective learning outcomes for students. The interview with Mary Carol Combs in Part I foreshadows recurring themes found in Parts II and III of the book. In response to the question of what teachers need to know in order to better accommodate the needs of English language learners, Combs suggests that a deeper understanding of social justice pedagogies will help teachers honor students' language rights and that knowledge of effective pedagogical strategies for English language learners will enable teachers to use students' languages as a resource in instruction. The recurring themes in the pedagogical chapters unpack the complexities of relationships between language rights and pedagogical practices and are closely aligned with Combs' advise and with what Cummins (2000) views as fundamental imperatives for changes in education.

Focusing on the "language as right-language as resource" dyad, Cummins (2000) views language rights as fundamental to pedagogical changes, noting that "the deep structure of educational change reflects the extent to which educators individually and collectively challenge the coercive power structure of the wider society" (p. 254). *Coercive relations of power*, says Cummins, "refer to the exercise of power by a dominant individual, group, or country to the detriment of a subordinated individual, group or country" (2000, p. 254).

In our reflections on the pedagogical chapters, we found that the authors advocated against coercive relations of power in favor of collaborative relations of power. *Collaborative relations of power*, according to Cummins (2000), is power used to enable or empower individuals or groups to achieve more. From this perspective, "empowerment" means the "collaborative creation of power which is generated through interaction with others" (p. 254). Rather than treating empowered students as a threat to the authority and curriculum of the schools, the prevalent view presented here is that the "more empowered one individual or group becomes, the more that is generated for others to share" (Cummins, 2000, p. 254). Rather than giving license to competitiveness and dominance, the authors of the pedagogical chapters emphasize collaboration and sharing.

A basic principle upon which these authors operate is that language as right is intimately tied to the students' sense of identity. Cummins puts it this way:

> Students whose schooling experiences reflect collaborative relations of power participate confidently in instruction as a result of the fact that their sense of identity is being affirmed and extended in their interactions with educators. They also know that their voices will be heard and respected within the classroom. Schooling amplifies rather than silences their power of self-expression. (2000: p. 253)

In keeping with the key tenets of SRTOL, the pedagogical chapters invite readers to reflect on how schooling failures for speakers of minority language are linked to minority languages as rights and to consider the manner and means by which coercive relations of power stem from negative language attitudes and the non-communal functions of classrooms. Alternatives to coercive power relations are offered by Katz, Scott, and Hadjoiannou in their presentation of research that shows a persistent pattern of negative attitudes toward language differences among developing and practicing teachers. Their alternatives to coercive power relations focus on integrating critical inquiry processes into teacher education programs. Nancy Rankie Shelton demonstrates success with integrating critical inquiry processes into teacher education courses with strategies that involve preservice teachers in a series of language-based, self-awareness activities that enhance preservice teachers' understanding of how languages and varieties of a language attain power and dominance.

Although these last mentioned authors indirectly treat issues of self-identity, other chapters confront the problem of self-identity directly. Valerie Kinloch demonstrates how to use critical literacy pedagogy to enhance students' awareness of different aspects of self-identity. David E. Kirkland and Austin Jackson show how even progressive approaches to language instruction for minority language/dialect speakers can inadvertently lead to problems with self-identity.

The chapters just described are found in Part II of the book and serve as a bridge between language policies and pedagogical practices. Importantly though, they make visible the sometimes invisible aspects of how language as a right can be treated in classroom settings. The pedagogical chapters in Part III treat language as resource, focusing particularly on how to use minority languages/dialects as learning resources.

In Part III, the authors suggest that the knowledge that many practicing teachers acquired while in training has often been insufficient for the challenges faced in today's classrooms. In our reflections on the sources of insufficient knowledge, we noted a common theme among authors—the view that minority dialects as problems can be replaced with strategies that demonstrate how to use minority languages as resources. As with Cummins, the authors share an overriding concern over how dominant group institutions have required non-dominant groups to deny their cultural identity and give up their languages as a necessary condition for success in the mainstream society (Cummins, 2000). Evidence that this unfair and inequitable exchange is ill advised is found in Beth V. Yeager and Judith L. Green's description of the multiple identities that are present in classrooms and their explicit suggestions of ways to use multiple identities to foster nurturing classroom environments.

Multiple strategies that enable teachers to employ students' language as resource are also revealed through the pedagogical chapters by way of dialect/language-specific strategies. For example dialect specific strategies are offered by Rebecca S. Wheeler in her discussion of code-switching activities. Language specific strategies are presented by Mari Haneda for English Language Learners and by Danling Fu for new Chinese immigrant students. The use of language as resource is also made available in chapters that treat adaptive strategies, i.e. existing strategies commonly used in the classroom that have been modified to fit the needs and interests of different students. For example, Laurie Katz and Tempii Champion demonstrate ways to adapt storytelling conventions to better utilize the storytelling conventions that children of African descent bring to the classroom. Jeane Copenhaver-Johnson, Joy Bowman, and Angela Rietschlin's literature-based strategies, the read-alouds described by Tamara L. Jetton, Emma Savage-Davis, and Marianne Baker, and the modified approaches to literature offered by Dorothea Anagnostopopoulos all provide ways to utilize language and dialect patterns as resources in classrooms.

Moreover, many of the alternative strategies have a better track record for yielding learning success than the reductionist strategies that are evolving in response to high stakes testing and the No Child Left Behind mandates, as explained by Dorothea Anagnostopoulos. Of particular note among the discussions in Part III is a strand of views that asserts the positive effects of bilingual education programs where all students become bilingual, not just the so-called English language learners.

The pedagogical chapters in Parts II and III of this book suggests that the benefits of minority language as a right and resource are numerous and should be considered to be just as important as learning the language of wider communication. A critical question to ask, though, is what fundamental changes are needed in values to realize the benefits of embracing the notion of language as right and resource. Should our educational systems place a higher value on language uniformity than on language diversity? On monolingualism than on bidialectism and bilingualism? Do the suggested pedagogical changes amount to the lowering of standards for excellence and performance? The authors of the pedagogical chapters suggest that policymakers and educators need to insist on standards that a) affirm students' rights to multiple language identities and b) utilize the varied and multiple resources of students' heritage languages for more effective teaching and learning. In doing so, policymakers and educators will be better able to differentiate between language standards that establish a framework for learning achievement and language standardization that calls for adherence to a single set of language patterns. Valuing only English or only Standard English elevates the language standardization process and impedes efforts to achieve higher learning outcomes for all students, including those from minority language/dialect backgrounds.

The ways in which this volume presents the theme of minority language as a right and as a resource raise questions about the low value placed on language diversity in general, and on minority dialects and languages in particular. In effect, the authors challenge readers to think introspectively about how we might more systematically honor and utilize the language that minority speakers bring to the classroom. As is consistently shown throughout the volume, employing pedagogical strategies that lead to sustained academic success for minority dialect/language speakers will require fundamental changes in the way the culture values the rights and resources of minority languages and dialects. The authors offer ample examples of what respect for language rights feels like and what utilizing the resources of languages/dialects looks like in classrooms. In the broadest sense, their examples feel and look like a pedagogy of success.

Globalization: A Way Forward with Practices and Policies

As indicated in the Preface, one of the main reasons for including a section on globalization in this volume was to enable readers to move from a localized to a global perspective of how language diversity is managed in the schools and how language policies support the preservation of indigenous languages, particularly in areas where early colonization has threatened the preservation of local languages. In our reflections on Part IV, a set of themes emerged that centered on lessons that can be learned in the United States from other nations.

One recurring theme is that experiences from abroad challenge some of the myths about language diversity and schooling problems that are addressed by SRTOL. The chapters in Part IV provide evidence that some of the myths held about language teaching and learning in the United States fail to hold up in settings where language diversity is accepted as the norm in schools and in society. For example, we might take the myth that the practice of teaching only one language or dialect in schools is the most expedient effective route to academic excellence for all. As demonstrated by Xenia Hadjioannou's experience in Greece, multiple dialects can be managed in school settings. As well, multiple languages can serve as the language of instruction, as shown by Gerda Videsott in her description of how the trilingual community in South Tyrol, Italy, employs three languages as the medium of instruction.

Other authors debunk the myth that communities have little to offer schools. Ana Christina DaSilva Iddings explains how a community in Brazil served as a useful venue for initiating changes in learning. Patrick H. Smith, Luz A. Murillo, and Robert T. Jiménez demonstrate how capitalizing on the ways that homes and schools connect in Mexico can serve as a resource for bridging home–school connections for new immigrant students in U.S. public schools. In essence, the chapters in Part IV not only debunk some of the common myths about language addressed in SRTOL, but they also demonstrate the ways that language diversity has been managed and vibrantly utilized in educational settings beyond the United States.

Viewing teaching practices and policies from a global perspective also offers insights into different organizational and governance structures that may be used in U.S. schools to better effect in managing both language instruction and learning generally. To be noted, of course, is that the policy practice problem everywhere is highly complex, not just in the U.S. but in other nations as well. This point is clearly articulated by Hall (2006) in *Reading across International Boundaries: History, Policy, and Politics.* Hall argues that educators and the public must not only become more literate about existing educational policies, but also become policy literate, i.e. able to see caveats in the development of policies and ways to strategically intervene before policies are finalized and translated into teaching practices. The caveats treated in the final chapters of this volume chart a path towards becoming more policy literate.

Caveats in the global community remind the reader of the need to be watchful along the path of developing policy literacy. Preserving indigenous languages is no easy task in colonized countries where English and other colonized languages have served as national languages. As Carole Bloch explains, despite constitutionally sanctioned policies protecting indigenous languages in South Africa, as in other countries, implementing language restoration programs are stifled by political, ideological, and economic barriers. Moreover, Nkonko M. Kamwangamalu suggests that invoking a sense of "justice" does not seem to be the strongest argument to use in support of language policies that elevate the status of indigenous languages in South Africa. He goes on to propose a mechanism for creating affirmative language policies and practices that is grounded in economic theories. How, then, does one create a balance between humanistic and economic goals for supporting the raison d'être of indigenous languages and their speakers? This is another caveat to be watchful of along the path of becoming policy literate.

Another caveat is how to treat the evolving *new* Englishes that do not conform to the standards of British and American English. Zarina Hock addresses the issue of new Englishes in India. She points to the expected evolution of an Indian English whose lexicon, phonology, syntax, and rhetorical styles are shaped by the context of indigenous languages and cultures. She explains that the complexities of the role of English in India are signaled by its various referents—English as the "Other Tongue," the "Auntie Tongue," and the "Mother Tongue."

In the global community, there is growing concern over "linguicism," characterized as using the languages imposed by outsiders as defining criteria and as the basis for creating sociolinguistic hierarchies among people. The reader is gently nudged into considering whether, indeed, it is feasible to create new norms of usage that differ from U.S. and British English norms in order to prevent highly problematic systems of social stratification based on language standards imposed on the "conquered" by those who once colonized them?

With this last caveat, we return our reflections full circle to the problem of English dialects that was the focus of the original SRTOL resolution. Will the context of how nonnative English speakers around the globe generate new structures and uses of the English language affect future views about how non-standard dialects are perceived in this nation? Further, if educators, scholars, and policymakers fail to consider patterns of language use that are normative in other nations (e.g. multilectalism and multilingualim), or if we fail to consider issues that are of concern to the global community, how likely are we to fall victim to the problem of overplaying our own presumptions of power and language dominance? There is much to suggest that U.S. citizens may overvalue the current status that English holds as a world language and undervalue the shifting geopoltical rela-tionships that might generate evolutionary, if not revolutionary, changes in language-related issues in the global community.

As we look to the future, it is important to ask again if the values accorded to viewing the United States as a monolingual society are noble or if they are uninformed and myopic. Will the coercive power of dominance continue to have the same force in the new world order? Would we be better off working toward collaborative powers created in concert with the global community, rather than coercive powers created from a dominance stance on language? These are the types of question that this book suggests should be addressed as grounding for future directions.

Speaking collectively for the editors and contributing authors of this book, we hope that readers of this volume will consider the two overarching themes of this book in their move forward. The first is presented in the Foreword of the book. David Bloome encourages the reader to rethink the basic proposition that language is about us as whole beings in all of our variety, rather than about some of us as three-fifths of some defaulted model of human worthiness. Human worthiness should be at the epicenter of the language policymaking agendas that serve to inform pedagogical practices. The second overarching theme is presented in this, the Afterword of the book. Values are the driving force for pedagogical changes that affirm students' rights to their heritage dialects and languages and to the use of their languages as resources in teaching and learning. Enacting changes in education that value minority dialects and languages as salient rights and worthwhile resources poses a challenge. The challenge is not simply to permit tolerance; it is to be proactive in preserving rights and in perceiving and using all of our resources to enable and facilitate learning, growth, and prosperity. Declaring a right, proclaiming a value, permitting a general possibility—we know now—are just not enough.

References

Cummins, J. (2000). "This Place Nurtures my Spirit": Creating Contexts of Empowerment in Linguistically-Diverse Schools. In R. Phillipson (Ed.). *Rights to Language: Equity, Power, and Education*. Mahwah, NJ: Lawrence Erlbaum Associates, Inc.

Fishman, J. A., & Fishman, G. S. (2000). Rethinking Language Defense. In R. Phillipson (Ed.). *Rights to Language: Equity, Power, and Education*. Mahwah, NJ: Lawrence Erlbaum Associates, Inc.

Hall, K. (2006). Literacy Policy and Policy Literacy: A Tale of Phonics in Early Reading in England. In R. Openshaw, & J. Soler (Eds.). *Reading across International Boundaries: History, Policy, and Politics*. Charlotte, NC: Information Age Publishing, Inc (pp. 55–67).

Author Biographies

Dorothy Aguilera is Assistant Professor in Educational Leadership Program and on the Advisory Council for the Tribal Educator's Program at Lewis & Clark College. Dorothy has worked as a consultant on national, state and local research and innovative program implementation projects with K-12 schools serving Native American communities in rural and urban areas. As an education activist her work centers on collaborating with tribal nation communities to establish ongoing streams of culturally responsive education through indigenously controlled schools. Her dissertation project was a comparison of school reform in 14 case studies involving schools serving Native American students, examining relationships among culturally responsive education, indigenous language immersion education, student achievement, and external student success indicators. Dorothy is of mixed heritage including Choctaw.

Dorothea Anagnostopoulos is Associate Professor of Teacher Education at Michigan State University. Her research interests are in the sociocultural analyses of educational policy and teaching and learning in urban high schools. Dr. Anagnostopoulos' teaching focuses on the preparation of teachers for urban schools. She is a co-director of the Future Teachers for Social Justice project which engages high school students in collecting a cross-generational oral history of schooling in Detroit, MI. Dr. Anagnostopoulos' research on educational policy and teaching and learning in urban high schools has been widely published in journals, including *Research in the Teaching of English, American Educational Reseach Journal, Journal of Curriculum Studies*, and *Educational Policy Analysis and Evaluation*. Her current research includes a study of the implementation of sexual harassment policies in high schools and a study of how preservice teachers engage in moral reasoning about social difference and inequality.

Marianne Baker is Assistant Professor of Reading Education in the Department of Early, Elementary, and Reading Education at James Madison University in Harrisonburg, VA. Dr. Baker teaches children's and adolescent literature courses, literacy acquisition courses, as well as graduate courses in reading. Her research focuses on the relationship between exposures to various genres of literature and literacy development and written expression. Recent publications include:

Cross-Age Book Clubs Demonstrate the Power of Reading. *JMU College of Education*, 3. Baker, M. I. (2006). The Payoffs of Early Literacy Practices. *Viewpoint: Bulletin of VAECE*, 3, 4. Baker, M. I. (2005) Ivey, M. G. and Baker, M. I. (2004). Phonics Instruction for Older Students? Just Say No. *Education Leadeership*, *61*(6), 35–39. Ivey, M. G. and Baker, M. I. (2004). Phonics Instruction for Older Students? Just Say No. *Education Leadership,* 61(6), 35–39.

John Baugh received his PhD in linguistics from the University of Pennsylvania (1979). Prior to joining Washington University in St. Louis as the Margaret Bush Wilson Professor in Arts and Sciences and Director of the African and African American Studies Program, he served as Professor of Education and Linguistics at Stanford University. Professor Baugh is the author of several books, including *Black Street Speech: Its History, Structure and Survival* (University of Texas, 1983); *Out of the Mouths of Slaves: African American Language and Educational Malpractice* (University of Texas, 1999); and *Beyond Ebonics: Linguistic Pride and Racial Prejudice* (Oxford, 2000). Professor Baugh is a sociolinguist who studies the social stratification of linguistic diversity in advanced industrialized societies, with particular attention to the linguistic plight of socially dispossessed populations. He also serves as Director of the American Linguistic Heritage Survey, an ongoing study sponsored by the Ford Foundation to examine the prevalence of linguistic profiling in the United States.

Carole Bloch coordinates the Early Literacy Unit of the Project for the Study of Alternative Education in South Africa, a multilingual education institute based at the University of Cape Town. She is also the central coordinator of the Stories across Africa Project, a core pan-African project of the African Academy of Languages, the official language organization of the African Union. For many years, she has been involved in helping to change policy and implement practices to improve the way in which young children are taught reading and writing in African multilingual contexts. Her work, and that of the Early Literacy Unit includes teacher training and training of trainers for mother tongue-based bilingual education, as well as materials development and research into young children's literacy learning. Her particular research interest is young children's emergent biliteracy learning. She has written much about early literacy and multilingual education in South Africa and Africa, including (a) co-authoring a chapter with Neville Alexander on the Battswood biliteracy research project "Aluta Continua: The Relevance of the Continua of Biliteracy to South African Multilingual Schools"; (b) in Hornberger, N. (Ed.) (2003). Continua of Biliteracy: An Ecological Framework for Educational Policy, Research, and Practice in Multilingual Settings; (c) a book on her daughters emergent writing development, *Chloe's Story: First Steps into Literacy* (1997); and (d) several picture books for young children.

David Bloome is Professor in the School of Teaching and Learning of the Ohio State University College of Education. Bloome's research focuses on how people use spoken and written language for learning in classroom and non-classroom settings, and how people use language to create and maintain social relationships, to construct knowledge, and to create communities, social institutions, and shared histories and futures. He is a former president of the National Council of Teachers of English and of the National Conference on Research in Language and Literacy. He is a former middle school and high school teacher. He is co-director of the Columbus Area Writing Project, co-editor of *Reading Research Quarterly*, and founding editor of *Linguistics and Education: An International Research Journal*. He is the co-author of four books, editor/co-editor of six books on language and literacy in education, and author or co-author of numerous journal articles and book chapters. Bloome's current scholarship focuses on four areas related to writing and reading education: (1) the social construction of intertextuality as part of the reading, writing, and learning processes, (2) discourse analysis as a means for understanding reading, writing, and literacy events in and outside of classrooms, (3) narrative development among young children as a foundation for learning and literacy development in schools, and (4) students as researchers and ethnographers of their own communities.

Joy Bowman is currently a first grade teacher at Western Elementary School in Lexington, OH. She works as a classroom-based researcher in collaboration with Dr. Jeane Copenhaver-Johnson of the Ohio State University at Mansfield and Angela Johnson Rietschlin of Olentangy Local Schools and is a lecturer at the Ohio State University at Mansfield. Her work on children's responses to read-alouds has been published in *Language Arts* and presented at national and international conferences.

Tempii Champion is Associate Professor in the Department of Communication Sciences and Disorders at Long Island University Brooklyn Campus. Dr. Champion's current teaching and research interests are in language development and language disorders among multicultural populations. She has made numerous presentations at professional meetings. Dr. Champion was Principal Investigator on a grant from NIH entitled "Language Intervention among AA Children." Dr. Champion has authored *Understanding of Narrative Structures Used among African American Children: A Journey from Africa to America*, published in 2002 by Lawrence Erlbaum Associates, Inc., Mahwah, NJ. Dr. Champion has articles and chapters published in various journals concerning the language skills of African American children.

Mary Carol Combs is an adjunct Associate Professor in the Department of Language, Reading and Culture, University of Arizona (Tucson) where she teaches graduate and undergraduate courses in bilingual education law and policy, ESL methods, and multicultural education. She is also on the faculty of the American Indian Language Development Institute (AILDI); her institute courses include indigenous language planning and policy, foundations of American Indian language education, and indigenous culture, language, and identity in film. Her current research focuses on the English language acquisition and literacy development of kindergarten and first grade English language learners in structured English immersion (SEI) classes. She is also participating in a study to assess the effect of state and federal immigration policies on undocumented students in K-12 schools in southern Arizona. The former director of the English Plus Information Clearinghouse, a national clearinghouse on language rights and public policy based in Washington, DC, Dr. Combs remains active in national networks concerned with policy developments in the education of ELLs in the United States. She received her PhD in language, reading and culture from the University of Arizona (1995), an MA in applied linguistics from Georgetown University (1983), and a BA in German from the University of Michigan (1978). She has published articles on the education of English language learners, bilingual education and language policy, and is co-author of the fourth edition of *Bilingual and ESL Classrooms* (2006, McGraw-Hill), with Carlos Ovando and Virginia Collier.

Jeane Copenhaver-Johnson is Assistant Professor in the School of Teaching and Learning at the Ohio State University at Mansfield. Her research focuses on issues of equity and social justice in classrooms, and she conducts classroom-based studies designed to (1) uncover the resources linguistically and culturally diverse children bring to literate events and (2) help teachers construct pedagogies of equity. Her work on young children's responses to interactive read-alouds explores how children's responses intersect with racial and cultural identities and understandings. She also conducts research on issues of social justice in teacher education, investigating ways to combat homophobia and heterosexism in preservice teacher education programs. Her work has been published in several journals, among them *Language Arts, Childhood Education, The New Advocate, The Early Childhood Education Journal,* and *Multicultural Perspectives.*

Danling Fu is Professor of Language and Culture, in the School of Teaching and Learning, College of Education in the University of Florida. In addition to teaching courses for both undergraduate and graduate students in the areas of language, literacy and culture, she has conducted research in the public schools with a focus on children's writing development and literacy instruction for new immigrant students. Her research has resulted in two books and over 60 journal articles, book chapters and book reviews. She gives speeches and conducts workshops on various issues pertaining to literacy education, writing transitions and biliteracies for English language learners across the continent in the United States.

Judith L. Green is Professor of Teaching and Learning in the Language, Literacy and Composition specialization at the University of California, Santa Barbara, in Santa Barbara, CA, where she also co-directs the Center for Literacy and Inquiry in Networking Communities and is Emphasis Leader in Teaching and

Learning, and Qualitative and Interpretive Research. Her research focus is the social construction of knowledge, ethnography and discourse analysis and literate practices as social accomplishments across disciplines. Professor Green's teaching and work with schools focuses on: (1) exploring learning in the contexts of teaching—ethnographic and discourse studies of learning in cultural and community contexts; and (2) understanding how the language of the classroom and classrooms as cultures-in-the-making support and constrain opportunities for learning and identity construction for students. She has written numerous articles on the social construction of knowledge and classroom discourse among linguistically and culturally diverse children and classrooms as cultures. Her previous books include Green, J. L., Camilli, G., & Ellmore, P. B. (Eds.) (2006). *Handbook of Complementary Methods in Education Research*; Green, J., & Luke, A. (Eds.) (2006). *Review of Research in Education, Vol. 30*; Beach, R., Green, J. L., Kamil, M., & Shanahan, T. (Eds.) (2005). *Multidisciplinary Perspectives on Literacy Research*; Green, J. L., & Harker, J. (Eds.) (1988). *Multiple Perspective Analyses of Classroom Discourse: Methods and Issues.*

Xenia Hadjioannou is Assistant Professor of Language and Literacy Education at the Lehigh Valley campus of Penn State University. Her research focuses on the study of classroom discourse and particularly the examination of speech genres that support student thinking and learning, the analysis of exemplary practices in the language arts classroom, and the theoretical and discourse/analytical examination of linguistic diversity in education. In her teaching, Dr. Hadjioannou works primarily with preservice teachers in an exciting course configuration which involves the merging of three separate methods courses (reading methods, writing methods and children's literature) into one integrated literacy block. Her most recent publications include: Bringing the Background to the Foreground: What Do Classroom Environments That Support Authentic Discussions Look Like?, an article published in the *American Educational Research Journal* (2007); *Talking about Books with First-Graders*, published in Scientia Paedagogica Experimentalis (2007); and Linguistic Variation in Greek Cypriot Elementary Education, published in *School Systems in Multilingual Regions of Europe*, a volume edited by W. Wiater and G. Vindesott (2006).

Mari Haneda is Assistant Professor of Foreign/Second Language Education as well as of Language, Education, & Society in the School of Teaching & Learning at the Ohio State University. In her research, she takes an ethnographic approach, together with the use of discourse analysis, drawing principally on cultural historical activity theory, new literacy studies, sociolinguistic studies of bilingualism and biliteracy, and critical linguistics and literacy. Her research has focused on: (a) the language use and the literacy practices of school-aged English language learners in and out of school; (b) the relationships among language, literacy, gender, ethnicity, class, and culture in the development of identity among language minority students; and (c) the processes through which second language students are socialized into academic discourse practices. Her articles have appeared in edited volumes and journals such as *Applied Linguistics, Linguistics and Education*, and *TESOL Quarterly*.

Zarina Manawwar Hock retired as Senior Editor and Director of Book Publications from the National Council of Teachers of English. Her advanced degrees in English literature, teaching English as a second language, and comparative literature steered her first into teaching college-level English, both in India and the United States, and ultimately into publishing. Before her appointment as Senior Editor, she managed NCTE's Editorial Department and coordinated the efforts of the Council's International Consortium. As Director of Book Publications and Senior Editor, she acquired, developed, and shaped manuscripts in English language arts, research, and pedagogy for publication in NCTE's Books Program. She compiled and maintained the house style manual for NCTE publications. She has made presentations on language usage and style, international English, and negotiating identity in a multicultural context. Her essay on world Englishes was published in the *Encyclopedia of English Studies and Languages Arts*. She currently works as an Editing Consultant at Illinois State University.

Ana Christina DaSilva Iddings is Assistant Professor of Language, Literacy, and Culture in the Department of Teaching and Teacher Education at the University of Arizona. In 2007, Dr. DaSilva Iddings became the Director of the Commission on Language that is part of the National Council for Teachers of English (NCTE). Her research interests are (a) language learning; (b) immigration and equity in education; and (c) the preparation and professional development of teachers to work with English language learners. Dr. DaSilva Iddings is the co-author of the edited volume *Cooperative Learning and Teaching in Second Language Classrooms* published by Cambridge University Press. In addition, her work has appeared in numerous refereed journals including the *Modern Language Journal, TESOL Quarterly, Bilingual Research Journal*, and the *Journal of Language, Identity, and Education*.

Austin Jackson is Assistant Professor in the Residential College of the Arts and Humanities at Michigan State University. His research areas include African American rhetoric, cultural studies, and the implications of critical ethnography for critical literacy and pedagogy in college compostion. Austin's teaching focuses on the rhetoric of racial liberalism; its relationship to structural inequality; and the potential for critical social theory and Black youth rhetorical and cultural production to help students produce and resist discourses of power, both inside and outside official classroom contexts. He has served as graduate coordinator for the My Brother's Keeper Program for At-Risk Black Males, and is co-author of several articles, including: From the "Lower Socio-Economic": Three Brothers and an Old-School Womanist Respond to Cosby (with David Kirkland, Jeffrey Robinson, and Geneva Smitherman, in *The Black Scholar*, 2005); "Black People Tend to Speak Eubonics": Race and Curricular Diversity in Higher

Education (with Geneva Smitherman, in *Strategies for Teaching First Year Composition*, 2002); and Making Connections in the Contact Zones: Towards a Critical Praxis of Rap Music and Hip Hop Culture (with Anthony Michel and David Sheridan, in *Black Arts Quarterly* (Ed. H. Samy Alim, Stanford University Press, Summer, 2001); Big D, Rufus, and Leroy: Ebonics on the Internet (with David Kirkland and Geneva Smitherman, in *American Language Review*, 2001).

Tamara L. Jetton is the Berrell Endowed Professor of Developmental Literacy at Central Michigan University, Mt. Pleasant, Michigan. Her research focus is adolescent literacy, and literacy in diverse media environments. Professor Jetton's teaching and work with schools focuses on teacher professional development in literacy, specifically reading comprehension and writing to learn. Her interest in adolescent literacy led to the publication of *Adolescent Literacy Research and Practice*. She has also written numerous articles that have been published in such journals as *Reading Research Quarterly*, *Review of Educational Research*, and *Journal of Educational Psychology*. She has published several chapters in books and volumes such as *Bridging the Achievement Gap: Improving Literacy Learning for Pre-Adolescent & Adolescent*, *Handbook of Discourse Processes*, *Handbook of Research on Literacy in Technology at the K-12 Level*, and *Handbook of Reading Research, Volume III*. She has served on the editorial advisory board of *The Reading Teacher*, *Reading Research Quarterly*, *Journal of Adolescent and Adult Literacy*, *Journal of Literacy Research*, and *Contemporary Educational Psychology*.

Robert T. Jiménez is Professor of Language, Literacy and Culture at Vanderbilt University. He teaches courses in research methods, second language literacy, and issues related to the education of Latino/Latina students. Jiménez has conducted research on the strategic processing of competent and less competent bilingual readers, and on the delivery of services and instruction to language minority students with learning disabilities or at risk for referral to special education. He is currently using an ecological framework to examine the literacies of linguistically diverse students. He is also interested in the potential of alternative literacy practices to promote these same students' personal, political, and economic goals. Previously, Jiménez was both a bilingual and a migrant teacher for 3 years in northern Illinois. His work has been published in several journals including the *American Educational Research Journal*, *Elementary School Journal*, *Reading Research Quarterly*, *The Reading Teacher*, and the *Journal of Adolescent and Adult Literacy*.

Nkonko M. Kamwangamalu is Professor of Linguistics and Director of the Graduate Program in the Department of English at Howard University in Washington, DC. He holds an MA and a PhD in linguistics from the University of Illinois at Urbana-Champaign, and has also received a Fulbright award. Prior to joining Howard University, Professor Kamwangamalu taught linguistics at the

National University of Singapore, the University of Swaziland, and the University of Natal in Durban, South Africa, where he was Director of the Linguistics Program. His research interests include multilingualism, code-switching, language policy and planning, language and identity, new Englishes, African American English, and African linguistics. He has published widely on most of these and related topics. He has also been an invited plenary or keynote speaker at a number of international conferences including, most recently, the 14th World Congress of Applied Linguistics (University of Wisconsin, 2005) and the Symposium in Honor of Joshua Fishman's Eightieth Birthday (University of Pennsylvania, 2006). Professor Kamwangamalu is Policy Editor for the series *Current Issues in Language Planning* (Multilingual Matters), member of the TOEFL Board, member of the editorial boards for *World Englishes* and *Language Policy*, and past editor-in-chief of *Southern African Linguistics and Applied Language Studies*.

Laurie Katz is Associate Professor of Early Childhood Education at the Ohio State University. Her research, teaching and service have focused on teacher preparation of early childhood educators, inclusion issues, relationships between families, communities and schools, and narrative styles and structures of young children. One of the key issues that she has been addressing in teacher education programs is how early childhood curriculum and instruction can be conceptualized to incorporate the broad diversity of children (birth to 8 years of age) including children from linguistic minority communities and children with disabilities. She is one of the co-editors of *Language Arts* published by the National Council of Teachers of English. Previously, she co-edited *Tennessee's Children*, a journal of the Tennessee Association for the Education of Young Children. She has served as past director of the Commission of Language within the National Council of Teachers of English.

Valerie Kinloch (PhD) is a Professor in Literacy Studies in the School of Teaching & Learning at the Ohio State University. Her research interests include the sociocultural lives, literacies, and collaborative engagements of urban youth and adults in and out of school spaces. She is the author of several journal articles, including "The White-ification of the Hood": Power, Politics, and Youth Performing Narratives of Community (2007, in *Language Arts*), Youth Representations of Community, Art, and Struggle in Harlem (2007, in *New Directions for Adult and Continuing Education Journal*), and Revisiting the Promise of *Students' Right to Their Own Language*: Pedagogical Strategies (2005, in *CCC*). Her co-authored book, *Still Seeking an Attitude: Critical Reflections on the Work of June Jordan*, was released in 2004, and her most recent book, *June Jordan: Her Life and Letters*, was published in 2006. Valerie was awarded a Spencer Foundation Research Grant and a Grant-in-Aid from the National Council of Teachers of English to support work on the literacy and activist practices of African American and Latino/a high school and first generation college students in Harlem (NYC). This work examines how community gentrification and a politics of place impact the lives, literacies, and cultural identities of urban youth of color.

David E. Kirkland is Assistant Professor in the Department of Teaching and Learning at the Steinhardt School of Education at New York University. His scholarship examines urban youth cultures and identities, adolescent literacies, and African American language and education. His past research has focused on literacy in the lives of six young Black men, who learned and practiced literacy squarely within (r)evolutions in African American, hip hop, and urban youth cultures. Based on this work, Dr. Kirkland has written substantially about the influences of hip hop and popular cultures on the educational experiences of urban youth. He has used his understandings to push for a new vision for English education, which he more clearly articulated in a recent volume of the *English Journal* (May, 2008). He also theorizes and contributes to new literacy, critical pedagogy, and African-centered perspectives on language and literacy in the lives of urban youth, particularly of urban adolescent Black males. Currently, Dr. Kirkland's research focuses on the influence of digital media and new technologies on urban youth literacies. In essence, Dr. Kirkland's scholarship aims to provide an intellectual forum for a complex set of conversations, where urban students' literacies, particularly those that take shape in non-traditional and digital contexts, can find expression, relevance, and acceptance in formal settings.

Margaret D. LeCompte is Professor of Education and Sociology at the University of Colorado-Boulder. She received her BA from Northwestern University in political science, and after serving as a Peace Corps Volunteer in the Somali Republic, earned her MA and PhD from the University of Chicago. She is internationally known as a proponent of qualitative and ethnographic research and evaluation in education. Her publications include *The Ethnographer's Toolkit* (1999), with J. J. Schensul, a seven-volume set of books on ethnographic research methods, *The Way Schools Work* (1999), a sociology of education text informed by critical theory, written with Kathleen Demarrais, and many other books and articles on research methods in the social sciences, empirical studies of school reform and school organization, and investigations of at-risk, ethnically diverse, gifted, artistically creative and language minority students. Dr. LeCompte was president of the Council on Anthropology and Education of the American Anthropology Association and served as editor of the AERA published journal, *Review of Educational Research*, from 2003–2006. She is the Founder and current President of the University of Colorado chapter of the American Association of University Professors, and Vice President of the Colorado Conference of the AAUP.

Rick Meyer is a Professor at the University of New Mexico in the Department of Language, Literacy and Sociocultural Studies. He taught for almost 20 years before earning his PhD in reading at the University of Arizona. His areas of research include teacher development, critical literacy, young children's literacy development, and literacy as a tool for agency. He teaches courses in critical literacy, written language development, family literacy, reading pedagogy and research. He is the director of the High Desert Writing Project, affiliated with the National Writing Project. Dr. Meyer has served as president of the Center for the Expansion of Language and Thinking and is currently on the board of that organization. His most recent books include *Reading and Teaching* and *Phonics Exposed: Understanding and Resisting Systematic Intense Direction Phonics Instruction*, both published by Lawrence Erlbaum Associates, Inc.

Luz A. Murillo is Assistant Professor of Reading at the University of Texas Pan American, where she teaches undergraduate and graduate courses in language arts, literacy, and writing. As an educational anthropologist, she uses ethnography to understand how minority languages and literacies are developed and practiced in schools and communities in Colombia, Mexico, and the U.S. Her current research focuses on the development of academic literacy skills among bilingual education teachers in the Rio Grande Valley, Texas. Professor Murillo's work has appeared in books and journals including the *Colombian Journal of Applied Linguistics, Lectura y Vida, Lenguas en Contexto, and Estudios de Lingüística Aplicada.*

Angela Johnson Rietschlin is currently a first grade teacher at Johnnycake Corners Elementary School in the Olentangy Local Schools in Ohio. She also is a doctoral student at the Ohio State University at Columbus and is a lecturer at the Ohio State University at Mansfield. She works as a classroom-based researcher in collaboration with Dr. Jeane Copenhaver-Johnson of the Ohio State University at Mansfield and Joy Bowman of the Lexington Local Schools. Her work on children's responses to read-alouds has been published in *Language Arts* and presented at national and international conferences.

Christina M. Rodríguez is Associate Professor of Law at the NYU School of Law, where she has been on the faculty since 2004. Her fields of research include language rights and language policy; immigration law and policy; citizenship theory; and constitutional law and theory. Her most recent scholarly works include: *The Significance of the Local in Immigration Regulation, Guest Workers and Integration,* and *E Pluribus Unum: How Bilingualism Strengthens American Democracy.* She teaches constitutional law, comparative constitutional adjudication, immigration law, and international refugee and asylum law, and she co-directs the NYU Public Law Colloquium, as well as the Bickel & Brewer Latino Institute for Human Rights at NYU. Before arriving at NYU, Professor Rodríguez served as a law clerk to Justice Sandra Day O'Connor of the U.S. Supreme Court and to Judge David S. Tatel of the U.S. Court of Appeals for the D.C. Circuit. Professor Rodríguez was born and raised in San Antonio, TX. She earned a BA in history from Yale College in 1995, a Master of Letters in modern history in 1998 from Oxford University, where she was a Rhodes Scholar, and a JD from Yale Law School in 2000, where she was an articles editor of the *Yale Law Journal*, and was awarded the Benjamin Scharps prize for the best paper by a third year student.

Jacqueline Jones Royster, Senior Vice Provost, Executive Dean for the Colleges of the Arts and Sciences, and Professor of English at the Ohio State University, has three complementary areas of research: the rhetorical history of women of African descent, the development of literacy, and contexts and processes related to the teaching of writing. She has authored numerous articles and books including: *Southern Horrors and Other Writings: The Anti-Lynching Campaign of Ida B. Wells-Barnett* (1997); *Traces of a Stream: Literacy and Social Change among African American Women* (2000); *Critical Inquiries* (2003); *Profiles of Ohio Women, 1803–2003* (2003); and a co-edited volume, *Calling Cards: Theory and Practice in the Study of Race, Gender, and Culture* (2005). In addition, she has filled various leadership roles in English professional organizations, including serving as chair of the Conference on College Composition and Communication and chair of the executive committee of the Modern Language Association's Writing Division. Her awards include: the CCCC Braddock Award (2000); the state of Ohio's Pioneer in Education Award (2000); the MLA Mina P. Shaughnessy Prize (2001); the Columbus YWCA Woman of Achievement Award (2004); the CCCC Exemplar Award (2004); the ADE/MLA Frances Andrew March Award (2006).

Emma Savage-Davis is Director of the Center for Education and Community and Associate Professor of Middle Grades Education at Coastal Carolina University. She began her career as an educator in the Chicago Public School system, where she taught for more than 11 years. Subsequently, she taught in higher education for the past 12 years in Tennessee, VA, and now in South Carolina which has broaden her perspective of diversity and educational needs. Savage-Davis has served on several national and state education associations. She is currently a site team member for the National Forum to Accelerate Middle Grades Reform Schools to Watch Program in South Carolina. Savage-Davis has worked in community outreach programs for more than 20 years and school-based community partnerships for 10 years. She is also a National Middle School Association Program Reviewer, Board of Director for the Association of Teacher Educators and President-Elect of the Southeastern Regional Association of Teacher Educators. She has previously published on topics relative to education, disadvantaged youth, and diversity and literature. Savage-Davis has also been awarded grant funding for programs that help underrepresented students get access to higher education and promote literacy with at-risk youth.

Jerrie Cobb Scott is Professor of Urban Literacy at the University of Memphis, where she also serves as Director of the Reading Center. Much of Scott's work is dedicated to making a positive difference in the pedagogical practices employed in our increasingly language and culturally diverse classrooms. She is an applied linguist, and her current research, publications, and service focus on language and literacy with special attention to diversity. She served as consultant and expert witness in the Ann Arbor Black English case, as well as in other language-related court cases. She is one of the co-editors of *Tapping Potential: English/Language Arts for the Black Learner*, widely published in the areas of language diversity and literacy. Scott is currently Lead Editor of *Tennessee's Children*, a state journal affiliated with the National Association for the Education of Young Children. She regularly serves as review editor for a variety of publishers, including NCTE's *Language Arts Journal* and *Reading Research Quarterly*, Sage Publishers, and *The Reading Teacher*. Scott's currently funded research includes a genre writing and question posing research project funded by the NCTE Research Foundation, and math, assistive Technology and reading, a professional development program funded by Tennessee Higher Education Commission. She is completing a book entitled *Pedagogical Choices for Language Diverse Classrooms*. Scott is Founder and Director of the National African American Read-In Chain, a 19-year literacy campaign supported by the National Council of Teachers of English, the International Reading Association, and other professional organization. Scott is dedicated to making literacy an important part of all children's lives, especially those who are least likely to have this type of support.

Nancy Rankie Shelton is Professor in Literacy Education at UMBC, where she teaches graduate and undergraduate courses in reading and writing. Her research focus is critical literacy, the writing process approach to teaching, and the affects of mandated curriculum on teachers and administrators. Professor Shelton's teaching and work with schools focuses upon: (1) creating holistic literacy learning environments and (2) understanding the sociocultural aspects of literacy development. Her recent publications and professional activities have centered on the writing process approach to teaching, critical literacy, and the affects of mandated curriculum on teachers and administrators. Her previous publications include *Rereading Fluency: Process, Practice and Politics* (Heinemann, 2007); A thing of beauty? Preservice teachers' experiences with cultural difference, literacy, and the arts. *Arts and Learning Research Journal*; Deconstructing Mr. Davis. *Talking Points*; Including students with special needs in a writing workshop. *Language Arts*; and First Do No Harm: Teachers' Reactions to Mandating Reading Mastery. In *Reading for Profit: How the Bottom Line Leaves Kids behind* (Ed. B. Altwerger; Heinemann).

Patrick H. Smith is Associate Professor of Biliteracy at the University of Texas at Brownsville/Texas Southmost College, where he teaches courses on literacy, bilingual education, and research design. His research focuses on language and literacy learning among diverse populations, and the funds of linguistic knowledge that Mexican-origin and transnational learners bring to schools in Mexico and the U.S. Smith's work on Mexican literacies has been published in leading literacy and applied linguistics journals in the U.S., Mexico, and Argentina, including *Reading Research Quarterly*, *Southwest Journal of*

Linguistics, The Reading Teacher, Lectura y Vida, and *Estudios de Lingüística Aplicada.*

Geneva Smitherman is University Distinguished Professor of English at Michigan State University (MSU) and Founder and Director of My Brother's Keeper, an MSU outreach mentoring program for Detroit middle school males. She serves on the Executive Committee and is co-founder of MSU's doctoral program in African American and African Studies, one of only eight such programs in the nation. Her research focuses on African American language and culture and language policy and education in the U.S. and South Africa. She was the chief expert witness for the children in King (the "Black English" Federal court case). Her books include the classic *Talkin and Testifyin: The Language of Black America* (Houghton-Mifflin, 1977), *Black Talk: Words and Phrases from the Hood to the Amen Corner* (Houghton-Mifflin, 1994, 2000), *Talkin That Talk* (Routledge, 2000), and *Educating Black Males* (co-author; Third World Press, 1996). Her most recent book is *Word from the Mother: Language and African Americans* (Routledge, 2006). Other publications include 125 articles and papers on language diversity and eight edited or co-edited books on language, culture and education. She was a member of the first CCCC Committee on Students' Right to Their Own Language. Professor Smitherman's awards include the 2005 NCTE James R. Squire Award, for her "transforming influence" and "lasting intellectual contribution" to the field of English studies. She has appeared in numerous media venues, seeking to raise public awareness on language issues, including *National Public Radio, The Today Show, Oprah, CNN, Phil Donahue Show,* and *CBS Reports.*

Joel Spring received his PhD in educational policy studies from the University of Wisconsin. He is currently a Visiting Professor at Queens College of the City University of New York. His major research interests are the history of education, multicultural education, Native American culture, the politics of education, global education, and human rights education. He is the author of many books. The most recent are *How Educational Ideologies are Shaping Global Society; Education and the Rise of the Global Economy; The Universal Right to Education: Justification, Definition, and Guidelines; Globalization and Educational Rights; Educating the Consumer Citizen: A History of the Marriage of Schools, Advertising, and Media,* and *A New Paradigm for Global School Systems: Education for a Long and Happy Life.*

Dolores Y. Straker (deceased) was the fourth dean of Raymond Walters College, a 2-year regional campus of the University of Cincinnati. Prior to coming to Raymond Walters, Dr. Straker was associate dean for academic affairs at the City University of New York (CUNY) central office where she managed three university-wide programs: the university's educational opportunity programs (SEEK and College Discover); the Freshman Year Experience Program; and the university's newly developed Writing Across the Curriculum Program.

Before becoming a member of the CUNY Central Office, Dr. Straker worked on the campus of York College for 25 years as a faculty member, director of the campus SEEK Program, and associate dean for academic affairs. Straker authored articles and reports on developmental education in higher education and gave conference presentations internationally, nationally, and locally on developmental reading, writing, language and literacy, and cross cultural communication at the National Council of Teachers of English (NCTE), the NCTE International Conference, the Conference on College Composition and Communication (CCCC), and the International Pragmatics Association. Straker participated on many committees and commissions of the National Council of Teachers of English and the Conference on College Composition and Communication and is currently a member of the NCTE Commission on Language.

Gerda Videsott is a scientific collaborator at the Free University of Bozen-Bolzano, Faculty of Education. Her research focus is on multilingualism, in particular on the interface between linguistics and didactics.

Aaron Welborn is formerly the project and editorial coordinator in African and African American Studies at Washington University in St. Louis, where he now works as a writer and editor for the University Libraries.

Rebecca S. Wheeler is Associate Professor of English Language and Literacy at Christopher Newport University in Newport News, VA. Her research focuses on bidialectalism, teacher and student attitudes, and linguistically informed methods for teaching Standard English in diverse classrooms. In the schools, Wheeler works with literacy coaches, communication specialists, and classroom teachers K-14 who want to know "what to do about all those missing -eds, -ss" in their students' writing. While her work currently focuses on helping teachers respond to African American student writers, the insights and methods she brings extend to any group of students who speak and write an everyday English differing from Standard American English (Cajun English, Native American English, Appalachian English, Southern English, Bronx English, international English, etc). Wheeler shows teachers how to build on what students do know— community English—as they add Standard English to their students' linguistic repertoires. She has consulted with schools in Chicago, New York, Baltimore, New Orleans, Arkansas, and Virginia and has published widely on linguistic insights and strategies to transform English instruction in diverse classrooms. Recent relevant publications include: Breaking the Code. *Educational Leadership* (forthcoming), Association of Supervision and Curriculum Development; Code-Switch to Teach Standard English. *English Journal*, 2005, 109–112; *Code-Switching: Teaching Standard English in Urban Classrooms* (NCTE, 2006), co-authored with urban elementary educator Rachel Swords.

Beth V. Yeager is Assistant Reseacher at the University of California, Santa Barbara, in Santa Barbara, CA, where she is also the Executive Director of the Center for

Literacy and Inquiry in Networking Communities. Her research focus is the social construction of knowledge, ethnography and discourse analysis, the social construction of academic identities across disciplines, and learning in the context of teaching. Dr. Yeager's research interests (and initial work as a teacher researcher) grew out of her professional experience as a bilingual teacher across 32 years, in pre-kindergarten, and at the second, fifth and sixth grade levels. Her current work, including her work with schools and teachers, focuses on: (1) exploring learning in the contexts of teaching, from ethnographic and discourse perspectives, and within and across academic disciplines; (2) understanding what supports and/or constrains the construction of networking communities across distances and contexts (including those using innovative broadband technologies; and (3) understanding how the language of the classroom and classrooms as cultures-in-the-making support and constrain what opportunities for learning and identity construction are afforded students. She has written many articles on teacher as researcher, and, with her colleagues, on the social construction of knowledge and classroom discourse among linguistically and culturally diverse students.

Author Index

Abbi, A. 368
Abedi, J. 48
Acevedo, M. 306
Achebe, C. 370
Adger, C. 44, 112, 180, 181, 278, 287
Ager, D. 336
Aguilera, D.E. 68, 71, 80
Akers Chacón, J. 303
Akinnaso, F.N. 350
Albuquerque Journal 64
Alexander, N. 331, 348, 349, 351, 352, 355, 356
Alim, H.S. 28, 133
Almasi, J.F. 225
Altwerger, B. 55
Amanti, C. 36, 55, 203, 233
Amatucci, K.B. 220
Anagnostopoulos, D. 266, 270
Anderson, E. 286
Anderson-Janniere, I. 137
Anderson-Levitt, K. 310
Anderson, R. 248
Andrews, A.B. 57
Andrews-Beck, C. 287
Angelou, M. 27
Antonio, S. 49
Anzaldua, G. 247, 254
Applebee, A.N. 269
Arnold, R.D. 77
Arvaniti, A. 276, 284
Arviso, M. 68
Arya, P. 225
Asmal, K. 346
Au, K.H. 111
August, D. 49

Baca, J.S. 56
Bailey, B.L. 134
Baker, B. 179

Baker, C. 348
Bakhtin, M.M. 140, 262, 263–4, 279
Balboni, P. 319
Bamgbose, A. 329, 345, 346, 347, 350
Banks, J.A. 221
Baquedano-Lopez, P. 234
Barnes, J. 111
Barnhardt, R. 71
Barrentine, S.B. 207, 213, 215
Barry, A. 207
Barton, D. 309, 346
Bateson, M.C. 206
Batt, L. 48
Baugh, J. 43, 49, 50, 134, 144, 179
Bauman, R.A. 200
Beck, I.L. 208
Beckstead, K. 315
Beeman, M. 233
Belardi, W. 319
Berliner, D. 55
Bernal García, M.E. 307
Bhatia, T.K. 362, 368, 371, 372, 373, 374
Bhatt, R.M. 366, 367
Biddle, B. 55
Biklen, S.K. 310
Birch, B. 179
Bloch, C. 347, 348, 349, 351, 352, 355
Blom, J. 285
Bloome, D. 107, 112, 113, 157, 160, 161, 193, 200
Bogdan, R. 310
Bomer, R. 61
Bourdieu, P. 309
Bovelsky, S. 103
Bowerman, S.A. 341
Bowman, J.T. 213
Brass, J. 270
Bridges, D. 222
Brilliant-Mills, H. 162

Brown, S. 112
Bruner, J. 353
Bunch, G. 120, 122
Bunting, E. 214
Busch, B. 353

Callahan, L. 254
Callahan, R. 235
Calliari, F. 319
Carew, J. 56
Carigiet, W. 322
Carlisle, J. 233
Carpenter, B. 178, 179, 183
Carrasco Altamirano, A. 305
Carter, S.P. 107, 112, 113, 157
Casper Star Tribune 61
Cathomas, R. 322
Cazden, C. 143, 216, 248
Cazden, C.B. 208
Champion, T. 193, 194, 195–6, 197, 200
Charalambopoulos 276
Charity, A.H. 179
Chhaba, V. 244
Chinn, P.C. 220
Christenbury, L. 177, 178
Christian, B.M. 107, 112, 113, 157
Christian, D. 44, 180, 181, 287
Christie, F. 162
Civil Rights Project at Harvard University 47
Clark, C. 106
Clay, M.M. 348
Cleary, L.M. 68
Cobarrubias, J. 332
Cockrell, D.H. 105
Cockrell, K.S. 105
Cohen, S. 315
Cole, M. 145
Coleman, E. 213, 214
Coles, G. 55, 62
Coles, R. 210, 213
Colinet, Y. 197
Collier, V. 36
Collier, V. P. 31
Columbus Dispatch xii
Combs, M.C. xx, 35–8
Commissioner of Indian Affairs 72, 73
Conly, J.L. 224
Conrad, A.W. 336
Conrad, N.K. 208

Constitution of the Republic of South Africa 332, 335
Cook, L.S. 220
Cooper, R.L. 330, 339
Copenhaver, J.F. 207, 209, 215
Copenhaver-Johnson, J.F. 213
Corbin, J. 208
Coulmas, F. 339
Coulthard, R.M. 278
Crawford, J. 44, 46, 48, 73, 76, 78
Crawford, L. 351
Crawford, T. 160
Crazzolara, E. 321
Cross, B. 106
Cummins, J. 68, 78, 194, 233, 243, 248, 381–2, 383

Dail, R. 194
Dalton, S.S. 234
Darling-Hammond, L. 44, 45, 47, 48
Dasgupta, P. 370, 373
Davis, J. 58
Davis, L. 233
Davis, M. 303
De Klerk, V. 341
De la Garza, Y. 305
De Luna, M. 303, 307
Deloria, V. 74
Delpit, L. 96, 133, 179, 278, 287
Demmert, W.G., Jr. 68, 73
Department of Education (South Africa) 334
Dewey, J. 90, 232
Deyhle, D. 68
Dick, G.S. 75
Dijan, J.-M. 345
Dillon, S. 45
Dixon, C. 154, 155, 156, 167
Donahue, P.L. 305
Donato, R. 245
Donelson, K.L. 221, 223
Donovan, C.A. 207
Dowdy, J.K. 133, 179
Du Plessis, T. 333*t*, 334
DuBois, W.E.B. xiv, 95
Dunbar, P.L. xvii
Durán, R. 156
Durand, J. 303

Echevarria, J. 36, 236, 237
Ecohealth 61

Edelsky, C. 346, 348
Edwards, D. 215
Edwards, V. 340
Egan, K. 348
Egan-Robertson, A. 160, 161
Ehri, L. 186
Elbow, P. 88, 96
Ellecosta, L. 321, 322
Elley, W. 353
Erickson, F. 157, 161, 287
Escamilla, K. 68, 105
Estell, D.W. 75
Estrada, J. 315
Estrada, P. 234

Fadiman, A. 61
Fagerberg-Diallo, S. 354
Fairclough, N. 139, 141, 143, 147, 148, 265
Farr, M. 314
Farris, P.J. 222
Fasold, R. 341
Fecho, B. 213, 262, 263
Federal Register 60
Feitelson, D. 207
Feldman, C. 68
Ferguson, C. 275
Ferguson, G. 340
Fernandez, R.M. 248
Ferreiro, E. 309
Ferrin, S. 79
Fillmore, L.W. 32
Fine, A. 224
Fisher, D. 207
Fishman, G.S. 377, 378, 379, 380
Fishman, J. 277
Fishman, J.A. 329, 336, 337–8, 340, 342,
    377, 378, 379, 380
Fix, M. 50
Flake, S.G. 224
Flood, J. 207
Flores Farfán, J.A. 310
Florez, V. 104
Floriani, A. 155, 167
Fogel, H. 186
Fox, D.L. 221
Frabboni, F. 324
Freire, P. 112, 114, 291, 294, 295–6,
    309
Frey, N. 207
Frost, J.L. 356
Fu, D. 247, 252

Fuller, B. 45, 46, 262

Gallimore, R. 233
Gamoran, A. 262, 269
Gandara, P. 234
Garan, E. 47
Garner, H. 233
Gautam, V. 367
Gay, G. 220
Gee, J.P. 95
Gesicki, K. 262
Gess-Newsome, J. 106
Giesbers, H. 285
Gilbert, S.L. 104
Gilyard, K. 143, 147, 148, 180
Godina, H. 222
Godley, A. 178, 179, 183
Goldberg, C. 233
Goldstein, Z. 207
Gollnick, D.M. 220
Gong, Y. 208
González, N. 36, 55, 89, 203, 233
Goodman, D. 110, 113, 179
Goodman, K. 347
Goodman, Y. 109, 179, 353
Government of India 366, 367, 369, 373
Granger, T. 357
Grant, C.A. 119
Graves, A. 36
Green, J. 155, 156, 160, 167
Greene, J. 63
Greenleaf, C. 106
Gregory, E. 352
Griffin, D.M. 179
Griggs, W.S. 305
Grin, F. 338, 339
Grisham, D. 277
Groff, C. 366, 367
Guba, E. 91
Guha, R. 366
Gumperz, J. 193, 285
Gupta, A. 277, 278
Guthrie, J. 286
Guthrie, L. 179
Gutierrez-Clellan, V.F. 200
Gutiérrez, K. 55, 64, 234
Guzman, M. 99

Hadjioannou, X. 276, 277, 286
Hairston, M. 222
Hakuta, K. 49

Hall, K. 385
Hall, N. 347, 351
Halliday, M.A.K. 134, 233
Hamilton, M. 346
Haneda, M. 235
Hardaway, N.L. 104
Harper, C. 277–8
Harris, P. 211
Harris, V.J. 207, 221
Harris-Wright, K. 137, 287
Hawkins, M. 233
Heath, S.B. 55, 177, 193, 209, 346, 352
Hefflin, B.R. 207
Henderson, D.L. 221
Henkin, R. 209
Henze, R. 245
Herron, C. 211
Hibbert, L. 335
Hickman, J. 208
Hicks, D. 262, 263
Hilliard, A.G., III 145
Hilpold, F. 324
Hinton, L. 75
Hock, H.H. 368
Höglinger, E. 324
Holdaway, D. 347
Hollins, E. 99
Holm, A. 68, 76
Holm, W. 68, 76
Holmes, K. 220
Holmes, S. 220
Holt, K.W. 224
Holtzmann, R. 324
Holzrichter, A. 307
hooks, b. 211, 212
Hull, G. 106
Humblet, I. 286
Hunger in America 61
Hymes, D. 43, 340

Inanda 113
Irsara, A. 321
Irvine J.J. 119, 215
Ivey, G. 269

Jackson, A. 140
Jackson, J. 27
Jennings, L. 154
Jetton, T.L. 220, 227
Jiménez, R.T. 306, 313
Jiménez, T.R. 29

Johannessen, L.R. 269
John-Steiner, V. 233
Johnson, A. 210
Johnson, A.C. 213
Johnson, D. 221
Joiner, C.W. 24, 135–6, 176, 188
Jones, S. 134, 209, 211
Jordan, J. 87–8, 89, 96
Joseph, B. 368
Jung, I. 345, 347

Kachru, B.B. 369, 370, 373
Kalman, J. 306, 309
Kamanä, K. 69
Kamwangamalu, N.M. 330, 331, 334, 338, 339
Kang, E. 262
Karp, S. 44, 63
Karyolemou, M. 276, 277
Katz, L. 193, 194, 200
Katz, S.R. 105
Kaufman, N.H. 57
Kavanaugh-Anderson, D.C. 211
Kawagley, A.O. 71
Kawai'ae'a, K. 70, 73
Kelly, G. 160
Kemmis, S. 208
Khubchandani, L.M. 365
Kids Count News 60
Kim, J. 48
Kimbrough, J. 307
Kinloch, V. 86, 89, 90, 95, 96
Kirkland, D. 140
Kita, B. 207
Kitchen, R. 62
Knoeller, C. 262, 263
Kohnert, K. 247
Koul, A. 362
Krashen, S. 31, 241, 249, 353
Kretzschmar, W. et al. 43
Kriel, M. 331
Kroon, S. 285
Kroovand, N. 103

Labov, W. 176, 178, 179, 188, 195, 195*t*
Lacoste-Caputo, J. 47
Lado, R. 181
Ladson-Billings, G. 119, 209, 244
LaFortune, R. 68
Lakoff, G. 55
Langer, J.A. 262, 269

Langman, J. 244
Lapp, D. 207
Larson, J. 55
Lasn, K. xv
Lave, J. 291, 293
Lawrence-Lightfoot, S. 58
Le Page, R. 341
Leap, W.L. 68
LeCompte, M.D. 68, 71
Lee, C. 47, 120, 122
Lee, M.G. 224
Lehr, S. 214
Leland, C.H. et al. 212
Lensmire, T.J. 262, 263
Leont'ev, D. 294
Lesestudie Südtirol Kurzfassungen 324
Lessow-Hurley, J. 36
Lester, N.A. 211
Liebrand, R. 285
Lincoln, Y.S. 91
Lindfors, J. 277, 278, 283, 285, 287
Lipka, J. 72
Lipton, M. 245
Litchner, J.H. 221
Lloyd, D.J. 88
Lomawaima, T. 80
López Austin, A. 307
López Luján, L. 307
Lowell, S. 212
Lucas, T. 245
Lytle, C.M. 74

McAllister, G. 119
Macaulay, T.B. 369, 370
McCabe, A. 193, 195, 195t, 197
McCardle, P. 244
McCarty, T.L. 62, 71, 73, 75, 77, 80
McClure, E. 179
McCoy, R. 222
McDiarmid, G.W. 105
McGuire, C.E. 212
McKeown, M.G. 208
McKissack, P. 111, 187
McLure, P. 214
McTaggart, R. 208
Macedo, D. 112, 309
Mahboob, A. 367
Mahiri, J. 89
Mair, C. 336
Major, E.M. 119
Mallikarjun, B. 365, 367

Mannheim, B. 222
Marcus, C. 111
Mark, D.L.H. 104
Marshall, J. 269
Martens, P. 56
Martínez-Léon, N. 306
Marzano, R. 183, 189
Massey, D.S. 303
Masten, A.S. 74
Matos, L. 120, 122
Matoush, M. 247
Matute-Bianchi, M. 248
May, J.P. 221
Mead, M. 348
Medicine, B. 75
Medina, C. 106
Mehan, H. 211, 283
Mellott, J. 219
Mercer, N. 215
Meyer, L. 55
Meyer, R. 55, 56, 59, 61
Middleton, J.N. 105
Minnicci, A. 178, 179, 183
Minow, M. 29
Moallem, M. 103
Moll, L. 36, 55, 89, 203, 233, 315
Moore, R. 148
Morales, R. 106
Morine-Dershimer, G. 164
Morton, M.B. 193, 200
Moschonas, 276
Mosley, M. 208
Muldrow, R. 193, 194, 200
Muñoz Cruz, H. 305
Myers, J. 62
Myers-Scotton, C. 285

Nambissan, G.B. 367
Naregal, V. 337
Nathenson-Mejia, S. 105
National Center for Educational Statistics 234
National Reading Panel 59, 62
Nation's Report Card 58
Native Language Network 68
Neff, D. 55
Nettle, D. 338
New Mexico Health Policy Commission 61
New Mexico Voices for Children 60, 61
Newkirk, T. 214
Ngugi Wa Thiong'o 347, 348

Nielsen, F. 248
Nieto, S. 179, 188
Nilsen, A.P. 221, 223
Nino, C.F. 86, 89–90, 92, 94, 95, 96
Noguera, P.A. 244
Norton, D.E. 220
Novak, J. 45, 46
Nystrand, M. 262, 263, 269

Oakes, J. 245
Obadiah, J.E. 105
Ochs, E. 117, 193
O'Donnell-Allen, C. 270
O'Flahavan, J.F. 225
O'Flavahan, J. 286
Ogbu, J. 42
Ohanian, S. 55, 62
Ohio Center for Curriculum and
    Assessment 194
Ohio Office of Early Childhood Education
    193
Okawa, G.Y. 107, 110
Okpewho, I. 197
Olson, D. 294
Orfield, G. 47
Ortiz, J. 74
Otto, S. 107, 112, 113, 157
Ouane, A. 345, 347
Ovando, C. 36
Oyler, C. 207

Padak, N.D. 221
Palacas, A.L. 137
Pandor, N. 334, 335
Papantoniou, Z. 278
Pataray-Ching, J. 211
Paulston, C.B. 338
Peacock, T.D. 68
Pennycook, A. 336
Peredo Merlo, M.A. 306
Perie, M. 304, 305
Perreault, G. 119
Peterson, C. 193, 195, 195t, 197
Philips, S. 62
Phillipson, R. 336
Pickering, D. 183, 189
Pierce, C. 56
Pierce-Gonzalez, D. 56
Piestrup, A.M. 180
Pinar, W.F. 305
Placier, P.L. 105

Pollock, J. 183, 189
Pool, J. 337
Portes, A. 33
Postman, N. 108–9
Powell, S. 220
Preston, D.R. 44, 118
Pullum, G. 181
Putney, L. 156

Quinn, R. 200

Rahman, T. 340
Raider-Roth, M. 286
Ramirez, J.D. 350
Rao, R. 370
Rappaport, D. 213
Rasinski, T.V. 221
Ravitch, D. 23
Redd, T.M. 178, 180
Reese, L. 233
Reeves, J. 235
Reifel, S. 356
Reilly, B. 106
Reynolds, R. 179
Rhymes, B. 55
Richardson, E. 104, 142, 178
Richebuono, B. 319
Richman, C.L. 103
Rickford, J. 27
Rickford, J.R. 134, 136, 138, 139, 143, 178,
    179, 188
Rickford, R.J. 134, 143
Rifesser, T. 321, 322
Ritchie, W.C. 368, 371, 372, 373, 374
Roberts, B.C. 210
Robertson, S.L. 264
Robinson, A. 351
Rockwell, E. 309
Rodríguez, A.J. 106
Rodríguez, C.M. xx, 28–34, 378
Rogers, R. 208
Rogoff, B. 232
Romaine, S. 338
Romero, M.E. 71, 73
Roos, P.D. 29
Rosales, M. 213
Rosenberg, P. 286
Rosenblatt, L.M. 209, 211, 215
Rouillard, J. 75
Rowe, D. 193
Rubal-Lopez, A. 336

Rubin, B.C. 244
Rubio-Marín, R. 34
Ruiz Ávila, D. 305
Rumberger, R. 234

Sablo, S. 89
Sankoff, G. 341
Savage-Davis, E. 220, 227
Scarborough, H.S. 179
Schieffelin, B.B. 117, 193
Schiffman, H.F. 337, 340, 360, 367, 368, 372, 373
Schilling-Estes, N. 179, 181, 188
Schlesinger, A., Jr. 20
Schmidt, R.J. 332
Schultz, J. 157
Schultz, K. 262, 263
Scollon, R. 200
Scott, J.C. 90, 105, 109, 111, 112
Scotton, C.M. 337
Seabrook, G. 286
Seberich, R. 321
Secretaría de Educación Pública 306, 312, 314
Sen, A. 365, 367
Shannon, D. 214
Sherrill, D. 103
Short, D. 36, 236, 237
Short, K.G. 221
Shuart-Faris, N. 107, 112, 113
Silva, P. 331
Sims, R.B. 220
Sinclair, J.M. 278
Sipe, L.R. 207–8, 212, 214, 215
Sipp, L. 208
Skutnabb-Kangas, T. 340–1
Slavin, R.E. 222
Sledd, J. 138
Sleeter, C. 119
Smagorinsky, P. 269, 270
Smit, U. 331
Smith, E. 137
Smith, F. 356
Smith, H.L. 134
Smith, M.W. 269
Smith, P.H. 306, 307, 313
Smith, R. 103
Smith, R.C. 305, 308
Smitherman, G. xvii, xx, 24–8, 85, 86–7, 89, 95, 96, 105, 113, 134, 137–8, 140, 145, 178, 287, 378

Smolkin, L.B. 207
Snow, C. 120, 122, 248
Solsken, J. 193
South African Broadcasting Corporation 334t
Southerland, S.A. 106
Souza Lima, E. 155–6, 157
Sparks, W.G., III 105
Spellings, M. 47, 59
Sperling, M. 269
Spharim, G. 233
Spinelli, J. 224
Spradley, J.P. 208
Spring, J. xix–xx, 18–23, 55
Srivastava, R.N. 367
Staples, S.F. 224
State Health Facts 61
Steffensen, M. 179
Stone, A. 68
Strauss, A. 208
Strauss, G. 339
Strauss, S. 55
Street, B. 193, 199, 346
Strizich, M. 68
Stromquist, N.P. 305
Su, Z. 104
Suárez-Orozco, C. 29
Suárez-Orozco, M. 29
Subedi, D. 270
Sullivan, T. 307
Sunday Times (Johannesburg) 341
Sunderman, G. 47, 48
Sung, B. 248
Sweetland, J. 178, 179, 183, 186
Swords, R. 176–7, 182–5, 186, 187, 372
Sychterz, T. 207

Tabouret-Keller, A. 341
Taibon, M. 319
Tarpley, N.A. 211
Tatter, P. 233
Tatum, B.D. 119
Taylor, D. 347, 348
Taylor, H. 137, 185
Teale, W.H. 207
Tedlock, D. 222
Tejeda, C. 234
Terrill, M. 104
Tharoor, S. 361–2
Tharp, R.G. 234, 241
Thomas, W.P. 31

Thompson, D.L. 214
Toribio, A.J. 315
Towner, J.C. 68, 73
Townsend, J. 277–8
Tracey, C. 47
Trezise, J. 211
Triebel, A. 345
Tse, L. 248–9
Tsiplakou, S. 276, 284
Tuirán, R. 303
Tuyay, S. 154, 155, 167, 173

U.S. Department of Education 55, 59, 78

Vacca, J. 103
Vaillancourt, F. 338, 339
Valdes, G. 120, 122, 236, 237, 245
Valenzuela, A. 305
Van de Craen, P. 286
Van Dijk, T.A. 145
Van Manen, M. 64
Vargas, M.A. 305, 306
Vaughn-Cooke, F. 137
Velázquez, D. 62
Verner, M.E. 105
Verra, R. 319, 321
Videsott, G. 319, 321
Virginia Department of Education 219
Vittur, F. 321
Vogt, M.E. 36, 236
Vygotsky, L.S. 145, 233, 240

Wagner, D. 346, 347, 355
Watahomigie, L. 75
Waters, M.C. 29
Webb, K. 178, 180
Webb, V. 331
Wee, L. 337
Weiss, E. 306
Wells, G. 220
Wenger, E. 38, 291, 293
Wertsch, J.V. 68
West, T, 103

Western Cape Education Department
  (WCED) 356
Wheeler, R. 372
Wheeler, R.S. 178, 179, 182, 183
Wheelis, A. 54
Wiater, W. 321
Wiley, T.G. 4
Wilhelm, J. 269
Will, G. 45
Williams, B. 71
Williams, F. 103
Williams, R. xi
Williams, Robert 26
Willis, A.I. 207
Wills, D. 56
Wilson, M. 106
Wilson, W.H. 69, 70, 73, 74, 75, 77
Winser, W.N. 211
Witt, E. 220
Wittgenstein, L. 325
Wolfe, P. 56
Wolfram, W. 44, 107, 109, 179, 180, 181,
  188, 277, 287
Wood, G. 44
Woodson, C.G. 134
Woodson, J. 212
Wortham, S. 262
Wortham, S.C. 356
Wright, J. 262
Wright, L. 208
Wright, S. 338

Yamamoto, A. 75
Yamauchi, L. 234
Yeager, B. 155, 156, 167
Yolen, J. 224

Zehr, M. 49
Zepeda, O. 75
Zhou, M. 33
Zimmerman, W. 50

Subject Index

AAL *see* African American Language

AAVE (African American Vernacular English) *see* African American Language

Academic English (AE) 49, 132, 133, 233, 241

Academic English Mastery Program (AEMP) 25

active language defense 379–80

Administration for Native Americans (ANA) 79, 80

Africa *see* literacy issues in Africa; South Africa: early literacy learning; South Africa: educational policies

African American English (AAE) *see* African American Language

African American Language (AAL) 132–49, 178–9; failures of progressive pedagogies 134–8; hip hop 28, 93–4; language, identity and power 132, 133, 134, 138–49; language rights 87, 88–9; and limited English proficiency 49–51; misconceptions 42, 44; students' views 132–3, 133*f*, 144–5; *see also* democratic engagements; Ebonics; Martin Luther King, Jr. Elementary School v. Ann Arbor School District Board (1979)

African American students 176–89; code-switching 95, 136, 183, 185, 186–8, 383; compulsory ignorance laws 4; contrastive analysis (CA) 183, 185, 186–8; correction 180; grammar 182, 183–5; key notions from applied linguistics 180–2; language policies 4, 5, 6, 24–8; language style 182, 183; plural patterns 183–4, 184*t*; possessive patterns 184, 185, 185*t*; reading acquisition 179, 187; slave legacy 42–3,

44; story-telling 195–6, 199–201; and traditional language arts methods 176–80; writing 185, 186, 187–8

African American Vernacular English (AAVE) *see* African American Language

Afterschool Study 194, 195–7

agency 294

American Indian Language Development Institute (AILDI) 75, 76

ANA *see* Administration for Native Americans

applied linguistics 180–2

Arabic 21

art xiv

assimilation 332

attitudes toward language 12–13, 181; effects of training 102, 105–7, 119; exposure to non-dominant language speakers 102, 104; implications for teacher education programs 107–14; language background 102, 103–4; Language Knowledge and Awareness Study (LKAS) 99–103; other studies 103–7; students' attitudes 13, 132–3, 133*f*, 144–5; teacher attitudes 102, 103

banking concept of education 295

basic interpersonal communication skills (BICS) 233

Basquecization 340

behaviorism 15

BIA *see* Bureau of Indian Affairs

bidialectalism 15–16, 137–8, 363

bilingual education 19, 30, 31–3; dual language programs 31–2, 383; language immersion programs 68–9, 70–1, 80; language maintenance programs 248;

teacher education 105; tribal schools 74–5; *see also* bilingualism; Chinese immigrant students; language of the classroom; multilingualism in classrooms: South Tyrol; South Africa: early literacy learning

Bilingual Education Acts 6, 19, 74, 76, 77, 78, 79

bilingualism 247–8; additive bilingualism 350; benefits 248–9; NCLB Act 54–5, 248; *see also* bilingual education; Chinese immigrant students; English language learners (ELLs)

Black English *see* African American Language

"Black English" case *see* Martin Luther King, Jr. Elementary School v. Ann Arbor School District Board (1979)

Brazil *see* Projeto Aprendiz

Britain: language policies 18–19

Brown v. Board of Education (1954) 5, 7, 41–2, 378; linguistic significance 42–4

Bureau of Indian Affairs (BIA) 72, 75, 76

CA *see* contrastive analysis (CA)

CALP (cognitive academic language proficiency) 233

Canada: language rights 29–30, 33

CASE (Chicago Academic Standards Exam) 264–6

Castañeda v. Pickard (1978) 33

CCCC *see* Conference on College Composition and Communication

Center for Applied Linguistics 31

Center for Research on Education, Diversity, and Excellence (CREDE) 234, 235, 241

Central Alaskan Yup'ik 70–2, 80

Chicago Academic Standards Exam (CASE) 264–6

children's rights 57

Chinese immigrant students 14, 247–60; becoming bilingual 254–9; benefits of bilingualism 248–9; code-switching 254–7; using first language for social studies 249–54; writing development 254–9, 254f, 255f, 256f, 257f

citizenship 32–4, 72

civil rights 6, 30, 75–7

Civilization Act (1819) 74

code-switching 111–12, 134, 137, 140, 141f, 285; African American students 95, 136, 183, 185, 186–8, 383; Chinese immigrant students 254–7; India 371–2; power relations 136; *see also* Greek Cypriot community

cognitive academic language proficiency (CALP) 233

cognitive view of learning 15

communicative competence 117, 130, 286

communities of practice 38

community languages 94–5

Conference on College Composition and Communication (CCCC) 10, 11, 85, 87–8, 89, 100, 120

constructivist pedagogy 15, 106

context 58

contrastive analysis (CA) 132, 134, 136–47, 137f, 142f; African American students 183, 185, 186–8; language and identity 143–5; language and power 136, 138, 147; language and society 145–6; language: definition 140; observations 140–3; research methods 138–40

cooperative learning groups 222

correction 180

CREDE *see* Center for Research on Education, Diversity, and Excellence

critical language pedagogy 142–3, 143f, 382

critical literacy 13, 61, 252; decoding *vs.* understanding 309; reflection 112–13; and social practices 212; teacher education 382; threat 213; *see also* democratic engagements; read-alouds

cultural competence 244

cultural rights 20, 22–3, 29–30, 88, 127

cultural values 179

culturally responsive education 68, 79, 80, 81, 206–7, 220

culture jamming xiv–xv

defining language: law and government policy xi–xii; music and art xiv; redefining language xiv–xv; social institutions xii–xiv

democracy: interpretive attitude 89–90

democratic engagements 90–7; SRTOL and "community language" 94–5; student perceptions of language rights 91–4

Denetclarence v. Denver Board of
Education (1973) 75
dialect prejudice 179, 188
dialects 181; bidialectalism 15–16, 137–8,
363; children's attitudes to 211–12;
comparative examination 287; and
reading 179, 187; standards 43–4;
United States 118–19, 277–8, 285;
utterances 279; *see also* Greek Cypriot
community
dialogue 111, 112, 294–5
digital literacy practices 297–8, 313–14
diglossia 275–7, 286
discussion 221–2; peer discussion 225–6,
227–9
double negative 181
Dred Scott v. Sandford (1857) 43
dual language programs 31–2, 383

Ebonics 26, 27, 92, 133f; *see also* African
American Language; Oakland Ebonics
debate
economic contexts 63
educational policies: South Africa 16,
329–42; United States 54–9, 305
educational rights 22–3, 24, 29, 33
EEOA *see* Equal Educational Opportunity
Act
elite closure 337–8
empowerment 64, 294, 382
English as a global language 18–19, 20,
21–2, 340–1, 369–70, 373; Anglo-
American conspiracy theory 336;
global grassroots theory 336–7
English language learners (ELLs) 12,
232–45; detracking 244; education
30–1, 232–5; equalizing learning
opportunities 235–43; factors
hindering instruction 28–9, 234–5;
funds of knowledge 36–7, 89;
implications for practice 243–5;
sheltered instruction 35–6, 236–43;
(teaching approach 237; strategies
237–40; lesson analysis 240–1;
standards 241–3); *see also* Chinese
immigrant students
English Only Movement 6, 247, 277, 301,
379; CCCC National Language Policy
Resolution (1988) 11; CCCC Position
Statement (1986) 10; EPIC response
(1987) 10–11; Hawaii 5, 69; and

instrumental language rights 34;
NCLB Act 19; policy 48, 49, 69, 78,
247
English Plus 11, 78, 373
English Plus Information Clearinghouse
(EPIC) 10–11
enrichment 88
Equal Educational Opportunity Act
(EEOA, 1974) 24, 76
equity pedagogy 106
Esperanto 18
ethnographic perspective 154–6
European language portfolio 322

Farrington v. Tukushige (1927) 5
first, second, third space 55
French 21
funds of knowledge 36–7, 89, 203, 233,
260

generative pedagogy 295–6
German 4, 5
grammar 177, 179–80, 182, 183–5
Greek Cypriot community 275–89;
dialect in United States 277–8;
diglossia 275–7, 286; discourse moves
280–3, 281t, 282f; Greek Cypriot
dialect (GCD) 276; Greek Cypriot
dialect in the classroom 275, 278–85,
279f, 280f, 281t; implications for
U.S. educational practice 285–7;
linguistic situation 276–7; Standard
Greek (SG) 276; students' perspectives
on GCD 283–5; *see also* Language
Knowledge and Awareness Study
(LKAS)

Haitian Study 194, 197
Hawaii 5, 50, 69–70, 77, 78, 79, 80;
see also indigenous students' rights
Hawaiian Pidgin English (HPE) 50
high stakes testing and literature
262–71, 357; accountability 264;
consequences of testing 262;
heteroglossia 263–4; monologic
instruction 266–8; reflective pedagogy
and dialogic assessment 268–70;
standardization of classroom talk
264–6, 268; standardization of social
languages 263–4
hip hop 28, 93–4

identity 13–14, 56–7, 88, 92, 95, 96, 178, 199–201, 252–3, 293, 382; *see also* contrastive analysis (CA); positionality; story-telling
immigrant populations: illegal immigrants 303; instrumental language rights 34, 378; language policies 4, 5, 6; segmented assimilation 32; *see also* English language learners (ELLs)
India: multilingualism 16, 360–74; constitutional privilege 365–8; diversity within unity 360; elitism to equity 372–3; English 18–19, 368–73; going to school: three stories 360–5; Hinglish 370–2; "minority" languages 366–7; official languages 366; Three-Language Formula 367–8
Indian Education Act (1972) 75
Indian Self-Determination and Education Assistance Act (1975) 76
Indigenous Language Institute 68
indigenous students' rights 7–8, 68–82; bilingual education legislation 74–5; Central Alaskan Yup'ik 70–2, 80; civil rights laws 75–7; English Only 78; Hawaii 5, 50, 69–70, 77, 78, 79, 80; hegemonic oppression 72–80; language immersion 68–9, 70–1, 80; language loss 68, 73; language preservation 80; language revitalization 68, 76, 77, 78; Native Americans 72–7, 78–80; political autonomy 81; recommendations for change 80–2; sovereign rights 74, 78–9; subsistence practices 70–2; treaty rights 82; U.S. Government Policy 72–4, 378–9
instructional approaches: contrastive analysis (CA) 132, 134, 136–7, 137*f*; critical language pedagogy 142–3, 143*f*, 382; inclusive approaches 106; inquiry orientation 110–13; progressive language pedagogies 134–8; questioning orientation 110–11; transmission orientation 110; *see also* contrastive analysis (CA)
instrumental language rights 34, 378
International Reading Association (IRA) 194
internationalization 332
Italy *see* multilingualism in classrooms: South Tyrol

Japanese 21

language 180–1
language awareness 13
language economics 338–40
language, identity, and power 132, 133, 134, 138–49
language ideologies 13
language immersion 68–9, 70–1, 80
Language Knowledge and Awareness Study (LKAS) 99–103; effect of training 102; exposure to non-dominant language speakers 102; findings 101–3; language background 102; methodology 100–1; questions 99–100; teacher attitudes 102
language loss 32, 68, 73, 248, 340–1
language of the classroom 14, 153–74, 383; academic study: *Watermelon Project* 162–3; consequential progressions 156; diversity 163; ethnographic perspective 154–6; initiating community 156–60, 158–9*t*; intertextual ties 161; language as resource 164, 167–73, 170–2*t*; metadiscourse 161, 163; opportunities for learning 155–6, 167–73; patterns of practice 161, 163–4, 165–6*t*; principles of practice 173–4; reformulating community 160–2; repertoire for action 161–2; text construction 157, 161
language policies: Africa 346; African American policies 4, 5, 6, 24–8; Britain 18–19; global policies 18–23; and inequalities among learners 18–19; minority language policies 4–7, 28–32, 378–9; and pedagogical practices 3–16, 24–5, 30–2; United States xi–xii, 19–34, 58–9, 377–81; *see also* defining language; South Africa: educational policies; Students' Right to Their Own Language Resolution
Language Positionality Project 120–30; approach 122–3; foundational knowledge 123–4; overview 120–2, 121*t*; reading and responding to SRTOL 125–9; students' responses 123–9; variations in own language 124–5
language preservation 80
language style 111–12, 182, 183
language transfer 181–2

language variation 180–1; *see also* attitudes toward language; code-switching; positionality

Lau v. Nichols (1974) 6, 28, 75–6

limited English proficient (LEP) students: definition 49–50, 73; *see also* English language learners (ELLs); No Child Left Behind Act

linguistic instrumentalism 337

linguistic suffering 7, 54, 56

literacy: autonomous model 346; digital literacy practices 297–8, 313–14; emergent literacy 346–7, 350, 351; ideological model 346–7; multiple literacies 346; oral literacy 193–4, 345–6, 348; *see also* critical literacy; literacy issues in Africa; read-alouds; reading; social construction of literacy; story-telling; writing

literacy issues in Africa 345–9; beliefs about literacy 346–7; language medium 346; literacy environments 347–9; oracy 345–6, 348; Stories across Africa Project 355–6; universal primary education (UPE) 347–8; *see also* South Africa: early literacy learning

literature: culturally conscious literature 206; novels 263–4; *see also* high stakes testing and literature; multicultural literature; read-alouds; reading

LKAS *see* Language Knowledge and Awareness Study

Mandarin 18, 21

Martin Luther King, Jr. Elementary School v. Ann Arbor School District Board (1979) 6, 24–5, 27–8, 135–6, 176, 178, 188, 378

mass media xiv, 334, 334*t*, 335, 336

Mexican communities *see* social construction of literacy

Meyer v. Nebraska (1923) 5, 29, 378

microaggressions 56–7

minority language policies (USA) 4–7, 28–32, 378–9

Modern Language Association (MLA) 85

multicultural education 20, 102, 105, 119, 219–20

multicultural literature 206, 219–30; cooperative learning groups 222; culturally responsive pedagogy 220;

discussion 221–2, 225–6, 227–9; high-quality adolescent literature 223–4; multicultural literature project 223–9; reading 220–1, 223–4, 227–9; selection criteria 221, 223; tandem stories 227–8; writing 222, 226, 227–9

multilingualism 15–16; *see also* India: multilingualism; multilingualism in classrooms: South Tyrol; South Africa: educational policies

multilingualism in classrooms: South Tyrol 319–26; bilingualism exam 325, 325*f*; elementary school 322; European language portfolio 322; evaluation 323, 324; integrated didactics program 322, 323; intermediate and high school 322, 323*t*, 324*t*; kindergarten 321; *paritetic* school system 320–3, 320*f*; teacher education 322

music and art xiv

National Assessment of Educational Progress (NAEP, 2005) 58, 58*t*

National Association for Bilingual Education (NABE) 49

National Clearinghouse for Bilingual Education (1977) 76

National Council of Teachers of English (NCTE) xvii, 10, 11–12, 85, 100, 194

National Indian Bilingual Center 76

National Indian Education Association (NIEA) 79–80

Native American Languages Act (1990, 1992) 77, 78, 79–80

Native Americans: compulsory Americanization 5; legislation 75–7, 78, 79–80; right to literacy 4; *see also* indigenous students' rights

NCLB *see* No Child Left Behind Act

NCTE *see* National Council of Teachers of English

negative liberties 378

New Mexico: counterportrait 60–1; economic context 63–4; English Plus 78; hope 64–5; politics and policy 58–9; possibilities 63–5; social context 60–1

NIEA (National Indian Education Association) 79–80

No Child Left Behind Act (NCLB, 2001) 28, 41–2; bilingualism 19, 54–5, 248;

criticisms of 44–5, 301, 378; linguistic significance 44–51; penalizing diversity 6–7, 23, 45–7; Reading First 54, 55; resource inequities 47–51; Spanish 22; testing regime 30–1, 41, 45, 58; *see also* indigenous students' rights

Oakland Ebonics debate 26–7, 132, 136–7, 372
oral literacy 193–4, 345–6, 348

peer discussion 225–6, 227–9
permissive language defense 377–9
phonics 55, 56
Plessy v. Ferguson (1896) 5, 42
plural patterns 183–4, 184*t*
pluralism 332, 365
Plyler v. Doe (1982) 38
positionality 117–30; approaches to changing teacher attitudes 119; Language Positionality Project 120–30, 121*t*; self-discoveries 117–19
possessive patterns 184, 185, 185*t*
power relations 118, 132, 133, 287; CA programs 138, 147; code-switching 136; coercive relations 382; collaborative relations 381–2; students' views 124, 212–13
preventive language defense 380
proactive language defense 380
progressive language pedagogies 134–8
Projeto Aprendiz 16, 291–301; community practices 296–300; (graffiti 298, 298*f*; internet café 297–8, 297*f*; newspaper and radio station 296–7, 297*f*, 300; workshops 299, 299*f*); community/ school 291–2; human agency and social change 294; implications for U.S. educational practice 300–1; individual and context 293–4; learning and identity 293; participatory learning 293; pedagogy of opportunities 294–6; practice to theory 292–4

race: children's race-focused talk 212–13; defining language xiii; symbolic racism 145; United States xiii, 26–7, 42, 73, 138; Whiteness 212–13, 220; *see also* high stakes testing and literature
read-alouds 206–16; call-and-response 211; child-centred approach 208;

cultural responsiveness 206–7; culturally conscious literature 206; directive response 212; ethnocentric notions of relevance 213–15; intertextual connections 210–11, 214; participant structures 211–12, 215; race-focused talk 212–13; research context 208–9; sense of community 209–13, 215; students' right to own language 207–9, 216; threat 213; time 215
reading: critical literacy 61, 112–13, 309; and dialect 179, 187; dialogic view 266; generic programs 62; high-quality adolescent literature 223–4; Mexico 306; multicultural literature 220–1, 223–4, 227–9; phonics 55, 56; Reading First 54, 55; social context 60–1; South Africa 352–6; as text reproduction 266
reflection 112–13
register shifting 112
Russian 21

Santa Barbara Classroom Discourse Group 155
SCWriP (South Coast Writing Project) 155
second language acquisition 48–9
Senegal 354
sheltered instruction 35–6, 236–43
social construction of literacy 16, 303–17; implications for U.S. educational practice 314–16; Mexican literacies in U.S. schools 304–5; Mexican literacies: research 305–6; study: Central Mexico 306–14; (context 307–9; theoretical framework 309; methodology 309–10; analysis 310; school-based literacies 310–12, 311*f*; family and community literacies 309*f*, 312–13, 312*f*, 313*f*; digital literacy practices 313–14; teacher training 314–15)
social contexts 60–1
social institutions: defining language xii–xiv
social justice 37–8, 104, 381
sociocognitive view of learning 15
sociocultural theory 155–6, 262, 263, 291
South Africa: early literacy learning 16, 345–57; Battswood Biliteracy Project 350–2; Culture of Reading Project 353–6; Free Reading in Schools Project

352–3; Language in Education Policy (LiEP) 349; literacy issues in Africa 345–9; research and practical interventions 349–56

South Africa: educational policies 16, 329–42; Afrikanerization 331; Anglicization 330; apartheid 329; assimilation 332; Bantu Education Act 331, 333; black elite closure 337–8; consequences of language policy failure 340–1; Dutchification 330; hegemony of English 330, 331, 332, 333, 334, 335, 336–7, 340–1; implementation failures 333–8, 340–1; indigenous African languages 329, 331, 332, 338–40; internationalization 332; language democratization 331–2; language economics 338–40; Language in Education Policy (LiEP) 349; language policy escape clauses 335–6; language practices 333–5; (education 333–4, 333*t*, 335, 336; media 334, 334*t*, 335, 336; government and administration 334, 335, 336); pluralism 332; social history and language policies 330–3; vernacularization 332–3

South Coast Writing Project (SCWriP) 155

sovereign rights 74, 78–9

Spanish 22

SRTOL *see* Students' Right to Their Own Language Resolution

Standard English: concept 43–4, 181; emphasis on xiii, 41, 42; grammar 177; student perceptions 92–4, 95–6

Standards for Effective Pedagogy 234, 235, 241; Cognitively Challenging Activities 234, 243; Contextualization 234, 242–3; Instructional Conversation 234, 243; Joint Productive Activity 234, 242; Language and Literacy Development 234, 242

story-telling 14, 192–204; evaluative analysis 195, 195*t*; integrating language variation 201–4; narrative patterns 195–201; oral literacy 193–4; social patterns for identity and relationships 199–201; standard format 192–3

Storytelling Project 194, 199–204

students' attitudes toward their own language 13, 132–3, 133*f*, 144–5

Students' Right to Their Own Language Resolution (SRTOL) 3, 8–12, 85–6, 120, 360; democratic engagements 89–97; position statement on English as the Official Language (1986) 10; position statement on SRTOL (1974) xv, 10; reaffirmation (2003) xvii–xviii, 11–12, 373–4, 376; redefinition 87–9

style-shifting 111–12, 182

tandem stories 227–8

teacher education xviii, 13–15, 35–8; bilingual education courses 105; discovering one's students 36–7; effects of training 105–7, 119; equity pedagogy 106; field-based v. non-field based courses 105; ideological barriers 106; in-service training 105; inclusive approaches 106; inquiry approach 106–14, 382; (rationale 108; development of inquiry stance 108–10; inquiry orientation to diversity instruction 110–13); prejudice reduction 105; reading groups 106; research implications 107–14; sheltered teaching strategies 35–6; social justice 37–8; *see also* multicultural literature

teacher expectations of students 119, 178, 179

To Kill a Mockingbird 262, 265–8

Treaty of Guadalupe Hidalgo (1948) 4–5

Tribal Restoration Act 6

U.N. Convention on the Rights of the Child 57

United States: dialect 118–19, 277–8, 285; educational policies 54–9, 305; English Only policy 48, 49, 69, 78, 247; indigenous language rights 72–4, 378–9; language policies xi–xii, 19–34, 58–9, 377–81; minority language policies 4–7, 28–32, 378–9; poverty 60–1; race xiii, 26–7, 42, 73, 138; Spanish 22

utterances 279

values 56–7, 376, 380–1, 383–4, 386

vernacularization 332–3

vernaculars 181

Voting Rights Act (1975) 33

World Englishes 20, 22, 369–70, 373, 386
writing: African American students 185,
  186, 187–8; authoring *vs.* scribal
  functions 309; Chinese immigrant
students 254–9, 254*f*, 255*f*, 256*f*, 257*f*;
Mexico 305–6, 311–12; response to
multicultural literature 222, 226,
227–9; South Africa 351